THE HANDBOOK OF LOAN SYNDICATIONS AND TRADING

THE HANDBOOK OF LOAN SYNDICATIONS AND TRADING

Editors:

ALLISON TAYLOR

ALICIA SANSONE

McGraw-Hill

New York Chicago San Francisco Lisbon London Madrid
Mexico City Milan New Delhi San Juan Seoul
Singapore Sydney Toronto

Copyright © 2007, by The McGraw-Hill Companies, Inc. All rights reserved. Printed in the United States of America. Except as permitted under the United States Copyright Act of 1976, no part of this publication may be reproduced or distributed in any form or by any means, or stored in a database or retrieval system, without the prior written permission of the publisher.

3 4 5 6 7 8 9 0   DOC/DOC   0 9 8 7

ISBN-13: 978-0-07-146898-5
ISBN-10: 0-07-146898-6

This publication is designed to provide accurate and authoritative information in regard to the subject matter covered. It is sold with the understanding that the publisher is not engaged in rendering legal, accounting, or other professional service. If legal advice or other experts assistance is required, the services of a competent professional person should be sought.

> —*From a declaration of principles jointly adopted by a committee of the American Bar Association and a committee of publishers.*

McGraw-Hill books are available at special quantity discounts to use as premiums and sales promotions, or for use in corporate training programs. For more information, please write to the Director of Special Sales, Professional Publishing, McGraw-Hill, Two Penn Plaza, New York, NY 10121-2298. Or contact your local bookstore.

This book is printed on acid-free paper.

Library of Congress Cataloging-in-Publication Data

   The handbook of loan syndications and trading / Allison Taylor and Alicia Sansone, editors.
      p. cm.
   ISBN 0–07–146898–6 (alk. paper)
   1. Bank loans. I. Taylor, Allison. II. Sansone, Alicia.
   HG1641.H26 2006

   332.1'753068—dc22   2006006606

CONTENTS

List of Contributors   xi
Preface   xv
Acknowledgments   xix

Chapter 1

An Overview of the Loan Market   1
*Scott Page, Payson Swaffield, Allison A. Taylor, Ruth Yang,
Peter C. Vaky, Steve Miller, Scott D. Krase, Elliot Ganz*

An Introduction to the Loan Asset Class   3
Evolution of the Primary and Secondary Leveraged
    Loan Markets   21
Introduction to the Syndicated Loan Market   39
Players in the Market   47
Interplay with Other Capital Markets   52
The LSTA and Its Role in the Promotion of the
    Corporate Loan Asset Class   61
The LSTA—A Regulatory and Documentation Review   75

Chapter 2

**Effects of the Legal Characterization of Loans under the
Securities Laws   85**
Tiziana M. Bason, Michael P. Kaplan, and Bradley Y. Smith

Chapter 3

Loan Structures   101
Steve Miller, Marc Hanrahan, David Teh, Dawn Pasquin

Basic Loan Structures   103
Second Lien Loans   108
Project Finance   137

Chapter 4

The Primary Market   155
Barry Bobrow, Mercedes Tech, Linda Redding, Alex Spiro, Elliot Ganz

An Introduction to the Primary Market   157
The Architecture of Information Distribution in the
  Loan Market   186
The Implications of the Use of "Syndicate Information"
  in the Loan Market   196

Chapter 5

Understanding the Credit Agreement   209
Richard Wight, Warren Cooke, Richard Gray

Introduction   211
Part 1. Making the Loan: Commitments, Loans, and
        Letters of Credit   211
Part 2. Making Money off the Loan: Loan Pricing and Fees   223
Part 3. Making the Borrower Repay the Loan: Amortization
        and Maturity   248
Part 4. Conditioning the Loan: Conditions Precedent and
        Representations   262
Part 5. Monitoring the Loan: Financial, Affirmative, and
        Negative Covenants   291
Part 6. Securing and Guaranteeing the Loan:
        Collateral Packages   327
Part 7. Enforcing the Loan: Events of Default
        and Remedies   336

Part 8. Keeping Peace Among the Lenders: Interlender, Voting, and Agency Issues 354

Part 9. Selling the Loan: The Assignments Clause 366

Part 10. Understanding the Boilerplate: All the Stuff at the End That No One Ever Reads 373

Part 11. The Borrower Can Have Rights, Too 386

Chapter 6

The Secondary Loan Market 393
Meredith Coffey, Robert Milam, Laura Torrado, Michele B. Piorkowski

An Introduction to the U.S. Secondary Loan Market 395

How to Trade Loans and the Strategies to Use 403

The Secondary Loan Market: Settling Loan Transactions 420

Chapter 7

Secondary Market Pricing
Theodore Basta, Tom Price, Jean Cho

Loan Valuation: The Origins of Secondary Market Pricing 459

The LSTA/LPC Mark-to-Market Process: Then and Now 464

The LSTA Trade Data Study: Measuring the Accuracy of Secondary Market Prices 470

Introduction to Model Pricing 479

Historical Secondary Market Price Performance, Distributions, and Volatility 484

Price Volatility and the Daily Value at Risk 493

Chapter 8

Analytics and Performance 507
Sean Kelley, Meredith Coffey, William Deitrick, Steve Bavaria, Neal Schweitzer, David Keisman, Steve Miller, Sam DeRosa-Farag

Analytics and Performance Overview 509

Measuring Loan Returns 510

Relative Value Analysis 513

Introduction: Rating Agencies in the Loan Market   521

Standard & Poor's Loan and Recovery Ratings   526

Loan Loss Given Default: Trends to Consider   533

S&P/LSTA Leveraged Loan Index: Overview   539

Description and Inclusion Rules of the Credit Suisse
    Leveraged Loan Index   541

Credit Suisse Institutional Leveraged Loan Index   548

Leveraged Senior Loan Performance Attribution   569

Chapter 9

Distressed Loan Investing   581
*Peter T. Santry, Joe Lamport, David Isenberg,
Gregory A. Bray, William R. Wagner*

Introduction to Distressed Loan Investing   583

Securities Law Concerns Related to a Borrower's
    Bankruptcy   594

Distressed Debt Investing—Risk Considerations   602

Distressed to Recovery: A Look at the Restructuring
    Process   625

Chapter 10

Vehicles and Products Derived from the Asset Class   643
*Philip Nisbet, Richard W. Stewart, Sam DeRosa-Farag,
Mark Herzinger*

Introduction   645

Collateralized Loan Obligations: A Primer   646

Using Loan-Only CDS in the Leveraged Finance
    Markets: Implications in an Increasing Volatility
    Environment   670

Bank Loan Total Return Swap Primer   680

Chapter 11

CDOs: A Primer   709
The Bond Market Association

Chapter 12

Loan Portfolio Management   785
Michael P. McAdams, Jack Yang, Howard Tiffen, Geoffrey A. Gold

Introduction   787
Loan Investment Strategies: An Overview   793
A Retail Loan Fund Manager's Perspective   799
Portfolio Management by Nonbank Loan Investors   803
Distressed Loan Portfolios   817

Chapter 13

Legal, Regulatory, and Accounting Issues   823
*Bala Ayyar, Wayne Lee, Seth Grosshandler, Kate A. Sawyer,
John C. Pattison*

Introduction to Accounting Standards Applicable to Loans:
    A Bank's Perspective   825
FAS 140 as Applied to Assignments and Participations   834
The Loan Market and Basel 2 Regulatory
    Capital Requirements   842

Chapter 14

The Globalization of the Loan Market   859
*Meredith Coffey, Clare Dawson, Philip Cracknell, Suraj Bhatia,
Jennifer Ashe, Mike Kerrigan, Steve Curtis, Ian Sandler*

Global Loan Market Review   861
The European Syndicated Loan Market   888
The Syndicated Loan Market in the Asia-Pacific Region   898
With Limited Options in the Domestic Loan Market,
    Japanese Investors Look to the United States for
    Investment Opportunities   903
Toward a More Integrated World: The Future of the Global
    Distressed Loan Market   917

Glossary of Terms   929

Index   949

LIST OF CONTRIBUTORS

Jennifer Ashe
Vice President and Head of
Research
The Sumitomo Trust & Banking
Co. Ltd., New York Branch

Bala Ayyar
Canadian Imperial Bank of
Commerce

Tiziana M. Bason
Davis, Polk & Wardwell

Theodore Basta
Vice President, Market Data
The Loan Syndications and
Trading Association

Steven Bavaria
Vice President and Head –
Syndicated Loan & Recovery
Ratings
Standard & Poor's

Suraj Bhatia
Senior Managing Director
The Sumitomo Trust &
Banking Co. Ltd., New York
Branch

Barry Bobrow
Managing Director
Loan Syndications
Wachovia

**The Bond Market
Association**

Gregory A. Bray, Esq.
Partner
Milbank, Tweed, Hadley &
McCloy

Jean Cho
Analyst
Markit Group

Meredith Coffey
Senior Vice President
Reuters Loan Pricing
Corporation

Warren Cooke
Partner
Milbank, Tweed, Hadley &
McCloy

Philip Cracknell
Standard Chartered

Steve Curtis
Partner
Clifford Chance LLP

Clare Dawson
Loan Market Association

William Deitrick
Vice President
Citigroup Global Market Inc.

Sam DeRosa-Farag
Managing Director, Global
Leveraged Finance Strategy
Credit Suisse

Elliot Ganz
General Counsel
The Loan Syndications and
Trading Association

Geoffrey A. Gold
Partner
Strategic Value Partners

Richard Gray
Partner
Milbank, Tweed, Hadley &
McCloy

Seth Grosshandler
Cleary Gottlieb Steen and
Hamilton LLP

Marc Hanrahan
Partner
Latham & Watkins LLP

Mark Herzinger
Director
Barclays Capital

David Isenberg, Esq.
Of Counsel
Milbank, Tweed, Hadley &
McCloy

Michael P. Kaplan
Davis, Polk & Wardwell

David Keisman
Moody's Investors Services

Sean Kelley
Tall Tree Investment
Management, LLC

Mike Kerrigan
Partner
Hunton & Williams LLP

Scott D. Krase CFA
Managing Partner
Oak Hill Advisors

Joseph Lamport
Counsel and Senior Advisor
Sandelman Partners

Wayne Lee
Canadian Imperial Bank of
Commerce

Michael P. McAdams
President and CEO
Four Corners Capital
Management, LLC

Robert Milam
Vice President
JPMorgan Securities

Steve Miller
Managing Director
Standard & Poor's Leveraged
Commentary & Data

Philip Nisbet
Director
Barclays Capital

Scott Page
Portfolio Manager
Eaton Vance Management

Dawn Pasquin
Managing Director
GE Energy Financial Services

John C. Pattison
Canadian Imperial Bank of
Commerce

Michele B. Piorkowski
Associate Director
Bear Stearns & Co. Inc.

Tom Price
Director
Markit Group

Linda Redding
Wachovia

Ian Sandler
Vice President
Morgan Stanley

Peter T. Santry
Managing Director
Banc of America Securities LLC

Kate A. Sawyer
Cleary Gottlieb Steen and
Hamilton LLP

Neal Schweitzer
Moody's Investors Services

Bradley Y. Smith
Davis, Polk & Wardwell

Alex Spiro
Associate General Counsel
Bank of America

Richard W. Stewart
Managing Director and Senior
Portfolio Manager
Nomura Corporate Research
and Asset Management Inc.

Payson Swaffield
Portfolio Manager
Eaton Vance Management

Allison A. Taylor
Executive Director
The Loan Syndications and
Trading Association

Mercedes Tech
Managing Director
Syndications
Société Générale

David Teh
Associate
Latham & Watkins LLP

Howard Tiffen
Managing Director
Van Kampen Investment
Advisors

Laura Torrado
Senior Managing Director
Bear Stearns & Co. Inc.

Peter C. Vaky
SunTrust

William R. Wagner
Kaye Scholer LLP

Richard Wight
Partner
Milbank, Tweed, Hadley &
McCloy

Jack Yang
Partner
Highland Capital Management,
LP

Ruth Yang
Director
Standard & Poor's Leveraged
Commentary & Data

PREFACE

The business of corporate loan syndications, trading, & investing has changed at an astounding rate over the last fifteen years. Back then, banks would lend large amounts of money to their corporate borrowers and hold the loans on their books. Today, these loans are sold to other banks, institutional investors, mutual funds, insurance companies, structured vehicles, pension funds and hedge funds. Loans are traded, similar to equity and bonds; indices are made on the performance of loans; loans are put into structured vehicles to attract different types of investors; credit derivatives are made when loans are the underlying instrument; and loans are bought and sold around the globe.

According to Reuters Loan Pricing Corporation, new issue corporate loan volume in the US reached $1.5 trillion in 2005. That is up from $137 billion in 1988. Secondary trading volume reached $177 billion in 2005, up form $8 billion in 1991. According to Standard & Poor's, the number of vehicles managed by institutional investors of loans reached 570 in 2005, up form 32 in 1995. The corporate loan syndication and trading market has exploded since it began in the late 1980's!

There have been a few small books written about the loan market over the last 10 years, but no one has endeavored to compose a comprehensive book on the loan market as a whole. For this project, we recruited forty-seven experts within different fields of the loan market to record: the evolution of the market, give a description of basic loan structures, offer a review of the syndication process, and the Credit Agreement, and present an analysis on how loans trade and settle. We examine the risks associated with investing in loans, report on the different types of vehicles that invest in loans, provide different views of portfolio management strategies and a look at the details of investing in distressed loans. And last but certainly not least, we have published the first comprehensive glossary of terms for the loan market.

WHO ARE WE?

Formed in 1995, The Loan Syndications & Trading Association, "LSTA", is the not-for-profit trade association for the floating rate corporate loan market, dedicated to advancing the interests of the marketplace as a whole and promoting the highest degree of confidence for investors in floating rate corporate loans. The LSTA's primary goals are to promote efficiency, transparency, and liquidity of the asset class. Unlike other trade associations, the LSTA's members are buy-side and sell-side alike, along with law firms and vendors to the market. In short, any firm that has a stake in the loan market is a member of the LSTA.

BUT, WHAT DO WE REALLY DO?

LOANS ARE NOT SECURITIES! You will read that many times throughout this Handbook. As a result, there is no regulatory authority that oversees and sets standards on how loans are sold and traded throughout the financial market, Consequently, the evolution of the loan syndication and trading market, the development of market standards and documentation have been created through a consensus building process within the loan market as a whole. The LSTA is at the heart of this consensus building process. The LSTA solves problems, the LSTA creates solutions, and the LSTA is a place to band together to deal with new challenges that arise in this ever changing and growing market.

WHY DID WE TAKE ON THIS MONUMENTAL ENDEAVOR?

Due to the astounding growth of the loan market since the late 1980's, in 2004, the LSTA added "education of the loan asset class" as an additional primary objective of the Association. Today, the

LSTA educates both new investors in the asset class, as well as new employees of firms already involved in the market. We added additional conferences and seminars to our agenda, but when we looked around, there was still a hole, and this still evolving market needed a reference guide, a how-to book on how it operates and a resource tool to learn about the risks and rewards of the asset class.

In May of 2005, the LSTA Board of Directors approved the initiative to begin the process writing what is now known as The Handbook of Loan Syndications and Trading. The forty-seven authors, who volunteered their own time to be a part of this Handbook, spent countless hours writing their chapters and sub-chapters. For them, I am eternally grateful. It is our hope that MBA students, law students, analysts, investors reviewing the asset class as a potential new vehicle for investing, and new employees at firms involved with the loan product now have a comprehensive guide to the U.S. corporate loan market and that it will educate them on this not so new, exciting, rewarding alternative investment. I would like to thank my Coeditor, Alicia Sansone for the many sleepless nights she spent pouring over this manuscript. Without her, this Handbook would not be published today.

I started my career in 1981 in the credit training department of Texas Commerce Bank. In my career, I have been a lender/structurer of loans, a seller, a trader, an analyst and a champion of the development of market standards. I have seen the corporate loan market grown from a sleepy, clunky, inefficient market to one that is transparent, streamlined and efficient. Yes, there is still a lot of work to be done, but everything that we have done along with hard work and the dedication of LSTA members, is to help shape a very exciting market to which we are proud to be a part of. We have developed a market in which bond and equity investors alike are clamoring to invest. We hope that after reading this Handbook, you will understand the risks and rewards of the corporate loan market and decide to be part of this market with us.

Allison A. Taylor
Executive Director
LSTA

AKNOWLEDGMENTS

If you're reading this, then we actually did it. Wow!

The Handbook of Loan Syndications and Trading was over a year in the making, and many people were involved in its creation. The phrase "It takes a village" has taken on a whole new meaning for me.

First and foremost I have to sincerely thank the 47 contributors who spent many hours of their precious spare time writing, and rewriting this book. Your commitment, knowledge and patience were inspiring, and this book is dedicated to you.

To the 2005/2006 LSTA Board of Directors, especially my Chair Scott Krase. Thank you for trusting me with this project, and all of the encouragement along the way.

Bridget Marsh and Savitia Iyer were invaluable in helping me get the original manuscript to the publisher on time. If it weren't for you two, I would probably still be stuck on Chapter 5! Many thanks.

To Allison Taylor and the entire staff of the LSTA, you guys are troopers. When I would walk into the office after working all night, practically wearing my pajamas, and I my motto was "you're lucky I showered," you didn't run and hide. I am truly grateful for your encouragement and support. You are *all* a bunch of Smarty Pants!

Stephen Isaacs and Daina Penikas at McGraw Hill, I definitely could not have gotten through this process without your guidance. I know it's all in a day's work for you guys, but I am forever in your debt.

Thanks to my all of my friends, especially Tom, Deb, Diane, Jimmay and Jean. You put up with not seeing or hearing from me for weeks at a time, but were cheering me on none the less. See, I told you, it's a really big book!

Finally, to Maureen Sansone, my Mom and biggest fan, thanks for *everything*.

Alicia Sansone
Senior Vice President
Communications, Marketing and Education
LSTA

CHAPTER 1

An Overview of the Loan Market

Scott Page
Portfolio Manager
Eaton Vance Management

Payson Swaffield
Portfolio Manager
Eaton Vance Management

Allison A. Taylor
Executive Director
The Loan Syndications and Trading Association

Ruth Yang
Director
Standard & Poor's Leveraged Commentary & Data

Peter C. Vaky
SunTrust

Steve Miller
Managing Director
Standard & Poor's Leveraged Commentary & Data

Scott D. Krase CFA
Managing Partner
Oak Hill Advisors

Elliot Ganz
General Counsel
The Loan Syndications and Trading Association

An Introduction to the Loan Asset Class

Scott Page
Portfolio Manager
Eaton Vance Management

Payson Swaffield
Portfolio Manager
Eaton Vance Management

In the investment profession, hard facts and conclusions about risk and return are notoriously difficult to establish. Time, data, statistics, definitions, prejudice, psychology, and who knows what else can form a fog in which even well-informed observers with the best of intentions may see only what they want to see, forming their own subjective conclusions.

With these caveats as a warning, we proceed in this section to discuss the risk and return profile of the relatively new bank loan asset class as it has emerged over the past 15 or more years. We believe that when the short history of this asset class is told both in words and in numbers, a useful mosaic of risk and return emerges.

The clearest conclusion is a simple one: historically, *this asset class has had modest but solid returns, with very low volatility and relatively low correlation with most other major asset classes.* On a risk-adjusted basis, bank loans are comparatively attractive.

A SHORT HISTORY OF BANK CREDIT RISK SINCE THE 1980s

Commercial Bank Credit Culture

When we graduated from college at or near the beginning of the 1980s and entered a rather difficult job market, we began in training programs at large commercial banks, most of which ran large credit-training programs at great expense, often with hundreds of trainees and scores of fully dedicated instructors. Accounting, risk analysis, cash flow projections, legal ramifications, and many other topics were taught over the course of almost a year before young analysts were deployed in one of the many lending departments of a bank.

Each of these departments created commercial loans, the large majority of which were designed to reside on the bank's balance sheet. The loans were sometimes syndicated, typically through the correspondent banking unit, but the process was rudimentary at best, particularly when compared to today's practices. Certainly, no one was concerned with creating instruments that would trade and be valued in a market. Corporate loans were then, and had always been private, customized contracts between the bank and its customer, not an asset class to be managed using the same portfolio management techniques that are applied to stocks and bonds. Banks held credit risk on their balance sheets in large and often undiversified pools that were driven by customer relationships, profit centers, excess capital, and other non-portfolio management considerations. Despite the best efforts of credit-risk management and the techniques passed down to young analysts through credit-training programs, this type of thinking led to repetitive and noteworthy credit debacles in real estate, oil and gas, sovereign debt, and, in the 1980s, excessive leveraged buyout (LBO) loans. These crises may have, in turn, led to the misperceptions that linger even today that bank loans are intrinsically risky and commercial bankers are accident-prone.

High-Yield Bonds Emerge as an Asset Class

With growing momentum during the 1980s, Michael Milken, Drexel Burnham Lambert, and the high-yield bond market produced a not very quiet revolution on the credit front. Drexel, of course, was an investment bank and sat on the other side of the Glass-Steagel wall that separated commercial banks and their credit cultures from investment banks and their unique cultures. Although decidedly one up on commercial bankers in many ways, investment bankers up until that time were largely credit puritans, focusing on creating and trading investment grade stocks and bonds. In addition, investment banks focused primarily on blue-chip companies, with the top firms predominantly serving their mostly investment grade-rated Fortune 500 customers. The emergence of the high-yield market changed everything, filling a vacuum that had defied nature for far too long. We are not financial historians, but, having lived through it, we believe it's hard to exaggerate the importance of the high-yield market as a catalyst for change in corporate finance, and for the emergence of the bank loan asset class.

Prior to the formation of the high-yield bond market, credit risk was something to be avoided, not something to be managed. The banking system—investment or commercial—rarely created noninvestment grade securities. In the case of commercial banks, loans were relationship-driven and held on balance sheets, and no one even considered external ratings profiles or other risk labels. In secondary markets, the noninvestment grade bonds that did exist were mostly the unfortunate products of downgrades—"fallen angels" that were shunned by respectable banks and investors. It seemed that the entire point of commercial banking training and culture was to avoid risk, not manage it, and although this thinking may seen a bit delusional by today's standards, it was the norm at that time. Commercial banks took on large positions in the belief that their credit prowess, honed and taught in credit-training programs, eliminated most credit risk. Portfolio management and diversification weren't nearly as important as conducting a thorough credit analysis, writing a properly structured loan agreement, meeting profit-center goals, and building customer relationships.

The Credit Buy Side Emerges

To our knowledge, the first explicit application of basic portfolio management techniques to credit-risk assets on any scale was done by Drexel's investor clients: S&Ls, insurance companies, and, most importantly, the mutual funds that came to dominate as consumers of high-yield bonds. What we mean by portfolio management is really quite simple: objective credit analysis that is not driven by customer relationships and includes diversification by issuer and industry. High-yield bond investors founded credit-risk portfolio management, thereby creating the buy side, from which the bank loan asset class eventually emerged. When Drexel's excesses unraveled the firm in 1990, to the private pleasure of many establishment banks and bankers on whose turf Milken had dared infringe, these same bankers ironically rushed to fill the void. Commercial and investment banks recruited teams of ex-Drexel bankers, establishing their own high-yield practices. After a few lean years in the early 1990s, the high-yield bond market recovered from the excesses of the 1980s, and investor conferences once again began to fill resort hotels in Scottsdale. As the 1990s progressed, the market grew stronger each year. At many of these conferences, generally taking the form of one or two panels in a small conference room, the buy- and sell-side communities surrounding *syndicated loans*, not bonds, began to gather and take form.

LEVERAGED LOANS: A NEW ASSET CLASS

An Idea Whose Time Had Come

Many have laid claim to having created the first structures on the buy side of the bank loan asset class, and it is difficult to determine with accuracy who did what first. It was an idea whose time had come, and different institutions worked on various vehicles and structures to bring this asset class to investors. Two broad classes of investors emerged and continue to exist today: structured vehicles, primarily in the form of collateralized loan obligations (CLOs), which are generally sold to institutions; and mutual funds, which are primarily sold to individual investors. The challenges of developing and marketing these vehicles were many. Few data on the risk and return profiles of bank loans existed, and the components and structuring features that are taken for granted today were still under development, being tested through educated trial and error. There was no market pricing or pricing service, no standardized settlement procedures or documentation, and no agreed-upon procedures for structuring and capitalizing CLOs. Trading was by appointment. There were no ratings of bank loan instruments. Many banks that originated paper were wary of the developing market and were at times cool to showing new investors any loans other than their riskiest, least attractive assets.

Fortunately, the largest and most influential banks understood the mutual benefit for both the buy and sell sides of the development of this new asset class. Manufacturer's Hanover, Bankers Trust, Chemical Bank, Continental Bank, Chase Manhattan, Citibank, and a number of other important institutions embraced the development of mutual fund and CLO investors. Each year saw the creation of more investors, and the concept gained greater acceptance by all banks. The HLT regulations of the early 1990s, a reaction by the Federal Reserve Bank to commercial bank involvement in the high-yield excesses of the 1980s, made holding high-yield loans more expensive and difficult for banks and became a catalyst for the further development of the institutional market. The B term loan was created, a crucial innovation favored by issuers that relaxed the high levels of amortization generally required by commercial banks. Many commercial banks would not or could not buy B term loans, despite their popularity with borrowers, and this void increased the market's reliance on nonbank institutional investors to successfully syndicate transactions.

As the 1990s passed, each year saw the development and refinement of the numerous components required for a full institutional asset class. The Loan Syndications and Trading Association (LSTA) was formed, and it became the forum in which important issues—documentation, pricing, trading standards, settlement issues—were debated and decided. The Loan Pricing Corporation, which began providing rudimentary pricing for a select number of issues, refined and built its pricing model in conjunction with the LSTA. Though initially reluctant to do so, rating agencies, agent banks, and issuers slowly embraced the concept of assigning ratings to bank risk.

New York money-center commercial banks merged and changed—Chemical with Manufacturer's Hanover, then with Chase Manhattan (and later with JP Morgan), Bankers Trust into Deutsche Bank—yet they maintained their dedication to the growth of the syndicated bank loan market. And in 1995, even the elite private investment partnership of Goldman Sachs (which had been active in the trading of distressed debt) launched and built a full bank loan syndication and trading effort—something that would have been unthinkable five years earlier, and an event that perhaps symbolically marked the point at which there was no turning back to the traditional commercial banking model. All of these elements combined, and at an unknown moment somewhere in the mid–1990s, a new investment asset class was born.

Risk, Returns, and Bank Loans

As new investors approached this new asset class, investment managers were required to describe its potential risks and returns. Nearly all of them emphasized three key features: seniority, security/collateral, and the floating-rate nature of returns. The first two components mitigated credit risk, and the third virtually eliminated interest-rate risk. When compared to the best-known asset class with credit risk, high-yield bonds (instruments that were generally subordinated and unsecured, and that came with fixed interest rates), bank loans were clearly less risky. But by how much? After all, leveraged bank loans were noninvestment grade, so how defensive could they be? It was hard to say with any precision.

Without data, institutional investors mostly shunned the asset class, causing a "chicken and egg" dilemma that is probably common to all new investment categories. Interestingly, it was the retail investment community that first and most vigorously pursued the opportunity through broker-sold mutual funds, not analysis-driven institutional investors, who were limited by lack of data.

Default versus Recoveries

Credit-risk studies by rating agencies and academics primarily focus on one key event: default. Although the subject of credit risk is approached in many different ways, nearly all credit analysts focus on predictions and probabilities surrounding events of *default*—the inability of a company to meet the terms of its debt obligations. Until very recently, research regarding recoveries in the event of default, a natural follow-on curiosity, has been pursued with much less energy, precision, and, frankly, logic. However, an analysis of recoveries is critical because of the simple equation that credit losses equal the incidence of default multiplied by one minus the recovery rate.

The treatment of the separate phenomena of default and recovery is an issue that rating agencies wrestle with even today. For investors in senior secured bank loans, recoveries are not a secondary consideration. After all, who really cares if a borrower defaults if an investor recovers all principal and is paid interest in the process? The degree of added safety created by seniority and security were the subject of debate as the asset class took full form. Data tracking recoveries were lacking, and even now are not definitive or clear, as the information relies heavily on investor experience and anecdotes. The degree of defense offered by a bank loan's seniority, security, and other protective features was then, and to some extent still is, in the eye of the beholder. Undoubtedly, the first investors in the asset class were experienced in and optimistic about the advantages of seniority and security in default recoveries.

Enterprise Value, Hard Collateral, and Bankruptcy

Early on, one of the most significant open questions about bank loans concerned the treatment of senior, secured classes in bankruptcy and reorganization. The answer to this question would heavily affect bankruptcy outcomes. Bankruptcies and out-of-court restructurings were nothing new to the financial landscape. What was new was the growing number of noninvestment grade companies that had been formed by the deliberate use of high-yield bonds, leveraged loans, and private equity. The default cycle in the late 1980s produced little transparent information about bank loan default and recovery, as the data had been cloaked by bank balance sheets and/or held tight by the nascent distressed bank debt community. Perhaps the data existed, but knowledge of the advantages of seniority and security was not widespread.

In addition, as the 1990s unfolded, deals were being structured with greater reliance on a new type of collateral that was not in the form of hard assets—accounts receivable, inventory, property/plant/equipment—but was in the more abstract form of enterprise value. Although a few wise souls may have predicted the outcome, one that is obvious only in retrospect, the enterprise value of firms in the growing service economy had never been tested on a large scale as collateral in the courts, and there was uncertainty. Had bankruptcy judges used their considerable discretion to rule against this form of collateral, the value of seniority and security in many loan agreements would have been greatly diminished, and the advantages of this asset class would have been diluted. Fortunately, as events unfolded, enterprise value was deemed highly significant in bankruptcy and restructuring situations. It's a useful reminder, however, that there was a time when the recognition of enterprise value was not a foregone conclusion in the minds of many investment managers.

RISK AND RETURN IN BANK LOANS: A HISTORICAL REVIEW OF THE NUMBERS

> *Conclusion:* The bank loan asset class is defensive, with modest yet solid returns and very low volatility, especially when compared to high-yield bonds and many other fixed income asset classes. Supporting data: risk versus return charts and Sharpe ratios. See Exhibits 1.1 and 1.2.
>
> *Conclusion:* As an asset class, bank loans have low correlations with most other major investment asset classes, creating a powerful instrument for dampening volatility in broader portfolios. Supporting data: correlation statistics. See Exhibit 1.3.

EXHIBIT 1.1

Bank loans: risk versus return compared to other major asset class indices. Bank loans have modest but solid returns and low volatility.

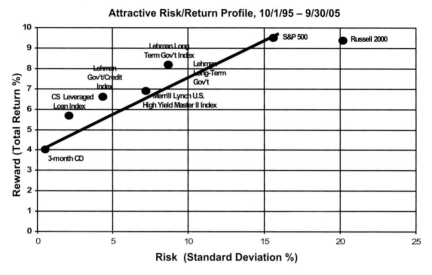

Source: Standard & Poor's Micropal, CS, Bloomberg.

EXHIBIT 1.2

Bank loans: Sharpe ratio compared to that for other major asset class indices. Bank loans have modest, stable returns, with an attractive Sharpe ratio over the last 10 years.

	10 Years Ending 9/30/05		
	Return	Risk (SD)	Sharpe Ratio
CS Leveraged Loan Index	5.67	2.14	0.93
Lehman Govt Credit Index	6.59	4.38	0.66
3-month CD	4.00	0.54	0.59
Lehman Long-Term Govt Index	8.18	8.70	0.52
Merrill Lynch High-Yield Master II	6.88	7.22	0.44
S&P 500 Composite	9.49	15.63	0.37
Russell 2000 Small Stocks Index	9.37	20.19	0.28

Source: Standard & Poor's Micropal, CS, Bloomberg.

Conclusion: Defaults come in waves, concentrated with regard to both time and industry. Average default rates are not as meaningful as peak default rates. In general, the episodic nature of credit losses and recoveries wreaks havoc

EXHIBIT 1.3

Bank loans: correlation with other major asset class indices. Low or negative correlations enhance risk-reduction benefit when loans can be combined with other asset classes in large portfolios.

Monthly Return Correlation Matrix 1/1992–9/2005

	3-Month Treasury Bill	1-Year Treasuries	5-Year Treasuries	10-Year Treasuries	30-Year Treasuries	High-Grade Corporate Bonds	High-Yield Corporate Bonds	S&P 500	Bank Loans
3-Month Treasury Bill	1.00	0.52	0.10	0.06	0.04	0.03	-0.08	0.09	0.04
1-Year Treasuries		1.00	0.71	0.60	0.47	0.57	0.01	-0.01	-0.16
5-Year Treasuries			1.00	0.96	0.86	0.86	0.03	-0.09	-0.16
10-Year Treasuries				1.00	0.92	0.88	0.06	-0.10	-0.13
30-Year Treasuries					1.00	0.88	0.17	-0.02	-0.06
High-Grade Corporate Bonds						1.00	0.42	0.15	0.07
High-Yield Corporate Bonds							1.00	0.49	0.49
S&P 500								1.00	0.14
Bank Loans									1.00

1. Correlations based on monthly returns for each category from 1/1991 through 9/30/05.

2. High-grade corporate bonds represented by the Lehman Brothers Credit Index.

3. High-yield corporate bonds represented by Merrill Lynch High-Yield Master II.

4. Bank loans represented by the CS Leveraged Loan Index.

5. It is not possible to invest directly in an index. Past performance does not predict future results.

Source: Standard & Poor's Micropal, Eaton Vance, Bloomberg.

EXHIBIT 1.4

Bank loan defaults versus high-yield bond defaults. Like defaults on high-yield bonds, bank loan defaults tend to be concentrated by time; there are short, intense credit storms offset by longer periods of relative calm.

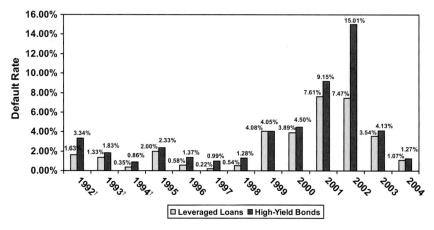

Defaulted loans defined as missed coupon, filed for Chapter 11, distressed exchange, or cross-defaults. *Semiannual default rate annualized.
†Estimate based on overall leveraged loan market cross defaults with high-yield bonds.

Source: CS, Moody's Investors Service.

with investment statistics, numbers that require higher-than-normal caution when interpreting. Supporting data: default data by year and by industry. See Exhibits 1.4 and 1.5.

Conclusion: Credit spreads in the bank loan market ebb and flow, but vary within a much narrower range than spreads in the high-yield bond market. Supporting data: history of bank loan spreads versus high-yield spreads. See Exhibit 1.6.

Conclusion: There are numerous ways of measuring and estimating annual credit losses in this asset class. The exact numbers depend on management style and skill, market entry and exit timing, and a number of other factors. When the actual credit experiences of a variety of public mutual fund managers, measured over various periods, are averaged into theoretical estimates from rating agency default/loss data and idealized loss studies, we believe that the best overall average estimate is approximately 60 basis points of annual credit loss. Variations from this point estimate can be considerable, driven most powerfully by market timing and investment style, but this estimate provides a starting point

EXHIBIT 1.5

Industry default data. Defaults on bank loans, like defaults on high-yield bonds, tend to be concentrated in specific industries.

	1995	1996	1997	1998	1999	2000	2001	2002	2003	2004	Average	Cumulative
Aerospace	0.0%	0.0%	0.0%	0.0%	0.0%	2.1%	0.0%	0.0%	2.3%	0.0%	0.4%	0.6%
Chemicals	0.0%	0.0%	0.0%	0.0%	0.0%	5.5%	0.4%	6.7%	0.0%	3.5%	1.6%	2.8%
Consumer durables	0.0%	0.0%	0.0%	0.0%	0.4%	0.0%	2.0%	0.0%	0.0%	0.0%	0.2%	0.6%
Consumer nondurables	0.0%	0.0%	0.0%	0.0%	3.1%	10.1%	6.3%	7.3%	2.8%	5.6%	3.5%	6.0%
Energy	0.0%	22.5%	0.0%	0.0%	0.0%	0.0%	0.0%	0.0%	0.0%	0.0%	2.3%	0.1%
Financials	0.0%	0.0%	0.0%	0.0%	0.0%	2.1%	0.0%	0.0%	0.0%	0.0%	0.2%	0.3%
Food and drug	15.0%	0.0%	0.0%	49.0%	0.0%	10.4%	0.0%	0.0%	8.6%	0.0%	8.3%	3.1%
Food/tobacco	0.0%	0.0%	0.0%	0.0%	5.2%	4.4%	2.6%	1.4%	6.4%	24.8%	4.5%	4.9%
Forest products	0.0%	0.0%	0.0%	2.0%	0.0%	1.9%	0.0%	0.0%	0.0%	0.0%	0.4%	0.3%
Gaming/leisure	0.0%	0.0%	0.0%	0.0%	0.0%	0.0%	8.3%	0.0%	0.0%	0.0%	0.8%	2.2%
Heath care	0.0%	0.0%	0.0%	6.1%	58.7%	12.4%	6.8%	0.7%	6.3%	0.0%	9.1%	11.3%
Housing	0.0%	0.0%	0.0%	0.0%	1.3%	0.0%	0.5%	1.8%	0.0%	0.0%	0.4%	0.7%
Information technology	40.1%	0.0%	0.0%	0.0%	6.0%	0.8%	7.2%	0.2%	11.6%	0.0%	6.6%	4.7%
Manufacturing	0.0%	0.0%	0.0%	0.0%	3.6%	2.9%	5.5%	6.3%	4.9%	0.0%	2.3%	4.5%
Media/telecom	0.0%	77.5%	0.0%	0.0%	16.5%	13.8%	37.5%	55.3%	31.7%	53.6%	28.6%	36.4%
Metals/mining	0.0%	0.0%	0.0%	42.9%	0.0%	4.3%	0.5%	3.2%	4.3%	8.6%	6.4%	3.2%
Retail	44.9%	0.0%	100.0%	0.0%	0.0%	0.0%	6.5%	0.0%	2.8%	0.0%	15.4%	2.7%
Service	0.0%	0.0%	0.0%	0.0%	1.2%	22.8%	10.4%	11.1%	11.7%	0.0%	5.7%	10.2%
Transport	0.0%	0.0%	0.0%	0.0%	4.1%	6.6%	5.6%	6.0%	0.0%	4.0%	2.6%	4.6%
Utility	0.0%	0.0%	0.0%	0.0%	0.0%	0.0%	0.0%	0.0%	6.7%	0.0%	0.7%	0.9%

Source: CS.

E X H I B I T   1 . 6

Risk versus return for major bank loan mutual funds. Bank loan spreads vary within a much narrower range than high-yield bond spreads.

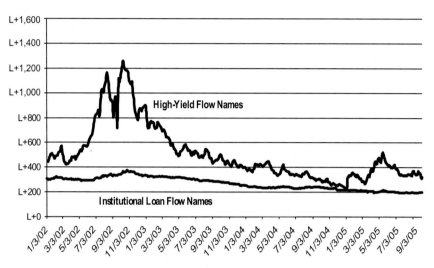

Average spreads of high-yield and institutional loan flow names. Loan spreads are spread to Maturity; HY spreads are spread to worst until 8/12/04, option-adjusted spreads thereafter, reverse swapped. Discounted spread is spread to maturity based on the bid level and stated amortization.

Source: Standard & Poor's LCD, Merrill Lynch High-Yield Index.

on which to base expectations. Of course, the future could be very different, but that's the basic experience so far, plus or minus.

Observation: The advantages of seniority and security are significant, but the statistics supporting this conclusion are weak. We have seen all kinds of numbers over the years, but reliability is difficult given measurement errors, apples/oranges-type data sets (for instance, senior, secured securities such as first mortgage bonds versus senior, secured bank loans), varying definitions of recovery, and other suspicious flaws in data. There may be clean numbers out there, but from what we have found thus far, the results are inconclusive. We have seen some studies that claim that recoveries are 100 percent and others that claim 50 percent. Based on our experience, we believe that senior secured recoveries applicable for the relevant range of bank debt used in most mutual funds and CLOs vary between 60 and 80 percent, with the best estimate of recoveries through a full cycle being approximately 70 percent.

Observation: Default probabilities increase geometrically as ratings decline into B/B2 and B-/B3 territory (or further), and generally there is not sufficient additional coupon to compensate for the much higher default risk *unless* (1) recoveries in the event of default are strong, and/or (2) investors hang tight through a downturn to experience the rebound on the other side. Interpreting the data supporting this observation is complex, and this is perhaps the most central debate among investors in all high-yield instruments (both bonds and bank loans). It is beyond the scope of this section to resolve this debate, other than to point out our belief that in the bank loan universe, at the very least, enhancing stability achieves more than chasing yield. The rolling, gentle, more predictable statistical topography of the more stable end of the bank loan asset class is one that most investors find preferable to the sudden, sharp peaks and valleys of the more aggressive end. But the debate is a worthy one, and in the end it remains a matter of investor preference. A talented credit manager and an investor with able market-timing skills and some guts can do well in the riskiest loans, evidenced perhaps best by the very strong results experienced by distressed bank loan investors in 2003. Supporting data: lots, but we will leave it to the Ph.D.s to sort out.

Observation: Various investment managers with public track records have approached this asset class quite differently, with results that vary widely. In the mutual fund arena, defensive managers who have moderate volatility relative to the index have better long-term results on a risk-adjusted basis. Mutual funds experience withdrawals during market declines, and aggressive funds that perform poorly in bear markets experience greater withdrawals. These withdrawals can negatively affect an investor's experience through the usual whipsaw of buy high and sell low. Supporting data: risk versus return charts, Sharpe ratios, and mutual fund flows. See Exhibits 1.7, 1.8, and 1.9.

Observation: The measurement techniques used by Lipper and Morningstar in the mutual fund arena, which highlight returns more clearly than risk, may push managers into

EXHIBIT 1.7

Bank loan mutual funds, five- and seven-year risk versus return. Added return requires significant increases in risk/volatility.

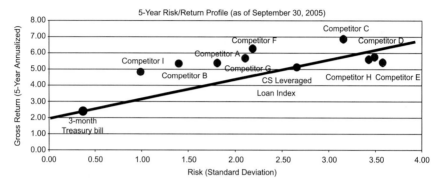

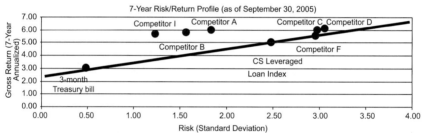

Competitor universe established by searching the Morningstar Datalab Bank Loan fund Universe for public funds with 5-year track records. For fund complexes with multiple share classes, the class B share product was selected. Specific performance experiences will vary. This information is for illustrative purposes only and sould not be considered investment advice or a recommendation to buy or sell any particular security. It is not possible to invest in an index. Past performance does not predict future results.

Source: Morningstar Datalab, CS, Eaton Vance.

taking greater credit risk. The episodic nature of credit risk, with short but intense down cycles and declining mutual fund net asset values (NAVs), combined with the usually much longer bull or calm portions of the credit cycle, has a tendency to tempt many risk managers to taking on greater risk. In other words, credit conditions are typically stable most of the time, and a manager will seek to gain yield and total return by taking on more risk, even unreasonable risk, which will move the manager up in Lipper's quintile rankings and gain Morningstar stars. These rankings will face sharp reversals during credit downturns, and some investors will suffer even more because of the whipsaw effect of fearfully withdrawing funds at market bottoms.

EXHIBIT 1.8

Sharpe ratios for major bank loan mutual funds. Sharpe ratios favor bank loan portfolios that stabilize risk relative to the index.

Name	5-Year Annualized Return (Gross)	5-Year Risk (SD)	5-Year Sharpe Ratio
Competitor I	4.80	0.99	2.53
Competitor B	5.32	1.40	2.16
Competitor A	5.36	1.81	1.69
Competitor G	5.65	2.11	1.59
Competitor F	6.26	2.19	1.81
Competitor J	5.12	2.66	1.06
CS Index	5.12	2.66	1.06
Competitor C	6.85	3.16	1.44
Competitor H	5.61	3.43	0.97
Competitor D	5.74	3.49	0.99
Competitor E	5.39	3.58	0.86

Competitor universe established by searching the Morningstar Datalab Bank Loan fund Universe for public funds with 5-year track records. For fund complexes with multiple share classes, the class B share product was selected. Specific performance experiences will vary. This information is for illustrative purposes only and sould not be considered investment advice or a recommendation to buy or sell any particular security. It is not possible to invest in an index. Past performance does not predict future results.

Source: Standard & Poor's Micropal, CS, Bloomberg.

EXHIBIT 1.9

Bank loan mutual fund assets under management. Investors withdrew funds from bank loan mutual funds during the 2001–2003 market downturn. Risk-seeking (versus the index) managers experienced greater withdrawals than risk-stabilizing managers.

	Total	Risk	Risk	
	Assets under Management $B	Stabilizing	Seeking	New
1996	$ 11.0	$ 2.3	$ 8.6	
1997	$ 13.9	$ 3.4	$ 10.5	
1998	$ 17.4	$ 4.8	$ 12.6	
1999	$ 23.4	$ 8.2	$ 15.2	
2000	$ 25.5	$ 9.5	$ 16.0	
2001	$ 23.8	$ 9.8	$ 14.0	
2002	$ 18.2	$ 7.9	$ 10.3	
2003	$ 14.2	$ 7.1	$ 7.1	
2004	$ 19.9	$ 10.3	$ 9.4	$ 0.2
2005	$ 30.1	$ 13.7	$ 13.9	$ 2.5
Bear-market drop in assets under management (2000–2003)	−44%	−25%	−56%	
Bull-market increase (2003–2005)	112%	93%	96%	

Source: Eaton Vance.

EXHIBIT 1.10

CLO assets under management as a percent of the total market. CLOs have grown more than mutual funds as consumers of primary syndicated bank loans.

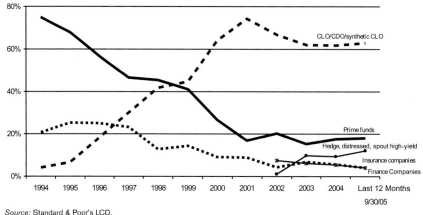

Source: Standard & Poor's LCD.

Observation: CLOs are generally structured to survive market declines, and most of them survived the sharp downturn in 2001 and 2002. Since investors cannot withdraw funds from CLOs during market declines unless structures are breached—a rare occurrence—and since CLOs are a significant and growing percentage of the asset class, the presence of CLOs is a stabilizing influence on the asset class, particularly during market declines. See Exhibit 1.10.

RISK AND RETURN IN BANK LOANS: THE NARRATIVE

In terms of risk and return, the bank loan asset class has been a success, at least so far. The advantages of seniority, security, and the floating-rate interest profile have attracted both institutional and retail investors in size. Although noninvestment grade, the asset class has proven to be quite stable, especially when compared to high-yield bonds. The asset class experienced its first real credit test in 2001 and 2002, and passed.

The Time Line of Risk/Return in Bank Loans

The decade of the 1990s started with high interest rates and quite stable credit markets. Although default tables show significant defaults in 1990 and 1991, weak credits remaining from the late 1980s LBO binge, these were well-identified and easy to avoid when the first bank loan funds were started. For most of the decade, defaults were extremely low, and the period proved an attractive one for bank loan investors. The only negative was the slow and relentless decline in interest rates, which progressed in fits and starts across the decade.

The late 1990s, starting say in 1997, saw significant weakening of credit standards in both the high-yield and bank loan markets, primarily through the creation of large exposures to technology and telecommunications companies with significant negative cash flow and poor collateral coverage. There were small wobbles in 1998 and 1999 with the Asia debt crisis and defaults of nursing home issuers. But these were small in comparison to what was to follow. Technology and telecommunications companies defaulted on bonds and loans in 2001 and 2002, creating a default and loss cycle larger than any seen since the Great Depression of the 1930s. This difficult period was followed quickly by large fraud-related defaults, most of which were by investment grade companies (Enron, WorldCom, and so on), that tested liquidity across debt markets and compounded the difficulties created by the technology and telecommunications defaults.

The First Credit Test

Given that all bank loan mutual funds started after the credit default cycle of the late 1980s and early 1990s, 2001 and 2002 were the first real tests for the bank loan market. The market passed. Mutual fund investors, perhaps lulled into a false sense that bank loan funds contained little or no credit risk because of the stability of NAVs during the 1990s, reacted to the volatility of 2001 and 2002 by withdrawing funds. Mutual funds that were more aggressively positioned had the largest NAV declines and experienced the largest withdrawals. Still, even the most aggressively positioned bank loan funds had negative total returns that were significantly less than those for high-yield bond funds. More conservative funds weathered the downturn with positive total returns throughout.

CLOs, vehicles that are leveraged 8 to 12 times, also largely survived the downturn. Although market-value funds experienced some instability as the market struggled to find levels at which to price risk during the cycle, cash flow CLOs that did not have market-value tests survived the period. The strength of CLOs during this period stood in stark contrast to the experience of investors in collateralized bond obligations (CBOs), vehicles that invested primarily in high-yield bonds. CBOs were not structured to survive a severe credit downturn, and many did not. Those that survived did so with significant damage to investors.

The Rebound of 2003

Following the downturn, 2003 was an extraordinary year in the bank loan market. Although many of the technology and telecommunication loans created realized losses that would never be recovered, the overall market, which had traded down in sympathy, did recover. Aggressively positioned bank loan mutual funds, many of which became even more aggressive as they met redemptions, snapped back and provided annual returns in 2003 that sometimes exceeded 20 percent. More conservatively positioned funds, which had probably resized their positions as their portfolios declined in size with redemptions, enjoyed less robust snapbacks, but they hadn't experienced as much of a decline in 2001 and 2002. Perhaps the most important development during the 2001–2003 period was the success of investors in distressed bank loans. Distressed loan investors, through dedicated private funds or general credit hedge funds, were aggressive buyers of senior, secured bank loans during 2001 and 2002, and their investments provided a handsome return during 2003. These funds bet on the advantages of seniority and security, and these successful and often debt-financed bets were the cornerstone of many of the legendary hedge fund returns experienced during 2003. The success of these investments may create better secondary market support for bank loans during the next credit decline.

The Current Market

Bank loans are now an official asset class that is attracting attention. They have moved from being private instruments created for the balance sheets of banks to being an asset class that is comparable to many others used in asset allocation models by both institutions and individuals. Strong Sharpe ratios and attractive low or negative correlations have made bank loans into perhaps the strongest risk-reduction asset class available in the capital markets. That is, if you build an asset allocation model; insert the risk, return, and correlation of most of the major asset classes; and start dialing back portfolio risk, the model will invariably pick bank loans as the most effective way to reduce volatility. Institutions have definitely taken notice and have increased their exposure to this investment class through CLOs, other leveraged vehicles, and separately managed accounts. Retail investors investing through mutual funds have maintained their interest in this asset class, and inflows in 2004 and 2005 have more than offset the 2001 to 2003 outflows.

Increased awareness of the virtues of bank loans has come at a cost, however. Spreads today have narrowed across the risk spectrum and are at historic lows. Although spreads now are only modestly below the levels experienced during the early and mid–1990s, they are significantly below the unusually wide spreads seen during the late 1990s and certainly during the credit crunch in 2001 and 2002. While it may be difficult to distinguish the normal ebb and flow of credit spreads through a credit cycle from a potential secular decline in spreads caused by greater familiarity with and interest in the asset class, there is probably an element of the latter. Once again, investment managers' ability to draw the line on risk is likely to be tested, although the results will not be known until the next credit downturn.

[Scott Page and Payson Swaffield are portfolio managers in Eaton Vance Management's bank loan group. The views and opinions expressed herein represent those of the above individuals as of the date hereof, and not necessarily those of EVM as a firm. This information is for illustrative purposes only and is not intended as investment advice or a recommendation to purchase or sell specific securities and may change at any time without prior notice. It should not be assumed that any of the strategies, securities, sectors, or industries listed were or will be profitable. Past performance does not predict future results.]

Evolution of the Primary and Secondary Leveraged Loan Markets

Allison A. Taylor
Executive Director, The Loan Syndications and Trading Association

Ruth Yang
Director, Standard & Poor's Leveraged Commentary & Data

AN ALTERNATIVE INVESTMENT CLASS

Leveraged loans are a unique alternative investment class because they carry a distinctly different risk/reward profile from traditional fixed income securities or equities, but have primary and secondary marketplaces that are far more efficient and liquid than many other alternative investment classes, such as private equity. As a result, investors use loans not only to diversify existing portfolios of equities and fixed-income investments, but also to build an array of investment vehicles, including collateralized loan obligations (CLOs) and collateralized debt obligations (CDOs) as well as loan funds available to both institutional investors and the retail market. Over the past decade, the leveraged loan market has grown significantly, not only in the United States, but also in Europe, and markets such as Latin America, Asia, and Eastern Europe have also begun to show signs of increasing activity.

What, then, are leveraged loans? They are a subset of the broad corporate loan universe consisting of loans that are speculative-grade (rated below BBB-) and usually syndicated among a group of bank and nonbank lenders. As speculative-grade instruments, leveraged loans are riskier instruments at the lower end of the ratings scale and thus are "high-yield" instruments, bearing interest rates higher than their safer investment grade counterparts. Since these are syndicated instruments, a single lender does not bear the entire risk of the loan, but rather a group, or syndicate, of lenders funds the borrower's needs.

Lenders take part in a syndicated loan through one of two methods: an assignment or a participation. In an assignment, the buyer becomes the direct lender of record and is entitled to all voting privileges of the other lenders of record. In a participation, the buyer takes a share of an existing lender's loan; participants generally do not have full voting rights. Participations can be riskier in times of credit stress, as the participant does not have a direct claim on the loan. In this case, the participant becomes a creditor of the lender and often must wait for claims to be sorted out to collect on its participations. (For further details, see Steve Miller's section, "Basic Loan Structures," in Chapter 3.) Investors in leveraged loans, however, engage in both assignments and participations because loans have an appealing risk/return investment profile. They not only provide a healthy interest income return but also have a high average recovery level in the case of default.

Leveraged loans are a floating rate asset class whose base rate, generally the London Inter-Bank Offered Rate (LIBOR), is usually reset at least every quarter and therefore keeps pace with changing interest rates. Additionally, the high-yield nature of these loans boosts that LIBOR income with an additional spread of 150 basis points or more.

Loans are also usually fully secured by the assets of the company, in addition to carrying covenant protection. As a result, in case of bankruptcy, the buyer of a leveraged loan will generally get most, if not all, of its money back. The covenant protection also allows the lenders to a troubled borrower to monitor and reset the conditions of the loan along the way if covenants are breached. As a result, investors find the asset class a much safer investment than, for example, high-yield bonds, which are primarily unsecured, do not provide meaningful covenant protection, and are interest-rate-sensitive.

ORIGINS OF THE PRIMARY MARKET

Corporate loans broadly support a variety of projects ranging from funding working capital needs to providing acquisition financing. Along with bonds and equity, they are one of the three legs of the corporate capital tripod. Banks, historically, have originated loans to companies, and to this day they remain the primary source of funds for corporations borrowing money through loans. However, syndicated loans have grown to the point where banks can syndicate, or sell off, pieces of loans to other banks or financial institutions as attractive forms of investment. Today, we refer to this form of financing as the *syndicated loan market*.

Many people believe that the syndicated loan market originated with the mound of debt issued by corporations during the 1980s. Robust economic activity at that time provided a great bull market, not only for the stock market, but also for the corporate loan market. Large, national money-center banks happily facilitated the symbiotic relationship between corporations hungry for loans and banks eager to lend. Loan underwriting and syndication grew on an unprecedented scale to fuel corporate expansion in response to the economic growth of that decade.

Acquisition financing, in particular, reached new heights in the latter part of the 1980s. No single bank could afford to underwrite and carry the large amount of debt necessary to support the new corporate grail—the leveraged buyout. As a result, banks sought to increase their profits but limit their risk by simultaneously underwriting larger dollar amount of loans and then syndicating those same loans, thus diversifying their portfolios. Loan syndication was not new to the banks, however. In fact, they had been selling corporate loans for years.

Evidence of this activity can be seen as early as the late 1970s. Penn Square Bank of Oklahoma's activities at that time have the dubious honor of being the predecessor of pre–1980 syndicated lending. While this was not one of the market's more celebrated events, it was one of the most memorable. Beginning in 1978, Penn Square Bank sold loans, primarily oil and gas loans, to other banks, including Continental Illinois and Chase Manhattan, in the form of loan participations. By early 1982, Penn Square had sold loan participations to a total of 53 different banks. The total amount of loan participations sold is unknown; however the FDIC believes that the amount exceeded $2.1 billion,[1] contrasting sharply with the $520 million in assets that the bank recorded on its books in mid–1982. Though improper loan documentation contributed to Penn Square Bank's demise on July 5, 1982, there is no doubt that its loan participation sales represented some of the market's earliest forays into syndicated lending.

The advent of acquisition financing in the 1980s fostered the development of large corporate loans with interest rates higher than the market had previously seen. These higher interest rates produced higher returns for investors, attracting traditional bond and equity investors such as credit corporations, insurance companies, and leasing companies. Retail mutual fund companies also began to structure funds solely for investing in corporate loans. Pilgrim Prime Rate Trust,[2] started in 1988, was the first mutual fund of this kind. These nonbank buyers increased demand for leveraged loan products, thereby enabling the larger agent banks to underwrite and distribute increasingly bigger loans.

As the number of institutional buyers of corporate loans began to grow, so did their appetite for a more liquid, transparent, and

---

[1] Federal Deposit and Insurance Corporation, *Managing the Crisis: The FDIC and RTC Experience* (Washington, D.C.: FDIC, 1998), p. 527.
[2] Pilgrim Prime Rate Trust is now ING Prime Rate Trust (NYSE: PPR). ING's predecessor business acquired the fund from Pilgrim Corp. in April 1995. It was also the first NYSE-listed loan fund (May 1992) and the first loan fund to utilize leverage for investment purposes (May 1996).

effective secondary market. During the 1990s, the secondary market for loans slowly began to mature into a much more efficient market. In 1995, the industry established a trade association to set guidelines for this growing market: the Loan Syndications and Trading Association (LSTA). The confluence of these events—a growing investor base and the establishment of market standards for practices—allowed the leveraged loan market to mature dramatically over the past nearly 20 years in the United States, and, today, the asset class continues to adapt and grow, both domestically and abroad.

DEVELOPMENT OF THE SECONDARY MARKET

Over the past decade, corporate credit markets have grown dramatically, but the growth of the corporate loan market has dominated that of markets for other asset classes. In 1994, at $389 billion[3] and $306 billion,[4] respectively, the primary issuances for the corporate loan and bond markets were about evenly sized. Today, however, corporate loan issuance is more than double that of corporate bonds. In 2005, the corporate bond market experienced an estimated $681 billion in primary issuance, approximately 2.2 times 1994's levels, while the corporate loan market had nearly double that amount: $1,648 billion in volume, 4.2 times its 1994 level. Leveraged loans have made a significant contribution to that growth (see Exhibit 1.11).

In 1998, primary volume for leveraged loans was $256 billion,[5] 30 percent of the corporate loan amount and 36 percent of the corporate bond amount for that year. In 2005, with $297 billion of issuance, leveraged loans' share of U.S. corporate loans had declined to 18 percent, but had grown to 44 percent of the corporate bond market. Clearly, corporate borrowers have taken advantage of the opportunities afforded them by this asset class.

However, the rapid development of the secondary market for syndicated loans has provided the most significant impetus to the maturation of this asset class. The secondary market has afforded

---

[3] Loan Pricing Corporation, "U.S. Lead Arranger League Tables," Jan. 17, 2006, http://www.loanpricing.com/analytics/league_table_us.htm.

[4] Thompson Financial Securities Data, "Corporate Issuance—High Yield and Investment Grade Monthly," Jan. 19, 2006, http://www.bondmarkets.com/story.asp?id=97.

[5] Standard & Poor's Leveraged Commentary & Data, "Leveraged Lending Review 4Q05."

E X H I B I T   1 . 1 1

Primary volume for corporate loans and bonds (in billions of dollars).

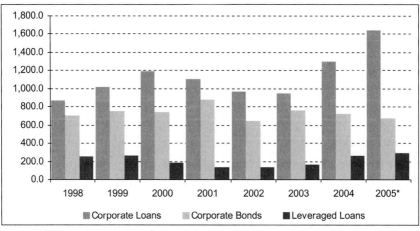

* Corporate bond volume reflects data through 11/30/05 annualized to a full year estimate.

Source: Loan Pricing Corporation (corporate loans), Thomson Financial Securities Data (corporate bonds), Standard & Poor's LCD (leveraged loans).

the opportunity for growth in the investor base, leading to innovation in the vehicles, including providing access to the retail investor. The healthy secondary market has allowed for the development of portfolio management tools, along with heightened transparency and increased informational efficiency. The development and rise of the secondary market for loans has been a significant contributor to the market as a whole because loan investors, banks and nonbanks alike, need liquidity. Liquidity is an essential tool of portfolio management. Without liquidity, portfolio managers would not be able to manage the credit-risk profiles of their portfolios.

The origins of the secondary market are difficult to determine; it is clear, however, that the presence of the secondary market did not lag long behind the primary. In 1991, the Loan Pricing Corporation estimated that there was $8 billion of secondary trading activity in loans. By 1998, this amount had grown nearly tenfold to $77.6 billion, and in 2005 it is estimated to top $170 billion (see Exhibit 1.12). A significant part of that growth came from the distressed market; that segment's development exemplifies the ability of this market to adapt to changing credit climates.

EXHIBIT 1.12

Secondary volume (in billions of dollars).

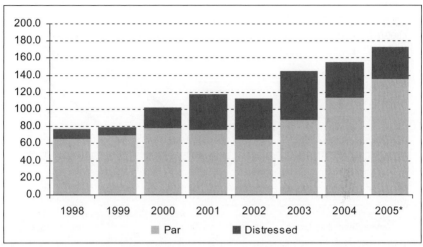

* 2005 volume reflects data through 9/30/05 annualized to a full year estimate.

Source: Loan Pricing Corporation.

The credit default cycle that started in late 1999 resulted in a deluge of paper from companies in default and bankruptcy entering secondary market. In 1997, according to Standard & Poor's research, speculative-grade credits experienced a default rate of 2.0 percent. In 1998 and 1999, this rate spiked to 5.5 percent and 5.8 percent, respectively. In 2001, however, the rate hit a nearly record high of 9.6 percent, closely followed by 2002's 9.1 percent.[6] A less-sophisticated secondary market would have ground to a halt in the face of this deluge of distressed paper. The leveraged loan market, however, continued to maintain its pace and even grow in the face of this development as distressed loan players stepped up to take advantage of the new opportunities afforded to them at that time.

Despite this recession and a historic default cycle, both the primary and the secondary loan markets have grown exponentially over the past decade. And while primary issuance is greater than secondary volume in terms of pure dollar amounts, growth rates for the secondary market have clearly dominated those for the primary. Today, the corporate loan market is approximately 80 percent

---

[6] Diane Vazza and Devi Aurora, "Quarterly Default Update and Rating Transitions," *Standard & Poor's Ratings Direct,* Nov. 1, 2002, pp. 1–2.

EXHIBIT 1.13

Volume growth of primary and secondary markets (base
date of 1998).

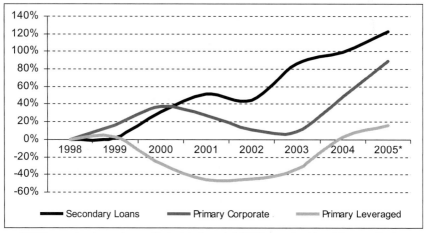

Secondary Loans   Primary Corporate   Primary Leveraged

*2005 secondary loan volume reflects data through 9/30/05 annualized to a full year estimate.

Source: Loan Pricing Corporation (secondary loans and primary corporate), Standard & Poor's LCD (primary leveraged).

larger than it was in 1998, and the leveraged markets have rebounded from their 2001–2002 default cycle lows. However, secondary
volume has more than doubled since 1998. See Exhibit 1.13.

The investor base for corporate loans has similarly grown and
diversified over the last decade. Banks used to be the dominant
buyers and holders of corporate loans, but today, institutional
investors are the primary funding source for leveraged loans. In
1994, banks (both domestic and foreign) purchased 71 percent of
the leveraged loans in the primary market, but over the next
decade, their share shrank to 30 percent and institutional investors
came to represent the lion's share of investment activity. As institutional investors rose in the ranks, however, banks did not exit
from the relationship. Their role in the market changed from pure
loan originators to arrangers and traders/dealers of loans.

The changing role of banks greatly facilitated the development of the secondary market. Back in the late 1980s, banks
focused almost exclusively on their role as originators because they
were reluctant, or even forbidden, to take the principal risk
required for trading loans. Instead, any secondary trading was bro-
kered; it was a negotiated transfer between a buyer and a seller and
did not require the broker to carry inventory or take principal risk.

In the early 1990s, banks began to establish trading groups that could hold inventory and take positions in names, thereby creating a significantly more liquid and active secondary market for loans. While brokers remain active in today's secondary loan market, traders are now the dominant players. Today, more than 30 institutions have full-time resources dedicated to loan trading activity—a significant growth over the estimated dozen of a decade ago.

This growth in secondary market activity is particularly notable in light of the fact that loans are not securities, but rather private placement instruments, which normally are extremely awkward to trade efficiently in a secondary market. For institutional investors, however, Rule 144a of the Securities Act of 1993 breaks down many of the barriers to efficient secondary market activity and greatly facilitates resale activity among that class of investors. As a result, these investors could help to build up secondary liquidity, which in turn also increased the appeal of leveraged loans as a viable alternative investment class. In 1997, approximately 40 institutional managers invested in leveraged loans, with approximately 1.6 vehicles per manager (64 vehicles). Less than 10 years later, the manager count has grown fivefold, and those managers oversee almost double the number of vehicles. In 2005, 225 managers participated in the leveraged market, with an average of 2.5 vehicles per manager (571 vehicles). See Exhibit 1.14.

EXHIBIT 1.14

Growth in institutional investors.

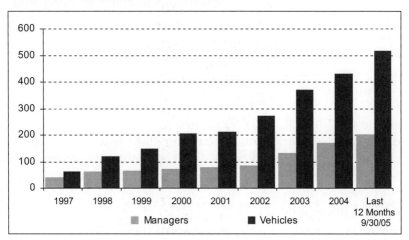

Source: Standard & Poor's LCD.

EXHIBIT 1.15

Primary and secondary market growth.

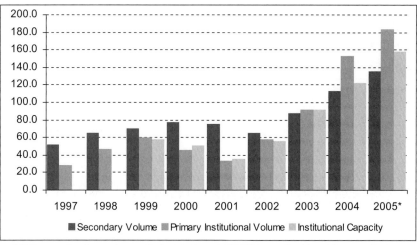

*2005 secondary loan volume reflects data through 9/30/05 annualized to a full year estimate.

Source: Loan Pricing Corporation (secondary volume), Standard & Poor's LCD (primary institutional volume and institutional capacity).

Capital from these investment vehicles has opened up a significant amount of capacity in the market over that time; institutional
capacity for 2005 is nearly $160 billion (see Exhibit 1.15).

Most institutional investors today restructure their loan portfolios into prime funds or structured vehicles such as CLOs/CDOs.
Insurance companies have participated in the leveraged market
from its beginnings in the early 1990s and continue to represent
about 5 percent of institutional money. Hedge funds entered the
market just a few years ago, but their share has ballooned from
barely 1 percent in 2002 to 12 percent in 2005. See Exhibit 1.16.

Unlike those of other players in the institutional market,
prime funds' share has both drastically and significantly declined
over the past decade. In 1997, prime funds represented nearly half
the institutional market, and today they take less than 20 percent.
To be fair, however, in absolute dollar amounts, the change is less
drastic. Though prime funds take fewer dollars today than they
did at their peak in 1999, their consumption is about even with
their 1997 dollar amount. The declining consumption rate of prime
funds over the past decade can largely be attributed to the recession. During the three-year period from 2001 to 2003, the Federal

EXHIBIT 1.16

Diversification of primary market by investor type.

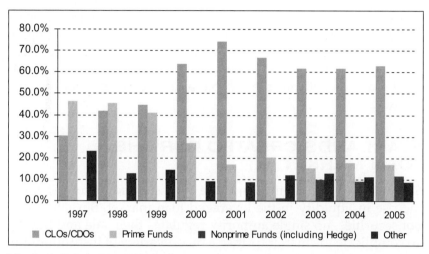

Reserve lowered interest rates 13 times, resulting in a 5 percent decrease in the fed funds rate. This, in turn, drove down LIBOR and reduced the interest income stream from prime funds. Furthermore, the recession was driven by record-setting default rates in 2000 and 2001, accompanied by a general decline in corporate credit quality, which resulted in increased market volatility. Both factors diminished the appeal of prime funds to retail investors, which, in turn, temporarily drove down their NAVs. As the economy has emerged from the recession and interest rates have risen, NAVs and the appeal of prime funds have also picked up.

The loan market has appealed to a broad range of investors, and the increasing capacity from CDOs/CLOs and the entrance of hedge funds, which have counterbalanced the relatively flat capacity from prime funds over the past decade, have also more than doubled total institutional capacity. In response, arrangers changed the structure of loans to meet this increasing demand and increased the availability of institutional tranches—fully funded term loans with longer maturities (eight to nine years) that pay slightly higher spreads than shorter-term, revolving or amortizing facilities. Thus, over the past decade, as secondary capacity and demand have increased, so has the institutional issuance volume.

The loan market itself has also matured to facilitate its growing capacity. Ten years ago, market participants established the LSTA to set up and oversee the standards and practices for trading loans, as well as certain processes such as mark-to-market pricing. In addition, an increasing share of loans has acquired ratings to support a standard framework for credit quality assessment. These developments, as well as others, have helped to build the leveraged loan market into the flexible and resilient market that it is today.

STANDARDS CREATED FOR THE LOAN MARKET

Standardized documentation is the most significant contributor to the rise in liquidity in the leveraged loan market. Since loans are not securities, no single authority regulates their sale and trading. To complicate the matter further, a broad variety of institutions buy loans—banks, mutual funds, finance institutions, hedge funds, pension funds, and distressed funds—and different authorities (e.g., the Federal Reserve, the SEC, ERISA) regulate these institutions. The market established the LSTA in 1995 out of the need to set standards for the rapidly growing loan sales and trading market, because participants recognized that the confluence of such varying interests and processes would result in a chaotic marketplace without any semblance of order. Later in this chapter under "The LSTA and Its Role in the Promotion of the Corporate Loan Asset Class," the LSTA's many accomplishments in terms of standard documents, guidelines, and market practices are discussed in detail.

The LSTA's primary goal has always been the promotion of the orderly development of a fair, efficient, liquid, and professional trading market for commercial loans. It is a not-for-profit trade association that has created more than 50 standard forms and market practices for the corporate loan asset class. These standard forms and market practices have been an integral part of creating a liquid and efficient loan market—both in the primary and in the secondary market.

The establishment of a centralized, mark-to-market process based upon dealer quotes was one of the LSTA's first accomplishments. In 1995, comptrollers and auditors of the banks that were trading loans requested a third-party, nonbiased pricing service so that they could verify the prices at which traders were marking positions on their books. In January 1996, the LSTA began collecting dealer quotes on approximately 155 secondary-traded loan facilities from a dozen dealers on a monthly basis. At the end of 1999, the frequency of pricing was increased to daily. Today, the LSTA, in conjunction with the Reuters LPC, gathers over 5,000 dealer quotes on over 2,400 U.S. based loan facilities from more than 30 dealers. Over the past decade, the service has also been transformed into a buy-side driven service: institutional investors, as opposed to traders, now drive what facilities need to be priced. As a result, the coverage of LSTA/LPC Mark-to-Market Pricing is broad enough to support the wide array of institutional investors in the marketplace.

The standardization of documents and practices, however, is the most significant responsibility of the LSTA. Over the past decade, the LSTA has established standard terms for nearly two dozen documents, including par and distressed trade confirms and purchase/sale agreements, as well as guidelines for processing such amendments. While the LSTA's work has primarily affected secondary market activity, it has also touched upon the primary market through model credit-agreement provisions and standard confidentiality language. There is no question that its activities have fostered the nearly fivefold growth in secondary market activity during its tenure. Today, the LSTA continues to drive market standards with the establishment of CUSIPs on loans and its public legal analysis of issues as diverse as IRS regulations, FASB rulings, and the Patriot Act.

Development of Ratings

While rating agencies have covered the bank loan market throughout the past decade of its growth, their coverage of this market has significantly increased over that time period. Standard & Poor's first began bank loan–specific coverage in 1996. Two years later, in 1998, S&P covered 56 percent of the leveraged loan universe; today, it covers more than 70 percent of the primary leveraged market and 77 percent of the institutional market (see Exhibit 1.17).

Not all loans have institutional tranches, and those that do have them are more likely to have ratings. This is due to the fact that institutional investors generally repackage their loan portfolios into structured vehicles or prime funds, both of which usually require collateral ratings. Ratings provide a standard framework

EXHIBIT 1.17

Growth in rated bank loan debt (in billions of dollars).

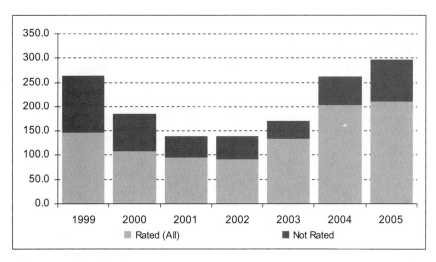

Source: Standard & Poor's LCD.

by which investors can evaluate the credit quality of the borrower. As a result, better-rated borrowers in the BB range pay lower interest rates than their lower-rated counterparts in the single-B range. Over the past decade, as ratings have become more prevalent and institutional investors have increasingly driven market demand, the risk premium for single-B borrowers has increased, although overall spreads have declined. In the first quarter of 1998, the average spread on an institutional tranche to a borrower rated BB/BB- was 261.78, 16 basis points (bps) lower than that to a B+/B borrower, whose average spread was 277.57. In the fourth quarter of 2005, the average spread for the BB/BB- borrower had fallen a point to 175.20, reflecting market preference for these better-rated credits. For the same time period, the average spread for B+/B credits was 262.51, providing the BB/BB- credits with an 87-bp premium for lower risk.

Besides serving as guidance to investors, ratings have also helped the loan market to grow and mature because they provide standardization in analysis and transparency. As the market innovates and grows into new territories and new products develop, ratings will help lenders to evaluate the risk/reward profiles of those changes.

RECENT DEVELOPMENTS IN THE LOAN MARKET

Second Liens

Second lien loans are one of the most significant innovations in the U.S. leveraged loan market in the past five years. They originated as a form of rescue financing—credit that distressed companies utilized to access funds when their access to the "traditional" senior secured market was problematic. Second liens are "first-loss" tranches in that, in case of default, they are paid after the senior secured portion, but before any other debt. As a result of their higher risk profile, they pay higher spreads than the senior portions. Those spreads, however, like all spreads in the leveraged market, have begun to decline in response to market pressures and increased demand for second lien facilities from a range of investors.

The increase in second lien loans in the United States since 2003 has been dramatic, serving in turn to whet the appetite of the investor market. In 2005, volume topped $16 billion, 35 percent greater than 2004's issuance (see Exhibit 1.18).

Over the past three years, the average spread for second liens has declined in response to market appetite. In 2003, they carried an average spread of 738 bps. In 2004, that spread fell almost

EXHIBIT 1.18

Primary volume for second lien tranches (in billions of dollars).

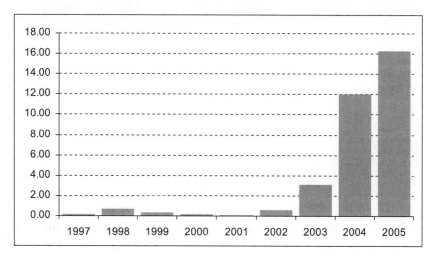

Source: Standard & Poor's LCD.

10 percent, to 672 bps, and in 2005, it declined a hair more, to 668 bps. However, second liens have held their pricing better than their first-lien counterparts. In 2003, second liens carried a premium of 276 bps over their first-lien institutional tranches. In 2004, that premium widened to 327 bps, and for the first nine months of 2005, it stepped out even further, to 367 bps.

The recovery levels on second liens, however, have yet to be tested through a credit crunch such as the market experienced in 2000 and 2001. The next downward cycle will challenge this new innovation in this constantly adjusting and developing loan market.

Globalization

The U.S. leveraged loan market has always been part of a global market. Over the past 15 years, Asian banks have played a significant role in the development of the leveraged loan market in the United States. Though their share has steadily declined to about 15 percent today, foreign banks represented 41 percent of the activity in the leveraged loan market in 1994. Globalization of leveraged loans, however, has continued, as the success of the U.S. market has pushed leveraged lending to other continents. Over the past decade, Asia, Eastern Europe, Australia, and Latin America have all shown signs of activity in leveraged lending, but it is Western Europe that has risen to be the second-largest market in the world.

Since the introduction of a standard currency (the Euro) in 1998, the European leveraged market, including the United Kingdom, France, Germany, Italy, Spain, the Netherlands, Switzerland, and the Nordic countries, has boomed. In 1999, the market had primary volume of about $33 billion, and in 2005, the market was 4.4 times that at $144 billion (see Exhibit 1.19).

During these years of growth, Europe has followed the U.S. pattern of an increasing institutional share and the introduction of second liens. And as in the U.S. market, the share of institutional investors has also increased.

Indeed, in 1999, institutional investors represented less than 12 percent of a market that had only $33 billion in volume. In 2005, they took over 40 percent of a market with volume in excess of $100 billion (see Exhibit 1.20).

Specifically, LCD (Leveraged Commentary & Data) estimates that there are now 53 loan managers in Europe managing 126 vehicles, with more than a dozen more vehicles in the pipeline, waiting

EXHIBIT 1.19

Primary volume for Europe (in billions of dollars).

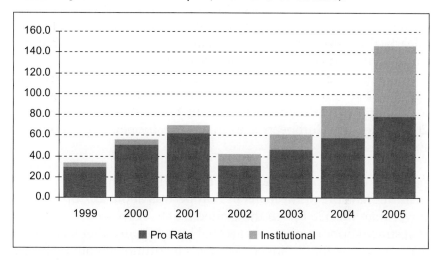

Source: Standard & Poor's LCD.

EXHIBIT 1.20

Diversification of investors in the primary market.

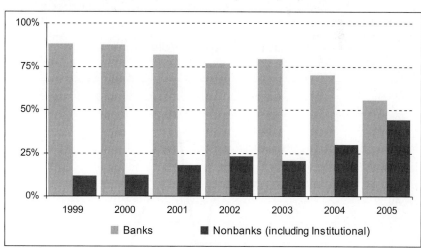

Source: Standard & Poor's LCD.

to be rolled out in the first half of 2006. Of these 53 managers, 26 manage portfolios in both the United States and Europe, up from 13 at the end of 2004 and just 6 at the end of 2003. In some of these cases, the managers started out in Europe and crossed over to the United States. A significant number of investors from the United States, however, have crossed over into Europe, either by starting up new investment groups in Europe or by acquiring existing ones. Clearly, the European leveraged loan market provides an attractive investment opportunity for leveraged loan investors worldwide.

The greatest appeal of the European market lies in its higher spreads. For most of the past decade, U.S. loan spreads carried a premium over European loans, but that changed at the end of 2003, when the European loan market really began to boom (see Exhibit 1.21).

In 1999, Europe's $4 billion in institutional volume paled compared to the U.S. volume of $60 billion. In addition, the average institutional spread for loans in Europe was about 267 bps, 72 bps lower than the 338 bps in the United States, representing a limited investment opportunity for potential investors in either location. In 2003, however, that changed; Europe's institutional volume hit $14 billion, and by the end of that year, the average institutional spread in Europe had risen to 298 bps while the U.S. average had fallen to 279 bps, a discount of nearly 20 bps. Today, even as European institutional pricing has moved down in response to investor demand,

EXHIBIT 1.21

Institutional spreads: U.S. premium/discount versus Europe (bps).

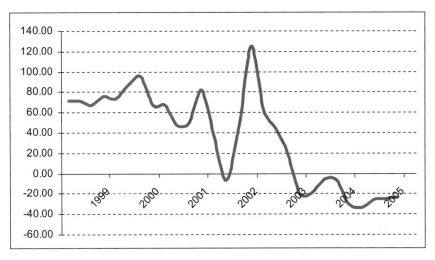

Source: Standard & Poor's LCD.

spreads remain 24 bps higher than the U.S. average. However, in light of the similarities between the two markets, that difference is likely to narrow as demand for European paper rises over the coming years.

CONCLUSION

Over the last 20 years, the corporate loan asset class has changed dramatically. It has developed from a primary-market and bank-oriented asset class into one with well-structured primary and secondary markets and a diversified investor base. Leveraged loans are a liquid, transparent, and efficient alternative form of investment, with opportunities available globally. That being said, the market continues to foster its own development through standards and market research in order that it may continue on its path to greater transparency and efficiency.

Introduction to the Syndicated Loan Market

Peter C. Vaky
SunTrust

In 1981, during the height of activity in the internationally syndicated loan market, a British merchant banker sardonically called the market a process whereby "the timid sold to the uninformed." Today the loan syndication market has evolved to a level scarcely imagined on London's Threadneedle Street. It is now a market that its predecessors would not recognize, particularly with respect to its size. Annual loan syndication levels now exceed US$1 trillion. And this enormous growth has fueled an increased sophistication in market conventions, the number of lenders and participants, the demand for standardized documentation, and ease of transferability, which, in turn, have fueled an active secondary market and a tiering/stratifying of market segmentation. All of this has led to a loan market whose product has emerged as the most flexible financing alternative available to corporate finance. The overall growth of the syndicated loan market is shown in Exhibit 1.22.

There are features of loans that corporate financiers find very attractive and lenders find comforting, and these have helped to foster the growth of this asset class. Loans can be prepaid without

EXHIBIT 1.22

Syndicated loan issuance, 1990–2005.

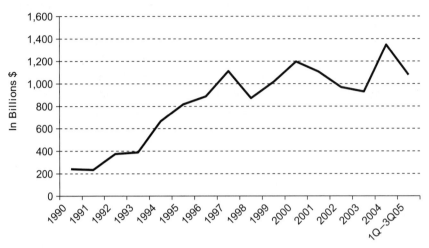

Source: Loan Pricing Corporation.

penalty. They are set forth in agreements containing covenant protections and/or security. Loans also have priority in value claims by
being at the top of the capital/liability structure. These characteristics have made the syndicated loan the preferred financing activity
of the debt capital markets. As a result, the growth of the syndicated loan market has made this financing activity more readily
usable for large financings, and a larger group of loan participants
has emerged.

GENERAL LOAN MARKET CHARACTERISTICS

Loans in the syndicated loan market have the following characteristics:

> *Floating interest rate:* The market convention today is a rate
> that is quoted as a spread over a floating-rate index. That
> index is the three- or six-month LIBOR (London Interbank
> Offered Rate). In the past, other indexes have been used,
> such as the prime rate, banker's acceptance rates, or even the
> fed funds rate.
> *Maturity:* Loans have maturities (also known as tenors) as
> short as six months for bridge loans, 360 days (one year) to

five years for working capital revolvers, and five to seven years for more leveraged term loans to corporations. There are also construction/project loans that are syndicated that can have maturities of ten to twelve years.

Prepayable without penalty: Since the loans are floating rate, they carry the "free option" of being "called." In other words, the loans can be repaid at any time without penalty. Those prepayments generally occur at interest payment dates to avoid the breakage cost of the index rate setting.

The syndicated loan market is classified into three subsectors:

- Investment grade
- Leveraged loans
- Middle market loans

These categories are defined by the credit rating, debt burden, pricing, and (in the case of middle market loans) size.

Investment Grade

The investment grade sector of the market represents 46 percent of the market and is made up of transactions for companies with public ratings from Moody's and Standard & Poor's of BBB-/Baa3 and above. Exhibit 1.23 shows the historical size of the investment grade market.

Most of the transactions in the investment grade market are revolving credit facilities ("revolvers") that finance the backup of commercial paper in the public market or are used infrequently when circumstances require short-term borrowings that are unavailable through public-market instruments. Since these revolvers are seldom utilized, lenders do not earn much return from interest income. Most of the return comes from a facility or "nonuse" fee. The public securities market offers investment grade companies efficient short-term funding alternatives through commercial paper and effective long-term funding through term bond issuance. As a result, loan outstandings under these revolvers are infrequent. The lower-rated investment grade companies (BBB/BBB-), which do not have as many public-market options, offer lenders an opportunity to have outstandings.

The general time period or maturity ("tenor") of loans or loan facilities to investment grade companies ranges from 360 days to

EXHIBIT 1.23

Investment grade versus noninvestment grade total syndicated loan issuance.

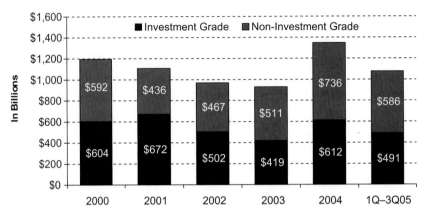

Source: Loan Pricing Corporation.

5 years. The irony of the investment grade loan market compared to the bond market is that tenors for investment grade loans are shorter than tenors for investment grade bonds. While investment grade bond issuers can issue 30-year bonds in the market, investment grade borrowers in the loan market almost never borrow beyond 5 years because lenders do not feel that they get an adequate return for the time risk. Lenders prefer the ability to use a time limit to reprice risk through fees or spread adjustments. For investment grade lenders, the returns are lower, but the risk is deemed to be low as well. The investment grade loan market can be characterized as a low-margin, high-volume business.

Leveraged Loans

In contrast to the investment grade market, the leveraged loan market is a higher-margin but lower-volume business. Leveraged loans are loans to companies that do not have an investment grade rating and/or that have a high level of contracted or outstanding debt. Within the leveraged market, there is a distinction between those companies that are just below investment grade (BB+ to BB, also known as "4B" or "crossover credits") and those companies that are considered highly leveraged (HLTs). The general measure of high leverage has been 3 to 4 times for senior debt to

EXHIBIT 1.24

Leveraged syndicated lending as a percentage of total
syndicated lending volume.

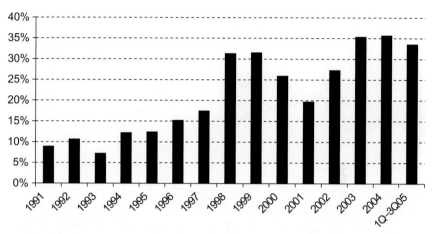

Source: Loan Pricing Corporation.

earnings before interest, taxes, depreciation, and amortization
(EBITDA) or 4 to 6 times for total debt to EBITDA. There are exceptions for the debt levels of finance and media companies, whose
leverage multiples are even higher. In terms of ratings, the more
highly leveraged companies tend to be rated B+ to B (single Bs) but
can drop to B- and CCC+ ("triple hooks"). The leveraged market
represents 34 percent of the total syndicated loan market, as shown
in Exhibit 1.24.

Leveraged loans are made to support companies that are borrowing to make acquisitions, spend on large capital expansions,
refinance and increase existing debt ("recap"), or make one-time
high dividend payments to shareholders. The market perceives
these loans to be more risky and requires a higher return in the
form of fees and loan spread. Traditionally, loans with spreads of
1.5 percent over LIBOR and higher have been characterized as
leveraged loans. Historically, these loan spreads have been above 2
percent and have reached as high as 4 percent. Exhibit 1.25 shows
the historical record of leveraged loan spreads.

Since the market perceives that there is more risk in leveraged
loans, these companies have fewer public-market alternatives. This
has resulted in the loan market being the best financing alternative
for leveraged borrowers. (The floating rate and lack of prepayment

EXHIBIT 1.25

(*a*) Drawn margins on leveraged pro rata loans. (*b*) Drawn margins on leveraged term loans.

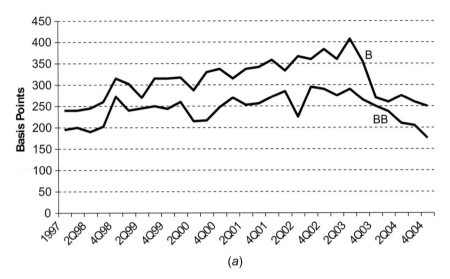

(*a*)

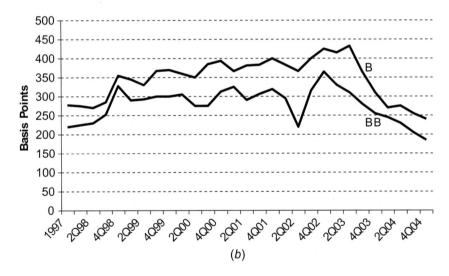

(*b*)

Source: Loan Pricing Corporation.

costs attract companies that want to increase their debt burden temporarily to buy other companies or recapitalize their balance sheets.) Lenders prefer the predictability of interest income from

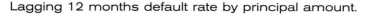

EXHIBIT 1.26

Lagging 12 months default rate by principal amount.

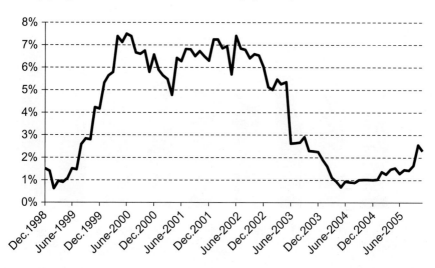

having loans outstanding and higher front-end fees, even though default rates are higher for leveraged loans (see Exhibit 1.26).

Middle Market Loans

The middle market is characterized by loans to companies whose size limits their access to capital. The rating agencies consider the size of a company to be the single most important element in determining the company's rating. As a result, companies with less than $500 million in sales and EBITDA levels of $25 to $50 million depend upon the loan market as their primary source of financing. The middle market loan volume accounts for 6 percent of the total market, as shown by Exhibit 1.27.

Size also affects the lenders' view of these borrowers. Since there are, by definition, fewer lenders providing smaller loans, lenders perceive the liquidity of these loans to be less than that of larger loans to larger leveraged companies. Less liquidity in these loans, in turn, has caused lenders to be more conservative in their structuring of debt for middle market companies. This conservatism can be seen in the lower leverage multiples of middle market loans relative to their larger counterparts. As a result,

Middle market outstandings as a percentage of all leveraged loans.

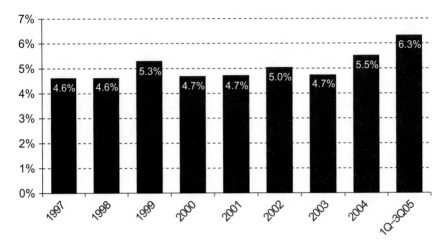

Source: Standard & Poor's LCD.

Recovery rates.

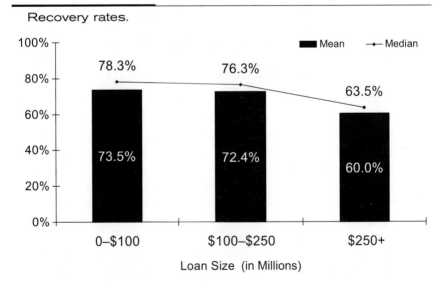

Source: Moody's Investors Service.

recovery rates for the middle market are slightly higher than those for the large leveraged corporate market. Exhibit 1.28 illustrates this.

These smaller-sized loan transactions with fewer borrowers needed to complete the syndication are often nicknamed "club deals." This name connotes a smaller number of closely familiar ("insider") lenders to the borrower and sometimes results in terms and conditions that are higher or lower than those for the broader, more publicized market.

Players in the Market

Steve Miller
Managing Director
Standard & Poor's Leveraged Commentary & Data

An issuer is, quite simply, a firm that issues a loan. In days of yore, issuers in the loan market were called borrowers, but as the loan market has matured, it has adopted many of the conventions and parlance of the bond market. As a result, companies that borrow money are now called issuers. There are three primary types of issuers in the syndicated loan market: investment grade, leveraged, and middle market.

> *Investment grade issuers.* Investment grade issuers are those rated BBB- or higher by Standard & Poor's, Baa3 or higher by Moody's Investors Service, and/or BBB- or higher by Fitch Ratings. These companies tend to be large, established firms with little balance sheet leverage and strong profitability. As a result, these issuers typically tap the syndicated loan market for unfunded credit to back seasonal borrowing needs, backstop commercial paper, or fund acquisitions on a short-term basis. These issuers do, on occasion, take funded term loans. But this usually happens only if they are facing liquidity concerns or a financial crisis. In most cases, it is less expensive for investment grade issuers to borrow in the public market via bonds or commercial paper than to borrow money from banks directly.
>
> *Leveraged issuers.* Leveraged issuers are generally those with noninvestment grade ratings. Standard & Poor's LCD defines these issuers as those that have either (1) loans that are rated noninvestment grade or (2) loans that are rated investment grade or not rated at all, but that are backed by security and have a spread of LIBOR + 125 or higher. There are several routes to noninvestment grade land. The

traditional path was as a fallen angel, an issuer that started as investment grade and was downgraded to noninvestment grade status as a result of earnings deterioration. One obvious recent example is General Motors, which was investment grade for decades before spiraling down to junk status in 2005. But these firms are only a fraction of the leveraged loan market, which is dominated by original-issue, noninvestment grade issuers that came to the market via a leveraged buyout, recapitalization, or acquisition. Leveraged firms, as the name implies, tend to have capital structures in which debt dwarfs equity. The classic definition was a balance sheet in which liabilities exceed equity by three times or more. As capital structure became more complicated and recapitalization techniques drove equity into negative territory, the definition of a leveraged issuer evolved to one that is cash flow–based. In general, leveraged issuers have debt-to-EBITDA ratios of three times or more. There are exceptions, of course, with many investment grade issuers—particularly those in the media sector—carrying lofty debt multiples. And, on the other side of the ledger, there are many cyclical issuers that even with debt multiples lower than three times are rated below investment grade.

Middle market issuers. By 2005, the consensus definition of a middle market loan in the syndicated loan market was one to an issuer with EBITDA of $50 million or less. These loans tend to be $200 million or less and generally fall into leveraged land. Middle market loans, as of 2005, had their own idiosyncrasies, however. They tend to be less liquid and lack a broad following among dealers or accounts. They are more likely to be nonrated. In 2005, for instance, 42 percent of middle market loan volume was rated compared to 71 percent for all leveraged loans. And they are more likely to be to private issuers than large corporate loans. As a result, they are generally priced with an illiquidity premium in the form of a higher spread.

SYNDICATORS

Syndicators serve the time-honored investment banking role of raising investor dollars for an issuer in need of capital. The issuer pays the arranger a fee for this service, and, naturally, this fee increases with the complexity and riskiness of the loan. Borrowers will issue a mandate to one or more syndicators to raise a loan. In general, there are three types of syndications: an underwritten deal, a "best-efforts" syndication, and a "club deal."

An underwritten deal is one in which the arrangers guarantee the entire commitment, then syndicate the loan. If the arrangers are unable to fully subscribe the loan, they are forced to absorb the difference, which they may later try to sell to investors. This is easy, of course, if market conditions, or the credit's fundamentals, improve. If not, the arranger may be forced to sell the loan at a discount and, potentially, even take a loss on it. Or the arranger may just be left with more than its desired hold level of the credit. So, why do arrangers underwrite loans? First, offering an underwritten loan can be a competitive tool to win mandates. Second, underwritten loans usually provide more lucrative fees because the agent is on the hook if potential lenders balk. Of course, with flex language now common, underwriting a deal does not carry the same risk that it did when the pricing was set in stone prior to syndication. Even so, full underwrites were increasingly rare by 2005, though partial underwriting was still common.

A "best-efforts" syndication is one for which the arranger group commits to underwriting less than the entire amount of the loan, leaving the credit to the vicissitudes of the market. If the loan is undersubscribed, the credit may not close, or major surgery may be needed to clear the market. Traditionally, best-efforts syndications were used for risky borrowers or for complex transactions. Since the late 1990s, however, the rapid acceptance of market-flex language has made best-efforts loans the rule even for investment grade transactions.

A "club deal" is a smaller loan (usually $25 to $100 million, but sometimes as high as $150 million) that is premarketed to a group of relationship banks. The arranger is generally a first among equals, and each lender gets a full cut, or nearly a full cut, of the fees.

LENDER TITLES

In the formative days of the syndicated loan market (the late 1980s), one agent usually syndicated each loan. "Lead manager" and "manager" titles were doled out in exchange for large commitments.

As league tables gained influence as a marketing tool, "co-agent" titles were often used to attract large commitments or in cases where these institutions truly had a role in underwriting and syndicating the loan.

During the 1990s, the use of league tables and, consequently, title inflation exploded. Indeed, the co-agent title has become largely ceremonial today, being routinely awarded for what amounts to no more than a large retail commitment. In most syndications, there is one lead arranger. This institution is considered to be on the "left" (a reference to its position in a tombstone ad). There are also likely to be other banks in the arranger group, which may also have a hand in underwriting and syndicating a credit. These institutions are said to be on the "right."

The different titles used by significant participants in the syndications process are administrative agent, syndication agent, documentation agent, agent, co-agent or managing agent, and lead arranger or book runner.

> *The administrative agent* is the bank that handles all interest and principal payments and monitors the loan.
>
> *The syndication agent* is the bank that handles, in purest form, the syndication of the loan. Often, however, the syndication agent has a less specific role.
>
> *The documentation agent* is the bank that handles the documents and chooses the law firm.
>
> *The agent* title is used to indicate the lead bank when there is no other conclusive title available, as is often the case for smaller loans.
>
> *Co-agent* or *managing agent* is largely a meaningless title that is used mostly as an award for large commitments.
>
> *The lead arranger* or *book runner* is a league table designation used to indicate the "top dog" in a syndication.

INVESTORS

There are three main groups of primary investors: banks, finance companies, and institutional investors.

> *Banks,* in this case, can be either commercial banks or the securities firms that usually provide investment grade loans. These are typically large revolving credits that are used to back up commercial paper, for general corporate purposes,

or, in some cases, for acquisitions. For leveraged loans, banks typically provide unfunded revolving credits, lines of credit (LOCs), and—although they are becoming increasingly less common—amortizing term loans, under a syndicated loan agreement.

Finance companies have consistently represented less than 10 percent of the leveraged loan market and tend to play in smaller deals—$25 to $200 million. These investors often seek asset-based loans that carry wide spreads and that often feature time-intensive collateral monitoring.

Institutional investors in the loan market are principally structured vehicles known as collateralized loan obligations (CLOs) and loan participation mutual funds (known as *prime funds* because they were originally pitched to investors as a money market–like fund that would approximate the prime rate). In addition, hedge funds, high-yield bond funds, pension funds, insurance companies, and other proprietary investors do participate opportunistically in loans. Typically, however, they invest principally in wide-margin loans (referred to by some players as "high-octane" loans), with spreads of LIBOR + 500 or higher. During the first half of 2005, these players accounted for roughly 8 percent of overall investment.

CLOs are special-purpose vehicles set up to hold and manage pools of leveraged loans. Such a special-purpose vehicle is financed with several tranches of debt (typically a AAA-rated tranche, a AA tranche, a BBB tranche, and a mezzanine tranche) that have rights to the collateral and payment stream in descending order. In addition, there is an equity tranche, but the equity tranche is usually not rated. CLOs are created as arbitrage vehicles that generate equity returns through leverage, issuing an amount of debt that is 10 to 11 times their equity contribution. CLOs are usually rated by two of the three major ratings agencies and impose a series of covenant tests on collateral managers, including minimum rating, industry diversification, and maximum default basket. By 2002, CLOs had become the dominant form of institutional investment in the leveraged loan market, taking a commanding 80 percent of primary activity by institutional investors.

Prime funds are mostly continuously offered funds with quarterly tender periods or true closed-end, exchange-traded funds. By mid–2005, there were a growing number of open-ended funds that were redeemable each day. While quarterly redemption funds and closed-end funds remain the standard because the secondary loan market does not offer the rich liquidity that is supportive of open-end funds, the open-end funds have sufficiently raised their profile that by mid–2005 they accounted for 15 to 20 percent of the loan assets held by mutual funds.

Interplay with Other Capital Markets

Scott D. Krase
Managing Partner
Oak Hill Advisors

INTRODUCTION

As the loan market asset class has continued to mature, buyers, sellers, issuers, and underwriters are challenged to navigate the complexities and advances that now permeate the market. Arrangers must make difficult decisions regarding the size and structure of the pro rata tranches of a credit facility. Today, loans may include a first, a second, and sometimes a third lien on the assets. These loans are often being substituted for a high-yield offering and create trade-offs for both issuers and buyers. In addition, borrowers may have the option of choosing to go directly to potential purchasers rather than working through more traditional syndication desks. Finally, the continued growth and development of the European market, both on the Continent and in the United Kingdom, provide borrowers, lenders, and arrangers with even more options for the structuring of a particular credit facility.

All of these developments have created a complex interplay between different types of bank loan buyers and sellers, as well as between bank debt and other capital markets. This section provides a brief overview of these dynamics (see Exhibit 1.29), which are discussed in more detail in subsequent chapters.

EXHIBIT 1.29

Simple Comparison of Characteristic of Leveraged Capital Markets

	Revolver/TLA	Institutional/TLB	Second Lien/TL	High-Yield Bonds
Coupon	Floating rate	Floating rate	Floating rate	Fixed rate
Ranking	Senior	Senior	Senior	Senior/senior subordinated
Spread (L+)	150–300 bps	150–350 bps	350–800 bps	7.5–12.0%
Security	Secured	Secured	Secured	Unsecured
Maturity (yrs.)	5 to 7	6 to 10	6 to 10	7 to 12
Covenants	Maintenance	Maintenance	Both	Incurrence
Repayments	Amortizing	Limited	Limited	Nonamortizing
Event-related	Required	Optional	Optional	No prepays
Callability	Callable, no fee	Callable, possible fee	Callable, possible fee	No call period, fee
Market	Private	Private	Private or public	Public
Funding	Company option	Fully funded	Fully funded	Fully funded
Information	Private	Mostly private	Mostly public	Public

Source: Bank of America, "The New Leveraged Loan Syndication Market," *Journal of Applied Corporate Finance*, 10(1), Spring 1997, pp. 79–88.

PRO RATA VERSUS INSTITUTIONAL TRANCHES

The pro rata tranches of credit facilities, known as revolvers and term loan As (TLAs), have traditionally been purchased by commercial banks and other relationship lenders. However, beginning in 2000, these institutions' ability to issue large-sized pro rata tranches began to change. Credit losses and regulatory pressures caused many banks and other financial institutions to dramatically curtail their lending activities, in both number and size of commitments (see Exhibit 1.30).

As a result of this phenomenon, the lending activity by nonbank buyers dramatically increased to fill the void left by traditional sources. Beginning in the late 1990s, nonbank institutional investors began buying fully funded, higher-priced, nonamortizing term loans, which are today known as term loan Bs or TLBs (see Exhibit 1.31). The increased presence of nonbank buyers has

EXHIBIT 1.30

Most active pro rata leveraged investors (lenders that made 10 or more primary commitments).

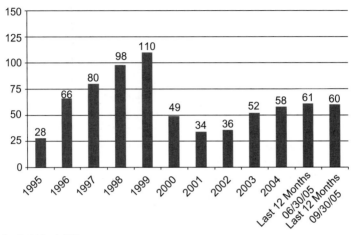

Source: Standard & Poor's LCD.

EXHIBIT 1.31

Primary market for highly leveraged loans by broad investor type.

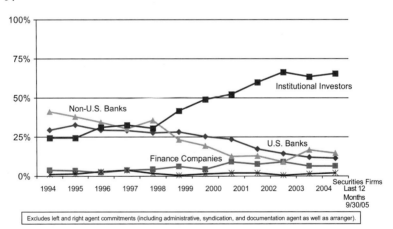

Excludes left and right agent commitments (including administrative, syndication, and documentation agent as well as arranger).

Source: Standard & Poor's LCD.

allowed commercial lending to evolve from a bilateral market to a primarily syndication- and distribution-driven model, much like the bond market.

Typically, pro rata tranches have lower stated spreads than other securities and therefore represent one of the few opportunities in the leveraged loan market to purchase debt in the secondary market at a discount. Therefore, despite the lower stated spread, investments in the revolver or term loan A tranches may generate incremental returns as a result of paydowns and prepayment priorities as compared to their institutional counterparts.

However, revolvers and term loan As often have less liquidity than institutional or term loan B tranches given the intensive accounting and the funding requirements, which investors sometimes view as onerous. Furthermore, many revolvers may be drawn in multiple currencies, further limiting the potential investor base, as many institutional lenders are not liquid in multiple currencies. Finally, borrower consent and minimum assignment sizes also may prevent certain investors from buying revolvers. As a result, revolvers are able to maintain an associated price discount.

BANK LOANS VERSUS HIGH-YIELD BONDS

An analysis of the interplay between these trillion-dollar markets involves two key elements: (1) a relative value comparison and (2) an examination of the gaps that remain as market convergence becomes a reality.

From a relative value perspective, comparing floating-rate loans to fixed-rate high-yield bonds involves a trade-off between seniority and callability. Floating-rate loans offer a senior secured position in the capital structure with better financial covenants. These benefits are offset by the borrower's option to prepay the loan at any time.

The reduced risk inherent in floating-rate loans' senior secured status results in a lower yield. The severity of this discount is reasonably determined by the expected cost of the issuer's prepayment option. Either in a more volatile interest-rate environment or where there is significant credit improvement, being "short" this call option can be very expensive for an unsophisticated investor.

High-yield bondholders pay a fixed rate based on a spread over a risk-free Treasury benchmark. In contrast, bank loans, while also priced over a risk-free benchmark, are floating-rate and therefore are priced against swaps or LIBOR. In comparing high-yield bonds to bank loans, an investor needs to derive a fixed-rate equivalent spread for floating-rate bank loans (or vice versa) by utilizing a swap-adjusted pricing model. The total spread over the average life of a bank loan will be the sum of the credit spread, the swap adjustment, and any price discount or premium.[7]

From underwriting to investing, over the last 10 years the loan and bond markets have substantially converged. As early as 1995, Martin Fridson, then chief high-yield strategist at Merrill Lynch, in a Merrill Lynch research report, addressed questions associated with the loan- and bond-market convergence and concluded that the proper focus of the convergence should be on why there are, and will continue to be, inconsistencies in comparing the two assets. He presented four basic reasons for the presence of these inconsistencies:[8]

1. Barriers to access for both investors and issuers
2. Incomplete dissemination of information related to pricing and the companies involved
3. Parochialism of intermediaries, who are first and foremost profit centers
4. Infeasibility of comparing prices on a consistent scale

Although most of these reasons have faded over time, an information gap remains between the "private" bank and "public" high-yield markets. Bank loan investors continue to enjoy access to more timely and complete information than high-yield bond investors receive. In response to regulators' concerns about private bank information traveling to public bond-trading areas, today many organizations physically separate their bank loan and high-yield departments and declare a trading desk to be either "private" or "public." Moreover, as technology has allowed more detailed information to travel faster and as the bank debt trading activity has exploded, managing the flow of information on both sides of the "wall" has become a critical compliance priority.

---

[7] Citigroup, "A Guide to the Corporate Loan Marks," *Leveraged Loan Handbook* (February 2004), p. 51.
[8] Merrill Lynch, "Why the Leveraged Loan and High Yield Bond Markets Must Converge," *Extra Credit: The Journal of Global High Yield Bond Research,* May/June 1995, pp. 4–7.

MIDDLE MARKET LOANS

Historically, middle market loans were dominated by mid-tier commercial banks and finance companies. These institutions viewed middle market loans as part of an overall business relationship with the issuing company or financial sponsor. This type of lending often consisted of a small syndicate of one to three investors, and little information was disseminated, which served to limit buyers in the secondary market and allowed borrowers to better control the lender group.

Today, however, there has been a substantial increase in the number of middle market loans that have been syndicated to the market at large. Such loans are characterized by their small size (in general, facilities of less than $150 million) and are often issued by companies with EBITDA generally below $50 million. Middle market loans often provide higher yields than traditional institutional term loans, and may offer up-front fees or discounts to compensate for the associated reduced liquidity and smaller size. Middle market loans may also include higher amounts of secured leverage because companies tapping this market typically would not also access the high-yield market. The appetite for middle market loans has increased as collateral managers seek loans with attractive spreads and as hedge funds continue their global search for yield (similar to the explanation for the increased growth in the second-lien market). This increased appetite has driven up the trading prices of these loans; however, in general, middle market loans continue to trade below larger, more liquid, and widely syndicated institutional term loans.

Institutional investors (and certain hedge funds) may be able to capitalize on the benefits of engaging in privately negotiated transactions, or direct lending. Perhaps the most notable advantage is the significant increase in the amount of information and access to the management available when making a credit decision. A direct lender is often less time-constrained and, without an intermediary to filter requests, may be able to obtain more data about a borrower's business, prospects, industry, and customers. Such a lender may also have direct communication with a company's management and arrange multiple meetings with it, as well as make multiple follow-up requests for information. The access to management and information provides opportunities for direct lenders to make more informed, and perhaps better, credit decisions.

Moreover, once the transaction is completed, a direct lender often continues to have the same level of access to management and information.

In addition to having access to information, direct lenders also often have the ability to structure the transaction to mitigate, or sometimes eliminate, documentation risk. This advantage may relate to structuring covenants, seniority, collateral, call protection, pricing, or a host of other legal issues. In short, direct lenders' ability to control documentation ensures that all of the negotiated items are acknowledged in the credit, intercreditor, and other operative agreements.

Finally, given the competition for assets in today's low-yield environment, direct lenders also benefit from the ability to control allocations. A direct lender can manage how much of a particular transaction it would like to own, possibly selling some exposure to other investors. Today, it is not unusual to see a few hedge funds coming together to invest in a company directly, effectively disintermediating larger syndicate desks.

THE U.S. MARKET VERSUS THE EUROPEAN MARKET

As we enter 2006, leveraged finance has become a global business. Driven primarily by demand from equity sponsor transactions, over the last four years, the supply of leveraged loans in Europe has grown to be one-third of all global leveraged volume (see Exhibit 1.32).

Historically, European banks have dominated the primary new-issue market in Europe, generally employing a buy-and-hold strategy that has hampered liquidity and trading opportunities. Today, however, as more lenders are trading on a global basis and more institutions have emerged, trading in Europe has become easier, and a greater flow of information and ideas has developed.

Since the sell-off in the high-yield market in the spring of 2005, more borrowers have relied on financing transactions solely with senior debt, extending the tranches through second liens and mezzanine debt. In some cases, borrowers are doing so to the exclusion of high-yield instruments. As a result, senior secured leverage levels have increased, with leverage levels in some transactions far exceeding those found in the U.S. primary market.

EXHIBIT 1.32

European leveraged loan volume as a percent of global volume.

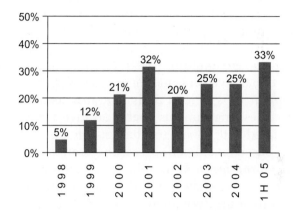

Source: Standard & Poor's LCD.

The spreads on the institutional tranches of European term loan Bs and term loan Cs (which typically are approximately 50 percent held by banks and 50 percent by institutions) have traditionally been higher than those on comparably rated U.S. tranches. The pricing on the typical bank structure (which is generally unrated) with a revolver, term loan A, term loan B, and term loan C has generally ranged from E + 225 to E + 325, with the term loan B and term loan C at E + 275 and E + 325, respectively. Pricing and maturity increase through the second-lien and mezzanine tranches. This pricing hierarchy provides a substantial pricing arbitrage on a loan with both dollar- and Euro-denominated debt, where enough spread differentials exist to cover the necessary hedging costs and to account for potential liquidity issues.

As dividend recaps, refinancings, and secondary LBOs are becoming more common in Europe, primary new issue spreads have compressed to reflect the lofty trading levels exhibited by the predecessor or comparable loans in the secondary market. The surge in investor demand for European loans, the previous lack of supply relative to demand, and a change from the buy-and-hold mentality to a portfolio management approach have all served to significantly increase the secondary trading activity.

As with most assets, factors specific to certain industries or issuers, and technicalities related to supply and demand, may cause an arbitrage between two currencies to exist, which an astute investor may be able to capture.

CREDIT DERIVATIVES

Loan derivatives are building a strong following among hedge funds, institutional investors, and insurance companies. Historically, the most popular type of loan derivative has been the total rate of return swap. These instruments enable an investor to purchase the returns associated with a loan, or a basket of loans, in exchange for a fee. The fee is based on either a spread on a loan to finance the derivative or an up-front fee built into the transaction. Regardless of the form, the fee is approximately 50 to100 basis points annually of the notional amount of the derivative.

Currently, the majority of credit derivatives are being issued in the form of a credit default swap (CDS). While the vast majority of the CDS market involves senior unsecured obligations, the "loan-only deliverable" market is developing. Dealers have begun to trade specific contracts using senior secured loans, including both revolvers and term loans. Loan CDS provide the opportunity for investors to purchase additional credit exposure without paying a large premium to par (which is significant for par callable loans). Since the CDS spread reflects the then-appropriate adjusted credit spread, investors can now make bearish credit bets using CDS and buy and sell exposure to the entire market via a basket of leveraged loan credit default swaps.

CONCLUSION

As described in this brief overview, developments and trends in the leveraged capital markets have provided an array of opportunities for borrowers and investors alike. As the leveraged asset class has evolved, lenders and arrangers have had the opportunity to access a variety of different structural options. Purchasers of debt have had the potential to capitalize on relative value discrepancies across currencies and jurisdictions and throughout capital structures to generate incremental returns. In addition, the vast expansion of the credit derivatives market has provided another opportunity for creating desired returns based on predetermined events and situations. The complex interplay within and among participants and structures in the overall leveraged capital markets has created a phenomenal convergence on a global basis.

The LSTA and Its Role in the Promotion of the Corporate Loan Asset Class

Allison A. Taylor
Executive Director, LSTA

The Loan Syndications and Trading Association (the LSTA or the association) was incorporated in 1995 because of the need to establish standards for the rapidly growing loan sales and trading market. In this section I will discuss the LSTA's history, review some of its significant accomplishments, and analyze its impact on the development of the loan asset class during the 1990s and 2000s.

The LSTA is the not-for-profit trade association for the floating-rate corporate loan asset class. It is dedicated to advancing the interests of the marketplace as a whole and promoting the highest degree of confidence among its many diverse investors. The LSTA undertakes the development of policies and market practices designed to promote fair principles. Through a consensus-building process, it promotes cooperation and coordination between the firms transacting in loans. The LSTA stands out among financial market trade associations because it represents all segments of the market it serves: both buyers and sellers of loans.

EARLY HISTORY

In 1991, the total volume of secondary trading of corporate loans was $8 billion. By 1995, the total volume of secondary trading of corporate loans had reached $34 billion in the United States, an increase of 325 percent in four years (see Exhibit 1.33). Settlement time, the time between trade date and settlement date, was reaching new highs, thereby causing buyers of loans to incur significant costs.

In 1995, as a secondary trader of performing loans called par/near par loans, I bought a $10 million piece of a very large, recently syndicated performing loan from a co-agent. The transaction took six weeks to close, i.e., to settle the loan from the trade

EXHIBIT 1.33

Secondary trading volume (in billions of dollars).

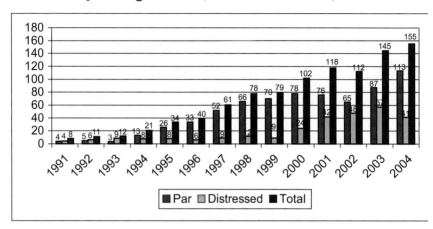

Source: Loan Pricing Corporation.

date. (By way of comparison, it took one day for stocks to settle from the trade date.) As the buyer, I owned the credit risk as of the trade date. So, if the company had gone into bankruptcy, for example, I would have owned a loan that was likely to be worth less than the price at which I had bought it. However, the seller of the loan was still the lender of record and was collecting and accruing interest, while having sold the risk.

If this had been an isolated incident, I would have moved on to bigger things. But it wasn't. This long settlement period was becoming more of a norm than an outlier. As a result, something needed to be done—standards were needed. I faxed a questionnaire to 15 other traders asking them if they also felt that we needed a standard settlement period on loans and, if so, what that standard settlement period should be.

Fourteen of the fifteen traders responded enthusiastically with *yes*. (The fifteenth trader was a trader of distressed loans. This trader believed that he would make more money if there were no standards in the market.) The entire market was losing too much money because of delayed settlements.

We knew that we needed a standard trade confirmation[9] in order to implement a standard settlement period. In addition, a stan-

---

[9] The trade confirmation is the agreement between buyer and seller that legally documents the exchange of the loan between buyer and seller.

dard trade confirmation would eliminate unnecessary arguments and disagreements between buyers and sellers. Delayed settlement equaled increased costs; increased costs decreased profits—time equals money!

In order to create a standard trade confirmation, it was necessary to hire a law firm to facilitate the consensus-building process between the traders and the in-house lawyers. And, as we all know, hiring law firms requires money. As a result, it became necessary for us to establish a trade association in order to achieve our goals. In the beginning, three firms—ING, Morgan Guaranty Trust Co. of New York, and Goldman Sachs—stepped up and contributed $100,000 each to fund the organization. Shortly thereafter, another nine firms joined the effort; each contributed $100,000, and the LSTA was formed. (The LSTA was originally called the Debt Traders Association. Its name was changed in 1996.) The additional nine firms were Bank of America, Bank of Montreal, Bankers Trust Company, Bear Stearns Cos., Inc., Chemical Bank, Citibank, First Chicago, Lehman Brothers, Inc., and Merrill Lynch & Co.

Prior to the formation of the LSTA, counterparties could end up in trade disputes over a variety of issues, including who would receive a paydown on a loan between trade date and settlement date, who would pay the assignment fee to the agent, and who would pay breakfunding costs. Today, as a result of the efforts of the LSTA to develop standard terms and conditions for loan trading, buyers and sellers are much less likely to end up in a trade dispute.

From its original membership of 12 institutions, the LSTA has grown to more than 200 members. Today, members include commercial banks, investment banks, mutual funds, CLO fund managers, hedge funds, distressed funds, buy-side institutions, sell-side institutions, law firms, accounting firms, brokers, and many others. Within these institutions, the following types of people have been active in the LSTA: loan traders, syndicators, commercial lending officers, portfolio managers, workout officers, and many others. Exhibit 1.34 shows the growth in LSTA membership by institution type. The diversification of LSTA members is a reflection of the loan market itself.

The association's main goal is to promote the orderly development of a fair, efficient, liquid, and professional trading market for commercial loans and other similar private debt.

As of this writing, the LSTA has 51 full members, 52 associate members, and 98 affiliate members. Founding members are leading

EXHIBIT 1.34

Breakdown of LSTA members.

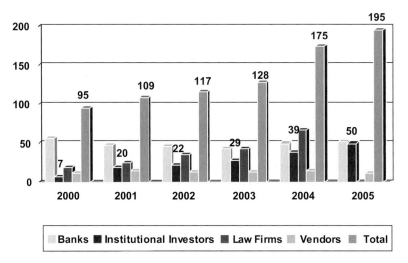

commercial banks and dealers; they are institutions that have been and will continue to be instrumental in developing the association, its agenda, and its initiatives. Full members are institutions that, directly or through affiliates, trade bank debt or invest in bank loans for their own account, such as dealers, commercial and investment banks, funds, and insurance companies. Associate members are market participants that trade or invest in commercial loan instruments, but are traditionally smaller and less active than full members. The affiliate member organizations have a general interest in the market; they include law firms, brokers, consultants, and advisors.

The LSTA originally began as a trade association of traders. Every year since its inception, however, the LSTA and its mission have expanded, matured, and evolved. Initially, the association worked exclusively on documents and products for the secondary loan market. Today, the LSTA's mission is to support the loan asset class as a whole. By producing standard documents and market practices for the primary and secondary markets, taking charge of regulatory matters when the need arises, and working with the FASB on issues that could potentially damage the treatment of loans or related products, the LSTA has evolved into a caucus for market participants to discuss and debate current issues affecting the market while continuing to increase the communication and education of the asset class. The LSTA is the principal advocate for the floating-rate loan asset class!

Each of the standard documents, market practices, and market products that have been adopted or created by the LSTA is the product of a consensus-building process. Depending on the issue, this process can sometimes take years, and the growing pains can be numerous. But once a consensus on a matter has been reached, it sticks. We proudly point to the fact that our documents and market practices are widely used and recognized by market participants, and that their success has inspired other international organizations to follow suit.

Since the inception of the LSTA, the loan market has grown a great deal in volume, depth, liquidity, and membership. In 1995, syndicated loan volume was $398 billion; in 2004, volumes exceeded $1.3 trillion. Secondary trading volume was $34 billion in 1995; in 2004, volume reached $155 billion. In 1995, there were 32 active loan investment vehicles; today there are 433. The LSTA's first pricing service obtained marks on 155 different facilities; today we receive marks on over 2,000 facilities. (The growth of facilities marked can be seen in Exhibit 1.38 later in this section.) Our membership is up from 21 members in 1995 to 200 members in 2005. This remarkable growth is reflected in Exhibit 1.35.

EXHIBIT 1.35

Percent growth of the loan market, 1995–2005.

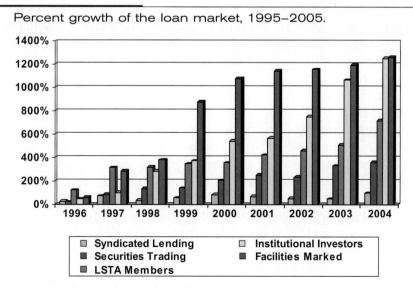

Source: Loan Pricing Corporation, Standard & Poor's, LSTA.

This growth was made possible through the structure and discipline that the LSTA and its membership have provided to the loan trading market. Gone are the days when you waited six weeks to close on an assignment of a performing large liquid loan. Gone are the days when you needed original signatures from the buyer, seller, agent bank, and borrower on assignment agreements. Gone are the days when an institutional investor could not get reliable prices on secondary loans. Gone are the days when a buyer and seller weren't legally bound to a trade over the phone. Gone are the days when the loan asset class did not have a unique identifier, just like every other tradable asset class. Gone are the days when the market had nowhere to go to deal with a problem in the market. The LSTA and its membership have changed all this.

Going forward, the LSTA's core mission is to continue to improve liquidity, efficiency, and transparency in the loan asset class. No one can argue the fact that loans are a great deal more liquid, efficient, and transparent today than they were in 1995 and that these improvements have helped attract a flood of new investors. According to Standard & Poor's, in 1995, banks purchased 71 percent of all leveraged loans in the primary market; today, institutional investors purchase 70 percent of these loans— an astonishing change.

Between 1995 and 2005, the LSTA produced more than 50 standard documents, market advisories, and market practices. In addition, many of these documents have been revised as many as seven times in order to keep them current with market practices.

The rest of this section will be dedicated to reviewing some of the most significant LSTA developments from 1995 to 2005 that have enhanced the liquidity and efficiency of the loan market. The standard documents and market practices adopted by the LSTA will be discussed in the next section. All of the LSTA documents and market practices are meant to be standards for the U.S. market. Practices around the globe may or may not be the same. For current documents and market practices, please go to www.lsta.org. Exhibit 1.36 outlines some of the more significant LSTA achievements from 1995 to 2005.

It is important to note that all procedures and forms are *recommendations* of the LSTA. The LSTA is not a regulatory authority. It has no authority to compel the use of any of its forms by any market participant. *Buyers and sellers of loans can always make modifications to the recommended forms and closing procedures.*

EXHIBIT 1.36

Significant LSTA standards that have improved liquidity.

Standard	Year
• Dealer Based Mark-to-Market Pricing service	1995
• Par/Near Par Trade Confirmation ⇒ (T + 10 established for par/near par loans)	1996
• Distressed Trade Confirmation	1997
• T + 20 initiated for distressed trades	1998
• Mark-to-market pricing moved to weekly basis	
• Faxes OK Master Confidentiality Agreement	
• Code of Conduct and Confidential Information Supplement	
• Mark-to-market pricing moved to daily basis	1999
• LSTA/LPC Mark-to-Market Pricing created; mark-to-market pricing moved from a sell-side business to a buy-side business	
• Distressed Purchase and Sale Agreements	2000
• Standard Assignment Provision and Model Assignment Agreement	
• *Wall Street Journal* begins reporting prices on secondary loans	
• LSTA licenses S&P to create LSTA/S&P Leveraged Loan Index	
• Standard Amendment Procedures	2001
• Enforceability of Oral Trades memo	
• Post 9/11 "liquidity letter" published by LSTA board	
• LSTA launches S&P/LSTA Leveraged Loan Index	
• First trade data study completed	2002
• Loan trading exception from New York State Statute of Frauds becomes effective	
• Distressed Purchase and Sale Agreements overhauled	2003
• Model Bank Book Legends and Guidance	
• JMPF Recommendations for Handling Non-Public Information by Credit Portfolio Managers	
• New Trade Confirmations	2004
– T + 7 for par	
– Major changes to distressed loan documents	
• Primary Market and Agent Transfer Practices	
– Document review period	
– Postclosing status update	
– Electronic delivery of closing documents	
– Allocation and commitment	
– Agent timeline–transferring funded loans	
• Patriot Act position paper	
• CUSIPs launched in the loan market	
• Primary Practice Standards	2005
– Market standard that agents close primary allocations within "F" + 10	
– No delayed compensation for settlement of primary allocations	
– Agents will provide lenders with the date of initial borrowing at lender's request–needed to calculate delayed compensation for "early day" secondary trades–accrues from "F" + 14 for secondary trades entered into "F" + 6 or earlier	

E X H I B I T   1 . 3 6   *(Continued)*

Standard	Year
• Confirmation for Primary Allocations to Institutional Investors–Exhibit A–2 to Primary Practice Standards	2005
– No documentation "out" except for subsequent changes	
– Nonreliance on arranger–lender performs its own due diligence and does not rely on the arranger	
– Acknowledgment that information may include material nonpublic information, which will not be used in violation of laws	
• Revised Model Assignment Provision in Credit Agreements	
– Clarified that increases in the amount of revolver exposure by an existing revolving lender, as well as sales to its affiliates, do not require agent consent	
– Made explicit that no transfers may be made to individuals ("natural" persons)	
– Minimum assignment amount–added a footnote for credit agreement drafter to consider whether in a given credit a minimum assignment amount lower than \$5,000,000 (but in no event less than \$1,000,000) is appropriate for revolving facilities	
• Multi-Allocation Assignment Agreement	
– Simplifies settlement of allocations to multiple subaccounts with a single agreement.	
– Added a new lender-assignee representation to the effect that it is sophisticated with respect to the bank debt market and is experienced in acquiring bank debt.	
– The new lender representation regarding nonreliance has been revised to explicitly contemplate circumstances in which a lender elects not to receive financial and other syndicate-level information that is material nonpublic information.	
• Market Guidance for Handling Private Information in a Public Market	2006

GENERAL MARKET INITIATIVES OF THE LSTA

Mark-to-Market Pricing Service

The very first accomplishment of the LSTA was the creation of a month-end secondary loan pricing service. As a reminder, in 1995, the LSTA was a trade association made up solely of traders from sell-side institutions. Prior to the creation of this service, traders faxed their list of holdings to all the other traders to obtain quotes on the bid/offer prices so that their controllers would have an outsider's view on the price the trader was recording on his books. However, traders did not like sharing this type of information with their competitors, and in reaction to their dissatisfaction, in November 1995, the LSTA arranged for an accounting firm to compile a list of loans that the traders were holding and a bid and an offer price for each of them. In December 1995, prices on 155 different facilities were disseminated to traders for their month-end price marks, and the old system was replaced for good.

In March 1997, the LSTA retained the Loan Pricing Corporation, a vendor that was familiar with the loan product. From 1997 to 1998, the number of *active* loan investment vehicles doubled from 64 to 122. Many of these new vehicles needed a robust secondary pricing service, so reporting frequency was increased to a weekly basis. The market still needed more, and in January 1999 the board of the LSTA identified the need to improve and enhance the existing mark-to-market (MTM) service as its highest priority.

The Loan Pricing Corporation was chosen to continue serving as the LSTA's vendor. In July 1999, the collection of secondary loan prices was increased to a daily basis. In September 1999, LSTA/LPC MTM Pricing was launched, and the service moved from a sell-side focus to a buy-side-driven business. No longer were we asking the traders which loans they wanted priced; we were now asking the institutional investors which loans they needed priced. This one act more than doubled the number of loans being priced. Another milestone was reached in January 2000 when the *Wall Street Journal* began publishing loan prices on a weekly basis.

Today the service collects prices on more than 2,400 loan facilities on a daily basis and services the vast majority of institutional investors in the market (see Exhibit 1.37). The creation and expansion of this pricing service has had a dramatic impact on the evolution of the loan asset class. With the creation of a reliable secondary pricing service, institutional investors now feel comfortable investing in loans as an alternative investment vehicle.

Some people believe that the growth in institutional investors' purchasing loans in the market is a direct result of the improved MTM service. Which comes first, the chicken or the egg—the improvement in the quality and quantity of the marks or the rise in investors? These two increases are illustrated in Exhibit 1.38.

S&P/LSTA Leveraged Loan Market Index

Another important development for the loan market was the creation of a leveraged loan index, which measures market returns

EXHIBIT 1.37

Number of facilities marked by MTM Pricing service.

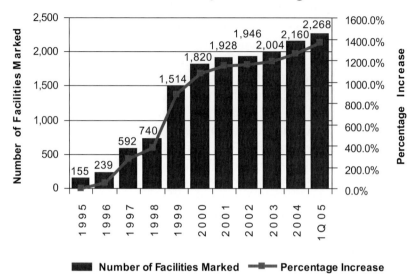

Source: LSTA/LPC Mark-to-Market Pricing.

EXHIBIT 1.38

Percent growth in institutional investors and number of facilities marked since 1995.

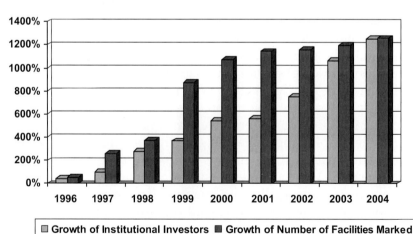

over time. Among other things, this is important for institutional investors that need to measure their own performance against that of the market as a whole.

EXHIBIT 1.39

Average annualized monthly return of S&P/LSTA Index versus other asset classes, January 1997 to September 2005.

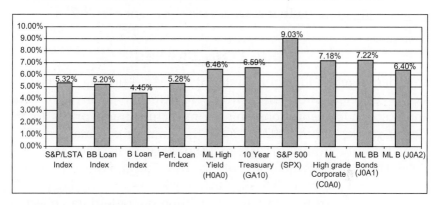

Source: Standard & Poor's, S&P/LSTA Index, Merrill Lynch, Bloomberg.

EXHIBIT 1.40

Historic trade volume.

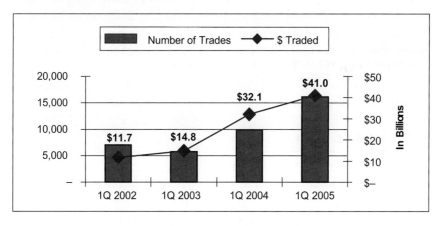

Source: LSTA.

In 1999 the LSTA board voted to establish a leveraged loan index in a partnership with Standard & Poor's (S&P). In August 2000, the LSTA signed a license agreement with S&P to create the S&P/LSTA Leveraged Loan Index. The index was launched in October 2001 and is used to track returns in the leveraged loan market. It captures a broad cross section of the U.S. leveraged loan market, including dollar-denominated, U.S.-syndicated loans to overseas issuers. It is available at Bloomberg page LCDZ.

The performance of loans relative to other investment alternatives will be discussed in more detail throughout the rest of this book. However, Exhibit 1.39 gives a snapshot of loan-market performance compared to other asset classes since January 1997.

Trade Data Studies

In order to get an idea of the integrity of MTM pricing, in 2002 the LSTA collected information from six institutional investors and three sell-side institutions comparing actual trade prices to the dealer marks. From 2002 to 2005, the number of data providers grew steadily, from 9 in 2002 to 12 in 2003, 16 in 2004, and 18 in 2005. The providers are from both the buy side and the sell side and include both par and distressed loan desks. As the number of data providers has grown, so has the volume of trade data collected. Data for the analysis, which covered only the first quarter of each year, consisted of $11.66 billion in 2002, $14.77 billion in 2003, $32.08 billion in 2004, and $40.97 billion in 2005 (Exhibit 1.40). In 2002, the study included 39 percent of Loan Pricing Corporation's estimated first-quarter secondary volume; in 2003, it included 46 percent; in 2004, 77 percent; and in 2005, a staggering 102 percent (meaning that the LSTA collected 2% more trades than Reuters LPC reported in 05).

The LSTA/LPC MTM Pricing service and related products continue to evolve and improve. The studies show that the relationship

EXHIBIT 1.41

Standard assignment amounts for term loans.

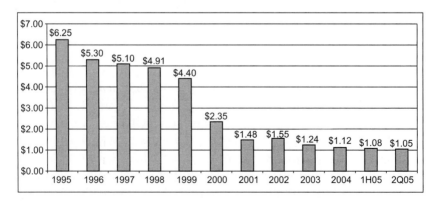

Source: Standard & Poor's and LSTA.

between MTM and trade prices has tightened, with the greatest variations being associated with the higher-risk loans that suffer from the most informational inefficiencies. However, where credit quality signals are clear and pricing information flows efficiently, the relationship is strengthening. So, while the relationship between MTM and trade price is not perfect, the highest degrees of variance show up where they are expected—in areas of illiquidity, uncertainty, and risk.

CUSIPs

Creating unique identifiers for loans has been the largest, most time-consuming, and most difficult initiative ever undertaken by the LSTA. Through the tireless efforts of individuals at JPMorgan and CS, CUSIPs on all syndicated loans were launched in January 2004. We envision that agent banks will ultimately be able to electronically alert their bank groups of interest payments, paydowns, and the like. The syndicate banks will one day be able to update all their books and records electronically, thereby reducing human error and substantially increasing the efficiencies of the loan asset class. The implementation of CUSIPs could prove to be the watershed event in the development of loan-market efficiency and transparency.

STANDARD DOCUMENTS AND REGULATORY MATTERS

The other major focus of the LSTA has been the development of standard documents and the management of major legal and regulatory matters of importance to the loan market. These developments will be discussed in the next section.

It's difficult to graph or demonstrate the success that the LSTA has had on the market as each initiative is adopted. That being said, we can show the effect that the LSTA's adoption of standard minimum assignment amounts had on the market.

In 2001, the LSTA adopted a new standard of a minimum assignment for term loans of $1mm and for revolvers of $5mm. By the end of 2001, the average minimum standard assignment for term loans reached $1.48mm, down from $6.25mm in 1995. See Exhibit 1.41.

EXHIBIT 1.42

Volume of syndicated lending and secondary trading since 1995.

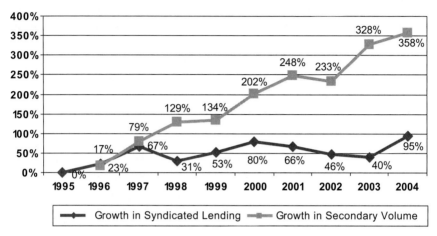

Source: Loan Pricing Corporation and LSTA.

EXHIBIT 1.43

LSTA Chairs 1995–2006.

Year	Name	Institution
1995–1998	Allison Taylor	ING-Barings
1998–1999	Danise Longworth	JPMorgan
2000	Bob Hevner	Deutsche Bank
2001	Mike McAdams	ING Capital
2002	Linda Bammann	Bank One
2003	Glenn Stewart	Bank of America
2004	Don Pollard	Credit Suisse First Boston
2005–2006	Scott Krase	Oak Hill

WHAT ELSE IS LEFT TO DO?

The loan market has changed dramatically over the last 10 years, and it will continue to change. Exhibit 1.42 highlights the rise of secondary trading compared to the rise of syndicated lending. Undoubtedly, all of the LSTA's standard documents and market practices will need to be revised from time to time to address market developments. But the LSTA won't stop there!

The LSTA expects to address many developing issues and challenges. It expects to be at the forefront of the global expansion of the loan market. It expects to play a significant role in the development of credit derivatives as a tool in the loan market. And, importantly, the LSTA expects to be a major source of education and training in the loan marketplace.

It is difficult to predict where the loan market will be headed in the next few years. But it is easy to predict that wherever it goes, the LSTA will be right at the cutting edge.

CONCLUSION

The LSTA is a consensus-building body of loan-market participants from both the buy side and the sell side. This is different from many similar trade associations that only represent one side of the market. I believe that this is one of the major reasons for our success. All the significant large players in the market, as well as many smaller players, are members. The LSTA solves problems, the LSTA creates solutions, and the LSTA is a place to band together to deal with new challenges that arise in the market. The LSTA is at the heart of the loan market.

The LSTA has always stood ready to deal with the most critical issues affecting the loan market at any given time. Its success is due to the time and dedication of its members. I want to take this time to sincerely thank all of our past chairs, board members, committee chairs, and, most of all, our members for the past 10 years of commitment to the loan asset class. (Exhibit 1.43)

I have found it very gratifying to serve the loan market, and the LSTA has made a substantial difference in shaping the loan market as we know it today. It will continue to influence its ever-changing landscape. I sincerely look forward to being a part of its continuing evolution.

The LSTA—A Regulatory and Documentation Review

Elliot Ganz
General Counsel, LSTA

From its inception, the LSTA has played a prominent role in the development of legal standards that have affected the loan market.

The LSTA's focus has been on five primary areas: (1) documentation and market standards, (2) best practices and policy, (3) legislation, (4) litigation, and (5) regulatory and accounting issues. This section will review some of the important legal developments driven by or addressed by the LSTA over the past 10 years.

DOCUMENTATION

Prior to the establishment of the LSTA, there were virtually no market standards for trading loans and no standardized documents. Closing even a par trade could take weeks or even months because each document, from the confirmation to the assignment agreement, had to be negotiated separately each time. Closing distressed trades was that much more difficult. In the past 10 years, the LSTA has spearheaded efforts to increase the liquidity, efficiency, and transparency of the loan market through the development of standard documents in both the secondary and primary markets.

The LSTA began its efforts to standardize documents at the most basic level: confirmations for secondary trades of performing, or par, loans. The process of reaching a consensus on a standard par confirmation involved negotiations and discussions, sometimes heated, among attorneys and businesspeople, most of whom worked in the trenches, i.e., the trading floors of major dealers.

This process has been followed repeatedly. Standardized documents have never been simply conjured up by a bunch of lawyers in a conference room; rather, the documents have been carefully crafted to reflect market consensus and, of course, what is possible at the time.[10] And it is also noteworthy that the process has not been stagnant. Many of the documents developed by the LSTA have been revised numerous times to reflect changing market practices and, often, increased efficiency (the par confirmation itself was revised five times between 1996 and 2005).

In 1996, one of the earliest decisions made through the consensus building process was the establishment of the market convention that there would be no "breakfunding" paid between buyers and sellers at the time of settlement of a secondary trade. Under

---

[10] For example, lawyers did not invent the concept of T + 10 for par loans; instead, they drafted documents that reflected the consensus of the market participants. Accordingly, as the market became more efficient, T + 10 was reduced, because of market consensus, to T + 7. This new consensus was then drafted into the documents.

most credit agreements, the borrower has the right to draw down multiple LIBOR contracts with different maturities. For example, under a $100mm Term Loan A facility, a borrower may choose borrow $20mm for 3 months using 3 month LIBOR, $50mm for 6 months using 6 month LIBOR and another $30mm borrowed for 1 month using 1 month LIBOR (the borrower makes these decisions based on it's perception of the direction of interest rates).

The lenders, in turn, are required to fund each of these contracts. Prior to the adoption of the market convention, the buyer of a loan in the secondary market would compensate the seller to the extent that LIBOR decreased between the original date of the LIBOR contracts and the date of funding of the secondary trade. This was known as "breakfunding".

The members of the LSTA decided that it would enhance the liquidity and transparency of the loan market if the convention of breakfunding were dropped.

The market also understood that whatever small amounts might be achieved by charging for breakfunding would, in the long run, likely be offset by the administrative costs saved in not having to calculate these costs, and in the timelier closing of trades.

In 1997, the LSTA went on to tackle much thornier issues. It implemented the concept of delayed compensation[11] and revised the par confirmation to reflect this convention. That same year, it developed, published, and revised a distressed trade confirmation. In the following year, the LSTA established T + 20 as the market convention for closing distressed trades and implemented delayed compensation on distressed trades. Also in 1997, forms for bilateral and multilateral netting were published.

In the years that followed, as the LSTA standards took hold and helped to increase market efficiency, the LSTA developed more complex standardized documents, such as confidentiality agreements, assignment agreements for par and distressed loans, and, later, distressed trade purchase and sale agreements (PSA). Developing the PSA was, of course, much more difficult, reflecting the complexities presented by distressed loan trading issues.

---

[11] Under delayed compensation, the seller of a funded loan pays the buyer the interest rate paid under a credit agreement, and the buyer pays the seller the cost of carry beginning after the designated market closing period, generally either T + 7 (for par loans) or T + 20 (for distressed loans). Delayed compensation is a "no-fault" system whose goal is to prevent parties from artificially shorting loans by simply delaying the closing of trades without cost.

The next area of focus for the LSTA was so-called primary loan documentation. These efforts to standardize the *underlying loan assets* were important because the more that basic loan documents could be made to look like one another, the more efficient and transparent it would be to trade them in the secondary markets. Over the years, model credit agreement provisions were adopted, as were, among other things, model transfer provisions, amendment provisions, an administrative questionnaire, and a form assignment and assumption agreement.

Finally, as the distressed loan trading market became more sophisticated and more global, the LSTA turned its attention to specific bankruptcy- and credit derivative–related situations. In 2004, the LSTA, together with the Bond Market Association, developed a Model NOL Order[12] to ensure continued liquidity in postpetition claims markets, and began the process of developing a Proceeds Letter to address issues that arise with respect to post-reorganization securities that are the proceeds of prepetition debt. In 2005, an ad hoc group of loan- and derivative-market participants began exploring the development of a "loan-only" credit derivative product. The LSTA expects to play a major role in the development of documentation that will address the requirements of that growing market. Finally, the LSTA, in partnership with the Loan Market Association, was also instrumental in helping to develop standard terms and practices that could be applied globally.

BEST PRACTICES AND POLICY

From the outset, one of the missions of the LSTA has been to develop market consensus around best practices from a legal and regulatory perspective. Because of the diverse nature of the participants in the loan market, the LSTA never sought to dictate specific policies or procedures; rather, it aimed to express general principles or guidelines that would be relevant to all market participants, no matter what their particular circumstances or makeup.

---

[12] The dual purpose of the Model NOL Order is to protect a debtor corporation's ability to use net operating loss (NOL) carryovers and other tax attributes without unduly restricting trading in the bankrupt corporation's debt. Recurring trading interruptions that were caused by broad NOL orders precipitated the need for a Model NOL Order. The problem was very serious, as some orders had the effect of either immediately halting or severely restricting trading. Cases involving such NOL orders include UAL, US Airways, Mirant, Conseco, and WorldCom. In 2005, the positive impact of the Model NOL Order was felt in such cases as Delphi, Delta Airlines, and Northwest Airlines.

The first efforts to develop such market principles occurred in 1998, when a Code of Conduct and a Confidential Information Supplement to the Code of Conduct were published by the LSTA. The purpose of the Code of Conduct was to establish general standards of trading conduct that would be acceptable to all market participants. As the code itself pointed out, "the Code is a set of standards and procedures, compliance with which is completely voluntary.... The Code is intended to promote compliance with and work in tandem with applicable legal requirements, and to provide guidance where such requirements do not exist." The code went on to make another important point that applies to all market pronouncements and recommendations made by the LSTA: "A market participant should implement the Code in a manner appropriate to the size, nature and complexity of the market participant and its participation in the loan market, as well as its business activities generally." In other words, "one size does *not* fit all."

Indeed, this principle was also applied to the Confidential Information Supplement. Rather than articulating strict policies and procedures for the management of confidential information, the supplement defined certain classes of information, such as "syndicate confidential information" and "borrower confidential information," and proposed broad guidelines that market participants were urged to follow in a manner appropriate to each of them given their particular circumstances.

In October 2003, the LSTA and several other trade associations published the Joint Market Practices Forum's "Statement of Principles and Recommendations Regarding the Handling of Material Non-Public Information by Credit Market Participants." The Statement of Principles provides guidance to credit market participants that use public securities and securities-based swaps to manage their credit portfolios. It outlines the proper handling of information obtained in the ordinary course of their private lending activities to ensure that this information is not inappropriately shared with or used by others within the same institution that have responsibility for managing portfolio credit risk. Once again, the principles are stated broadly enough to cover the particular facts and circumstances that affect the wide range of market participants.

More recently, the LSTA has been developing principles for the use of material nonpublic information that apply to loan market participants who also participate in the public securities markets.

LEGISLATIVE INITIATIVES

The third area of focus for the LSTA has been on legislative initiatives.

During its first 10 years, the LSTA was rarely involved in direct efforts to bring about specific legislation. The one exception was its successful effort to amend the New York State Statute of Frauds law to exempt loan trading, so that oral trades are binding so long as all material terms of the trade have been established. Prior to the amendment, when a buyer and a seller orally agreed to a loan trade, they did not have a legally binding contract until the confirmation was signed. This was unlike transactions involving most other asset classes, where oral trades are legally binding. In June 2001, the LSTA undertook a legislative effort to amend the New York State Statute of Frauds to create an exemption for loan trading. In June 2002, the Statute of Frauds Bill passed both houses of the New York State Legislature, and in August Governor Pataki signed the statute of frauds legislation. In October 2002 the loan trading exemption from the Statute of Frauds became effective, a milestone accomplishment for the LSTA.

The application of the Statute of Frauds to loan trades posed substantial risks, especially in the distressed market, where prices can change rapidly. Thus, working to amend the statute was an important exercise for the LSTA.

LITIGATION

During its first 10 years, the LSTA has participated as an *amicus curiae* ("friend of the court") four times. In each case, the decision to file was made on an ad hoc basis, but, in late 2005, the LSTA adopted a policy and procedure for filing *amicus* briefs.

The relevant paragraph in the policy states that an "*amicus* brief... may be filed with any court of competent jurisdiction if the legal issues presented are ripe for consideration and *raise serious policy issues that broadly affect any one, or all, of the markets and market participants represented by the Association*" [emphasis added].

The LSTA's first *amicus* brief was filed in connection with an appeal of a U.S. District Court decision[13] that held that §489 of the New York State Judicial Law permitted an obligor on a claim to

---

[13] *Elliott Associates, L.P. v. Republic of Peru*, 1998 WL 477436 (S.D.N.Y. Aug. 6, 1998) ("*Elliott v. Peru*").

defend an enforcement action on the basis that the holder acquired the claim with the intent and for the purpose of bringing a legal action thereon.[14] Applied to the market for secondary loan trading, however, this interpretation of the statute could have wreaked havoc. Accordingly, the LSTA filed an *amicus* brief and the U.S. Court of Appeals for the Second Circuit, agreeing with the position of the LSTA, reversed the lower court's decision.[15]

A second *amicus* brief was prepared on behalf of the LSTA in a case where the plaintiff attacked the enforceability of the LSTA's own distressed debt confirmation. However, the plaintiffs amended their pleadings to drop this allegation before the *amicus* brief was actually filed.

In December 2004, the LSTA and the Clearing House Association filed an *amici* brief with the U.S. Court of Appeals for the Third Circuit supporting the reversal of a district court decision that granted "substantive consolidation" in bankruptcy proceedings involving Owens Corning.[16]

Substantive consolidation would have allowed the company to substantively combine its assets and liabilities with those of its subsidiaries, a move that would have effectively wiped out the structural seniority positions held by a group of bank lenders that had obtained repayment guarantees from a number of the company's subsidiaries. After consolidation, the banks would have had to share the benefits of the subsidiaries' guarantees equally with all other unsecured creditors.

The appellate court affirmed the LSTA's position in a strongly worded opinion.[17] The Third Circuit opinion stated that "no principled, or even plausible, reason exists to undo the [borrower's] and the banks' arm's-length negotiations and lending arrangement" and that to do so would cause "chaos in the marketplace." The Owens

---

[14] In *Elliott v. Peru*, Elliott Associates, L.P. ("Elliott") purchased in the secondary market from ING and Swiss Bank $20.5 million face amount of working capital debt of two Peruvian banks, for which it paid approximately $11.5 million. Peru guaranteed to repay the entire amount. When Elliott sued to enforce payment of the indebtedness and to collect on the guarantee, the defendants asserted as a defense to payment New York's champerty statute, New York Judiciary Law §489. The so-called champerty statute was a relic of the medieval practice of lawyers purchasing claims for nominal consideration for the sole purpose of bringing suit thereon and collecting legal fees from the obligor.
[15] See *Elliot Associates, L.P. v. Republic of Peru*, 194 F. 3d 363 (2nd cir. 1999).
[16] 316 B.R. 168 (Bankr. D. Del. 2004). The appeal was brought by Credit Suisse First Boston on behalf of a syndicate of lenders that had extended a $2 billion unsecured loan to Owens Corning and certain of its subsidiaries.
[17] *In re Owens Corning*, No. 04–4080 (3d Cir. August 15, 2005).

Corning case is another example in which the LSTA intervened for compelling policy reasons.

In December 2005, the LSTA agreed to join an *amici* brief with three other trade associations to oppose a ruling by the Bankruptcy Court in the Southern District of New York that a claim in bankruptcy in the hands of an innocent holder who purchased for value is subject to equitable subordination[18] on the ground that a previous holder of that claim engaged in improper conduct that harmed other creditors.

The LSTA concluded that the court's ruling could have a very detrimental effect on the liquidity and transparency of the market for loans because, among other reasons, it is impossible for an innocent holder of bankruptcy claims to conduct proper due diligence on the so-called bad actors.

The LSTA will, no doubt, continue to get involved in appropriate cases that raise important policy issues for the market.

REGULATORY AND ACCOUNTING ISSUES

The LSTA has frequently taken positions on regulatory and accounting issues that are of importance to the loan market. For example, in April 2001, the LSTA issued a position paper regarding the application of the SEC's Regulation FD[19] to the syndicated loan market. The memorandum analyzed the application of Regulation FD to the syndicated commercial loan market, and concluded that the practices currently in place in the market should protect companies seeking access to the syndicated loan market from violations of Regulation FD.[20]

In 2004, the LSTA produced a position paper[21] on the Patriot Act Customer Identification Procedure (CIP). The paper was designed to set forth guidance for the syndicated lending market on

---

[18] Section 510(c)(1) of the Bankruptcy Code provides that, after notice and a hearing, the court may "under principles of equitable subordination, subordinate for purposes of distribution all or part of an allowed claim to all or part of another allowed claim or all or part of an allowed interest to all or part of another allowed interest."

[19] 17 C.F.R. 243.100–243.103.

[20] The regulation provides, *inter alia*, that when an issuer, or a person acting on its behalf, discloses material nonpublic information to certain enumerated persons (in general, securities market professionals and holders of the issuer's securities, who may well trade on the basis of the information), it must make public disclosure of that information.

[21] On the LSTA Web site, www.lsta.org

Patriot Act CIP verification, the enhanced anti-money-laundering compliance procedures issued under the Patriot Act that became effective in October 2003. The guidance was designed to serve as a helpful reference point as firms developed and implemented procedures to satisfy the CIP verification requirements. The principal conclusion of the guidance was that the relationships between agents and lenders and between trading counterparties in the secondary loan market generally do not give rise to "accounts" or "customer" relationships as contemplated by the regulations and, accordingly, do not require any special compliance procedures.

The LSTA has also actively advocated accounting positions that are important to the loan market.[22] The LSTA has sought to modify accounting positions espoused by the Financial Accounting Standards Board (FASB) that could have negatively affected the syndicated loan market or related products. In August 2002, the LSTA met with the SEC in response to the FASB's Exposure Draft on SPE Consolidation. In September 2002, the LSTA submitted a comment letter to the FASB regarding the SPE consolidation and subsequently participated in a roundtable discussion on the matter.

More importantly, during 2004 and 2005, the LSTA spent a great deal of time advocating that the FASB's proposed amendment to *FAS 140* should not go so far as to end sales treatment for loan participations. The FASB's decision on this issue was of critical concern to the LSTA because of the adverse impact that a change in *FAS 140* standards could potentially have had on the loan participation market. In no small part because of the LSTA's advocacy, the FASB determined that loan participations in the United States will continue to receive sales accounting treatment under *FAS 140* so long as the transfer constitutes a "true sale at law."[23]

On February 28, 2003, the Internal Revenue Service adopted final regulations regarding tax return disclosure, registration, and list-keeping requirements relating to tax shelters. After considering industry comments, including an LSTA comment letter, the final regulations cut back substantially on the scope of previously issued and widely criticized temporary regulations that would have imposed burdensome compliance requirements on many routine transactions.

---

[22] The accounting-related activities of the LSTA are recounted in this section because the accounting standards in question are informed to a large extent by legal issues.

[23] To qualify for sales accounting treatment, a legal conclusion that a "true sale" has occurred will be sufficient; a legal opinion will not be required in all cases, however.

Nevertheless, the final regulations still imposed some risk unless certain prophylactic measures were taken. Consequently, to aid the loan market in adopting so-called nonconfidentiality clauses that could effectively mitigate the risk, the LSTA published a memorandum explaining the regulations in detail and providing suggested sample risk-mitigating provisions for the various documents used in connection with typical loans.

CONCLUSION

From its inception, the LSTA has been at the forefront of legal efforts to support and defend the loan asset class and promote liquidity, transparency, and efficiency in the marketplace for loans. It is likely that the LSTA's legal focus will grow along with the asset class and will continue to play a major role in its development.

CHAPTER 2

Effects of the Legal Characterization of Loans under the Securities Laws

**Tiziana M. Bason, Michael P. Kaplan, and
Bradley Y. Smith**
Davis, Polk & Wardwell

The syndicated loan market was founded on the assumption that loans are not "securities" under the federal or state securities laws, and that therefore the underwriting, syndication, and trading of loans are not regulated by such laws. Although this assumption has come under increased scrutiny in recent years, it remains fundamental to the market's development and operation, and there has been no reported judicial decision to the contrary. What are the main advantages of the current legal categorization of loans? What changes would need to be made to the underwriting, syndication, and trading practices of our members if loans were considered securities subject to the laws applicable to securities? This chapter analyzes these questions and provides practical suggestions for our members to consider if the legal climate changes.

LEGAL BACKGROUND

To appreciate the significance of loans not being characterized as securities for purposes of the securities laws, one must first have some appreciation of those laws and their application to capital-market transactions involving the offer and sale of securities.

Regulation under the Federal Securities Laws

The public and private sale of "securities" is governed by the Securities Act of 1933 (as amended, the '33 Act) and the Securities Exchange Act of 1934 (as amended, the '34 Act and, together with the '33 Act, the Acts), together with, in each case, the rules and regulations thereunder. The Acts regulate the process by which securities may be issued and sold by "issuers," "underwriters," and "dealers" (as these terms are defined in the '33 Act) and subject each of them to the antifraud provisions of the '34 Act.

The '33 Act focuses on the initial distribution of securities by issuers and underwriters, not secondary trading (other than by underwriters), and its primary purpose is to ensure that investors are given full and fair disclosure about the issuer and the securities offered before making an investment decision. The '34 Act, on the other hand, provides protection to buyers and sellers in the secondary markets by requiring issuers to keep their information current through periodic reporting requirements.

As a general matter, the sale of a security by an issuer or an underwriter may be made only if the Securities and Exchange Commission (the SEC) has declared a registration statement relating to the sale effective or if either the security itself or the transaction in which the security is being sold is exempt from the registration requirements. Exemption from registration does not, with limited exceptions, exempt the sale of a security from the relevant antifraud provisions of the '34 Act. The exemptions from registration that are most relevant to the discussion in this chapter are the Section 4(2) "old-style" private placement exemption and the safe harbor provided by Rule 144A.

Section 4(2) Exemption

Section 4(2) of the '33 Act provides an exemption from the registration and other requirements of the '33 Act for any issuance of securities by an issuer "not involving a public offering." While the cases are varied, from the first Supreme Court case on the issue (*SEC v. Ralston Purina*), the key to the exemption has been whether the offering is made solely to those who are able to fend for themselves and therefore do not need the protection that registration would afford to investors. In addition, buyers cannot purchase with a view to broad distribution. As a result, transactions relying solely on Section 4(2) for an exemption from registration are generally limited to offerings to very large institutional investors. In these transactions (often referred to as "old-style" private placements), each purchaser enters into a contract directly with the issuer to acquire the securities. If an investment bank is involved, it agrees only to use its best efforts to identify purchasers as a placement agent for the issuer and does not take any underwriting risk. The placement agent generally restricts contacts to customers with which the agent has a preexisting relationship, keeps records on the number of offerees contacted, and limits the number of offerees. Because of the sophistication and bargaining power of the potential purchasers, each purchaser undertakes its own due diligence of the issuer, and the only "disclosure" document may be a term sheet for the securities offered and, depending on the issuer, whatever information is publicly available.

Both the terms of the offering and the terms of the purchase agreement are the subject of significant negotiation among the issuer, its placement agent, and the potential purchasers. If the group of institutions is large, those making smaller purchases typically rely on the one or two largest purchasers to take the lead in negotiations. Counsel to the purchasers is expected to deliver an opinion at closing that no registration of the offered securities is required under the Securities Act, but a 10b-5 disclosure letter is rarely provided.

The purchasers in these old-style private placements generally expect to hold the securities they acquire for a substantial period of time. Because Section 4(2) is a transaction exemption that exempts only the initial sale of securities by the issuer to the initial purchasers, these purchasers acquire what are commonly referred to as *restricted securities*. These purchasers then must establish a separate exemption for any resale of the securities, as long as the securities they hold remain restricted. Any resale that is not pursuant to an exemption could retroactively vitiate the exemption of the initial placement.

Rule 144A Exemption

Rule 144A supplements the statutory private placement exemption with an exception for resales of restricted securities, and by doing so has created a highly liquid market for privately placed securities.

Rule 144A accommodates important variations from the old-style private placements just described. First, it permits investment banks to perform their customary underwriting function without requiring them to register the sale of securities. Second, the rule facilitates secondary trading of securities after the initial placement of securities to the syndicate by permitting resales to sophisticated institutional investors without limitations on time or volume. It is important to note that Rule 144A provides an exemption for the resale of the securities, not the original purchase from the issuer. Thus, in an underwritten offering of debt securities, investment banks rely on the Section 4(2) exemption for the initial sale of the securities by the issuer to them, and rely on Rule 144A for their resale of the securities (as well as for resales by investors).

Rule 144A clarifies that an investment bank that resells securities acquired from an issuer in a private placement under Rule 144A will not be deemed a dealer under Section 4(3) of the '33 Act or an underwriter under Section 2(11) of the '33 Act, thus permitting investment banks to perform the functional role of underwriter without causing them to become "underwriters" or "dealers," which would make their purchase of securities subject to the '33 Act. The rule also permits resales of securities, without limitation of time, to persons whom the seller reasonably believes are "qualified institutional buyers," so long as reasonable steps are taken to ensure that the potential purchasers are aware that the seller may rely on the rule for an exemption from registration.

Practice under Rule 144A

A Rule 144A offering typically involves (1) business and legal due diligence by the investment bank and its outside counsel, in order to enable counsel to provide a 10b-5 disclosure letter; (2) preparation of an offering document (typically referred to as an offering memorandum or circular) with input from counsel and auditors; (3) preparation and negotiation of the underwriting papers (typically referred to as a purchase agreement) and related documents; and (4) negotiation with auditors and counsel regarding the contents of comfort letters and legal 10b-5 disclosure letters. With respect to the contents of the offering document for a Rule 144A offering, although such an offering does not have to comply with the strict letter of the SEC's extensive requirements for a registration statement, the antifraud provisions of the federal securities laws, as well as the common law of fraud, apply to disclosures made in connection with the marketing of unregistered securities. As a result, Rule 144A offering documents tend to include (or incorporate by reference from the issuer's SEC filings, if eligible) all the disclosure that would have been required if the offering were registered under the '33 Act.[1]

Advantages of Loan Characterization

The fact that loans currently are not characterized as securities for purposes of the securities laws affords both borrowers and arrangers of syndicated loan facilities greater flexibility in accessing sources of debt capital. This flexibility results from two related legal considerations: first, the absence of any requirement either to go through the registration process with the SEC or to ensure that the transaction satisfies all technical requirements for an exemption from the registration requirements of the securities laws, and

---

[1] At a minimum, Rule 144A requires availability of current basic financial information about the issuer upon request by an investor.

second, the absence of exposure to antifraud liability under the securities laws, which is discussed in more detail in the next section of this chapter. These legal considerations translate into important practical benefits: There is no need, either as a legal matter or as a matter of market practice, to create a prospectus or similar offering document that satisfies detailed SEC disclosure requirements, and there is no need for some of the traditional due diligence elements of a securities offering—accountants' "cold comfort" letters and lawyers' 10b-5 disclosure letters—that can add both time and expense to the transaction and in certain cases make it impossible to consummate a securities offering within a particular time frame.

IF LOANS WERE SECURITIES

If loans were to be considered securities for purposes of the securities laws, the impact on loan-market participants would be twofold. First, loan-market participants would have to satisfy themselves that the origination, syndication, and trading of loans were effected in a manner that did not contravene the registration requirements of the '33 Act. Second, loan-market participants would need to reexamine their approach to disclosure and due diligence issues in light of the potentially greater risk of liability under the antifraud provisions of the securities laws. Finally, certain other regulatory regimes, including state securities laws and regulations by the National Association of Securities Dealers, Inc. (the NASD), would also affect practice.

Compliance with Registration Requirements

Under current market practice, the initial underwriting and placement of a syndicated loan facility, considered apart from secondary trading, would probably qualify for an exemption from registration requirements under Section 4(2) of the '33 Act. The transaction does not involve a public offering because the purchasers of the securities are very large and/or sophisticated investors. Although the range of institutions that invest in syndicated loans has broadened since the early days, when loan-market participants were exclusively commercial banks, such institutions are nevertheless sophisticated investors of the type that can (and do) fend for themselves. The problem with this analysis, however, is that the legal issue cannot be considered apart from secondary trading in the loans, which is an integral part of the loan market, and, as noted earlier, Section 4(2) does not provide an exemption from registration requirements for resale of restricted securities (indeed, resales can retroactively taint the exemption afforded for the initial purchase). Therefore, loan-market participants would have to turn to Rule 144A.

To establish the availability of the Rule 144A exemption, loan-market participants would need to consider adoption of the following procedures:

- They would need to confirm that the issuer is eligible for the Rule 144A exemption. Investment companies are not, and if an issuer is not a reporting company under the '34 Act or a foreign private issuer that voluntarily furnishes certain information to the SEC pursuant to Rule 12g3-2(b) under the '34 Act, the issuer must agree to provide certain current information to potential investors who request the information.[2] It would need to screen potential investors that would be solicited during the syndication process to ensure that the loan-market participant has a reasonable belief that all investors are qualified institutional buyers (QIBs) as defined in Rule 144A. (In general, qualified institutional buyers are institutions that have $100,000,000 or more invested in securities of unaffiliated issuers.) Reasonable belief may be established by certification from potential buyers, but the certification does not have to relate to a specific transaction. Reasonable belief may also be established through recent publicly available information about the prospective purchaser. Thus, certain professional services publish lists of investors that have been identified as qualified institutional buyers, and most investment banks have solicited certifications from their clients as to their status, on which they rely.
- They should notify the potential syndicate members that the seller may be relying on the exemption from '33 Act

---

[2] To ensure compliance with the informational requirement of Rule 144A, members could include in the bank book for any borrower that is not a reporting company three years of financial statements and a brief business description. The financial statements need not be audited (or include footnotes) to the extent that an audit is not reasonably available.

registration requirements provided by Rule 144A. The following language could be included in the bank book:

> The Borrower and the Arranger intend that the term loans should not constitute "securities" for purposes of U.S. securities laws. If the loans are deemed to be securities, potential lenders are hereby notified that the Borrower and the Arranger may be relying on the exemption from registration under the Securities Act provided by Rule 144A thereunder in connection with the loans.[3]

- As to documentation, while securities offerings typically include elaborate representations by the issuer concerning compliance with Rule 144A (e.g., absence of integration with another securities offering, general solicitation, and so on), the general representation by the borrower in the credit agreement should be that the execution and delivery of the credit agreement and the notes (if any are issued) do not violate applicable laws and that no consents are required in connection therewith. If members wish, they could add an explicit reference to the securities laws and Rule 144A in the representation. With respect to trading, the credit documentation could require that lenders certify in the assignment documentation that any assignment of a loan is done in compliance with applicable law.[4]

- Finally, in order to comply with the requirement that a private placement be conducted in a manner that does not involve a "general solicitation," no party involved—the

---

[3] This legend is drafted on the assumption that a change in the law in this area will be evolutionary: a case or two will decide on its facts that the loans in question are securities, with the consequence that loan-market participants will as a matter of prudence alter their practices on the assumption that loans will be held to be securities without necessarily wishing to concede that for purposes of future litigation.

[4] Technically, the arranger of a syndicated loan facility does not need to police resales to effect an initial valid Rule 144A placement, so it is not necessary to specifically restrict resales to QIBs, although it is customary to do so in securities offerings. (Note that this assumes that the initial loan is made by the arranger, who then assigns portions of it to other lenders.) However, any subsequent lender that wishes to assign its loan (including the arranger if it intends to make a market in the loans) will need to make sure that its resales comply with applicable law. If the loans are deemed to be securities, then lenders would need to resell using Rule 144A or another exemption. This suggestion is a middle ground between ignoring resales altogether and adding securities-type transfer restrictions, which would appear unusual in a credit agreement.

borrower, the members arranging the syndicate, or the members acting as agents for the syndicate—should talk publicly, including to the press, about the loans prior to the completion of syndication. Disclosure in a press release consistent with that permitted under Rule 135c of the Securities Act (which permits a brief announcement of the transaction and the use of proceeds, without naming any arranger or agent bank) would be permitted, as would discussions with rating agencies in order to obtain a rating of the facility.

Antifraud Liability Considerations

The more difficult question, and potentially the greater change in current market practice, concerns the approach to disclosure and due diligence issues if loans are held to be securities for purposes of the antifraud provisions of the securities laws.

Under the current legal regime, regardless of whether loans are securities, loan-market participants are liable for common law fraud for material misrepresentations in connection with the syndication of loans. While the specific elements of common law fraud may vary among jurisdictions, generally, a plaintiff will need to establish that (1) the defendant made a material false representation, (2) the defendant knew that the representation was false, and made it with the intent to defraud ("scienter"), (3) the plaintiff reasonably and justifiably relied on the false representation, and (4) the plaintiff suffered damage as a result of such reliance. The exposure of a member arranging a syndicate (the arranger) to liability for material misstatements may be mitigated by representations from the loan-market participants that they have done their own due diligence with respect to the borrower and are not relying on the arranger with respect to credit decisions, which have been upheld by some courts as evidence of lack of justifiable reliance.[5] However, courts have not always respected such representations and disclaimers. For example, when loan-market participants do not have sufficient access to the borrower and its records to complete their own due diligence, or when the arranger has made

---

[5] See, e.g., *Banque Arabe et Internationale d'Investissement v. Maryland Nat'l Bank*, 57 F.3d 146 (2d Cir. 1995); *UniCredito Italiano SPA v. JPMorgan Chase Bank*, 288 F. Supp. 2d 485 (S.D.N.Y. 2003).

independent oral representations to the loan-market participants that are not specifically covered by the mitigating representations or disclaimers, courts have found that such mitigating representations or disclaimers are not sufficient to render the reliance of the loan-market participants on the misstatements made by the arranger unjustified.[6]

If loans were considered securities, loan-market participants would be subject to the antifraud provisions of Rule 10b-5 under the '34 Act, in addition to the common law fraud liability for material misrepresentations described previously. Rule 10b-5 generally prohibits the use of a materially misleading statement or omission in connection with the purchase or sale of a security. Courts have long recognized an implied private cause of action for violations of Rule 10b-5 and have imposed liability based on material misstatements and omissions in connection with purchases and sales of securities in contexts where a statutory remedy is not permitted under Sections 11 and 12 of the '33 Act (which impose liability for material misstatements or omissions in connection with registration statements and prospectuses in a registered offering). As civil liability under Rule 10b-5 is judicially inferred, courts have generally required the same elements as under common law fraud to establish liability. However, with respect to scienter, courts have relaxed the requirement, so that affirmative intent to deceive may not be necessary, and reckless disregard for the truth or falsity of the statements in question may be sufficient. Therefore, Rule 10b-5 violations may be easier to prove than common law fraud. In addition, the use of representations and disclaimers in syndicated loan documents to limit the liability of the arranger for misstatements in the common law fraud context previously discussed is undermined by Section 29(a) of the '34 Act in the Rule 10b-5 context. Section 29(a) voids any "condition, stipulation or provision binding any person to waive compliance with any provision" of the '34 Act. Although some courts have held that nonreliance clauses do not violate Section 29(a), other courts have reached the opposite conclusion.[7] While nonreliance clauses in agreements between sophisticated parties may be evidence of nonreliance, the nonreliance clause is

---

[6] See, e.g., *Hitachi Credit America Corp. v. Signet Bank*, 166 F.3d 614 (4th Cir. 1999).

[7] Compare *AES Corp. v. Dow Chemical Co.*, 325 F.3d 174 (3rd Cir. 2003) and *Rogen v. Ilikon Corp.*, 361 F.2d 260 (1st Cir. 1966) [use of nonreliance clause to bar fraud claims was inconsistent with Section 29(a)] with *Harsco Corp. v. Segui*, 91 F.3d 337 (2d Cir. 1996) [nonreliance clause did not run afoul of Section 29(a)].

but one factor to be considered in determining whether reliance is justified. Therefore, in Rule 10b-5 cases, the ability to rely on contractual representations and disclaimers to rebut claims of justifiable reliance may be even more limited than in common law fraud cases.

The central question, then, is whether, in light of the potential increase in liability exposure, the current practice with respect to offerings of debt securities under Rule 144A would be imported wholesale into the loan syndication market, or whether instead the loan syndication market would continue to follow a different and less rigorous path. The addition of an SEC-style disclosure document to the loan syndication process, coupled with due diligence backups in the form of auditors' cold comfort letters and outside counsel's disclosure letters, would represent a significant change from current market practice, and would decrease flexibility and add transaction costs to the loan syndication process. Whether this will in fact happen is difficult to say, as it will ultimately reflect a judgment as to the degree of legal risk and the cost of mitigating that legal risk as opposed to compliance with any particular requirement of statute or regulation. As noted earlier, the Section 4(2) private placement market has traditionally operated without these features. On the other hand, the dynamic of the loan market seems more analogous to the Rule 144A market, and it would be hazardous to predict that the prevailing practices in the latter would not ultimately be adopted in the former if the legal underpinning for the current difference in practice—the conclusion that loans are not securities—no longer held.

Regulation under State Blue-Sky Laws and the NASD Rules

If loans were considered securities, then, in addition to the regulation under the Securities Acts, they would be subject to other regulatory regimes applicable to offers and sales of securities, including state securities or blue-sky laws and the rules and regulations of the NASD.

Under the state securities or blue-sky laws, it is unlawful to offer or sell securities unless the securities are either registered or exempt from registration. As a general matter, there are self-executing exemptions (i.e., no filings are necessary) for (1) securities listed on certain major U.S. stock exchanges (e.g., the New York

Stock Exchange, Nasdaq National Market, and American Stock Exchange) and securities that rank senior or equal to securities so listed, and (2) sales to certain classes of institutional purchasers ("institutional sale exemptions"). The institutional sale exemption of every state exempts offers and sales to banks, insurance companies, pension funds, and registered investment companies. However, there is no uniformity in the state securities laws with respect to exemptions for sales to other classes of institutions (e.g., large corporations, hedge funds, investment partnerships, and so on). Certain states also have limited offering exemptions, but some of these exemptions require a preoffer or presale filing. Therefore, loans of publicly listed companies are exempt from state blue-sky laws. In addition, sales to traditional institutional purchasers of loans would probably fall within the institutional sale exemptions. In Rule 144A offerings, underwriters typically have internal procedures in place to ensure that securities are distributed in a manner that complies with the institutional sale exemptions. Members may consider adopting similar internal procedures in connection with loan syndications.

The NASD is a self-regulatory member organization of broker-dealers that is subject to oversight by the SEC. NASD Regulation, Inc. (NASDR), a wholly owned subsidiary of the NASD, (1) proposes rules and regulations on how member firms conduct their business as underwriters and broker-dealers, (2) sets qualifications and administers testing for persons seeking to become registered representatives, (3) has the power to institute disciplinary proceedings against member firms and registered representatives, and (4) conducts arbitrations of disputes between member firms and their representatives and customers.[8]

---

[8] Note that the NASD rules and regulations apply only to activities of registered broker-dealers. Even if loans were considered securities, trading of loans by regulated commercial banks is unlikely to require registration of such banks as broker-dealers under the '34 Act, as even under the current regime, trading of debt securities by a bank (or any other person) for its own account would generally not require registration as a dealer. In addition, there are exceptions to the definitions of *broker* and *dealer* with respect to purchases and sales by a bank of "identified banking products," which include loans, and loan participations that are sold to certain "qualified investors" or other investors that have access to material information and are capable of evaluating such information (based on their financial sophistication, net worth, and knowledge and experience in financial matters). Therefore, trading of loans (if they were considered securities) by banks is unlikely to be affected by the NASD rules and regulations.

In general, NASD Rule 2710 requires a broker-dealer to file all SEC-registered and other public offerings of securities with the Corporate Financing Department of NASDR and prohibits unfair or unreasonable underwriting or other terms or arrangements in connection therewith. NASD Rule 2720 imposes restrictions on a broker-dealer's participation in an offering if it is deemed to be an affiliate of the issuer or is deemed to have a conflict of interest with the issuer. However, securities exempt from registration with the SEC pursuant to Section 4(1) or 4(2) of the '33 Act are also exempt from NASD Rules 2710 and 2720. Therefore, generally, loans, even if they were considered securities, would be exempt from NASD Rules 2710 and 2720 to the extent that they fell within the Section 4(1) or 4(2) exemption (including through compliance with Rule 144A).

However, various other NASD rules would continue to apply to the conduct of broker-dealers in connection with secondary trading of loans (if they were considered securities) even if the initial syndication of the loans fell within the Section 4(1) or 4(2) exemption. For example, NASD Rule 2230 requires a broker-dealer to give its customer, at or prior to the completion of a transaction, a written confirmation, which discloses (1) whether the broker-dealer is acting as a broker for the customer, as a dealer for its own account, or as a broker for a third party or for both the customer and a third party and (2) if the broker-dealer is acting as a broker for a third party or for both the customer and a third party, either the name of the person from whom the security is purchased or to whom it is sold and the date and time of such transaction or the fact that such information will be furnished upon request, and the source and amount of any commission or other remuneration received by the member in connection therewith. NASD Rule 2310 prohibits a broker-dealer from making recommendations to a customer unless the broker-dealer has "reasonable grounds for believing that the recommendation is suitable for such customer upon the basis of the facts, if any, disclosed by such customer as to his other security holdings and as to his financial situation and needs."

NASD Rule 2440 (the "markup rule") provides that in over-the-counter transactions, a broker-dealer must sell or buy a security to or from its customers at a fair price, in the case of a principal transaction, or charge a fair commission, in the case of an agency transaction, taking into consideration all relevant circumstances, including market conditions with respect to such security at the time of the transaction, the expense involved, the fact that the broker-dealer is entitled to a profit in the case of a principal transaction, and the value of any service rendered by reason of the broker-dealer's experience and knowledge of such security and market in the case of an agency transaction. The NASD has adopted a general policy that markups or commissions in excess of 5 percent of the prevailing market price of a security are prohibited. However, each transaction must be examined based on its own facts and circumstances, and markups or commissions of 5 percent or less may still in certain circumstances be considered unfair. The relevant factors include (1) the type of security involved, (2) the liquidity of the security, (3) the price of the security, (4) the amount of money involved in the transaction, (5) disclosure, (6) the pattern of a broker-dealer's markups, and (7) the nature of the broker-dealer's business. In the absence of other bona fide evidence of the prevailing market, a broker-dealer's own contemporaneous cost is the best indication of the prevailing market price of a security. The NASD has proposed an interpretation that would further limit how the prevailing market price for a debt security would be established, allowing broker-dealers to look beyond contemporaneous costs only in specified circumstances. This proposal has been subject to criticisms from industry participants and has not yet been adopted.

To the extent that loans are considered securities, a broker-dealer who trades loans in the over-the-counter market must therefore comply with the markup rule. Generally, the broker-dealer should not charge a markup or commission of more than 5 percent over the prevailing market price in selling loans (or a markdown in the case of a purchase of loans). However, a broker-dealer must also consider each trade based on the factors listed previously in determining a fair markup (or markdown) or commission. For instance, thinly traded loans that require additional effort or cost to buy or sell may justify a higher markup than more actively traded loans. A loan with a high prevailing market price may require a lower markup, whereas a transaction involving a small loan principal amount may justify a higher markup. To the extent possible, the broker-dealer should look to its own contemporaneous cost for the type of loans being traded in determining the prevailing market price. Generally, in connection with sales of loans by a broker-dealer from its inventory, the broker-dealer should not consider its historical basis in such loans in determining the prevailing market price. If the broker-dealer is engaging in a "riskless" transaction (e.g., buying a loan in order to fill a previously received order to buy the same from a customer), the broker-dealer should ensure that the markups/markdowns charged in both transactions are reasonable in relation to each other.

Ms. Bason and Messrs. Kaplan and Smith are partners in the Corporate Department of Davis Polk & Wardwell. The authors gratefully acknowledge the assistance of Albert Cua and Ian Walker, associates of Davis Polk & Wardwell.

CHAPTER 3

Loan Structures

Steve Miller
Managing Director
Standard & Poor's Leveraged Commentary and Data

Marc Hanrahan
Partner
Latham & Watkins LLP

David Teh
Associate
Latham & Watkins LLP

Dawn Pasquin
Managing Director
GE Energy Financial Services

Basic Loan Structures

Steve Miller
Managing Director
Standard & Poor's Leveraged Commentary and Data

Most loans are structured and syndicated to accommodate the two primary syndicated lender constituencies: the sell-side banks (domestic and foreign) and the buy-side institutional investors (primarily mutual funds and insurance companies). Leveraged loans consist of the following:

- *Pro rata debt* consists of the revolving credit and an amortizing term loan (TLA), which are packaged together and, usually, syndicated to banks. In some loans, however, institutional investors take pieces of the TLA and, less often, the revolving credit as a way to secure a larger institutional term-loan allocation.

- *Institutional debt* consists of institutional term loans. In most deals, these facilities are packaged together and sold to institutional investors, but there are also some banks that buy institutional term loans.

In addition to banks and institutional investors, finance companies also play in the leveraged loan market, buying both pro rata and institutional tranches. With banks increasingly withdrawing from the market, however, and with institutional investors playing an ever-larger role, by 2002 most executions were structured as simply revolving credit/institutional term loans, with the TLA falling by the wayside.

TYPES OF SYNDICATED LOAN FACILITIES

There are four main types of syndicated loan facilities: a revolving credit (within which are swingline, multicurrency-line, competitive-bid option, term-out, and evergreen structures), a term loan, a letter of credit (LOC), and an acquisition or equipment line (a delayed-draw term loan).

A *revolving credit line* allows borrowers to draw down, repay, and reborrow. The facility acts much like a corporate credit card, except that borrowers are charged an annual commitment fee on unused amounts regardless of usage (the facility fee), which drives up the overall cost of borrowing. Revolvers to noninvestment grade issuers are often tied to borrowing-base lending formulas. This limits borrowings to a certain percentage of collateral, most often receivables and inventory. Revolving credits often run for 364 days. These revolving credits—called, not surprisingly, 364-day facilities—are generally limited to the investment grade market. The reason for what seems like an odd term is that regulatory capital guidelines mandate that, after extending credit under a revolving facility for one year, banks must increase their capital reserves to take the unused amounts into account. Therefore, banks can offer issuers 364-day facilities at a lower facility fee than that for a multiyear revolving credit. There are a number of options that can be offered within a revolving credit line:

- A *swingline* is a small, overnight borrowing line, typically provided by the agent.
- A *multicurrency line* allows the borrower to borrow in several currencies.
- A *competitive-bid option (CBO)* allows borrowers to solicit the best bids from its syndicate group. The agent will conduct what amounts to an auction to raise funds for the borrower, and the best bids are accepted. CBOs are typically available only to large, investment grade borrowers.
- A *term-out* allows the borrower to convert borrowings into a term loan at a given conversion date. This, again, is usually a feature of investment grade loans. Under the option, borrowers may take what is outstanding under the facility and pay it off according to a predetermined repayment schedule. Often the spreads ratchet up if the term-out option is exercised.
- An *evergreen* is an option allowing the borrower—with the consent of the syndicate group—to extend the facility each year for an additional year.

A *term loan* is simply an installment loan, like the loan one would use to buy a car. The borrower may draw on the loan during a short commitment period and repays it either through a scheduled series of repayments or in a one-time lump-sum payment at maturity (bullet payment). There are two principal types of term loans:

- An *amortizing term loan* (term loan A, or TLA) is a term loan with a progressive repayment schedule that typically runs six years or less. These loans are normally syndicated to banks along with revolving credits as part of a larger syndication. Starting in 2000, TLAs became increasingly rare, as issuers bypassed the less accommodating bank market and tapped institutional investors for all or most of their funded loans.

- An *institutional term loan* (term loan B, C, or D) is a term-loan facility carved out for nonbank institutional investors. These loans came into broad usage during the mid–1990s as the institutional loan investor base grew. Until 2001, these loans were, in almost all cases, priced higher than amortizing term loans, because they had longer maturities and back-end-loaded repayment schedules. The tide turned, however, in late 2001, and through 2005 the spread on a growing percentage of these facilities came into parity with (and in some cases even lower than) the spread on revolvers and term loan As. This is especially true when institutional demand is running high.

Letters of credit (LOCs) differ in nature, but, simply put, they are guarantees provided by the bank group to pay off debt or obligations if the borrower cannot.

Acquisition/equipment lines (delayed-draw term loans) are credits that may be drawn down for a given period to purchase specified types of assets or equipment or to make acquisitions. The issuer pays a fee during the commitment period (a ticking fee). The lines are then repaid over a specified period (the term-out period). Repaid amounts may not be reborrowed.

ASSET-BASED LENDING

Asset-based lending is a distinct segment of the loan market. Asset-based loans are secured by specific assets and usually governed by a borrowing formula (or a "borrowing base"). The most common type of asset-based loans is backed by receivables and/or inventory lines. These are revolving credits that have a maximum borrowing limit, say $100 million, but also have a cap based on the value of an issuer's pledged receivables and inventories. Usually, the receivables are pledged, and the issuer may borrow against 80 percent of them, give or take. Inventories are also often pledged to secure borrowings. However, because they are obviously less liquid than receivables, lenders are less generous in their formula. Indeed, the borrowing base for inventories is typically in the 50 to 65 percent range. In addition, the borrowing base may be further divided into subcategories—for instance, 50 percent of work-in-process inventory and 65 percent of finished goods inventory.

In many receivables-based facilities, issuers are required to place receivables in a "lock box." That means that the bank lends against the receivables, takes possession of them, and then collects them to pay down the loan.

In addition, asset-based lending is often based on specific equipment, real estate, car fleets, and an unlimited number of other assets.

BANKERS ACCEPTANCE

A bankers acceptance (BA) is a money market instrument—a short-term discount instrument that usually arises in the course of international trade. Before we explain BAs, let's introduce some more basic concepts.

A *draft* is a legally binding order by one party (the *drawer*) to a second party (the *drawee*) to make payment to a third party (the *payee*). A simple example is a bank check, which is an order directing a bank to pay a third party. The three parties don't have to be distinct. For example, someone might write himself a check as a simple means of transferring funds from one bank account to another. In this case, the drawer and the payee are the same person. When a draft guarantees payment for goods in international trade, it is called a *bill of exchange*.

A draft can require immediate payment by the second party to the third upon presentation of the draft. This is called a *sight draft*. Checks are sight drafts. In trade, drafts often call for deferred payment. An importer might write a draft promising payment to an exporter for delivery of goods, with payment to occur 60 days after the goods are delivered. Such drafts are called *time drafts*. They are said to mature on the payment date. In this example, the importer is both the drawer and the drawee.

In cases where the drawer and drawee of a time draft are distinct parties, the payee may submit the draft to the drawee for confirmation that the draft is a legitimate order and that the drawee will make payment on the specified date. Such confirmation is called *acceptance*—the drawee accepts the order to pay as legitimate. The drawee stamps "ACCEPTED" on the draft and is thereafter obligated to make the specified payment when it is due. If the drawee is a bank, the acceptance is called a *bankers acceptance* (BA).

A bankers acceptance is an obligation of the accepting bank. Depending on the bank's reputation, a payee may be able to sell the bankers acceptance—that is, sell the time draft accepted by the bank. It will sell for the discounted value of the future payment. In this manner, the bankers acceptance becomes a discount instrument traded in the money market. Paying discounted value for a time draft is called *discounting the draft*.

In international trade, bankers acceptances arise in various ways. Consider two examples:

1. An importer plans to purchase goods from an exporter. The exporter will not grant credit, so the importer turns to its bank. Both parties execute an acceptance agreement, under which the bank will accept drafts from the importer. By doing so, the bank extends credit to the importer, who agrees to pay the bank the face value of all drafts prior to their maturity. The importer draws a time draft, listing itself as the payee. The bank accepts the draft and discounts it, paying the importer the discounted value of the draft. The importer uses the proceeds to pay the exporter. The bank can then hold the bankers acceptance in its own portfolio or sell it at discounted value in the money market.

2. In an alternative arrangement, the exporter may agree to accept a letter of credit from the importer's bank. This specifies that the bank will accept time drafts from the exporter if the exporter presents suitable documentation that the goods were delivered. Under this arrangement, the exporter is the drawer and payee of the draft. Typically, the bank will not work directly with the exporter, but will work with the exporter's correspondent bank. The exporter may realize proceeds from the bankers acceptance in several ways. The bank may discount it for the exporter, the exporter may hold the acceptance to maturity, or the exporter may sell the acceptance to another party.

DEBTOR-IN-POSSESSION FINANCING

Debtor-in-possession financing (DIP financing) is financing arranged by a company that is in the Chapter 11 bankruptcy process. DIP financing is unique among financing methods in that it usually has priority over existing debt, equity, and other claims. (Chapter 11 gives the debtor a fresh start, which is, however, subject to the debtor's fulfillment of its obligations under its plan of reorganization.)

Second Lien Loans

Marc Hanrahan
Partner
Latham & Watkins LLP

David Teh[1]
Associate
Latham & Watkins LLP

INTRODUCTION

What Is a Second Lien Term Loan?

A typical second lien loan is a term loan B secured by a lien on sub-stantially all of the borrower's assets.[2] In some cases, the second lien term loan may be secured equally and ratably with a pari passu tranche of secured bonds or other debt. Alternatively, the second lien term loan might be the only second lien loan in the cap-ital structure. In either case, the second lien term loan lenders will almost certainly be sharing the capital structure with at least one other credit facility of a more traditional variety—possibly just a revolver, or possibly a term loan and revolver—secured by a first lien on substantially the same collateral. The second lien term loan is denominated "second" because the two classes of creditors agree that, in the event that any of their shared collateral is ever sold in a

---

[1] This article is adapted from a Latham & Watkins Client Alert, "Second Lien Financings—Answers to the Most Frequently Asked Questions," April 15, 2004.

[2] Term loan Bs are a variation on the type of term loans (which are now often called term loan As) traditionally made by banks and other financial institutions that want both a steady return of principal (through periodic amortization) and interest payments. Term loan Bs are targeted at, and typically held by, hedge funds and other institu-tional investors with a longer-term investment strategy. As a result, term loan B lenders generally require only nominal, if any, principal repayment on their term loan Bs until the maturity date (or the year prior to maturity), and have the right to refuse all or a specified portion of optional prepayments made by the borrower. If both a term loan A and a term loan B are made to the borrower in the same transaction, the interest rate on the term loan B generally will be higher than that on the term loan A. If a credit facility contains both a term loan A and a term loan B, any optional pre-payment amounts not applied to prepay the term loan B typically will be applied to prepay the term loan A. Term loan Bs bear interest at a floating rate (typically), some-times with specified minimum rates, and have covenant packages that are derived from (and substantially similar to) those found either in the borrower's traditional bank credit agreement or, in an increasing number of cases, in the borrower's high-yield bond indenture.

foreclosure or other enforcement action, either before or during a bankruptcy proceeding, the first lien debt (and all other first lien obligations, if any, that are then outstanding) will be entitled to be paid in full from the proceeds of the shared collateral before any of the proceeds from the shared collateral are distributed to the second lien term lenders. As discussed later in this article, second lien loans are not contractually subordinated in the traditional sense (i.e., holders are not subordinated in terms of payment, as high-yield bondholders might be), but are subordinated only in their claim to the proceeds of the shared collateral.

Prior to 2003, second lien loans were not commonly sold into or traded in the broadly syndicated loan market. Things have changed dramatically since then, and second lien loan financings are now a widely used financing tool, often selected by borrowers in lieu of unsecured high-yield debt or traditional unsecured mezzanine financing. Exhibit 3.1 illustrates the rapid growth of second lien loans over the last four years.

EXHIBIT 3.1

Number of second lien loans, 2002–2005

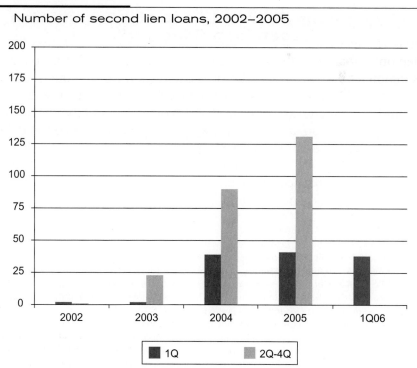

Source: Standard & Poor's Report, "1Q06 Second Lien Lending Review"

There are several kinds of second lien loans, and it is important to note that there are often significant differences between second lien loans that are structured as "club deals," which are less
broadly syndicated, and second lien loans sold to a broader range
of investors. Club deals involving second lien loans tend to be
more "hand sewn" and can contain varying provisions that usually result from more extensive negotiations among the smaller number of lenders involved. It is also important to recognize that the
second lien loan product, like any new financing product, continues to evolve. Over time, we would expect many of the variations
currently found in second lien loan financings to settle out into a
market norm (as was the case with the junk bond market in the
1980s). Until that time, however, borrowers, investors, arrangers,
and lawyers should be careful not to assume a uniformity in
approach to all issues raised by second lien loans. Nevertheless,
the second lien market is shaking itself out, and there has been considerable progress over the last couple of years in settling around
market norms.

What Are the Pros and Cons of a Second Lien Loan for a Borrower?

Second lien loans are attractive to borrowers for a number of reasons. Because of the benefits of secured creditor status, a borrower should get better pricing on second lien loan financing than it
would if it incurred unsecured debt on substantially the same
terms. In addition, a borrower may get broader access to the debt
markets because of the tremendous interest in second lien loans
across a range of institutional investors, including financial
institutions, insurance companies, mutual funds, collateralized debt
obligation (CDO) and collateralized loan obligation (CLO) funds,[3]

---

[3] CDOs and CLOs are structured vehicles that issue asset-backed securities, generally
secured by debt obligations that may include term loans. These vehicles have become
major players in the secondary debt markets and have played an important role in
developing a liquid secondary market for term loans and high-yield bonds. For tax
reasons, these vehicles do not invest in the primary debt offering, but they will often
acquire debt in the secondary market within a few days after the initial offering. Since
2003, CDOs and CLOs have been incorporating second lien term loans in their portfolios. As investors, rating agencies, and other market players have become more
familiar with second lien financings, their treatment in CDOs and CLOs has been
evolving and continues to evolve. Nevertheless, second lien term loans are, and are
expected to continue to be, a part of the portfolios of many CDOs and CLOs.

and hedge funds. For some borrowers, this deeper level of market interest can make the difference between being able to complete a financing package and not having requisite access to the capital markets. Some borrowers may also perceive second lien lenders to be potentially less volatile in a distress scenario than unsecured creditors to the extent that the holders of second lien loans believe that they are sufficiently secured to successfully weather a period of poor financial performance. To the degree that a borrower's alternative to a second lien loan is a high-yield bond or mezzanine debt, the borrower may also be attracted to the relatively modest call protection typically found in the second lien loan market.[4]

However, there are also costs to the borrower associated with providing collateral to second lien lenders. First, the covenant package applicable to second lien loans is likely to impose a more restrictive cap on the amount of additional first lien loans that may be incurred in the future than might appear in an unsecured high-yield bond indenture, which tends to have looser covenant structures. In addition, depending on the value of the collateral and the cash flow of the enterprise, the borrower's ability to obtain additional first lien financing in the future may be impaired by the presence of a significant tranche of second lien secured debt on its balance sheet. Further, the total amount of additional second lien loans that may be incurred in the future will probably be capped, usually based on a maximum leverage ratio or other limitations. The existence of a second lien loan in its capital structure may also make it harder for a borrower to obtain unsecured debt in the future because future unsecured creditors of the borrower would be effectively subordinated to the second lien loan. Finally, there may be some incremental costs associated with providing collateral to second lien lenders (e.g., filing fees, title insurance costs, and local counsel opinions), although these costs alone rarely result in borrowers deciding against a second lien loan.

---

[4] Second lien loans distributed in the broadly syndicated market are often subject to pre-payment premiums during the first two or three years after funding at relatively modest levels (e.g., 103, 102, 101). By comparison, high-yield bonds are typically subject to "no call" provisions for the first five years, with higher call premiums thereafter. A borrower anticipating a refinancing in a short period of time may find the difference to be of major significance in choosing a second lien loan rather than alternative financing such as a high-yield bond.

Why Would a First Lien Lender Want to Permit a Second Lien Loan Deal?

Historically, first lien lenders have not been inclined to provide collateral to junior creditors. The concern in times past has been that the existence of other secured creditors and their rights in collateral could result in complications for first lien lenders in the event of a workout or bankruptcy. However, in some cases, the proceeds from the second lien deal are needed to make a transaction feasible, are earmarked to pay down first lien loans, or will effectively limit the amount of first lien loans needed to capitalize the borrower. With a lower level of credit exposure, the first lien lenders may become significantly more flexible, and the increased cushion provided by the second lien loans may make the remaining first lien loans easier to syndicate. In addition, the first lien lenders can protect their interests through intercreditor arrangements that limit or control the secured creditors' rights that second lien lenders might otherwise exercise to the detriment of the first lien lenders. Such an arrangement leaves the second lien lenders with what is sometimes referred to as a "silent second" lien. The term *silent second* refers to the concept that, under the applicable intercreditor arrangements, the second lien lenders will not interfere in any way with the exercise of secured creditors' rights by the first lien lenders (i.e., they will remain truly silent while the first lien lenders exercise their rights). However, as discussed later, the evolution of the second lien loan market and the resulting requirements of second lien lenders have made the term "quiet" or "well-behaved" second more applicable, in many cases, than silent second.

Why Would a Junior Creditor Be Willing to Accept a Second Lien?

A second priority lien, even a silent second, gives a second lien lender effective priority over trade creditors and other unsecured creditors, to the extent of the value of its interest in the collateral. In terms of payment priority, second lien status does not affect the value of being secured—a second lien lender is always better off in this regard than it would be if it were unsecured (as further discussed later in this article). In addition, under applicable intercreditor arrangements in most deals, the second lien lenders expressly reserve many, if not all, of the rights of an unsecured creditor, subject to some important exceptions discussed later.

SOME IMPORTANT BACKGROUND INFORMATION

So far, we have established that second lien lenders get paid second when it comes to the proceeds of collateral. We have also said that second lien loans are usually silent seconds (or at least quiet or well-behaved seconds). So where's the controversy? Well, the key question is, "How silent is silent?" How well behaved must second lien lenders be vis-à-vis first lien lenders? Market participants from the old school of senior lending believe that second lien lenders should speak only when they are spoken to. The new school of players in the second lien loan market today is not as demure as the old school lenders would like. In today's market, second lien lenders are willing to defer to first lien holders on various matters up to a point or for a limited period of time, but no more than that. The action in the structuring and negotiating of second lien deals revolves around the determination of the relationship between the rights of first lien lenders and second lien lenders under what are commonly referred to as intercreditor arrangements. In order to address the critical questions of how and why those intercreditor arrangements are being sorted out in the loan market today, we need to explore some background information about what it means to be a secured creditor in the first place. We will then discuss which of these rights second lien lenders may be willing to part with.

What Is the Difference between Debt Subordination and Lien Subordination?

Basics

In traditional debt subordination, the debt claim itself is subordinated. If a holder of subordinated debt obtains anything of value in a bankruptcy from any source, it agrees to turn it over to the holders of senior debt until the senior debt is paid in full. In the case of second lien loans, only the liens are subordinated; the underlying debt claim is not. What this means is that the holder of the second lien loan agrees only to turn over proceeds from sales of shared collateral to the first lien lenders. The holder of a second lien loan does not have to turn over to the first lien lenders funds distributed to it from other sources.

Priority vis-à-vis the Trade

In its simplest terms, debt subordination places the subordinated debt behind the senior debt, but does not place it ahead of any other debt of the borrower (unless the holders of that other debt agree, in turn, to subordinate their debt to the subordinated debt). By contrast, although lien subordination does place the second lien loans behind the first lien loans to the extent of the value of the first lien lender's interest in the collateral, it also places the second lien loans ahead of trade and other unsecured creditors to the extent of the value of its interest in the collateral. This is the key benefit for the second lien lenders.

Payment Blockage Issues

Unlike traditional subordinated debt, second lien loans are not typically subject to payment blockage provisions of any kind. Thus, even in a distress scenario, the holders of second lien loans are entitled to receive scheduled payments of principal and interest, and payment thereof cannot be blocked by the first lien lenders.

Remedy Standstill Provisions

The remedy bars in second lien deals typically apply only to remedies associated with the collateral. Most second lien deals specifically preserve all or almost all of the remedies that would be available to an unsecured creditor, with a few exceptions (as we will discuss later).

In a Bankruptcy, What Rights do Secured Creditors Gain?

In a bankruptcy proceeding, secured creditors have a variety of meaningful rights that unsecured creditors don't have. As a result, secured creditors enjoy significantly higher recovery rates in bankruptcies and other reorganizations than unsecured creditors.

Priority vis-à-vis Trade and Other Unsecured Creditors

Under the bankruptcy code, creditors' claims can generally be divided into three basic classes: (1) secured claims, (2) priority unsecured claims, and (3) general unsecured claims.[5] A second lien lender's claim is treated as a secured claim to the extent of the value of its interest in the collateral. For example, assume that the company in bankruptcy owes $50 to a first lien lender and $200 to a second lien lender and that both the first- and second lien loans are secured solely by liens on an asset worth $150. In this case, the first lien lender will have a $50 secured claim and no unsecured claim. The second lien lender, in turn, will have a secured claim of $100. The second lien lender's residual $100 claim will be treated as a general unsecured claim. As a result, an "undersecured" creditor will hold both secured and unsecured claims. Under the bankruptcy code, secured claims are entitled to receive value equal to the full value of their interest in the collateral before any value is given to holders of unsecured claims, and any priority unsecured claims are entitled to receive the full value of their claims before any unsecured claims receive any value. To the extent that a secured creditor is undersecured (i.e., the value of its collateral is less than the amount of its prepetition claim), that undersecured creditor will share pro rata with other general unsecured creditors (including trade creditors) in the amount, if any, remaining after repayment in full of both secured claims and priority unsecured claims.

Postpetition Interest
A secured creditor is entitled to postpetition interest under the bankruptcy code to the extent that the value of its interest in the collateral securing its claim is greater than the amount of its pre-bankruptcy claim. An undersecured creditor is not entitled to postpetition interest. As a result, in the example discussed previously, the first lien lender's $50 secured claim will increase during the

---

[5] Under the bankruptcy code, unsecured claims are not all treated equally. Certain unsecured claims, called priority unsecured claims, have the right to be paid in full before any of the residual unsecured claims, called general unsecured claims, are paid. Priority unsecured claims include:
- Postpetition administrative expenses needed to operate the bankrupt company (such as employees' wages and other ordinary course operating expenses) or to pay lawyers, accountants, and other professionals hired by the bankrupt company or certain types of creditors
- In an involuntary bankruptcy, "gap" claims, which are ordinary course unsecured claims incurred between the bankruptcy filing date and the entry of an order for relief
- Certain prepetition employees' wages
- Certain contributions to employee benefit plans
- Certain types of tax claims

pendency of the bankruptcy proceeding to the extent of any accrued interest that is not paid currently, thereby reducing the likely recovery by the second lien lender.

Adequate Protection Rights

Under the bankruptcy code, a secured creditor has the right to be protected against declines in the value of its interest in the collateral following the date of the bankruptcy filing. This is a very broad right and entitles a secured creditor to a voice in any actions taken in a bankruptcy proceeding that could affect the value of its collateral (including the use of cash collateral, sales of collateral, substitutions of collateral, or the grant of a priming lien on collateral to secure a DIP financing). Upon request, a secured creditor is entitled to assurance that its interest in its collateral is adequately protected if there is a serious risk of the value of its interest diminishing. This "adequate protection" may take the form of a court-ordered grant of additional or substitute collateral or the provision of periodic cash payments to the secured creditor or any other form providing the secured creditor with the "indubitable equivalent" of its interest. The bankruptcy court has broad discretion in fashioning an appropriate remedy in this regard.

Right to Object to Use of Cash Collateral

Cash collateral is a defined term in the bankruptcy code and includes cash, negotiable instruments, securities, deposit accounts, and other cash equivalents in which a prepetition creditor has a security interest. Under the bankruptcy code, a company in bankruptcy is not permitted to use cash collateral unless each creditor that has a security interest in the cash collateral consents to its use or the bankruptcy court authorizes its use, after notice and a hearing. This gives each secured creditor a say on the use of cash collateral, unless the bankruptcy court orders otherwise.

Right to Approve Asset Sales

Under the bankruptcy code, a company in bankruptcy can sell assets, free and clear of all liens, in various circumstances. However, under certain circumstances, the consent of a secured creditor to a sale of its collateral may be required. If more than one party has a lien on the collateral, each of the secured creditors may be required to consent to the sale.

Right to Approve Secured DIP Financings

A company in bankruptcy needs funds with which to operate. For obvious reasons, many bankrupt companies have negative or marginal cash flow, which prompts the need for debtor-in-possession (DIP) financing arrangements. DIP financings can be secured or unsecured, but they are generally secured on a first-priority basis. The bankruptcy code authorizes the bankruptcy court to provide for a DIP loan to be secured by a lien that is senior or equal to the liens held by the other secured creditors, as long as those other secured creditors are given adequate protection or consent to the prior or equal liens. As a result, creditors secured by all or substantially all of the bankrupt company's assets will have a strong say with regard to the company's ability to obtain a priming DIP loan.

Harder to Be "Crammed Down"

In a bankruptcy, the creditors in each class of impaired claims have the right to vote on any proposed plan of reorganization. However, in certain circumstances, a plan of reorganization can be confirmed over the objections of a particular class of creditors. A class of creditors that is forced to accept the terms of a plan that it voted against is said to be "crammed down." It is generally much harder for a class of secured creditors to be "crammed down" in a bankruptcy than a class of unsecured creditors. Under the bankruptcy code, a class of creditors can be crammed down only if the plan of reorganization is "fair and equitable" to that class. The standard for what is fair and equitable is higher for secured creditors than it is for unsecured creditors, which gives secured creditors greater leverage at the bargaining table in bankruptcy plan negotiations.

More Leverage in Plan Negotiations

The combined effect of these various rights of secured creditors is to give secured creditors far more leverage than unsecured creditors in negotiating and shaping the plan of reorganization.

What Rights Do Unsecured Creditors Have outside of Bankruptcy?

Unsecured creditors (as well as secured creditors) have several important rights outside of bankruptcy, including the following:

- The right of any three unsecured or undersecured credi-tors to put a company into an involuntary bankruptcy[6]
- The right to accelerate their debt and sue for payment
- The right to challenge the validity, enforceability, or priority of any liens on the company's assets

What Rights Do Unsecured Creditors Have in a Bankruptcy?

Unsecured creditors (as well as secured creditors) have other meaningful rights during a bankruptcy, including the following:

- The right to request the appointment of a trustee in bank-ruptcy (e.g., because the bankrupt company is mismanag-ing the business)
- The right to propose a plan of reorganization at the end of the 120-day (or longer) time period in which the bankrupt company has the exclusive right to propose a plan
- The right to vote on a plan of reorganization
- The right to challenge the validity, enforceability, or priority of any liens on the bankrupt company's assets
- The right to challenge or dispute any other actions taken or not taken, or any motions made, by the bankrupt com-pany, any secured creditor, or any other interested party

Although, generally, the rights of an unsecured creditor in bankruptcy are significantly less than those of a secured creditor, they are enough to give unsecured creditors a seat at the table in the plan negotiations.

What Are the Relationships between Multiple Secured Creditors at Law absent an Intercreditor Agreement?

Order of Priority
The general rule is first in time, first in line. Under that general rule, as between two secured creditors, unless otherwise agreed by

---

[6] Any three unsecured or undersecured creditors can commence an involuntary bankruptcy case against a company if the total value of their claims against the company is at least $11,625 more than the total value of their interests in assets of the company pledged to secure those claims.

those creditors, the first to "perfect" its security interest in an asset gets the first-priority lien on that asset. The second in time is second in line.[7] Priority is important because it determines the order of repayment when the collateral is sold or otherwise disposed of.

Control over Enforcement Actions

If two creditors are secured by liens on a particular asset, the general rule under the Uniform Commercial Code (UCC) and other applicable laws is that either creditor has the right to foreclose on the asset. If the first lien lender forecloses on the asset, the second lien lender is not entitled to any of the foreclosure proceeds until the first lien lender has received the full value of its claim. If the second lien lender forecloses on the asset, the first lien remains in place on the sold asset, and the second lien lender is entitled to the foreclosure proceeds. However, as a practical matter, few buyers in a foreclosure sale are willing to buy an asset subject to a first lien, and few first lien lenders are willing to release their first liens unless their debt has been repaid in full. As a result, it is common for the agreements between creditors to provide that the first lien lenders have the right to control the disposition of collateral (possibly subject to time or other limitations).

Restrictions on Dispositions of Collateral

A secured creditor does not have an unfettered right to dispose of collateral. The interests of the debtor and other secured creditors are protected by a variety of rules designed to protect those interests in the value of the collateral, if any, remaining after repayment in full of the claims of the secured creditor that forecloses on the collateral. Most of these rules can't be waived by a debtor or other pledgor or may be waived by a debtor or other pledgor only under an agreement entered into after a default has occurred. In addition, in certain cases, particularly where the first lien lender has agreed to serve as agent for the second lien lender, a first lien lender may owe fiduciary duties to the second lien lender.[8] These rules

---

[7] There are numerous exceptions to this general rule, including liens securing purchase money debt and certain tax, ERISA, and other statutory liens. In addition, with respect to many types of collateral, certain methods of perfection, such as possession or control, may be entitled to priority over an earlier security interest that is perfected solely by the filing of a financing statement.

[8] We are not aware of a general fiduciary duty owed by a senior secured creditor to a junior secured creditor simply by virtue of having a senior lien on common collateral.

effectively limit the ability of a secured creditor to conduct collateral "fire sales."

Rules Governing Foreclosure on UCC Collateral

The UCC (Uniform Commercial Code) contains a variety of substantive and procedural requirements governing foreclosure on personal property collateral that is subject to the UCC.[9] Most important, under the UCC, every aspect of a disposition of collateral must be "commercially reasonable." A secured party is liable to the debtor and other parties with a security interest in the same collateral if it fails to comply with this standard or if it fails to comply with any of the notice or other requirements surrounding foreclosure imposed by the UCC. These UCC requirements also effectively limit the ability of any secured creditor to sell collateral at a fire sale.

Rules Governing Foreclosure on Real Property Collateral

The substantive and procedural requirements that govern foreclosure on real property collateral vary from state to state. In most states, a secured creditor can foreclose on real property through a judicial foreclosure, supervised by a state court. In some states, a secured creditor can also enforce remedies against real property outside of the court system through a nonjudicial foreclosure in which a trustee or referee conducts the sale. If the sale is conducted through a judicial foreclosure, the secured party will typically have to satisfy procedural requirements intended to ensure that the sale is conducted in a public forum to protect against a sale of the real property below fair market value.

Fiduciary Duties in the Zone of Insolvency

Directors and officers of a company owe a fiduciary duty to the company's shareholders to act in what they reasonably believe to be the best interests of the shareholders. However, if the company

---

[9] The UCC covers most types of tangible and intangible personal property. Some of the significant categories of property that are not covered by the UCC include:
- Real estate (other than fixtures)
- Some types of intellectual property
- In most states, insurance policies and any claims under those policies (other than as proceeds of other collateral)

enters the "zone of insolvency," those fiduciary duties are additionally, and primarily, owed to the company's secured and unsecured creditors. A company in bankruptcy clearly falls within the zone of insolvency. However, a company can also be in the zone of insolvency as it approaches bankruptcy. As a rule of thumb, a company is in the zone of insolvency if it can't generally pay its debts as they become due or if the fair market value of its assets is less than the fair market value of its liabilities. These fiduciary duties to creditors are a further limit on the likelihood that collateral will be disposed of in haste at significantly below its fair market value.

Bankruptcy Code Restrictions

The bankruptcy code imposes its own set of restrictions on asset sales. During a bankruptcy, with limited exceptions, a secured creditor generally does not have a right to compel sales of collateral. As a general matter, the company in bankruptcy decides which assets to sell (albeit, in practice, following discussions with its secured creditors). Asset sales are governed by Section 363 of the bankruptcy code. These "363 sales," as they are commonly known, are subject to overbidding and bankruptcy-court scrutiny and approval, with a view to achieving the best available sale price.

STRUCTURING SECOND LIEN LOANS

With that background discussion behind us, we will now turn to a series of specific issues relating to the structure of second lien loans financings in the broadly syndicated loan market today.

What Makes a Second Lien Loan Silent/Quiet/Well Behaved?

The terms *silent, quiet,* and *well behaved* all refer to degrees to which the second lien lenders agree not to exercise (or restrict the exercise of) some or all of the special rights that they would otherwise enjoy by virtue of their secured creditor status. The arrangements to forgo or restrict their rights are usually set out in an agreement entered into by the representatives of the various classes of creditors (typically a collateral trust agreement or an intercreditor agreement). While the degree to which second lien lenders agree to give up their rights may vary from deal to deal, the categories of restrictions at play may be summarized as follows:

- Prohibitions (or limitations) on the right of the second lien holders to take enforcement actions with respect to their liens (possibly subject to time or other limitations)
- Agreements by the second lien lenders not to challenge enforcement or foreclosure actions taken by the holders of the first liens (possibly subject to time or other limitations)
- Prohibitions on the right of the second lien holders to challenge the validity or priority of the first liens
- Waivers of (or limitations on) other secured creditor rights by the holders of second liens loan in and outside of bankruptcy
- Acknowledgments by the second lien lenders of the first lien lenders' entitlement to first proceeds of the shared collateral.

What Restrictions Do the Second Lien Lenders Typically Agree to with Respect to the Period before a Bankruptcy Filing?

The answer to this question depends on the context. In the case of a truly silent second, the first lien lenders generally control all decisions regarding the enforcement of remedies against the collateral as long as any first lien loans are outstanding. As a result, following a default on the first lien loans, subject to the UCC, the bankruptcy code, and other legal limitations discussed previously, the first lien lenders typically decide, among other things,

- Whether and when to exercise remedies against the collateral
- Which items of collateral to proceed against, and in which order
- Whether the sale should be a public or a private sale
- To whom collateral should be sold, and at what price

In today's second lien loan market, second lien lenders do not typically agree to remain truly silent. Generally, second lien lenders will agree to refrain from exercising their secured creditor rights only for a limited period of time, typically 90 to 180 days. This period of time is often referred to as a "fish-or-cut-bait" or "standstill" period. At the end of the standstill period, the first lien lenders lose their monopoly on the exercise of secured creditor remedies. In some deals, if the first lien lenders have not taken steps to exercise remedies against the collateral when the standstill period expires, they forfeit any further right to take remedies, giving the second lien lenders the monopoly on remedies. There are many variations on the scope and duration of these standstill arrangements, and they are often one of the more heavily negotiated sections of an intercreditor agreement.

In addition, under most intercreditor arrangements, second lien lenders typically waive their right to challenge the validity, enforceability, or priority of the first liens and acknowledge the first lien lenders' entitlement to receive the proceeds of the collateral until all first lien obligations are repaid in full.[10]

What Restrictions Do the Second Lien Lenders Typically Agree to in a Bankruptcy Proceeding?

The short answer is all of the rights that they waive before bankruptcy (as discussed earlier), plus some others. The longer answer depends, again, on the context. The following waivers and consents (to varying degrees) are commonly seen in intercreditor agreements in the second lien loan market:

- Adequate protection waivers
- Advance consents to use of cash collateral
- Advance consents to sales of collateral
- Advance consents to DIP financings

Waiver of the Right to Seek Adequate Protection

Second lien lenders will typically (and should) reserve their adequate protection right to ask for a junior lien on any property on

---

[10] The first lien lenders generally do not provide a reciprocal waiver of their right to challenge the second liens. As a practical matter, first lien lenders will often be reluctant to challenge the second liens out of concern that a challenge could boomerang. The first and second liens tend to be granted at the same time under the same set of security documents or under separate but substantively identical security documents. If there is a flaw in the security documents that impairs the second liens, there is a good possibility that it will also impair the first liens.

which the bankruptcy court grants a lien to secure first lien loans, as long as the new junior lien is subject to the same lien subordination arrangements as the original second lien. This right is critical to avoid erosion of the second lien lenders' bargained-for collateral. Most security agreements contain an "after-acquired collateral" clause that grants the secured creditor a lien on all then-owned collateral and on any collateral acquired in the future. However, under the bankruptcy code, liens created prior to a bankruptcy generally do not attach, or apply, to assets acquired or arising after the commencement of the bankruptcy proceeding. As a result, it is customary for secured creditors to agree to permit uses of the cash proceeds from sales of their collateral consisting of inventory, accounts receivable, or other similar classes of "quick assets" only if the court permits them to obtain a lien on quick assets created or acquired after the commencement of the bankruptcy. In general, the first lien lenders can be counted on to make this request (typically in connection with the debtor's request for authority to use cash collateral to obtain debtor-in-possession financing, or it may be phrased as an adequate protection motion). However, the second lien lenders need to be able to tag along in order to preserve their second liens on quick assets acquired after the commencement of the bankruptcy, or they will lose the benefit of their bargain.

In some cases, particularly where there are second lien term loans with similar (or even identical) covenants, the second lien term loans will waive their adequate protection rights for as long as any first lien loans are outstanding. However, in many cases, there is strong resistance by some participants in the syndicated loan market to agreeing to any adequate protection waivers.

The practical significance of these adequate protection waivers depends on the facts of the case. Excluding the ability to have a say in the use of cash collateral and DIP financings (which we will discuss later), the principal benefit of adequate protection is the right of a secured creditor to ask for additional or substitute collateral to protect against declines in the value of its interest in the collateral after the date on which the bankruptcy commenced. This right is of critical importance to a holder of liens on quick assets (as discussed earlier), and it is also meaningful if the company in bankruptcy has valuable unencumbered or partially encumbered assets on which additional or replacement liens can be granted to protect the value of the original liens. The remedy is of more limited utility to a second lien lender that already has a lien on all of the borrower's assets.

In most cases, the borrower will have some unencumbered assets, and the grant of a lien on those assets to compensate for deterioration in the value of the second lien holder's original collateral may materially enhance the second lien lender's ultimate recovery. The value of the second lien lender's interest in any additional or substitute collateral obtained to secure its obligations protects, dollar for dollar, against erosion of the value of second lien lenders' interest in their collateral. As a result, giving up the opportunity to obtain additional or substitute collateral in the name of adequate protection could have a real-world cost. On balance, however, if the second lien lenders preserve their right to obtain a second lien on any new collateral provided to the first lien lenders in the name of adequate protection, their waiver of the right to seek other forms of adequate protection on their own will not prove to be an imprudent concession in most real-world circumstances.

Waiver of the Right to Oppose Adequate Protection for the First Lien Loans

Second lien lenders typically waive any right to dispute actions taken by the first lien lenders to seek adequate protection with respect to the collateral securing the first lien loans. This waiver is not particularly controversial and is not usually subject to any time limitation.

Advance Consent to the Use of Cash Collateral

Second lien lenders typically give an advance consent to any use of cash collateral approved by the first lien loans (effectively waiving their right to oppose the company's proposed use of cash collateral on adequate protection grounds). Under the bankruptcy code, a debtor may use cash collateral with the secured lender's consent. Absent such consent, the debtor may obtain an order of the bankruptcy court authorizing the use of cash collateral. To obtain the order, the debtor must demonstrate that the secured creditor is adequately protected. The primary benefit to a secured creditor of the right to consent to the use of cash collateral is that it allows the secured creditor to leverage how the company uses its cash. As a borrower in bankruptcy invariably cannot operate without access to cash and other cash collateral, secured creditors can, and frequently do, condition their consent to the use of these funds on adoption by the company in bankruptcy of a satisfactory operating budget. As a result of this advance consent, the second lien lenders will almost certainly be required to rely on the first lien lenders to handle these budget negotiations.[11]

Advance Consent to Sales of Collateral

Second lien lenders are often asked in the context of intercreditor negotiations to agree not to object to any court-approved asset sale that is also approved by the first lien lenders as long as liens attach to the proceeds of the sale in accordance with the lien priorities agreed to in the intercreditor agreement. In those deals in which second lien lenders agree to such a request, the second lien lenders may condition their advance consent on the use of all or a specified portion of the sale proceeds to permanently reduce the first lien loans. However, second lien lenders often resist agreeing to such a request, since, if they provide an advance consent to asset sales, they no longer have any say as to sales of collateral approved by the first lien lenders. If the second lien loans are undersecured, second lien lenders may be relying on a successful reorganization of the debtor for repayment of their loans, and selling assets may frustrate that goal. The first lien loans, on the other hand, are more likely to be oversecured and may want a quick liquidation of the bankrupt company's assets, without regard to the company's prospects of emerging from bankruptcy. This opens the door to the possibility for mischief, such as a fire sale of assets at below fair market value or a sale of key income-generating assets or other material assets whose sale might eliminate the possibility of a

---

[11] In the early stages of a case, a debtor may have no source of liquidity for operations other than cash collateral. As a result, if the debtor is denied the use of cash collateral, it may be required to cease operations and liquidate. As a practical matter, if a bankruptcy court is faced with either permitting the use of cash collateral over a secured creditor's objection or causing the debtor to liquidate, the bankruptcy court will routinely permit the use of cash collateral. Thus, as discussed in the text, first lien lenders tend to concentrate their efforts not on seeking to prevent such use, but rather on requiring that such use be conditioned on the debtor's adherence to a tight operating budget.

successful reorganization. However, there are other protections for the second lien lenders—the sale still has to be approved by the bankruptcy court and must be conducted through an auction process, at which the second lien lenders can bid,[12] and the fiduciary duties and other legal requirements discussed earlier should prevent most of the potential for mischief from ever coming to fruition. Because of these competing perspectives, the issue of restrictions on the ability of second lien lenders to object to a court-approved asset sale remains at play in the second lien loan market.

Advance Consent to DIP Financing Approved by the First Lien Lenders

Second lien lenders typically agree to some form of agreement not to object to DIP financings consented to by first lien lenders. This agreement by second lien lenders appears in various permutations:

- Unconditional agreement not to object to any DIP financing approved by the first lien lenders, with no cap on the amount of the DIP financing
- Conditional agreement to any DIP financing approved by the first lien lenders, subject to a dollar cap (which may include a cushion to allow "protective advances") on the amount of the DIP financing
- Conditional agreement to any DIP financing approved by the first lien lenders, but only if the liens securing the DIP financing rank prior or equal to the liens securing the first lien loans

---

[12] Unless the court orders otherwise, at the auction, the second lien lenders can "credit-bid" (i.e., reduce dollar for dollar the cash price payable by the second lien lenders for the auctioned asset by an amount equal to) the value of their interest in the collateral in excess of the value of the first lien lenders' interest in the collateral. For example, assume that the bankrupt company owes $50 to the first lien lenders and $200 to the second lien lenders. Both the first and second lien loans are secured solely by liens on an asset worth $150. If a third party makes a cash bid of $120 for one of the bankrupt company's crown jewels, and there are no other bidders, the first lien lenders are likely to favor the sale because they will get paid off in full. With credit bidding, the second lien lenders are required to cash-bid only $50 (the value of the first lien lenders' interest in the collateral) and can credit-bid up to the full amount of their $200 debt. Credit-bidding allows second lien lenders to lower the cash component of their bid, which gives them a competitive advantage over other bidders without credit-bid rights.

The third permutation is becoming increasingly popular in the second lien loan market. It is attractive to second lien lenders because it requires the first lien lenders to "share the pain" and thereby reduces the chances of an overly generous DIP, and it is acceptable to first lien lenders and borrowers because it does not arbitrarily cap the amount of the DIP financing. This permutation is generally found to be a reasonable and fair compromise from the perspective of all parties involved. Some second lien lenders require certain quid pro quos in exchange for an agreement of this type, including the reservation of a right to propose a competing DIP financing and the right to object to any aspects of the DIP financing that may constitute a sub rosa plan of reorganization.

Is There a Preferred Way to Document These Intercreditor Arrangements?

Some deals reflect the intercreditor arrangements just described in a document called a *collateral trust agreement*, while others use a document called an *intercreditor agreement*. Substantively, the choice of document is a distinction without a difference—it doesn't affect the terms of the intercreditor arrangements themselves. If the parties prefer to have separate collateral agents hold the first and second liens on behalf of their respective lender groups, the intercreditor arrangements are usually documented in an intercreditor agreement. An intercreditor agreement is currently the document more commonly used in the syndicated loan market.

Are Intercreditor Agreements Enforceable?

Courts are generally willing to enforce intercreditor agreements between a debtor's creditors, even when the borrower is in bankruptcy. The bankruptcy code specifically provides that a subordination agreement is as enforceable in a bankruptcy as it is outside of bankruptcy. As a general matter, an agreement containing the types of intercreditor provisions discussed here should be enforceable under state law, both before and during a bankruptcy. In practice, most bankruptcy courts will not monitor compliance with every aspect of the advance waivers and consents contained in an intercreditor agreement, but the final plan of reorganization is likely to give effect to the agreement's priority waterfall provisions by treating first and second lien lenders as separate classes for plan purposes.[13] As a court of equity, a bankruptcy court may allow the second lien lenders to assert rights that they agreed to waive in the intercreditor agreement, leaving the first lien lenders to sue the second lien lenders in state court for breach of contract damages. In practice, that course will probably not be appealing to the first lien lenders absent repeated and flagrant disregard of the original bargain by the second lien lenders.

Does a Second Lien Lender Ever End Up Worse Off than an Unsecured Creditor?

Typically, an intercreditor agreement expressly states that, both before and during a bankruptcy, the second lien lenders can take any actions and exercise any rights that they would have had if they were unsecured creditors, except any rights that they expressly waived in the intercreditor agreement, such as with respect to challenges to sales of collateral, DIP financings, and the lien priority of the first lien loans.[14] We think these limitations are appropriate. We have seen instances in which first lien lenders go even further, however, and request advance agreements by the second lien lenders regarding how they will vote on a plan of reorganization. These voting agreements generally come in two basic forms: (1) an agreement not to support or vote in favor of a plan unless the first lien lenders vote in favor of the plan or the plan meets certain conditions (e.g., that the first lien loans get repaid in full), and (2) an agreement not to oppose a plan supported by the first lien lenders. These voting agreements are more controversial and may not be enforceable.

---

[13] In theory, the court could construct a plan providing for first and second lien lenders to share in a defined pool of value and leave them to sort out their intercreditor relationship after the plan is confirmed and consummated. That is not a likely result in practice, since it would be difficult to obtain the approval of the creditors affected by such a classification.

[14] In reality, waiving the right to challenge the first liens may not be as big a concession as it might appear to be at first blush. As discussed in note 10, the first and second liens are often granted at the same time and under either a single set of security documents or separate sets of nearly identical security documents. If the first liens can be successfully challenged, there is a reasonable chance that the same case can be made against the second liens.

The right to vote on a plan of reorganization provides significant protections for a secured creditor. First and second lien lenders have very different interests, and they frequently (and often strongly) disagree on the merits of a proposed plan. Furthermore, unsecured creditors almost never agree to limit their voting rights in a plan, and including such a provision in a lien subordination agreement could cause the second lien lender to have significantly less bargaining power than an unsecured creditor in plan negotiations. These factors may explain why restrictions on the right to vote for or against particular plans of reorganization are almost never agreed to by second lien lenders.

Do Second Lien Lenders Have the Right to Purchase the First Lien Loans?

In some second lien financings, the first lien lenders give second lien lenders an option to purchase the first lien obligations. The exercise price in such arrangements is generally the par value of the outstanding first lien loans plus accrued interest and other amounts due. Usually, the option can be exercised during an agreed-upon time period starting on the date on which the company files for bankruptcy and/or the first lien lenders take any action to foreclose on their collateral. Some second lien lenders view the purchase option as a "must-have" provision. First lien lenders generally view the purchase option as acceptable, since, if it is exercised, it allows them to exit from a troubled credit at par.

The purchase option has some value for the second lien lenders because, once it is exercised, the second lien lender will no longer be subject to any of the intercreditor arrangements discussed earlier and will be free to exercise all the rights of a secured creditor. As a result, the second lien lenders will have increased leverage in the plan or out-of-court restructuring negotiations, which may translate into a higher net recovery for the second lien lenders. However, in any restructuring where the second lien lenders are sufficiently organized and are able and willing to buy out the first lien position at par, an amicable arrangement is likely to be within easy reach. As a result, many market participants do not attribute significant value to including this option in the original documentation.

Do We Need Two Sets of Security Documents?

Because of a single unfortunate case from 1991,[15] there is some debate as to whether the first and second liens can be granted in a single set of security documents (containing separate grants of security interests for the first and second liens) rather than in separate sets of security documents. Some first lien lenders are concerned that they may prejudice their right to postpetition interest unless the first and second liens have completely separate security documents. We believe that, if properly prepared, a single set of security documents should work to ensure that the first- and second lien lenders hold separate secured claims. Each security document should contain two separate granting clauses and a clear statement of an intention to create two separate classes of secured creditors.

How Do Various Classes of Creditors Vote?

As we discussed earlier, the first lien lenders generally control (at least for some period of time) many of the key decisions relating to the collateral. Typically, the collateral agents are authorized to take action only if instructed to do so by first lien lenders holding more than 50 percent of the total amount of the outstanding first lien loans. Often, the amount of unfunded commitments is not counted

---

[15] The case is called *In re Ionosphere Clubs, Inc.*, 134 B.R. 528 (Banker, S.D. N.V. 1991). In that case, three series (series A, B, and C) of creditors had a security interest in the same assets of the bankrupt company. The security interest for each of the series A, B, and C creditors was granted in the same security agreement. The security agreement contained a single "granting clause" that granted one security interest in favor of the series A, B, and C creditors. The issue at stake in the case was whether the series A, B, and C creditors held three separate secured claims or were co-owners of a single combined claim. The answer would determine whether the series A creditors were entitled to postpetition interest. In bankruptcy, only an oversecured creditor is entitled to postpetition interest. A creditor is oversecured if the value of its interest in its collateral exceeds the amount of its claim. If the series A, B, and C creditors each held a separate secured claim, the series A creditors would be oversecured and the series B and C creditors would be undersecured. However, if the series A, B, and C creditors were co-owners of a single combined secured claim, the entire class, including the class A creditors, would be undersecured.

The bankruptcy court held that the series A, B, and C creditors were co-owners of a single secured claim because the series A, B, and C creditors were secured by a single security interest. The court stated that, if the three series had been secured by three separate liens on the collateral, there would have been three separate secured claims.

for voting purposes in connection with the exercise of remedies, on the theory that only the holders of funded first lien loans have "skin in the game."

If there is more than one tranche of first lien loans outstanding, the first lien lenders need to decide among themselves how the various tranches of first lien loans will vote together as a single class. There are two general approaches to this conundrum. The first is the electoral college system, under which each tranche of debt within a class votes as a block in favor of (or against) the proposed action. The block vote of each tranche is determined by a majority (or supermajority) of the holders of that particular tranche. The second approach is the popular vote system, in which all of the debt in a class (regardless of tranche) votes together as a single class. The popular vote system tends to be less attractive because it does not address the situation in which different tranches of debt have different voting requirements to approve a particular action. One tranche of debt may require majority approval for a particular action, while another tranche of debt may require supermajority approval for the same action. By lumping all the tranches of debt into a single voting group, the voting requirements for the various tranches of debt may be effectively replaced with a single uniform voting standard that is not consistent with the parties' bargained-for intent.

Apart from Intercreditor Agreements and Collateral Documents, What Other Documents Are Involved in a Second Lien Loan Transaction?

In addition to the intercreditor agreements and security agreements discussed previously, second lien loans are governed by a loan or credit agreement that sets out the other applicable commercial terms of the debt (e.g., principal amount, interest rate, repayment provisions, conditions, representations and warranties, covenants, events of default, and so on).

Early in the development of the second lien loan product, certain transactions used one credit agreement for both the first lien loans and the second lien loans. In today's market, it is becoming increasingly popular to document the first lien loans and second lien loans in separate credit agreements. This trend is largely due, we think, to the nature of the covenant packages that typically apply to second lien loan transactions. Second lien loan covenants generally include most of the same categories of controls as first lien loan covenants, but they are usually less restrictive. For example, a typical first lien credit agreement might include two or more financial covenants (e.g., interest coverage ratio and leverage ratio), while a typical second lien credit agreement might include only one financial covenant (e.g., a leverage ratio). In addition, the second lien loan covenant package will be less restrictive than the analogous provisions in the first lien covenants (e.g., the leverage ratio in the second lien covenant package may be 10 to 20 percent wider than the leverage ratio in the first lien covenant package).

The looser covenant packages for the second lien loans are designed to give the first lien lenders more control in the event of a deterioration in a borrower's credit. Because the first lien lenders' covenants are tighter, the first lien lenders' rights to enforce remedies or to "bring the borrower to the table" may be triggered prior to the rights of the second lien lenders and give the first lien lenders greater ability to control the outcome of the process.

Because of the differences in covenant packages, first and second lien lenders in today's market tend to prefer to have separate credit agreements so that they can better control their own destinies. If the respective covenants of first and second lien lenders are contained in one document, it becomes more difficult to ensure that determinations of the two constituencies can be made independently. For example, in the case of amendments or determinations regarding the exercise of remedies, if both first and second lien lenders are governed by a single credit agreement, particular care must be taken to ensure that one constituency or the other is not given control of decisions that the other constituency feels it should have a voice in. While some first and second lien loans are still documented in a single credit agreement, the majority of deals now use separate credit agreements to ensure that decisions of the two lender groups can be made independently.[16]

What else is unique regarding the loan documentation used in second lien loan transactions? The following sections give a brief description of certain provisions that are commonly seen today.

---

[16] Standard & Poor's reports that during the first two quarters of 2005, of the second lien loans it tracked, over 90 percent were documented under separate credit agreements. See Standard & Poor's Report dated August 22, 2005, "Second Lien Evolution Creates Higher Recovery Prospects—At First Lien Lender's Expense."

Are There Any Limits on the Amount of Future First Lien Loans?

Yes. In order to protect the second lien lenders from losing the value of their accrued claims, the typical covenant package in a second lien deal will fix the maximum principal amount of first lien loans that may be incurred. The cap is typically fixed at a specified dollar amount (which may include a cushion to allow protective advances), but it may sometimes be a function of a maximum leverage ratio or other financial test.

Are There Any Limits on the Amount of Future Second Lien Loans?

Yes. In order to protect the second lien lenders from being diluted, the typical second lien covenant package will cap the borrower's ability to incur additional second lien loans. The cap is often based on a maximum leverage ratio or other financial test, although it could be expressed as a dollar cap.

Are There Other Permitted Prior Liens?

The phrase *second lien loan* is a shorthand statement of the relative priorities of the liens securing first and second lien loans. It is not an absolute statement of the priority of the liens securing second lien loans. In reality, the liens securing second lien loans may be junior to both the liens securing the first lien loans and certain other liens, sometimes called *permitted prior liens*, which are permitted to rank ahead of the second liens (and possibly the first liens) under the terms of the security documents. The payment of creditors secured by permitted prior liens will generally be baked right into the priority waterfall provisions for distributions of collateral sale proceeds contained in the intercreditor agreement.

As a general rule, permitted prior liens fall into four categories:

- Liens securing the first lien loans (and all related obligations)
- Liens that predate the second liens (which, in some deals, may include liens that the borrower inherits if, for example, it acquires assets in the future that are subject to liens)

- Liens securing a specified amount of purchase money debt
- Liens that are not voluntarily granted by the borrower but arise by operation of law and are entitled by law to priority over the second liens (for example, certain tax and ERISA liens)

Not every one of these categories is appropriate in every deal. The exact definition of permitted prior liens will need to be negotiated appropriately to suit the context of each deal. The obligations secured by permitted prior liens can be material and may affect the successful marketing of the transaction.

Can Second Lien Loans Be Voluntarily Prepaid Prior to First Lien Loans?

Generally not. In most first lien loan agreements, the borrower is contractually prohibited from voluntarily prepaying second lien loans prior to repayment of first lien loans in full.

What Sort of Mandatory Prepayments Typically Apply to Second Lien Loans?

Generally, the same categories of mandatory prepayments that are applicable to the first lien loans (e.g., asset sales, equity proceeds, and excess cash flow) apply to second lien loans. However, almost all second lien deals provide that such mandatory prepayments of second lien loans are not required to the extent that the relevant proceeds are required, under the terms of the first-lien loan documentation, to be used to repay first lien loans.

Are There Any Unique Restrictions on the Assignability of Second Lien Loans?

No. In typical second lien loan documents, the assignment provisions are the same as those found in first lien loan documents. The point to be aware of is that, in any given first/second lien loan transaction, the same investors may own both the first lien loans and the second lien loans. It is possible that a group of investors could control decisions and the exercise of remedies for both the first lien loans and the second lien loans.

Are the Second Lien Loans Cross-Defaulted to the First Lien Loans?

In most transactions, in the event of a covenant default under the first lien loan agreement, a default under the second lien loan agreement is not immediately triggered through a cross-default provision. To do so would deprive the first lien lenders of the earlier triggers they receive by virtue of their tighter covenant package, described earlier. However, in many second lien loan agreements, the second lien loans are cross-defaulted to a first lien loan default if such default is not cured or waived within a specified period of time (usually 45 to 60 days). The theory behind such a provision is that, if the first lien loan default cannot be dealt with within the prescribed period, it must mean significant trouble for the borrower, and the second lien lender should be entitled to a seat at the table under such circumstance. This provision is somewhat peculiar to the second lien loan market, and it remains to be seen how it may change over time.

SUMMARY

Second lien loan financings appear to be here to stay. These financings can provide some companies with access to the syndicated loan market where they would otherwise not have access at all, and their popularity with a range of institutional investors from CLOs/CDOs to hedge funds is fueling their growth. However, there can be costs associated with second lien loan structures, and a careful borrower will want to think through the consequences of issuing second lien loans for its ability to tap the debt markets in the future.

Traditional first lien lenders are not predisposed to favor second lien loan deals, but they have been required to take a more flexible approach to these new financing structures to help reduce their own exposure or to accommodate their customers' desire to raise capital in this new way. We do not expect first lien lenders to ever be vocal advocates for securing the claims of their junior cousins in the capital structure, but they can no longer simply ignore these new products.

Second lien lenders are inching their way toward consensus on many of the key structuring points that find their way into intercreditor arrangements that define the rights of second lien lenders in these deals, but we have not yet reached a market equilibrium on every point. Moreover, the second lien loans that have proliferated during the favorable economic climate in which they were developed have not been thoroughly tested in a down-cycle. Anecdotal evidence from the relatively few recent bankruptcies involving second lien loans indicates that they can add significant additional complexity in bankruptcy, notwithstanding an extensive intercreditor agreement. How the bankruptcy courts (and the lienholders) ultimately resolve those complexities may affect senior lenders' and borrowers' appetite for these products in the future.

Project Finance

Dawn Pasquin
Managing Director
GE Energy Financial Services

Project finance is a financing technique used to fund a discrete project with limited recourse to the equity investors in the project. Project finance loans have unique characteristics compared to traditional corporate loans. In most greenfield projects, the borrower is not a going concern, and in many cases, the project hasn't even been constructed when the loan is made. Recourse to the equity investors, who do not guarantee repayment of the loan, is limited to their respective ownership interests in the project. The collateral takes the form of a series of contractual arrangements designed to ensure that the project is built, operates, and generates sufficient future cash flow to cover costs, to repay loan-market participants, and to provide a return to equity investors during a finite period. For these reasons, project finance transactions must be viable on a stand-alone basis.

Project finance transactions are structured by allocating each risk to the counterparty best equipped to manage that risk. The risk allocation is made in the form of contractual arrangements between the borrower and the project counterparties—collectively, the project documents. There are usually no historical data available for the project, and the transaction is generally not rated by rating agencies. Loan-market participants need to complete a thorough due diligence of the project participants and project documents to be satisfied that risks are adequately mitigated.

Credit agreements include standard clauses for pricing, amortization, final maturity, security package, and other standard corporate loan-like terms and conditions. In addition, the credit agreements include provisions to ensure that the project documents work as expected and to provide an early warning mechanism for potential problems. The credit agreements may also include credit enhancements to further protect loan-market participants against project-specific risks if the provisions included in the project documents are deemed unsatisfactory.

This article will first discuss the key project participants and project documents in a typical project finance transaction. It will then highlight the major categories of risk to be analyzed during the due diligence process. It will introduce customary provisions included in the credit agreements, and will summarize the potential roles of a bank or financial institution during the project finance life cycle.

PROJECT PARTICIPANTS AND KEY PROJECT DOCUMENTS

A simplified project finance structure, with key project participants and documents, is shown in Exhibit 3.2. Parties involved include:

EXHIBIT 3.2

Standard project finance structure.

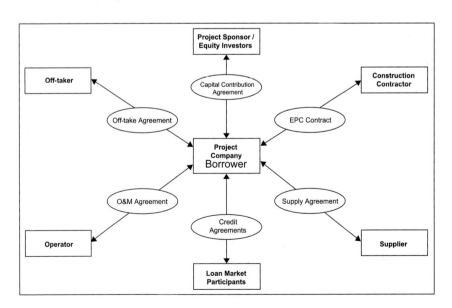

The borrower: A special-purpose project company, capitalized through a combination of debt and equity, is established to implement the project. The borrower is the entity that enters into the various project documents with the other project participants, thereby limiting the risk to the equity investors.

Project sponsor: During the development phase, a project sponsor performs all tasks necessary to implement the project. This includes securing the transaction, obtaining permits and approvals, environmental due diligence, negotiating documents, implementing an insurance program, and arranging the financing.

Equity investors: Equity investors invest cash equity in the borrower, with the amounts and timing being specified in a capital contribution agreement. Equity investors may be the project sponsor, other project participants who share in the equity upside as a performance incentive, or pure financial investors seeking dividend income.

Loan-market participants: In order to maximize returns, equity investors leverage projects with debt capital. The loans are typically provided on a senior, secured basis. The acceptable leverage ratio will depend on many factors and is discussed in more detail in the next section of this article.

Construction contractor: If the project is not yet built, an engineering, procurement, and construction contractor is hired to build and complete the project. The construction contractor should be experienced in the technology being utilized, with a strong track record of completing projects on time and within budget. Projects provided on a turnkey basis under lump-sum, date-certain contracts can be used to minimize the risk of cost overruns or completion delays.

Suppliers: Feedstocks or other inputs required for the production process should be contracted for with an experienced and creditworthy supplier on a long-term basis at an agreed-upon price, quantity, and quality. This will ensure adequate supply during the life of the project and will minimize operating cost volatility.

Operator: Once the project has been completed and feedstock is delivered, an operator is responsible for operation and maintenance of the project. Performance standards and a budget are agreed on in an operation and maintenance agreement. The operator may be paid a fixed fee or be compensated on a cost-plus basis.

Off-taker: In order to ensure a stable and predictable revenue stream from the project, the borrower may enter into long-term off-take contracts with creditworthy counterparties for ideally all of the project's output. The off-taker agrees to purchase a specified amount of capacity and output for a fixed price on a "take-or-pay" basis—in other words, the off-taker is obligated to pay for delivered production, whether it is needed or not. In some industries, hedges can be used in lieu of take-or-pay off-take agreements. The contracted revenues should be sufficient to cover at a minimum all fixed and variable operation and maintenance costs as well as interest and principal due to loan-market participants (with some level of cushion).

Project participants should be compensated appropriately for the respective level of risk taking. This will minimize the risk of a participant defaulting on its commercial obligations over the project life. Terms and conditions that are too favorable for the borrower will not necessarily improve the project's chance of success. Exhibit 3.3 provides a summary of the risk/reward trade-off of key project participants.

EXHIBIT 3.3

Role	Risk	Reward
Project Sponsor	• Development capital	• Development fee
Equity Investor	• Equity capital	• Dividend return
	• Contingent capital contributions	• Gain on sale of equity interest or asset
	• Project risks (subordinated to lenders)	• Other interests in project (e.g., contractor or operator)
Construction	• Cost over-runs	• Net margin
Contractor	• Performance guarantees	• Bonuses
	• Damages for nonperformance	
Operator	• Performance guarantees	• O&M fee
	• Loss of fees for nonperformance	• Bonuses
Suppliers	• Sufficient quantity provided to specification	• Margin
Off-takers	• Take or pay obligations	• Security of supply
Lenders	• Loss of principal	• Margin/fees

PROJECT FINANCE RISK CATEGORIES

Loan-market participants rely on the adequacy and thoroughness of project documents that are negotiated and executed, but not implemented or tested, prior to the loan's being made. In order to ensure that the project performs as expected and to predict the certainty of cash flow, a thorough due diligence of project-specific risks should be performed. The main categories of project finance risks are described here. A project finance due diligence checklist can be found in Exhibit 3.4.

Financial Structure

The appropriate debt-to-equity ratio is determined by taking into account the certainty of cash flow necessary to cover operation and maintenance costs and debt service. Projects in noninvestment grade countries may command higher equity levels to reduce loan-market participant exposure. The base-case cash flow projections should demonstrate an acceptable level of debt service coverage ratios (defined as cash available for debt service during a defined period divided by interest and scheduled principal due during the same period). Liquidated damages to be paid by the construction contractor or operator in case of construction delay or performance shortfalls should be sufficient to preserve the base-case economics. In addition, standby funding in the form of contingent equity obligations or standby lines of credit should be available to cover unforeseen costs. The maximum tenor of the loan will be determined in part by loan-market participants' appetite as well as by the economic life of the assets (assuming adequate capital expenditures), but is usually shorter than the term of the off-take agreements. The security package should include a first-priority, perfected interest over all of the project's assets and accounts. The project should include reserve accounts to overcome short-term liquidity problems arising out of unplanned events or to smooth uneven cash flow streams. The exposure to interest-rate fluctuations needs to be managed to minimize fluctuations in cash flow.

Counterparty Credit Risk

Each of the various project counterparties should have sufficient financial wherewithal to meet its obligations under its respective project documents. Moody's or Standard & Poor's ratings can be

E X H I B I T   3 . 4

Financial Structure	• Debt to Equity Ratio • Debt Service Coverage Ratio • Liquidated Damages • Contingency Funding • Loan Tenor • Security Package • Reserve Accounts • Interest Rate Risk
Counterparty Credit Risk	• Project Sponsor / Equity Investor Credit Risk • Construction contractor Credit Risk • Off-taker Credit Risk • Operator Credit Risk • Supplier Credit Risk • Insurance Provider Credit Risk • Hedge Provider Credit Risk
Construction Risk	• Construction contractor experience / reputation • Technology Risk • Delay Risk • Cost Overrun Risk • Environmental Risk • Insurance • Force Majeure
Operation Risk	• Operator experience / reputation • Technology Risk • Operation & Maintenance Budget • Operator Fee Structure • Environmental Risk • Insurance • Force Majeure
Economic Risk	• Market Risk • Competitive Position • Foreign Exchange Risk • Inflation Risk • Supply Risk
Legal Risk	• Governing law • Enforceability • Change in law • Documentation risk • Permits, Approvals, consents
Structural Risk	• Ownership Structure • Account Structure • Taxation
Sovereign Risk	• Hark currency rating of Borrower's host country • Ability of project of operate without interference from the government

used to determine counterparty creditworthiness. Consideration should also be given to the timing of the financial obligations. For example, do the equity investors make capital contributions up front, on a pari passu basis with loan disbursements, or at the end of the construction period? Is the construction contractor's progress payment schedule front- or back-ended, or is there a retention payment that is withheld until project completion? Additional financial support in the form of parent-company guarantees or bank letters of credit may be requested by loan-market participants if they are unsatisfied with the counterparty's credit on a stand-alone basis. The project documents and credit agreements often include a provision requiring the borrower or counterparty, as applicable, to replace credit enhancements and guarantees in case of a credit-quality deterioration.

Construction Risk

A construction contractor must be able to demonstrate a long-term successful track record in completing the same type of project on time and within budget. The probability of the project's achieving the technical performance levels in the base-case financial model will be determined in part by the complexity of the technology utilized. Fixed-price, date-certain construction contracts should clearly specify performance standards, quantity and quality of output, and delivery points for feedstock intake and product output. Some level of contingency is usually included in the construction budget to cover cost overruns or change orders. Performance guarantees ensure that the project will produce the right quantity and quality of products. Liquidated damages should be required to keep the base-case economics whole in case of construction delay or performance shortfall. The construction contractor may also get a bonus as an incentive to complete the project ahead of schedule. In highly technical projects, it is beneficial for the construction contractor to also assume the role of a long-term maintenance or service provider for its equipment. An independent engineer is typically engaged to assist loan-market participants in evaluating construction and technical risk, and to provide opinions on the status of construction during the construction period.

An environmental impact assessment is usually prepared by a third-party consultant to identify preexisting environmental problems at the project site. Any such issues need to be adequately addressed to ensure that there is no negative financial impact on the project.

An insurance consultant usually prepares a report confirming that an adequate insurance package is in place to cover property damage up to the replacement value of the asset in case of catastrophic events. In addition, business interruption insurance should be maintained to cover loss of revenues in case of late completion.

Operation Risk

The operator should be an established company with a proven track record of successfully operating comparable types of projects within budget. If the operator is a special-purpose company, then its owners should provide support through advisory and technical support agreements. The risk of technical obsolescence of the project during the loan tenor should be clearly understood.

The level of budgeted operation and maintenance costs in the base case should be reasonably conservative and well documented. The borrower should be able to replace the operator if it is not performing, and budgeted operation and maintenance costs should be sufficient to replace the operator without having to increase the budget.

The roles of the contractor and the operator need to be clearly delineated to avoid potential disputes. If the operator is also an equity investor, loan-market participants may request any fees payable to the operator to be subordinated to debt service.

As during the construction period, environmental risk and the adequacy of the insurance program need to be assessed.

Competitive Landscape

The exposure of the project to market risk should be analyzed. Expected cash flow from a project with all of its production sold under long-term fixed-price contracts with creditworthy off-takers is obviously more stable and predictable than cash flow from a project selling commodity products into an open market. The structure of pricing, including inflation, exchange-rate, and other potential adjustments, for contracted projects should be considered. Growth assumptions, market share, and competitive position should be analyzed in pure market-risk transactions. Understanding the project's position in the market, relative cost structure, barriers to entry, and regulatory framework are important even in fully contracted deals in case the project documents are terminated prematurely.

Another component of market risk is feedstock supply. If long-term arrangements for the project's feedstock requirements cannot be made, the project's ability to withstand commodity price volatility should be tested. Feedstock supply consultants with industry expertise and experience may be hired to manage the supply chain. Cash reserve funds or revolving lines of credit can be used to provide extra liquidity to cover price movements for noncontracted feedstock.

Legal Risk

There should be sufficient precedent in the law governing the transaction documents, such as U.S. or U.K. law. Enforcement of the contractual obligations and security in case of default should be easy, and arbitration proceedings in western jurisdictions or acceptable international arbitration forums should be included. The exposure of the project to changes in law should be mitigated in the project documents. The project documents should also provide for clear dispute resolution and arbitration procedures. Mismatches in definitions and key clauses between project documents should be minimized. The transaction structure shown in Exhibit 3.2 is relatively simple. Additional complexities, such as split construction contracts, conduit funding structures, multiple operation and maintenance contracts, or multiple tranches of debt with different risk-sharing arrangements, increase the documentation risk. To the extent possible, all permits, approvals, and consents required to construct and operate the project should be in place prior to the loan's being made.

Structural Risk

Projects with clear direct relationships between the equity investors and the borrower (i.e., a direct subsidiary) are less risky than projects with ownership structures involving various layers of subsidiaries and cross shareholdings. The level of control of the loan-market participants in the allocation of cash throughout the tenor of the loan is important. The exposure of the project to tax risk during construction and operation, including withholding tax on interest, can be mitigated by passing tax liabilities through in the revenue stream.

Force Majeure Risk

The project documents should include complete definitions of force majeure (natural and unavoidable catastrophes that might impede the successful completion of a project), and mismatches in force majeure definitions between documents should be avoided. The borrower should be able to claim for time extension and cost cover in case of uninsurable force majeure events.

Sovereign Risk

Sovereign risk is the ability of the borrower's host country to meet its financial obligations as well as the ability of the project to operate without interference from the government. Sovereign risk can be measured by the foreign currency rating (usually provided by Moody's or Standard & Poor's) of the country in which the borrower is domiciled.

If loan-market participants are not satisfied with the risk allocation in the project documents, additional credit enhancements may be factored into the credit agreements.

STRUCTURING THE CREDIT AGREEMENTS

Since the project's future cash flow is the only source of repayment, loan-market participants typically require more control over the use of funds and more stringent covenants than is usual in corporate loan transactions. Credit agreements include standard conditions precedent to disbursement, representations and warranties made by the borrower and, in some cases, by the equity investors, affirmative and negative covenants, and specific events of default and cure periods. Rather than provide an exhaustive outline of a credit agreement, this section aims to highlight particular clauses that are applicable to a project finance transaction.

Security Package

Loan-market participants are usually secured by a first-priority, perfected security interest in all assets of the project, including real property, fixtures, leases, inventory, cash accounts, machinery, and equipment. The rights of the borrower under each of the project documents, governmental approvals (if assignable), and all insurance proceeds are assigned to the loan-market participants. It is also prudent to receive consents to such assignment from the project counterparties. In addition, loan-market participants should receive a pledge of equity investors' shares in the borrower. This will enable the loan-market participants to step into the rights and obligations of equity without having to otherwise enforce security. It is not uncommon for the loan-market participants to share the security package with interest-rate or foreign-exchange-rate hedge providers, since the project benefits from reduced cash flow volatility as a result of the hedges. A collateral trustee normally holds the security.

Capital Contributions

In addition to their base capital contributions, equity investors may be responsible for contingent capital contributions during the construction or operation phases. Any such contingent capital contribution would be specific, capped, and limited to particular events.

Cash Flow Projections and Annual Budget

As part of the due diligence process, loan-market participants review financial projections demonstrating the borrower's ability to cover operation and maintenance costs and service debt over the loan tenor. The projections include detailed calculations for revenue growth, operating performance, and fixed and variable operation and maintenance costs, including amounts for working capital and contingencies (especially during the construction period). The projections should also include reasonably conservative views on inflation, interest rates, and foreign exchange rates, or should include the impact of any hedges used to reduce interest-rate or foreign-exchange-rate volatility. The base-case projections should demonstrate an acceptable level of debt service coverage ratios. Sensitivity analysis is then run off the base case to ensure that the project can sustain realistic decreases in revenue as well as cost increases. Breakeven sensitivities are run to determine the worst-case scenario for key industry drivers.

The operation and maintenance budget and financial projections should be updated on an annual basis, with explanations of significant deviations from the prior year. In addition, spending above budget is limited, with capped annual capital expenditures.

Conditions Precedent to Disbursement

All proceeds from debt and equity are deposited in a bank account held by a collateral trustee. During the construction period, the collateral trustee releases funds from the account to make progress payments to the construction contractor, pay interest to the loan-market participants, or cover other documented costs included in the construction budget. Disbursements are usually made on a monthly or quarterly basis, subject to the independent engineer's confirming that the project is on schedule and that there are sufficient funds available to complete the project. Disbursements during construction are usually further conditioned upon no default, no material adverse change, all insurance and permits and consents in place, and other project-specific conditions.

Cash Flow Waterfall

All cash proceeds, including construction financing, revenues from sales contracts, insurance proceeds, and all other amounts due to the borrower, are deposited in a bank account held by a collateral trustee or lead bank. All disbursements from the account are made according to a specified order of priority, called the *waterfall*. The priority of disbursements after completion will depend upon the nature of the project, but the following order would generally apply:

1. *Operation and maintenance expenses.* All fixed and variable operation and maintenance costs required to operate the project are paid first (except any subordinated fees to the operator) according to the annual operation and maintenance budget. This would include wages, feedstock

supplies, insurance costs, legal and accounting fees, taxes (if applicable), and so on. Loan-market participants reserve the right to approve or deny payment of expenses that exceed the annual operation and maintenance budget.

2. *Senior debt service.* This would include fees, interest, and scheduled principal payments on senior, secured debt as well as fees to the administrative agent and the collateral trustee.

3. *Funding of debt service reserve account.* Loan-market participants typically require a cash reserve account to cover at least six months' forward-looking interest and principal payments. This allows loan-market participants to continue to get paid during temporary liquidity shortfalls. The construction budget typically includes an amount sufficient to fund the debt service reserve account just prior to commercial operation, when operating hiccups are most likely to occur. However, timing of funding of the debt service reserve account is agreed between the borrower and the loan-market participants. In lieu of cash, loan-market participants may sometimes agree to an acceptable letter of credit posted by equity investors until the project generates enough cash to replace this amount. Any withdrawals from the debt service reserve account in one period would need to be topped up in subsequent periods prior to other disbursements in the waterfall.

4. *Funding of other reserve accounts.* Loan-market participants may require additional reserve accounts depending upon the nature of the business. For example, if the project is unable to purchase its feedstock on a long-term contracted basis or implement hedges to decrease the volatility of expenses, it would be prudent to keep a minimum amount of cash on hand to cover unforeseen cash outflows. Similarly, highly technical projects may require periodic capital investments with high costs every fifth or sixth year. A reserve account can be used to smooth out the capital expenditures over the cycle instead of stressing cash in one particular year.

5. *Subordinated debt service.* Interest and principal payments to third-party lenders subordinated to first lien loan-market

participants are paid last in the waterfall. In some cases, equity investors may make their capital contributions in the form of subordinated debt for tax efficiency. Such subordinated debt payments to equity investors would not be made at this level in the waterfall, but would instead be subject to the same restrictions as payments of dividends (as described next).

Excess cash at the bottom of the waterfall can be distributed to equity investors in the form of dividends provided that defined distribution tests have been met.

Dividend Distribution Tests

No dividend distributions are allowed if there is a potential default or an actual event of default or if any of the reserve accounts are not funded. Most credit agreements also block dividends if the debt service coverage ratio falls below a minimum level or if the borrower's consolidated debt-to-equity ratio is higher than the maximum permitted. The credit agreement usually requires cash to be retained in a separate account and be used to prepay debt on a mandatory basis if the dividend distribution tests are not met for an extended period of time.

Financial Covenants

Unlike most corporate borrowers, project finance borrowers usually do not have to meet various financial covenants except for purposes of dividend distribution tests.

Additional Indebtedness

The borrower will not be allowed to incur additional indebtedness, although carve-outs for specific items in the ordinary course of business, such as trade payables of less than 90 or 180 days, are usually permitted. The borrower may also be allowed to incur additional indebtedness on a second-lien or subordinated basis if substantial capital investments are required in order to comply with existing laws or a change in law. The borrower usually reserves the right to refinance existing indebtedness provided the terms and conditions are not better than the existing debt.

Additional Liens

The borrower will be prohibited from placing liens on any of the assets that form part of the security package. Carve-outs consistent with permitted indebtedness are generally allowed.

Intercreditor Arrangements

Intercreditor agreements determine the rights of various lenders if there is more than one class of lender. If different classes of lenders share in the security on a pari passu basis, then the intercreditor arrangements specify voting rights and may include standstill periods. At a minimum, second lien or other subordinated lenders must agree not to impair the ability of the first lien lender to enforce its security. Specific intercreditor provisions can be highly negotiated. A thorough legal due diligence is recommended to ensure that first lien lenders' rights are maintained during a bankruptcy.

Insurance Proceeds

Casualty insurance proceeds from catastrophic events should be paid directly to loan-market participants and used to prepay the loan on a mandatory basis. In case of a partial loss, loan-market participants usually make insurance proceeds above a threshold amount available for rebuilding or repair subject to the independent engineer's confirmation that (1) the facility can be rebuilt to its original capacity and performance standard, and (2) the insurance proceeds together with other cash available are adequate to complete the repairs.

Sale of Assets

In order to preserve the value of the security, there are limitations on the borrower's ability to sell or dispose of material assets, usually expressed as an annual maximum and a consolidated total during the tenor of the debt. Sale of defective or obsolete assets, or assets sold in the ordinary course of business, is typically allowed if the assets are not replaced. Proceeds from asset sales would be used to prepay debt on a mandatory basis to reflect the decrease in the value of the security.

Amendments to Project Documents or Credit Agreements

The borrower will not be allowed to terminate, amend, modify, or waive any clauses in either the project documents or the credit agreements without loan-market participants' consent. Loan-market participants often reserve the right to include input from outside consultants, especially for technical, legal, and insurance matters, upon a request for amendment, modification, or waiver.

Limitations on Business

The borrower will not be allowed to engage in any business other than the business initially intended by the project, and is limited in its ability to enter into new documents. Similarly, the borrower is restricted in its ability to create or acquire subsidiaries.

Related-Party Transactions

All transactions between the borrower and any affiliated companies must be handled on an arms-length basis and on market terms and conditions to ensure that there are no conflicts of interest.

Ownership

The initial equity investors are generally restricted from selling their equity interests in the project below a controlling level, especially during the construction period. Some flexibility may be given for minority shareholders, or if transfers of ownership interests are to companies with creditworthiness and experience similar to those of the original equity investor, provided that loan-market participants have the right to approve such transfers. Any contingent equity obligations would need to be provided by the new equity transferee, together with any required credit enhancements.

Voting Rights

Consent from a subset of loan-market participants, with the voting percentage defined (e.g., 51 percent or $66^2/_3$ percent), will be necessary for most amendments and waivers. Certain amendments or waivers, such as changes in interest rate, tenor, amortization schedule, loan amount, or security package, will always require 100 percent loan-market participant consent.

Assignment

Loan-market participants typically want the right to freely assign or sell their participation in the loan without the borrower's consent. This is usually agreed, provided there is no increased cost to the borrower.

ROLE OF LOAN MARKET PARTICIPANTS DURING PROJECT LIFE

Project finance transactions have three primary phases: development, construction, and operation. The development of a project can be time-intensive, requires substantial financial resources, and is characterized by high execution risk. The construction phase requires regular monitoring to ensure that the project remains on schedule and within budget. Once the project commences operation, the commercial risk drops significantly. An administrative agent manages the project on behalf of the lending group, while a collateral trustee holds the security and manages the waterfall.

Development

During the development phase, a project sponsor may hire a bank or financial institution to act as a financial advisor and/or lead arranger. The financial advisor would assist in structuring the transaction and negotiating the project documents to ensure that risks are mitigated to the satisfaction of the equity investors and the ultimate lending group. The lead arranger would underwrite the deal at market terms and conditions, prepare the bank loan book, and syndicate the transaction to a larger bank group. Other than allocation of human resources and the opportunity cost of other deals, a bank or financial institution's risk during the development phase is limited. Out-of-pocket expenses, such as consultant costs and legal fees, are reimbursed either by the project sponsor or from the proceeds of the financing. Depending upon the creditworthiness of the project sponsor, loan-market participants may request prepayment for out-of-pocket expenses during the development phase. Since development capital is the riskiest form of capital, it is not unusual for the investors to earn an appropriate development fee for this effort.

Construction

An independent engineer, working on behalf of the administrative agent and the loan-market participants, typically reviews monthly construction reports to ensure that the project is on schedule, confirms that sufficient funds are available to cover outstanding costs, and witnesses performance testing. Once a loan-market participant makes its commitment, it is obligated to fund provided that all conditions precedent to disbursement have been met. No loan-market participant is required to make a disbursement for another if such other loan-market participant defaults on its funding obligation. However, it may be prudent for the remaining loan-market participants to step up if sufficient funds would not otherwise be available in order to see the project through to completion. Loan-market participants typically earn only interest during the construction period, and may be requested to capitalize interest during construction into the loan principal amount.

Operation

Repayment of principal generally commences 6 to 12 months after completion. Loan-market participants assign an in-house portfolio manager to handle incoming cash flow and to process credit amendments and waiver requests. Substantial portfolio management resources will be required in case of an event of default and when security is enforced.

In conclusion, project finance is a useful technique when considering financing alternatives for large- to medium-scale greenfield projects. When structured properly, project finance offers a means for a project sponsor, equity investors, and other parties to share risks, costs, and benefits in an economically efficient manner.

CHAPTER 4

The Primary Market

Barry Bobrow
Managing Director Loan Syndications
Wachovia

Mercedes Tech
Managing Director Syndications
Société Générale

Linda Redding
Wachovia

Alex Spiro
Associate General Counsel
Bank of America

Elliot Ganz
General Counsel
The Loan Syndications and Trading Association

An Introduction to the Primary Market

Barry Bobrow
Wachovia

Mercedes Tech
Société Générale

Linda Redding
Wachovia

INTRODUCTION

In the primary market for syndicated loans, issuers and investors come together to price, structure, and invest in one of the oldest of financial instruments—bank loans. While parts of the loan market have evolved significantly over the past few decades and now resemble the markets for other fixed-income products more closely, the primary market for syndicated loans retains some unique attributes that are distinct from those of other debt markets. Some of those distinguishing attributes are set forth here:

- *Flexible structuring.* Loans remain one of the most customized credit products in the capital markets, with highly negotiated packages of covenants and other structural elements. Arrangers compete by creating unique structures, and investors are willing to accept these unique structures as long as they believe that the structures represent an acceptable risk. The primary market for loans accommodates this structural flexibility with highly negotiated term sheets and documentation.
- *Revolving loans.* Unlike other fixed-income markets, the loan market remains heavily weighted toward revolving loans. Nearly every company has at least some amount of unfunded revolving loan in its capital structure that allows it to manage the fluctuations in its cash levels caused by working capital and other needs. The need to accommodate requirements for revolving credit is a structural challenge that is unique to the loan market.
- *Floating rate/callable.* Loans are generally floating-rate instruments and as such do not have the interest rate and

inflation risk inherent in fixed rate debt. In addition, because loans are priced on a floating rate basis, generally at a spread over the 30–90 day London Interbank Offered Rate (LIBOR) index, loans do not have the same prepayment breakage costs as fixed rate debt, where pricing is based on longer term Treasury rate indices. For this reason, loans are generally callable at par at any time. In recent years, some loans have included call protection features, where the loan is callable, but a slight premium is payable during the first year or two. This is still very different from the bond market, where the debt generally has a lengthy non-call period and prepayment penalties designed to discourage early termination.

- *Relationship underpinnings.* Much of the loan market is still made up of relationship-oriented banks making loans to their corporate clients and holding those loans on their balance sheets. Because corporate issuers expect their core relationship banks to provide and hold credit in order to be eligible to provide other products, banks are critical investors in the loan market. This is in contrast to other fixed income markets, where investment decisions are made purely on a risk/return basis, and issuers are not reliant on their investors for other financial services.

- *Private market.* Though there are an increasing number of institutional investors participating in the loan market on a public basis, the loan market is still primarily a private market, and the majority of market participants generally prefer the greater amount of information afforded private investors in order to complete their credit analysis. For this reason, the primary loan market provides significantly more information than is typically available for public securities, including detailed historical analysis and projections. Private investors are not permitted to actively trade other securities of the issuer while they are in possession of the private offering materials. In addition, the principal regulatory oversight comes from bank regulators such as the Office of the Comptroller of the Currency. There is no direct SEC regulation, as bank loans are not considered securities.

LOANS—A BRIEF HISTORY

As recently as the mid–1980s, loans to corporate borrowers were made almost exclusively by banks. These loans held the first-priority position in the issuer's capital structure, and the credit exposure represented by the loans formed the cornerstone of the broader banking relationships between banks and their clients. These credit facilities were used for a wide range of corporate purposes, including the financing of working capital, capital expenditures, and acquisitions and as backstops for commercial paper programs. Banks tended to hold the entire loan for their own account, and in those rare situations where they needed to limit their credit exposure to a particular borrower, they typically contacted other banks to share the loan with them. The process of forming a syndicate of lenders at that time was relatively informal and completely opaque to public view. Hold levels were high, trading was nonexistent, and loans were not viewed as a financial-market instrument. There were none of the features typically associated with a primary market, such as information memoranda, a sales/marketing process, credit ratings, and secondary market trading. The clear delineation between arrangers and investors that we see today did not exist, as most banks played both roles as necessary. Public data on the size of the loan market or the relative position of the various players was not available. Similarly, there was no publicly available analysis on the relative value of loans compared to other credit markets. In addition, because much of the large bank consolidation had not yet occurred, the market was much more fragmented than it is today, with many more banks active as lenders to the corporate arena than there are today.

The leveraged market is the market segment that has undergone the most change over the past two decades, and it is the primary focus of this book. Numerous events occurred over the past two decades to create the primary loan market as it exists today. Consolidation of banks created a small number of large banks that had long and deep relationships with their corporate clients. Hold levels became much more disciplined as part of the banks' portfolio management practices, and the consolidated banks were not willing to hold all of the loans on the balance sheets of their acquired banks. In addition, the substantial amount of financing needed to support the leveraged buyout business that emerged in the late 1980s required larger and more risky loans. The need to distribute loans reliably in order to permit the large banks to manage their balance sheets and act as arrangers for their corporate clients led to the creation of formal capital markets and loan sales functions.

As banks began acquiring securities capabilities during the mid–1990s, the leading investment banks also entered the loan business as arrangers, primarily as a defensive measure to protect their other capital raising businesses from being taken from them by the much better capitalized commercial banks.

Beginning in the early 1990s, banks and investment banks alike sought to broaden their distribution networks by actively marketing the merits of loans as a distinct asset class to a broad range of alternative investors, including offshore banks, insurance companies, and pension funds. They also created new types of loan buyers by helping to structure collateralized loan obligations (CLOs), collateralized debt obligations (CDOs), prime-rate funds, and synthetic funds that could serve as outlets for the loans they originated and traded. With these new types of investors came an expanded need for public data on loans, including performance measurements and market quotes. By the late 1990s several entities had begun creating and publishing formal research on the loan asset class. Today the relative stability in value of loans compared to other debt asset classes is well documented and understood by a wide range of parties. The research available on loans today includes the issuance by the major rating agencies of a new category of ratings specific to bank loans. Throughout all of these changes, secondary market volumes have increased exponentially as the new investor classes have actively traded their portfolios through the rapidly growing ranks of traders and brokers.

MARKET SIZE AND SCOPE

There is no consistent definition of what the "loan market" encompasses, and because it is a private market, it is impossible to know with complete certainty what the actual size and scope of the market are on an annual basis.

The Federal Reserve defines a syndicated loan as any loan in excess of $20 million that has two or more participants ("investors"). As part of its annual Shared National Credit Exam, which reviews the credit quality of all syndicated loans owned by member banks, the Federal Reserve publishes an estimate of the total amount of commitments and loans outstanding that it considers to be syndicated.

EXHIBIT 4.1

Total commitments outstanding, Shared National Credit
Exam, 1995–2005.

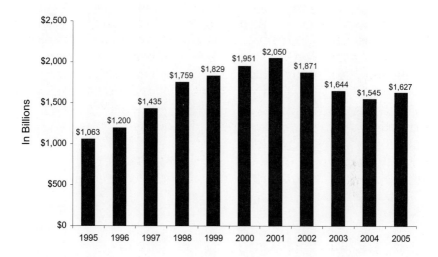

Source: Federal Reserve.

According to its 2005 exam, the total syndicated loan market was $1.6
trillion in terms of commitments outstanding, which is consistent
with the 10-year average for this report (see Exhibit 4.1).

There are many distinct submarkets within the total market,
each of which has unique structuring characteristics, and which
feature different arrangers and investors. As in the public bond
markets, the loan market can be divided into two broad categories
in terms of ratings quality. As shown in Exhibit 4.2, approximately
45 percent of the overall market was rated investment grade, and
28 percent was below investment grade (the leveraged market),
based on a trailing five-year average. The remaining 27 percent of
the market includes nonrated financings.

The investment grade market consists largely of unfunded
revolvers used by investment grade companies to backstop their
commercial paper programs and provide for working capital and
other general corporate purposes. It is used less frequently for event-
driven transactions such as acquisitions. This market is characterized by high dollar volume, and it is not unusual to see revolvers run
into the billions of dollars for a single issuer. Transactions are more
consistently structured than in other market sectors of the loan

EXHIBIT 4.2

Syndicated loan volume by rating, 1999–2005.

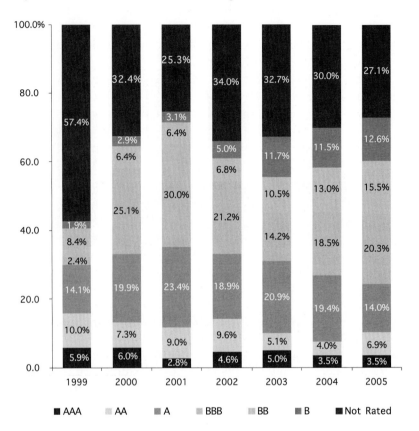

Source: Loan Pricing Corporation.

market in terms of financial covenants and borrowing mechanics. Banks are the primary investors in the investment grade loan market, and their investment decisions are often driven by overall relationship considerations.

By comparison, the leveraged loan market is much more complex in terms of its structure and players. Transactions in this market sector are typically smaller than those in the investment grade loan market, but activity is higher in terms of deal count. Deal activity is heavily influenced by event-driven transactions such as leveraged buyouts and corporate acquisition financing. Structurally, the leveraged loan market is more heavily reliant on funded term loans than on large revolving credit facilities, as many leveraged issuers have higher funded debt needs and/or less access to the public bond market. Leveraged loans tend to be much more structured than investment grade loans, and generally include more comprehensive collateral packages, financial covenants, and borrowing/repayment mechanics owing to the higher credit risk. The investor base includes both bank and nonbank investors.

Leveraged new issue volume is driven primarily by M&A and other transactional activity (see Exhibit 4.3). M&A accounted for $129 billion in 2005, or over 44 percent of total new-issue volume of US$-denominated leveraged loans in 2005, compared to $117 billion in 2004. A significant portion of this growth was driven by LBOs, which aggregated over $65 billion in 2005 compared to $50 billion in 2004.

Sponsor-related transactions have represented an increasing portion of leveraged volume. In 2005, new-issue sponsor volume aggregated $145 million, representing 26 percent of total volume, compared to $115 billion in 2004. From 2000 to 2003, sponsor-related volume was less than $60 billion per year.

Practitioners in the leveraged loan market typically draw a distinction between larger issuers and middle market issuers. The definition of middle market varies widely; it can be based on either the size of the issuer (generally measured by EBITDA) or the size of the

EXHIBIT 4.3

Total new-issue volume by purpose, 2005. Volume: $295 billion.

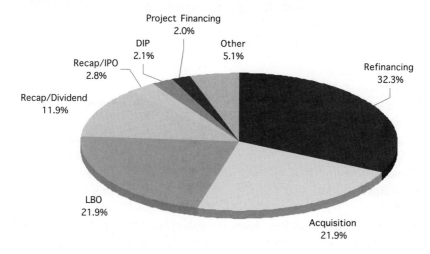

Source: Standard & Poor's Leveraged Lending Review 4Q05.

transaction. Broadly speaking, issuers are considered to be middle market when EBITDA is less than or equal to $50 million, or when the overall transaction size is less than or equal to $250 million (note that this would not include add-on transactions to larger deals). On a relative basis, middle market loans are more stringently structured than their higher-rated leveraged counterparts, and they often carry a pricing premium to compensate investors for the assumed higher risk associated with smaller issuers as well as the relative illiquidity of middle market transactions in secondary trading.

LOAN MARKET PLAYERS: ISSUERS, INVESTORS, AND LEAD ARRANGERS

Issuers

Companies seek syndicated loans to finance their working capital needs or to finance a wide variety of activities, including funding capital expenditures and financing acquisitions. Companies may also seek syndicated loans to construct new facilities or for stand-alone real estate development projects. Given the primary purpose of the loan market, which is to facilitate the distribution of loans among financial institutions, any loan that exceeds the desired hold level of the originating institution is a candidate for syndication.

Private equity funds are also prominent players in the loan market. These funds finance the acquisition of companies through a combination of debt and equity. The debt portion typically relies heavily on debt raised through the syndicated loan market. These transactions, known as leveraged buyouts, are a key driver of activity in the leveraged loan market.

Investors

There are many types of investors in the loan market today, ranging from traditional banks that participate in loans for relationship reasons, to highly sophisticated institutional investors, including hedge funds, that invest in the asset class for return and for diversification of their fixed income portfolios. Exhibit 4.4 shows the breakdown of the investor base for leveraged loans as of the end of 2005.

Generally speaking, loan investors can be broadly classified into two distinct segments; Pro Rata Investors and Institutional Investors. These segments are further described below.

EXHIBIT 4.4

Primary market for highly leveraged loans by investor type.

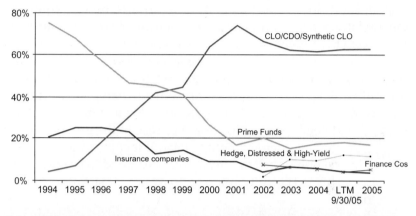

To provide a more realistic view of institutional buying habits in today's market, we add to the CLO tally the institutional commitments held by the arranger at close. For tax purposes of course, CLOs tend to participate as primary assignees and therefore are often left off the "at close" allocation list. In addition, beginning in 2002, we have made a better effort to track hedge funds and other investors in this analysis. As a result, we can only provide data for finance companies and hedge distressed & high-yield funds starting in 2002.

Source: Standard and Poor's Leveraged Lending Review 4Q05

Pro Rata Investors

Bank investors, often referred to as *pro rata investors*, are the traditional investors in loans. This investor class includes commercial banks, universal banks, and investment banks. Historically, banks, including investment banks, participated in loans as a way to augment their banking relationships with issuers. Banks may also use syndicated loans as a way to boost loan outstandings and therefore drive incremental interest income. Bank investors have become increasingly sophisticated in the way they manage their loan portfolios, and some banks will actively trade all or a portion of their loan portfolio to manage credit risk or portfolio return; however, because of issuer relationship reasons, many banks still attempt to maintain significant positions in the loans of their important clients as a demonstration of support. Bank investors are able to invest in revolvers, as they have the back office to support repeated advances and repayments, and they also invest in term loans. Banks have very flexible funding sources, consisting of the deposits and other core activities of the lending institution. These fund sources are generally very stable and not subject to significant fluctuations based on market conditions. The combination of a revolving loan and a term loan is referred to as a prorata commitment.

Institutional Investors

The institutional, or nonbank, investor class is a diverse mix of investment vehicles, including structured funds known as CLOs, mutual funds known as prime-rate loan funds, finance companies, insurance companies, hedge funds, distressed investors, and high-yield funds. This investor class invests in loans as a way to diversify fixed-rate portfolios and generate returns on their own equity capital. These investors, described more fully in the following list, typically have less flexible funding sources than banks, and therefore have a strong desire for fully funded loans with longer tenors, with limited need for amortization. Because of the great liquidity in the institutional lender segment, a typical leveraged loan structure will include a nonamortizing term loan designed to be sold to these investors. This is typically referred to as the "institutional" or "B" term loan.

Over the last decade, loans have become an increasingly popular asset class for institutional investors. According to Standard & Poor's, institutional investor participation in the loan market has grown 179 percent since 1992. As shown in Exhibit 4.5, the composition of the institutional segment of the leveraged loan market has changed markedly over time. In its initial phases the market was dominated by prime-rate funds. As it has grown, CLOs have become the dominant form. The major components of the institutional market are explained further below.

- *CLOs* are the largest segment of the institutional market, accounting for over 60 percent of total market share in 2005, according to Standard & Poor's. CLOs are special-purpose vehicles that invest in leveraged loan portfolios. Like other types of institutional investors, CLOs generally have portfolio limits prescribed with respect to minimum ratings, diversification, and defaults through the indenture agreement with the structure's underlying investor base. CLOs are funded through a combination of debt and equity raised from third-party investors, and as such, are highly susceptible to market conditions.
- *Prime-rate funds*, which represented 17 percent of the institutional market in 2005, are mutual funds that invest solely in bank loans. Originally known as "loan participation funds," these vehicles were originally marketed as an alternative to money market funds to investors

EXHIBIT 4.5

Primary Institutional Market by Investor Type.

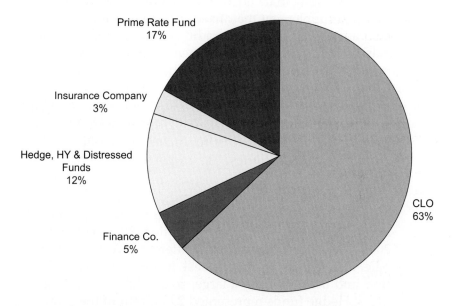

Prime Rate Fund 17%

Insurance Company 3%

Hedge, HY & Distressed Funds 12%

Finance Co. 5%

CLO 63%

To provide a more realistic view of institutional buying habits in today's market, we add to the CLO tally the institutional commitments held by the arranger at close. For tax purposes of course, CLOs tend to participate as primary assignees and therefore are often left off the "at close" allocation list. In addition, beginning in 2002, we have made a better effort to track hedge funds and other investors in this analysis.

Source: Standard and Poor's Leveraged Lending Review 4Q05.

seeking returns that tracked the prime rate. Bank loan funds can be structured as open-ended, with daily redemption or periodic tender periods, or closed-ended and are generally listed securities. The investment objectives and restrictions with respect to diversification and so on are included in the individual fund's prospectus as for any other mutual fund. Prime-rate funds are funded by the investment activities of the underlying investors (generally individual investors), and therefore are subject to cash inflows and redemption activity. Most prime-rate funds offer only quarterly redemption periods, but some funds offer daily redemptions. As a result of this, prime-rate funds are highly subject to fluctuations in market conditions.

- *Insurance companies,* which represented 3 percent of the institutional market in 2005, are among the oldest non-bank investor classes in the loan market. As traditional investors in traditional privately placed bonds, insurance companies began investing in the loan asset class in the early 1990s as a way to supplement their fixed-income portfolios. Insurance companies have traditionally invested in the loan market via their general investment accounts; however, they are increasingly investing in the loan market via self-structured CLOs as well.

- *Finance companies,* which represented approximately 5 percent of the institutional market in 2005, invest in both the pro rata market and the institutional market, often with a focus on smaller facilities.

- *Other:* A variety of niche investors are also active in the loan market, including hedge funds, high-yield funds, and other investors. Together, these investors represented approximately 12 percent of institutional loan volume in 2005. Each investor class has a different investment rationale. Hedge funds generally seek income and diversification, and therefore play a larger role in higher-yielding loans. Hedge funds represented 29 percent of the primary market for institutional loans with spreads of LIBOR + 400 basis points or higher in 2005. High-yield funds generally are not active investors, but will occasionally invest in a loan rather than investing in the bonds of a specific issuer for return or security reasons.

Institutional market participants currently provide approximately 70 percent of the liquidity in the leveraged market, compared with approximately 30 percent in 1995 (see Exhibit 4.6). This market share has been taken primarily from domestic banks, which held 12.3 percent in 2005 compared with 33 percent in 1995; European banks, which held 8.5 percent in 2005, compared to 19 percent in 1995; and Asian banks, which held 3.1 percent in 2005, compared to 14 percent in 1995. According to Standard & Poor's, since 2004, there have been less than 60 active pro rata participants compared to over 100 as recently as 1999.

Continued acceptance of leveraged loans as an asset class and the performance of these loans relative to that of comparable asset classes has encouraged increasing levels of institutional involvement. New entrants to the market have driven this change. There are currently over 400 active institutional loan investment vehicles

EXHIBIT 4.6

Primary Market for Highly Leveraged Loans by Investor Type

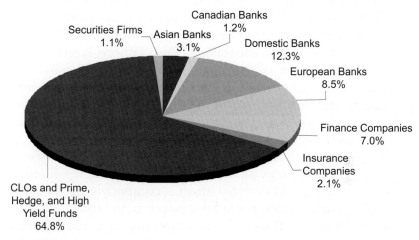

Source: Standard and Poor's Leveraged Lending Review 4Q05:

managed by approximately 170 active manager groups, compared to 205 active investment vehicles in 2000 and only 32 in 1995.

CREDIT ANALYSIS

Credit analysis is a fundamental determinant of the structure and pricing of a syndicated bank loan. Credit analysis determines the probability that a borrower will make its scheduled interest payments and repay the debt at maturity. It includes an assessment of the relevant industry characteristics and trends; assessment of the borrower's business fundamentals, competitive position, and strength of management; and a thorough financial analysis.

The analysis of the relevant industry includes an assessment of industry strength and prospects for growth or decline as a result of economic cycles, product cycles, technological change, labor situation, and regulation, among other factors. In addition, the nature of the competitive environment, the number and relative position of existing competitors, barriers to entry for new competitors, and key success factors will be analyzed. The borrower's business fundamentals—its competitive position in the industry (which is often measured by market share, but may also be assessed with respect to strength in a particular niche)—will also be analyzed. Competitive strengths can include price, product quality, service, and trademarks or branding. While a company's size does not directly correlate with its competitive strength, size often affects a company's market advantage in terms of breadth of product line and extent of distribution capabilities. Furthermore, larger companies generally benefit from a greater degree of diversification, which can mitigate the effects of market volatility. Further business analysis will include the borrower's relative strength with respect to marketing and distribution, technological expertise, operating efficiency, and risk management.

Management's strength and track record of success are critical components of credit analysis, since management's financial plans and policies will directly affect a company's performance and credit quality. Breadth of management is an important factor because of the inherent risk of reliance on one or a small number of individuals.

A financial analysis of a potential borrower includes an analysis of certain financial statistics that are used to measure and compare credit risk—for example:

- Profitability measures (gross margin, EBITDA margin, return on capital)
- Leverage ratios (debt to capitalization, debt to EBITDA)
- Coverage ratios (EBITDA to interest, fixed charge coverage)
- Liquidity tests (working capital, current ratio)

Credit risk standards for various financial statistics vary substantially across industries. Profitability and coverage measures indicate a company's ability to generate cash flow, withstand economic cycles, and obtain external capital. Leverage and liquidity measures are further evidence of financial flexibility. In addition, a financial analysis includes an assessment of accounting quality, including methodologies used for basis of consolidation, income recognition, capital expenditures and depreciation, and financing, especially off-balance-sheet obligations. Management's policies with respect to financial risk are also a critical factor. Finally, specific loan terms and conditions will be factored into a fundamental credit analysis. The quality of the collateral security provided for a syndicated loan improves the probability of repayment under a distressed scenario. Furthermore, financial covenants provide lenders with protection through an early warning of credit deterioration.

THE SYNDICATION PROCESS

Syndication effectively begins with an issuer selecting a lead arranger for a particular loan. The selection of a lead lender is based on a number of factors, including the proposed terms and conditions of the facility, the willingness of the lender to hold a designated amount of the loan after the syndication, the reputation and experience of the potential lead lender, the relationship between the issuer and the potential lead lender, and the ability of the lead lender to execute and support other types of capital markets products for the company. In the process of competing for a mandate, lending institutions evaluate the viability of taking the borrower into the loan market, and generally do this using their capital markets desks. The capital markets process involves an assessment of a potential borrower's financing requirements and credit quality to determine the optimal financing structure to meet the borrower's objectives.

Often, more than one institution is selected to play a leading role in a given transaction. Because of the rules established by the numerous league table rankings, a fairly stratified title assortment is granted to these lead institutions. Titles will be discussed in the next section.

Lead Arrangers and Agents

In most transactions, the lead arranger will also act as the administrative agent and be responsible for the ongoing administration of the loan. The titles "syndication agent" and "document agent" are often awarded in conjunction with large commitments, but the actual responsibilities that go with these roles may be shared or handled by the administrative agent or the lead arrangers.

Titles such as "co-agent" or "managing agent" may be awarded on a case-by-case basis, generally to bank loan investors with significant commitments; however, these titles have less significance for league-table purposes and no functional responsibilities.

League Tables

Market share in the syndicated loan market is quoted in league tables published by several companies, including Loan Pricing Corporation (LPC), Bloomberg, and Thomson Financial.

The lead arranger is essentially the middleman in the syndication process. Up to two institutions may receive league-table credit for acting as the lead arranger. In most transactions, the lead arranger structures the term sheet; interfaces with the client and with investors; prepares, negotiates, and closes documents; and manages the syndication process. Consequently, the lead arranger generally receives premium compensation, the title of lead arranger is the most coveted title from a league table standpoint.

The bookrunner title, which designates the lender or lenders who are managing the syndication sales process, is usually given to one or more of the lead arrangers or agents.

Agent Titles

In most deals, there are up to five lenders given with agent titles that signify important roles in a syndicated loan financing: administrative agent, syndication agent, and documentation agent. These titles may or may not correspond to actual roles performed with respect to a loan.

- *Administrative agent.* The administrative agent generally represents the bank and manages all funding of interest, principal, and other loan payments.
- *Syndication agent.* The syndication agent handles the syndication of the loan (up to two positions can be offered).
- *Documentation agent.* The document agent handles the documentation governing the loan, including security agreements (up to two positions can be offered).

Co-Agent Title

Often the titles of managing agent, senior managing agent, or co-agent are used to give special treatment to lenders committing at a level just below the agent tier, but above the untitled lenders in the syndicate. These less prestigious titles are not limited in number.

According to LPC, in 2005, the top three arrangers (Bank of America, JP Morgan, and Citigroup) represented 47 percent of the total market for syndicated loans (see Exhibit 4.7). However,

EXHIBIT 4.7

The LPC League Table for 2005 U.S. Corporate and
Institutional Transactions.

2005 U.S. Lead Arranger

Rank	Bank Holding Company	Lead Arranger Volume (US$)	Number of Deals	Market Share
1	Bank of America	272,915,148,945	948	20%
2	JP Morgan	420,814,461,091	912	19
3	Citigroup	255,836,672,373	377	8
4	Wachovia Corp	88,999,421,213	344	7
5	PNC Bank	10,184,350,131	174	4
6	Wells Fargo & Co	27,328,641,166	164	3
7	General Electric Capital Corp	18,596,569,000	154	3
8	ABN AMRO Bank NV	19,677,905,229	143	3
9	Credit Suisse First Boston	39,284,309,730	141	3
10	Deutsche Bank AG	50,349,621,115	102	2
10	KeyBank	15,513,018,831	102	2
12	Bank of New York Co Inc	9,497,215,540	70	1
13	National City Corp	5,480,099,508	66	1
14	BNP Paribas SA	15,461,350,000	65	1
14	Goldman Sachs & Co	27,421,586,500	65	1
14	Lehman Brothers	26,194,650,018	65	1
14	Merrill Lynch & Co Inc	13,780,488,600	65	1
18	UBS AG	12,096,763,500	62	1
19	Barclays Bank Plc	26,112,371,000	58	1
19	Harris Nesbitt	7,861,946,078	58	1
19	Royal Bank of Scotland Plc	15,053,466,942	58	1
19	SunTrust Bank	16,062,106,648	58	1
23	Mitsubishi UFJ Financial Group Inc	9,197,111,101	53	1
24	CIBC World Markets	8,091,136,975	52	1
25	US Bancorp	5,362,772,930	45	1
26	Scotia Capital	9,389,279,457	34	1
27	Bear Stearns Cos	7,684,500,000	33	1
28	Madison Capital Funding LLC	1,745,150,000	32	1
29	Morgan Stanley	15,512,361,298	31	1
30	CIT Group	1,890,600,000	27	1

concentration has decreased. The top three leads represented 65 percent in 2004. In the leveraged market, the top three arrangers represented less than 38 percent of total leveraged volume. Furthermore, competition is stronger than the league-table statistics might suggest. Beyond the top three lead arrangers, there are a significant number of other banks and securities firms that compete, often with particular expertise in specific niches. There are more than 25 arrangers that led financings aggregating over $5 billion in 2005, maintaining strong competition.

Pricing

Loan pricing is defined as the interest rate charged on the loan, plus any associated fees required as part of the financing package. Loans in the domestic syndicated loan market are generally priced via a floating interest rate, such as LIBOR plus a percentage, or *spread*, that reflects the risk of the issuer relative to the market and to other issuers with a similar profile. Generally, the spread, also known as the *applicable margin*, is shown either as a percentage (LIBOR + 3.50%) or, more commonly, in basis points (LIBOR + 350 basis points).

Most often, loan pricing is negotiated between the lead arranger(s) and the issuer during the initial negotiation of the loan, along with the other key structural and pricing issues, including fees, tenor, and covenants. These terms are summarized in a term sheet, which will be discussed in greater detail later. In situations where the loan is being underwritten by the arranger(s), the term sheet will be accompanied by a commitment letter and a fee letter, the execution of which affirms the mandate.

Loan pricing is influenced by a number of factors, including the following:

- The credit profile of the issuer
- Prevailing market conditions
- Comparable deals in the market
- Comparable prior transactions (i.e., similar industry, use of proceeds, size of company, and so on)
- Investor relationships
- Ancillary business opportunities
- Relative value
- Secondary market trends

E X H I B I T   4 . 8

Sample pricing grid based on debt/EBITDA ratio.

Debt/EBITDA	Pro Rata	Term Loan B
≥=5.50X	L + 325	L + 375
<5.50X, ≥=4.00X	L + 300	L + 350
<4.00X, ≥=3.50X	L + 275	L + 325
<3.50X, ≥=3.00X	L + 250	L + 300
<3.00X	L + 225	L + 275

Unlike other fixed income products, where the pricing is set for the life of the instrument, loan pricing is frequently expressed in a matrix or pricing grid, where the LIBOR spread will vary depending on certain post closing conditions. These conditions are intended to capture changes in the relative risk or performance of the company and can include many different criteria. Several common examples of the criteria include public ratings, leverage ratios, and coverage ratios. An example of a performance-based grid is shown in Exhibit 4.8

Pricing Flex

Historically, loans were priced by the arrangers at the time the mandate to lead the loan was granted and did not vary as they came to market. This is in contrast to bonds, which are typically priced at the time the offering is completed, based on the pricing required to "clear the market" and sell the entire issue. Over the past decade, the pricing mechanism on loans has come to more closely resemble that of bonds through the inclusion of pricing "flex." Arrangers and issuers agree on a targeted and often a maximum price for the issue, but the actual pricing is determined through the loan marketing process. Loans are announced with a target price, but the price will either flex up or flex down depending on demand and on general market conditions. While the inclusion of price flex has limited the risk to the arrangers of pricing a deal incorrectly during the pitch and negotiation process, it has not eliminated the risk entirely. The degree of price flex permitted to the arrangers is often one of the most heavily negotiated elements of a commitment letter.

Different Types of Fees

A key part of the syndication strategy involves determining the fee payout structure to the investors that make up the loan syndicate. An "up-front fee" is a fee paid to investors to augment the return on their portion of the loan. While most institutional term loans are sold at par (i.e., no closing fees are paid), the pro rata portion of loans typically has an up-front fee associated with it. The fee will vary from transaction to transaction, and will frequently vary within the same transaction based on the level of commitment offered by an investor. In this case, investors will be paid a one-time fee based on the level of their commitment. In transactions where the loan is oversubscribed and investors' commitments are being reduced through allocation, the actual fee they receive will be based on their allocated amount.

Non-Use Fee

Revolving loans pay interest on the amount of the facility that is actually used. In order to compensate investors for making the unused commitment available at all times, they are typically paid a commitment or non-use fee. This fee is payable either monthly or quarterly in arrears based on the daily amount of the commitment that is undrawn. Often these fees will vary based on the same criteria used in the loan pricing grid.

SYNDICATION STRATEGY

By forming a syndicate of investors, the arrangers are fulfilling the objectives of the borrower—to raise the required amount of financing on the required timetable—while also fulfilling their own objectives—maximizing the revenue from the transaction and further developing relationships with the investors. The strategy for meeting these objectives will vary widely from one transaction to another. In formulating the strategy, the arrangers take a wide range of factors into consideration, including the following:

- *Underwritten versus best efforts.* The borrower may decide to ask its lead bank either to underwrite a loan or to simply arrange it on a best efforts basis. In an underwritten loan, the arrangers are taking on themselves the risk that syndication will not be successful and that they may need to hold more of the loan than they had originally intended. In a best efforts arrangement, this syndication risk is taken on by the issuer. An underwriting is more expensive to the issuer, but when issuers do not have strict timetable requirements or when they feel that it is not worth paying for the certainty of receiving funds, they will opt for a best efforts arrangement.

- *Timing to close.* Syndication can take several weeks to complete, even after it is launched. If there is insufficient time to complete the syndication, the arranger can opt to close the transaction first and syndicate afterwards. Alternatively, a two-step syndication could be conducted, where a small group of relationship lenders closes the transaction and jointly syndicates afterwards. Issuers typically pay a premium to have their arrangers close a loan prior to completion of syndication.
- *Size of transaction.* Larger transactions require more investors and larger holding levels in order to complete.
- *Anticipated investor demand.* The assessment of how many investors may be interested is based on a wide variety of factors, including
  - The number of existing lenders for this borrower typically considered to be attracted to this type of transaction
  - The aggressiveness of the loan in terms of pricing and structure compared to other transactions currently in the market
  - Leverage
  - Ratings
  - Complexity of the story and structure
  - Current supply and demand factors in the market for similar transactions
  - Desire of the borrower to have its bank loan held widely and trade well

After considering all of these factors, the arrangers will determine what they feel is the optimal strategy, including the timetable, titles, and requirements of potential participants in terms of fees and commitment levels.

RATINGS PROCESS

While banks still rely primarily on their internal credit analysis as the primary tool for determining their interest in making a particular loan, structured vehicles such as CLOs and CDOs are required by their indentures to balance the levels of loans with various ratings within their portfolios. The rapid growth in CLO investors has therefore given rise to a need for loans to receive ratings (either public or private) from the major rating agencies. The agencies have, in turn, developed significant expertise in the loan asset class. As of 2004 year end, the leading agencies have provided ratings for over 1437 different loans.

The process for obtaining a rating for a loan is very similar to that for obtaining a rating for other debt instruments. The agencies undertake a multistep process. First, they evaluate the issuer's overall risk of default on its financial obligations, and assign one of their traditional letter ratings (AAA, AA, A, BBB, and so on). This analysis can be done with or without a presentation from the company, but for leveraged loans, where ratings are thought to be critical in the syndication process, it generally involves a formal meeting between the company and the rating agency analyst and a presentation by the company. The analyst will then undertake a deal-specific analysis of the loan itself, which looks beyond the risk of default to factor in the likelihood of ultimate loss and recovery. This analysis considers not only the overall creditworthiness of the borrower, but also the unique features of the loan instrument, such as collateral, covenants, and other structural features that may determine how much loan investors are ultimately repaid in a post-default scenario. This may result in a loan rating that is "notched" up from the issuer's rating or from other debt of the same issuer.

Arrangers typically attempt to have the ratings available at the beginning of the syndication process to assist investors in making credit and pricing decisions. Frequently the loan rating is obtained simultaneously with the rating for other layers of a firm's capital structure, including bonds and preferred stock. In addition to the actual ratings, the agencies will issue detailed commentary on their ratings and on the assumptions and expectations they formed during the ratings process. These commentaries are often of critical importance to potential investors.

As with other debt products, after an initial rating, investors generally want ongoing surveillance and updates from the rating agencies. For this reason, issuers may choose to meet regularly with their agency analysts to make sure that the analysts have the best available information when issuing their ratings and updates.

OFFERING MATERIAL AND PREPARATION

Once the transaction has been mandated, the lead arranger will begin working with the issuer to draft the offering materials that will be distributed to potential investors. The information provided for a leveraged loan can be extensive, and the drafting process can often be lengthy. While the arrangers work extensively with the issuer on the preparation of the information memorandum, the finished product is considered to be delivered from the issuer to the investors. Generally, the final information memorandum will include a statement from the company that it has approved the information contained within the memorandum and that the information is accurate and complete. In addition, investors acknowledge that they have done their own independent credit analysis and are not relying on specific representations made by the arrangers.

Typical sections included in an information memorandum are

- *Executive summary*—a high-level summary of the transaction, the company, and the financial sponsor (if any)
- *Investment considerations*—selling points of the transaction
- *Terms and conditions*—a summary of the term sheet agreed to by the arranger(s) and the company
- *Business overview*—an in-depth review of the company's business
- *Management overview*—short biographies of the company's officers
- *Industry overview*—an overview of the company's industry
- *Historic financial overview*
- *Projected financial overview*

As appropriate, the information memorandum may contain appendices with additional information on the issuer, including annual reports, SEC filings, product descriptions, and so on. In addition to this information, the information memorandum will contain a schedule of the syndication timing, including information regarding the investor meeting, commitment deadline, and scheduled closing. The information memorandum typically also includes housekeeping information, such as contacts for the arrangers and the issuer for questions and an administrative questionnaire for investors. Finally, the information memorandum will include a release letter signed by the issuer and a confidentiality agreement.

While much of the information in a typical information memorandum can be drawn from the public filings of a company, not all borrowers file public statements. In addition, many loan investors require information that is not public in order to make their credit decisions. For this reason, the primary market for loans includes processes whereby investors must declare themselves to be on either the public side or the private side prior to reviewing any information. If they choose to remain public and review only the public information provided by the company, they are entitled to continue trading in the other securities of the company throughout their review process. Private side investors may receive information that is beyond the available public information, such as projections, but they are then restricted in their ability to trade the public securities of the company. Arrangers must prepare two sets of memoranda for these investors and make sure they have the opportunity to declare their preference before they receive information. Market practice is that investors must police themselves on their trading activities once they have made a public declaration.

LENDER MEETING (INCLUDING PUBLIC AND PRIVATE)

A key part of the syndication process is known as the *bank meeting* or the *investor meeting*. This meeting generally consists of a presentation by the issuer's management team to investors that are interested in participating in the transaction. The purpose of the meeting is to give investors the opportunity to meet the issuer's management.

Typically, an investor meeting agenda will include the following:

- Introduction and overview of the transaction (this is usually managed by the bookrunner)
- Management introduction

- Management presentation
- Business overview
- Strategy
- Industry
- Financial review
- Projected financial performance

There will also generally be a discussion of the merits of investing in the loan and an overview of the credit facility. These latter sections are generally conducted by the lead arrangers. In the event of a meeting with both public and private investors in attendance, the audience for the projected financial performance discussion will be limited to private investors. The bank meeting may also include facility tours, if applicable.

SALES PROCESS

The sales process is generally conducted by the sales desks of the arranging banks, which have divided up their coverage of the investor universe. Generally the salespeople will receive a briefing on the loan from the origination side of the deal team prior to the actual launch. A determination will be made as to how many investors to invite and which investors are deemed to be most suitable or potentially interested in a particular loan offering. The sales process will be launched with calls from the sales team to investors inviting them to review the loan. The salesperson is responsible for making sure that investors' questions are addressed, and that the feedback he or she is getting from investors gets back to the origination and capital-markets teams.

FUNDING AND BREAKING INTO THE SECONDARY MARKET

When the sales process is complete, the arrangers will allocate the facility among the committed investors. The announcement of this allocation is the point at which the primary syndication is completed, and the loan will immediately break into a secondary market. The loan may then begin trading, even though it may not have actually closed. This preclosing trading is called "when-issued" trading.

FORMS USED

Commitment Letter

The commitment letter is used to document the agreement between the arrangers and the borrower with respect to the basis for and conditions of the arrangers' commitment. In addition to specifying the amount and tenor of the loan, the commitment letter will generally include a brief description of the purpose of the financing to set the basic understanding of the deal. The commitment letter will also specify conditions for the commitment, which may include

- Completion of due diligence
- Absence of material adverse change in the business, financial condition, or prospects of the borrower
- No material adverse change in the loan syndication or capital market
- Negotiation of documentation by date certain
- Payment of fees and expenses

Furthermore, the commitment letter will define certain rights and responsibilities of the borrower and the arrangers with respect to the syndication process. For example, the commitment letter will specify the borrower's obligation to provide requested information for the bank book and to participate in meetings with potential bank loan participants. The commitment letter will also define certain legal protections for the benefit of each party, including indemnification, confidentiality provisions, jurisdiction, governing law, and so on.

Fee Letter

The fee letter will specifically identify the type and amount of fees payable in connection with a syndicated loan, including arrangement and structuring fees or underwriting fees, administrative agency fees, collateral agent fees, and other amounts payable to the arrangers. As discussed previously, the fee letter will also generally include market flex language, which details certain provisions of the facility that may be subject to change if necessary to complete syndication (for example, the structure of the facility and its terms or pricing).

Term Sheet

The term sheet provides a summary of the terms of the loan financing, which will be documented in more detail in the credit agreement, which provides the definitive documentation for the financing, as described in more detail in Chapter 5. The term sheet will generally include the following types of provisions:

- *Parties to the financing.* Definitions of the borrower(s) and guarantor(s) (if any), as well as the arrangers and lead agents.
- *Terms and amounts of the facilities.* A description of the type (e.g., revolving credit, term loan, and so on), amount, currency, and tenor of the facility.
- *Payment provisions.* A description of the fees and interest rates, optional prepayment provisions, and mandatory amortization and prepayment requirements.
- *Collateral.* A description of any security interests to be provided to the lenders.
- *Conditions for availability.* A list of any actions to be taken by the borrower or items to be delivered by the borrower to the administrative agent and any other requirements that must be satisfied in order for the credit to be available. This may include, for example, receipt of the executed loan documentation, compliance with covenants, satisfactory legal structure, perfection of security interests if applicable, receipt of financial statements and other required information, receipt of all required government and third-party consents, and opinions of counsel.
- *Representations and warranties.* A description of the types of representations and warranties (with appropriate materiality and reasonableness standards) that will be included in the credit agreement, which may include accuracy of the financial statements, absence of undisclosed liabilities, no material adverse change, corporate existence, compliance with law, corporate power and authority, enforceability of credit documentation, no conflict with law or contractual obligations, no material litigation, no default, ownership of property, indebtedness, liens, intellectual property, taxes, government

regulations, ERISA, purpose of loans, subsidiaries, environmental matters, solvency, investments, labor matters, accuracy of disclosure, leases, creation and perfection of security interests, and status of the credit facilities as senior debt.

- *Affirmative covenants.* A description of the covenants of the borrower, i.e., covenants regarding the delivery of financial statements, reports, accountants' letters, projections, officers' certificates, and other information reasonably requested by the senior lenders; payment of other obligations; continuation of business and maintenance of existence and material rights and privileges; compliance with laws and material contractual obligations; maintenance of property and insurance; maintenance of books and records; right of the senior lenders to inspect property and books and records; notices of defaults, litigation, and other material events; compliance with environmental laws; further assurances (including, without limitation, assurances with respect to security interests in after-acquired property); terms of leases; and interest-rate protection to be agreed upon.

- *Financial covenants.* Details of the measures of credit quality that the borrower will be required to maintain for the tenor of the loan. Examples of financial covenants include (1) minimum consolidated EBITDA/ consolidated interest expense, (2) minimum consolidated EBITDA/consolidated fixed charges, and (3) maximum consolidated total debt/consolidated EBITDA, minimum net worth, and minimum current ratio.

- *Negative covenants.* Details of the negative covenants imposed on the borrower. These may include limitations on indebtedness; liens; guarantee obligations; mergers, consolidations, liquidations, and dissolutions; sales of assets; capital expenditures; dividends and other payments in respect of capital stock investments, loans and advances, optional payments, and modifications of subordinated and other debt instruments; amendments to material contractual obligations; transactions with affiliates; sale and leasebacks; changes in fiscal year and organizational documents; negative pledge clauses; and changes in lines of business.

- *Events of default.* Generally, events of default will include nonpayment of principal when due; nonpayment of interest, fees, or other amounts after a grace period; material inaccuracy of representations and warranties; violation of covenants (subject, in the case of certain covenants, to certain grace or notice and cure periods); default under other credit documentation; bankruptcy events; cross-defaults with respect to outstanding indebtedness; material judgments; certain ERISA events; termination or amendment of certain material agreements if such termination or amendment could reasonably be expected to have a material adverse effect; actual or asserted invalidity of any guarantee or security document, subordination provisions, or security interest; and a change of control (the definition of which is to be agreed upon).
- *Other documentation matters.* The term sheet will also usually detail provisions with respect to voting requirements for amendments, assignments and participations, expenses and indemnification, yield protection, and governing law.

CONCLUSION

The primary market for bank loans has evolved significantly over the past 30 years, and has become more and more similar to the markets for other types of fixed income debt. Most of the changes have been in the direction of increased liquidity and transparency of the market, and toward the development of a robust secondary market for loan assets. Importantly, the pace of change has accelerated over time, and shows no signs of slowing. The size of the market alone ensures that the market will continue to attract new entrants and new service providers, all of whom will push the pace of change. Despite all of these changes, though, the market retains many unique characteristics, rooted in the issuers' need to reliably access revolving loans and the banks' need to cross-sell other products. The complex relationship between issuers and investors in the bank loan market, combined with the overall attractiveness of this market to new investors, ensures that this market will remain distinct from other fixed income markets, even as it continues to evolve.

The Architecture of Information Distribution in the Loan Market

Alex Spiro
Bank of America

INTRODUCTION

This article describes the architecture for identifying, sorting, and distributing information in the loan syndication and trading market and identifies the reasons that architecture has evolved. These reasons largely fall into two categories: architecture responsive to borrowers' desire to protect their confidential and sensitive information, and architecture that accommodates certain loan-market participants' desire to participate in both the loan market and the securities markets.

The architecture for handling borrower information first evolved in response to borrowers' interest in controlling their private information. Lenders generally require private information regarding a borrower prior to making a lending decision and then require periodic reporting of private information once a loan has been made. Borrowers' interest in protecting the dissemination of their private information caused confidentiality undertakings to be a common element of the borrower-lender relationship.

The loan market is a unique capital market in the United States, inasmuch as it is the only significant capital market that involves a nonsecurities product (as discussed in Chapter 2). However, while syndicated loans are not securities, many loan-market participants (LMPs, lenders, or prospective lenders) also participate in the securities markets. LMPs' participation in the securities markets requires the loan market to address certain information flow issues that are key to the securities market.

Specifically, securities-market participants cannot make investment decisions with respect to securities based on material nonpublic information (MNPI). LMPs often have the contractual right to receive borrowers' private information, which may include MNPI from or regarding a borrower. A borrower may also be an issuer of securities. LMPs who participate in both the loan market and the securities market may obtain MNPI as a result of their involvement in the loan market and must wall off that information from those making investment decisions with respect to securities. However, some LMPs, so-called public LMPs, wish to simultaneously participate in the loan market and obtain borrowers' private information, which may constitute MNPI, and trade the borrowers' securities without the necessity for ethical walls. In order to accommodate public LMPs, the loan market has developed an architecture to sort information between that which is appropriate for public LMPs and that which is appropriate for all other LMPs, to distribute that information in a manner that identifies the type of information, to put LMPs on notice of the possible receipt of MNPI, and to obtain LMPs' acknowledgment that they will comply with the law, including securities laws, in connection with the handling of that information.

Other driving influences on the architecture of information distribution include Regulation FD (Reg FD) and lenders' duty of confidence to their borrowers.

ARTICLE ORGANIZATION

This article first clarifies some definitional confusion regarding information in the loan market. Next, it describes the legal issues that inform the handling of borrower information in the loan market. Finally, it describes documentation practices with widespread market acceptance that address information distribution issues and provide for reasonable protection of information in order to address borrowers' expectations concerning the handling of their private information, protect against the misuse of MNPI in the securities markets, and enhance the ease of compliance by borrowers with Reg FD.

DEFINITIONAL ISSUES

There is some market confusion as to how to identify the different types of information that are present in the loan market. The terms *public* and *private* are used frequently and would seem to have straightforward meanings. Unfortunately, that is not always the case.

The main definitional confusion arises because *public* means one thing in the securities context and another in the loan context. While the information definitions described here are not universally accepted in the loan market, they are helpful in identifying the types of information that are in the market.

Public Information

There are two types of public information. The first is information that is understood as public consistent with the securities laws, e.g., information that is readily available to the affected investor community for a reasonable period of time. The most obvious example of this is something that is posted on the Securities and Exchange Commission's EDGAR service.

The other type of public information is the type of information that is contained in a public bank book (as described in a later section). That type of public information is information that does not contain MNPI. It consists of public information as understood in the securities law context and also includes information as to which a determination has been made (usually by the borrower) that none of the information constitutes MNPI. We call this subset of information *bank loan public information*. Importantly, bank loan public information may include confidential and sensitive, private information. As described later, public bank books virtually always include a confidentiality undertaking, so bank loan public information, unlike public information, is almost always subject to a confidentiality undertaking.

Why is it important to understand that there are two types of public information? Because bank loan public information is not really public—you may not be able to harvest it from public sources. If some disinterested third party or "man on the street" requested it, the answer would almost certainly be no, since the information is subject to a confidentiality undertaking.

Private Information

The next category of information is private information. Private information is not synonymous with MNPI; it is information that is either covered by a confidentiality undertaking or subject to a bank's duty of confidence to a borrower and accordingly is treated as private and shared in a manner consistent with the contractual undertaking and/or duty. Most credit agreements' confidentiality provisions (as well as the LSTA's credit agreement form confidentiality provision) indicate that information must be marked as confidential for it to be subject to the confidentiality provision; however, some credit agreements may be more expansive, so many LMPs presumptively treat information arising from the lender-borrower relationship as confidential. LMPs also tend to be conservative in making the assessment of whether information is private because of the possibility that the duty of confidence may apply to the lender-borrower relationship and the nonpublic information shared as a result of that relationship. Private information often includes MNPI, but it also includes a much broader set of information.

Material Nonpublic Information

The last category of information is MNPI. In brief, MNPI is information that is, with respect to the borrower, material and not plainly in the public domain. *Material* has been variously defined: information as to which there is a substantial likelihood that a reasonable investor would consider the information important in making an investment decision, information with respect to which disclosure would change the total mix of information available, or information with respect to which disclosure is reasonably certain to have a substantial effect on the market price of the security.

WHAT INFORMS THE LOAN MARKET'S PRACTICES REGARDING INFORMATION DISTRIBUTION?

There are four general reasons that explain how and why the industry cares about corralling private information:

Borrowers' Desire to Protect Confidential Information

The cornerstone of how the industry handles borrowers' private information is abiding by borrowers' desire to protect their confidential information. That desire is usually evidenced by a confidentiality provision contained in the credit agreement.

Common Law Duty of Confidence

Banks and other lenders generally may have a common law duty of confidence to their borrowers; if banks disseminated a borrower's confidential information to third parties without obtaining a confidentiality undertaking, they would risk breaching that duty.

Regulation FD

For borrowers with tradable securities outstanding, Reg FD may be applicable. In essence, Reg FD (17 C.F.R. 243.100–243.103) requires that information either be made available substantially simultaneously to the market or be distributed to certain classes of entities (including lenders) under a confidentiality undertaking. Accordingly, even for bank loan public information, many borrowers insist on a confidentiality undertaking because the absence of such an undertaking would require the borrower to determine whether the distribution of the information is compliant with Reg FD. Borrowers often believe that the confidentiality undertaking makes the distribution of information Reg FD compliant without further analysis.

Securities Law Concerns

United States securities laws and regulations impose significant prohibitions on trading securities on the basis of MNPI. Rule 10b–5 prohibits certain persons who are aware of MNPI regarding a company or its securities from trading in the securities without appropriate disclosures. In addition, tippers and tippees may also be liable under Rule 10b–5. A tipper is a person who, in violation of a duty and for his or her own direct or indirect benefit (including intangible benefit), discloses MNPI to another person with the expectation that that person might trade on the information, even if he or she does not trade. A tippee is the recipient of the MNPI and may violate Rule 10b–5 if he or she knew or should have known that the MNPI was provided by the tipper in violation of a duty owed to a third party. Because many LMPs also trade securities and are affected by these laws, distributors of loan product information generally use three tools to cause recipients of information to comply with and be on notice of these laws: (1) confidentiality undertakings, pursuant to which recipients of information agree to maintain the confidentiality of that information, (2) securities law compliance provisions, pursuant to which recipients of information acknowledge that they will handle information in accordance with the securities laws, and (3) explicit notices, pursuant to which recipients of information are warned that they may be receiving MNPI.

CONTRACTUAL PROVISIONS THAT CORRAL PRIVATE INFORMATION

The loan market reasonably provides for compliance with the matters described in the previous section (borrowers' expectations, lenders' duties, Reg FD, and securities law issues) through an architecture that captures virtually all LMPs who may come into contact with the loan asset class. This architecture requires most LMPs to agree to both a confidentiality undertaking and a securities law compliance provision. In addition, most LMPs are given prominent notice of the type of information that they may receive by virtue of considering becoming a lender under a credit agreement.

For greater clarity, a confidentiality undertaking is simply a contractual obligation of a recipient of information to maintain the confidentiality of the information in accordance with the terms of the undertaking. A securities law compliance provision is an acknowledgment by a recipient of information that the information received may be material, private information and that the information will be treated in accordance with the securities laws.

DOCUMENTS CONTAINING PROVISIONS THAT CORRAL PRIVATE INFORMATION

The bulwarks of segregating private information are embedded in five key documents that have widespread use and acceptance in the loan market: Master Confidentiality Agreements, trade confirmations, bank books (also known as confidential information memoranda), credit agreements, and splash pages (also known as click-through screens—the first page viewed prior to entering a Web-based document distribution site).

Master Confidentiality Agreements

The LSTA has adopted a Master Confidentiality Agreement that has widespread market acceptance. The document is entered into between frequent loan trading partners and provides for the sharing of confidential information from a seller of a loan with a buyer of a loan so that the buyer can perform due diligence on the loan. It permits the sharing of information on a confidential basis and ultimately provides contractual comfort to a borrower that its private information will be shared only among the lending syndicate, potential lenders, and certain other entities that have a need to know it. The agreement contains both confidentiality undertakings and a securities law compliance provision.

Note that the confidentiality undertaking in the Master Confidentiality Agreement is frequently superseded by a particular confidentiality provision in a credit agreement. Generally, if the credit agreement that is the subject of the Master Confidentiality Agreement has more restrictive terms than the Master Confidentiality Agreement, the credit agreement confidentiality undertaking will govern. Accordingly, any LMP that obtains information relating to a borrower under a Master Confidentiality Agreement will be subject to a confidentiality undertaking and a securities law compliance provision.

If a Master Confidentiality Agreement is not used, a "one-off" confidentiality agreement with similar provisions, providing the same protection, is generally executed.

To put the use of the Master Confidentiality Agreement in a practical context, suppose that an LMP is considering purchasing a loan and decides that in order to prudently do so, it requires information that the borrower provides under the credit agreement. The credit agreement will typically provide that in order for a lender to share the borrower's private information with a potential purchaser of the loan, the potential purchaser must be bound by a confidentiality undertaking. If the potential purchaser is bound by the Master Confidentiality Agreement, it will be obligated to maintain the confidentiality of the information and acknowledge that the information it will receive may include material, private information. In addition, it will agree to act in accordance with applicable law, including the securities laws. Ultimately, this is powerful contractual protection against the potential purchaser's improper use or dissemination of the private loan information.

Standard Trade Confirmations

The LSTA has also adopted a form of Standard Trade Confirmation that has widespread market acceptance (trade confirmations are discussed in greater detail in Chapter 6). When a lender sells a loan, it usually does so by first agreeing to trade with a counterpart on the phone and then, shortly thereafter, exchanging a market Standard Trade Confirmation. The trade confirmation has standard terms, and among those terms are a confidentiality undertaking and a securities law compliance provision.

So, in a practical context, if an LMP purchases a loan following the execution of a Standard Trade Confirmation, the LMP has agreed to keep the borrower's information confidential and has acknowledged the applicability of the securities laws. Again, this is powerful contractual protection against an LMP's improper use or dissemination of the private information.

Bank Books

Bank books (also known as confidential information memoranda) are the materials distributed to the potential lending syndicate. Typically they are compiled by arrangers and approved for distribution by borrowers. The LSTA has adopted several form documents that appear at the beginning of bank books. The form documents consist of a Special Notice to Recipients, a Notice to and Undertaking of Recipients, and an Authorization Letter. The special notice informs recipients as to the nature of the information in the bank book, i.e., whether it is private information or public information. The Notice to and Undertaking of Recipients fulfills many functions but is essentially a series of undertakings and acknowledgments by recipients of the bank book that the recipient must agree to in order to review the bank book. The Authorization Letter provides the borrower's instruction to the arranger to distribute the bank book to LMPs that are considering becoming lenders. While the LSTA forms are not universally used, they have widespread acceptance. If the LSTA forms are not used, something very similar is usually used in their place.

There are two kinds of bank books: traditional bank books, which may contain MNPI, including the borrower's financial projections, and so-called public bank books—bank books that do not contain MNPI. The LSTA forms for private bank books contain a securities law compliance provision; it is embedded in the Special Notice to Recipients that appears on the cover of the book and is consistent with other such provisions discussed earlier. The special notice informs recipients of the bank book that the book may contain MNPI and that recipients agree to use the information in accordance with applicable laws, including the securities laws.

The LSTA forms for the public bank book do not contain a securities law compliance provision. In this case, the special notice indicates that the book does not contain MNPI. Accordingly, it is not necessary to include a securities law compliance provision for the simple reason that since the book does not contain MNPI, there is no need for the recipient to acknowledge that it will handle information in accordance with the securities laws. However, some arrangers have adopted the practice of including a version of the securities law compliance provision out of an abundance of caution.

A note on how information in bank books is sorted to determine whether a book contains MNPI or not: There are two practices in this regard. The market practice that is becoming prevalent is for the borrower to provide some type of written comfort to the arranger and to prospective lenders that the borrower has reviewed the materials and that the materials do not contain MNPI. The other market practice, used by some arrangers on occasion, is for the arranger to review the information and determine whether any of the information in the book constitutes MNPI.

All bank books contain a prominent confidentiality undertaking.

In sum, bank books also provide powerful contractual protection against an LMP's improper use of the private information, inasmuch as they contain a clear warning when the bank book contains MNPI, a confidentiality undertaking, and, when appropriate, a securities law compliance provision.

Credit Agreements

While syndicated credit agreements are not standardized documents, the vast majority share certain characteristics. Also, the LSTA has issued model credit agreement provisions for certain "boilerplate" provisions of syndicated credit agreements that have widespread market acceptance. Virtually all credit agreements under which private information is shared, and the LSTA standard provisions, include a confidentiality provision. There is also an emerging trend to include a securities law compliance provision in credit agreements.

Splash Pages and Related Matters

In addition to the four basic documentary methods of isolating private information discussed here, since the advent of Internet distribution of documents, the loan market has adopted an important fifth documentary protection against the mishandling of private information. The text on the Internet splash page, the page that precedes access to information on a Web-based document delivery system such as IntraLinks or SyndTrak (the two dominant providers of Web-based document delivery systems used in the loan market), almost always contains a confidentiality undertaking and often contains a securities law compliance provision. The LSTA has a group that is considering adopting industry-standard text for splash pages, and both provisions are certain to be recommended by that group.

In addition, many lead arrangers' splash pages warn LMPs that the site (the documents posted within it) may contain MNPI and that if they do not wish to obtain MNPI, they should not access the site. Recently, IntraLinks and SyndTrak have introduced sites that are partitioned, with a public side and a private side. Splash pages for these sites generally also warn LMPs that if they do not wish to obtain MNPI, they should review only information that is contained on the public side of the site.

To be clear, these splash pages constitute binding contractual agreements in the same way that the other forms of documentary protection do. Before accessing a site, LMPs must click on "I Agree," or something similar, before proceeding. The act of clicking on the "agree" button creates a binding contract.

In addition to the splash page, at industry urging, IntraLinks and SyndTrak have each rolled out new product versions that have an optional function that permits LMPs to select their content preferences. That is, after agreeing to the terms of a splash page, LMPs may select content that consists of only public information or content that consists of all information, including information that may constitute MNPI. This architecture provides a convenient accommodation for public LMPs so that they can be reasonably confident that the information on the public portion of the site will be MNPI-free and accordingly will not restrict any securities activities they may be engaged in relating to the applicable borrower.

Generally, the lead arranger puts information on these web sites with the borrower's consent. Importantly, the public portion of the web site generally includes only information that is demonstrably in the public domain (for instance, information taken from the SEC's EDGAR service), information for which the borrower has provided comfort that the information does not include MNPI, or information for which the arranger has determined that the information does not include MNPI. In practice, sometimes the arranger's and the borrower's desire to increase the quality of the information on the public side of a site may cause the borrower to make a public announcement or a filing with the SEC before posting certain information on the public side of a site in order to be confident that the information at issue does not constitute MNPI.

CONCLUSION

These five documents (master confidentiality agreements, trade confirms, bank books, credit agreements, and splash pages) and the emerging trend of partitioning web sites into public and private sides are the basic building blocks of how private information is contractually corralled within the loan market and how the loan market provides reasonable protection against the improper use and dissemination of private information. These documents and practices, when implemented in an orderly fashion, provide reasonable confidence that no matter how an LMP enters the loan asset class, it will be obligated to treat borrowers' confidential information in a manner consistent with the borrowers' objectives and with the securities laws.

The Implications of the Use of "Syndicate Information" in the Loan Market

Elliot Ganz
General Counsel, LSTA

INTRODUCTION

The antifraud and related provisions of the U.S. federal securities laws generally restrict the use of material nonpublic information (MNPI) about an issuer or its securities when entering into securities transactions. In order to comply with these laws, firms in the financial services industry have long employed informational "walls" to separate different parts of a firm, so that persons engaged in securities sales and trading activities (so-called public-side activities) do not have access or exposure to MNPI about customers with publicly traded securities that is routinely available and an integral part of the business in other parts of the firm, such as investment banking (so-called private-side activities). These are well-established practices that are sanctioned by the rules of the Securities and Exchange Commission (SEC).

Loans are originated, maintained, and distributed on the basis of the borrower's providing its lenders with confidential information about the borrower's business that may contain MNPI (Syndicate Information). Certain loan-market participants (LMPs), however, have a business model in which personnel who are engaged in securities (or securities-related derivatives) sales and trading also engage in transactions in interests in loans. Accordingly, this requires compliance procedures to ensure that such personnel do not have access or exposure to Syndicate Information containing MNPI on borrowers that also issue securities in which the firm may trade. Additionally, such LMPs must have procedures ensuring that nontrading personnel or representatives receive, handle, and make decisions with respect to Syndicate Information that is provided to all lenders.

KEY CONCEPTS WITH RESPECT TO INFORMATION IN THE LOAN MARKET
Syndicate Information

Syndicate Information is confidential information that a borrower provides (typically through an administrative agent or arranger) to lenders or prospective lenders. Syndicate Information is provided subject to specific confidentiality undertakings contained in credit agreements, evaluation materials, and stand-alone confidentiality agreements. Syndicate Information can be more extensive than the information that is publicly available and in certain circumstances may constitute MNPI. Syndicate Information may be provided orally or in writing. It typically consists of (1) information made available by a borrower in connection with the origination of a loan,[1] (2) information periodically made available by or on behalf of the borrower to the entire syndicate of lenders in accordance with the terms of the applicable credit agreement, and (3) information periodically made available by the borrower to the entire syndicate of lenders regarding developments or other special circumstances; this may include borrowing requests and amendments and waivers.

---

[1] In some circumstances, Syndicate Information may include the credit documentation.

Confidentiality provisions in credit agreements also contemplate and permit the disclosure of Syndicate Information by an LMP to prospective LMPs in connection with a proposed secondary sale of an interest in a loan, subject to the prospective LMP itself agreeing to an appropriate confidentiality undertaking.

Borrower Restricted Information

As used herein, Borrower Restricted Information refers to confidential information, including MNPI, that is made available by or on behalf of a borrower that is not Syndicate Information because the borrower has not made such information available to all the members or potential members of the syndicate. Borrower Restricted Information might include, for example, MNPI provided privately by a borrower to an agent or to a limited number of syndicate members (often referred to as agent-only information) or information made available to a steering committee or certain creditors during the course of a restructuring. Borrower Restricted Information often is later communicated to the entire syndicate and thus becomes Syndicate Information.

Material Nonpublic Information

Syndicate Information and Borrower Restricted Information may contain MNPI. Information has been defined as "material" under the U.S. federal securities laws when (1) there is a "substantial likelihood" that a "reasonable investor" would consider the information important in making an investment decision, (2) the disclosure of the information would be "viewed by the reasonable investor as having significantly altered the 'total mix' of information made available,"[2] or (3) the disclosure of the information is "reasonably certain to have a substantial effect on the market price of the security."

A determination of materiality is a fact-specific inquiry, requiring careful assessment of the inferences that a reasonable person would draw from a given set of facts and the significance of those inferences. The same information may be material in one context but not material in another.

According to the SEC, (1) information is nonpublic if it has not been disseminated in a manner that makes it available to investors

---

[2] Suggest commencing sub-clause (ii) by referencing the "substantial likelihood" qualifier.

generally,[3] (2) insiders must wait a "reasonable" time after disclosure of MNPI before trading, and (3) what constitutes a reasonable time depends on the circumstances of the dissemination.

The Public and Private Sides

LMPs are said to participate in the loan market in one of two ways: either on the private side or on the public side of information barriers. The private side refers to the side of information barriers on which individuals may have (or may be deemed to have) access to Syndicate Information and possibly MNPI. Typically, business units of LMPs that arrange, originate, and syndicate loans or engage in advisory activities are likely to be on the private side of information barriers because these activities routinely result in the receipt of Syndicate Information and possibly MNPI.

The public side refers to that side of information barriers on which individuals do not have access to MNPI; they are "walled off" from individuals and information on the private side. Traditional securities sales and trading activities are normally conducted on the public side. This model is frequently followed by LMPs for those parts of its loan business where the same personnel are also making decisions with respect to securities transactions.

Those LMPs that have elected a public side model for business areas that acquire loans either in the original syndication or in the secondary market have elected to make decisions with respect to such loan interests without information that is available to LMPs that conduct such activities on the private side. By definition, such information may be material. The public-side LMP needs to be cognizant of the risk it is taking by engaging in transactions without access to information that is otherwise available to the market in which the LMP is transacting.[4]

---

[3] Public information is information that is broadly disseminated to the public via a press release from the company that has been picked up on a national news service, a news story disseminated by a national news service, or a public filing with the SEC or a court.

[4] It is important to note that most (if not all) arrangers of syndicated loans will rely on the borrower and its counsel to determine whether information is free of MNPI. If a borrower fails or refuses to authorize information to be distributed to the public side, then arrangers will act accordingly and distribute it only to the private side. Arrangers will not reevaluate the borrower's decision or analyze the information independently. Public-side LMPs may choose to establish vetting procedures within their firms to receive syndicate-level information and have qualified private-side personnel determine for the LMPs themselves whether the information constitutes MNPI. However, the risk of deciding incorrectly will rest with the public-side LMP.

Confidentiality Arrangements—the Basis for the Private-Side Loan Market

Borrowers furnish syndicate information to lenders and prospective lenders on the basis of confidentiality arrangements undertaken by the recipients. During the primary syndication of a loan, the confidentiality arrangement may take the form of a confidentiality agreement contained in a "splash page" for an electronic workspace set up by an agent or contained in the underlying evaluation materials. In the secondary market, the governing confidentiality agreement[5] is typically between the seller and the prospective lender. Once a primary syndication closes and a credit agreement is signed, or once a secondary trade closes and the buyer becomes a party to or participant in the credit agreement, the confidentiality provisions of the credit agreement itself generally govern. It is important to note that information that is not MNPI may be confidential from a borrower's point of view (for example, where it might be useful to competitors). Accordingly, *all prospective lenders or purchasers of loans, whether on the private side or on the public side, are subject to the terms and conditions of confidentiality arrangements,* whether or not they come into possession of MNPI.[6]

ADDRESSING THE ISSUES

In order to address the issues that arise from the fact that many LMPs also transact in the securities markets, LMPs should consider some of the following principles.

LMPs Should Implement and Maintain Information Controls and Related Policies and Procedures for Handling Syndicate Information in Order to Avoid Entering into Securities Transactions on the Basis of MNPI

Each LMP must establish information controls and related policies and procedures appropriate to its particular business activities and organizational structure to help it control, limit, and monitor the

[5] The LSTA published a Master Confidentiality Agreement in November 1999 that is widely used by participants in the loan market.
[6] It is also worth noting that some investment grade loans may not contain confidentiality provisions because the borrowers provide only public information to the lenders. These syndicated loans do not raise any of the issues addressed in this article.

communication and use of MNPI. The primary objectives of such policies and procedures should be to (1) prevent the inappropriate communication of Syndicate Information and the execution of securities transactions on the basis of MNPI in violation of applicable law, and (2) avoid violation of any nondisclosure duties and undertakings that the firm may owe to clients or companies from which the Syndicate Information was obtained.

Information controls and related policies and procedures have been recognized by securities and banking regulators as appropriate mechanisms for handling the receipt of MNPI in accordance with applicable legal restrictions. Indeed, the SEC has provided safe harbor protection for persons who establish appropriate information controls in order to ensure that they are not in possession of MNPI at the time they enter into a transaction in the relevant security. LMPs should design policies and procedures to ensure that people who are engaged in securities sales and trading activities do not have access or exposure to MNPI that may be contained in Syndicate Information communicated to the LMP as a result of its loan positions.

A Firm's Information Controls and Related Policies and Procedures Should Be Tailored to the Nature and Scope of Its Business Activities and Operations

Each firm's policies and procedures for handling MNPI should be tailored to the unique structure and circumstances of the firm's activities. Given the significant differences among firms in terms of, for example, the types and scope of their loan market and securities activities and the location of and relationship between such activities, it is neither possible nor desirable to develop uniform or standardized policies and procedures for all LMPs.

LMPs Should Consider Including Certain Key Elements in Their Information Controls and Related Policies and Procedures

In designing or reviewing their information controls, LMPs should consider including the following elements, which incorporate certain regulatory guidance regarding information controls as well as the views of the LSTA as to recommended loan market practices.

Restricted Lists and Watch Lists

Many LMPs that are simultaneously engaged in securities transactions have found it useful to maintain some combination of
restricted lists and watch lists for purposes of restricting certain
transactions and reviewing compliance with their firms' information controls, although the nature and scope of such lists vary
from firm to firm.

A *restricted list* is a list of securities, other traded instruments, or
issuers for which a firm has restricted proprietary, employee, and certain customer securities transactions. The restricted list is generally
distributed to sales and trading personnel as necessary to prevent
inappropriate transactions. Securities, other traded instruments, or
issuers may be placed on the restricted list for a variety of reasons,
including compliance with applicable laws and avoiding conflicts of
interest or the appearance of such conflicts.

One example of a situation in which a restricted list might be
relied upon by an LMP that is simultaneously engaged in loan and
securities activities is where a firm that has access to Borrower
Restricted Information that includes MNPI with respect to a borrower or its loans may choose to restrict trading in that borrower's
securities because it has decided to disclose such information to
one or more of its public-side personnel (who are said to "cross the
information wall") for the purposes of obtaining such personnel's
particular market expertise. Another example might be a situation
in which the MNPI was so sensitive that, although the firm could
properly rely on its information barriers, it would restrict the trading of securities in order to avoid even the appearance of conflicts
of interest.

A *watch list* is a list of securities or issuers for which trading or
marketing is not prohibited but is subject to close scrutiny by the
firm's compliance or legal department. The dissemination of the
watch list is usually limited to persons performing legal or compliance functions, to permit the review of trading activities without
signaling the firm's possible possession of MNPI.

Firms that maintain such lists should also have criteria and
procedures for the addition of securities and issuers to and their
deletion from the lists and for controlling access to the watch list.

Information Barriers

Firms can also establish information barriers between departments
that may have access to MNPI and those that do not. Functional and

physical separation of these departments can assist in defining and maintaining these walls. Functional separation might include, for example, separate employees, lines of authority, databases, record keeping, and support groups. Physical separation may include limiting or restricting access to files, offices, computers, and data.

Other elements of information control that support the critical elements might include (1) written and formalized policies and procedures, (2) an independent compliance function, (3) procedures for communicating across information barriers, (4) record-keeping requirements, (5) education and training requirements, and (6) review and approval of policies and procedures by senior management.

LMPs Should Consider Structuring Their Information Controls and Policies and Procedures to Address the Following Special Issues That May Be Posed Depending on Whether They Conduct Their Loan-Market Activities on the Private Side, the Public Side, or a Combination of Both

Receipt of MNPI by Private-Side LMPs

Firms that conduct some or all of their loan activities on the private side of information barriers (whether those activities include, for example, structuring, arranging, and/or acting as agent for syndicated loans for borrowers that are issuers of public securities; trading or dealing in the secondary market for such loans; involvement in restructurings regarding such loans; or simply lending) may receive MNPI from borrowers in the course of these activities. These firms should have policies and procedures designed to prevent the misuse of MNPI, including the analysis thereof (whether in the form of Syndicate Information or Borrower Restricted Information), in their investment decisions relating to securities.

Receipt of Information by Public-Side LMPs

Firms that conduct all or a portion of their loan market activities on the public side of the information wall, whether these activities include lending or trading in the secondary market, should implement policies and procedures designed to ensure that those employees involved in lending and trading decisions (Public-Side

Employees) receive only Public Evaluation Materials (as defined below) and information that the LMP has ascertained does not contain MNPI. In addition, such firms should implement policies and procedures that enable them to impose ad hoc information barriers or restrict the purchase or sale of securities of borrowers by Public-Side Employees who have either (1) inadvertently received MNPI or (2) deliberately chosen to receive MNPI. Such firms should also designate either employees who are not Public-Side Employees or external advisors to receive periodic Syndicate Information (as described in more detail below).

Production of Evaluation Materials

In connection with an arranger's structuring or syndication of a loan, a borrower will typically provide the arranger with detailed information about its business and operations for distribution by the arranger to prospective LMPs. Some of this information may, from time to time, constitute MNPI. This information, often compiled by the arranger into a confidential evaluation memorandum and other evaluation materials (collectively, Evaluation Materials), is intended to be made available to all prospective LMPs who are evaluating the loan.[7]

However, many prospective LMPs may wish to remain on the public side of the information barrier with respect to the evaluation of the loan. In order to address this segment of the loan market, the borrower and/or arranger may compile an evaluation memorandum and other Evaluation Materials that do not contain MNPI (Public Evaluation Materials).

Consequently, firms that are arrangers may consider establishing policies and procedures addressing the production of Evaluation Materials. Elements to consider in policies and procedures for preparing Evaluation Materials can include (1) using legends and undertakings (including, without limitation, splash pages) to remind all recipients of Evaluation Materials of their confidentiality obligations and their responsibility to use any information they contain in a manner consistent with securities laws, and (2) procedures for working with borrowers that are best suited to produce Public Evaluation Materials that do not contain MNPI for distribution to

---

[7] It is important to note that the information compiled by the agent is provided by the borrower and its advisors and that the borrower typically represents to the agent that the information is accurate and complete.

public-side LMPs. The procedures for developing Public Evaluation Materials could include a requirement that borrowers affirmatively identify all information that is to be provided to public-side buyers (other than information, such as public securities filings, that is demonstrably public) as either public or nonmaterial.

Distribution of Evaluation Materials

Written Evaluation Materials are typically communicated by the arranger or syndicator of a loan to potential purchasers via electronic workspaces and disseminated subject to the recipient's making certain representations and agreeing to certain undertakings. These representations and undertakings are usually enumerated on a splash page, i.e., the first electronic screen that is visible to an LMP who wishes to access the Evaluation Materials. The recipients indicate their agreement to the representations and undertakings by clicking on an "agree" button on the splash page.

Firms that are arrangers or syndicators of loans may implement procedures that require potential recipients to make certain representations and agree to certain conditions before any Evaluation Materials are disclosed. The representations and undertakings that an arranger could require might include (1) an agreement that the recipient maintain the confidentiality of the Evaluation Materials in accordance with the terms of (a) the confidentiality provisions of the underlying credit agreement (assuming that the recipient is already a party thereto), (b) the confidentiality provisions set forth on the splash page itself, or (c) the confidentiality provisions included within the Evaluation Materials; (2) an acknowledgement that the Evaluation Materials may contain MNPI; (3) a representation that the recipient has developed compliance procedures regarding the use of MNPI; (4) an undertaking that MNPI will be handled in accordance with applicable law; (5) an acknowledgment that the arranger makes no representation as to the designation of information as public or private, but instead has relied on the borrower; and (6) an agreement that the underlying borrower may rely upon all the representations and undertakings agreed to by the recipient.

Distribution of Evaluation Materials to Public-Side Purchasers

Electronic workspaces may require LMPs evaluating a loan to indicate whether they are interested in Evaluation Materials that are

designated as private-side information or whether they are interested in receiving only information that is designated as public-
side information. Firms that are arrangers or syndicators of loans
may consider establishing procedures that clearly mark and identify on the workspace those Evaluation Materials that have been
determined (typically by the borrower) to be Public Evaluation
Materials. Alternatively, an arranger may establish procedures by
which a party who declares that it is a public side purchaser is
automatically denied access to any information on the workspace
other than what has been determined to be Public Evaluation
Material.

Receipt by Public Side LMPs of Public Evaluation Materials

Firms that evaluate syndicated loans on the basis of Public
Evaluation Materials only should consider establishing policies
and procedures addressing the receipt and use of Evaluation
Materials. These policies and procedures might include (1) a
requirement that public-side employees be permitted to access and
view only Public Evaluation Materials, (2) compliance surveillance
or audits designed to ensure that public-side employees' access is
limited to Public Evaluation Materials only, and (3) restricting trading in the securities of a borrower in cases where (a) MNPI inadvertently comes into the possession of public-side employees or (b)
the mere knowledge of the existence or purpose of a proposed loan
to a borrower could constitute MNPI (for so long as such information constitutes MNPI). Procedures might also include the ability to
designate an individual or individuals within the firm (or external
advisors of the firm) who are not involved in the decision-making
process and give them authorization to receive private Evaluation
Materials and draft transaction documentation (in cases where a
borrower does not specifically indicate that such documentation
does not constitute MNPI).

Periodic Distribution of Information Relating to Borrowers

After a syndicated loan is closed, Syndicate Information is periodically communicated to all the members of the lending syndicate by
the agent on behalf of the borrower. This Syndicate Information typically concerns the borrower and/or the loan and is communicated

either as part of the routine administration of the loan or under special circumstances relating to the borrower and/or the loan. Such Syndicate Information may contain MNPI. Firms that conduct their loan market activities on the public-side of the information wall may choose not to have periodic Syndicate Information communicated to their public side employees. Nevertheless, such firms must frequently act upon such information (for example, by voting on an amendment or funding a loan). Consequently, LMPs that choose not to have periodic Syndicate Information communicated to their public-side employees should designate other individuals (either employees who are not public-side employees or external advisors) to receive periodic Syndicate Information, and agents should implement procedures to honor these requests.

CONCLUSION

Most LMPs have adopted and enforce vigorous policies to manage the communication and use of Syndicate Information. The maintenance of robust compliance procedures is crucial to the continued growth and transparency of the loan market.

CHAPTER 5

Understanding the Credit Agreement

Richard Wight
Partner
Milbank, Tweed, Hadley & McCloy

Warren Cooke
Partner
Milbank, Tweed, Hadley & McCloy

Richard Gray
Partner
Milbank, Tweed, Hadley & McCloy

INTRODUCTION

This chapter is intended to address some of the basic questions that a lender (or lender's counsel) may confront in understanding a standard credit agreement. It is broken into 11 parts.

There are some key assumptions to keep in mind when reading this chapter. First, we address only bank-led syndicated credit agreements for nonbankrupt borrowers. We will not address the unique issues that arise in the context of debtor-in-possession financings or in conduit lending. Second, although we discuss some of the issues that arise with non-U.S. borrowers, the principal thrust of this chapter will be issues raised when lending to domestic companies. Third, we presume (unless indicated otherwise) that the credit agreement will be governed by New York law. We do not, in particular, address issues that would arise under an English-law credit agreement. Last, for ease of reading, we generally refer throughout this chapter to provisions applicable to the "the borrower." Other than in the context of the making of loans, the term should nevertheless be understood to include subsidiaries of the borrower; and it should be noted that many provisions, including representations and warranties, covenants, and events of default, apply as well to other parties (guarantors, pledgors, and others) that support the credit.

Part I. Making the Loan: Commitments, Loans, and Letters of Credit

CREDIT VARIANTS

Loans

In its simplest form, a credit agreement will provide merely for loans; in its more complex forms, it may encompass letters of credit, bankers' acceptances, and deposit facilities as alternative ways of making credit available to borrowers. Over many decades, the financial markets have developed a number of loan variants, as well as other devices by which lenders can provide financing to borrowers. These we discuss here.

Revolving Credit versus Term Loans

Revolving credit loans, as their name implies, "revolve" within "commitments" established by the lenders. The borrower may borrow, repay, and reborrow the loans during the term of the commitments, so long as the applicable lending conditions are satisfied. By contrast, term loans, once borrowed and repaid, may not be reborrowed. This is not to say that term loans cannot be made available under commitments that contemplate multiple drawdowns (a so-called "standby term loan facility"), but simply that once the loan has been repaid, the borrower has no ability to reborrow the amount repaid. An easy analogy is to equate revolving credit loans to credit card debt and term loans to a home mortgage.

A and B Loan Tranches

Term loans have evolved over time into two types: a so-called A loan tranche and B loan tranche. A loans are generally understood to be term loans that are made by bank lenders (as opposed to funds or other institutional investors), have a tenor equal to the term of any revolving credit commitments in the credit agreement, and are entitled to the benefit of real amortization, i.e., installments that over the term of the loan will represent sizeable (and not just nominal) paydowns of the facility. By contrast, B loans will typically be made by funds or other institutional lenders, have a maturity longer than any related A loan (usually six months to a year longer), and have only nominal amortization until the last year, i.e., typically 1 percent per year until the last year or the very final installment. Revolving credit and A loans are often referred to as the *pro rata tranches*; B loans are referred to as the *B tranche*. The latter is true even though a credit agreement may have multiple series of B loans (Series B, Series C, Series D, and so forth). Thus, any tranche that is in the mold of a B tranche will be referred to as a B tranche, even though the name assigned to that tranche uses another letter of the alphabet (other than, of course, A).

Competitive Bid Loans

As will be discussed in greater detail later under "Pricing" in Part 2, a credit agreement may also provide for so-called competitive bid or competitive access facilities. Facilities of this kind are most often offered to borrowers with high credit quality and are tied to revolving credit facilities. Lenders do not commit to making competitive bid loans; rather, these loans may be offered by the lenders at their individual option within the aggregate limits of the revolving credit commitments of all revolving credit lenders. A lender can thus lend *more* than the amount of its own revolving credit commitment, so long as the aggregate of all revolving credit loans (including all competitive bid loans) does not exceed the aggregate of the revolving credit commitments of all the lenders. The purpose of competitive bid loans is to allow the lenders (if they choose) to provide loans to a borrower at rates lower than those otherwise available under the agreed pricing set out in the credit agreement.

The normal mechanism in a competitive bid facility is for the borrower to request its revolving credit lenders to make offers to make loans for specified periods (usually corresponding to the permitted durations of interest periods) at specified interest rates or at specified margins over LIBOR. The lenders then compete to provide loans by making the best offer they can. The borrower has the option to accept (or reject) the offers made, though the credit agreement will stipulate that, if the borrower wishes to accept any bids, it will accept them in ascending order, i.e., it will accept the offers for the lowest rates first. Whether a lender submits an offer is within its sole discretion, so there is no requirement that the amount of a competitive bid loan offered by a lender be limited to that lender's revolving credit commitment. The only condition will be that the aggregate of all competitive bid loans and all revolving credit loans may not exceed the aggregate amount of the revolving credit commitments.

Swingline Loans

Swingline loans are loans made available by a "swingline lender." They are an adjunct to the revolving credit facility. One purpose is to give the borrower faster availability to loans than would otherwise be permitted under the notice periods prescribed in the credit agreement, which will typically require at least three business days' notice for LIBOR loans and one business day's notice for base rate loans. Even in cases where same-day availability is allowed for base rate loans, a swingline facility will permit loans to be made later in the day. The reason swingline loans can be made on such short notice is that they are being advanced by only one lender, usually the lender serving as the administrative agent (though some agreements will contemplate more than one swingline lender). A second purpose is to give the borrower access to loans of lower minimum amounts than would otherwise be required for a syndicated borrowing from all the lenders participating in the revolving credit facility.

Swingline facilities have several key features. First, the swingline lender will customarily be obligated to make swingline loans only within the limit of its revolving credit commitment. Second, a maximum amount of swingline loans will be specified. Third, swingline loans will normally be required to be repaid in a very short time, typically within five business days or two weeks and, sometimes, concurrently with the next regular borrowing under the credit agreement. Finally, in the event that for any reason the borrower does not repay the swingline loans within their prescribed maturity (including by reason of an intervening event of default or even bankruptcy), the other revolving credit lenders will be unconditionally obligated to purchase participations in the swingline loans so that the risk of the swingline loans is shared ratably among all revolving credit lenders.

Letters of Credit

Often a credit agreement will provide that the revolving credit facility is available not only for loans, but also for letters of credit, with the maximum for both loans and letters of credit not to exceed the amount of the revolving credit commitments. Typically, the aggregate amount of letters of credit must be within a sublimit of the revolving credit commitments.

The content of the letter of credit provisions in a credit agreement is driven in large part by the nature of letters of credit. A letter of credit is an undertaking by the issuer of the letter of credit (virtually always a bank, although legally it can be anyone) to pay the beneficiary of the letter of credit a specified sum upon delivery of documents during the term of the letter of credit. The issuer is *unconditionally* obligated to honor a drawing under the letter of credit if the proper documents are presented, without any requirement on the part of the issuer to verify the truth of statements in the documents. So long as the documents "strictly comply" with the terms of the letter of credit, the issuer is obligated to pay. The borrower (in letter of credit terminology, the "account party") will in turn be unconditionally obligated to reimburse the issuer for the amount paid by the issuer as a result of any drawing under the letter of credit.

Letters of credit can be either commercial letters of credit (if they support the shipment of and payment for goods) or standby or performance letters of credit (if they support an obligation of the borrower to make payments to a third party under a separate contract). Standby or performance letters of credit may be issued to support, say, a borrower's obligation to an insurance company for workers' compensation payments or franchise obligations by a cable television company to a municipality or an infinite variety of other obligations.

Letters of credit issued under syndicated credit agreements will rarely have an expiration date more than one year after issuance, though market practice has adopted the concept of an "evergreen" letter of credit. In an evergreen letter of credit, the initial expiration date will automatically be extended for an additional year (or other period) unless the issuer notifies the beneficiary within, say, 30 days that the letter of credit will not be renewed. Commercial letters of credit are typically for shorter terms; standby letters of credit are of longer duration and will, if appropriate, employ the evergreen option. A credit agreement will normally not allow letters of credit to have an expiration date (taking into account evergreen renewals) beyond the termination date of the commitments.

The credit agreement will commonly require the borrower to reimburse the issuer of a letter of credit on the day upon which a drawing under the letter of credit is honored by the issuer (or, at most, one business day later). Sometimes the credit agreement will state that the reimbursement claim automatically converts into revolving credit loans, with the lenders obligated to fund their portion of the loans so that the issuer obtains full reimbursement for the drawing.

To ensure that the exposure to the borrower associated with each letter of credit is shared by all of the revolving credit lenders ratably in accordance with their revolving credit commitments, the credit agreement will commonly provide that each revolving credit lender is deemed to have acquired a participation in the letter of credit upon its being issued. Payment for such participation is not required unless the borrower shall for any reason (including bankruptcy) fail to reimburse the issuer, at which point the revolving credit lenders will be unconditionally obligated to pay for their previously purchased participations in the related reimbursement claim.

A point that sometimes arises in negotiating letter of credit provisions is what happens if the issuer wrongfully honors (or dishonors) a drawing made under a letter of credit. The customary approach is to provide that the issuer may dishonor any drawing that does not "strictly" comply with the provisions of the letter of credit, but to require the borrower to reimburse the issuer for any drawing honored by the issuer that "substantially" complies with the requirements of the letter of credit. Letters of credit normally require that documents strictly comply, but to protect the issuer against close judgment calls in reviewing documents, the "substantially complies" standard is applicable as between the issuer and the borrower.

Letters of credit cannot be unilaterally paid off. If the borrower wishes to refinance the loans under a credit agreement, it can do so easily just by prepaying the outstanding principal with interest. However, since a letter of credit is an unconditional obligation of the issuer to the beneficiary, it cannot be cancelled by the issuer without the beneficiary's consent. The only way it can be "refinanced" is by causing a replacement letter of credit to be issued to the beneficiary and having the beneficiary consent to the termination of the letter of credit under the credit agreement. To coordinate this at a closing can be cumbersome, especially if there are many letters of credit outstanding at the time. An alternative custom that has developed is for the letters of credit under the credit agreement to continue even following a refinancing and for the borrower either to post cash collateral for its reimbursement obligation or to post a backup letter of credit from another institution to support the reimbursement obligation. In either event, the amount of cash posted or the face amount of the backup letter of credit will normally be 102 to 105 percent of the potential reimbursement obligation, in order to cover letter of credit fees and any default interest accruing on the reimbursement obligation. The borrower would then undertake to replace all backstopped letters of credit within some relatively short period.

Bankers' Acceptances

In a bankers' acceptance facility, the lenders will allow the borrower to draw *time drafts* on the lenders, which the lenders agree will then be "accepted" by the lenders. This is akin to having the borrower write a check that is certified by a bank, with the exception that a check is payable "at sight" (i.e., immediately), whereas a time draft will be payable after an agreed-upon period of time. Following acceptance, the borrower will be free to sell the accepted draft at a discount into the bankers' acceptance market, although the typical acceptance facility will provide for the accepting lender itself to purchase the draft at an agreed-upon discount and commission. While they were historically common, bankers' acceptance facilities are today rarely seen in syndicated credit agreements.

COMMITMENTS

Several Liability

A commitment represents the obligation of a lender, at the request of the borrower, to make loans or issue letters of credit (or, in a bankers' acceptance facility, to accept and discount bankers' acceptances). In a syndicated credit facility, each lender undertakes a separate commitment to the borrower; its commitment may be part of a tranche in which a number of other lenders participate, but each lender is individually obligated (i.e., *severally* obligated) to make loans to the borrower. It is not, in other words, a condition to a lender's obligation to make a loan that other lenders are also making their loans; no lender is excused from making its loan if the conditions to lending are satisfied, even though one or more other lenders in the same tranche are refusing, or defaulting on their obligation, to lend.

Reducing Commitments

Just as term loans can amortize (i.e., have required installments for repayment), so also can a revolving credit commitment "amortize." Such a facility is a so-called reducing revolving credit facility. The installments will be phrased as reductions of the commitments coupled with a requirement that whenever the aggregate outstanding loans and letters of credit exceed the amount of the commitments, the borrower must prepay the excess. The borrower will also typically be allowed to reduce the commitments at any time, subject to giving prior notice (although it is customary to limit the ability of the borrower to reduce the commitments to the unutilized portion of the commitments).

Terminating Commitments

The credit agreement will virtually always give the borrower the option to terminate commitments for any tranche of loans at any time, and, of course, the remedies provisions of the agreement will provide that the commitments terminate (either automatically or at the election of the lenders) upon the occurrence of any event of default.

Increasing Commitments: Incremental Facilities and Accordion Features

Many credit agreements will accord the borrower the right to increase the amount of credit available under the agreement after the closing. No lender will at the outset commit to providing any increase (the credit agreement will be explicit on this point), but all of the lenders will in effect agree that, if the borrower is able to obtain the agreement of one or more lenders to step up for increased credit exposure, no further consent of the lenders is required to permit the *increasing* lenders to commit to the increase. The increase will thus be automatically entitled to the benefit of any guarantees or collateral security to which the closing date facilities are entitled.

Increases under a credit agreement can be offered in two forms, either as so-called incremental facilities or as accordion features. An accordion feature is the simpler of the two. It is normally available only for increases to revolving credit facilities and will contemplate that the amount of the revolving credit commitments may go up (usually up to some specified maximum) if the lenders are willing. The interest, maturity, and other terms of an increase will be identical to those applicable to the existing (and increased) revolving credit facility. The accordion mechanism will provide that, upon any increase, the borrower will adjust the loans (through appropriate borrowings and prepayments) so that the loans in the increased facility are held by the lenders ratably, a requirement discussed in more detail in "Pro Rata Treatment" in Part 8, "Keeping Peace Among the Lenders."

Incremental facilities, in comparison, do not contemplate an increase in existing commitments, but rather contemplate that entirely new commitments or tranches can be established. The credit agreement may even allow for more than one incremental facility, although these are always capped at a dollar maximum. Depending upon the flexibility afforded to the borrower, the new tranches may be either revolving credit or term facilities. The terms of an incremental facility, unlike an increase pursuant to an accordion, do not necessarily need to be the same as those of any other tranche in the credit agreement. The up-front fees, interest rate, maturity, and amortization will be specified at the time the incremental facility is established. Accordingly, an incremental facility providing for term loans may result in either A or B loans. The incremental commitments themselves will be set forth in a separate, usually very short, two- or three-page "incremental facility agreement" executed by the borrower, any guarantors, the administrative agent, and the lenders that are to provide the facility.

In the case of increases under an accordion or an incremental facility, the lenders that provide the increase or incremental facility will not typically be limited to those that are already party to the credit agreement. Any institution that is willing to provide the increase or incremental facility will be allowed to step up. However, the identity of any new institution will be subject to the consent of the borrower, the administrative agent, and any issuer of letters of credit under the facility to the same extent that the consent of those parties would be required if the new institution were taking an assignment of loans.

Conversion of Revolving Credit Commitments

Sometimes a credit agreement will provide that, at the commitment termination date for revolving credit commitments, any outstanding revolving credit loans will convert into term loans (sometimes called a "term-out" option). This type of conversion is normally automatic (i.e., not subject to a bring-down of representations or the absence of a default), but in some agreements those conditions will be required to be satisfied.

MULTICURRENCY FACILITIES

Credit agreements will sometimes provide for loans to be made (or letters of credit to be issued) in currencies other than U.S. dollars. Normally, the available currencies will be specified at closing, with an option to add currencies later, subject to agreement of each relevant lender and the conditions that the currency be freely convertible and no central bank or other approval be necessary for the loans or letters of credit to be made or repaid.

Multicurrency facilities can be structured in a variety of ways, depending upon the needs of the borrower, the depth of the market for the currency, and tax and other considerations. The following are some common structures.

Ratable Committed Loans

In the ratable committed loan structure, the relevant lenders in a tranche will ratably commit to make loans in dollars and in specified foreign currencies. Sometimes sublimits will be imposed on the amount of any particular foreign currency. This structure has the advantage of being easy to administer, but the disadvantage that each lender in the tranche must have access to each of the specified currencies. This may limit the universe of lenders to which the tranche can be syndicated. The size of any sublimit will also be subject to the depth of the market for the currency.

Nonratable Committed Loans

In this structure, a subgroup of lenders in a dollar tranche will agree to make loans in the currencies specified. There may be different lenders in each subgroup. This structure enhances the number of foreign currencies that can be made available to the borrower, since not every lender is required to have access to all currencies, but it has the disadvantage of being difficult to administer, since loans end up being made on a nonratable basis. It also has the disadvantage of not spreading the credit exposure ratably among the lenders; which subgroup holds exposure at any time is a function solely of which currencies were borrowed.

Local Currency Tranches

In a local currency structure, a separate tranche is created for each foreign currency, with specified lenders making loans directly to the relevant borrower out of local offices in the relevant foreign country. This eliminates the administrative disadvantage of the nonratable committed loan structure, and has the advantage of increasing the number of currencies that may be made available. Given that the loans are made out of local offices, it may also have the advantage of eliminating any withholding taxes. It has the dis-advantage of breaking the total credit available under the facility into discrete segments; thus, unused commitments in one currency cannot be accessed in other currencies. It also does not solve (and may, in fact, exacerbate) the problem of the credit risk not being spread ratably among the lenders. The latter risk is sometimes eliminated by having the local currency tranche be supported by a letter of credit issued under the credit agreement, but this can raise the cost to the borrower of accessing the foreign currency.

Competitive Bid Loans
In the competitive bid loan structure, nondollar loans are made available to the borrower under the competitive bid facility. See the previous discussion in "Competitive Bid Loans." Each lender is given the option to offer to make loans in the currencies requested by the borrower, but is not obligated to make an offer. This struc-ture solves many of the problems previously enumerated, but has the disadvantage of not giving the borrower guaranteed access to any particular foreign currency. It works best for investment grade borrowers.

MINIMUMS, MULTIPLES, AND FREQUENCY

A borrower will sometimes push to have complete freedom to des-ignate the amount of any loan, regardless of whether that results in an extremely small loan or a loan with an odd value. It will want as much freedom to borrow $23.37 as to borrow $10,000,000. More frequently, a borrower will push to be able to have any number of separate LIBOR loans (i.e., separate LIBOR interest periods) out-standing at any time. Arguably, since the invention of computers, none of this should be an issue. However, both administrative agents and lenders want to be spared the administrative nuisance of very small loans. In the context of LIBOR loans, a small prin-cipal is inconsistent with the principle of "match –funding," dis-cussed in "LIBOR" in Part 2, "Making Money off the Loan," since most deposits taken into the London interbank market are in min-imums of $5,000,000. It also forces the administrative agent and the lenders to track a potentially very large number of LIBOR loans with distinct interest periods and distinct interest rates. Accordingly, most credit agreements will require that loans have relatively large minimums ($5,000,000 is typical for LIBOR loans, with somewhat smaller figures for base rate loans) and that the aggregate number of LIBOR loans be limited (10 is typically the maximum). Both of these constraints will operate to reduce the frequency of borrowings under the credit agreement.

MECHANICS OF FUNDING

In syndicated credit agreements, most remittances between the borrower and the lenders will pass through the administrative agent. Thus, when a loan is to be made, the lenders will be required to remit funds to the administrative agent, who will then disburse the funds to the borrower. This is usually the case even with competitive bid loans, though not necessarily for swingline loans (where the credit agreement may provide that the swingline lender remits proceeds directly to the borrower).

The administrative agent is the agent of the lenders, not the borrower, and, consequently, the loan is not made when funds are received by the administrative agent. Rather, the loan is made only when the administrative agent transfers funds to the borrower. The discussion in "The Clawback Clause" in Part 8, "Keeping Peace Among the Lenders," addresses what happens if a lender does not provide the administrative agent with its portion of a loan, but the administrative agent, not being aware that the lender has failed to remit funds, nevertheless forwards to the borrower an amount representing that lender's loan.

The credit agreement will require that the borrower give advance notice of any borrowing to the administrative agent, who will then notify the relevant lenders. Except in rare cases, notices will be required to be delivered on "business days," and in the case of LIBOR loans, will be required to be delivered at least three business days prior to the date the loan is to be made. Base rate loans, depending on the number of lenders in the facility, may require one business day's or same-day notice. The credit agreement will almost always specify a time of day by which notices are to be given and a time of day by which the lenders are to provide funds to the administrative agent. It will not ordinarily specify a time of day for the administrative agent to remit funds to the borrower, since the administrative agent does not have control over when it will receive funds. All notices will be irrevocable, because it will be presumed that the lenders will have allocated funds for the anticipated lending, and were the borrower to decline to take the loan, the lenders would not have an alternative for redeploying the funds that were to have been lent to the borrower.

In some cases, when the borrower requires loan proceeds to make an acquisition and needs funds in the morning of the closing day, the parties may enter into a "prefunding" agreement, under which the lenders will deposit funds with the administrative agent the business day preceding the anticipated closing date and the borrower will agree to pay interest on such funds until the closing date as if the loans had been made. If for any reason the closing does not occur on that day, the deposited funds would be returned to the lenders by the administrative agent. This mechanism enables the administrative agent to know at the opening of business on the closing date that it has been put in funds by all lenders.

Prefunding agreements are also sometimes used when a borrower wishes to take down LIBOR loans at closing and has not yet executed the credit agreement (this is normally the case, since most credit agreements are not in fact executed until the initial funding, even though the language of the credit agreement will invariably contemplate that the funding is to occur some days after execution). Since the credit agreement is not yet in effect, there is no agreement under which the borrower can give notice (and no agreement under which it is obligated to make "breakfunding" payments if for any reason the borrowing does not occur). See the discussion of breakfunding in "Breakfunding" in Part 2, "Making Money off the Loan." The prefunding agreement will bridge this gap by having the borrower undertake that, if the closing does not happen when expected, it will make breakfunding payments as if the lenders had received a valid notice of borrowing.

Part 2. Making Money off the Loan: Loan Pricing and Fees

PRICING

Interest

Credit agreements provide more variability in pricing than bond indentures or private placements, where interest is calculated at a constant rate for the life of the deal. The interest rate on U.S.

dollar–denominated loans under credit agreements is normally expressed as the sum of (1) a base component, usually either the base rate or LIBOR (explained more fully later), that is reset from time to time, plus (2) a margin that is either fixed for the life of the transaction or subject to change based upon preagreed criteria.

Typically, a borrower can elect to borrow either base rate loans or LIBOR loans, or both simultaneously, under a credit agreement, and the borrower can switch back and forth between the two types of loans. Switching from one type to another is referred to as *conversion*. By way of example, a company might initially borrow $100,000,000, consisting of $10,000,000 of base rate loans and $90,000,000 of LIBOR loans; three months later, convert all of the base rate loans, so that the full $100,000,000 is outstanding as LIBOR loans; and six months further on convert some or all of the LIBOR loans back into base rate loans. In addition, as noted in "Credit Variants" in Part 1, "Making the Loan," some credit agreements offer high-grade borrowers competitive bid or competitive access facilities, where the interest on loans is determined according to a bidding process among the lenders. The key pricing options generally made available to borrowers are discussed here.

Base Rate

The base rate (sometimes referred to as the "alternate base rate" or "ABR") is typically defined as the higher of (1) a specified bank's (normally the administrative agent's) publicly announced benchmark "base rate" or "prime rate" and (2) 50 basis points over the federal funds rate. Some banks prefer calling their publicly announced rate their "base rate" and others prefer "prime rate," but the two terms mean essentially the same thing. This is the primary benchmark rate publicly announced by the bank for interest on its loans.

The base or prime rate is unilaterally determined by the bank based upon its cost of funds, competitive pressures, and other factors. Even though it can be changed at any time, banks are reluctant to change it to reflect seasonal or other short-term increases in their cost of funds because of its economic (and sometimes political) importance. Thus, the second component of the base rate, the market-based federal funds rate, serves to protect lenders at times when the base or prime rate is not adjusting quickly or frequently enough to reflect the increased cost of funds. (The addition of the

50 basis points is done to bring these two rates closer to parity.) The federal funds rate for any day is usually defined as the average rate on overnight federal funds transactions for the preceding business day, as published by the Federal Reserve Bank of New York. If that rate is not published, it will be determined by the administrative agent based upon actual quotes from federal funds brokers.

LIBOR

LIBOR (sometimes referred to as "LIBO Rate") is an acronym for London Interbank Offered Rate. It refers to the London-based wholesale market for jumbo U.S. dollar deposits between major banks. Since such deposits are often referred to as Eurodollar deposits, the terms *Eurodollar* and *LIBOR* are often used interchangeably; some credit agreements may refer to "LIBOR (or LIBO Rate) loans," while others refer to "Eurodollar loans." The applicable LIBOR interest rate for a loan under a credit agreement is the prevailing interest rate offered by banks for a matching Eurodollar time deposit. This rate is usually determined by reference to a "screen quote" from Reuters or Telerate or, if a screen quote is not available, specific banks named in the credit agreement as "reference banks."

As will be discussed further in the section "Breakfunding," the assumption underlying the pricing provisions for LIBOR loans is that each lender will fund its loan by accepting a Eurodollar time deposit on which it will have to pay interest at a certain rate, and that it will relend the funds to the borrower at the same rate (plus a margin representing profit). This is so-called match funding. This assumption drives many provisions of credit agreements, both substantive and mechanical, conforming LIBOR loans to the market practice for Eurodollar deposits.

Perhaps the most important mechanical feature is fixing the interest rate on LIBOR loans for specific periods, referred to as "interest periods," that correspond to the tenor of the "matching" Eurodollar time deposits. The durations for interest periods are normally limited to the tenors for deposits commonly available in the Eurodollar market. The desired duration among these options is then selected by the borrower. The most common tenors, and therefore the most customary interest periods available to borrowers, are one, two, three, and six months. Other interest periods are also often available, but when they include tenors where the

Eurodollar market is less liquid, such as nine or twelve months, or shorter than one month, unanimous consent of the affected lenders is usually required because of the difficulty of finding matching deposits.

The beginning and end dates of interest periods are also subject to rules that may seem somewhat arcane, generally pertaining to what happens if the last day of an interest period would otherwise fall on a nonbusiness day or when the relevant months do not have corresponding days (for example, is February 30 the three-month anniversary of November 30?). These rules are driven by the corresponding market conventions for Eurodollar deposits. At the borrower's election, it may have LIBOR loans with different interest periods outstanding simultaneously, with the maximum number of allowed interest periods limited as described in "Minimums, Multiples, and Frequency" in Part 1. Because by market convention the interest rate for a Eurodollar deposit is set two business days before the deposit is accepted (i.e., its value is two business days forward), the interest rate for a LIBOR loan is set two business days before the interest period begins. For the meaning of "business day," see the discussion in "Business Day Conventions" later in Part 2.

The interest rate for a LIBOR loan is fixed for the duration of its interest period, given that the interest rate for the matching Eurodollar deposit is also fixed for that period. If the borrower repays the LIBOR loan or converts it into a base rate loan in the middle of the interest period, the lenders are still obligated to maintain any matching Eurodollar deposit. They could therefore incur a funding loss if interest rates have declined since the beginning of the interest period and they are unable to cover the interest they are paying on the matching Eurodollar deposit by redeploying the proceeds of the repayment for the remainder of the interest period. Credit agreements require the borrower to indemnify the lenders for these losses (see the section "Breakfunding" later in Part 2). A few credit agreements prohibit voluntary repayments and conversions of LIBOR loans in the middle of interest periods. Virtually all credit agreements prohibit repayments of competitive bid loans prior to their maturity. Similarly, borrowers are sometimes prohibited from selecting interest periods that would extend beyond the final maturity of the credit agreement or that would straddle scheduled amortization dates if the amortization could force a repayment of LIBOR loans in the middle of an interest period.

At the end of each interest period for a LIBOR loan, the borrower is required to elect whether that loan will be converted into a base rate loan or be continued (or "rolled over") as a LIBOR loan (and, if the latter, to specify the new interest period). If the borrower fails to do so, the credit agreement will normally provide one of two fail-safes: either the LIBOR loan will be automatically converted into a base rate loan or the LIBOR loan will be rolled over into another LIBOR loan with an interest period of one month. There are advantages to each fail-safe. The advantage to the borrower of an automatic conversion into a base rate loan is that its oversight may be corrected immediately without breakfunding, rather than waiting until the end of a one-month interest period. The advantage to the borrower of continuing the loan as a one-month LIBOR loan is that LIBOR is likely to be lower than the base rate and will therefore result in lower interest charges. Breakfunding is never an issue for base rate loans, since base rate loans do not have interest periods; they continue as base rate loans forever until they are repaid or converted into LIBOR loans.

When a base rate loan is converted into a LIBOR loan, or when a LIBOR loan is rolled over or converted into a base rate loan, it is normally *not* considered a new borrowing that requires the satisfaction of conditions precedent. It is treated merely as the resetting of interest on an outstanding loan, similar to the resetting of the interest rate from time to time on an adjustable-rate home mortgage loan.

Because the pricing of LIBOR loans is premised upon the assumption that lenders fund those loans with matching Eurodollar deposits, lenders consider this pricing to be "cost-plus." They require compensation for any direct or indirect costs of funding LIBOR loans above the interest they pay on the Eurodollar deposits. Most of these items are described in the section "Yield Protection" later in Part 2, but one, reserve requirements, merits special mention here. When a bank is required to maintain reserves against a deposit, it will not have the full amount of the deposit available to it to lend to its customers. By way of example, if a bank is required to maintain a reserve equal to 3 percent of a deposit, it would have only $9,700,000 available to lend from a $10,000,000 deposit. This means that in order to make a $10,000,000 LIBOR loan, it would have to fund itself with (and pay interest on) a larger Eurodollar deposit (in this example, a deposit of $10,000,000 *divided by* 0.97, or $10,309,000).

Lenders are generally compensated for the additional cost by one of two methods. The first method is for the definition of the interest calculation to include a gross-up for the reserve requirement. The definition (sometimes referred to as "adjusted LIBOR" or the "adjusted Eurodollar rate," if the gross-up is not contained in the definition of LIBOR itself) is written arithmetically as follows:

Adjusted LIBOR = LIBOR$/(1 - R)$

The R in this definition means the maximum gross rate at which reserves are required to be maintained against Eurocurrency liabilities, as defined in Regulation D of the Federal Reserve Board. Because this method provides for recovery according to the maximum possible reserve rate, it is referred to as compensation for reserves on a "statutory maximum" basis. Lenders prefer this method because it is straightforward and easy to calculate, since it implicitly assumes that the full amount of the matching Eurodollar deposit is a "Eurocurrency liability." In fact, the calculation of Eurocurrency liabilities for a bank under Regulation D is more complex and can change daily. Lenders that are not subject to any reserve requirements (or are subject to lower reserve requirements) will be overcompensated. For this reason, some borrowers insist upon indemnifying lenders for reserve costs only on an "as incurred" basis. When calculated on an as incurred basis, the compensation would be based upon the individual position of each lender.

All of this notwithstanding, the reserve rate for Eurocurrency liabilities has been zero for more than 15 years. Nevertheless, negotiations continue to take place over these provisions in credit agreements because it is always possible that the reserve rate could be reset to a level higher than zero.

It should be apparent that the need for LIBOR loans to follow certain conventions of the Eurodollar market reduces the flexibility of this pricing option for borrowers. There are also other typical restrictions that further limit flexibility. For example, the fact that Eurodollar deposits are priced two London business days prior to the delivery of funds means that the typical credit agreement will require notices of borrowings, prepayments, and conversions for

LIBOR loans at least three business days in advance. The question thus arises, why do borrowers elect LIBOR loans over base rate loans? The answer is easy: the interest on LIBOR loans is invariably lower. Indeed, the more apt question is, why do borrowers ever elect base rate loans? Here, the answer does go back to the need for flexibility in certain circumstances. For example, in the context of an acquisition with a moving closing date or another urgent need for financing without much advance notice, the three business days requirement for borrowing LIBOR loans may not be practicable. Similarly, a borrower's cash management may result in frequent borrowings and repayments, and the advance notice requirements and restrictions on repayments of LIBOR loans in the middle of interest periods (or the requirements for breakfunding if such repayments do occur) may lead a borrower to maintain at least a portion of its loans as base rate loans.

Competitive Bid Loans

As noted in the section "Competitive Bid Loans" in Part 1, "Making the Loan," some credit agreements offer high-grade borrowers competitive bid or competitive access facilities, where the interest on loans is determined according to a bidding process among the lenders. To initiate the process, the borrower makes a formal request of the administrative agent to solicit offers from the lenders to make competitive bid loans. The borrower specifies (1) the total amount of loans needed, (2) whether the offers should be expressed as a margin above LIBOR or should be expressed as a flat rate, (3) if the offers are for LIBOR-based loans, the tenors for which offers are solicited (which generally must conform to the same conventions described earlier for interest periods for LIBOR loans), and (4) if the offers are solicited for flat-rate loans, the tenors for which offers are solicited (which generally are between 7 and 180 days).

Lenders at their option may provide offers in response to the borrower's request, and the borrower may at its option accept any offers made (although if it does accept offers, it must accept them in ascending order, i.e., the offers for the lowest rates first). Any offers accepted by the borrower result in competitive bid loans by the respective lenders on the terms of the accepted offers. The interest rate for competitive bid LIBOR loans is calculated by adding the accepted margin to the relevant LIBOR determined two business days before the loans are made, in accordance with the Eurodollar convention discussed earlier. The interest rate for flat-rate loans will be the flat rate accepted by the borrower.

The interest rate is fixed for the tenor of the loan, which will normally be called an interest period, even though competitive bid loans are not necessarily LIBOR-based. The loans will generally not be prepayable during the interest period, and the lender will be entitled to breakfunding if the loans are nevertheless paid during the interest period. The principal difference between competitive bid loans and the loans otherwise available under the credit agreement is that competitive bid loans become due and payable on the last days of their interest periods. They may not be converted or continued as new competitive bid loans. If the borrower wishes to roll over a competitive bid loan, it must borrow new competitive bid loans (which, of course, will be subject to the satisfaction of conditions precedent and the bid procedure described earlier) and apply the proceeds to repay the maturing competitive bid loans.

Other Pricing Options

Over the years, the bank loan markets have seen a variety of other pricing options tied to various indices. These have included pricing determined by reference to certificate of deposit rates and term federal funds rates. LIBOR has spawned HIBOR (Hong Kong), SIBOR (Singapore), and IBOR (indeterminate global markets). The pricing options explained here reflect the predominant preferences in today's markets. There will doubtless be other preferences that come in and out of vogue over time.

Applicable Margins

As noted earlier, the interest rate on each base rate loan and each LIBOR loan includes an additional margin, sometimes also referred to as the *spread*. The applicable margin is in some cases a flat rate that is fixed for the life of the agreement, but in other instances it increases over time or is dependent on the credit ratings and/or leverage of the borrower. Whichever approach is taken, the applicable margin for LIBOR loans is always higher than the applicable margin for base rate loans in order to bring the two rates closer to parity. The difference is usually 100 basis points in today's market, although the applicable margin for base rate loans would not be less than zero even if the applicable margin for LIBOR loans were less than 1 percent.

A flat margin or one that increases over time is rather straightforward and requires no further explanation. When the applicable margin is dependent on the credit rating and/or leverage of the borrower, the various rates are set forth in the credit agreement in the form of a grid that varies by type of loan (by tranche and by pricing option) and the relevant financial measure (hence the term *grid pricing*).

When grid pricing is based upon credit ratings, the relevant parameters will include reference debt (sometimes referred to as the "index debt"), the identity of the credit rating agencies to be relied upon, and the treatment of split ratings (when the rating agencies assign different ratings to the same index debt). The index debt can be the loans under the credit agreement, a specific issue of debt securities of the borrower, or unspecified non-credit-enhanced, publicly issued debt of the borrower. Often, when there is a split rating, the higher of the two ratings will be used, but when the ratings differ by more than one level (with each movement from "−" to flat to "+" constituting a level), the most standard approach is to split the difference by using the level immediately above the lower of the two ratings. Typically, any change in the applicable margin takes place either when the borrower notifies the administrative agent of the change in the rating or simultaneously when the change in rating occurs. If the index debt is rated by only one of the rating agencies or ceases to be rated at all, the applicable margin reverts to the highest rate in the grid.

When grid pricing is based upon leverage, the relevant date on which to test leverage is the end of the borrower's most recent fiscal quarter, and changes therefore occur no more frequently than quarterly. The administrative agent is dependent upon receiving the pertinent information from the borrower, typically a certificate by the borrower showing the leverage calculation (usually the ratio of EBITDA to indebtedness) and the related financial statements of the borrower. The applicable margin customarily changes upon delivery of that information or within two or three business days thereafter. Any adjustment in the applicable margin based upon leverage ceases to apply when either (1) the borrower furnishes information for its subsequent fiscal quarter, in which case the applicable margin is reset (or continues) based upon the new information, or (2) the borrower fails to furnish that information for the next quarter on a timely basis, in which case the applicable margin reverts to the highest rate in the grid.

Regardless of the form of grid pricing, many credit agreements will provide that, during the existence of an event of default, the applicable margin will bump up to the highest level on the grid. This will be in addition to any default interest payable, described later.

Interest Payment Dates

The credit agreement will specify the dates on which interest is to be paid. In the case of base rate loans, most credit agreements will specify quarterly payment dates (often at the end of calendar quarters or on quarterly anniversaries of the closing date). In the case of LIBOR loans and competitive bid loans, interest will be payable on the last day of each interest period and, if any interest period is longer than three months, on each quarterly anniversary of the first day of the interest period. The result is that if the borrower has multiple LIBOR loans outstanding, it may be paying interest frequently during the course of a quarter as interest periods come and go. Most credit agreements will also provide that, for all loans, interest is payable on the date that the principal is paid or the loan is converted to a different type. In some cases, the latter rule will not apply to base rate loans, on which interest may be payable only at quarterly dates.

Default Interest

There are two principal approaches to default interest (an increased interest rate by reason of default) taken in credit agreements. One approach requires default interest to be paid only on amounts that are not paid when due. If the overdue amount is the principal of a loan, then the interest rate on that amount is increased to the default rate, described later. For example, if loans in the amount of $100,000,000 are outstanding and the borrower fails to pay an installment of $10,000,000, then the increased interest rate would apply only to the overdue amount of $10,000,000. (Of course, if all of the loans are accelerated because of the payment default, then all of the loans would be overdue and would therefore attract the higher interest rate.) When the overdue amount is something other than principal, say interest or fees, then interest is paid on that overdue amount at the default rate.

A second approach requires that interest be paid at the default rate on the entire amount of the loans whenever an event of default exists, regardless of whether the event of default involves nonpayment. Thus, using the previous example, if loans in the amount of $100,000,000 are outstanding and the borrower fails to pay an installment of $10,000,000 (or, indeed, if a financial covenant is breached), and such failure (or breach) constitutes an event of default, then the increased interest rate would apply to the full $100,000,000. Since it is not feasible to apply interest to accruing obligations like interest and fees until they are overdue, even when an event of default exists, the default interest rate would apply to the amount of these obligations only if they are not paid when due.

The default rate of interest for the principal amount of any loan under both approaches is usually 2 percent above the then-applicable rate for that loan. The default rate of interest for other amounts is usually 2 percent above the then-applicable rate for base rate loans. This increase of 2 percent is in addition to what-ever applicable margin is in effect. It is customary that interest accruing at the default rate be payable on demand rather than on the regularly scheduled dates otherwise provided in the credit agreement.

Another aspect of interest in a default scenario is worth not-ing. When an event of default exists, it is possible that lenders may become concerned about the likelihood of repayment. They may consider accelerating the maturity of loans. They may be willing (indeed, eager) to accept repayments of LIBOR loans in the middle of an interest period rather than risk waiting until the end. However, in order to avoid the funding losses referred to earlier, they may prefer to structure the credit agreement to minimize the likelihood that interest periods for LIBOR loans are outstanding when these problems exist. Accordingly, credit agreements typi-cally limit the borrower's ability to request LIBOR loans when an event of default exists. Some credit agreements provide that when an event of default exists, LIBOR loans automatically convert into base rate loans on the last days of their respective interest periods, and the borrower is precluded from having additional LIBOR loans. This approach may present difficulties for an administrative agent, who may or may not know of the existence of the event of default. Accordingly, the more common approach is for these limitations to apply only after notice that an event of default exists has been delivered to the borrower by the administrative agent.

Fees

There are four main types of fees seen in credit agreements: commitment fees, facility fees, utilization fees, and letter of credit fees. Administrative agency fees and up-front fees are not covered in this discussion because they are generally provided for in fee letters rather than in credit agreements.

Commitment Fees

Commitment fees accrue at an agreed per annum rate on the daily average unused commitments of the lenders. They constitute compensation for the lenders' contractual commitment to make loans. They are most often paid on the unused portion of revolving credit commitments. Whether or not they are paid on unused term loan commitments varies by transaction and may depend on the length of the period for which the term loan commitments are available. The rate at which commitment fees are payable is generally either flat for the duration of the credit agreement or subject to grid pricing.

In calculating the unused amount of revolving credit commitments, all outstanding loans, undrawn letters of credit, and outstanding reimbursement obligations for payments under letters of credit are considered utilizations of the revolving credit commitments. In credit agreements with swingline loans, the amount of outstanding swingline loans is generally not deducted for purposes of calculating commitment fees (even though it is considered a utilization of the revolving credit commitments for other purposes). This is so because the lenders that have not advanced swingline loans nevertheless remain committed to extend credit to the borrower in the amount of those loans, whether by funding participations in the swingline loans or by making revolving credit loans for the purpose of repaying the swingline loans. Accrued commitment fees are generally payable quarterly in arrears.

Facility Fees

In contrast to commitment fees, which are computed on unused commitments, facility fees are computed on the total amount of revolving credit commitments, both used and unused. Facility fees generally do not apply to term loan facilities, and commitment fees and facility fees are mutually exclusive—the same revolving credit facility would not attract both. Facility fees are most often seen either where the usage of a revolving credit facility is expected to be low or where the facility provides for competitive bid loans. Like commitment fees, facility fees are either calculated at a flat rate or subject to grid pricing and are generally payable quarterly in arrears. Some credit agreements provide that facility fees are payable only until the revolving credit commitments terminate. Others, however, provide that facility fees are payable until the later of the termination of the revolving credit commitments or the repayment in full of the loans and termination of the other extensions of credit. This latter structure is designed to avoid a reduction in the aggregate cost of the facility when the commitments expire. After termination of the revolving credit commitments, the fee is payable on the total amount that would be considered utilization of the revolving credit commitments.

Utilization Fees

In transactions where the revolving credit commitments are not expected to be heavily utilized, the commitment fee or facility fee may be lower than in other comparable transactions. However, to address the possibility that utilization may in fact turn out to be high, the credit agreement may provide for an additional fee to be payable if utilization exceeds a certain percentage, say, 30 percent or 50 percent, of the commitments. On each day when this percentage is exceeded, the utilization fee is payable on all utilizations of the revolving credit facility, i.e., not merely on the portion in excess of the 30 percent or 50 percent threshold.

In contrast to the approach used to calculate the commitment fee, utilization for this purpose is more likely to be defined broadly, including not only outstanding revolving credit loans, letters of credit, and reimbursement obligations, but also swingline loans and competitive bid loans. Like commitment fees and facility fees, utilization fees are either calculated at a flat rate or subject to grid pricing. Approaches vary as to whether accrued utilization fees are payable quarterly in arrears or concurrently with payments of interest on the related loans, although quarterly payments are more common. Utilization fees are characterized under some credit agreements as additional interest on loans because interest may receive more favorable treatment than fees under the Bankruptcy Code.

Letter of Credit Fees

As letters of credit are issued under a revolving credit facility, all of the revolving credit lenders share in the credit exposure because, even if they are not the letter of credit issuer, they have participations in the letters of credit. Accordingly, borrowers are obligated to pay to each revolving credit lender a letter of credit fee accruing at an agreed per annum rate on its participation in the undrawn amount of each outstanding letter of credit. In the case of the issuer of each letter of credit, its participation therein for purposes of this calculation is deemed to be its remaining credit exposure after subtracting the participations of the other revolving credit lenders. It is very common for the rate for the letter of credit fees to be the same as the applicable margin for LIBOR loans, taking into account the use of any applicable grid pricing.

Even though all revolving credit lenders share in the credit exposure to the borrower, the letter of credit issuer bears an additional risk—the risk that one or more of the revolving credit lenders might not fund their participations in a letter of credit if the borrower fails to reimburse it. Letter of credit issuers are compensated by borrowers for this additional risk in the form of a fronting fee (so called because the issuer "fronts" the letter of credit for the other revolving credit lenders). The fronting fee accrues at a modest agreed per annum rate on the undrawn amount of each outstanding letter of credit, and the rate is generally flat rather than based on grid pricing.

These letter of credit fees and fronting fees are customarily payable quarterly in arrears, although they are often paid two or three business days after the quarterly period ends in order to give the administrative agent sufficient time to make the necessary calculations. In addition to these fees, the letter of credit issuer may impose administrative charges for issuing, amending, and making payments under letters of credit.

Computation of Interest and Fees

There are two generally used methods of calculating accruing interest and fees under a credit agreement. The first method calculates the accruing amount on the basis of a year of 360 days and actual days elapsed. For example, if the formula for determining interest on a LIBOR loan results in a rate of 6 percent per annum, then the effective interest rate would be 6% × 365/360 = 6.08% per annum. The second method calculates the accruing amount on the basis of a year of 365/366 days and actual days elapsed. This method does not result in any adjustment to per annum rates determined in accordance with the applicable formulae.

The first method just described is the one used in the market for Eurodollar deposits. It is universally used when calculating the interest on LIBOR loans and competitive bid LIBOR loans. It is also customarily applied to competitive bid absolute-rate loans. There is less uniformity in the method used for calculating interest on other types of loans and for calculating accruing fees, since policies are not consistent among lenders.

There is also a third method of calculating interest, although it is more prevalent in bond indentures than in credit agreements. This method calculates interest on the basis of a year consisting of twelve 30-day months. If the stated interest rate is 6 percent per annum, then the rate for any calendar month would be 6% × 1/12 = 0.5%, regardless of how many days there actually are in that month (28, 29, 30, or 31). This method results in the same amount of interest being payable over an entire year as would result from the application of the second method (i.e., a year of 365/366 days), but it results in a "distortion" for any individual month with other than 30 days.

Accrual Conventions

When calculating interest and fees, one final overarching principle should be borne in mind. If a loan is made on a Monday and repaid on Tuesday, for what day is interest payable? Stated another way, if the base rate is 6.00 percent on Monday and 6.25 percent on Tuesday, what is the interest rate on the loan? Market convention is that interest (with the exception of that on intraday loans, which are beyond the scope of this chapter) is charged for the day on which the loan is made and each day thereafter that it is outstanding, but *not* for the day on which it is repaid. In this example, therefore, interest would be payable at 6.00 percent. Fees are calculated on a similar basis.

BUSINESS DAY CONVENTIONS

The definition of "business day" in any credit agreement will typically have two components. First, it will set out a general rule as to what constitutes a business day in the jurisdiction in which the administrative agent is located. Second, if LIBOR loans are to be available, it will lay out the rules applicable for determining LIBOR business days. The definition of business day will determine notice periods for borrowings and prepayments and other actions to be taken under the agreement, and will also determine when loans are to be made available or payments to be made. Loans will, for example, be made and repaid only on business days.

In a New York–law agreement, the general rule will state that a business day is any day other than a day on which banks are required or authorized to close. Note that this is *not* equivalent to days on which the stock exchanges are open (the approach customarily seen in bond indentures), nor will it include Saturdays. Even though many banks may be open on Saturdays, they are in fact authorized to close, so Saturdays, under the definition, will not constitute business days. Days upon which banks are authorized to close may happen unexpectedly if, for example, there is a blackout or some other disaster and the governor issues an order that banks are authorized to close. Sometimes a borrower will push to have the business day definition specify the jurisdiction in which it is located, so that, for example, the base definition will consist of New York and Kentucky business days. Administrative agents generally resist this approach because of the complications it creates when determining LIBOR business days.

If the credit agreement includes LIBOR borrowings, the second part of the definition will provide that, insofar as it relates to LIBOR, the term will refer to any New York business day (as determined in accordance with the general rule) that is *also* a day on which dealings in dollar deposits (or other relevant currency) are carried out in the London interbank market. Thus the typical notice period for a LIBOR loan (three days) will need to allow for three full New York and London business days. Thus, a request for a LIBOR borrowing made on a Thursday where the Friday is a holiday in New York and the Monday is a holiday in London will result in the borrowing's not being available until Thursday of the following week.

LENDING OFFICES

Lenders (at least bank lenders) have traditionally specified different "lending offices" for different classes of loans. When the LIBOR market first developed, banks almost uniformly specified a domestic office for base rate loans and nondomestic offices for LIBOR loans. Most credit agreements now give lenders the flexibility to use whatever lending offices they choose. Thus, a typical provision would allow each lender at its option to make a loan through any domestic or foreign branch or affiliate of the lender, as specified by the lender. Lenders have a variety of internal considerations (including income tax issues and internal regulatory concerns, among others) that may lead them to elect to fund LIBOR loans from offices outside of the United States.

YIELD PROTECTION

Yield protection clauses, as the name implies, are intended to protect the yield to the lender from making a loan to the borrower. With some exceptions (the taxes clause being the principal one), they are designed to address yield issues as they relate to LIBOR loans. Yield protection clauses do not protect base rate loans, the theory being that changes affecting the underlying cost of base rate loans can generally be passed on to borrowers immediately by the relevant institution changing its prime rate.

The focus of yield protection clauses on LIBOR borrowings is a product of how LIBOR loans are (nominally) funded. As described earlier, the theory underlying a LIBOR loan is that a bank takes in a deposit for a relatively short term (say, three or six months) in London and lends the proceeds of the deposit to its customer for a longer term (say, five or seven years). The interest rate on the loan will simply be the sum of the interest paid by the lender on its deposit *plus* an interest margin. LIBOR will be adjusted every three or six months as deposits are renewed or "rolled over" by the lender in London to maintain the loan outstanding to its customer, and any change in pricing (whether higher or lower) will be passed on to the customer. Hence LIBOR loans are, in essence, a cost-plus loan product.

When the LIBOR market first developed, this practice was nearly universally employed by banks that made LIBOR loans. It is described as "match funding," i.e., the funding for a loan is "matched" to a deposit. Today, with the LIBOR market having developed to the point where many tens of billions of deposits are traded each day, few banks will match fund. Nonbank lenders will not in any event match fund because they do not take deposits. Nevertheless, the principle of match funding still lives in the yield protection clauses of credit agreements as a way of protecting the lenders against unexpected events during the term of a LIBOR deposit that would adversely affect their ability to make, maintain, and earn money from LIBOR loans.

In decades past, yield protection clauses were the source of long, agonizing negotiations between borrowers and lenders. In recent years, the language has become more settled. The LSTA's Model Credit Agreement Provisions include market-standard yield protection clauses. Although yield protection clauses can vary widely, they almost always consist of the following provisions and are included in credit agreements even though (apart from breakfunding) the number of times that lenders have invoked the clauses since the creation of the LIBOR market can probably be counted on one hand. Lenders remain convinced that the potential damage to them from omitting the clause far outweighs any detriment to requiring borrowers to cover lenders for unknown costs if a yield protection event were ever to occur.

Increased Costs

An early concern of lenders was that the cost of a deposit taken into their London branches to provide funds for a loan might change during the term of the deposit by reason of a change in law, such as through the imposition of a tax, a new reserve, or some other regulatory requirement. The increased costs clause of a credit agreement was therefore invented to protect the lender against this risk (again, consistent with the cost-plus assumptions of LIBOR loans) by allowing it to pass on those costs to the borrower in the event of a "regulatory change" or a "change in law." Those terms were defined broadly to pick up not only changes in law, rules, and regulations, but also requests, guidelines, or directives from a government authority "whether or not" these have the force of law. The latter was intended to address the approach taken by central banks (particularly the Bank of England) of using "persuasion" to induce banks to take action (such as maintaining reserves) rather than setting out the requirements in explicit published regulations. "Costs" for these purposes are not limited to out-of-pocket cash costs, but also include reductions in the return for a lender (as would be the case if it were required to maintain reserves against a deposit that funds the loan).

This clause generally provides that the amount of the cost incurred by a lender (and which it will therefore pass on to a borrower) is within the good faith determination of the lender (or, alternatively, that it will be conclusive "absent manifest error," or words of similar import). The clause may, in some cases, require the lender to deliver supporting calculations for its determination. However, given the difficulty for an institution with many hundreds of millions (or billions) of offshore deposits with different tenors, located in different legal jurisdictions and in different currencies and funding many different loans, the general consensus is that it is not appropriate to require a detailed analysis of the cost determined by the lender for reimbursement from a borrower. Reliance on the lender's acting in good faith is generally deemed sufficient.

Sometimes a borrower will attempt to limit a lender's ability to seek compensation from the borrower to situations in which the lender is seeking similar compensation in similar amounts from other customers "similarly situated." Apart from the difficulty of determining what "similarly situated" means, the general consensus is that requiring "equal" or "similar" or "comparable" treatment among customers is not appropriate. It is also nonstandard. If incorporated, it puts a lender in the difficult position when a yield protection event occurs of having to review potentially hundreds or thousands of agreements to determine whether there are individual variances that require different steps to be taken vis-à-vis different borrowers.

Another issue generally addressed in the clause will be the ability of a lender to seek retroactive reimbursement for increased costs. One concern that lenders have is that, because of the difficulty of working through the implications of regulatory changes for an institution with a loan portfolio in the billions, they may discover after the fact that an increased cost event has occurred. A common resolution is to allow the lender to seek recovery for costs for some retroactive period from, say, 90 to 180 days prior to the effectiveness of the regulatory change. Costs incurred prior to that period will be solely for the account of the lender.

Capital Costs

Capital costs are usually dealt with in a clause separate from the general increased costs clause (the LSTA Model Credit Agreement Provisions are consistent with this approach) because the provision seeks reimbursement for costs suffered not only by the lender, but also by the lender's holding company (capital adequacy rules often apply at the bank holding company level). Capital costs are an example of costs that reduce the rate of return for a lender by requiring it to increase the amount of capital to be maintained by the lender or its holding company against its assets (including, of course, the loan). Capital costs are imposed on any class of loans made by the lender; they are not confined to LIBOR-based loans.

Eurodollar Disaster

Another concern when banks first started making LIBOR-based loans was the possibility that some "disaster" could occur in the LIBOR market that would result in the lenders being unable to obtain LIBOR quotes at the end of an interest period, or that, although they could obtain quotes, those quotes would not adequately reflect the cost to the lenders of making the loan. The solution was the so-called Eurodollar disaster clause, under which the borrower's ability to obtain LIBOR loans would be suspended until the "disaster" was over. The clause is normally triggered in one of two ways: *first*, if the administrative agent determines that rates are not available in the Eurodollar market in the relevant amounts or for the relevant maturities, and, *second*, if the required lenders of the relevant tranche make the determination that the rates quoted in the LIBOR market do not adequately cover the cost to the lenders of obtaining funds to make the loans. If the credit agreement contemplates both base rate and LIBOR pricing, the clause will simply require that any LIBOR loan requested by the borrower be made instead as a base rate loan. If the credit agreement does not provide for base rate pricing (as would normally be the case with offshore borrowers), then the clause will contain a detailed procedure for the borrower and the lender to negotiate a "substitute basis" upon which to price the loans. Absent agreement within a defined period of time, the borrower would be required to repay the loan.

Illegality

With some historical justification, when the LIBOR loan market first developed, lenders were concerned that making or continuing a loan based upon LIBOR could be made illegal. The fear was that a regulatory change could give rise to more than just increased costs; it might involve a flat prohibition against pricing loans based upon offshore deposit taking. One area of concern arose in the late 1960s when Interest Equalization Regulations were issued by President Nixon. It was feared at the time that the newly developing LIBOR market would be perceived as circumventing these regulations and, thus, that the U.S. government might prohibit U.S. banks from making LIBOR loans. Under the illegality clause, if a regulator outlaws pricing based on LIBOR, either interest will be shifted to a different interest rate (the base rate or a substitute basis as described in the section "Disaster"), or the borrower will be obligated to repay the loan immediately. Of course the illegality would probably still arise if the borrower were unable to repay, but at least the lender could argue that it had done everything possible to adhere to the law and that any violation by it was solely attributable to a pesky borrower in breach of its agreement.

Notwithstanding all this, there is an emerging consensus that, given the tremendous growth in international financial markets since LIBOR loans were first created, it is almost inconceivable that a government or regulator would declare LIBOR-based loans unlawful in the manner contemplated by the clause. As a consequence, some credit agreements today no longer include an illegality clause.

Breakfunding

Under the theory of match funding, if a borrower repays a LIBOR loan in the middle of an interest period (which notionally corresponds to the term of a deposit taken in by the lender), the lender will be deprived of an interest stream (namely, the one on the loan) necessary to service the payments that the lender must make to its depositor at the end of the deposit term. Similarly, a borrower might request a LIBOR loan and then, for whatever reason, decline to take down the loan. The lender will have obtained a deposit in London two business days prior to the anticipated borrowing date and yet find itself in the position of having the deposit proceeds not being put to work. In either case, the lender would be forced to find an alternative use spanning the balance of the deposit term for the money repaid to it by the borrower. The alternative use might yield a lower interest coupon than the amount that was to be paid by the borrower.

The breakfunding clause is intended to address the possibility that the source of funds for interest on the deposit (namely, the anticipated interest payments to be made by the borrower on its loan) is "broken" in the middle of the deposit term. The breakfunding clause will, in essence, allow the lender to be compensated for any shortfall between the amount of interest that would have accrued on the loan (usually not including the margin) for the balance of the interest period and the amount of interest that the lender is able to earn by reinvesting the prepaid proceeds into alternative assets.

Breakfunding clauses take two basic forms. One form allows the lender in its good faith to specify the cost suffered by it through having to redeploy the repaid loan proceeds. This approach is consistent with that used in the increased costs clause in that no detailed mathematical calculation of the loss to the lender will be made. The clause will customarily permit the lender, in determining its loss, to assume that it funded each LIBOR loan by taking in a deposit in the London interbank market in an amount, and for a term, equal to the interest period for the LIBOR loan. In other words, the lender shall be deemed to have match-funded all of its LIBOR loans.

Another form of the clause simply sets out an arithmetical formula for calculating the minimum amount that should be payable to the lender as a result of the breakfunding event. The formula assumes match funding, but because the math is explicit, a statement confirming the assumption is not express. The formula also assumes that the lender reinvests the funds in the LIBOR market. Sometimes the shortfall payable to the lender will include the interest margin, but in most cases, the borrower is required to make up for the difference in LIBOR only for the two periods, i.e., the original interest period and the remaining portion of the interest period following the breakfunding event.

An illustration of the calculation may be useful. Assume that a $1,000,000 LIBOR loan has a six-month interest period and a rate of 6 percent, consisting of LIBOR for the interest period of 5 percent and an interest margin of 1 percent. Assume next that the borrower prepays the $1,000,000 in full at the fourth month. Finally, assume that at the time of the prepayment, LIBOR for a two-month interest period is 4.5 percent. The lender will be unable to reinvest the funds at a sufficient rate to cover the hypothetical six-month deposit that it took in to fund the loan. The borrower will, therefore, be required to pay breakfunding of $833, which represents 5 percent *minus* 4.5 percent, or the difference in LIBOR rates, *times* $1,000,000 (the amount prepaid) *times* 2/12 (the number of months of the original interest period remaining *divided by* the number of months in a year). If the lender were to be compensated for the loss of interest margin as well, the amount payable by the borrower would increase to $2,500, which represents (6 percent *minus* 4.5 percent) *times* $1,000,000 *times* 2/12.

Taxes

As noted previously, the taxes clause is not confined to compensating a lender for LIBOR-related costs. Rather, the clause is intended to protect the lender against taxes that would reduce its yield on the loan. Net income taxes (and comparable taxes, however denominated) imposed by the jurisdiction of the lender's organization, its principal office, or the lending office for the loan would be excluded. Certain other exclusions for taxes resulting from lender activities unrelated to the specific loan are sometimes also negotiated. The primary concern relates to taxes that the borrower would be required to withhold from the stated interest that it would otherwise pay to the lender. The typical approach of the taxes clause is to require the borrower to "gross up" the interest payment so that the lender realizes an amount in cash that, after deduction for the withheld taxes (including further withholding taxes on the gross-up payments), is equal to the stated interest on the loan.

An illustration of this may be helpful. Assume that interest on a loan made by a bank located in the United States is equal to 6 percent. Assume also that the borrower is in a jurisdiction that imposes a withholding tax of 30 percent on interest payments made to the United States. Absent a gross-up, the lender will receive only 4.2 percent per annum on its loan, i.e., (100 percent *minus* 30 percent) *times* 6 percent. The taxes clause will, accordingly, gross up the interest payment to an amount equal to 8.571 percent (i.e., 6 percent *divided by* 0.70). When the 30 percent withholding is then applied to the 8.571 percent, the lender will receive 6 percent (8.571 percent *times* 0.70 = 6.0 percent) in cash.

The lender in this situation may, of course, be entitled to claim a foreign tax credit on its U.S. tax return for the amount withheld from its grossed-up interest (the full amount of which, i.e., the 8.571 percent, is included in gross income). Typically, lenders resist agreeing to reimburse the borrower for the benefit derived from foreign tax credits because of practical and administrative difficulties in tracing credits to particular loans. There is also a certain rough justice to this because borrowers typically refuse to cover the lender's additional net income taxes resulting from the payment of the larger grossed-up amount (a so-called spiral gross-up or super-gross-up), even when the lender cannot obtain benefit from the additional foreign tax credits (for example, because the lender otherwise already has more credits than it can use, given the complex limitations that apply).

A lender may also in the future receive a refund from the foreign jurisdiction of the 2.571 percent paid to that jurisdiction if more than the amount required by law was withheld. The taxes clause may provide that if a refund is received from the foreign jurisdiction that, in the discretion of the lender, can be associated with the loan made to the borrower, then the borrower will be entitled to receive an amount equal to the proceeds of the refund (net of any related expenses incurred).

The taxes clause will protect both domestic lenders that make loans to foreign borrowers and foreign lenders that make loans to domestic borrowers. The rate of withholding by a country (the United States is no different on this score) is usually determined on a country-by-country basis and is dependent upon whether the payor country and the recipient country have a tax treaty. Thus, interest paid by a U.K. borrower to a U.S. lender is generally not subject to withholding. In contrast, interest payments by a Canadian borrower to a U.S. lender are subject (with some exceptions) to withholding at a rate of 15 percent.

If loans by a particular lender to a borrower are going to result in withholding, the borrower probably will not allow that lender into the syndicate. Most taxes clauses, therefore, provide that a lender is entitled to be grossed up only if at the inception of the loan (i.e., closing or the date on which the lender acquired a loan by assignment), the lender is exempt from withholding. The clause thus becomes, in effect, merely a change in law provision, designed to address the circumstance of new taxes or changes in treaties. Of course, the borrower may sometimes have no choice if its jurisdiction does not have in place relevant tax treaties that reduce the withholding rate to zero. A borrower located in such a jurisdiction may have to gross up lenders at inception (not merely based on a change in law) as a cost of obtaining financing.

INTEREST SAVINGS CLAUSES

Many credit agreements will contain a so-called interest savings clause. The provision addresses what happens if, for any reason, the stated rate of interest on the loans exceeds the maximum rate (the usury rate) allowed under applicable law. This could happen if the interest rate under a credit agreement were higher than the permitted usury limit in the borrower's jurisdictions. In many cases, for example, usury laws will treat up-front fees as "interest." In such a case, if on syndication the borrower paid a 1 percent up-front fee to each lender and the initial loan interest rate is 10 percent, the actual stated rate of interest should the loan be repaid in 30 days would be 22 percent.

Some usury laws, if violated, can have Draconian effects on lenders. Lenders might, for example, be required to return *all* interest (not just the excess interest) or even a multiple of the interest paid. Fortunately none of this is a problem under New York law, which in essence provides that any loan of $2,500,000 or more, or any loan made under a facility providing for aggregate loans of $2,500,000 or more, is not subject to New York's usury limitations. A question may remain as to whether the New York rule applies (even for a New York–law credit agreement) if the borrower is not located in New York. Although interest limitations for banks that are federally regulated are determined by the jurisdiction from which a loan is made, this is not necessarily the case for nonbank lenders.

To deal with these concerns, an interest savings clause will provide that any interest paid on the loans in excess of that permitted under applicable law will be deemed to have been a prepayment of principal and not a payment of interest. There are few court decisions confirming that this approach works, but it has developed as the market-standard solution to the usury problem.

Part 3. Making the Borrower Repay the Loan: Amortization and Maturity

PAYMENTS GENERALLY

Immediately Available Funds

Credit agreements will almost universally require that payments be made (and loans advanced) in so-called immediately available funds. Immediately available funds are funds that are immediately available in the place of payment. Payment by check would generally not be in immediately available funds, since, before the recipient can have access to the funds represented by the check, they must first be collected (which may take several business days, depending upon where the bank on which the check has been drawn is located). Payments made by the borrower directing that the administrative agent debit an account of the borrower at the administrative agent itself will be immediately available for this purpose.

Time of Payment

Credit agreements generally require that payments be made at a particular time on the date of payment. Absent specification of a time, a borrower would be able to make payment at any time up to the close of business. Receiving funds so late in the day would probably make it impossible for the lenders to reinvest those funds. It would also probably be too late for investment by the administrative agent if, in reliance on the clawback clause, discussed in the section "The Clawback Clause" in Part 8, "Keeping Peace Among the Lenders," it has forwarded funds to the lenders. Not designating a specific time may also confuse the setoff rights of the lenders by making it unclear when during the day the borrower first goes into default.

Extensions for Nonbusiness Days

Under New York law (General Construction Law, Article 2, §25), if a payment is due on a day that is not a business day (such as a Sunday), the payment will automatically be extended to the next succeeding business day (i.e., Monday), but (unless the parties have otherwise agreed) no interest will be payable for the period of the extension. Credit agreements are almost universally structured so that payments are due on business days to avoid this rule. Nevertheless, since nonbusiness days can occur unexpectedly (see the discussion in the section "Business Day Conventions" in Part 2, "Making Money off the Loan"), credit agreements will also state that if any extension should ever occur, interest will be payable during the extension.

SCHEDULED REPAYMENT

Lenders ultimately want their loans to be repaid, and the credit agreement will, accordingly, always include a maturity date. The exact date is determined by negotiation, and there is no general custom as to what the maturity should be, except that revolving credit and A loan tranches (discussed in the section "Credit Variants" in Part 1, "Making the Loan") will almost never extend beyond seven years and B loan tranches will rarely extend beyond eight years. Additionally, B loan tranches will nearly always mature at least three months after any revolving credit or A loan tranche set out in the same credit agreement.

   Although revolving credit commitments can be repayable in installments by providing for reductions in accordance with a commitment reduction schedule, in most cases a revolving credit commitment will have a bullet maturity, i.e., the entire commitment will be available until maturity, and then the whole amount will terminate. By contrast, both A loan and B loan tranches will invariably provide for installments of principal to be paid prior to maturity. As noted earlier (see the section "Credit Variants" in Part 1, "Making the Loan"), the installments for a B loan tranche will be nominal until the final year; the installments for an A loan tranche will be larger, so that the loan is substantially repaid by the time it matures.

ADVANCING THE MATURITY DATE

In the "Commitments" section in Part 1, "Making the Loan," we described the so-called accordion feature that allows commitments to be increased at the option of the borrower (assuming that it finds willing lenders). To confuse things, bankers also use the term *accordion* to describe a quite different feature whereby the maturity date for a loan will be advanced because of an intervening bond maturity. An example might arise when a loan is made with, say, a seven-year maturity, while a large subordinated bond indenture, scheduled to mature in five years, is outstanding. As a credit matter, most lenders will find this situation unacceptable. Of course, the expectation of the borrower will be that it will refinance the bonds in advance of their maturity, so that no conflict between the lenders and the bondholders will ever occur. To ensure that the borrower in fact completes the refinancing in a timely fashion, the credit agreement may provide that, if the bonds are still outstanding on the date six months prior to their maturity, the maturity date for the loans will automatically be advanced to that date. Hence, the "accordion."

364-DAY FACILITIES

One very common category of credit agreement is the so-called 364-day facility. These facilities originate from Federal Reserve capital rules to the effect that banks are not required to hold capital against any commitment having a term of one year or less. A lender can, therefore, offer more advantageous financing to borrowers because the cost to the lender is lower. Although Federal Reserve rules stipulate that the zero capital requirement applies for any facility of one year or less, the market practice is for these facilities always to expire one day earlier than a full year, i.e., on the 364th day.

364-day facilities are made available primarily to investment grade borrowers and will almost always provide a mechanism for extension of the facility at its expiration. The Federal Reserve has issued only very general guidance as to how such extensions must be effected in order that the facility not lose zero-capital treatment. Perhaps as a consequence, the market practice is to lay out in the credit agreement explicit extension procedures by which the lenders can extend their commitments. The Federal Reserve recognizes (and the customary extension procedures reflect) that from the standpoint of business practicality, a borrower will want to know prior to the very expiration of the commitments whether or not they have been extended. The LSTA Model Credit Agreement Provisions include language that has been approved by the Federal Reserve for extensions of 364-day facilities. Under this language, lenders are allowed to commit to an extension as early as 30 days prior to the expiration date, even though the resulting commitment could have a term of 395 days. With certain exceptions, the Federal Reserve will also allow the borrower to request the extension as early as 45 days prior to the expiration date.

STRIPPED LOAN FACILITIES

"Stripped" loan facilities are largely a historical anachronism, but a few credit agreements may from time to time still adopt this format. Basically, in a stripped loan facility, each loan matures at the expiration of its interest period (base rate loans will be given an "interest period" of 30 or 90 days). If the borrower wants to continue a loan, it must reborrow the principal at the end of the interest period. This works fairly easily in the context of a revolving credit facility. For a term loan facility, the typical approach requires revisions. In a normal (not stripped) term loan facility, the commitments will expire after the loans are made. In a stripped term loan facility, the commitments continue until the final maturity date so that loans can be rolled over at the end of each interest period. The commitments would be structured so as not to unintentionally convert the term loan facility into a revolving credit facility, usually by having any unused term loan commitment automatically terminate.

Borrowers generally do not like stripped loan facilities because they are required to satisfy the truth of representations and the absence of default conditions in order to obtain each rollover of a loan, although when the stripped loan concept was in use, certain representations and defaults were excluded if the aggregate exposure under the rollover did not increase. Lenders initially adopted the stripped loan structure in the belief that it afforded accounting benefits when loans were assigned or participated on a short-term basis.

VOLUNTARY PREPAYMENTS

The general rule under New York law is that a loan may not be prepaid without the consent of the lender. The theory is that the lender has contracted for a loan of a particular term, and that it would constitute a breach of that contract were the borrower to be allowed to pay early. Credit agreements will nearly always expressly override this general rule and allow the borrower to prepay loans at any time at its option. There are exceptions, such as with respect to competitive bid loans (most credit agreements will not permit those to be prepaid), and, of course, any payment of a LIBOR loan prior to the expiration of its interest period will need to be accompanied by a breakfunding payment (described in the section "Yield Protection" in Part 2, "Making Money off the Loan"). In contrast, the typical bond indenture or private placement often will not allow prepayments for the first three or four years, and will allow them thereafter only if a premium is paid.

In the case of the prepayment of a loan that is otherwise payable in installments, the prepayment provision will address how the prepayment is to be applied to the installments. Absent specification, under New York law the borrower would be free to apply the prepayment to whichever installments it chose. Lenders will prefer to have prepayments applied to installments in inverse order (which is to say, starting with the last installment and then working forward), so that the credit exposure is shortened and the borrower remains subject to the discipline of having to make the regular agreed-upon installments of principal initially contemplated by the parties. Borrowers will prefer the opposite, namely, that prepayments be applied to installments in the direct order of maturity. Some agreements will compromise on the two extremes by stipulating that prepayments are applied to installments ratably. Other twists are also seen, such as applying prepayments first to the next four installments and then ratably or in inverse order. There are no limits here to what the parties can negotiate.

Another allocation issue that credit agreements may from time to time address is between loans within a particular tranche. This might occur, for example, if the loans outstanding under a tranche were broken into three classes, base rate loans, LIBOR loans with an interest period expiring in a week, and other LIBOR loans with an interest period expiring in four months. To minimize breakfunding costs, the borrower will of course want to prepay the base rate loans first and then the LIBOR loans with the interest period expiring in one week. Credit agreements will invariably allow the borrower to pick and choose among these loans to minimize its costs, since the lenders are essentially indifferent as to which loan is repaid. Sometimes, however, the credit agreement will lock in this type of allocation by an express statement that base rate loans are paid first and then LIBOR loans are paid in the order in which interest periods expire.

Voluntary prepayments may usually be made only upon notice given by the borrower to the administrative agent (who then advises the appropriate lenders). For a LIBOR loan, the notice period is typically three business days; for a base rate loan, the notice period will normally be one day in advance and in some cases on the day of the prepayment. A notice, once given, will be irrevocable because it is presumed that the lenders, in reliance on the notice, will have committed to redeploy the funds to be repaid to an alternative asset (though a borrower will often be allowed to issue a revocable notice of prepayment in connection with an anticipated refinancing).

As with the making of loans, prepayments will be required to be in certain minimum amounts (and sometimes multiples in excess of those minimums) to ease the administrative burden of dealing with small funds transfers.

MANDATORY PREPAYMENTS

Mandatory prepayments, as the term indicates, *mandate* that the borrower prepay loans upon the occurrence of specified events. Mandatory prepayments should be contrasted with the corresponding requirements in bond indentures, where a required prepayment (which is normally confined to asset sales and changes of control) will be structured as an "offer to prepay" made to all bondholders rather than as an obligation that bonds be prepaid or redeemed. There are at least two substantive differences between the credit agreement approach and the bond indenture approach. First, in a credit agreement, the prepayment is usually required to be made immediately (or virtually so). In a bond indenture, the process can take up to 90 or more days, with the issuer being given 30 or more days in which to make an offer, the bondholders being given another 30 or more days to accept the offer, and the issuer being granted yet more time in which to make payment. The second major difference is that in a credit agreement, the lenders (with the exception for B loan tranches, as described later in this part in "Prepayment Opt-Outs") will not be given the opportunity to opt out of a prepayment. In the bond indenture context, whether or not a particular bondholder is prepaid is purely a function of whether it elects to be prepaid by accepting the offer to prepay.

Revolving Clean-Downs

In a revolving credit facility, a clean-down requirement would force the borrower, typically for a period of 30 days during each calendar year, to have no outstandings under the revolving credit commitments. This type of mandatory prepayment would customarily be inserted for a seasonal business, where, if its business is successful, a borrower should not require any borrowings during a particular time of year (such as, in a retail business, during the months of January or February following an intense holiday sale season). The prepayment is in effect a control against adverse developments in the borrower's business.

Borrowing Base

Borrowing bases are typically found only in secured agreements with revolving credit facilities. If the credit agreement has a borrowing base, the availability of revolving credit loans will be tied to an agreed valuation (the "borrowing base") of the collateral security. Hence, if, giving effect to a borrowing, the amount of the loans and letters of credit exceeds the borrowing base, the lenders will not be obligated to honor the borrowing request. Similarly, if the amount of the borrowing base falls below the aggregate outstanding loans and letters of credit, the borrower would be required to immediately repay a sufficient amount of the loans to eliminate the shortfall.

Borrowing bases, which occur primarily in so-called asset-based deals, are usually structured around the value of easily liquidated collateral, such as accounts receivable and inventory. The percentage "advance rates" to be lent against each type of collateral will be determined by the lender after extensive analysis of the assets in the borrowing base. The typical borrowing base definition will apply the advance rates only to "eligible" accounts receivable and inventory to improve further the chances that the borrowing base, when liquidated, will be sufficient to repay the secured loans. The prepayment has an effect very similar to that of the clean-down prepayment described previously. Thus, in a seasonal business, when the borrower is flush with cash (and therefore when its receivables and inventory are relatively low), shrinkage in the borrowing base will force it to reduce its outstanding loan balance.

Asset Sales

The asset sale prepayment will force the borrower to prepay loans upon any sale of assets that is out of the ordinary course of business and, usually, is over an agreed-upon threshold. The asset sale prepayment is often redundant of the asset sale covenant in that a sale that requires a prepayment is frequently also a sale that must first be consented to by the lenders. As a consequence, lenders are almost always in a position to impose conditions on their consent to a sale (such as requiring prepayment), whether or not the credit agreement incorporates a mandatory prepayment. See the discussion in the "Fundamental Changes" section of Part 5, "Monitoring the Loan."

Typically, the asset sale prepayment will also allow the borrower a period within which to reinvest the proceeds before being required to make the prepayment. The reinvestment will normally be required to be made into replacement or equivalent assets, although the covenant will sometimes permit the reinvestment to be applied to "capital expenditures" generally. See the discussion regarding capital expenditures in the "Capital Expenditures" section in Part 5, "Monitoring the Loan." Lenders frequently grant the borrower up to a year to make a reinvestment. Only if a reinvestment does not occur within that time frame will the borrower be required to make a prepayment. In highly leveraged, fully secured deals, the borrower will either be required to pledge the proceeds with the administrative agent (or collateral agent) pending reinvestment, or be required to apply the proceeds to revolving credit loans until they are borrowed to make a reinvestment.

One of the things that lenders must address when drafting asset sale prepayment provisions is that the covenant not be inconsistent with the asset sale provisions of any outstanding bond indentures. For example, if the bond indenture specifies a reinvestment period of 180 days, the credit agreement will not want to specify a longer period; otherwise the bonds would conceivably be paid before the loans. Similarly, if the bond indenture specifies dollar thresholds over which prepayments are to be made, the dollar thresholds in the credit agreement should not be higher.

The asset sale prepayment will customarily be required to be in the amount of the net proceeds of the sale. "Net proceeds" will be defined as all cash proceeds received by the borrower net of transaction costs (including transfer taxes) and typically also net of income taxes that the borrower anticipates having to pay by reason of the sale. The borrower is normally allowed to estimate these taxes in "good faith," even though there may be potential for abuse in that regard. Net proceeds may also include promissory notes or deferred installments received in connection with a sale, as and when the cash realized on the notes or installments is actually remitted to the borrower. The fundamental changes covenant (see the "Fundamental Changes" section of Part 5, "Monitoring the Loan"), however, will often control the amount of noncash consideration that the borrower can receive. This is another instance in which the credit agreement will not want to be looser than any outstanding bond indentures.

Casualty Events

Somewhat akin to the asset sale prepayment, a casualty event prepayment will require the borrower to prepay the loans, generally out of insurance or condemnation proceeds, in the event that property (over a threshold value) is destroyed or is taken by a governmental entity. The prepayment will normally allow the borrower a period, again similar to that for the asset sale prepayment, in which to reinvest the proceeds of the casualty event into replacement assets.

Debt and Equity Issuances

In highly leveraged deals, or in transactions in which the credit agreement is in effect a bridge to a bond or equity offering, the agreement will include a debt or equity prepayment requirement. In agreements with both types of prepayments, the borrower will often be afforded greater flexibility to keep a portion of the proceeds of an equity issuance than of a debt issuance. It is thus not uncommon to see the borrower be obligated to apply to the prepayment of the loans 100 percent of the proceeds of a debt issuance, but only 50 percent of the proceeds of an equity issuance.

Excess Cash Flow

Lenders may ask to receive earlier repayment if a borrower is doing well. The cash flow prepayment is one device to accomplish this. It stipulates that some percentage (the number is strictly up for negotiation, although 50 percent and 75 percent are common) of the borrower's excess cash flow will be applied to prepay the loans. "Excess cash flow" will be defined in such a way as to capture the "excess" cash being thrown off by the borrower's business. Thus, the definition will typically start with EBITDA and then subtract interest, scheduled principal payments, capital expenditures, scheduled dividend payments, and taxes, to name a few items. It may also pick up changes in working capital, so that if working capital increases from the beginning to the end of the year, excess cash flow is reduced and, conversely, if working capital decreases, excess cash flow increases.

One of the issues that this kind of prepayment provision should address (not all credit agreements do) is how voluntary prepayments of term loans should be treated. Logically, if the borrower is flush with cash in July because the first six months have been strong, the lenders will want the borrower to prepay the term loans immediately (there may be no revolving credit loans outstanding at the time). The excess cash flow prepayment is not typically required to be made more than once a year, and then only when the audited financial statements are delivered. So, in this example, the borrower would not be obligated to make a prepayment until the end of March in the year following, nine months after July. The solution is to induce the borrower to prepay in July by giving it full dollar-for-dollar credit against the excess cash flow prepayment that would be required to be made in March of the year following. Thus the borrower will not have a disincentive to make a prepayment in July because it knows that what it pays in July will reduce its March obligation on a dollar-for-dollar basis.

Change of Control

Credit agreements vary as to whether a change of control should be an event of default or a mandatory prepayment. Since the borrower may regard such an event as being outside its control, many borrowers prefer that it be a prepayment event rather than a default. By contrast, the near-uniform practice in bond indentures is to require the issuer to make an offer to prepay upon the occurrence of a change of control rather than have it trigger a default. The change of control prepayment (or default) derives from the fundamental principle that a lender wants to "know its customer," including who ultimately controls that customer. If the customer should change, or if control of the customer should devolve upon a new entity, the lenders may want the right to exit the facility.

In the case of a privately owned company, the lenders will typically require that all or a majority of the borrower's stock continue to be owned by the individuals, financial sponsors, or companies that own the borrower at the inception of the facility. The lenders will trust the current owners' integrity, competence, strategy, policies, and management style and will not want them replaced. In some cases, the "change of control" definition may simply require that voting power be retained; in other cases, the lenders may require that the existing owners continue to have sufficient "skin in the game" and thus also trigger the default upon a sale of nonvoting stock. (If the sponsor or investor has already realized its target return on the investment, it may have less incentive to support the borrower in the future.)

In the case of a public company, the definition will be triggered if any person or group obtains control by acquiring a percentage of the outstanding shares greater than a negotiated threshold (20 to 30 percent is typical). The assumption is that so long as the borrower's shares are widely held, its character will not change. A change of control in a public company may also be triggered by changes to the board of directors, such as if a majority of the board cease to be "continuing directors" (usually defined as new directors that have been approved by incumbent directors). This might occur if a competing shareholder or group were to attempt to take over the borrower through a proxy fight.

Although the concept of a change of control provision sounds entirely lender-favorable, certain classes of borrowers may actually want a change of control provision to be included in a credit agreement, viewing it as a form of "poison pill"—another hurdle that a potential acquiror of the borrower would need to overcome if it wanted to make a hostile bid for the borrower.

Currency Adjustments in Multicurrency Deals

As with a purely U.S. dollar credit agreement, a credit agreement with a tranche available in both U.S. dollars and one or more other currencies will normally delineate the amount of credit available under the tranche by reference to a U.S. dollar commitment level. Thus, although loans may be available in euro, the credit agreement will typically state that the borrower can borrow euro only up to the U.S. dollar equivalent of, say, U.S. $100,000,000. The credit approvals obtained internally by each lender will then reflect this limit upon their exposure. Of course, if the euro equivalent of U.S. $100,000,000 is borrowed at closing and the euro subsequently increases in value against the U.S. dollar, then the aggregate exposure of the lenders will have effectively been increased. The same mismatch can occur if nondollar letters of credit are issued.

To address this risk, a credit agreement will customarily require a periodic calculation (typically quarterly, but sometimes more frequently) of the aggregate amount of loans and letters of credit under a multicurrency credit agreement, taking into account any fluctuations in currency values. The normal approach is to require a prepayment down to an exposure level equal to 100 percent of the commitments to the extent that the aggregate exposure (the U.S. dollar equivalent of outstanding loans) exceeds 105 percent of the commitments.

In a credit agreement where the only currency available under a particular tranche is a designated foreign currency, these issues do not arise, since it is presumed that the initial credit approval of the lenders was couched in terms of the particular foreign currency.

APPLICATION OF PREPAYMENTS AMONG TRANCHES

In addition to specifying how mandatory prepayments are to be applied to loan installments, the credit agreement will specify how prepayments are to be applied among loan tranches (assuming that there are multiple tranches). The normal approach is to require that prepayments be applied first to the term loan tranches (ratably) and then to revolving credit tranches. This is driven by the borrower's desire not to lose the liquidity afforded by the revolving credit commitments until the term loans have been paid in full.

If the revolving credit commitments provide for letters of credit, the prepayment provisions will also typically specify that revolving credit loans are paid in full first before any prepayment proceeds are applied to provide cover for letters of credit (see the discussion in the next section, "Cover for Letters of Credit").

COVER FOR LETTERS OF CREDIT

As noted in the section "Letters of Credit" in Part 1, "Making the Loan," letters of credit cannot be unilaterally repaid. A letter of credit is an irrevocable undertaking on the part of the issuer owing to a third party, with the borrower being obligated to reimburse the issuer only in the event of a drawing. Since the reimbursement obligation is not payable until the drawing is made, it cannot be paid or prepaid prior to a drawing. To enable letters of credit nevertheless to be "repaid" (or "prepaid" upon a mandatory prepayment event), credit agreements will contemplate that the borrower "cover" its contingent reimbursement obligation by posting cash collateral with the administrative agent in an amount equal to the face amount of the letter of credit. If the facility is being repaid in full, this amount may be a higher percentage of the face amount (102 or 105 percent) in order to also cover future fees and costs. The agreement will typically provide that any posted cash be invested solely in very short-term Treasury securities (though many credit agreements are silent on investment). Because of the negative arbitrage implicit in posting cash in this manner, mandatory prepayment provisions will normally stipulate that all loans are paid in full before cover is posted for any letters of credit.

PREPAYMENT OPT-OUTS

As noted previously, one of the basic differences between the prepayment provisions of a credit agreement and those of a bond indenture is that in the credit agreement, all lenders of a particular tranche will be prepaid, and there is no ability to elect or not elect a prepayment. B loan tranches are one exception to this general rule that has developed in the market. B loan lenders will sometimes be given the right to opt out of a mandatory or optional prepayment if there are A loans outstanding. The monies that would otherwise be applied to the B loans are instead applied to the A loans. Whether B loans are afforded this option is strictly a question for negotiation. Borrowers may resist the lack of flexibility that the opt-out entails for them.

PREPAYMENT PREMIUMS

In addition to any breakfunding payments that may need to be made upon a prepayment (see the discussion in "Breakfunding" in Part 2, "Making Money off the Loan"), in some cases the borrower will also be required to pay an additional fee (a prepayment premium) in a percentage equal to the amount of principal being prepaid. In a bond indenture or private placement, the premiums may start as high as 5 or 6 percent of the amount of the prepayment and descend to zero over a period of years. In a credit agreement, the prepayment premiums, if specified at all, will normally apply only to the B loans, will be in much lower amounts (2 percent descending to 1 percent), and will apply only to prepayments made in the first or second year following the closing. In addition, some agreements provide that a premium is not payable at all unless the source of the prepayment is a refinancing by the borrower with cheaper debt—this approach is a so-called soft call. The theory behind the soft call is that if the borrower is prepaying B loans from the proceeds of an asset sale, earnings, or just cash on hand, it should be free to do so without paying the premium, and that only if the borrower is fleeing to cheaper financing should it be forced to pay a premium.

MULTIPLE BORROWERS

Some credit agreements, rather than having loans made to a single borrower under the guarantee of one or more subsidiaries or parent entities, will provide instead that the loans are deemed to be made to multiple borrowers, with each borrower being jointly and severally obligated to repay all loans. This is sometimes referred to as a "co-borrower arrangement." There is little practical legal difference between having a single borrower with guarantees and having a co-borrower structure, but some believe that the co-borrower structure may provide a slight advantage under fraudulent conveyance rules (see the section "Solvency" in Part 4, "Conditioning the Loan"), in that it may be easier to argue that each co-borrower received the full amount of the loan proceeds. It is unclear, however, whether a bankruptcy court would give much credence to this argument if it can be shown that the proceeds in fact went to a particular borrower or subsidiary.

Part 4. Conditioning the Loan: Conditions Precedent and Representations

CONDITIONS PRECEDENT

The conditions precedent in a credit agreement are in essence a simplified closing list. They specify what the borrower must deliver to the lenders (or the administrative agent), what actions it must take, and what other circumstances must exist in order for credit to be available. Normally the conditions will be broken out into two types: those to be satisfied at closing, and those to be satisfied at both closing and each borrowing thereafter (the latter are the so-called ongoing conditions).

Normally, a majority vote will be required to waive any of the conditions precedent, although some credit agreements will require unanimity for any changes to the closing-date conditions. However, unless the lenders have waived a condition by an appropriate vote, any lender that believes that a condition has not been satisfied is still free to take up a dispute with the borrower; a disagreement with the borrower by one lender will not affect the obligation of any other lender.

The following are some key conditions that are contained in basically every credit agreement.

Execution

The credit agreement (and other related agreements) must be executed by all parties. In rare cases, the parties may gather together in a conference room to sign all relevant documents, but most closings do not occur this way. In practice, most signatures are sent in by telecopy or by scanned e-mail. See the discussion in the section "Electronic Execution" in Part 10, "Understanding the Boilerplate," of the issues raised by telecopied signatures.

Lenders may not be identifiable and commitments may not be allocated until just prior to (or, in some cases, the day of) the closing. This problem is most common where the credit agreement includes a B tranche. A practice that has developed to address this situation is the use of "lender addenda." Lender addenda allow a credit agreement to be executed between the borrower and the administrative agent, with each lender becoming a party to the credit agreement by signing a short lender addendum in which the add-on party agrees to be a "lender" under the credit agreement with a "commitment" in an amount specified in the lender addendum. Delivery of lender addenda is no different in legal concept from returning signed signature pages, except that lender addenda have the advantage of referring to a particular agreement (not always the case with a signature page) and also specifying the amount of the lenders' commitments.

Corporate and Organizational Matters

The borrower must, of course, exist as a legal entity (corporation, limited liability company, partnership, or other creature), and the credit agreement must also be appropriately authorized and duly executed by the borrower. The president of a corporation (or the managing member of a limited liability company or the general partner of a partnership) probably has sufficient authority under general legal principles to bind the borrower, even for a very large financing. However, most credit agreements are not in fact signed by the president, managing member, or general partner, but rather by a treasurer or chief financial officer. In the case of a corporation, execution of an agreement that is "material" to the borrower normally requires board of directors approval, so it is inadvisable in that context to rely just on the "apparent authority" of the president. Similar action may be necessary for execution by a limited liability company or limited partnership.

Accordingly, the conditions precedent should require evidence of authorization. That evidence will normally consist of a certificate by an officer of the borrower, attaching appropriate organizational documents (in the case of a corporation, these would be the certificate of incorporation and bylaws), attaching the relevant board or shareholder resolutions, and setting forth a certificate of incumbency and specimen signatures of the officers that will be executing the credit agreement. Delivery of a false certificate will typically be an event of default. In addition, delivery of a false certificate to a bank could violate the Federal Bank Fraud statute, which makes it a felony to knowingly obtain monies from a bank by means of "false or fraudulent" representations.

Government Approvals

In cases where the credit agreement, or borrowings thereunder, requires government approval, it is customary for the conditions to state expressly that evidence of approval has been delivered to the lenders (usually also supported by a legal opinion). Evidence will normally consist of a copy of the approval certified by an officer of the borrower. A requirement for government approval in the context of domestic credit agreements is infrequent, but it does occur from time to time, such as with respect to borrowings by certain public utilities. It is much more common in the context of non-U.S. borrowers. See the discussion in the later section "Special Conditions Applicable to Non-U.S. Borrowers."

Opinions

It is customary for lenders to require, as a condition to closing, that formal written legal opinions, dated the closing date, be delivered affirming the legality, validity, binding effect, and enforceability (collectively, *enforceability*) of the credit agreement. One opinion is typically rendered by the borrower's legal counsel, addressed to the administrative agent and the lenders, and covering matters such as due organization of the borrower, its power to enter into the financing, its authorization of the transaction, and the like ("corporate" matters), as well as enforceability. Sometimes all or portions of the borrower opinion are given by the borrower's internal counsel. This may be acceptable to the lenders, given that the internal counsel is, in most cases, likely to be closer to the internal authorization process than outside counsel, although the independence of outside counsel is an important countervailing factor that tends to argue for an outside opinion.

A second opinion is generally given by the firm that is identified as legal counsel to the administrative agent or the lead bank, and is typically limited to enforceability. Although the more frequent formulation is that the opinion is rendered by counsel for the administrative agent, stating that the firm is counsel for the lead bank may actually more accurately reflect the realities of the typical role of the counsel.

Legal opinions speak as of their date, and the opining firm has no obligation to update the opinion unless it otherwise agrees to do so.

The required opinions expand and multiply with the circumstances of particular financings. For example, if there are ancillary agreements such as guarantees and security agreements, the closing opinions will cover these as well; and if the parties are in multiple jurisdictions, counsel in each relevant jurisdiction will generally be required to deliver an opinion.

The language of the typical closing opinion is the product of many years of developing custom, and opinion givers endeavor to ensure that the scope and language of their opinions are consistent with customary practice as well as with their internal policies (most law firms have opinion committees that establish what may be said in a closing opinion and what due diligence is required to say it). Among the principal sources of opinion practice today are published reports by New York's "TriBar" Committee, which began its existence as a group formed by three New York bar associations but today includes representatives from a number of states and Canada. Despite the emphasis on customary practice, however, there is still considerable divergence in approach from one law firm to another, and discussion of opinion forms for a particular transaction is often needed.

Typically the proposed forms of legal opinion will be attached to the credit agreement as exhibits. This helps assure that the lenders are aware of their content prior to signing, and provides certainty to the borrower that an opinion in the prescribed form will satisfy the conditions.

In a secured credit facility, an opinion may be required to confirm the creation of the relevant security interests (such a "creation" opinion is regarded as distinct from an opinion that the security agreement is enforceable), and sometimes to confirm the perfection of the security interests (although many firms are reluctant to give perfection opinions, and such opinions generally in any event require a number of exceptions and qualifications). The manner in which a security interest is perfected, and which law governs its perfection, will vary with the kind of collateral involved and various other factors, and the question of perfection of a security interest is not necessarily governed by the same law as determines the enforceability of the credit agreement or even of the security agreement. In general, law firms do not render legal opinions on the priority of a security interest, except in certain limited circumstances (for example, an opinion may be given that the pledgee of certificated securities is, subject to certain assumptions, a "protected purchaser" as that term is defined in Article 8 of the Uniform Commercial Code, an opinion that is equivalent to a first-priority lien opinion).

In many transactions, the legal opinions will cover other specialized matters. For example, an opinion may be required to cover the status of the borrower under the Investment Company Act of 1940, matters relating to the Federal Communications Act, or issues arising under other regulatory statutes.

Legal opinions express legal conclusions and do not generally cover factual matters, such as the accuracy or completeness of financial statements. One exception is the so-called no-litigation opinion, in which the opinion giver confirms that there is no pending or threatened litigation or proceedings against the client. However, recent litigation against law firms alleging negligent misrepresentation is making no-litigation opinions, at least by outside counsel, a rare phenomenon, and many firms will not give them under any circumstances. (So-called negative assurance in 10b–5 opinions in connection with securities transactions and law firm responses to audit letters, each of which may address the question of material litigation, involve considerations that are not present in the typical loan financing, and are beyond the scope of this chapter.)

The rationale for obtaining legal opinions at a credit agreement closing goes beyond giving the lenders a law firm to sue in the event that the conclusions set out in the opinion are incorrect. Delivering an opinion forces the opinion giver to go through a due diligence process that should have the beneficial result of making the conclusions accurate by, for example, forcing any corporate deficiencies to be fixed, clarifying board resolutions, obtaining necessary third-party consents, and the like. It is not enough, in other words, that the opinion giver believes that a legal conclusion is correct; it is more important that the conclusion in fact be correct, and the due diligence required for an opinion helps assure that. There are at least two other reasons for an opinion to be required at closing. First, bank regulators often expect to see an opinion in the loan file. Second, an opinion from the borrower's counsel can be valuable in the event that, at enforcement of the loan, the borrower tries to raise defenses that are addressed by the opinion. For example, a borrower might contend that the transaction had not been properly authorized or that it violated some law or contract; the opinion, in this context, could have significant estoppel value if it covered the same points.

Conditions Relating to Perfection of Collateral

The conditions precedent will require evidence that each security interest granted to the lenders has been perfected, which means in general terms that steps have been taken to give public notice of the security interest. If a security interest is not perfected, it may be set aside if the grantor files for bankruptcy. An unperfected security interest is often regarded as valueless.

Perfection may involve a number of different steps. Security interests in most kinds of personal property collateral (as distinct from real property) may be perfected by filing a simple "financing statement" under the Uniform Commercial Code, normally at a designated central location in the state of organization of the grantor of the collateral. For some kinds of collateral, such as collateral consisting of instruments (such as promissory notes or bankers' acceptances) or certificated securities (such as stock certificates), perfection may also be accomplished by taking possession of the collateral. For certain categories of collateral (such as deposit accounts and letter of credit rights), however, neither of these steps perfects the security interest, and the secured party must take "control"—a technically defined term—of the collateral. Some kinds of personal property collateral are sufficiently related to real estate that a filing in the real estate records is required in order to perfect the lien against competing interests in the real estate; and of course a mortgage (or, as the terminology has it in certain states, a "deed of trust") on real estate must be duly recorded in the real estate records. Lastly, in the case of real estate collateral, title insurance is often obtained (basically, third-party insurance that the mortgage lien has been perfected and ensuring its priority).

The conditions precedent will require evidence that the relevant steps required for perfection have been taken. Even when a security interest has been perfected, the lenders will also concern themselves with the question of priority: a security interest, though perfected, may rank behind an earlier perfected security interest. The conditions precedent will therefore often require evidence that the relevant security interests are "subject to no equal or prior lien or security interest." With respect to collateral perfected by filing, this may be accomplished by conducting a search under the Uniform Commercial Code of the filing records in the relevant jurisdiction or jurisdictions, with a view to determining whether any existing, perfected lien covers the collateral. There is no public record of a security interest perfected by control, so with respect to such security interests, it is necessary to rely upon representations and warranties and certificates of the grantor and third parties.

Promissory Notes

Most credit agreements today are so-called note option deals: promissory notes are not executed to evidence loans under the credit agreement unless a lender requests them. Few lenders actually do, although some banks have a policy that all loans must be evidenced by notes. Some fund investors may under their organizational instruments be required to obtain a note in order to pledge the loans as security for financing being provided to the fund. One potential advantage of obtaining promissory notes is that if they qualify as "instruments for the payment of money only," they entitle the holder to summary enforcement under Section 3213 of the New York Civil Practice Law and Rules (CPLR).

Promissory notes may be somewhat more common in cross-border deals because they may give the lenders an enhanced ability to enforce payment of the loan in the borrower's home jurisdiction. However, in other instances, a promissory note may attract stamp taxes, so whether to obtain a promissory note if the borrower is foreign is normally examined on a case-by-case basis.

In a revolving credit facility, the form of promissory note is typically a so-called grid note. In a grid note, the face of the note will specify a dollar amount that corresponds to the commitment of the lender, but the text of the note will provide that the real amount payable is the aggregate of all the loans actually advanced and outstanding. These are often set forth in a schedule (or grid) attached to the note. To deal with the possibility that a borrower may object to the amount entered on the grid, the credit agreement (and the note) will usually provide that the entries on the grid are "prima facie" accurate or accurate "absent manifest error." This has the effect of shifting to the borrower the burden of establishing that the notations were wrong.

The MAC Condition

The representations in a credit agreement will typically include a material adverse change (MAC) clause. Although there are many possible formulations of the MAC clause, a typical provision might read as follows:

> The Borrower hereby represents and warrants that since [specify date], there has been no material adverse change in the business, condition (financial or otherwise), assets, operations or prospects of the Borrower and its subsidiaries, taken as a whole.

As noted in the section "Ongoing Conditions" later in this part, the continued accuracy of representations will generally be a condition precedent to new loans under a credit agreement. Thus, if a material adverse change has occurred, the MAC representation cannot be truthfully made, and the obligations of the lenders to make new loans would therefore be suspended for so long as the material adverse change continues (unless the condition is waived).

The typical MAC provision tests whether a material adverse change has occurred since a particular date. The date specified is generally the date of the most recent audited financial statements of the borrower delivered to the lenders prior to signing the credit agreement. The audited financials are, of course, the most reliable financial information, forming the basis of the lenders' credit decision to enter into the credit agreement. Referencing this date protects the lenders against both deterioration in the borrower's condition that becomes material over time as well as a single dramatic event that is material by itself. By way of example, if a borrower requests a loan in the fourth year of a five-year credit agreement, whether it could satisfy the material adverse change condition would commonly be determined by comparing its condition at the time of the requested borrowing against its condition four years earlier.

The MAC clause removes some of the certainty that the borrower can access funds under the credit agreement. Borrowers may sometimes seek to reduce any uncertainty by changing the benchmark date against which a material adverse change is measured. For example, instead of specifying a fiscal date that occurred prior to the closing date, a MAC condition might look to whether a material adverse change has occurred "since the date of the latest financial statements delivered to the lenders under this agreement." Since financial statements are usually delivered quarterly, this would mean that the MAC clause would test whether there has been a material adverse change over a period of generally no more than 90 days before the borrowing. Changing the benchmark date in this manner may deprive the lenders of protection against a steady, incremental deterioration in the borrower's condition. It may also allow the borrower to wipe out a catastrophic adverse change simply by delivering a new set of financials. For example, if a category 5 hurricane were to destroy all of the borrower's manufacturing facilities, the borrower could arguably eliminate the resultant MAC by simply serving up financials that reflect a reduction in book value of fixed assets to zero.

Just as a borrower may seek to reduce its risk by changing the benchmark date for testing a material adverse change, it may alternatively request a cutoff date for the period over which a material adverse change is measured. It might, for example, request that the clause measure whether a material adverse change has occurred from a fiscal end date (prior to the closing date) to the closing date. Changing the standard MAC clause in this way can be even more detrimental to lenders, since it excludes from the MAC clause any material adverse change that occurs after the cutoff date (in this example, the closing date). This type of MAC clause will most often be found in a revolving credit facility used as a backup line for commercial paper or the like, since rating agencies may consider a more traditional MAC condition as rendering the facility too conditional to support a desired credit rating. The same result could be obtained by explicitly excluding the MAC clause from the list of representations that must be accurate as a condition precedent to each borrowing. This is often done in the case of strong investment grade borrowers.

The litany of items to be tested for a material adverse change—in the previous example, "business, condition (financial or otherwise), assets, operations or prospects"—is intentionally broad and overlapping. The term that is most often the subject of discussion is "prospects." A MAC clause that includes prospects protects lenders against a material adverse change affecting a borrower's future performance (and therefore its ability to repay the loans) that has not yet resulted in measurable consequences. Examples might include the permanent loss of a material license or the borrower's pulling a principal product from the market, the consequences of which are the loss of future revenues only.

Borrowers occasionally request other exceptions to the MAC clause. A frequent plea is that the MAC provision exclude changes arising from general macroeconomic circumstances, or changes affecting the borrower's industry generally. Notwithstanding the fact that such events or circumstances are general in nature and not particular to the borrower, they could nevertheless have a material adverse impact on the borrower's ability to repay the loans. For this reason, lenders often resist these exclusions. Whether they (or any other exceptions) are included in any given transaction will depend on how the parties believe that these risks are most appropriately allocated.

The entities to be covered by a MAC clause are those companies whose creditworthiness is the basis of the lending decision. These companies are usually the borrower and its subsidiaries, and any guarantor and its subsidiaries, but in an acquisition financing, the target company and its subsidiaries may also be included. In the context of an acquisition, it is not uncommon for the language of the MAC clause to follow the corresponding language in the acquisition agreement, since a borrower will not want to be contractually bound to complete a purchase if lenders have suspended funding on the basis of a different MAC clause for the target.

Whether a material adverse change has occurred is generally a question of fact, and there can be no legal certainty as to whether any given set of circumstances constitutes a material adverse change. The few court decisions that exist tend to be in the acquisition or merger context. An example is a recent Delaware case (*IBP*) where the court looked to two elements to decide whether a MAC existed. One was whether the event was something "unknown" to the lenders at the time of the closing (if the event is covered by a covenant or representation, it may not be considered unknown). A second was whether the event threatened the company's overall earnings potential in a "durationally-significant" fashion (as opposed to representing a decline in earnings as a result of business or commodity price cycles). These principles are generally consistent with other court decisions that have construed the term.

Special Conditions Applicable to Non-U.S. Borrowers

In the case of a non-U.S. borrower, certain additional conditions precedent may be included. The most significant of these is the delivery to the lenders of evidence (in addition to the required legal opinions of non-U.S. counsel) that the borrower has obtained all necessary foreign exchange licenses and other governmental approvals in order that it (and any other non-U.S. party) are entitled to make necessary payments in the prescribed currencies. There can be serious legal risks in proceeding with a cross-border financing without assurance as to compliance with the governmental requirements of the relevant non-U.S. jurisdictions.

Other Conditions

Other conditions that are from time to time inserted into credit agreements include the following.

Appraisals

Appraisals are typically required only in credit agreements that are secured and where a borrowing base (see the section "Mandatory Prepayments" in Part 3, "Making the Borrower Repay the Loan") measured by the value of inventory, receivables, or other assets is employed to limit the amount of credit available. The appraisal will frequently be undertaken by an affiliate of the lead bank. An appraisal may also be required if the loan is being made against the value of real estate. In this instance, the Financial Institutions Reform, Recovery and Enforcement Act of 1989 (FIRREA) requires that any federally regulated bank obtain an appraisal of the real estate before making the loan. FIRREA appraisals are not required where real property is merely part of a lien on the overall assets of an operating company or is obtained out of an excess of caution.

Environmental Due Diligence

Lenders often require an environmental due diligence report with respect to properties owned or leased by the borrower, particularly in situations where the nature of the business poses environmental risks or where there is real estate collateral. Such a report, which is generally undertaken by an engineer, can either be a so-called Phase I Report (where the engineer looks at public records and performs a physical inspection of the property) or a Phase II Report (where the engineer may conduct groundwater testing, take sample borings, and perform other investigations). Typically, unless a Phase I Report raises major concerns, a credit agreement will not require a Phase II Report. In many cases, the lenders will rely solely on a representation from the borrower as to environmental matters and will not conduct independent due diligence or request an engineer's report.

Insurance

If the borrower is required under the insurance covenant to maintain insurance, the conditions in a credit agreement may require that the borrower deliver evidence of the insurance and that (if mandated by the covenant) the administrative agent has been designated as the loss payee. Although evidence normally consists of a certificate issued by the borrower's insurance broker, in certain circumstances, the credit agreement may require delivery of the actual policy and all endorsements.

The Catchall

Credit agreements generally include a catchall condition that allows the administrative agent to request additional documents that it reasonably concludes are appropriate. Borrowers sometimes question the inclusion of this condition, but from the standpoint of the lenders, it provides a method to obtain satisfaction on matters discovered during the closing process. These might include issues raised as closing documents are being assembled, issues arising out of information set out on a disclosure schedule, and issues arising from an intervening change in law. In many closings, this condition is irrelevant, since the credit agreement will be signed and closed at the same time. However, when the credit agreement is signed in advance of the closing, the condition can provide substantial insurance against being required to close in the face of late-developing facts.

Effectiveness

Unless otherwise stated, the credit agreement becomes effective as a contract when all parties have executed and delivered counterparts. However, the effectiveness of the lenders' obligation to extend credit will be conditioned on the borrower's satisfying the conditions precedent. The administrative agent has an important role in confirming the satisfaction of the conditions, and will normally send out a confirmation, although the role of the administrative agent (and confirmations of effectiveness) will commonly be limited to the stated documentary conditions. The administrative agent will not be responsible for conditions that are nondocumentary, such as the standard condition that there is no actual or incipient event of default, that the representations of the borrower are correct, or that the lenders themselves are satisfied as to particular matters (the credit agreement will typically provide that the administrative agent may presume that each lender is satisfied in the absence of notice to the contrary).

Ongoing Conditions

The previous sections have described the conditions to be satisfied at the closing in order for the lending commitments to become effective. For each extension of credit (not just the initial one), the credit agreement will also require that all representations be true and that no actual or incipient event of default exist. These conditions become particularly important if the credit agreement allows for multiple drawdowns. Invariably, a senior officer (usually the chief financial officer) of the borrower will be required to deliver a certificate to this effect (the truth of representations and the absence of defaults) on the closing date, but will not normally be required to deliver a certificate at later borrowings. Credit agreements do not normally allow the mere delivery of a certificate to satisfy the condition itself; rather, the condition will go to the underlying facts, so that, if the lenders have reason to believe that the certificate is inaccurate, they are not barred from asserting that the condition has not been satisfied. Conversions of loans from one pricing option to another are not normally subject to a bring-down of ongoing conditions (but see the discussion in the section "Stripped Loan Facilities" in Part 3, "Making the Borrower Repay the Loan").

Some key principles should be borne in mind when reading the ongoing conditions provision of a credit agreement.

Representations

The condition will generally require that all representations be true and complete on the date of a borrowing "as if made on and as of that date." In other words, if a borrowing is requested in July following a closing date in March, the representations must be true in July as if they were being made in July (being true in March is not sufficient). There is one exception to this general rule. It is customary for representations that refer to a specific date (such as a list of the subsidiaries of the borrower "on the [signing date]") to be true only as of that specific date. This allows borrowings to be made without updating those representations (for example, a representation listing all subsidiaries of the borrower as of the signing of the agreement would not fail to be satisfied at a later date because of the establishment of new subsidiaries).

Some credit agreements will require that representations need be true and complete only "in all material respects." This can lead to potential interpretation issues and may be redundant when the representations themselves are already qualified by materiality, but it has become fairly standard in the market.

In credit agreements for investment grade borrowers, and where the facility is to backstop commercial paper, this condition may expressly exempt the material adverse change clause and the litigation representation for any borrowing being made after the closing date. Thus, the borrower would be permitted to borrow even though a material adverse change or material adverse litigation has occurred.

Defaults

The ongoing conditions will also include a requirement that no default or event of default exist at the time of or giving effect to a borrowing. The distinction between a default and an event of default is discussed in the section "Events of Default" in Part 7, ("Enforcing the Loan." The basic rule is that, although the loans may be accelerated only if an event of default occurs, the lenders are entitled to not increase their exposure (i.e., by making additional loans) if a mere default exists.

REPRESENTATIONS

The representations in a credit agreement affirm the fundamental understandings upon which the lenders are extending credit.

Although the items outlined in this section refer to the borrower, each credit party will normally provide appropriate representations as to itself and the ancillary documents that it signs. The representations address legal and financial issues, matters relating to the business and capital structure of the borrower and its subsidiaries, and various other matters of concern to the lenders. To the extent required to enable a borrower to make a particular representation, an appropriate qualification will be set out in a disclosure schedule. The disclosure schedules, when complete, end up being a very useful tool with which to understand the borrower's business.

Some representations, particularly those relating to legal condition, will also be covered by the opinion of the borrower's counsel. The representations and the legal opinion will to that extent provide double confirmation of the same underlying issues. There is a difference, though, between the two. If a legal opinion is inaccurate, the lender's remedy, if any, is against the counsel that delivered the opinion. If a representation is inaccurate, the lender's remedy is more powerful: it can demand payment of the loans. See the section "Inaccuracy of Representations" in Part 7, "Enforcing the Loan."

Certain representations are qualified by reference to materiality, eliciting whether a circumstance "could" or "would" or "could reasonably be expected to" or "would reasonably be expected to" result in a material adverse effect. Although credit agreement drafters will sometimes negotiate passionately over which of these approaches to take, there may in fact be little difference between the two. If there is any consensus as to what they mean, it is grounded in the distinction between *can* and *will*. "Could" asks whether there is any circumstance (regardless of how likely) in which a material adverse effect could occur. Thus a patently frivolous lawsuit for $1 trillion has the potential, if lost (i.e., *can*), result in a material adverse effect. The borrower would therefore be unable to represent that there is no litigation that *could* result in a material adverse effect. "Would" asks whether the suit is likely to be lost, i.e., taking into account the strength of the case against the borrower, does it appear likely (i.e., *will*) it will be lost, and, if lost, will it result in a material adverse effect? "Could reasonably be expected to" or "would reasonably be expected to" probably just soften (or confuse) the distinction by requiring that any determination be "reasonable." This may cut both ways. It may prevent the borrower from being too carefree in making these determinations, but it also may allow the borrower to argue that a determination of likely materiality must be reasonable, i.e., that the frivolous $1 trillion lawsuit should be ignored (even if the word *could* is used) because it is, well, frivolous.

Lenders will much prefer the "could" formulation because it allows them to make a credit judgment based upon the worst-case scenario, that the outcome of all litigation will be adverse to the borrower. Borrowers naturally prefer the "would" formulation because it relieves them from listing litigation that they conclude will be decided favorably. Any related disclosure schedule thus becomes much shorter, although this approach may limit the usefulness of the representation as a disclosure device to enable the lenders to learn as much as possible about the borrower and its business.

Legal Matters Representations

These representations will address the legal status of the borrower and its subsidiaries.

Due Organization

The borrower, whether a corporation, limited liability company, partnership, or some other kind of entity, will affirm that it is duly organized under applicable law and has the power to enter into the credit agreement and to undertake the transactions contemplated by the credit agreement. It will also affirm that it is qualified to do business in all relevant jurisdictions. The latter point can be important, as many states will not allow an entity organized elsewhere to enforce contracts (such as accounts receivable) unless it is qualified to do business in the state and is in "good standing" (i.e., has made all necessary annual filings and paid all applicable taxes). The good standing representation will normally be qualified with reference to materiality.

Due Authorization

The borrower will confirm that it has taken all necessary action to authorize the credit agreement and the transactions that it contemplates. See the discussion in "Corporate and Organizational Matters" earlier in this part.

Due Execution

The borrower will affirm that it has duly executed and delivered the credit agreement and other relevant documents. Thus, the borrower will confirm to the lenders that the officers who have been granted authority by the resolutions are in fact the ones that executed the documents.

Enforceability

The borrower will confirm that the credit agreement and other agreements are "legal, valid, binding and enforceable." These words have achieved near religious status for both representations and legal opinions. The representation may include qualifications for bankruptcy and similar events (in a case under federal bankruptcy law, all enforcement becomes subject to bankruptcy court approval), as well as for "equitable remedies" (this refers to remedies such as ordering "specific performance," that are in a court's discretion).

No Conflict

This representation will cover three classes of potential conflicts. The first is legal conflicts, to the effect that the credit agreement does not violate any law (for example, that it does not breach applicable usury laws or regulatory restrictions). The second is governance conflicts (for example, that the credit agreement does not violate the organic documents of the borrower). The preferred stock provisions of a charter, for example, may prohibit secured debt in excess of a given percentage of the equity capital of the borrower; violation of such a restriction could affect the enforceability of the credit agreement and lead to other adverse consequences for the borrower (such as a shift of board control to the holders of preferred stock). Lastly, the representation will address conflicts with other contracts to which the borrower is subject. It would, for example, have the borrower confirm that there is no debt limitation in a bond indenture or other agreement that would be violated by the borrowings contemplated by the credit agreement. The latter addresses the concern that the credit agreement could, for example, subject the lenders to a claim that they had interfered tortiously with holders of the borrower's bonds.

One risk arising from a breach of any of these representations is the potential impact on the borrower's credit profile. For example, breaching a debt covenant in a bond indenture or violating a government regulation could dramatically affect the borrower's ability to service the loans if the bonds are accelerated or a compliance proceeding is instituted by a regulatory agency against the borrower.

Government Approvals

The borrower will confirm that all necessary government filings and approvals have been obtained. In an acquisition context, this would include reference to any necessary Hart-Scott-Rodino approval by the Justice Department and, in a secured financing, would include reference to filings to perfect any security interests. In the case of a non-U.S. borrower, the representation would also list any central bank approvals or foreign exchange or other approvals.

Compliance with Law: Licenses

This representation will affirm that the borrower has obtained all licenses necessary for it to operate its business (at least in all material respects). This representation is different from the governmental approvals representation described in the preceding section. The former addresses approvals necessary for the credit agreement itself; the latter addresses approvals necessary for the borrower to operate its business.

Investment Company Act

Here the borrower is asked to confirm that it is not an "investment company," or otherwise "affiliated with" an investment company, as those terms are defined in the Investment Company Act of 1940. If a borrower were an investment company or an affiliate of an investment company, then a loan made in violation of the Act would, with some exceptions, be void.

Public Utility Holding Company

Although the provisions of the Public Utility Holding Company Act of 1935 requiring prior SEC approval for any borrowing by a holding company were repealed effective February 8, 2006, most existing credit agreements will still include a representation to the effect that the borrower is not such a holding company. This representation should in short order become a historical anachronism.

Foreign Assets Control Regulations

Under the Trading with the Enemy Act, the United States has pro-
mulgated regulations prohibiting any kind of transaction between
a U.S. citizen (and various other entities, including entities that are
headquartered or do business within the United States) and a number of countries, such as Cuba and North Korea. These regulations
would make illegal, among other things, any loan by a U.S. lender
(or a foreign lender with an office in the United States) to an entity
in or controlled by any prohibited country, or any loan that
"involves" property in a prohibited country. It would also make
illegal any loan that is made "on behalf of" or "pursuant to the
direction of" a prohibited country. A foreign assets control representation is common in private placements, but is rarely seen in
credit agreements, probably because banks have historically tended to have a closer day-to-day relationship with their customers
than institutional investors, and so the representation has been
perceived as unnecessary.

USA Patriot Act

Credit agreements may in rare instances require the borrower to
represent that it is not identified as, or affiliated with, a terrorist or
a terrorist organization on U.S. Department of Treasury lists. This
is not common practice, however. The more typical approach in
this regard is for the credit agreement to include the notice referred
to in the section "USA Patriot Act" in Part 10, "Understanding the
Boilerplate."

Margin Regulations

This representation will have the borrower confirm that the loans
will not violate Regulations U and X of the Federal Reserve Board.
Regulation U applies to banks and certain other lenders; Regulation
X applies to borrowers. Sometimes the borrower will also make the
same representation with respect to Regulation T (which applies to
brokers and dealers). Typically the representation states that the
loan proceeds will not be applied to "buy or carry" margin stock
(the definition of which is discussed later in this section) and that
the loans will not be secured "directly or indirectly" by margin
stock. To "carry" margin stock basically means to refinance other
debt originally incurred to purchase margin stock.

    The basic rule of Regulation U is that no lender may make a
loan to enable a borrower to buy or carry margin stock if the loan

is "directly or indirectly" secured by margin stock, unless the amount of the security is twice the amount of the loan. Note that the loan must *both* be made to buy margin stock and be directly or indirectly secured by margin stock before it is required to satisfy the 2-to-1 collateral coverage ratio. Thus, neither borrowing against the shares of a public company to buy a new factory nor borrowing against a factory to buy the shares of a public company requires compliance with the ratio. If a loan violates the margin regulations, it may be void.

"Margin stock" is defined, with limited exceptions, as any equity security publicly traded on the domestic markets, including warrants and debt that are exercisable for publicly traded equity securities. A loan is "directly or indirectly" secured by margin stock not only in the situation where the borrower grants a lien on margin stock to the lenders to secure the loans, but also where there is any restriction upon the borrower's ability to create liens on margin stock in favor of third parties or to sell margin stock to third parties. However if not more than 25 percent of the assets of the borrower and its subsidiaries subject to the restriction consist of margin stock, the loan will not be deemed to be indirectly secured by margin stock by reason of such restrictions.

In the event that a loan is directly or indirectly secured by margin stock, the lender is required, under Regulation U, to obtain from the borrower an appropriately completed Form U–1.

Regulations U and X can be particularly constraining when a credit agreement is financing a tender for outstanding publicly traded shares of a target. In this instance, where the value of the margin stock will by definition be equal to the amount of the loans, it is necessary to resort to interpretive rulings issued under Regulation U that describe how the nonmargin assets of a borrower may supplement the margin stock collateral pool and allow the requirements of Regulations U and X to be satisfied.

Financial Condition Representations

These representations address the financial or other business condition of the borrower and its subsidiaries.

Financial Statements

In preparing the credit agreement and obtaining the necessary internal credit approvals, the lenders will have examined recent financial statements of the borrower, typically the most recent annual audited statements and, if available, the most recent interim unaudited statements. All of these statements will almost certainly be included as part of any confidential informational memorandum. In many cases they will include "consolidating" as well as consolidated statements.

The financial statements representation has the borrower affirm that all of these statements have been prepared in accordance with GAAP, and that they are "complete and correct" (or, alternatively, that they "fairly present" the borrower's financial condition) in "all material respects." "Complete and correct" is perhaps more precise; "fairly present" is the phrase generally used by accountants when writing their audit report. For a discussion of GAAP, see the section "Definitions Generally; GAAP" in Part 5, "Monitoring the Loan."

The financial statements representation will also generally include language to the effect that the statements and footnotes reflect all material liabilities or unusual forward or long-term commitments of the borrower. This language is included because not all potential liabilities or commitments are required under GAAP to be disclosed in the financial statements or footnotes. For example, the fact that a borrower has agreed to supply oil to third parties at $20 a barrel when the cost of producing the oil has jumped to $40 a barrel and the market price is $60 a barrel probably will not appear anywhere in the financial statements or the footnotes. Sometimes borrowers will request that this language be qualified by reference to GAAP, i.e., that the statements reflect all material liabilities and unusual commitments *required to be disclosed under GAAP*. This approach generally defeats the purpose of addressing these liabilities and commitments in the first place.

The financial statement representation will typically include the MAC representation. See the section "The MAC Condition" earlier in this part regarding the material adverse change representation.

If the credit agreement is to finance an acquisition, the representation may cover pro forma financial statements (financial statements for a period, usually consistent with one of the periods covered by the financial statements referred to previously) prepared as if the acquisition had occurred at the beginning of the period.

Projections

In some instances, projections will have been delivered to the lenders. Borrowers are normally reluctant to make the same kinds of representations with respect to projections as they make with respect to historical financial statements. The typical credit agreement will, accordingly, soften the representation by simply requiring the borrower to state that any projections have been prepared in good faith based upon assumptions that the borrower has deemed reasonable. There may also be a statement to the effect that no assurances can be given that the projections will accurately reflect future financial condition or performance.

Taxes

The taxes representation will have the borrower confirm that all income, franchise, property, and other taxes (at least to the extent that a failure to pay the same would be material) have been paid. Property taxes, if not paid, raise concerns because unpaid property taxes give rise to a lien (in many cases senior to all other liens, including preexisting mortgages) on the particular property being taxed. Franchise taxes are of concern because failure to pay a franchise tax could result in the dissolution of a corporation or the failure of a company to qualify to do business (with the consequences described in the section "Due Organization" earlier in this part). Failure to pay income taxes can give rise to a lien in favor of the IRS on all of the borrower's property. The IRS tax lien is not automatically senior to all other liens, but it may nevertheless capture property not covered by a lien in favor of the lenders and, certainly, in an unsecured deal will give the IRS the status of a lien creditor while the lenders are unsecured.

Pension and Welfare Plans

Under the Employee Retirement Income Security Act of 1974 (ERISA), to the extent that a company is obligated to pay retired employees a defined pension benefit, the company will be required to pay into a trust an amount sufficient to cover future benefit obligations. ERISA establishes a government corporation (the Pension Benefit Guaranty Corporation, or PBGC) to assure retired employees that their pension payments will be made. In turn, the PBGC is granted, under ERISA, a lien equivalent to the tax lien granted in favor of the IRS described in the previous section,

"Taxes." Thus, the lenders have an interest in knowing that the borrower is complying with the requirements of ERISA.

In cases where the borrower has no employee benefit plans subject to ERISA, the representation may simply be a statement to this effect.

Solvency

The solvency representation was originally intended for those situations in which a transaction gave rise to concerns under fraudulent conveyance or fraudulent transfer laws—for example, when the proceeds of the loans were to be applied to pay an extraordinary dividend or distribution to shareholders. Similarly, such a concern might exist if the loans were to be guaranteed by subsidiaries. However, many lenders now include solvency representations as a matter of course, regardless of these structural issues. Sometimes a credit agreement will go further and require the borrower to deliver a professional evaluation from an independent appraisal firm, known as a "solvency opinion," that confirms that the borrower (or a guarantor) will not be rendered insolvent by the financing.

Fraudulent transfer laws originated by statute many centuries ago. They have been continued as legislation in every state and have also been incorporated into the Federal Bankruptcy Code. They are intended to capture a transaction in which (1) an entity undertakes an obligation or transfers property without receiving "reasonably equivalent" value and (2) the entity is insolvent at the time of, or would be rendered insolvent as a result of, the transaction. An illustration of the potential abuse that the fraudulent transfer laws prohibit might be the case of a penniless musician who sells his valuable Stradivarius to his brother for $1.00 and then declares bankruptcy. A fraudulent transfer will have occurred, since both tests of the law will have been met: first, $1.00 is probably not a "reasonably equivalent" value for the sale of a Stradivarius, and, second, the musician is insolvent at the time of the sale to his brother.

In the corporate lending context, these issues arise in a variety of ways. For example, if the proceeds of the loans will finance the payment of a dividend or distribution, the borrower is probably not receiving reasonably equivalent value for the payment; in fact, it is likely to be receiving no value at all. In the case of a guarantee of the loans by a subsidiary, unless the entire amount of the loan proceeds is being advanced to the subsidiary, the subsidiary also is not likely to be receiving reasonably equivalent value, since it will be guaranteeing the full amount of the loans but receiving only a portion (or none) of the proceeds. Restructuring a deal to eliminate the dividend or the upstream guarantees is not terribly practical.

The solution most often adopted in credit agreements is to attack the second prong of the fraudulent transfer test by having the borrower represent that it is "solvent." The term *solvent* will be defined as the obverse of the term *insolvency* as used in fraudulent transfer laws. A borrower is insolvent (1) when its liabilities (including contingent liabilities) exceed its assets, (2) when its property or capital is unreasonably small in relation to its business or the obligations being undertaken under the credit agreement, or (3) when it undertakes the obligations under the credit agreement with the intent to "hinder, delay or defraud" creditors. Occasionally the solvency representation will be further supported by a solvency opinion, as described earlier. While this was common in leveraged acquisitions in the early 1990s, the more common practice today is for the lender to conduct its own independent analysis of the borrower's solvency.

Representations and Disclosures Regarding the Business

While the financial condition representations address the financial or other business *condition* of the borrower, the representations set forth in this section address particular *facts* about its property or business. Not every credit agreement, of course, contains all of these representations, although in a highly leveraged transaction it would not be unusual to see them all.

Capitalization

Here the borrower, usually by reference to a disclosure schedule, will represent to the lenders what its capital structure is, including the amounts and classes of capital stock and other equity that have been authorized and are outstanding; in the case of a privately held company, the identity of the owner; and in all cases whether or not any extraordinary equity rights (such as an obligation to buy in equity from a shareholder) are outstanding. The disclosure schedule can thus be used as a base to determine whether a change of control has occurred.

Subsidiaries

The subsidiaries representation will normally make reference to a disclosure schedule. The disclosure schedule will typically set forth details regarding the various types of equity interests of each subsidiary that are outstanding, and which entity (the borrower or some other subsidiary or entity) owns those equity interests. The schedule will customarily have sufficient detail for the lenders to understand the ownership structure of the borrower and its subsidiaries and thus determine whether, in structuring the agreement, they have taken the right guarantees from subsidiaries and the correct pledges of subsidiary equity. Some credit agreements will go further and require that the borrower attach an organizational chart displaying the ownership structures of all subsidiaries.

Existing Debt and Liens

The borrower will be asked to affirm a disclosure schedule setting out any existing debt or existing liens. These items will then be "grandfathered" in the debt and liens covenants described in "Negative Covenants" in Part 5, "Monitoring the Loans." They will also enable the lenders to determine that they find acceptable the amount of other debt and other liens they will be competing with if the borrower sinks into financial difficulties.

Real Property

A disclosure schedule will list all real property owned or leased by the borrower. In a deal secured by mortgages, this list becomes a basis for confirming that mortgages on the relevant real property interests are being granted in favor of the lenders.

Litigation

The purpose of the litigation representation is to force the borrower to identify any "material" litigation or threatened litigation (including arbitrations and regulatory proceedings) to which the borrower or any of its subsidiaries is subject. Once the disclosure schedule is complete, the lenders can then make an independent judgment as to whether or not to proceed with the loan.

One of the problems that a borrower will confront in completing the disclosure schedule is determining whether an item of litigation needs to be listed, i.e., whether it rises to the level of materiality. Some borrowers throw up their hands and just list all litigation to which they are party. This may not be particularly helpful to the borrower, since it may in effect be conceding that a $500 lawsuit is material. Borrowers may try to overcome this conundrum by stating expressly in the disclosure statement that the mere listing of an item of litigation does not concede that it is in fact material. This latter approach, of course, can produce a problem for the lenders. A lender, if informed of material litigation, may feel that it is compelled to investigate thoroughly the nature of the litigation and whether it might eventually impair the borrower's ability to satisfy its obligations under the credit agreement. Overinclusive listing by borrowers makes this task much more difficult.

Title to Property
In a sense, the title representation covers some of the same territory covered by the liens representation. The title representation, however, goes beyond the mere existence of liens and addresses additionally whether the borrower has taken the actions necessary to give it proper ownership of its properties. An example might include purchasing real property from an entity that did not have adequate title to sell (perhaps a Native American tribe asserts ultimate ownership of the underlying land). Another example might be an FCC license purportedly issued to the borrower, but mistakenly issued to a subsidiary.

Labor Matters
This representation will typically have the borrower confirm that there is labor peace with its employees. To the extent that the borrower's employees are unionized, the representation may affirm that the borrower has made copies of all collective bargaining agreements available to the lenders.

Intellectual Property
Ultimately, every borrower has some important intellectual property (if nothing else, its name). For a borrower such as a chemical company that is heavily dependent on patents or a wine and spirits company that is heavily dependent on trademarks, intellectual property can be vital. This representation, therefore, has the borrower affirm that it has all intellectual property (patents, trademarks, and copyrights) necessary for it to operate its business.

Environmental Matters

Lenders may be concerned that environmental problems (current or former) of the borrower may adversely affect its credit quality. Under federal superfund legislation, for example, any past or present contributor of hazardous materials to a superfund site is jointly and severally liable for the entire cleanup cost. As a practical matter, the so-called de minimis contributors are allowed off the hook with relatively small payments. Nevertheless, credit agreements routinely ask the borrower to identify on a disclosure schedule any environmental exposure it may have (including current and past noncompliance).

When listing environmental matters on its disclosure schedules, the borrower (and lenders) may be faced with some of the same materiality questions that were discussed in "Litigation."

No Burdensome Restrictions

This representation is intended to elicit from the borrower whether it is subject to agreements that materially constrain its business. Examples might be a contract that limits its ability to use a patent to compete against a new product on the market, or a contract requiring the borrower to purchase a product from a supplier at above-market rates.

Completeness of Disclosures

This representation, similar to a 10b–5 representation in a securities underwriting agreement, makes the borrower confirm that the information supplied by it to the lenders in connection with the credit agreement (including all financial statements and other disclosures, and including any confidential information memorandum), when taken as a whole, is accurate and complete and does not omit any information necessary to be not misleading. This representation provides overarching comfort to the lenders that the borrower is not selectively supplying information that, individually, is perfectly accurate but that, in the aggregate, is deceptive.

Status as Senior Indebtedness

In transactions where the borrower may have outstanding subordinated indebtedness, it may be useful for the lenders to obtain an affirmation from the borrower that its obligations under the credit agreement constitute "senior indebtedness" for purposes of the subordinated debt. The same conclusions would normally also be confirmed in an opinion of counsel. Both the representation and the opinion may be stating the obvious (typically the status of the credit agreement under the definition of senior indebtedness will be apparent). They nevertheless give the lenders an argument (if any subordinated debtholder should assert otherwise) that they acted in good faith in believing that their loans are senior.

Perfection and Priority of Security

A security interest in property is created when an appropriate security agreement is signed, value is given by the lenders (the commitment to lend is "value" for this purpose), and the debtor has "rights in the collateral." Representations will typically be included in the credit agreement, or in the security agreement, to the effect that the relevant security agreement creates a valid security interest in the collateral, that such security interest has been perfected (depending on the nature of the collateral and other factors, a variety of steps may be required to perfect a security interest covering different kinds of collateral), and that such perfected security interest has first priority, subject to no equal or prior security interest (unless a different priority has been agreed). The priority representation may have to be qualified in some respects.

Representations for Foreign Borrowers

For a borrower that is not organized in the United States, the credit agreement may contain certain additional representations covering matters unique to nondomestic borrowers, including the following.

Immunity
This is a representation that the borrower's participation in the transaction constitutes commercial activity and is subject to civil and commercial law. As noted in the section "Waiver of Sovereign Immunity" in Part 10, "Understanding the Boilerplate," a "foreign state" under the U.S. Sovereign Immunity Act of 1976 is entitled to immunity from court jurisdiction, and its property from attachment and execution, in the United States. A foreign borrower that

at closing is private would acquire immunity if it were later to be acquired by the government of its country. A "commercial activity" representation thus affords the lenders a basis upon which to defeat a claim of sovereign immunity being raised by a borrower (even one that starts out privately held).

Pari Passu Ranking

This is a representation to the effect that the obligations of the borrower under the credit agreement rank at least pari passu with all other obligations of the borrower (this provides assurance that the laws of the borrower's country do not grant senior status to other claims that might "trump" the lenders' rights). An example of the latter was the legal rule in Argentina a number of years ago that non-Argentine creditors always ranked junior in priority to Argentine creditors in the insolvency of an Argentine borrower. Other countries have at times created special structural priorities, such as between notarized and nonnotarized documents.

Legal Form

This is a representation to the effect that the credit agreement and other relevant documents are in proper legal form for enforcement in the country in which the borrower is located. This will address, for example, whether the credit agreement is properly notarized and consularized, and whether it needs to be translated into a local language to be enforceable in a local court.

Taxes

This is a representation to the effect that the loans and the credit agreement are not subject to tax by the borrower's country. In many cases, of course, the borrower's country will impose a with-holding tax on payments of interest and on some other payments by the borrower, and may require payment of a stamp or other documentary tax in order for a creditor to enforce the documents in court; in such cases, the representations will be tailored so as to correctly reflect the tax position.

Sovereign Borrowers

In the case of a loan to a sovereign borrower (a government, central bank, or majority-owned government agency), this representation states that the borrowing country is a member in good standing of the International Monetary Fund and is eligible to use the resources thereof (among other things, this confirms the ability of the country to access IMF funding in certain circumstances), and possibly includes similar representations as to other applicable multilateral organizations. If the borrower is the country itself, it is also customary to have the borrower represent that its obligations under the credit agreement are entitled to the "full faith and credit" of the country, i.e., that the loan is not payable solely from a narrow source of funds, but rather is payable from the general revenue of the country.

Part 5. Monitoring the Loan: Financial, Affirmative, and Negative Covenants

SOME GENERAL PRINCIPLES

Covenants can be divided into three categories: financial covenants, affirmative covenants, and negative covenants. Many credit agreements will create a separate overarching section or article for each category, but frequently financial covenants are treated as negative covenants. There is no substantive effect to these classifications; they are purely a matter of convenience of reference.

All covenants are independent of one another. Thus, a transaction that the borrower wishes to undertake that is captured by more than one covenant must be allowed under each covenant. Simply because the transaction is permitted under one covenant does not carry with it any claim or argument that it is ipso facto to be permitted under another covenant. An illustration of this might arise in the context of the borrower's wanting to guarantee the debt of a valued customer. Guarantees of this type are likely to be controlled by the debt covenant (since this is a guarantee of debt) and by the investments covenant (since guarantees of the debt of a third party are normally also treated as an investment in the third party). To issue the guarantee, the borrower would therefore need to find a basket or other exception in each of the debt and investments covenants.

CATEGORIZING SUBSIDIARIES

Subsidiaries Generally

Most credit agreements will apply not just to the borrower, but to the borrower and its subsidiaries, the theory being that the financial strength of the borrower is only as good as the strength of the entire group. A subsidiary will normally be defined as any entity that either is consolidated with the borrower in the preparation of financial statements or a majority of whose voting equity is owned or controlled by the borrower or another subsidiary. Thus, the term *subsidiary* will include a limited partnership where the sole general partner is wholly owned by the borrower, even though the limited partnership interest is held by an unrelated third party and constitutes 99 percent of the equity. A sole general partner will by definition control the partnership.

Restricted and Unrestricted Subsidiaries

Bond indentures frequently have a concept of "restricted" and "unrestricted" subsidiaries. Credit agreements make this distinction less frequently. In those agreements that incorporate the concept, the motivation is to create a class of subsidiary (unrestricted subsidiaries) that is free from the representations, covenants, and events of default to which subsidiaries would otherwise be subject. Thus, for example, the borrower can allow an unrestricted subsidiary to incur debt (and secure it, if desired), make acquisitions, and undertake riskier, even nonperforming business activities without having to worry about the impact upon financial tests and without using the negotiated, dollar-limited baskets in negative covenants.

In a credit agreement with both restricted and unrestricted subsidiaries, the restricted subsidiaries will be subject to all of the representations, covenants, and defaults, while unrestricted subsidiaries will typically be subject to none of these. An exception will be made, however, for those representations, covenants, or defaults where an event or condition at an unrestricted subsidiary could affect the consolidated group, such as a failure of an unrestricted subsidiary to pay tax or ERISA liabilities (which, under applicable federal law, become the joint and several liability of every entity in the consolidated group). In these instances, unrestricted subsidiaries will not be treated differently from restricted subsidiaries.

The flip side for the borrower's having the greater flexibility of unrestricted subsidiaries is that unrestricted subsidiaries are treated essentially the same way as unrelated parties. Thus, for example, investments in unrestricted subsidiaries will be controlled and the EBITDA (positive or negative) of unrestricted subsidiaries will not be included in the EBITDA of the borrower and its restricted subsidiaries. Unrestricted subsidiaries will be treated as affiliates for purposes of the affiliate transactions covenant, forcing transactions with unrestricted subsidiaries to be on an arm's-length basis.

Designation of subsidiaries as restricted or unrestricted is usually at the discretion of the borrower. The mechanism for designation in credit agreements is typically less formal than that in bond indentures (a bond indenture will usually require a board resolution), but many of the other conditions for designation will be employed, such as the requirement that the investment in a subsidiary designated as unrestricted be within whatever limits are imposed in the agreement upon investments in third parties. Any designation of a restricted subsidiary as unrestricted (or vice versa) will typically be conditioned upon the absence of any default after giving effect to the designation. Subsidiaries of unrestricted subsidiaries will always be treated as unrestricted.

Significant Subsidiaries

If the borrower is a large corporation with many subsidiaries, it will often push for a concept of "significant subsidiaries." A significant subsidiary will typically be any subsidiary that meets the definition of a "significant subsidiary" under the SEC's Regulation S-X, although other definitions are possible. In general, this definition captures any subsidiary that has 10 percent or more of the assets or 10 percent or more of the income of the borrower's consolidated group. In its narrowest application, the definition of significant subsidiary will be used only in a bankruptcy default, i.e., the insolvency of a subsidiary will give rise to an event of default only if the subsidiary is significant. Other agreements will expand the concept further to certain of the representations or, in its broadest application, to many of the affirmative covenants. The

underlying theory is that the lenders should not be concerned with
bad events or conditions at subsidiaries that do not rise to the level
of being significant. The concept may not be appropriate if a borrower, though large, has many subsidiaries, none of which rise to
the level of being significant under Regulation S-X.

COVENANT DEFINITIONS

Definitions Generally; GAAP

In any agreement, definitions are the building blocks upon which
all other provisions are based. This is particularly true when
it comes to covenants. The operative principle to keep in mind
(at least when reading definitions that are relevant for negative
covenants) is that definitions are often worded to have sweeping
effect. Verbosity is deliberate here, motivated, to a great extent, by
bad court decisions, where a court (to illustrate) may have ruled
that a reference to a "car" cannot have meant an SUV or a van or
even a taxi or a limousine or a rental. Thus, the definition of "lien"
will not just cover liens as they are normally understood, but will
also include all charges, security interests, pledges, mortgages,
encumbrances, assignments, and other similar arrangements and
so forth ad nauseam. Similarly, the definition of "dividend" will
refer not just to dividends and distributions, but to purchases of
stock, sinking funds for that purpose, and even "phantom stock"
arrangements.

Perhaps the most basic building block is the definition of
GAAP. Credit agreement covenants, when being set by the administrative agent and the borrower, are normally based upon the borrower's historical and projected financial statements. These will be
required by the credit agreement to be prepared upon the basis of
generally accepted accounting principles "consistently applied."
That is to say, if the borrower delivered financial statements for its
two most recent fiscal years, the statements will not have employed
one set of principles in one year and a different set of principles in
the second year. To take an example, the statements will not calculate inventory on a first-in, first-out (FIFO) basis in the first year
and on a last-in, first-out (LIFO) basis in the second.

Thus, the *historical* financial statements delivered to the
lenders must be "consistent" and will be used as the basis for determining financial covenants and other levels. This then raises the

question of what is to happen after the closing. Is the borrower to be free to change accounting principles from year to year—to switch from LIFO to FIFO, for example? Borrowers may want precisely this flexibility. They may also want to prepare statements based upon generally accepted accounting principles as applied from time to time, i.e., reflecting changes in principles required by the accounting profession. Conversely, the lenders will want the principles used in calculating covenants to remain stable and not to reflect changes if those changes would affect the outcome of covenant compliance.

The definition of GAAP in a credit agreement, therefore, will address either one or the other of these approaches. One variant (preferred by borrowers) is to have GAAP defined as generally accepted accounting principles "as in effect from time to time." The other variant (preferred by lenders) is to have GAAP frozen in time to those principles that were in effect at closing and were used in preparing the statements upon which financial covenants were determined. A borrower may object that this requires it to prepare two sets of financial statements. The solution often adopted is discussed in the section "Fiscal Periods and Accounting Changes" later in this part.

Key Financial Definitions

To state the obvious, financial definitions are in large part accounting-based and heavily negotiated. Nevertheless, in looking at definitions to decipher covenants, some twists should be kept in mind.

Debt

The definition of debt will invariably pick up balance sheet indebtedness, but will not normally pick up current accounts payable and accrued expenses. Obligations with respect to capital leases (but not operating leases) will thus be counted as debt. The definition will also encompass guarantees of other debt, even though guarantees are normally footnoted in financial statements and are not carried as a liability on a balance sheet. In a similar vein, it will include all letters of credit (although trade letters of credit will normally be excluded). Obligations of third parties secured by a lien on assets of the borrower will be treated as debt, even though the obligations have not been assumed by the borrower. Sometimes the amount of such obligations will be deemed to be limited to the value of the property subject to the claim. That may not, however, be the correct result given Section 1111 of the Federal Bankruptcy Code, which in some circumstances will allow a creditor to submit a full claim against the borrower in a bankruptcy proceeding even if the borrower has not assumed the debt.

Finally, many credit agreements will state that debt includes obligations under hedging agreements, even though this may lead to time-consuming calculations for the borrower in determining leverage ratios. For example, to establish the amount of a hedging agreement, a borrower cannot simply look at an internal statement of account. Instead, it would need to ascertain from market quotes the hedge's termination liability. This could change daily. Many credit agreements avoid this problem by treating hedges as investments (see the discussion in the section "Investments" later in this part).

EBITDA

EBITDA stands for earnings before interest, taxes, depreciation, and amortization. The term is important for financial covenants, for interest margins (to the extent that margins are determined with reference to a debt ratio that incorporates EBITDA as one of its elements), and for an excess cash flow prepayment provision contained in the credit agreement. Some agreements will use the term *cash flow* or *operating cash flow* in lieu of EBITDA, though substantively the terms will be the same.

The purpose of the term is to capture the amount of cash thrown off by the borrower's business before taking into account nonoperating cash expenses, such as interest and taxes. Depreciation and amortization are added back because, although they reduce earnings, they do not reduce the amount of cash generated during any calculation period. EBITDA is intended to be a predictor of the ability of a borrower to pay interest and, ultimately, to repay principal. The debt ratio, interest coverage ratio, debt service coverage ratio, and fixed charges coverage ratio, discussed in greater detail later in this part, each of which has EBITDA as a component, test the amount of cash available to the borrower against its debt service needs.

FINANCIAL COVENANTS

Date-Specific versus Performance Covenants; Annualized and Rolling Periods

Financial covenants can be divided into two categories: those that test the borrower's financial position at a particular date (such as a net worth or current ratio covenant) and those that test its performance over one or more fiscal periods (such as a fixed charges or interest coverage covenant). A variant of the second category could be those covenants that contain both date-specific and performance elements, such as a debt ratio covenant testing the ratio of debt at a particular date to earnings for a specified fiscal period.

A performance-based covenant will in rare cases test performance on a quarter-by-quarter basis, i.e., measure earnings only for the most recent fiscal quarter. It is much more common for the relevant fiscal period to consist of the four most recent fiscal quarters, a so-called rolling four-quarter period. Thus, when testing the covenant at the end of December, the relevant test period would be the four quarters ending December 31. When testing again at the end of March, the relevant period would be the four quarters commencing on April 1 of the preceding year and ending on March 31 of the current year. The benefit of this approach (from the standpoint of both the borrower and the lenders) is that it avoids the borrower's falling into default because of seasonality issues, which might otherwise occur if only the most recent single fiscal quarter were tested. Retail businesses, for example, frequently have much lower earnings in the first fiscal quarter of the year than in the last fiscal quarter of the year.

Performance may also be "annualized." An example might be the case where a "debt ratio" is defined as the ratio of debt to earnings for the most recent fiscal quarter *times* 4 (or the two most recent fiscal quarters *times* 2). This approach can be useful for a start-up borrower, where earnings are expected to start low but grow quickly from quarter to quarter. Of course annualizing is technically not necessary—the lender could simply adjust the maximum permitted debt ratio—but cosmetically (and cosmetics often matter when crafting a credit agreement) it looks better to have a debt ratio maximum of 5 to 1 rather than 20 to 1.

Phase-In and Pro Forma Treatment

An issue that comes up in the context of credit agreements that finance acquisitions is how to deal with the impact of an acquisition upon performance-based covenants. For example, if an acquisition will double the borrower's business, it may make little sense to measure EBITDA on a strictly historical rolling four-quarter basis, since much of the rolling four quarters will reflect a lower preacquisition EBITDA. Similarly, testing interest expense only for that period will understate the borrower's future interest costs as a result of the increased acquisition borrowing. The solution typically adopted in credit agreements will be to calculate performance numbers (such as EBITDA, interest expense, capital expenditures, debt service, and taxes) on a hypothetical (or pro forma) basis as if the acquisition had occurred at the beginning of the rolling four-quarter period. An alternative approach is to annualize the figures until a full four quarters have elapsed after the acquisition.

For interest expense, a variant that is frequently used is to take interest expense for the period from the closing to the test date and multiply it by an appropriate fraction to bring it up to a full 365-day year. Thus, if an acquisition occurs on February 17 of a year, interest expense for March 31 would be annualized by multiplying the actual interest for the 42-day period between February 17 and March 31 by a fraction, the numerator of which is 365 and the denominator of which is 42.

Performance-Based Financial Covenants

Debt Ratio

Typically this term (frequently referred to as the *leverage ratio*) will be defined as the ratio of debt at a given date to EBITDA for the rolling four quarters most recently ended prior to that date. The debate in negotiating the credit agreement will be between whether the debt ratio is tested only at the end of a fiscal quarter (i.e., only at the end of the relevant rolling period) and whether the ratio is tested each day during the year. The former would allow the ratio during a fiscal quarter (i.e., between fiscal quarter ends) to exceed the maximum otherwise required at the end of the quarter. The latter would prevent this and certainly should be feasible from an accounting standpoint if you assume that a borrower can keep track of its outstanding debt at any given day even while measuring EBITDA only at fiscal-period ends.

Interest Coverage Ratio

The interest coverage covenant tests the ratio of EBITDA to interest expense during a fiscal period (typically the most recently ended rolling four quarters). "Interest expense" will normally be defined to include only cash interest. Thus PIK (pay-in-kind) interest and capitalized interest charges will be excluded. However, "cash interest" will not be literally confined to interest paid in cash during a particular period, but rather will include interest payable in cash during the particular period. To provide otherwise would potentially allow a borrower to manipulate interest expense by paying interest a day before the beginning (or a day after the end) of a fiscal period. Finally, interest expense will normally reflect payments made (or cash received) under interest hedging agreements.

Debt Service Coverage Ratio

The debt service coverage covenant measures the ratio of EBITDA to debt service during a fiscal period (as with interest coverage, the period is typically the most recently ended rolling four quarters). "Debt service" will consist of interest expense and *scheduled* principal payments. The latter will not normally include mandatory prepayments (such as excess cash flow, disposition, or debt and equity issuance prepayments). It will also not include voluntary prepayments. It will, however, include scheduled reductions of revolving commitments if that requires a payment of debt.

Fixed Charges Coverage Ratio

The fixed charges coverage covenant measures the ratio of EBITDA to fixed charges during a fiscal period (again, as with interest coverage and debt service coverage, this is typically the most recently ended rolling four quarters). "Fixed charges" will start with debt service, but will go further by picking up capital expenditures and often (but not always) taxes and dividends (particularly regular, scheduled dividends).

Capital Expenditures

Although frequently included in the financial covenants section of a credit agreement, the capital expenditures covenant is perhaps more accurately characterized as a negative covenant than as a performance-based covenant. The restriction limits the aggregate capital expenditures that the borrower may make during a fiscal quarter or fiscal year. "Capital expenditures" will be defined as any expenditure in respect of a capital asset of the borrower, i.e., an expenditure that does not flow through the borrower's income statement. Repairing a building thus would probably not be a capital expenditure; erecting a new building probably would. The covenant is calculated for discrete fiscal periods (one quarter or one year), rather than on a rolling basis. Once the maximum levels are set, the debate between the borrower and the lender will revolve around carryovers: how much of one period's unused capital expenditure capacity may be carried forward into a future period. The borrower will, of course, push for unlimited carryforwards, while the lender will wish to limit carryovers to one or two years (or permit none at all).

Lease Payments

Credit agreements will sometimes limit the aggregate payments that may be made during a fiscal period with respect to operating leases (as distinct from capital leases, which will normally be captured by the definition of debt and thus included in the interest coverage, debt service coverage, or fixed charges coverage covenant). Sometimes the limit will be phrased in terms of an aggregate dollar cap. In other instances, the credit agreement will create a concept of "attributable debt," where, even for operating leases, the future rental stream is discounted to present value to produce an attributable dollar amount. The aggregate of such attributable debt will then be limited by the debt covenant.

Date-Specific Financial Covenants

Net Worth

The net worth (or, more frequently, tangible net worth) covenant will test the balance sheet shareholders' equity of the borrower at a specific date (normally a fiscal quarter or fiscal year end). "Tangible net worth" will start with shareholders' equity as set out on the balance sheet, but will then adjust the figures to exclude intangibles (such as goodwill, research and development costs, and licenses) carried on the balance sheet. Tangible net worth will typically also exclude treasury shares.

Current Ratio/Working Capital

The current ratio covenant will test the ratio of current assets to current liabilities at a given date. The working capital covenant will measure the excess of current assets over current liabilities at a given date. Though these covenants have fallen out of favor in recent years and thus are incorporated in relatively few credit agreements, they may still be seen in asset-based financing transactions.

AFFIRMATIVE COVENANTS

Disclosure Covenants

Once lenders have made (or purchased) loans under the credit agreement, they will want to monitor the performance of the borrower. Credit agreements will therefore require delivery of annual audited and quarterly unaudited financial statements. In the case of foreign borrowers, where quarterly financial statements may not be regularly prepared, the covenant may limit the required financial statements to semiannual or perhaps only annual statements. In specialized situations (such as highly leveraged or asset-based facilities), financial statements may be required to be delivered monthly.

Delivery has traditionally been made by the borrower's sending statements directly to lenders. However, in recent years, as the size of lending syndicates has expanded and Web-based posting services (such as Intralinks) have become popular, financial statements are made available to lenders through posting on Internet web sites. These web sites will normally contain a warning identifying those areas of the site that contain material nonpublic information, so that public-side investors can elect not to receive private-side information.

The financial statements to be delivered will normally be "consolidated" (will consolidate the borrower with its subsidiaries) and, in some cases, will also be "consolidating" (will show how the balance sheet and the results of operations for each entity in the consolidated group were added together to produce the consolidated statements). Consolidating statements are considered particularly useful because they show more clearly which entities in the consolidated group are responsible for the assets and earnings. It is thus another method by which the lenders can determine that they have guarantees and security from the proper entities in the consolidated group.

Annual financial statements will be required to be audited by the borrower's independent public accountants; interim financial statements need only be certified by an officer of the borrower. One issue that arises is whether delivery of financial statements with a "going concern" qualification can satisfy the covenant. Borrowers frequently resist the requirement that no such qualification exist, reasoning that, if a particular condition is not a default under the financial covenants or other provisions of the agreement, it should not become a default through the inability to deliver unqualified financial statements. In other words, they argue, whether the borrower is in default should be determined by reference to the negotiated tests incorporated in the credit agreement and not by whether the accountants have determined that a going concern qualification should be taken.

Concurrently with the delivery of quarterly or annual financial statements, the borrower will typically also be required to prepare a compliance calculation for financial and other number-based covenants. The credit agreement will normally require that all financial statements and any compliance calculations be certified by the chief financial officer or a senior financial officer of the borrower. Since the enactment of the Sarbanes-Oxley Act, a practice of requiring that two officers make these certifications has been developing. In bond indentures, by contrast, it has long been the practice that all certifications are made by two senior officers, customarily defined as "responsible officers." In some instances, the credit agreement may require that the certification be made by the borrower's public accountants. Accountants resist this approach and are normally unwilling to say anything about a covenant unless it relates to "accounting matters." They may also charge an additional fee to make the certification.

The disclosure covenant will almost always include a general catchall allowing the lenders to request additional financial or other information from the borrower. Sometimes the request can be made individually by any lender, although often it may be made only through the administrative agent. The right to request additional information from the borrower can be important if the lenders have reason to believe that the borrower's financial condition may have deteriorated.

The credit agreement will typically include a requirement that the borrower notify the lenders of any default and of other material events. Thus, the borrower would be required to notify the lenders of the institution of any litigation that, if lost, could result in a MAC, of any ERISA or environmental claim that exceeds a specified dollar threshold (or could result in a MAC), and of any other event that results or could be expected to result in a MAC. Borrowers often negotiate for this covenant not to be triggered unless a senior officer, or group of senior officers, has "actual knowledge" of the existence of the event requiring disclosure.

Visitation Rights

Potentially one of the most important rights granted by borrowers to lenders is the so-called visitation or inspection right. This right is important for two reasons. First, it affords the lenders the right to visit and inspect the borrower's properties and books. This right can potentially be very significant if there is reason to believe that the borrower may be in default, although borrowers often try to limit the inspection right to situations where a default is known to exist. Conditioning the right in this manner undercuts the purpose of an inspection right in the first place (i.e., to determine whether or not the borrower really is in default). Second, bank regulators consider the visitation or inspection right important and may look to see if the lenders have been accorded this right in the credit agreement.

Maintenance of Insurance

Almost every credit agreement (except perhaps for credit agreements with investment grade borrowers) will include an insurance covenant. In its simplest form, the covenant will require the borrower to maintain insurance in a manner consistent with that maintained by other businesses in the same industry. The exact types of insurance, appropriate deductibles, limits on self-insurance, and covered risks will not be specified. In its more complex form, such as in highly leveraged secured transactions or project financings, the covenant will be detailed as to the risks to be covered and the deductibles or self-insurance to be permitted and will specify the qualifications for insurance carriers and that the lenders (or the administrative agent) must be named as "loss payees" or "additional named insureds." The covenant may also provide for the borrower to deliver an annual insurance compliance certificate to the administrative agent, demonstrating that all insurance required to be maintained under the covenant continues in effect and that all applicable premiums have been paid.

Sometimes, credit agreements will also require that the borrower obtain key-man life insurance on one or more senior officers or key employees. The purpose of key-man life insurance is not to have a pot of money from which to pay the loan, but rather to ensure that the borrower has at hand a ready source of cash to pay an incentive bonus or the like to induce a replacement from another company to step in and take over for the officer or employee who has died.

Motherhood and Apple Pie Covenants

A number of affirmative covenants in effect require the borrower to do nothing more than any right-minded borrower would do in the first place. The covenants are nevertheless included to guard against those situations in which a borrower is so abjectly sloppy or incompetent that it fails to run its business in the manner customarily expected of any good management team. The following are some examples of these covenants.

Books and Records
A credit agreement will normally expressly mandate that the borrower maintain appropriate books and records. Few borrowers fail to do this, but if, in exercising its inspection rights, a lender were to determine that inadequate books and records were being maintained, the lenders could obviously point to this covenant as a basis for taking remedial action.

Properties
This covenant will require maintenance of all properties, subject invariably to a materiality qualifier. It is hard to see how any borrower would ever trip this covenant, but in an egregious case, it could be important.

Existence and Franchises
This covenant will require the borrower to maintain franchises and licenses necessary for the conduct of its business, although there is usually a materiality qualifier. Of course, if the business is heavily dependent upon licenses (such as FCC licenses if the borrower is a

television station or wireless company), the credit agreement will probably deal more explicitly, usually in the defaults, with what happens if any material licenses are revoked or not renewed.

Compliance with Law

This covenant will require the borrower to comply with laws, at least if failure to do so would materially adversely affect its business. Sometimes the covenant will explicitly state that the laws the borrower is to comply with include environmental laws (in case there were any doubt), but otherwise it simply obligates the borrower to do something that it should be doing already. Including the covenant in the credit agreement may give the lenders an argument that they acted in good faith in extending credit to the borrower and that they should not therefore be responsible if a government authority should seek to charge them with aiding and abetting the borrower's violation of law.

Payment of Taxes and Other Obligations

This covenant is much like the compliance with law covenant, i.e., it merely obligates the borrower to do something that it should be doing already. It will normally be qualified by materiality. Absent that qualification, the covenant might be a back-door cross-default without the customary thresholds and notice and grace periods. The covenant will typically allow the borrower not to pay its taxes and other obligations if it is contesting the payment "in good faith" and keeping "adequate reserves" against the obligation.

In theory, the requirement that the borrower pay taxes has some marginal utility, given that defaulted taxes can result in a lien upon property; however, in practice, any such lien would be captured by the negative pledge covenant and so is already controlled. As with the compliance with law covenant, this covenant may help insulate the lenders against any claim by a taxing authority or party to a contract that the lenders were aiding and abetting the borrower's failure to pay taxes or breach of contract. The lenders will be able to point to the covenant and say that they have acted in good faith vis-à-vis the borrower.

Government Approvals

If the borrower is a non-U.S. entity, the credit agreement will frequently include a covenant requiring the borrower to maintain in force any government licenses and approvals necessary to permit it to pay the loans and perform its other obligations under the credit agreement.

Substantive Consolidation

Where loans under a credit agreement are being made to a borrower that is part of a larger consolidated group of companies, the lenders may be concerned with substantive consolidation in bankruptcy. "Substantive consolidation" arises out of a line of bankruptcy court cases that treats a group of affiliated entities as if they were a single company, so that the assets of each of the affiliated companies are deemed to be owned by one entity and the creditors of each of the affiliated companies are deemed to be creditors of one entity. If in making their original credit analysis, a group of lenders relied upon the borrower having particular assets and liabilities, substantive consolidation in a bankruptcy of the borrower and the other members of the affiliated group could run roughshod over the lenders' careful analysis. Credit agreements will, therefore, sometimes include a covenant requiring that the borrower take appropriate actions to minimize the risk of substantive consolidation. These include such things as (1) observing corporate formalities (in other words, keeping the borrower's assets identified and separate from affiliates' assets), (2) not commingling borrower cash with affiliates' cash (unless done pursuant to a cash management agreement that precisely lays out the rights and liabilities of each entity that is a party to the agreement), (3) dealing with customers under the borrower's name (and not using a common name for the group of companies as if they were all one entity) and (4) maintaining books and records separate from those of its affiliates.

A recent Federal court decision (*Owens Corning*) emphasizes the desirability of lenders' performing a separate credit analysis of the borrower and each entity obligated on the loans as another tool to avoid substantive consolidation. The case suggests that assessing the strength of each support party and including in the credit agreement appropriate restrictions emphasizing their "standalone" value (such as those described in the preceding paragraph), and allowing lender visitation rights at the level of each support party, will make it less likely that a bankruptcy court will order substantive consolidation.

Use of Proceeds

The use of proceeds covenant ensures that the borrower will in fact use the loan proceeds for the purpose it specified at the time the credit agreement was entered into. Of course, if the credit agreement is providing funds for a major financing, the conditions themselves will control the actual disbursement of proceeds, so there is little likelihood that the borrower could stray. Most agreements will provide that the proceeds of term loans will be used only for one-time expenditures, such as acquisitions or capital expenditures, or to repay other debt, and that revolving credit facilities will be available for the working capital needs and general corporate purposes of the borrower. "General corporate purposes" is customarily construed broadly to allow the use of revolving loan proceeds to finance acquisitions, repay debt, or pay dividends, though the term may not permit transformational acquisitions or extraordinary dividends of a substantial portion of a borrower's capital. The term may, as a result, have little practical effect in constraining the borrower's use of the loans.

The use of proceeds covenant may also require that loan proceeds be used in accordance with applicable law (including Regulations T and U, discussed in the section "Representations" in Part 4, "Conditioning the Loan"). This language, as with the compliance with law covenant, may help give the lenders an argument that they were not, in making the loans, assisting the borrower to use the proceeds for an unlawful scheme or other purpose.

Hedging Transactions

As noted in the section "Negative Covenants" later in this part, the credit agreement will frequently restrict the borrower from entering into hedging transactions for "speculative" purposes. At the same time, the credit agreement may compel the borrower to undertake a certain minimum amount of interest hedging in order to guard against swings in interest rates that could jeopardize the borrower's ability to service interest on the loans. The normal approach will be to require that a percentage of the borrower's overall debt (including loans under the credit agreement) be hedged so that the aggregate portion of its floating-rate debt (taking into account the hedge) does not exceed a percentage (usually somewhere around 50 or 60 percent) of its total debt. Note that this gives the borrower credit for fixed-rate bond or private placement debt, since that will be treated as "hedged" for these purposes.

Hedging covenants are typically phrased fairly loosely: they will obligate the borrower only to enter into the appropriate hedges within some period (commonly three months or so) of the closing and set out only general parameters as to the manner of the hedge (though the administrative agent or the required lenders will sometimes have approval rights over final terms). The borrower will also typically not be required to maintain the hedge for more than two or three years after the closing.

Further Assurances

This covenant is most often seen in security documents as an undertaking on the part of the borrower to execute additional agreements and take other action in order that the lenders have good liens on collateral. In that context, the covenant will apply only to the property that is specified as "collateral" in the relevant security document. When a further assurances covenant is contained in a credit agreement, it will be more expansive, setting out overarching rules that govern what entities are to guarantee the loans and what types of property are to constitute collateral. This covenant is where any negotiated exceptions or thresholds will be specified, such as which subsidiaries will be deemed sufficiently immaterial to escape becoming guarantors and which real properties will be deemed too low in value to be subjected to a mortgage. The covenant may also prescribe mini-closing conditions that must be satisfied whenever any new subsidiary becomes a guarantor, requiring that the lenders be provided the same corporate assurances (resolutions and opinions, for example) as were provided on the closing date by the borrower and the initial guarantors.

NEGATIVE COVENANTS
Negative Pledge

The negative pledge (which will typically be found in the credit agreement under a section heading of "Liens") restricts the borrower's granting of security interests in its assets (and not only "pledges," a term which actually refers to possessing security interests only). The term *liens* will be defined expansively to include all manner of liens, charges, encumbrances, pledges, security interests, and the like and will also typically include the interest of a lessor under a lease and of a vendor in a conditional sale. The term may also refer to "any other type of preferential arrangement;" this is intended to capture the circumstance in which, without granting a lien, the borrower agrees to set aside or designate certain revenues for the benefit of a lender (a practice that is not infrequent in international trade or project financings). Lastly, the term may, in the case of securities, pick up purchase and call options and other similar third-party rights. The purpose of the covenant is to limit the number of creditors that will enjoy a preferential status in a bankruptcy or insolvency of the borrower. Secured creditors normally vote as a separate class in a bankruptcy and thus can have significant bargaining leverage in addition to their right to be paid the entire proceeds or value of the property in which they have a lien.

The previous paragraph describes the lien covenant normally seen in credit agreements, i.e., a covenant that prohibits liens except to the extent that they fall into one or more exclusions. In the context of most bond indentures and some credit agreements, the lien covenant may take a different approach: rather than prohibiting liens directly, it will simply provide that, if liens (other than "permitted encumbrances") are granted by the borrower to a third party, the lenders must be "equally and ratably" secured. This is the so-called equal and ratable sharing clause.

There is basically no law and only very little lore concerning what an equal and ratable sharing clause means. The general consensus seems to be that, at least prior to acceleration or insolvency, "sharing" requires only sharing of the lien and does not require sharing control over the collateral. Thus the tag-along debt (the debt that contains the equal and ratable sharing clause and that, therefore, is entitled to be equally and ratably secured by reason of liens being granted to a third party) would have no right to consent to a release of collateral; that right would reside exclusively with the lenders triggering the clause. Further, there would be no requirement (again, absent acceleration or foreclosure) that the tag-along debt be entitled to approve a sale of collateral or share in the proceeds of a sale. In fact, there may not even be a requirement that the tag-along debt be entitled to initiate foreclosure, that right again residing solely with the debt whose lien triggers the clause. In effect, an equal and ratable sharing clause requires only the sharing of proceeds when and if they arise. The clause thus affords much less protection than a straight lien covenant and consequently is not normally seen in credit agreements.

With liens being defined so broadly, it naturally follows that the negative pledge covenant will contain numerous exceptions. Customary exclusions include among others:

Lender Liens
Liens in favor of the lenders. In most cases, this exception will automatically include liens securing increases under the credit agreement.

Grandfathered Liens
Liens that were in existence on the closing date (normally listed in a disclosure schedule if they exceed a dollar threshold). The agreement may permit these liens to be "extended, renewed, or refinanced," though it typically bars the affected lien from spreading to new property.

Permitted Encumbrances
"Permitted encumbrances," usually defined to sweep up a wide variety of liens that any business enterprise cannot avoid incurring in the ordinary course of business, such as easements and rights of way, warehouse liens, workers' compensation liens, mechanics' liens, utility pledges, rights of offset, and the like. Inchoate tax liens may also be permitted if the tax is not yet due or is being contested in good faith by the borrower.

Purchase Money Liens
Liens covering property that secure financing for the purchase price of the property. The lien could thus be in favor of the seller of the property or in favor of a bank that supplied funds to enable the property to be purchased. Typically, the lien will not be allowed to exceed the cost of the property (or sometimes a percentage of the cost) and must be incurred within some short period (say 90 days) of the property's being acquired. In addition, to qualify as a purchase money lien, the underlying obligation may not be secured by any other property of the borrower. Purchase money liens would

not include liens in existence on the property at the time it was acquired; those liens would need to fit into the acquisition lien basket, discussed next.

Acquisition Liens
Liens are liens that were in existence on property (or on property of a subsidiary) at the time the property (or subsidiary) was acquired. Liens created in anticipation of the acquisition will not qualify.

Lien Basket
Additional liens permitted without restriction up to a negotiated dollar threshold (included in many, though not all, credit agreements).

Negative Negative Pledge

A negative pledge, as described previously, limits the ability of the borrower to grant liens on its assets. A "negative negative pledge" takes this one step further and limits the ability of a borrower to enter into negative pledges with third parties. Thus, if an agreement has a negative negative pledge, the borrower would be prohibited from agreeing with a third party that its ability to grant liens is constrained (an equal and ratable sharing clause, discussed in the section "Negative Pledge," may count as a negative negative pledge for these purposes). The principal reason why a lender would want a negative negative pledge is to ensure that the borrower is free to grant security to the lender in the future without having to obtain consent from any third party.

Since a borrower can be expected to be subject to many lien restrictions in the ordinary course of its business, a negative negative pledge covenant will normally contemplate a long list of exclusions. Thus, for example, there will be exclusions for preexisting limitations and exclusions for contracts to which the borrower is a party that cannot be assigned or pledged without the consent of the counterparty. Similarly, there will be exclusions for property subject to permitted liens in favor of third parties and for leases (lessors customarily limit the ability of a lessee to grant liens on the leased property). Exclusions also may be permitted for contracts of sale where, pending a closing, the prospective purchaser of an item of property or division will want to limit the borrower's ability to grant liens on the property or division.

Debt

The debt covenant restricts the incurrence by the borrower and its subsidiaries of "debt." As with many definitions used in negative covenants, the term *debt* is defined expansively. The objective of the covenant is to ensure that the borrower does not take on more debt than it can service, given the cash being thrown off by its business. Customary exceptions include:

Lender Debt
Loans and letters of credit under the credit agreement; as with liens, this will automatically include any increases under the credit agreement.

Grandfathered Debt
Debt is debt that was in existence on the closing date; it is normally listed in a disclosure schedule if it exceeds a dollar threshold. One issue that will frequently be addressed is whether grandfathered debt includes extensions, renewals, and refinancings. Generally, to the extent that these are allowed, the credit agreement will state that the principal amount of the debt that is extended, renewed, or refinanced not be increased (other than for accrued interest and premiums). Any increase would, therefore, force usage of another basket.

Purchase Money Debt
Debt that finances the purchase price of property, whether in favor of the seller or in favor of a bank that supplies funds to enable the property to be purchased. Since this debt is normally secured by the underlying property, the exception may cross-reference to the purchase money basket in the lien covenant.

Working Capital Debt
Debt that provides working capital (at least in cases where the credit agreement does not have a revolving credit facility and is not supplying all necessary working capital liquidity to the borrower). Since working capital debt can often be short term or even payable

on demand, the credit agreement will typically impose limitations on the amount of such debt and the institutions from which it may be incurred. It may also limit the basket to particular subsidiaries, such as foreign subsidiaries.

Acquisition Debt
Debt that exists at the time an entity becomes a subsidiary. As with acquisition liens, debt created in anticipation of the purchase will not qualify.

Intercompany Debt
Debt between and among the borrower and its subsidiaries. In some instances, the credit agreement will provide that debt of the borrower to subsidiaries (as distinct from debt of subsidiaries to the borrower and intersubsidiary debt) must be subordinated to the claims of the lenders under the credit agreement. This is to prevent the subsidiaries (or, more importantly, creditors of a subsidiary that becomes insolvent) from competing with the lenders in obtaining payment of claims against the borrower.

Subsidiary Debt
Third-party debt of subsidiaries, although sometimes the credit agreement will limit the aggregate amount of this debt to avoid "structural subordination." The term refers to the fact that all claims against a subsidiary must be paid in full before any money may flow up to a shareholder, i.e., the borrower. If the credit agreement permits a subsidiary to have a large amount of debt, then (unless the subsidiary is also a guarantor of the loans) all debt of the subsidiary must be paid in full before any cash can be upstreamed to the borrower to service the loans. The lenders would, therefore, be effectively subordinated to the debt of the subsidiary.

Additional Debt
Additional public or quasi-public debt, such as a senior or subordinated high yield bond. Normally debt of this type will be subject to constraints as to aggregate amount, tenor (typically not earlier than 90 days after the maturity of the loans under the credit agreement), weighted average life to maturity (not earlier than that for the loans under the credit agreement), and redemption requirements and

covenants. Sometimes the latter will be required to be approved by the required lenders, but more frequently the credit agreement will simply mandate that they satisfy the market standard in effect at the time the debt is issued.

Debt Basket

As with the lien basket, a basket for debt that does not fit into any of the other listed exceptions. Sometimes the portion of the basket debt that may be utilized by subsidiaries is limited because of the structural subordination issues described previously.

Disqualified Stock

Although this is not normally a separate covenant, some credit agreements will control the issuance of "disqualified stock." The concept, which is very common in the bond indenture context, restricts the amount of debtlike equity, such as preferred stock that is entitled to mandatory redemption at a future specified date. Generally, if that date is within a defined period (typically 90 days or a year) *after* the maturity date for loans under the credit agreement, the lenders will want to treat the preferred as equivalent to debt. It will thus be controlled by the debt covenant and will be included in leverage tests.

Fundamental Changes

A fundamental change covenant will typically control three types of actions: mergers, acquisitions, and dispositions. The objective is to prevent transactions that would change the business or assets of the borrower upon which the lenders' initial credit decisions were made in some fundamental way. Sometimes a credit agreement will break these out into three separate covenants.

Mergers

The limitation on mergers will restrict the ability of the borrower to merge or consolidate with other entities. There will be exceptions. Almost universally, a credit agreement will permit mergers and consolidations of subsidiaries into the borrower if the borrower is the surviving or continuing corporation. Less frequently, a credit agreement will permit nonsubsidiaries to merge with the borrower if the borrower is the surviving entity *and* if the merger itself would be permitted under the acquisition limitation. The requirement that the borrower always survive contrasts with the approach typically found in bond indentures, where mergers are permitted even in cases where the issuer is not the survivor. A bond indenture will nevertheless still constrain the issuer by requiring that the surviving entity assume the issuer's obligations under the indenture and that the survivor satisfy certain other tests, such as being organized in the United States, not having a reduced net worth, and being able to incur at least $1.00 of additional debt.

Acquisitions
A limitation on acquisitions will control the ability of the borrower to acquire another business. It will thus control not just acquisitions of the equity of another company, but also acquisitions of a business or division of another company. As with the limitation on mergers, an exclusion will be made for "acquisitions" that are transfers of assets between and among subsidiaries or by subsidiaries to the borrower.

Dispositions
A covenant limiting dispositions will usually be in one of two forms: either it will limit sales by the borrower of "all or substantially all" assets or it will limit sales of "any assets." Although there are few court decisions illuminating what "substantially all" means, analogizing to the way the term is used in other contexts (such as state corporation law), there is a general consensus that a sale of "substantially all" of the assets of an entity could occur with a transfer of as little as 50 percent of the assets, or of assets representing as little as 45 percent of the revenue. Thus, if assets representing a mere 50 percent of the balance sheet book value are responsible for 90 percent of the borrower's EBITDA, a court could easily hold that a sale of those assets is a sale of "all or substantially all" of the assets of the company.

The "all or substantially all" restriction, of course, is considerably more flexible from the viewpoint of the borrower than an "any assets" covenant. The latter will need (and will customarily incorporate) exclusions for sales of inventory in the ordinary course of business and for sales of worn-out or obsolete property or equipment (the latter usually being capped at a dollar maximum).

Although it may seem redundant, credit agreements will regularly require prepayments from the proceeds of asset sales where the asset sale is itself not permitted under the credit agreement. Traditionally, there was logic to this approach, since the asset sale covenant could be waived by the required lenders, but changes in the prepayment covenant required the approval of a higher percentage (or all) of the lenders. Voting provisions tend to no longer be crafted in this manner, and credit agreements now routinely provide that prepayment requirements, unless they adversely affect one lender or tranche when compared to others, can be modified with the consent of the required lenders. The double treatment of asset sales (as a prepayment and in the fundamental changes covenant) is nevertheless continued in most credit agreements.

Sale-Leasebacks

Very common in bond indentures, sale-leaseback covenants are sometimes also incorporated into credit agreements. The basic purpose is to control a transaction in which the borrower sells an asset and then immediately leases it back under a capital or operating lease arrangement. It restricts, in sum, a form of secured financing. Of course, in the context of a credit agreement (but perhaps not in the context of a bond indenture), each of the elements of a sale-leaseback transaction should already be controlled by other covenants (among them the negative pledge, debt, and fundamental changes covenants), and so, from a technical standpoint, the restriction may be unnecessary. Nevertheless, it is sometimes inserted into credit agreements to cover the situation in which a sale-leaseback transaction might otherwise fit within an applicable basket.

Investments

From the standpoint of a lender, the objective of an investments covenant is much like that of the fundamental changes covenant: to control material changes to the business or assets of the borrower upon which the lender's initial credit decision was made. There is considerable overlap between the two covenants (a purchase of 100 percent of the stock of a corporation would, for example, constitute both an investment and an acquisition, and therefore any such purchase would need to satisfy the conditions of both covenants).

The definition of the term *investments* will, like other definitions, be perhaps overexpansive and encompass not just the acquisition of securities, but also extensions of credit, issuance of guarantees, and, sometimes, entering into hedging agreements. The term will normally not include extensions of credit by the borrower to customers in the ordinary course of business, i.e., the customary credit terms given by a borrower for payment of inventory or services (though sometimes credit terms longer than 90 or 180 days will be treated as investments). Expansiveness leads, in turn, to a variety of exceptions, including:

Grandfathered Investments
Investments in existence on the closing date (usually listed on a disclosure schedule if they exceed a dollar threshold). Grandfathered investments will not normally need to cover subsidiaries or cash equivalents, since each is customarily covered by other exceptions.

Permitted Investments
"Permitted investments" normally defined to mean a variety of liquid investments of high credit quality, such as commercial paper with high ratings from Moody's and Standard & Poor's, short-term Treasuries (or short-term repos on Treasuries), short-term certificates of deposit, and money market funds that primarily invest in other securities fitting within the definition of permitted investments. The term is intended to capture investments that can be treated essentially as equivalent to cash. Accordingly, equity securities are not included because of the potential for market volatility. Longer-term bonds (even if given the highest rating by Moody's and Standard & Poor's) and longer-term Treasury securities are normally not included because interest-rate volatility can adversely affect their market value.

Subsidiaries
Investments in subsidiaries (whether by the borrower or by other subsidiaries). In cases where the credit analysis of the borrower is based upon its being an operating entity with operating assets, the lender may want to control the movement of assets from the

borrower into subsidiaries and will, therefore, impose a dollar cap. The concern for the lender is allowing itself to be structurally subordinated to creditors of a subsidiary, which are entitled to be paid in full from the assets of the subsidiary before any money flows up to the borrower. Allowing the borrower to put money into subsidiaries may simply be supporting creditors of the subsidiaries. Sometimes this concern can be dealt with by having the subsidiaries guarantee the loans under the credit agreement. Another possible solution is to require that investments in subsidiaries be in the form of debt rather than equity. Claims by the borrower as a creditor with respect to the intercompany debt should then compete (in theory) with the other creditors of a subsidiary (though in some cases in a bankruptcy, the claims of a borrower against a subsidiary will be equitably subordinated). See the discussion of structural subordination in the section "Debt" earlier in this part.

Ordinary Course Items
Investments that any company cannot avoid in the ordinary course of business, such as operating deposit accounts with banks (sometimes subject to a requirement concerning the size or creditworthiness of the deposit institution) and security deposits with utilities in the ordinary course of business.

Acquisitions
Investments constituting acquisitions that are permitted under the fundamental changes covenant.

Basket
Investments that are not allowed under the other exceptions, usually up to some agreed dollar threshold.

Lines of Business

Consistent with the concerns described in the section "Fundamental Changes" earlier in this part, lenders make a credit analysis of the borrower based upon the nature of its current business. To take an example, the lenders will not want to see a cable television company enter the fast-food business. Not only may the borrower's management be unfamiliar with the operation of a fast-food business, but the financial covenants may no longer appropriately measure how the company is performing. As a result, many credit agreements will contain a line of business covenant that will require that a borrower not enter in any material respect into lines of business different from those in which the borrower is engaged at the closing of the credit agreement.

Derivatives

As discussed in the section "Affirmative Covenants" earlier in this part, lenders will often require a borrower to enter into hedging agreements (particularly interest hedges) in connection with the execution of the credit agreement. At the same time, however, the lenders may be concerned that the borrower could "overhedge" (speculate) in currencies, commodities, interest indices, or any of the numerous other products available in the derivatives markets. Accordingly, credit agreements will frequently control the hedging transactions into which the borrower may wish to enter beyond those required by the lenders in the affirmative covenants. These limitations can be found in a number of places. Sometimes hedges are deemed to be debt and thus are limited by the debt covenant. A second approach is to treat hedges as investments. A third approach is simply to deal with hedges in a stand-alone covenant.

Regardless of how hedges are controlled, it is often not terribly practical to limit hedge exposures to a dollar cap, since that would require daily recalculation of the exposure under a hedge as interest and other indicators change. The more customary approach, therefore, is to avoid dollar caps and allow hedges so long as they are entered in the ordinary course of the borrower's financial planning and not for speculative purposes.

Guarantees or Contingent Liabilities

Guarantees are frequently controlled by both the debt covenant (by treating guarantees of debt of a third party as debt of the guarantor) and the investments covenant (by treating guarantees of obligations of a third party as an investment in the third party). Some credit agreements will also control guarantees and other contingent liabilities with a separate covenant as well. "Guarantees" for these purposes, as in the debt and investments covenants, will be defined very broadly to pick up not just a simple guarantee, but also a broad variety of other arrangements, such as the borrower's causing a bank to issue a letter of credit to support the obligations of a third party or the borrower's agreeing to protect a third party against loss arising out of a commercial transaction. So-called take or pay agreements would also be captured, where, for the benefit of a creditor of a third party, the borrower agrees to purchase products (such as oil or processed chemicals) from the third party whether or not the third party is able to deliver the products to the borrower. Similarly, support arrangements where the borrower agrees with the creditor of a subsidiary to maintain the net worth of the subsidiary regardless of adverse events would be treated as a guarantee. If the net worth must always be positive, the borrower has in effect guaranteed the indebtedness of the subsidiary. The breadth of the definition stems from the expectation that borrowers will have an infinite capacity to be creative in structuring deals, and so the broader (and more verbose) the guarantee concept, the better.

The amount of a guarantee will be deemed to be equal to the amount of the stated limit. The amount of the guarantee will not be reduced by the fact that other parties are jointly and severally obligated with the borrower and that, therefore, the borrower can seek reimbursement from other parties for any payment by it in excess of its pro rata share.

Dividends

The dividend covenant in a credit agreement will limit dividends and distributions by the borrower. It will not, as is typically the case in bond indentures, be part of a broader category of "restricted payments" that limits both investments and dividends. A credit agreement will customarily control dividends and investments in separate covenants.

As with other definitions employed in other negative covenants, the term *dividend* or *dividend payment* will be defined expansively. It will not only pick up the layman's understanding of periodic dividends declared by the borrower's board, but also capture any other device by which money could leave the borrower and be paid to equity holders. Thus, it will include distributions, sinking fund payments, purchases of stock, and even "phantom stock" payments, i.e., where a creditor or employee is entitled to an equity-like return as if it held stock without actually owning any equity. It will include those actions if they are undertaken by the borrower; it will also include those actions if they are undertaken by subsidiaries (the theory being that a repurchase of *borrower* stock by a subsidiary is still money out of the consolidated group). Customary exceptions include:

Employee Stock Plans
Dividend payments arising when the borrower repurchases stock from employees upon their death or retirement. The aggregate repurchases in any single year are usually subject to a dollar cap.

Intercompany Dividends
Dividend payments by subsidiaries of the borrower to the borrower and to other subsidiaries. In the case where a subsidiary is not wholly owned, the exception will simply require that dividend payments be made ratably by the subsidiary to all of its shareholders.

Stock Dividends
Dividends paid through the issuance of additional shares of stock (other than disqualified stock; see the discussion in "Disqualified Stock" earlier in this part). Stock dividends will almost always be permitted without limit (frequently by carving out stock dividends from the definition entirely), since they do not represent money leaving the borrower's consolidated group.

Preferred Dividends
Dividends on preferred stock. Normally the exclusion will permit dividends only at the level in effect at the closing date and will not provide for dividends on future issuances of preferred. Normally also, this type of dividend will be blocked during an event of default.

Parent Company Debt
If the parent of the borrower has outstanding debt, dividend payments to the extent necessary to pay interest on such debt, so long as no event of default exists. As with preferred dividends, the amount of dividends permitted will normally be locked in at the

closing date and will not be increased if additional parent debt is issued.

Dividend Basket

A dividend payment basket based on a simple per annum dollar amount, a percentage of net income or cash flow, or some other figure negotiated among the parties, so long as no event of default exists. Sometimes also there may be a requirement that the borrower deliver an officer's certificate with a supporting calculation demonstrating that the borrower is in compliance at the time of the dividend and will continue to be in compliance after payment of the dividend.

Tax-Sharing Payments

If the borrower is a domestic corporation that is more than 80 percent owned by another domestic corporation, under the U.S. Internal Revenue Code, it will be consolidated with its ultimate parent for tax purposes. This means that the ultimate parent will be the entity that actually pays taxes to the government. Of course the parent will look to its subsidiaries (including, in this case, the borrower and its subsidiaries) for funds to make the tax payments. Credit agreements sometimes limit the aggregate amount of payments that may be made to a borrower's parent to an amount deemed to be "fair" from the standpoint of the borrower. The parent might, for example, have other subsidiaries that are generating substantially more current income than the borrower; in these circumstances, it would not be appropriate (arguably) for the borrower to pay more to its parent than the amount it would have been required to pay had it been an independent taxpayer. The restriction on tax-sharing payments is typically not a separate covenant, but is incorporated into either the dividend or the affiliate transactions covenant.

Dividend Blockers

A dividend blocker relates to a dividend covenant in the same way that a negative negative pledge relates to a negative pledge covenant. In other words, a dividend blocker will prohibit the borrower from agreeing with third parties that dividends and distributions by subsidiaries to the borrower are constrained. The covenant will also typically restrict other kinds of limitations on money or property going "upstream," such as through sales or mergers or other transfers. Lenders are concerned, in this context, that the borrower's access to funds may be dependent upon money flowing upstream from subsidiaries. Restricting that flow could impair the borrower's ability to pay the scheduled principal and interest on the loans.

As with the negative negative pledge, there are a number of customary exceptions that will be incorporated into the dividend blocker covenant, including exclusions for preexisting limitations and exclusions for contracts of sale of a subsidiary where, pending a closing, the prospective purchaser of the subsidiary will want to freeze dissipation of the assets of the subsidiary by means of upstream transfers.

Modification and Prepayment of Other Debt

Loans under the credit agreement are often not the borrower's only debt. Subordinated debt and other senior debt may be outstanding, whether in the form of a private placement held by insurance companies, a bond indenture, or other debt issuance. The credit analysis of the borrower by the lenders will, of course, have taken into account the borrower's closing date capital structure, including the maturity of any other debt and the terms and conditions applicable to the other debt. Changes in the other debt, such as to shorten the maturity, tighten covenants, increase interest rates, or the like, may adversely affect the credit profile of the borrower.

Credit agreements deal with these issues by controlling amendments to other debt and by limiting the ability of the borrower to prepay other debt. Sometimes the restriction on amendments will apply only to "nonmaterial" modifications. However, this approach can lead to difficulty in determining whether a change rises to the level of materiality that requires lender consent. One issue that will often be addressed is whether debt may be refinanced. When this is permitted, the credit agreement will typically set out a detailed set of criteria, including criteria with respect to amortization and maturity, interest rate, covenants, and redemption or repurchase events, that will be applicable to any refinancing indebtedness.

The prepayments limitation will apply only to voluntary pre-payments of other debt; it will not apply to scheduled principal or interest payments or to mandatory prepayments. The reason for this latter approach is the doctrine of "tortious interference." Courts will generally not permit parties to enter into an agreement if compliance with that agreement would require a breach of another agreement by which one of them is bound. Thus, a court would probably not allow a borrower to enter into a credit agreement with a group of lenders if compliance with the credit agreement would constitute a breach of a covenant in another debt agreement (such as by restricting the borrower's ability to make required debt payments). If the lenders did not carve out required payments or mandatory prepayments, they could expose themselves to liability to the holders of the other debt.

Affiliate Transactions

The affiliate transactions covenant restricts transactions between the borrower and its affiliates. "Affiliates" will typically be defined with reference to the SEC standard, i.e., whether an entity is "controlled" by voting power, contract, or otherwise. Anyone controlling the borrower or under common control with the borrower will be an affiliate. The definition may in some cases deem a percentage ownership (5 or 10 percent) to constitute control. If the borrower is closely held, the term may also sometimes expressly include family members of controlling parties.

The rationale for the covenant is the fear that an entity or individual controlling the borrower may be able to unduly influence the terms of transactions with that entity or individual (or with other entities that it or the individual controls). In a sense, the affiliate transactions covenant is another leg of the dividend covenant, in that it controls money going out of the system to equity holders. Thus, while a dividend covenant might prohibit the payment of dividends to the owner of a privately held company, absent a restriction on affiliate transactions, there would be nothing to prevent that company from purchasing pencils at a price of $1,000 each from the owner or from the owner's wife or son. Of course, in a public company, the securities laws will provide a measure of legal protection that may make this kind of abuse less likely.

Normally a credit agreement will allow transactions between the borrower and affiliates for the purchase or sale of property in the ordinary course of business if the transaction takes place on terms not less favorable to the borrower than terms that would be applicable to a transaction between two disinterested parties. This is the so-called arm's-length exception. Credit agreements will rarely adopt the approach taken in bond indentures, which will apply the arm's-length exception to any transaction (not just for the purchase and sale of property) and determine compliance with the arm's-length standard based upon either a board resolution or, if the transaction exceeds a dollar threshold, upon a third-party appraisal.

An affiliate transactions covenant will also normally contain exceptions for transactions otherwise expressly permitted under the credit agreement, such as the payment of dividends, and, because directors and senior officers may be deemed to be affiliates, for compensation to directors and officers, loans and advances to officers, and stock and bonus plans.

Amendments to Organic Documents and Other Agreements

Credit agreements may sometimes limit amendments to the borrower's charter, bylaws, or other organic documents. The fear is that the borrower might amend these instruments in a manner adverse to the lenders, such as by authorizing the issuance of preferred stock that benefits from mandatory dividends or redemption provisions. In most agreements, these concerns will be addressed by other covenants (in this example, the debt and dividend covenants), so including a limitation on amendments to organic documents is relatively rare.

Credit agreements may also sometimes limit amendments to material agreements. Modifications to other debt documents is one example and is discussed in "Modification and Prepayment of Other Debt" earlier in this part. Other examples might include a purchase and sale contract pursuant to which a major acquisition financed by the proceeds of the loans was consummated. In this case, the lenders may limit the ability of the borrower to waive rights it may have under the indemnification provisions of the contract. Similarly, if a supply contract is an important source of raw materials for the borrower, or if sales under a requirements contract provide funds critical to servicing the loans, modifications to those contracts could be restricted by the covenant.

One qualification that is frequently inserted into the covenant, as applied to either organic documents or other material agreements, allows the borrower to effect modifications without the consent of the lenders if the modification is "not adverse" or "not materially adverse" to the lenders, or if the modification will not adversely affect the rights of the borrower under the contract. From the borrower's perspective, this allows it to effect *de minimis* changes (such as modifications to the notice provisions or other routine matters) without having to obtain the consent of the lenders. There is considerable logic to this type of exclusion (especially since agents and lending syndicates typically do not want to be bothered with nonmaterial modifications), so many credit agreements carve out nonmaterial changes. This is so despite the difficulty of determining what is material in any particular circumstance (though some agreements will permit the administrative agent to decide whether a change is material, and only if it is material will a vote of the required lenders be taken).

Fiscal Periods and Accounting Changes

Financial covenants are often prepared with a view to step-ups or step-downs occurring at times of the year corresponding to fiscal quarter or fiscal year end dates. This makes determining compliance with the covenants straightforward for both the borrower and the lenders. To permit the borrower to change fiscal end dates would either require the lenders to guess whether the borrower is in compliance or force the borrower to prepare one-off, less reliable financial statements at a date that does not correspond to a fiscal period end. Credit agreements, accordingly, frequently restrict the ability of a borrower to change fiscal end days.

As noted earlier in the discussion of GAAP, the financial covenants set forth in a credit agreement are usually prepared on a base set of "generally accepted accounting principles" that have been "consistently applied." Changes in the application of those principles to the financial statements of the borrower, whether at the borrower's own initiative or as a result of changes in GAAP, could mean that the financial covenants no longer adequately measure business performance. The lenders, of course, fear that a change might make compliance too easy; the borrower fears that compliance will become too difficult. Credit agreements will thus often include a requirement that all financial covenants be calculated in a manner consistent with the generally accepted accounting principles used when the lenders made their initial credit analysis leading up to the closing. To minimize the expense of the borrower having to prepare two sets of financial statements, the agreement will contemplate that, in the event of a change in GAAP, the parties will negotiate appropriate changes to the financial covenants so that the required covenant levels reflect the changed GAAP. Absent agreement, the financial covenants will be calculated in accordance with original closing date GAAP.

INCORPORATION BY REFERENCE

From time to time, a credit agreement will incorporate covenants from another agreement. When necessary, these provisions will also incorporate related definitions and specify any necessary changes in terminology. For example, if the covenants being incorporated are set out in a bond indenture, the incorporation will need to stipulate that references in the covenants to "notes" and "noteholders" will be deemed to refer to "loans" and "lenders."

One key question that the incorporation provision will address is whether covenants are to be incorporated "as amended from time to time" or "as in effect" on the date of incorporation. The former removes the ability of the lenders to consent to changes to the incorporated covenants. The latter gives the lenders an independent consent right. Of course, even if incorporated "as amended from time to time," the covenant will still need to address what happens if, say, the bond indenture from which the covenants are incorporated is terminated. In that instance, the incorporation provision will normally provide that the indenture covenants are incorporated "as last in effect."

Part 6. Securing and Guaranteeing the Loan: Collateral Packages

GUARANTEES AND SECURITY GENERALLY

The obligations of a borrower under a credit agreement are frequently guaranteed, either by its parent or by its subsidiaries or other affiliates. The obligations of the borrower and guarantors are also frequently secured. Whether guarantee and security provisions are set forth in the credit agreement or in a separate agreement varies. Guarantees are often set out in the credit agreement (primarily for ease of reading); security provisions, except perhaps in the asset-based lending context, are rarely set forth in the credit agreement.

GUARANTEES

Guarantees Generally

A guarantee is a secondary obligation, meaning that the guarantor generally becomes obligated to make payment only if the primary obligor (the borrower) fails to do so. With some exceptions (such as California), there is no comprehensive statute governing guarantees (as there is, for example, under the civil code in many countries), and guarantees are therefore governed by common law decisions of the courts of the various U.S. states. At common law, guarantors were favored. As a result, court decisions have established a number of qualifications to the obligations of guarantors that, unless waived in the guarantee itself, can present pitfalls and traps for the lender. These qualifications drive much of the language that is seen in the typical guarantee.

Guarantee of Payment versus Guarantee of Collection

Guarantees are almost always structured as guarantees of payment rather than guarantees of collection. A guarantee of collection would require the lender to exhaust all remedies against the borrower before making a claim under the guarantee (and then only for the ultimate shortfall not paid by the borrower). By contrast, a guarantee of payment obligates the guarantor to pay the lender immediately upon the default of the borrower, regardless of whether the borrower has been notified of the default, whether a demand has been made on the borrower, or whether the lender has taken any other action against the borrower. This can be a very important right if, for example, the borrower is in bankruptcy and the guarantor is not. If a lender were required to take action against the borrower as a precursor to making a demand on a guarantor, it would be in a hopeless situation, since taking action against the borrower would violate the Bankruptcy Code's automatic stay. Accordingly, the typical guarantee will very explicitly have the guarantor waive any requirement that the lender first take any action against the borrower so that the lenders receive a guarantee of payment.

Waivers

At common law, the granting of extra time to the borrower, waiver or amendment of its obligations, the release of security, the release of other guarantors, and a host of other actions by a lender could have the effect of releasing a guarantee. Guarantees, therefore, routinely state that they are "absolute and unconditional" and include waivers of these common law defenses. Case law in California counsels that these waivers be as explicit as possible, resulting in detailed waiver provisions; in New York, it is common for guarantee waivers to refer specifically to only a few of the circumstances that could release the guarantor at common law, and to rely otherwise on a "sweep-up" phrase waiving "any other circumstance whatsoever that might otherwise constitute a legal or equitable discharge or defense of a guarantor or surety."

Subrogation

If a guarantor makes payment, it may at common law be "subrogated" to the rights of the payee to the extent of the payment. In other words, the guarantor would step into the shoes of the lender with respect to the loan paid by the guarantors. Customary guarantee provisions allow such subrogation, but require that any exercise of subrogation rights by the guarantor (which, at that point, would make the guarantor a competing creditor of the borrower) be postponed until the lenders have received full payment of their claims.

Reinstatement

If a borrower were to make payment on a loan within 90 days of filing for bankruptcy, the payment could potentially be recovered from the lenders as a "preference" under Section 547 of the Bankruptcy Code. To avoid the lenders' having to argue with the guarantor as to whether or not the borrower's original payment (now reversed) discharged the guarantee, guarantees generally include an express "reinstatement" clause, to the effect that a guarantee is automatically revived if a payment by the borrower is reversed or recaptured. The reinstatement clause will typically also require the guarantor to indemnify the lenders for any costs that they may incur in resisting the preference claim, the theory being that the lenders' fight in this regard is, in substance, a fight for the account of the guarantor.

Insolvency of Borrower

Lenders may make a demand on a guarantor only for amounts that have not been paid by the borrower when due. What happens if the borrower declares bankruptcy and the automatic stay operates to prevent an acceleration of the loans or if any other court order prevents acceleration? (See the discussion of the automatic stay in the section "Insolvency" in Part 7, "Enforcing the Loans.") To prevent the guarantee's being rendered worthless because there is nothing payable by the borrower that can be demanded from the guarantor, guarantees will include a provision that, if an event of default occurs and for any reason the lenders are prevented from accelerating the loans, the loans are nevertheless deemed to be due and payable for purposes of any claims on the guarantor. Thus, even though the loans are not accelerated as against the borrower, the loans are accelerated as against the guarantor.

Continuing Guarantee

A guarantee will typically specify that it is "continuing," i.e., that it covers not only obligations outstanding at the time the guarantee is issued, but also future obligations of the borrower incurred from time to time. Absent this language, the guarantee arguably would not cover future advances, for example, loans and letters of credit made under the revolving credit facility after the closing.

Summary Procedure

Sometimes a guarantee that is stated to be governed by New York law includes a provision that the guarantee is "an instrument for the payment of money only" within the meaning of Section 3213 of

New York's Civil Practice Law and Rules. An instrument that so qualifies may be enforced by expedited (or summary) procedure under Section 3213. It is not clear that saying that a guarantee is such an instrument makes it so (many guarantees include a variety of undertakings beyond the obligation to pay money), but there is some authority in New York that an express consent by the parties to enforcement under Section 3213 will be given effect.

Downstream, Cross-stream, and Upstream Guarantees

Guarantees can be "upstream" (a subsidiary guaranteeing the debt of its parent), "cross-stream" (a subsidiary guaranteeing the debt of a "sister" company, where both are ultimately owned by the same parent), or "downstream" (a parent guaranteeing the debt of a subsidiary). An upstream or cross-stream guarantee may be vulnerable to attack under federal and state insolvency laws because, except to the extent that the guarantor received the proceeds of the guaranteed loans or other "reasonably equivalent value," one of the two requirements for a "fraudulent conveyance" or "fraudulent transfer" will have been established. If, after giving effect to the guarantee, the guarantor is "insolvent," then both requirements will have been established. See the discussion in the section "Solvency" in Part 4, "Conditioning the Loan."

Credit agreements deal with this risk in two ways. Some will incorporate a so-called solvency cap or savings clause, where the agreement will limit or cap the guarantee at the maximum amount (but not one penny more) that would allow it to be enforced without resulting in a fraudulent conveyance. To take a simplified example, if a subsidiary has an excess of assets over liabilities of $10,000,000, and it guarantees debt in a face amount of $10,000,000, the aggregate amount of the guarantee would be limited automatically to $9,999,999 (leaving an excess of assets over liabilities of $1.00). Thus, even though the subsidiary may not receive any of the proceeds of the loans, it would not be rendered insolvent by reason of the guarantee, and so no fraudulent conveyance will arise. One weakness of the solvency cap is that it makes the amount of the guarantee unclear.

Other credit agreements will insert a so-called cross-contribution concept, where the borrower and each of the other guarantors agree that if any guarantor makes payment under a guarantee greater than the excess of its assets over its liabilities, it will be entitled to be reimbursed by the borrower and each other guarantor for the amount of the excess. The effect of this structure is to give the guarantor an additional asset (namely, the contingent reimbursement claim against the borrower and any other guarantors), which is designed to make the guarantor solvent at the time the guarantee is undertaken. The solvency representation (discussed in the section "Solvency" in Part 4, "Conditioning the Loan") will verify that the borrower and guarantors (together with their subsidiaries) as a whole are solvent (and thereby confirm that the contingent reimbursement claims are in fact money good).

Neither of these solutions may work if an upstream or cross-stream guarantee is being given by an entity organized outside of the United States. Many countries have so-called financial assistance rules that carry much more severe consequences than the fraudulent conveyance and fraudulent transfer doctrines in the United States. If a guarantee would render a guarantor insolvent, violation of these rules can result in personal liability (and even, in some cases, criminal liability) for managers or directors. Often, savings and cross-contribution clauses such as those described previously will be ineffective. As a result, even in situations where the tax problem described in the section "Deemed Dividends" later in this part does not exist, guarantees from foreign subsidiaries may become a patchwork of full guarantees, dollar-capped guarantees, and no guarantees—altogether a confused structure when compared to guarantees from U.S. subsidiaries.

COLLATERAL PACKAGES

Whole treatises have been written about the legal intricacies of collateral security. This chapter will not do so, but will focus briefly only on how collateral security affects the drafting of a credit agreement. In some cases, the parties may set forth the full set of security provisions in the credit agreement rather than placing them in a separate security agreement. As noted previously, this approach is quite rare. In most cases, therefore, taking collateral security affects only a few discrete provisions of a credit agreement including the following.

Conditions

The conditions precedent will typically include a requirement that the liens be perfected and that evidence (such as Uniform Commercial Code or title search results) of the priority of the liens be delivered to the administrative agent. In the case of a mortgage on real property, the conditions may also include the delivery of title insurance and surveys. If other particular kinds of collateral are to be included, such as collateral located outside of the United States, the conditions may be explicit as to the action that must be taken under relevant local law.

Representations

The credit agreement may include a representation that all action to perfect the liens has been taken (though, more frequently, this representation will be incorporated into the security documents).

In some cases, credit agreements will adopt an approach used in secured bond indentures of requiring the borrower to deliver an annual certificate (sometimes accompanied by an opinion of counsel) to the administrative agent confirming that all actions necessary to continue the perfection of liens has been taken. The agreement may also include similar annual confirmations that all insurance required to cover collateral is being maintained.

Affirmative Covenants

The further assurances covenant will typically be more expansive, including a description of action to be taken with respect to future acquired property (particularly real estate).

Defaults

The defaults clause may provide that an event of default will occur if the underlying security documents shall for any reason be unenforceable or if the lien on the collateral shall for any reason fail to be perfected.

Voting

The voting provisions will address the votes required to release collateral (usually, only releases of all or substantially all of the collateral require unanimous consent; otherwise consent of the required lenders is sufficient).

Expenses

The expenses provision may include an express statement that the borrower is obligated to pay the costs of perfecting liens (including recording taxes and the cost of title insurance).

SPRINGING LIENS

In some cases, the lenders will not take security at closing, but will enter into an understanding with the borrower that upon specified adverse events occurring in the future, the borrower will grant security to the lenders. Often the adverse event is the occurrence of an event of default, but in other instances it is an adverse develop-ment in a financial ratio short of an event of default. The future, contingent lien that this structure contemplates is a so-called springing lien.

Springing liens are relatively rare; if collateral security is important, the parties normally create and perfect it at closing. Lenders, in particular, do not want something as significant as security to be dependent upon the future cooperation of the bor-rower. If the adverse event that is to trigger the springing lien is an event of default, the borrower may see little advantage in granting the liens at the time required unless the default is concurrently being cured (most springing lien clauses do not so provide). Of course, assuming that the borrower cooperates and grants the rele-vant liens, the lenders are still not home free. A lien that "springs" will necessarily secure an antecedent (preexisting) debt, and thus the lenders benefiting from such a lien will not be fully secured until the Bankruptcy Code preference period (90 days for non-insiders) has passed. If the borrower commences a bankruptcy case prior to the ninetieth day, the liens may well be undone by the Bankruptcy Code. (See the discussion in "Reinstatement" earlier in this part.)

TRUE-UP MECHANISM

In certain circumstances, it is not possible to secure all tranches equally and ratably. For example, if a credit agreement has a revolving credit commitment provided to the borrower in the United States and a term loan commitment provided to a subsidiary in Europe, collateral security granted by the European subsidiary may be able to secure only the term loan because of either the financial assistance rules described in "Downstream, Cross-stream, and Upstream Guarantees" earlier in this part or the tax issue to be discussed in the next section, "Deemed Dividends." Another example is sometimes confronted in New York, where there is a very severe mortgage recording tax for liens on real property. In New York, if a term loan is secured by real property, the recording tax need be paid only once. If a revolving credit loan is secured by real property, the tax is payable on each drawing (at least, that is the uniform position of New York State recording offices). To minimize taxes, the parties would want to stipulate that only the term loans are secured by the mortgage.

Notwithstanding these dynamics, a successful syndication may be dependent upon the credit agreement's being structured to allow all lenders to share equally in all collateral. The mechanism that is often used is the so-called true-up. In a true-up, taking the first example, each tranche, upon realizing on the collateral for its loans, would purchase participations in the other tranche. Thus, the lenders that have made term loans in Europe would purchase participations in the revolving credit loans made in the United States, and the revolving credit lenders would, similarly, purchase participations in the term loans. The net result is that the risks and benefits of the collateral security for both tranches of loans will be shared equally among all lenders. In the second example, the term loan lenders would purchase participations in the revolving credit loans so that the proceeds of any foreclosure on mortgaged property in New York would be shared equally among all lenders.

DEEMED DIVIDENDS

A loan to a U.S. borrower that is guaranteed by a non-U.S. subsidiary may raise the so-called deemed dividend problem. Under Section 956 of the U.S. Internal Revenue Code, a guarantee of this type is generally deemed to be a dividend by the subsidiary to its

U.S. parent (up to the amount of the guarantee) of the earnings and profits of the subsidiary. Although it is not something that affects the enforceability of the guarantee, a deemed dividend can have potentially terrible tax consequences for the U.S. parent, since the parent will have to include the subsidiary's earnings and profits as taxable income without receiving any cash to pay the associated taxes. As a consequence, most guarantees of debt of a U.S. borrower will be restricted to U.S. subsidiaries.

The deemed dividend problem can also surface if a U.S. borrower pledges the equity of a non-U.S. subsidiary. Under the U.S. Internal Revenue Code, a pledge of more than 66 $\frac{2}{3}$ percent of the total combined voting power of the non-U.S. subsidiary will be deemed to be a dividend to the same degree as a guarantee by the subsidiary. To avoid this result, security agreements customarily limit the percentage of equity pledged to 65 percent (though 66 $\frac{2}{3}$ percent is the number actually set out in the tax rules). Customarily also, the carve-out above 65 percent will apply to all equity capital of the non-U.S. subsidiary, although the tax rule refers only to voting stock.

Part 7. Enforcing the Loan: Events of Default and Remedies

EVENTS OF DEFAULT

Events of default are events or circumstances that suggest a decreased likelihood that the borrower will be able to pay its obligations under the credit agreement and that may lead the lenders to want to terminate the credit. Although some events of default, such as the commencement of a bankruptcy proceeding, constitute serious and urgent problems, events of default are more often signs of incipient difficulties. Credit agreements include the event of default concept to give the lenders a hammer over the borrower should it breach the agreement or if certain other specified events occur.

Some breaches or events will result in immediate events of default; others ripen into events of default only after notice is given or time has elapsed (or in some cases both notice is given and time has elapsed). Prior to the point that a breach or event ripens into an event of default, it is commonly referred to as a "default" or "unmatured default." As will be discussed in greater detail in the section "Remedies" later in this part, lenders may accelerate the loans only once an actual event of default occurs; they may not do so upon the occurrence of a mere default. The lenders' remedy during the period when a breach or event is merely a default is to decline to make additional loans or issue additional letters of credit (and, perhaps, to sue the borrower or make a demand on the guarantors).

A breach or event should be a default or event of default only so long as it is continuing (though some credit agreements are not written clearly on this point). For example, if a borrower fails to pay an installment of principal when due, that will constitute (at least in most credit agreements) an immediate event of default. If the lenders take no action to accelerate the loans and the borrower later pays the defaulted principal, the event of default is cured, and the lenders may no longer accelerate the loans. See the discussion in the section "Remedies" later in this part for what happens if the lenders accelerate the loans prior to the payment of the defaulted principal.

Not all events of default are within the control of the borrower. For example, a borrower will typically have no control over its shareholders' selling their stock in the borrower and thus will have no ability to prevent a change of control. Similarly, a non-U.S. borrower probably will not have any ability to prevent nationalization of its property, or a moratorium affecting outstanding debt of its home country, both of which are common events of default for borrowers in non-OECD countries.

If the borrower is a reporting company under the Securities Exchange Act of 1934 and the credit agreement is deemed "material," it is required to disclose any acceleration and may be required to disclose the occurrence of a default or event of default even if it does not result in acceleration.

The events and circumstances that are normally listed in the events of default clauses under credit agreements include the following.

Default in Payment

Generally, the failure to pay when due the principal of a loan or the reimbursement obligation that arises upon a drawing under a letter of credit is an immediate event of default. A default in the payment of interest, fees, and other amounts will typically enjoy a grace period of from two to five business days (with two or three business days being the most common) before ripening into an event of default. A short grace period avoids an event of default based on wire transfer difficulties or administrative error. In contrast, the typical grace period for a payment default in a bond indenture is 30 days, whether for principal or interest. The longer grace period for bonds reflects the practical reality (at least historically) that, if a default occurs, there is greater difficulty in first locating and then obtaining waivers from a disparate and anonymous bondholder group than from lenders under a credit agreement. A similar rationale may explain the longer grace periods for covenant breaches under a bond indenture.

Inaccuracy of Representations

An event of default will arise if a representation is incorrect in any material respect when it is made or deemed to be made. The default will typically extend not only to the representations in the credit agreement, but also to those in related agreements, such as security agreements, intercreditor agreements, guarantee agreements, and the like. The default will also typically include statements made "in connection with" the credit agreement, which will sweep in representations made in amendments and in certificates and other documents furnished under the credit agreement (including preclosing commitment letters). Inaccuracies in closing certificates will therefore, if material, give rise to events of default.

The default is normally predicated upon the relevant representation being inaccurate *when made* (or when deemed made, such as upon the making of a loan). It is not a default if a representation that was initially correct later becomes incorrect. Thus, if at the closing of a single-draw term loan, the borrower is not a defendant in any material litigation, but subsequently is sued for a material amount, no default based upon a misrepresentation will arise, inasmuch as the representation was true when made.

The default is also predicated upon the inaccuracy's being *material*. Thus, an inadvertent failure to list an inactive subsidiary with no assets, no liabilities, and no operations is probably not a default. A failure to list an active subsidiary that has significant assets and liabilities and is also the holding company for a number of other listed subsidiaries probably would be material. Sometimes borrowers will push for an added "materiality" qualification by requesting that the default arise only if *material* representations are *materially* inaccurate. This approach is problematic, although it may be seen in rare cases. The difficulty is that it implies that some representations are not material. Taken to its logical conclusion, the qualifier could just as easily be inserted into the covenant default (i.e., that an event of default will occur only if a *material* covenant is breached) or even into the payment default (providing that an event of default occurs only if a *material* payment is not made).

Borrowers occasionally request that they be afforded a grace period to cure an inaccurate representation. It is unusual to see this concept incorporated into a credit agreement. However, if it is included, it will normally afford a grace period only for representations that are curable; most are not. The qualifier is in any event largely unnecessary. A borrower is much more likely than the lenders to know that a representation is inaccurate and, if it is so easily curable, can fix the problem itself even before being required to notify the lenders.

Breach of Covenants

Events of default based upon covenant breaches generally fall into two categories: those that are immediate and those that first require a grace period to run or notice to be given. As to who must give the notice, agreements differ. Some require that it be given by any lender; others prescribe that only the administrative agent or the required lenders are permitted to do so.

Commonly, breaches of negative covenants, financial covenants, and certain affirmative covenants (such as the agreement to maintain corporate existence and the undertaking that all subsidiaries shall be guarantors) will be immediate; others will require notice, lapse of time, or both. There is, however, no completely uniform approach for all credit agreements. In many instances the parties will negotiate to include or exclude a grace period for particular covenants. Factors that are weighed in determining what is appropriately an immediate event of default include (1) whether a breach, if it occurs, is susceptible of cure, (2) whether the covenant is so important that the lenders should have the right to act without delay, and (3) whether a breach, if it occurs, will be the result of intentional action of the borrower. One seemingly benign covenant—the borrower's obligation to notify the lenders promptly after obtaining knowledge of a default—is generally an immediate event of default, even if the underlying event or circumstance would not constitute an event of default until after notice or a grace period. The reason is simple: if the lenders do not know that a breach or other event has occurred, they are unable to deliver a notice or monitor the lapse of any grace period.

Bond indentures (in contrast to credit agreements) usually have longer grace periods (30 or 60 days is customary) and will require that notice be given before the grace period commences; in other words, there are no immediate events of default based on covenant breaches. As noted in the section "Default in Payment" earlier in this part, this more borrower-favorable approach is probably a function of the greater difficulty (historically) in locating and then obtaining waivers from a group of bondholders.

Cross-Default; Cross-Acceleration

The cross-default clause in a credit agreement is one of the most misunderstood provisions; it is also one of the most powerful tools that the lenders have to avoid being disadvantaged as against other creditors. Certain key principles need to be kept in mind when analyzing cross-default clauses.

Why a Cross-Default?

When a borrower defaults on indebtedness owed to other creditors, lenders may have at least three separate concerns. First, the default may indicate that the borrower is having credit-related problems that may also affect the borrower's ability to repay the loans. Second, the borrower is at risk of the other indebtedness being accelerated. Acceleration might not only jeopardize its ability to repay the lenders, but also subject it to other remedial actions, such as foreclosure on collateral (if the other creditors are secured) or a bankruptcy filing. Third, the borrower may enter into negotiations with the other creditors for a waiver or amendment that would eliminate the default or forestall the exercise of remedies. These negotiations could involve the restructuring of the other indebtedness by the borrower in a way that provides advantages to the other creditors over the lenders, such as the granting of collateral security, changing the average life of the other indebtedness, increasing compensation, or other concessions. As a result, the default in respect of other indebtedness may create intercreditor issues.

What Indebtedness Is Crossed?

In most credit agreements, the cross-default will be triggered if debt or hedging and other derivative obligations under another agreement go into default. Sometimes the definition is narrower, covering only indebtedness for borrowed money. Frequently, a term such as *material indebtedness* is used, which will set forth thresholds that the other debt must exceed to trigger the cross-default. The threshold for hedges and other derivatives is typically measured by reference to the amount payable by the borrower if the arrangement were terminated, rather than by reference to the amount overdue or to the notional amount, and is negotiated based upon the size of the borrower and the amount of other debt outstanding or permitted to be outstanding.

Meaning of Cross-Default and Cross-Acceleration

The term *cross-default* is often used loosely to describe both cross-default and cross-acceleration clauses. "Cross-default" refers more accurately to a provision that allows the credit agreement to be accelerated whenever a default occurs in another instrument, *whether or not* the debt under that other instrument may be accelerated. "Cross-acceleration" refers to a provision that allows the credit agreement to be accelerated only when the other debt has actually been accelerated. Some agreements will contemplate a third, in-between, category that is perhaps best described as "cross-accelerability" or "cross–event of default," i.e., a provision allowing the credit agreement to be accelerated when the other debt may be accelerated immediately without any further notice (other than mere demand) or lapse of time.

Using this terminology, the cross-default clause is more protective of the lenders than the cross-acceleration clause. However, from the perspective of the borrower, the cross-default may have the effect of wiping out grace periods and thus prevent it from being able to cure a default or to work out a problem with other creditors. Thus, if the credit agreement and another debt instrument each have a cross-default clause, when a default (but not yet an event of default) occurs under one instrument, an event of default will immediately occur under the other. By reason of the cross-default in the first instrument, this means that an event of default will now exist there as well. Thus the borrower suffers events of default under both agreements for a breach that was, under each, intended to have a grace period.

Conversely, a cross-acceleration is viewed by lenders as very weak. It arguably defeats the whole purpose of the clause, since it is triggered only when other creditors *actually* accelerate their indebtedness, rather than merely being entitled to do so. The cross-acceleration clause allows those other creditors to threaten and cajole and obtain additional favorable terms without according the lenders any matching bargaining power unless an acceleration actually takes place. Because indebtedness is rarely accelerated, this provides substantially less protection to lenders and is usually seen only in credit agreements for the most highly rated borrowers. It is also the approach taken in virtually all public debt indentures.

The cross–event of default clause may strike a middle ground between the two extremes of the cross-default clause and the cross-acceleration clause. By not triggering an event of default until all grace periods have run on the other debt instrument, it avoids the borrower's concern of losing its grace periods, and it avoids the lenders' losing leverage in a workout. The clause should, however, provide that clemency be available only for the original grace period in the other debt instrument and not for any extensions. In other words, once the original grace periods have run, a default should arise; "grace" should not include lengthy periods of repeated deferrals designed precisely to keep the lenders away from the negotiating table.

Cross-Payment Defaults

Because of their obvious importance, credit agreements frequently deal with payment defaults separately from other defaults. A typical clause, often called a "cross-payment default," reads as follows:

> The Borrower or any of its subsidiaries shall fail to make any payment (whether of principal or interest and regardless of amount) in respect of any Material Indebtedness, when and as the same shall become due and payable.

The reference to "regardless of amount" in this language is intended to make clear that it is *not* the amount of the payment default, but rather the principal amount of the debt *in respect of which* the payment default occurs, that determines whether the cross-payment default is triggered. The seriousness of the default is best measured by the amount of indebtedness that can be accelerated rather than by the amount needed to effect a cure.

Mandatory Prepayments

A cross-default clause will often carve out secured debt that becomes due prematurely as a result of the permitted sale or transfer of property or assets securing that debt. This is intended to exclude normal mandatory prepayment events that do not reflect adversely on the borrower.

Insolvency

The insolvency default is generally phrased broadly to pick up not merely bankruptcy proceedings against the borrower, but a host of other insolvency-related events (liquidation, reorganization, the appointment of a custodian or receiver, and the like) that have an effect similar to that of a bankruptcy filing. If the borrower or any of its subsidiaries is a bank or an insurance company, the default will also be triggered by a receivership or conservatorship (the equivalent terms for those entities). The default is normally divided into three categories: those based on actions by the borrower (the voluntary default), those based on actions of third parties (the involuntary default), and those based upon an admission of insolvency by the borrower (the admissions default).

Voluntary

The voluntary default will be triggered when the borrower commences a voluntary bankruptcy or insolvency proceeding (including applying for a custodian or receiver for its property). It will also be triggered if the borrower rolls over and plays dead when any of these actions are instituted by third parties. In most cases, the default will include the borrower's taking action (such as a board or shareholder meeting) to effect any of the listed items. Because all of these actions are voluntary, they constitute immediate events of default, and the borrower does not benefit from any grace period. As will be more fully discussed in the section "Remedies" later in this part, they also result in an automatic termination of commitments and automatic acceleration of the loans.

Involuntary

The involuntary default normally encompasses all of the actions listed in the voluntary default, if instituted by a third party against the borrower or its property. Because these actions may be without merit, the borrower is allowed a grace period, typically 60 days, to have the action dismissed. If dismissal has not been obtained upon expiration of the grace period, the involuntary filing would ripen into an event of default. As with the voluntary default, if an involuntary default becomes an event of default, commitments will be automatically terminated and the loans will be automatically accelerated.

Admission

The third category of insolvency default is triggered if the borrower "becomes unable, admits in writing its inability or fails generally to pay its debts as they become due." This language is an element of proof required for an involuntary bankruptcy proceeding to succeed, and so an admission of this type by a borrower may place it in immediate jeopardy of a bankruptcy case being commenced. Also, from a purely practical standpoint, if a borrower makes this type of admission, it is probable that payment and other defaults are imminent. It constitutes an immediate event of default, with no grace period, but will customarily not result in automatic termination of commitments or acceleration of loans.

Judgment Default

The litigation representation addresses whether any material suit or proceeding is pending against the borrower. The judgment default addresses what happens after the suit or proceeding has been lost and converted into a judgment. The default is triggered by an *unpaid* and *unappealed* judgment; the mere loss of a lawsuit and resulting obligation to pay monetary damages is not itself an event of default. There is typically a grace period of 30 or more days to allow the borrower to pay the judgment or to obtain a stay of enforcement by appealing. Failure to pay a judgment gives rise to concerns similar to those that arise when a cross-default occurs. It may indicate that the borrower is unable to meet its financial obligations and that the judgment creditor may be on the verge of exercising remedies such as obtaining and enforcing a judgment lien or instituting bankruptcy proceedings.

Like the cross-default, the judgment default also generally has a minimum dollar threshold. Since the credit considerations in this context are similar to those for the cross-default, it is quite common for the two thresholds to be the same. However, in the case of the judgment default, the amount covered by insurance is sometimes excluded on the theory that the borrower will not actually need to go out-of-pocket in the event that the judgment ultimately must be paid. Judgment defaults that exclude portions covered by insurance may sometimes require that the insurer be creditworthy and have first accepted responsibility for the judgment.

ERISA Events

As discussed in the section "Pension and Welfare Plans" in Part 4, "Conditioning the Loan," to the extent that a company is obligated to pay retired employees a defined pension benefit, the company will be required under the Employee Retirement Income Security Act of 1974 (ERISA) to pay into a trust an amount sufficient to cover future benefit obligations. If a business fails to meet this obligation, the Pension Benefit Guaranty Corporation (PBGC) may be entitled to a statutory lien on the assets of the company. This lien would cover not just the borrower, but subsidiaries that are 80 percent or more owned. In addition, ERISA provides that, in certain circumstances, any funding deficiency of the plan can become immediately due and payable, rather than being paid over a period of years. Acceleration of the deficiency could result in a sudden, unanticipated burden on a company's resources.

The typical ERISA event of default is triggered if any of these events occurs *and* if the result would be material. Materiality is often measured by reference to a dollar threshold or to a percentage of the borrower's net worth (or some other balance sheet item). In other instances, materiality is determined by a more subjective standard, i.e., whether the event would result in a "material adverse effect." In this latter case, many credit agreements will allow the required lenders to determine whether the event can be expected to produce a "material adverse effect."

Environmental Events

An event of default tied to possible environmental liabilities will typically be inserted in agreements for a company engaged in manufacturing or processing. It is normally triggered upon the assertion of liabilities against the borrower under environmental laws, including fines, penalties, remediation costs, and damage claims by private persons, that could have a material adverse effect upon the borrower or its business. An obvious example would be an assertion that the borrower either owns a superfund site or has contributed hazardous materials to a superfund site. As noted in the section "Environmental Matters" in Part 4, "Conditioning the Loan," under federal superfund legislation, any past or present contributor of hazardous materials to a superfund site is jointly and severally liable for the entire cleanup cost.

In the typical credit agreement, the assertion of an environmental liability will not be an event of default unless it can be expected to have a material adverse impact on the borrower, taking into account the likelihood of the claim's being successful. Given the subjective nature of this test, some credit agreements will provide that the required lenders determine whether the materiality standard has been met, rather than leaving it to dispute between the parties.

Change of Control

As noted earlier, a change of control may be treated as either a prepayment event or an event of default. Probably more credit agreements treat a change of control as a default than treat it as a mandatory prepayment. For a more complete discussion of change of control, see the section "Change of Control" in Part 3, "Making the Borrower Repay the Loan."

Invalidity of Guarantees or Liens

If the loans either have been guaranteed by subsidiaries or other parties or are secured by liens on property of the borrower or guarantors, the credit agreement will frequently include an event of default triggered by the failure of the guarantees or liens to be enforceable. In the case of liens, the event of default may also be triggered by the lien's not being perfected or entitled to the agreed-upon priority. In some instances, the mere assertion by the borrower or a guarantor of any infirmity will result in an event of default.

With one exception, it is difficult to conceive how this event of default could be triggered in the absence of deliberate acts by the borrower or a guarantor. The exception would be a failure to perfect a lien. This could happen with particular items of property if the parties simply do not bother to take cumbersome additional steps (such as noting the lien on certificates of title for motor vehicles, or implementing control agreements with respect to the borrower's deposit accounts). Recognizing this, borrowers will sometimes request a carve-out for collateral not having a material value in relation to their property as a whole. Sometimes also, borrowers will request a carve-out for a failure to perfect based upon actions by the administrative agent (such as its losing possessory collateral). The latter point is infrequently conceded, though, on the theory that it is the responsibility of *both* the borrower and the administrative agent to maintain perfection.

Foreign Borrowers

Loans made to a non-U.S. borrower or guaranteed by a non-U.S. guarantor carry greater political risk than comparable transactions with purely domestic companies. The risk is thought to be less if the borrower or guarantor is located in an OECD country. For borrowers located in emerging markets, lenders will be concerned with the possibility of (1) expropriation (the taking by a foreign government of property of the borrower or guarantor), (2) moratorium (the prohibition by a foreign government of local companies servicing external debt), (3) loss of any necessary local licenses or approvals (such as foreign exchange approvals) necessary to perform obligations under the credit agreement, and (4) the home country's inability to access the resources of the International Monetary Fund if foreign exchange reserves are depleted. Borrowers frequently argue that such events of default are unnecessary because, if the covered events are truly problematic, the lenders would be protected by their eventual manifestation as payment defaults. Lenders, on the other hand, consistent with their views on other events of default, wish to be able to take action at the earliest reasonable time to mitigate adverse consequences.

Specialized Events of Default

Credit agreements often include additional events of default that are specific to the borrower. For example, if a borrower is in a regulated industry (such as wireless telecommunications), it may be appropriate to include an event of default based upon the loss of a material portion of the governmental licenses necessary for its business. Similarly, if the borrower's success is dependent on one or more specific contracts remaining in effect, the credit agreement may contain an event of default triggered by the termination of any of those contracts or the default by one of the parties.

Material Adverse Change

In rare cases, particularly in asset-based lending transactions or in cross-border loans, a credit agreement will include an event of default based upon a material adverse change. (See the section "The MAC Condition" in Part 4, "Conditioning the Loan," for a discussion of the meaning of material adverse change.) Domestic borrowers strenuously resist a MAC default. It is arguably inconsistent with the principle that the financial covenants test the performance of the borrower. It may cause the borrower's accountants to classify the loans as short-term. It may also produce an element of business uncertainty akin to the loans being payable on demand. If the borrower is located outside the United States, however, the MAC clause may supplement the specialized events of default for non-U.S. borrowers discussed in the section "Foreign Borrowers" earlier in this part and is more frequently seen.

REMEDIES

When an event of default occurs, the lenders may be entitled to exercise a range of remedies against the borrower under both the credit agreement and any related security agreements. We will discuss here the remedies available under the credit agreement; the rights of the lenders vis-à-vis collateral security are beyond the scope of this chapter.

Whether to exercise remedies upon the occurrence of an event of default is not always an easy determination. To begin with, before taking any action, the lenders should be absolutely certain that an event of default has in fact occurred, and that it is of sufficient materiality to justify the proposed remedies. Other considerations come into play as well. Accelerating loans, for example, rarely results in the loans' being immediately repaid by the borrower; if it were that simple, the borrower would presumably have retired the loans before the default ever occurred. Acceleration can also have adverse effects on the borrower, the lenders, and other creditors. It typically results in an immediate filing by the borrower for protection under the Bankruptcy Code and is likely to result in significant legal and other costs. Bankruptcy may also shunt the borrower into a long period of uncertainty as the case progresses and will subject many nonordinary course decisions to cumbersome court approval. As a consequence, absent evidence of fraud or rank incompetence on the part of the borrower's management, it is almost always better for the parties to agree to an out-of-court restructuring of the loans.

The remedies afforded to the lenders under a typical credit agreement are discussed next, in ascending order of severity.

Stop Lending

As discussed in the section "Ongoing Conditions" in Part 4, "Conditioning the Loan," it is a condition to the making of any loan (or the issuance of any letter of credit) that no default or event of default exist. Any individual lender therefore has the right, absent waiver of the event of default, to refuse to make additional loans under the credit agreement; exercising this right is not dependent upon a determination by the required lenders to stop lending. Of course, once the default or event of default is cured or waived, assuming that all other conditions are satisfied, the lenders again become obligated to lend.

Terminate Commitments

Upon an event of default, the lenders may at their option terminate any outstanding commitments. This remedy is not typically exercisable by a lender alone, but is a right available only to the required lenders. In some credit agreements, the administrative agent will also be given the authority to terminate commitments on its own initiative (though only in the most extreme circumstances would an administrative agent want to do this without authorization from the required lenders). Most credit agreements will allow the lenders to terminate the commitments independent of accelerating the loans, thus affording a remedy short of a "nuclear option" to send a signal to the borrower. Most credit agreements will also provide that, if the event of default is based upon an insolvency, the commitments will automatically terminate without action by any party. See the following section, "Accelerate," for the rationale for this.

Accelerate

Upon an event of default, the lenders have the right to declare the loans due and payable. As with the termination of commitments, this right is almost never exercisable by an individual lender, but requires action by the required lenders. By way of contrast, bond indentures and private placements will frequently permit acceleration to be effected by a vote of less than a majority of the noteholders (25 percent is a figure that is often seen). In some credit agreements, the administrative agent will be permitted to accelerate the loans on its own (though, as with the termination of commitments, only in extreme circumstances would an administrative agent exercise this right). Granting this power to an administrative agent can nevertheless be important. Acceleration by the administrative agent is much speedier than acceleration by the required lenders and thus can enable setoff rights to be quickly exercised or other protective actions rapidly taken.

In the case of a credit agreement with competitive bid loans, the definition of "required lenders" will be adjusted to stipulate that, for purposes of acceleration, the lenders vote not in accordance with their outstanding revolving credit commitments, but in accordance with their outstanding loans. This avoids a scenario in which a competitive bid lender with the only outstanding loan under a facility is unable to declare the loan due and payable because the lenders as a group decline to vote their unused commitments in favor of acceleration.

Most credit agreements will provide that an event of default based upon the borrower's insolvency results in an automatic acceleration of all loans. This is intended to avoid the automatic stay under Section 362 of the Federal Bankruptcy Code, which decrees that a filing of a voluntary or involuntary petition against a debtor results in an automatic injunction against anyone in the world taking action against the debtor. Among other things, the stay may bar sending a notice of acceleration or other demand to a borrower. By having the acceleration occur automatically, the theory goes, no violation of the stay occurs, since no notice or other action is being taken by the lenders. Whether lenders would be in any less advantageous position in a bankruptcy proceeding if their loans were not accelerated is questionable, but when the Bankruptcy Code was originally enacted, it was deemed important that lenders have an already-liquidated claim at the start of a proceeding. Another (arguably more persuasive) justification is that automatic acceleration allows a full claim to be made against a guarantor (assuming that the guarantor is not itself in bankruptcy). The typical guarantee will of course also include language to the effect that if acceleration is for any reason prohibited, a full claim may nevertheless be made on the guarantor. See the discussion in the section "Insolvency of Borrower" in Part 6, "Securing and Guaranteeing the Loan."

Sometimes lenders will ask that automatic acceleration be expanded beyond insolvency defaults to all events of default. This might seem superficially appealing. It would avoid any vote by the lenders or initiative by the administrative agent, and it might serve as an added incentive for the borrower's not breaching the credit agreement in the first place. However, such an approach would have the disadvantage of removing control from the lenders. The lenders would no longer have the option of ignoring a default (which they might choose to do, even though they decline to waive the default, because the default is not sufficiently serious). It might also trigger cross-default or cross-acceleration clauses contained in other debt instruments. Except in rare cases, credit agreements will as a consequence provide for automatic acceleration only in the context of insolvency.

Demand Cover for Letters of Credit

If there are letters of credit outstanding at the time that an event of default occurs, the lenders can demand that the borrower provide "cover" (cash collateral) for any future reimbursement obligations that will arise upon drawings under the letters of credit. Demanding cover overcomes the structural difficulty that a letter of credit may not be accelerated or repaid in the same sense that loans can be accelerated and repaid. Nothing is due to the issuer until a drawing is made by the beneficiary. See the discussion in the section "Cover for Letters of Credit" in Part 3, "Making the Borrower Repay the Loan." Therefore, to create an obligation that can become due and payable upon an event of default, credit agreements routinely provide that the lenders have the right to demand that cash collateral be posted by the borrower in an amount equal to the future reimbursement obligations that will be payable upon drawings under the letter of credit. If the borrower does not immediately post the cash, the lenders then have a claim to which they can apply the proceeds of any collateral or that they can demand be paid by the guarantors.

Institute Suit

If a borrower defaults in the payment of any amount under the credit agreement, the lenders can institute suit against the borrower to compel payment. Suit can be an alternative to accelerating the loans and thus avoid the risk of precipitating a protective bankruptcy filing by the borrower (though once a judgment is issued and the lender starts taking action to collect money, a bankruptcy filing becomes more likely). Suing for a past-due payment is a remedy available to individual lenders; a credit agreement will not normally require that approval of the required lenders be obtained.

Demand Payment from Guarantors

To the extent that the credit agreement is guaranteed or secured by collateral provided by third parties, a payment default (or acceleration) will permit the lenders to demand payment of the guarantor or commence the exercise of lien remedies. Making a demand upon a guarantor is normally a right exercisable by each lender. Since liens are normally granted to the administrative agent (or a collateral agent), exercising remedies against collateral requires either the initiative of the administrative agent (or collateral agent) or the instruction of the required lenders; an individual lender would not normally have the right to start this process.

RESCISSION

The remedies clause of a credit agreement will sometimes give the required lenders the right to rescind an acceleration after it has occurred. This right will normally be subject to a number of conditions, including requirements that the borrower has cured the original event of default upon which the acceleration was based, there being no other intervening default or event of default, any default interest accrued on the accelerated principal during the period of acceleration having been paid, and (in some cases) the lenders not having commenced the exercise of judicial remedies. A rescission right is routinely included in bond indentures and private placements; it is rarely included in credit agreements.

WATERFALLS

The "waterfall" refers to the provision found in some credit agreements that specifies how monies are to be applied to obligations when the borrower pays an amount that is less than the full amount owing. Traditionally waterfalls were inserted only into mortgages, security agreements, and the like, but with the increase in credit agreements with multiple tranches, waterfalls have become more common. The typical structure provides for the fees and expenses of the administrative agent (or any collateral agent) to be paid before any other claims, for interest (and breakfunding payments) to be paid before principal, for term loans to be paid before revolving credit loans, and for revolving credit loans to be paid before cover for any outstanding letters of credit (except that during a default, the waterfall will require all principal and cover among all tranches of loans and letters of credit to be paid ratably).

SETOFF

A lender that has a monetary obligation to a borrower, such as a deposit liability or an obligation under a derivative contract, may be able to effect payment on the loan by canceling, on a dollar-for-dollar basis, the lender's obligation to the borrower against the borrower's loan obligation to the lender. The right to do this is referred to as the right of "setoff."

The right of setoff arises under common law, as created by court decisions in each state. The key requirement is that the two obligations be "mutual." Among other things, this means that the two parties must be in the same legal capacity. There would, for example, be no mutuality in the case of an obligation of the borrower to a bank, on the one hand, and an obligation owed by the bank *in a fiduciary capacity*, on the other. In addition, common law restricts the right of setoff in a variety of ways; for example, common law setoff requires that both obligations be matured, and perhaps that they be in the same currency. There may be questions as to whether an obligation payable at one branch of an international bank may be set off against a loan booked at a different branch.

For these reasons, credit agreements generally include an express contractual right of setoff. Such a contractual right may validly extend setoff rights beyond the rights provided by common law (although it is not clear that a clause purporting to depart from the rule of mutuality would be given effect by a court).

Although lenders are customarily afforded the right of setoff, the borrower itself is normally denied setoff rights through a credit agreement clause requiring that all payments by the borrower be made "without deduction, setoff, or counterclaim."

In addition to common law and contractual rights of setoff, a lender may, in some jurisdictions, benefit from statutory setoff rights. Such a statute is Section 151 of the New York Debtor and Creditor Law, which creates a powerful right of setoff by a bank, and permits such setoff even after the bank is served with an attachment or garnishment order.

Exercise by a lender of its right of setoff in a syndicated credit agreement will typically trigger an obligation on its part to share the proceeds of the setoff with other lenders. See the discussion in the section "Sharing of Setoffs and Other Claims" in Part 8, "Keeping Peace Among the Lenders."

Part 8. Keeping Peace Among the Lenders: Interlender, Voting, and Agency Issues

AGENCY PROVISIONS

Some Basic Principles

A syndicated credit agreement will, with rare exceptions, have an administrative agent. The role of the administrative agent is to interface between the borrower and the lenders, and among the lenders themselves. Thus, the administrative agent will receive financial and other reports from the borrower and ensure that they are made available to the lenders (typically by posting them on a web site). It will take delivery of and forward notices. The administrative agent will also receive and disburse between the borrower and the lenders the proceeds of loans and payments of principal, interest, and fees.

Except for purposes of maintaining the loan register (see the discussion in the section "Loan Register" in Part 9, "Selling the Loan"), the administrative agent is the agent of the lenders and *not* of the borrower. Thus, the borrower has no right to instruct the administrative agent to take, or refrain from taking, any particular action. The administrative agent is also solely an agent—it is not a trustee or fiduciary for the lenders. The duties of the administrative agent should not be confused with the leadership role often assumed by the lead bank (though that is normally the same institution as the administrative agent). Recommendations made by the lead bank to a syndicate are just that: recommendations of the bank, not of the administrative agent. Stated another way, the job of the administrative agent is ministerial only. Although it may have the authority to take actions on its own initiative to accelerate the loans, to commence enforcement actions, or to realize on collateral, it would not normally be obligated under the credit agreement to undertake any of these (as would be the case with a trustee for a bond indenture).

Remembering these basic principles will help in understanding the agency provisions set forth in the typical credit agreement. For reference, the LSTA Model Credit Agreement Provisions include market-standard agency language.

Appointment

The lenders that are parties to the credit agreement will appoint an institution (as noted, this will normally be the lead bank) as the administrative agent. Any lender that joins the credit agreement at a later date by postclosing assignment will, through operation of the clause, also be appointing that institution as administrative agent. The appointment will be stated to be irrevocable, even though later provisions in the agency clause will allow the administrative agent to resign. The appointment is made irrevocable so that no lender in the future will question the administrative agent's continuing authority. The credit agreement will also explicitly state that the institution functioning as administrative agent has in its individual capacity all of the same rights as any other lender.

In most cases, if the credit agreement is secured, the administrative agent will hold the liens for the benefit of the lenders. In some cases, however, it may be useful for there to be a distinct collateral agent role (this might be the case if the collateral security is being granted by the borrower equally for the benefit of the lenders and a separate group of creditors). In those cases, all of the same rights and privileges set forth in the agency provisions will apply to the collateral agent as well.

No Fiduciary Duty; Exculpation

As noted earlier, an administrative agent is not a fiduciary for any lender. The agency provisions will normally state that the administrative agent is not required to do anything under the credit agreement unless other provisions of the agreement expressly require it to act. Furthermore, the agency provisions will free the administrative agent from any liability for action taken by it at the instruction of the appropriate group of lenders (either the required lenders or each lender).

The exculpation will also make clear that the administrative agent is not under any duty to ascertain whether or not the borrower is complying with the provisions of the credit agreement. Nor will the administrative agent be responsible for determining whether the representations are true, whether documents delivered at the closing are accurate, whether the credit agreement is enforceable and (in most agreements), whether any of the conditions have been satisfied.

The one limitation to the exculpation will cover instances in which the administrative agent is grossly negligent or commits willful misconduct. The argument for not requiring the administrative agent to be liable for mere negligence but rather only for gross (really bad) negligence is that a court or jury presented with an error as a result of a confused set of facts can too easily be persuaded that the administrative agent is somehow responsible. A similar fear underpins other uses of the "gross negligence and willful misconduct" standard in the credit agreement (see, for example, the discussion in the section "Borrower Indemnification; Consequential Damages" in Part 10, "Understanding the Boilerplate").

In the same vein, no lender will be entitled to rely upon the administrative agent in any respect for matters relating to the credit agreement. The customary approach is to affirm that each lender takes full responsibility for its own credit decisions with respect to the borrower and for obtaining such information as the lender deems appropriate in extending credit to the borrower and monitoring the loan. The administrative agent will not be under any duty to disclose any information relating to the borrower or any of its affiliates that it obtains in any capacity. The administrative agent will not be deemed to have notice of any default (even payment defaults) unless it has been delivered notice to such effect by the borrower or a lender. Some agency provisions will require that any such notice, to be effective against the administrative agent, be prominently identified as a "NOTICE OF DEFAULT."

Reliance

The administrative agent will be permitted to rely upon notices, certificates, and other documents that it believes to be genuine and sent by the proper, authorized person. The ability to so rely extends to oral communications as well as written communications. The administrative agent will be permitted to consult with counsel (which can include the borrower's counsel) and is typically exculpated from any action it takes in reliance upon advice from counsel. Most agency provisions will also allow the administrative agent to assume that a lender believes that conditions to the making of a loan have been satisfied unless the administrative agent has received notice to the contrary prior to making funds available to the borrower. See the further discussion on this topic in the section "The Clawback Clause" later in this part.

Delegation

Since the administrative agent may be required to act through its own agents (such as employees or, if collateral security is involved, local trustees or subagents), the agency provisions will make clear

that the administrative agent may in fact carry out its responsibilities in this manner. Some agency provisions will also make
explicit that the administrative agent shall not be liable for the
actions or omissions of subagents so long as they were selected by
the administrative agent in good faith.

Filing Proofs of Claim

Although the authority granted to administrative agents in standard agency provisions is certainly expansive enough to include
filing proofs of claim on behalf of the syndicate, some credit
agreements will include an express statement to this effect. From
the standpoint of all parties (the borrower, the lenders, and the
administrative agent), it is in any event preferable that the administrative agent file claims arising out of the credit agreement; it
ensures accuracy, minimizes legal costs, and is normally insisted
upon by bankrupt debtors. Even though it may be inadvisable for
an individual lender to opt out of agent filing, the agency provisions will not normally require that all proofs of claim be submitted by the administrative agent. The bankruptcy court, though,
may insist on this.

Successor Agents

One of the key concerns of an administrative agent is that it be able
to exit its job as an administrative agent if it determines that this is
appropriate. Standard agency provisions will, therefore, include a
right of resignation, allowing the administrative agent to notify the
borrower and the lenders that it no longer wishes to continue in
this capacity. The resignation will typically be contingent upon a
successor agent's having been appointed by the required lenders
and having accepted the role as administrative agent. If no qualified institution is willing to serve as a successor, the administrative
agent is given the authority to appoint a successor. This latter right
may be more illusory than real for an agent that truly wants to
resign. Simply having the right to appoint a successor does not
mean that any successor that is willing to serve can be found.
Credit agreements try to deal with this provision either by allowing the administrative agent to resign anyway and devolve its
responsibilities upon the lenders individually (not always terribly

practical) or by stipulating that the borrower pay whatever agency fee the market requires in order to find a willing successor.

Often borrowers will request that they be given approval rights over a successor administrative agent. Although superficially there is some logic to this, it is somewhat inconsistent with the concept that the administrative agent is an agent of the lenders and not of the borrower. Accordingly, most agency provisions (including the LSTA Model Credit Agreement Provisions) will require only consultation with the borrower. If a consent right is granted to the borrower, it will normally only apply so long as no default or event of default exists.

Removal rights (the ability of the required lenders at their option to remove an administrative agent) have largely disappeared in recent years as a result of resistance by administrative agents.

Syndication and Other Agents

It is of course typical for a larger syndicated credit agreement to have many agency roles in addition to that of administrative agent. These other agency roles (syndication agent, documentation agent, managing agent, and the like) are frequently identified on the cover page of the credit agreement, and, in some cases, the respective agents will sign the credit agreement in those capacities. Whether or not other agents execute the credit agreement, it has become customary in recent years that the agency provisions set out an express statement that none of these other agents has any duties or responsibilities under the credit agreement. It is a means of affirming that their role is for naming purposes only.

LENDER INDEMNIFICATION

The general rule in a credit agreement is that the borrower is obligated to indemnify the other parties against any loss, liability, or other cost. However, in the case of the administrative agent and, if there is one, the issuer of letters of credit, it is customary also for the lenders to provide similar indemnification. In the case of a letter of credit, this indemnification will generally come only from the lenders participating in the letter of credit itself, i.e., solely the revolving credit lenders. The indemnification will typically be on the same terms as that provided by the borrower: it will not indemnify either the administrative agent or a letter of credit issuer for its gross negligence or willful misconduct.

VOTING

Basic Rule

The voting provisions of a credit agreement are superficially very simple. They mask, however, considerable market custom (and some law).

The basic rule is that the "majority" or "required" lenders must approve any modification, waiver, or supplement to any provision of the credit agreement. "Majority" or "required" will normally mean lenders holding more than 50 percent of the aggregate credit exposure, i.e., unused commitments and outstanding loans and letters of credit. In some agreements the percentage will be higher (66 $^2/_3$ percent is typical), but this is generally resisted by borrowers, since obtaining consents to changes may become more difficult. Sometimes the credit agreement will break out particular issues and require a so-called supermajority vote for changes. Borrowing base issues are an example of this. In so-called club deals (a credit agreement with only a very small number of lenders), the definition of "required lenders" may include a concept that a minimum *number* of lenders, as well as a minimum *percentage* of loans, vote in favor of a change.

Multitranche Agreements

In a multitranche agreement, one issue that will be addressed is whether the lenders vote as a single pool, or whether each tranche votes separately. The nearly universal practice that has developed in recent years is that all lenders vote together as a pool. This approach can, however, pose a potential risk to revolving credit lenders. For example, if the term loan lenders constitute a majority of the pool, there is nothing to prevent them from agreeing to delete the material adverse change clause if that would remove from the revolving credit lenders a basis upon which to refuse to lend. The solution that addresses this in the typical credit agreement is a clause that requires a separate majority vote of a tranche if a change would adversely affect that tranche without equally affecting all other tranches. Other, more explicit, language seen in many agreements states that no tranche can be required to make loans as a result of an amendment without the consent of a majority of that tranche. In this case, the waiver is still effective to eliminate an event of default, but is not effective for purposes of the conditions precedent.

The "Affected Lender" Concept

Although the general rule in all agreements is that no modification, supplement, or waiver can be effective unless it is approved by the required lenders, the typical voting provision will go on to lay out some exceptions where the consent of additional lenders is required. Thus, for example, changes to money terms (interest rate, amortization, amount of commitments, and the like) also require the consent of any "affected" lender. An "affected" lender does not mean each lender in the particular tranche, but only those lenders affected by the change in terms. Thus, an extension of a subset of revolving credit commitments can be effected through consent of the required lenders and those particular revolving credit lenders whose commitments are being extended. Lenders whose commitments are not being extended have no consent right (other than to participate in the required lender vote).

Other changes require the consent of *all* lenders. Examples include changes to the pro rata provisions of the credit agreement and certain changes to the voting provisions. Lastly, any modification that will affect the rights or obligations of the administrative agent (or of any swingline lender or letter of credit issuer) will require the consent of that party.

Collateral Security

Matters relating to collateral security and guarantees will usually be separately addressed in voting provisions. As to security, the most common approach requires the consent of each lender (except in the circumstances described in the next paragraph) to release all or substantially all of the collateral security or all or substantially all of the subsidiary guarantees. (See the previous discussion in the "Fundamental Changes" section of Part 5, "Monitoring the Loan," for the meaning of "all or substantially all.") Unanimous consent will also be required if the borrower wants the collateral to secure additional obligations, unless the additional obligations have a lower lien priority (in which case the general rule, i.e., the consent of only the required lenders, would apply). Absent language to the contrary, "additional obligations" in this context will not normally include increased credit under the credit agreement itself (which will normally be allowed to be secured *pari passu* with other loans so long as the increased credit is otherwise permitted under the credit agreement, or consented to by the lenders).

Voting provisions will also address releases of collateral in the context of asset sales that are permitted under the dispositions covenant, or to which the appropriate lenders have consented. Most credit agreements will authorize the administrative agent (or the collateral agent, if there is one) to release collateral in this context without any separate consent from any lender. In other words, the fact that a sale is permitted under the fundamental changes covenant or has been consented to by the required lenders (or other percentage) is deemed to carry with it full authorization to the administrative agent to release on its own any liens on the assets to be sold.

Finally, voting provisions will sometimes specify that any modification of a security document (not just releases of collateral) requires the consent of each lender. This can be extraordinarily cumbersome in many instances (most amendments to security documents are technical in nature), and the market practice seems to be moving away from this approach.

PRO RATA TREATMENT

A general principle in virtually all credit agreements is that the lenders are treated on a "ratable" basis. Thus, lenders in a tranche make loans of that tranche "ratably" in accordance with their commitments (with the exception for competitive bid loans discussed in the section "Competitive Bid Loans" in Part 1, "Making the Loan"). Similarly, principal and interest are paid and prepaid "ratably" in accordance with the outstanding amounts of the relevant tranche. Commitments are reduced, and commitment and facility fees are paid, "ratably" in accordance with the commitments of the particular tranche. Much of this is self-operative, since payments are almost always made directly to the administrative agent, and it is the administrative agent that keeps track of the status of outstanding commitments and that will remit funds paid by the borrower to the lenders. If a lender should in any circumstance receive more than its pro rata share of any payment, the provisions of the sharing clause discussed in the next section may be triggered.

SHARING OF SETOFFS AND OTHER CLAIMS

As noted in the preceding section, all payments to lenders of principal and interest of a particular tranche are to be made ratably within the tranche. An individual lender may nevertheless receive a payment without the other lenders receiving their ratable share. This could happen if a payment were made by the borrower directly to a lender (perhaps by mistake, or perhaps to prefer one lender over other lenders), if a lender exercises a right of setoff with respect to deposit accounts of the borrower maintained with a lender, or if a lender receives proceeds from an exercise of other remedies. The sharing clause is designed to ensure that the lender receiving the nonratable payment share the proceeds with the other lenders, either through the purchase of participations or through the acquisition of assignments from the other lenders, so that all lenders receive the benefits of the proceeds on a ratable basis.

The borrower will be required to consent that any lender that acquires a participation or other interest in this manner may in turn exercise a right of setoff with respect to the participation interest. This concept is sometimes referred to as the "black hole" provision. An illustration of the way it works may be useful. Assume that a lender has $1,000,000 in loans in a $5,000,000 syndicate (i.e., it has 20 percent of the total loans). Assume also that it holds $1,500,000 of deposits from the borrower. After exercising its right of setoff against the deposits and before purchasing participations from the other lenders, it will have $0 in loans and $500,000 of deposits. However, when it purchases participations from the other lenders so that everyone receives the benefit of the setoff ratably, it will have $800,000 of loans ($800,000 representing 20 percent of $4,000,000). Under the "black hole" clause, it will then be entitled to set off the remaining $500,000 of deposits, leaving it before the second round of participations with $300,000 in loans and $0 in deposits. Following the second round of participations, it would hold $700,000 of loans ($700,000 representing 20 percent of $3,500,000). In practice, if the black hole clause is ever employed, the various stages of setoff and purchases of participations would be effected in one single action, though they would be deemed to have occurred in separate stages as described here.

THE CLAWBACK CLAUSE

As noted in the section "Mechanics of Funding" in Part 1, "Making the Loan," in syndicated credit agreements, all funding passes through the administrative agent. The clawback clause addresses what happens if a lender does not provide its portion of a loan to the administrative agent, but the administrative agent nevertheless forwards to the borrower the full amount of the loan (including the portion that was to have been provided by the defaulting lender). The concern is an everyday issue because of the near impossibility of an administrative agent's ascertaining whether it has actually received funds from lenders before forwarding them on to a borrower. The funds transfer system does not operate in real time; in many cases it takes hours for a transfer to wend its way through the payments system, and then further hours before the administrative agent is able to confirm receipt. If administrative agents always waited until they knew with certainty that funds had arrived, most loans would not be made until either very late in the day (probably too late for the borrower to use them) or on the next business day.

Under the clawback clause, an administrative agent will be entitled to presume that a lender is remitting funds to the administrative agent, unless that lender has otherwise informed the administrative agent (customarily at least one business day prior to the date of the borrowing). If the lender fails to so inform the administrative agent and the administrative agent remits that lender's portion of the loan to the borrower, then the lender is unconditionally obligated to pay such funds immediately to the administrative agent. The clawback clause will also require the borrower to return those funds to the administrative agent on demand, although expressly reserving any rights that the borrower may have against the lender for having defaulted on its obligation to make the loan.

Most clawback clauses will also address the obverse situation, i.e., what happens if the borrower is to make a payment to the lenders but does not in fact remit appropriate funds to the administrative agent. Again, because of delays in the payments system, the administrative agent probably will not know whether the borrower has in fact made payment. The clawback clause will allow the administrative agent to presume that, unless the borrower advises it otherwise, the borrower has remitted the appropriate amount to the administrative agent. Further, the lenders will be obligated to return to the administrative agent any funds that the lenders are sent without the administrative agent's having received monies from the borrower.

Note that in either of these cases the administrative agent is *not required* to remit funds to the borrower or to the lenders; sending on money to either is completely within its sole discretion. Sometimes lenders will push the administrative agent to agree that it will not remit funds to the borrower unless it can confirm that all conditions have been satisfied. Consistent with the discussion in the section "Ongoing Conditions" in Part 4, "Conditioning the Loan," administrative agents resist this (and, accordingly, it will not be written into the credit agreement) because it in effect places the administrative agent in the position of watching the credit for the benefit of the lenders. Such a responsibility would be inconsistent with the concept (discussed in the section "Agency Provisions" earlier in this part) that the administrative agent's duties are ministerial only and that each lender takes full responsibility for monitoring the borrower and the agreement.

In all cases, for each day that a lender or the borrower has failed to remit relevant funds to the administrative agent, the credit agreement will specify an appropriate interest rate to be payable to the administrative agent on the defaulted amount.

ACCESS TO THE LOAN REGISTER

Pursuant to the assignments clause of a credit agreement (discussed in detail in the section "Assignments" in Part 9, "Selling the Loan"), the administrative agent may be required to maintain a register of loans identifying the names and addresses of the lenders and the amounts of their respective commitments and loan balances. See the LSTA Model Credit Agreement Provisions for an example of this provision. Although there may be exceptions, most of these clauses (the LSTA provisions included) will provide that the administrative agent make the register available for inspection by the borrower and any lender (usually at "reasonable" times and upon "reasonable" notice). This can be an important right for both borrowers and lenders in workout situations, even though, as a practical matter (since loan participations will not be logged in the register), it will not be a complete list of all interested parties if participation interests have been sold.

Part 9. Selling the Loan: The Assignments Clause

DISTINGUISHING ASSIGNMENTS AND PARTICIPATIONS

Credit agreements will typically control both assignments and participations. Understanding the legal distinction between the two is important. Assignments create direct contractual rights between the borrower and the assignee. That means that if the borrower defaults in payment of the loan, the assignee can sue the borrower. If the assignment is of a revolving credit commitment and the assignee breaches its obligation to make a loan, the borrower can sue the assignee. The assignee becomes a "lender" under the credit agreement, with full voting and other rights. If a lender transfers a portion of its commitment to an assignee, the lender will be relieved of its obligation vis-à-vis the borrower with respect to the portion sold, and the purchaser will become obligated with respect to that portion.

A participation does not create direct contractual rights between the borrower and the participant. Rather, the participant's rights and obligations vis-à-vis the borrower are derivative of the rights and obligations of the seller of the participation. The participant will not become a "lender" under the credit agreement, will not have voting rights, and will not be obligated directly to the borrower to make loans. The seller of the participation will remain fully obligated to the borrower for the full amount of its commitment and will not be relieved of the portion of its commitment sold to the participant. The borrower has no right to sue the participant directly. The participant will be entitled to receive only its applicable proportion of monies paid to the seller of the participation by the borrower. If the participant wants to sue the borrower, it must do so by persuading the seller of the participation to institute suit.

Because of the greater rights of an assignee as compared to a participant, assignments are normally subject to borrower consent (discussed in more detail in later sections), while participations generally may be made without consent.

ASSIGNMENTS

Most contracts (credit agreements are no different) specify that the agreement is binding upon the "successors and assigns" of the parties. A "successor" arises when a party merges with another entity; the survivor will be the successor. An "assign" arises when a party sells or assigns its interest to a third party. Assignments are, technically speaking, assignments only of rights and not of obligations, though many agreements will refer to an "assignment" of obligations. What this language really means is that rights have been *assigned* to a new party and that obligations have been *assumed* by the new party.

Consent Rights

From the standpoint of a lender, the ability to assign or participate interests in loans under a credit agreement is essential to preserving its access to liquidity. Consequently, a credit agreement will normally stipulate that the lenders are free to assign their rights and obligations under the credit agreement without the consent of any other party. The general rule will be subject to some exclusions that will dictate limited circumstances in which the borrower, the administrative agent, any swingline lender, and the issuer of letters of credit will have a consent right. Some general principles are that:

- The borrower will lose whatever consent rights it has after the occurrence of any (or certain specified) event of default.

- The borrower will have no consent rights if an assignment is to another lender or an affiliate (including, in the case of a fund, other commonly managed funds).

- The administrative agent, each issuer of letters of credit, and each swingline lender will have a consent right over any assignment of a revolving credit commitment.
- The administrative agent will have a consent right over any assignment of term loans.
- Each of these consent rights will be qualified by a requirement that the consent not be unreasonably withheld or delayed.

Sometimes the consent right granted to the issuer of letters of credit and swingline lenders is absolute, i.e., not subject to the requirement that the consent not be unreasonably withheld or delayed. The theory is that, since a letter of credit issuer or swingline lender is taking the direct credit risk of other lenders who participate in the issuer's or swingline lender's exposure, the issuer or swingline lender should not have to debate in front of a court whether a credit decision made by it with respect to the assignee was "unreasonable" or "delayed."

Although there is constant pressure from the market to remove borrowers' and administrative agents' consent rights, their removal may raise other legal issues. For example, borrowers and lenders both have an interest in loans continuing to be treated as a commercial debt relationship and not as securities under federal and state securities laws. Borrowers' and administrative agents' consent rights can, in this context, be a significant factor in determining whether loans are covered by the securities laws. See the discussion in the section "Are Loans Covered by the Securities Laws?" later in this part.

Eligible Assignees

Some credit agreements will introduce a concept of "eligible assignees"—entities that are not "eligible" may not (even during a default) acquire loans under the credit agreement without the consent of the borrower. The definition of what entities are "eligible" will normally include banks, financial institutions, and funds (and thus pick up all of the usual suspects that will want to hold loans, including B loans). Nevertheless, incorporating a definition of eligible assignee has become less frequent. The LSTA Model Credit Agreement Provisions, for example, leave who can become a lender to the determination of the borrower and the administrative agent, without defining an underlying class of entities that are permissible holders of loans and commitments.

Minimums

The assignments clause will almost always specify some minimum amount for an assignment, typically $5,000,000 or more for revolving credit loans and A loans and $1,000,000 or more for B loans. One of the issues that arises is whether the $1,000,000 figure applies to each individual fund in a family of funds that may be buying into the credit agreement, or whether it applies to the family as a whole. The market standard appears to be moving toward lumping together family funds for purposes of determining whether the minimum has been met.

Transfer Fees

A credit agreement will normally provide for a transfer fee to be paid to the administrative agent upon the occasion of each assignment of a loan. Who pays the fee will be left to negotiation between the assignor and assignee and will be specified in the assignment agreement.

Loan Register

Under the typical assignments provision, the administrative agent will be required to maintain a register of loans identifying the name and address of each lender and the amounts of their respective commitments and loan balances. The credit agreement will normally state that the loan register is conclusive and thus is the definitive determinant of who must consent to modifications to the agreement and who are the required lenders.

Are Loans Covered by the Securities Laws?

As noted previously, borrowers and lenders both have an interest in loans continuing to be classified as obligations that arise in a commercial debt relationship, and not as securities under federal and state securities laws. For example, treating loans as "securities" could trigger higher capital requirements for investment banks and could also impose formalities that increase execution time without meaningfully improving the basis upon which a sound credit judgment is made. Ultimately, such treatment could blur the distinction between the loan syndication market and the bond market and thus remove flexibility from the credit system.

The Securities Act of 1933 and the Securities Exchange Act of 1934 define "security" in slightly different ways, although courts have interpreted the definitions similarly. The Securities Act of 1933 defines a security, in addition to stock, bonds, debentures, and a long list of other instruments, as including "a note." Superficially, the definition could be read to include loans under a typical credit agreement since the term *note* is read broadly to include any evidence of indebtedness (including, therefore, noteless loans).

The courts have developed a number of tests to determine whether "notes" are securities. The latest word, adopted in 1990 by the Supreme Court (in the *Reves* case), is the so-called family resemblance test. Under this test, a note is presumed to be a security unless it looks like a non-security. More precisely, a note is presumed to be a security unless, examining it against the four factors described in the next paragraph, shows a "strong resemblance" to one of the types of non-securities on a list that has been judicially created over the years. The list of non-securities includes (1) a note with a maturity of less than nine months, (2) a note delivered in consumer financing, (3) a note secured by a mortgage on a home, (4) a short-term note secured by a lien on a small business or some of its assets, (5) a note evidencing a "character" loan to a bank customer, (6) a short-term note secured by an assignment of accounts receivable, (7) a note that simply formalizes open-account debt incurred in the ordinary course of business, and (8) a note evidencing a loan made by a commercial bank to finance current operations.

If a note that is not on the list of non-securities comes before a court, the court will look at four factors to determine if it is a security. *First* is the motivation for the parties to enter into the transaction. If the purpose of the issuer/borrower is to raise money for the general use of a business enterprise or to finance substantial investments, and if the purchaser/lender is primarily interested in the profit that the note will generate, the instrument is likely to be considered a security. If, however, the note advances a commercial or consumer purpose (such as facilitating the purchase and sale of a minor asset or to correct for the cash flow difficulties of the issuer/borrower), the note is probably not a security. *Second* is the plan of distribution. Is the note an instrument in which there is "common trading for speculation or investment"? *Third* is the reasonable expectations of the investing public. A court will consider instruments to be securities on the basis of public expectations, even when an economic analysis might suggest that the instrument is not a "security" in a particular transaction. *Fourth* is whether there is some element, such as the existence of another regulatory scheme, that significantly reduces the risk of the instrument, thereby rendering the application of the securities laws unnecessary.

In the context of a credit agreement, the second and third of these factors are most important (i.e., the plan of distribution and the expectations of the trading public). Helpfully, there are a number of provisions in a typical credit agreement that are not compatible with a plan of distribution for "common trading for speculation or investment." These include (1) reliance by the borrower on the credit and liquidity of the lender to make advances, (2) reliance by the administrative agent on indemnities and clawbacks from lenders, (3) lenders having the right to receive periodic information that goes beyond public information, including computations of covenant compliance, (4) lenders having visitation rights to obtain information, (5) lenders having the right (subject to confidentiality undertakings) to furnish nonpublic information to potential purchasers, (6) assignments being subject to administrative agent and, absent certain defaults, borrower consent, and (7) purchasers being required to be financial institutions or otherwise familiar with the credit judgments required in the commercial loan market. While not every commercial loan has all these provisions, most commercial loans have some combination of many of them.

As to the expectations of the investing public, credit agreements are quite different from private placements and bond indentures, where the issuers and the purchasers clearly expect and intend that the notes or bonds will be securities. Those instruments will typically use securities-like terminology. Most credit agreements, however, are carefully constructed to use loanlike terminology and avoid language such as "accredited investors," "qualified institutional buyers," "purchase without a view to distribution," and other securities law buzzwords. Use of the latter, by building in provisions designed to create securities law exemptions, could create the expectation that the agreement gives rise to securities in the first place. Accordingly, unless done very carefully, exemption wording can have an effect exactly opposite to the desires of the borrower and the lenders.

PARTICIPATIONS

As noted previously, participations (unlike assignments) do not give the participant any direct rights against the borrower, nor do they give the borrower any direct rights against the participant. The seller of the participation remains fully obligated on its commitment (including the portion sold). As a consequence, participations can generally be sold without the consent of any party.

Since a participant does not become a "lender" under the credit agreement, it is not directly entitled to voting rights, nor will the borrower typically want the participant to have voting rights. A participant could, of course, easily circumvent this by contractually restricting the seller of the participation from consenting to amendments or waivers without authorization from the participant. Participation provisions of credit agreements will as a consequence commonly limit the ability of a participant to control the seller's voting rights to matters that would adversely affect money terms (such as reductions of interest or principal, maturity, and the like) or terms where changes require unanimous lender consent. These limitations may, however, be more of a mirage than real. Given the development of loan trading in today's market, sellers and buyers of participations are in continual contact on both the buy and sell side of trading activity. They will naturally consult upon modifications and, although a participant may not have a legal right to force its seller to vote in a particular way, as a practical matter the seller will give great weight to the views of its participant.

One frequent exception to the rule that participants do not have direct rights against the borrower is with respect to yield protection and taxes. In this instance, the typical participations clause will permit a participant to make claims directly against the borrower (usually capped by the amount of the claim that the seller could have made had the participation not been sold).

LOAN PLEDGES

Many lenders will want to have the flexibility to pledge loans to support their own funding needs. Banks may want to pledge loans to the Federal Reserve under Regulation A to obtain short-term or emergency credit, and B loan lenders may need to pledge the loans held by them to secure financing provided to the lender. A restriction on the assignment of loans could be construed as a restriction on a pledge of loans. Although the Uniform Commercial Code as enacted in all 50 states should override any such restriction, the conventional assignments clause will still expressly allow a lender to pledge any loans held by it, with the qualification that no pledge will relieve the pledgor of any obligations under the credit agreement. One of the issues that these provisions leave open is what happens if the pledgee forecloses on the pledge and seeks to take title to the loan. In this instance, any necessary consents otherwise required in the assignments clause would arguably need to be obtained.

Part 10. Understanding the Boilerplate: All the Stuff at the End That No One Ever Reads

NOTICE PROVISIONS

The notice provisions set out the contact information for each party to the credit agreement, although, with respect to lenders, current practice is for the information to be specified in administrative questionnaires collected by the administrative agent during the syndication process or when a lender joins the credit agreement by assignment. Administrative questionnaires avoid the hassle of completing a notice schedule to be appended to the credit agreement in the last minutes prior to the closing.

In the recent past, notification provisions have begun to take into account electronic communication, i.e., e-mail, web site postings, and the like. As of this writing, however, most agreements do not lock in detailed procedures for electronic notification. The LSTA Model Credit Agreement Provisions, for example, contemplate that the administrative agent will independently prescribe procedures for the delivery of electronic communications, which it can change as technology and market practice develop.

NO DEEMED WAIVERS

One concern of lenders is that acquiescence in a breach by the borrower will, if continued, establish a course of conduct that might be viewed by the borrower or a court as an implied waiver. Lenders also fear that the act of making the loan might itself constitute a waiver if a borrower could charge them with knowledge of a breach at the time a loan is made (by, for example, asserting that the lenders are aware of facts that should lead to a recognition of the breach).

The "no deemed waivers" provision of the credit agreement attempts to address these issues by having the borrower agree at inception that no waivers will be deemed to arise in any circumstance unless they are expressly agreed in writing by the requisite lenders. Of course, there is no legal certainty that the provision will have the desired effect if it is ever presented to a court, so the closing date legal opinions will typically take a qualification for the clause. In addition, whenever lenders are aware of a breach that they are neither waiving nor using as a basis to exercise remedies, the borrower will often receive a "friendly" reminder from the administrative agent that acquiescence does not constitute waiver.

CUMULATIVE REMEDIES

The typical credit agreement will state expressly that the lenders are entitled to exercise remedies "cumulatively"—that if a medley of actions is available to the lenders, taking one action now does not preclude taking other actions later. Thus, setting off against deposit accounts immediately following acceleration should not preclude later suit or foreclosure; commencing suit against the borrower in New York does not preclude later suit against a guarantor in Canada.

Some states will not recognize a cumulative remedies provision. California's so-called One Form of Action Rule is an example. The One Form of Action Rule provides that, if a lender is secured by real property, it must foreclose on the property before or at the same time as bringing any other type of legal action to recover a debt. The rule also requires that any judicial action brought by a secured creditor to collect on its debt must include all real property security. If a lender does not include all real property in the action, any lien on nonincluded real property may be waived. The One Form of Action Rule may not be waived in advance of a default.

EXPENSES

The expenses provision will obligate the borrower to bear several different categories of costs. First, the borrower will agree to reimburse the administrative agent for costs incurred in connection with negotiating and closing the credit agreement or amendments. Second, in a secured deal, the borrower will agree to pick up costs, such as recording taxes, title insurance, and the like, that must be paid in order for the liens in favor of the lenders to be perfected and enforceable. Third, the borrower will undertake to pay costs and expenses associated with enforcement actions.

Credit agreements tend to be wordy on this latter point because of concern that the term *enforcement* has not been universally interpreted to include negotiations in connection with a workout or restructuring, or in connection with litigation over the expenses clause itself.

As to who is entitled to reimbursement in the context of enforcement, credit agreements take two approaches. Some credit agreements, in response to pressure from borrowers, permit only enforcement expenses of the administrative agent to be reimbursed; other agreements cover the expenses of any lender (the LSTA Model Credit Agreement Provisions take this approach). Regardless of the language in any particular credit agreement, there may be little practical difference between these two approaches. In the context of a workout, the borrower will invariably request a consent of some form, and thus the lenders will be free to insist that their legal costs be covered as a condition to granting their consent.

BORROWER INDEMNIFICATION; CONSEQUENTIAL DAMAGES

It is customary for lenders to obtain from the borrower a general indemnification against loss or liability suffered by the lenders in connection with the credit agreement. This indemnification is separate from the borrower's agreement (discussed in the section "Expenses" earlier in this part) to reimburse costs and expenses incurred directly in connection with the credit agreement. Reflecting the tendency of courts to construe indemnities narrowly, it will contain a long list of items for which the borrower is to indemnify the lenders: "losses, claims, damages, liabilities and related expenses" is the litany in the LSTA Model Credit Agreement Provisions. The indemnity will also expressly cover any of those items arising out of a claim by the borrower itself. The latter is intended to override a 1989 New York case (*Hooper*) that held that, unless an indemnification is explicit, it does not cover disputes between the parties to the contract itself, but covers only claims asserted by third parties.

Traditionally, credit agreements did not include a general indemnification from the borrower. However, when the practice of banks financing hostile acquisitions became widespread, and targets began suing lenders providing funds to the hostile bidder, indemnification clauses began to appear. No good idea goes unpunished, and the clauses soon became routine, to the point where their inclusion is now the market standard.

The borrower indemnity is deliberately broad and will cover not only the lenders, but affiliates of the lenders (such as securities affiliates that may have acted as arrangers of the credit facility) and their officers, directors, professional advisors, and others. The indemnity will also cover a broad range of events that might give rise to losses, including costs of investigations and litigation, regardless of origin. Normally, the clause will explicitly cover any environmental claims that might be asserted against the lenders in the event that they take over property from the borrower. However, it will typically exclude liability based upon "gross negligence" or "willful misconduct," as finally determined by a court of competent jurisdiction. Some borrowers may additionally seek to exclude liability for breach of contract by the lenders. The latter can be a sensitive point, since it is most likely to arise in a crisis situation, such as where the lenders refuse to honor a borrowing request because they believe that a "material adverse change" has occurred. The LSTA Model Credit Agreement Provisions provide that the indemnification is lost in this context only if there is a breach "in bad faith" by the indemnified party of its obligations under the credit agreement. Thus, if a lender determines that a

MAC has occurred and a court later holds that it was wrong, the indemnity is not lost so long as the determination was made in good faith.

Because of concerns arising out of court cases involving "lender liability," it is common for an indemnity to state that the lenders shall have no liability for any "indirect, consequential or punitive damages." The words *indirect* and *consequential* are alternative ways of referring to damages that were not reasonably in the contemplation of the parties when the contract was made. For example, if the failure of a lender to make a loan results in the borrower's not being able to consummate an acquisition, consequential damages might be the resulting loss of future profits for the borrower from not owning the business it sought to acquire. Punitive damages are damages of unpredictable amount, beyond any actual damages, that are awarded by juries to punish what they see as a party's wrongful behavior. One New York court has said that punitive damages are appropriate only where necessary to deter parties from engaging in conduct that may be characterized as "gross" and "morally reprehensible" and of such "wanton dishonesty" as to imply a criminal indifference to civil obligations. It is difficult to see how such behavior could arise in the context of a credit agreement, or that a waiver of punitive damages could even be enforceable, but it is customary nevertheless to address the issue in credit agreements. The LSTA Model Credit Agreement Provisions take this approach.

GOVERNING LAW

A credit agreement—indeed, virtually every contract—will include a "choice of law" provision, by which the parties agree as to the jurisdiction whose law will be applied to determine the validity of the contract and its interpretation. The contractually chosen law will not govern such matters as the borrower's existence and its power to enter into the financing (which are matters that are governed by the law of its jurisdiction of organization). It will also not govern issues such as perfection or priority of security interests (here the relevant governing law is determined by statute). It will, however, determine which jurisdiction's contract law applies as well as various other matters, including such issues as applicable usury limitations.

A provision choosing the law governing a contract is different from a "submission to jurisdiction" clause (see the discussion in the next section). The latter relates to the possible locale for litigation, while the former relates to which state's substantive law will be applied in whatever locale is used. Courts are accustomed to applying the law of other jurisdictions where required.

As a general principle, the law chosen by the parties to govern a contract must, if it is to be applied, bear a reasonable relation to the transaction. What constitutes a "reasonable relation" is not well defined, but the choice of New York law in a financing where the loans will be disbursed, and payments made, in New York and where the administrative agent or lead lenders are in New York, probably satisfies the reasonable relation standard. However, for any transaction of $250,000 or more, a New York statute (Section 5–1401 of New York's General Obligations Law) allows the parties to choose New York law regardless of whether there is a reasonable relation to New York.

New York law is extensive, stable, and relatively "creditor-friendly," and this fact, coupled with the enactment of Section 5–1401 of the General Obligations Law, makes it a favored choice as the governing law of credit agreements. Nevertheless, some agreements may choose other jurisdictions. For example, transactions led and managed outside the United States are often governed by English law, for many of the same reasons that New York law is considered attractive. It is *not*, however, considered advisable in cross-border lending to provide that the credit agreement be governed by the law of the borrower's jurisdiction. Selecting the borrower's jurisdiction forces the lenders into the difficult position of having to understand how a different legal regime would construe the standard provisions of a credit agreement, and perhaps subject the lenders to increased risk of changes in the applicable substantive law. It may also be against many lenders' internal credit policies.

A typical choice of law clause provides that the agreement "shall be governed by and construed in accordance with the law of the State of New York." Sometimes the clause goes on to exclude "conflicts of law" rules out of concern that the chosen jurisdiction's choice of law rules may direct the court to a different law (for example, the law of the borrower's jurisdiction). This is both unnecessary and undesirable. The better view is that the reference to "the law" of the chosen jurisdiction means that jurisdiction's *internal* law. Excluding conflicts of law principles could exclude the doctrine that the intentions of the parties should be given effect, not to mention (in the New York context) Section 5–1401 of New York's General Obligations Law. Some credit agreements adopt an alternative and better, though wordier, approach, excluding those conflict of law rules "that would otherwise direct application of the law of another jurisdiction."

ENFORCEMENT PROVISIONS

Submission to Jurisdiction; Process Agents

Lenders always prefer to enforce a credit agreement, should it come to that, in New York or some other "home" jurisdiction. Commencing litigation in the borrower's jurisdiction can entail incremental travel and other expenses, be less certain of a proper outcome, and of course eat up more lender officer time. This is particularly true when the borrower is organized outside of the United States, where additional factors come into play, such as the difficulty of communication with local counsel and the possibility that a local court would favor a local company and perhaps misconstrue New York law.

Court jurisdiction comes in two shapes and sizes: "subject matter" and "personal." "Subject-matter jurisdiction" refers to the power of a particular court to hear a particular kind of case. "Personal jurisdiction" refers to the power of a court over a particular entity.

For the most part, subject-matter jurisdiction cannot be created by agreement among the parties, and thus a submission to jurisdiction clause will not to this extent be enforceable. Parties cannot by agreement, for example, force a tax or customs court to hear a landlord-tenant dispute. Parties to a credit agreement could not require the New York Family Court to pass judgment on an interest-rate provision. The subject-matter jurisdiction of a federal court in the context of a commercial loan generally depends on the circumstance of "diversity of citizenship," a concept in the U.S. Constitution that requires that, in any litigation, the plaintiffs and defendants be from different jurisdictions (and that there not be "aliens" on both sides of the controversy). There are other sources of federal subject-matter jurisdiction, including where the borrower is a "foreign state" (see the discussion in the section "Waiver of

Sovereign Immunity" later in this part) and where litigation involves a U.S. national bank or other entity organized under U.S. federal law (12 U.S.C. §632).

State courts (except for specialized courts, such as family courts, traffic courts, and landlord-tenant courts) have far fewer limitations on their subject-matter jurisdiction. As a result, even though a particular dispute cannot be heard in a federal court, it may nevertheless be heard in a state court. Thus, a dispute under a credit agreement where the borrower is a non-U.S. corporation and there are many foreign banks in the lending syndicate can nevertheless be heard in New York State courts even though there are "aliens" on both sides of the dispute. However, even state courts of general jurisdiction may have limitations. For example, a so-called door-closing statute in New York precludes an action in a New York State court by one non-New York entity against another unless, among other exceptions, the contract is performable in New York (loans payable in New York probably satisfy this requirement).

Personal jurisdiction, which as noted previously refers to the power of a court over a particular defendant, consists of two components, each of which can be established by contract. First, there must be a "basis" for jurisdiction, and, second, notice must have been given to the defendant. A basis for personal jurisdiction over a borrower may be created simply by having the borrower consent (or "submit") to the court's jurisdiction. Most credit agreements will, therefore, include a formal submission to jurisdiction by the borrower. The submission will customarily be "nonexclusive," i.e., the parties will not be forced to litigate in the selected jurisdiction, but will be free to commence suit before any other court having the proper subject-matter and personal jurisdiction. This preserves for the lenders the right to sue the borrower in its home jurisdiction.

Notice can be effected in any manner agreed to by the borrower. For a borrower in the United States, the typical approach is simply to have the borrower consent to being advised of a suit by mail delivered to its "address for notices" specified in the credit agreement. For non-U.S. borrowers, credit agreements usually adopt a more formal approach of having the borrower appoint an agent in New York to which notice can be given (referred to in legal jargon as "service of process"). The agent will then be defined as a "process agent." This more formal approach for non-U.S. borrowers is designed to avoid a foreign court's refusing to enforce a New York judgment on the grounds that notice was inadequate.

Venue and *Forum Non Conveniens*

In addition to the concept of subject-matter jurisdiction, federal and state courts are typically also subject to "venue" requirements. Thus, although a federal court might have subject-matter jurisdiction to hear a suit, the venue statute might stipulate that only a court where one of the parties has a place of business may take on the suit. Venue requirements are generally waivable, and so it is customary in credit agreements for there to be a waiver of venue on the part of the borrower.

Even if a court has subject-matter jurisdiction and venue is proper (or has been waived), the court may still have the discretion not to hear a case if it thinks there is a more convenient forum for the suit. This is the so-called *forum non conveniens* doctrine. A court might thus force transfer of the case if that would be more convenient for the parties, taking into account such factors as the location of documents and witnesses, the place where relevant events occurred, and the like. It is customary to require the borrower to waive objection on *forum non conveniens* grounds, although the court is still free to transfer the case despite a waiver. A New York court, however, is precluded from granting a transfer (Section 327 of the New York Civil Practice Law and Rules) if the credit agreement provides for loans of $1,000,000 or more and contains both a choice of New York law and a submission to New York court jurisdiction.

Waiver of Sovereign Immunity

Sovereign immunity refers to the special status that a borrower has if it is a "foreign state" under the U.S. Foreign Sovereign Immunity Act of 1976, namely, immunity from court jurisdiction and immunity of its property from attachment or execution. Thus, a foreign state cannot be forced to appear in a U.S. court (federal or state) and cannot have its property in the United States seized to pay a judgment. The Act permits sovereign immunity to be waived. Accordingly, credit agreements with foreign states almost universally have the borrower relinquish whatever rights it has under the Act.

The term *foreign state* is defined broadly. It includes not only a foreign government, but any agency of a foreign government. It also sweeps in any entity that is majority-owned by a foreign country (if it is organized under the laws of that country). Because even a private company becomes entitled to sovereign immunity if a majority of its shares are acquired by its home country after the closing, sovereign immunity waivers are standard in all cross-border credit agreements, whether or not the borrower starts out governmental.

Waiver of Jury Trial

Unpredictable jury awards in "lender liability" cases have led lenders for many years to require borrowers to waive the right to trial by jury, so that any litigation will be before a presumably more sophisticated judge. The right is set out in the U.S. Constitution as well as in many state constitutions and statutes. Insofar as federal law is concerned, a waiver that is "knowing" will generally be enforceable. A waiver will almost certainly be knowing in the context of commercial credit agreements where the borrowers are sophisticated and represented by counsel. It is also more likely to be enforceable if the waiver is mutual, i.e., if *both* the borrower and the lenders waive their right to a jury trial. The LSTA Model Credit Agreement Provisions adopt the mutuality approach. In a few states, a waiver of the state constitutional jury right may not be enforceable even if it is knowing and mutual (California is an example).

Judgment Currency

A judgment currency clause will be inserted either when the credit agreement provides for nondollar loans or when it provides for dollar loans and the borrower is located outside the United States. It addresses the problem of transporting a judgment rendered by a court in one country to a second country that has a different currency. An example might arise if a borrower that is organized and has all of its assets in Germany is obligated on a loan denominated in U.S. dollars made available in New York by a group of U.S. lenders. If a judgment for U.S. $1,000,000 is rendered against the borrower in New York, the lenders will probably need to present the New York judgment to a German court and request that it order the borrower to pay. A German court, however, will probably render its own judgment in euro in an amount equal to the equivalent of U.S. $1,000,000. Between the time that the German court issues a judgment and the borrower actually pays the stipulated euro, the value of the euro may fall, and thus, when the lenders convert those euro into U.S. dollars, they may end up short. The judgment currency clause allows the lenders to go back to the New York court and request a new judgment in the amount of the shortfall, which could then be similarly enforced in Germany against the borrower.

As of this writing, no court in New York has yet upheld the concept (as contemplated in the judgment currency clause) that a lender can go back to court to obtain a supplemental judgment if currency fluctuations render the initial judgment amount insufficient. Accordingly, legal opinions delivered at closing will normally include an exception as to the enforceability of the clause.

SEVERABILITY; COUNTERPARTS; INTEGRATION; CAPTIONS

Severability

Some court decisions have ruled that, if the illegality of one provision "destroys" an agreement, the whole agreement will be nullified. If, however, the illegality does not destroy the agreement, the illegal provision can be severed and the balance of the agreement enforced. This concern can be particularly acute in cases where the borrower is located in a jurisdiction other than the governing law of the agreement. Would, for example, an entire New York law credit agreement fail because, say, the indemnification clause might be unenforceable in Arizona? Severability clauses are thus inserted into agreements as an expression of intent that the parties do not want the normal rule described above to apply.

Counterparts

The counterparts clause is one of those provisions that is frequently overlooked, but that has great practical significance. It permits a credit agreement to be executed by each party signing a different copy, or an individual signature page, and then assembling all of the respective copies or signature pages into one, single agreement. This practice is quite different from the method used in many foreign jurisdictions, where a contract, to be enforceable, must include the signatures of all parties on a single document that is executed at a single time.

Integration

The integration clause will stipulate that the credit agreement reflects the entire understanding between the parties and that it supersedes all prior agreements (including commitment or engagement letters or any "side letters," and including also oral understandings) executed between the parties. Frequently fee letters will be excluded, since not all fees are incorporated into the credit agreement. The LSTA Model Credit Agreement Provisions take this approach.

Superseding oral conversations can be particularly important. For example, when a deal goes sour, a borrower might allege that there were prior understandings as to whether and when remedies might be invoked. A borrower may even want to bring a lender liability claim against the lenders for breach of alleged prior conversations. The integration clause can be a shield against the borrower's raising these types of arguments.

Captions

The table of contents and the section and paragraph headings of a credit agreement can be extraordinarily useful in moving around and finding relevant provisions in the document. However, since captions could potentially be used by a borrower to help a court misconstrue the meaning of the words of a credit agreement, the captions clause provides that captions and the table of contents are not to have interpretive effect and are inserted for "convenience of reference" only.

ELECTRONIC EXECUTION

Lawyers may worry whether receipt of a telecopy signature page of an agreement is sufficient. For more than a century, a legal doctrine, the so-called best evidence rule, has required that if a party wishes to enforce a contract, it must produce an original of the contract or the "best evidence" of the execution by all parties of the contract. Revisions to the best evidence rule in both New York and federal courts now treat a telecopy or photocopy as equivalent to the original, so this concern has largely disappeared. Nevertheless, a telecopy or photocopy may still be challenged if genuine questions are raised as to the authenticity of the original.

SURVIVAL

Under traditional legal doctrine, once a closing occurs, the representations and warranties set forth in a contract lapse and cease to have any continuing force. The purpose of the survival clause is to overcome this traditional rule by providing that all representations survive throughout the entire term of the credit agreement. It is consistent with the principle underlying the no deemed waivers provision (see the section "No Deemed Waivers" earlier in this part) that simply because a lender may be aware of a breach when making a loan does not mean that the lender has waived the breach.

The survival clause will also explicitly state that indemnification and yield protection provisions will survive the repayment of the loans and termination of the credit agreement. Such survival is important, given that a lender will not necessarily know at the time of payoff whether it may suffer future claims or losses with respect to matters that the borrower has agreed to cover. The survival clause will not restore security or guarantees that the lenders have released, but it will at least preserve for the lenders a claim against the borrower for indemnification and the like that arise after payoff.

USA PATRIOT ACT

Shortly following the attacks of September 11, 2001, the United States enacted the so-called USA Patriot Act. The term abbreviates the rather meandering "Uniting and Strengthening America by Providing Appropriate Tools Required to Intercept and Obstruct Terrorism Act of 2001." Under the Act, the Treasury Department is required to prescribe regulations setting out procedures for financial institutions to verify the identity of customers, maintain records relating to customers, and consult lists of known or suspected terrorists or terrorist organizations to determine whether customers appear on the list. The regulations issued by the Treasury Department require that customers be advised that the financial institution will be collecting this information. The term *customer* does not include a public company or any existing customer of a bank, so notice is in fact not legally required in most cases. Nevertheless, for simplicity's sake it has become common for credit agreements to include a Patriot Act notice for all borrowers.

Part 11. The Borrower Can Have Rights, Too

THE RIGHT THAT LENDERS MAKE LOANS

As was discussed earlier (see the section "Several Liability" in Part 1, "Making the Loan"), when a group of lenders undertakes to make loans to a borrower, each lender is individually obligated, assuming all relevant conditions are satisfied, to extend credit up to the full amount of its commitment. These obligations are "several," i.e., the failure of one lender to make its loan does not relieve any other lender of its obligation.

Any lender that fails to make a loan requested by the borrower when all conditions precedent are satisfied will be in breach of its commitment under the credit agreement. The borrower may, as a consequence, suffer damages and may seek to recover those from the defaulting lender. Although the standard indemnification provisions in a credit agreement (see the discussion in the section "Borrower Indemnification; Consequential Damages" in Part 10, "Understanding the Boilerplate") will normally constrain the borrower's ability to assert consequential damages against the lenders for any breach, the borrower may still claim *actual* damages. In this context, actual damages might include the costs (higher interest, up-front fees, and other costs) of the borrower's procuring alternative financing.

THE RIGHT THAT LENDERS MITIGATE COSTS

Credit agreements will normally require that any lender requesting compensation under the increased costs or taxes clauses use "reasonable" efforts to book loans at a different branch or transfer loans to an affiliate if either action would reduce or eliminate these costs. The purpose, of course, is to minimize what costs are passed on to the borrower. The obligation to use "reasonable efforts" typically provides that any action taken not be "otherwise disadvantageous" to the lender. This is intended, among other things, to override any requirement that the lender book a loan in a particular jurisdiction if that would violate an internal lender policy. Some lenders, for example, have a policy that all LIBOR loans be booked in offshore offices and thus would not want to move those loans to a domestic office.

THE "YANK-A-BANK" PROVISION

If mitigation by a lender (as described in the preceding section) is not feasible, what is called the "yank-a-bank" provision (usually captioned "Replacement Lenders") will permit a borrower to replace a lender that requests reimbursement for increased costs or taxes. As normally written, the borrower will be responsible for finding a replacement lender and also for paying any associated transfer fees; the new lender will take an assignment of loans and commitments from the lender being replaced. Typically, replacement must result in a reduction of costs that the borrower would otherwise be required to pay. The replaced lender will be entitled to the full amount of its principal, interest, and any related breakfunding costs or fees (or, if applicable, premium).

Sometimes the yank-a-bank provision will allow a borrower to replace a lender that has declined to consent to a proposed amendment. With this provision, if an amendment needs unanimous approval, no small group of lenders will be in a position to extract a higher amendment fee or other concession, since the borrower could always replace those lenders with more compliant institutions. In many cases (though the market appears to be moving toward greater flexibility on this score), the aggregate percentage of the lenders that may be so replaced will be limited (5 percent is frequently seen), and typically also replacement will be allowed only for issues that require unanimous consent (as opposed to the mere concurrence of the required lenders).

THE RIGHT THAT LENDERS ACT IN GOOD FAITH

It is a general principle of New York law that every contract contains an implied covenant of "good faith and fair dealing." No party to an agreement may do anything that will have the effect of destroying or injuring the right of the other parties "to receive the fruits of the contract." In the context of credit agreements, some worry that lenders might not be acting in good faith if they accelerate loans based upon a technical or nonmaterial default. Breach by a lender of the implied covenant of good faith could potentially expose a lender to liability to the borrower (or, at a minimum, make a court reluctant to allow a lender to exercise remedies).

THE RIGHT TO DESIGNATE ADDITIONAL BORROWERS

Credit agreements sometimes permit the borrower to designate subsidiaries as additional borrowers. This right is most often granted with respect to foreign subsidiaries, where for tax or other reasons the subsidiary needs direct access to funds. Typically, the obligations of the subsidiary borrowers will be guaranteed by the borrower; absent such a guarantee, any such designation would normally require an independent credit approval (and hence consent) by each affected lender.

CURE RIGHTS

As discussed in the section "Events of Default" in Part 7, "Enforcing the Loan," a breach of the credit agreement will constitute an event of default only so long as the breach continues. By way of example, if a borrower fails to pay an installment of principal and then 10 days later pays the full amount that is past due, the event of default that originally arose upon failure to pay no longer continues, since it has been cured.

Certain types of breaches cannot be cured. If a borrower defaults on an interest coverage covenant at the end of a fiscal quarter, no cure is possible absent going back in time. In rare cases, however, a credit agreement may expressly allow a borrower to wipe out a financial covenant default after the fact, even though it is otherwise incurable. Of course, lenders are normally reluctant to agree to cure rights in a credit agreement because they disrupt the benchmarks that the covenants are designed to measure. Cure rights are consequently not commonly granted unless a parent holding company or other equity holder invests additional monies into the borrower as equity or subordinated debt. Thus, in the example just described, the borrower might be allowed to cure an interest coverage default if (1) its parent puts in additional cash equity capital, (2) the borrower applies the proceeds to repaying debt, and (3) the interest coverage ratio, when recalculated on a pro forma basis (as if the amount of debt outstanding during the period covered by the covenant were reduced by the amount of the repayment), at least equals the level required at the end of the relevant period. Normally, if cure rights are granted at all, they are subject to additional limits, such as being exercisable only within a relatively short period after the breach is discovered (and not in consecutive fiscal quarters), and are not available more than three or four times during the life of the agreement.

CONFIDENTIALITY

Confidentiality

Credit agreements require borrowers to deliver a substantial amount of financial information to lenders. Much of this may not be publicly available. Examples include projections, consolidating financial statements, product-line and divisional detail, and information delivered to the lenders in response to inquiries. Borrowers will want this information kept confidential. Disclosure could adversely affect their position with customers, competitors, and employees. For public companies, there is the added concern of the SEC's Regulation FD, which prohibits selective disclosure of material nonpublic information. Although revealing information to lenders without disclosing it publicly could be deemed "selective," Regulation FD contains an exemption for information delivered pursuant to a confidentiality agreement. The confidentiality clause serves that purpose.

The clause customarily requires that the lenders and administrative agent maintain the confidentiality of all "information" supplied by the borrower. Information will generally encompass any information that relates to the borrower or its business and that (although credit agreements are not uniform on this) is identified as confidential by the borrower at the time it is delivered to the lenders. There will, of course be exceptions that allow, among other things, disclosure to agents, accountants, and counsel; disclosure to other lenders and to prospective lenders (but only if they also agree to maintain the confidentiality of any information received by them); disclosure to regulators; disclosure in response to a proceeding or in connection with enforcement; and disclosure of information that becomes public other than through a breach by a lender.

The LSTA Model Credit Agreement Provisions sets out a confidentiality clause that incorporates these basic principles.

Use Restrictions

Sometimes, as part of a confidentiality clause, borrowers will request that lenders agree to a so-called use restriction, i.e., that information disclosed to lenders be used only "in connection with" the loans or the credit agreement. This can be problematic. Most banks have a single internal credit review function for all business dealings with a borrower, including loans, derivatives transactions, cash management services, letters of credit, deposit services, and the like. Revealing information to a credit officer in connection with a credit agreement will necessarily mean the information is being used for other purposes as well. In addition, lenders will use all information available to them in their overall portfolio management, arguably a use that is not "in connection with" a specific agreement. Thus, from the standpoint of the lenders, use restrictions are not terribly practical, and so they are rarely seen in credit agreements. To the extent that it is included at all, a use restriction may simply have the lenders affirm that they are aware of their responsibilities under applicable securities laws and will not use any information "in contravention of" the securities laws. Even the latter is not required under Regulation FD if a confidentiality agreement is in force, as the SEC has made clear in its Manual of Publicly Available Telephone Interpretations.

CONCLUSION

The discussion of the credit agreement set out in this Chapter 5 is intended to be solely an overview of the most common provisions found in a credit agreement for a domestic company. It does not encompass the tremendous variety of provisions that will be found in credit agreements since borrowers and arrangers each have an infinite capacity for creativity and negotiation. What is typical practice today will certainly evolve over time as new covenants are invented, new court decisions are rendered (requiring new waivers to be inserted) and new tax structures evolve. We hope, nevertheless, that the reader will find the discussion here useful as a resource when reviewing or drafting the next credit agreement that comes across his or her desk.

Richard Wight, Warren Cooke, and Richard Gray are partners at Milbank, Tweed, Hadley & McCloy specializing in bank financing.

CHAPTER 6

The Secondary Loan Market

Meredith Coffey
Senior Vice President
Reuters Loan Pricing Corporation

Robert Milam
Vice President
JPMorgan Securities

Laura Torrado
Senior Managing Director
Bear Stearns & Co. Inc.

Michele B. Piorkowski
Associate Director
Bear Stearns & Co. Inc

An Introduction to the U.S. Secondary Loan Market

Meredith Coffey
Senior Vice President
Reuters Loan Pricing Corporation

One of the most profound and influential changes in the syndicated loan market over the past years has been the emergence of a true secondary loan trading market. Its development has both supported and spurred the growth of the nonbank lender community, the rise of active portfolio management, and the increase in market participants' ability to sell loans in a downturn, thus allowing banks to clean up their balance sheets far more quickly and efficiently than ever before.

Since the early 1990s, secondary loan trading has grown at an exponential rate in both the par and the distressed areas, the two main categories of loan trading. While there are several definitions, for the purpose of this introduction, *par trading* is the purchase or sale of loans at or above 90 cents on the dollar; *distressed trading* is the purchase or sale of loans at below 90 cents on the dollar. As Exhibit 6.1 illustrates, trading activity has grown dramatically since the early 1990s, and the types of loans traded have changed over time. In the early 1990s, the little trading that did occur was mostly in distressed loans, reflecting banks' attempts to sell loans that had deteriorated during the downturn. However, the share of trading represented by distressed trading declined through much of the 1990s, as a bullish market and benign conditions limited the amount of distressed debt available to trade. Then, as credit quality deteriorated again in the early 2000s, distressed trading grew once more. Exhibit 6.2, which compares the volume of distressed trading to the volume of loans that the Shared National Credit (SNC) Review classified as substandard, doubtful, or loss, illustrates this relationship. As the share of troubled loans increased, so did the amount of distressed trading—and not just because there were more troubled loans. Indeed, a market in which to trade these loans has now developed, to the benefit of banks, as they can now sell their loans rather than spend years in workouts. Banks can

E X H I B I T   6 . 1

Secondary loan trading grows 15-fold since early 1990s

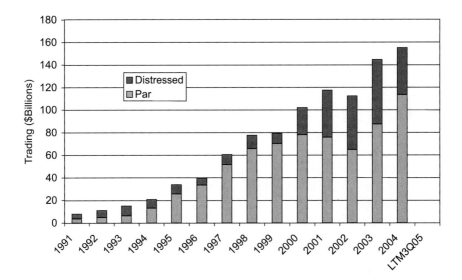

E X H I B I T   6 . 2

Distressed trading vs. SNC loans classified as substandard, doubtful, or loss

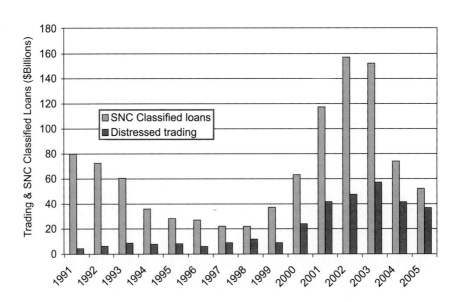

now clean up their balance sheets rapidly, and this may have helped them come through the 2000–2002 downturn relatively quickly, despite a spike in default rates. Further to this, banks were also quickly ready to lend to corporate customers again.

Distressed trading has ebbed and flowed with the fortunes of the credit cycle, but par trading, by contrast, has experienced a steady growth during the past years, save for a blip in 2002. The increase in nonbank lenders is a major reason for this growth. Nonbank lenders, such as collateralized loan obligations (CLOs), loan mutual funds, insurance companies, and hedge funds, actively manage their portfolios, and they need a secondary market in which to do so; thus secondary par trading and institutional issuance have grown hand-in-hand. In fact, this is a virtuous cycle: The development of a sophisticated nonbank lender base facilitates (and increasingly is contingent upon) the development of a liquid secondary loan market. In the late 1990s, an increasingly liquid secondary market encouraged more nonbanks to enter the loan market. As they entered the loan market, they traded more, thereby increasing the liquidity of the secondary loan market, which in turn encouraged more nonbank lenders to enter the loan market. This virtuous cycle continues to this day, and Exhibit 6.3 indicates just how much progress has been made. U.S. par trading volume totaled $130 billion in the 12 months ended third quarter 2005, up

EXHIBIT 6.3

Par versus institutional issuance

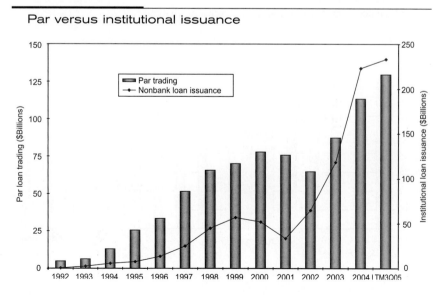

dramatically from the $5 billion tallied in 1992. Similarly, the issuance of term loan Bs soared past $230 billion, up from less than $1 billion in the early 1990s.

FACILITATORS OF SECONDARY TRADING

The rate of primary loan issuance has been contingent upon the secondary market's becoming more liquid, and liquidity has come not just from the sheer amount of loans traded, but also from the ease with which loans are traded. One metric of this is the average trade size. As Exhibit 6.4 indicates, the average trade size shrank from nearly $5 million in 2000 to just over $2.5 million in the fourth quarter of 2004. This decline indicates the greater granularity and liquidity in the secondary loan market.

Another measure of liquidity is the bid-ask spread. As Exhibit 6.5 illustrates, the spread between the average bid and average ask of nearly all loans narrowed significantly between 2002 and 2005. Part of this compression is due to the general improvement in market expectations since 2002 (the average bid has climbed considerably, and higher bids are correlated with narrower bid-ask spreads). However, Exhibit 6.5 looks at bid-ask spread by credit rating. Presumably a Ba1/Ba2 loan today is of no better quality than a Ba1/Ba2 loan from 2002, but the average bid-ask spread for

E X H I B I T   6 . 4

As liquidity grows, average trade shrinks

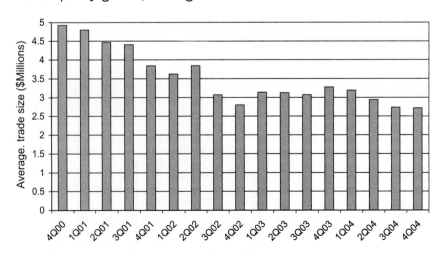

EXHIBIT 6.5

Loan bid-ask spread by rating

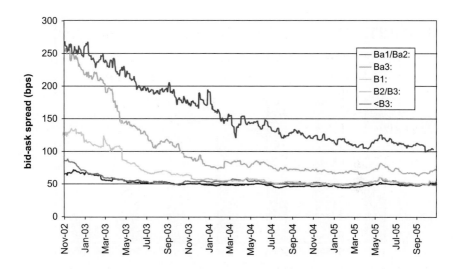

Ba1/Ba2-rated loans narrowed from more than 65 bps in 2002 to less than 50 bps in mid–2005.

While these metrics suggest that liquidity has improved for secondary loans, this did not just happen naturally. Indeed, many individuals and institutions have worked diligently to improve secondary market liquidity and have been instrumental in fostering the kind of environment that allows for sustained growth in secondary trading. Fundamental to this is leveraged loan documentation, which has changed to improve the tradability of loans (loans are traded through assignments or participations). Through the late 1990s, the typical minimum assignment amount was $5 million, which effectively required trades to be at least $5 million. The fact that the minimum trade size was so large had a deleterious effect on liquidity and trading activity. However, since the late 1990s, the standard loan documentation has been changed to reduce the minimum trade size for an institutional loan to $1 million. As Exhibit 6.6 indicates, the lower assignment minimum is correlated with a higher trading volume. In addition, the LSTA has been critical in developing trading and settlement norms, all of which lead to greater—and faster—trading, which, in turn, facilitates more trading.

EXHIBIT 6.6

Falling assignment minimums aid liquidity, facilitate trading

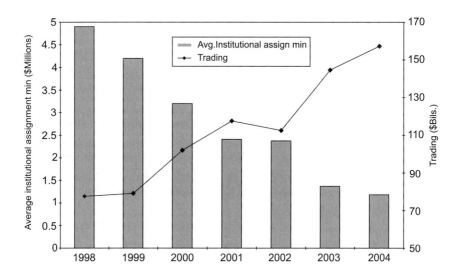

MARK-TO-MARKET PRICING, TRANSPARENCY, AND LIQUIDITY

While improvements in loan documentation and trading norms were critical in developing liquidity in the loan market, the availability of pricing information also was an important driver of increased secondary market liquidity.

Mark-to-market pricing (the process of valuing loans at their secondary market price) has had a long and storied history in the United States, and a much shorter (but faster) development in Europe. In the United States, market dynamics taking shape in the 1990s set the stage for the emergence of commercial pricing services. By the mid–1990s, a growing class of asset managers recognized bank loans as a relatively stable, senior secured asset class. However, many of these nonbank lenders wanted (or needed) to value their loan investments on a regular (often daily) basis. In the early days of loan investing, there was no service that provided valuations. Initially, originating banks (which came to be thought of as primary dealers, or brokers, as in the bond market) were increasingly asked by their nonbank clients to provide "indicative marks," known as the indicative "bid" (the level at which the dealer might buy the loan) and the indicative "ask" (the level at which the dealer might sell the loan). This process was typically accomplished by faxing "ax sheets" containing indicative prices back and forth between clients and individual dealers. Clients would then need to manually aggregate prices from several dealers in order to value their portfolio holdings. As this clearly was a cumbersome and inefficient process, pricing services developed to meet the market's need for a reliable, independent source of prices.

While these services were initially developed with a view toward providing net asset values (NAVs) for nonbank lenders, they actually ended up serving more than that purpose, aiding greatly in creating transparency in the secondary market. An ever-increasing number of loans were being priced in the secondary market, and ratings and terms and conditions on these loans were often available. Thanks to the pricing services, asset managers could research and evaluate loans and find buying opportunities. They could also use these prices for risk management purposes, to validate past actions, to track the performance of investment vehicles, and to keep watch lists of possible investment opportunities. The increased transparency in the market also facilitated the development of secondary trading. As Exhibit 6.7 indicates, there is a close correlation between the number of loans marked (in this case, by LSTA/LPC Mark-to-Market Pricing) and the amount of trading taking place.

EXHIBIT 6.7

Trading versus MTM

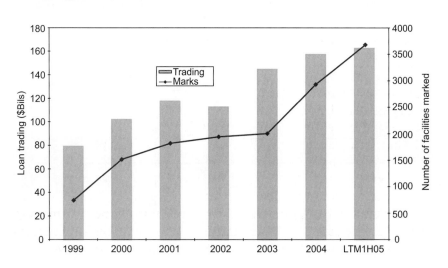

EUROPE AND BEYOND

The institutional and secondary loan market emerged first in the United States, but Europe has taken the lessons of the U.S. experience and evolved far more quickly. Whereas the U.S. secondary loan market developed gradually over a decade, the European market has grown rapidly over the last few years to reach trading volumes of more than €40 billion in 2004.

Exhibit 6.8 shows the remarkable development of the European appetite for secondary market information. Starting with fewer than 100 facilities in early 2002, Reuters LPC European Mark-to-Market Pricing was providing daily pricing on over 1,500 European loan tranches by mid–2005. New banks have established secondary trading desks over the last several years, bringing increased liquidity to the interbank market or the street.

Moreover, the nature of trading has changed. For most of its existence, the U.S. secondary market traded mostly leveraged loans. In contrast, in the early years, much of Europe's secondary market activity involved investment grade trading. This area was at the heart of the growth in loan trading, especially as banks traded in and out of the large telecom financings. During 2004, the focus for serious street traders switched from investment grade loans to leveraged debt. This was driven by the better returns available in the leveraged

EXHIBIT 6.8

European bid counts climb 15-fold since 2002

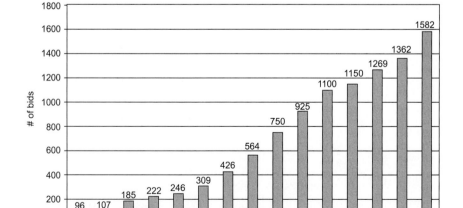

arena, and by vigorous interest from institutional investors in LBOs and leveraged corporate debt. Europe has seen many new funds starting up, with U.S. investors being especially interested in buying European debt for diversification and attractive yields.

The recent experience in Europe—which was certain that it would not adopt a U.S. model—might suggest that liquidity and transparency are an attractive development path for the global loan market.

How to Trade Loans and the Strategies to Use

Robert Milam
Vice President, JPMorgan Securities

The most important step in loan trading, as in any other form of trading in the capital markets, is to know and understand the basics of the product in question and the conventions of the market. At first glance, it might seem that loans trade much like high yield bonds. After all, they are cash instruments, and they trade on a dollar price as a percentage of par. As in the high yield market, sell-side dealers in the loan market, made up of commercial and investment banks, show prices for bids and offers, which could be either indications or firm prices at which the dealer will buy or sell the particular loan referenced. Dealers may advertise for trading business via telephone, e-mail, Bloomberg, or Web pages, just as in the bond markets, and, similarly, loan market participants may also make reverse inquiries.

However, there are several differences between loans and high yield bonds, and these come into play in the trading of these instruments. For one thing, loans are usually structured with very different maturities, average lives, and coupons from bonds, and this affects the way they trade compared to bonds. High yield bonds will often be issued with an eight- to ten-year maturity, no amortization schedule, and a fixed-rate coupon (although floating-rate coupon bonds are issued occasionally). By contrast, a loan, and in particular, an institutional term loan, will often have a five- to seven-year maturity and will nearly always mature before a bond. Loans also typically amortize quarterly, and this, combined with their shorter maturities, gives them significantly shorter average lives than bonds, and therefore a much stronger pull to par than is observed in bonds. Most loans feature LIBOR-based, floating-rate coupons rather than the predominantly fixed-rate coupons seen in bonds. Loans therefore have much lower interest-rate durations than bonds and as a result will be much less sensitive to changes in price caused by rising or falling interest rates. Fundamentally, loan prices should be affected only by interest-rate moves that are large enough to affect interest expense and therefore credit quality in a meaningful way.

Another major difference between loans and bonds lies in their respective collateral and security. While investment grade rated companies generally have loans and bonds that are pari passu, senior unsecured claims with equal rights to payment, subinvestment grade companies tend to have loans that are senior secured and bonds that are senior unsecured and senior subordinated. In the event of a default, this means that the loans will have first priority on any recovery available to the debtholders. As a result, the implied recovery rate of the loans is much higher than that of the bonds, and the risk to principal is therefore much lower on the loan side The additional risk to principal embedded in the bonds explains in large part why an unsecured bond will generally be issued with a higher coupon, or interest rate, than a senior secured loan for the same borrower, and also why, on the trading side, the bonds will have significantly more downside risk than loans.

Additionally, while bonds are commonly issued with strong call protection, loans often have little or no call protection at all, making refinancing risk a common concern for loan market participants. For example, a bond may be noncallable for half of its term, and then step down each year from a price as high as 110 or 115. By contrast, a loan with "strong" call protection would be noncallable for a year and then callable at 102 and 101 for years two and three, respectively—a great deal lighter than the standards set for high yield bonds. Of course, the amount of call protection on any given loan deal is often a sign of how strong the demand for the loan was in the primary market, and is also dependent upon general primary-market conditions (greater call protection reflects a deal that was a harder sell to the market, and vice versa for lighter call protection). As a result, loans exhibit significant negative convexity when trading near par, especially relative to bonds. Practically speaking, if a loan trades too far above par, it is in danger of being refinanced by the borrower. A loan for a well-performing borrower that is trading north of 101 or 102 in price without call protection is at risk of being called at any time, while a bond trading at 110 for the same borrower could quite conceivably trade to a price of 120, depending on the call protection. In general, in the secondary loan market, it is very rare to see a loan trade more than 1 or 2 points above either par or the current call protection price.

When trading loans, there are also a few settlement issues that are important to note. First, par loans trade on a "settle without accrued interest" basis, as opposed to bonds, which trade on a "settle with accrued interest" basis. When the coupon for a loan is paid, the agent bank, usually the original underwriter of the loan, will distribute to each holder the interest accrued in its name over the course of the accrual period for whatever amount of time it was a holder of record. This differs from bonds, where the bond trustee will pay the holder the entire coupon as of the record date. It also means that from the perspective of the bank loan investor, there is rarely a reason to calculate a "clean" or "dirty" price as is done in the bond market, and figuring accrued interest is not part of the settlement process. In distressed situations, if the borrower is keeping the bank debt current, as is normal for senior secured loans, the bank debt will continue to trade settle without accrued. If the borrower is no longer paying a coupon, as is normal for unsecured loans, the loans will trade "flat." This is similar to the terminology used when trading distressed or defaulted bonds: if a coupon is paid at some point in the future, the entire sum is for the benefit of the loan buyer.

A second important settlement issue to be aware of at the time of the trade is the documentation that will be used. Loans may trade and settle on either par or distressed documents, and the type selected generally depends on the financial condition of the borrower. Traditionally, a loan market participant would look to use distressed documents when trading a loan below a dollar price of 80. This has changed in recent years, however. Currently an informal dealer poll, often conducted by an interdealer broker, will generally determine the settlement documentation used and the official record date for a change from par to distressed documents. Typical events that would cause a switch include the aforementioned sub–80 trading price, a market belief than a restructuring of the credit is imminent, and an event of default such as a failure to pay or a bankruptcy, even if the paper is trading at or near par at the time. Distressed documents require the seller to make additional representations and warranties to protect the buyer from purchasing a claim that has been damaged, is tainted, or is otherwise not market-standard. Practically speaking, however, from the perspective of the loan market participant, settlement documentation is particularly relevant with regard to settlement timing, as current market convention is T + 7 for par and T + 20 for distressed (seven and twenty days past the date of issue, respectively), and overall closing costs, as distressed documents generally require additional legal expenses to be incurred. If a name is distressed, either the transaction may be impossible to complete using par documents or the buyer may demand a lower price for the embedded risk of not having the usual representations or warranties.

The overall settlement process and back-office requirements for loan trading are also much more cumbersome than those for bonds and other securities. Settlement usually requires multiple documents to be signed, some by multiple parties, thereby requiring significant paperwork. Furthermore, electronic settlement is still a work in progress. For a loan trade to close, both counterparties must sign a written confirmation of the trade, and then process an assignment agreement and eventually the funding memos. In fact, just processing the assignment agreement can take a significant amount of time. First, both counterparties must sign the document, after which it is sent to the agent bank, typically the original lead or underwriter of the loan, for another signature. In many cases the agent must then receive consent from the borrower which the credit agreement typically states is not to be unreasonably withheld, after which the agent bank can process the assignment. The funding memos are straightforward; they are simply a calculation of the amount of money changing hands, which reflects both the purchase price and any truing up of potential interest payments or funding costs should the loans be settling on a date later than the market-standard T + 7 or T + 20, known as "delayed compensation." The purpose of delayed compensation is to ensure that the owner of the loan receives the appropriate compensation, i.e., coupon, for the risk embedded in the investment. In the case of loans that are not paying a current coupon, the owner still has to fund the investment itself. Before delayed compensation, if a loan trade took two weeks or two months past the original settlement date to close, the owner of the loan received no carry for the entire time it was actually at risk.

When completing a trade, both counterparties should know the borrower, the tranche, and the notional amount being traded as well as the price, the settlement documentation being used, the treatment of accrued interest, assignment fees, and any other details that are unique or relevant to the particular transaction. Some examples of the latter include nonstandard representations or warranties being made in the case of a distressed trade, terms for the settlement process assignments or participations, and any negotiation of potential voting rights or requirements for collateral. Good trading practice recommends that no trade be completed without a full verbal confirmation of these items at the time of the trade (in fact, this is a good practice for all trading, not just bank loans). Take the following statement by way of example: "JPMorgan sells $5 million of Delphi term loan B at 100, distressed documents, T + 20 settlement, assignment fees waived, best efforts for an assignment, otherwise a no-voting-rights participation." The complete statement is important for a few reasons. First, for trading purposes, verbal confirmations are considered binding, while e-mail and Bloomberg messages may not be as enforceable. Second, the complete summary gives both counterparties one more chance to be clear with each other as to the exact details of the trade, which can be important for both preventing and potentially resolving future disputes resulting from a disagreement concerning the original trade terms.

For those loan market participants that are actively managing bank loan portfolios and therefore are frequently trading in the secondary market, measuring the volatility of this asset class, both alone and relative to other securities, is an important challenge and can be a helpful predictor of market moves. In fact, in recent years, understanding the impact of price movements in a company's equity or bonds has become more and more relevant. Typically a loan market participant should anticipate that the price movement of a senior secured loan will be approximately 20 to 25 percent of that of an unsecured bond for the same borrower. Since April 2003, statistical data show that loans have on average demonstrated a volatility 22.6 percent that of bonds in the same capital structure and consistently stayed in a range of 20 to 25 percent (see Exhibit 6.9). Practically speaking, this means that if a company's bond price changes by a point, the price of the company's bank loan will usually move about a quarter of a point in the same direction. However, this relationship will most likely fail in two instances. First, when

EXHIBIT 6.9

Loan versus Bond Volatility

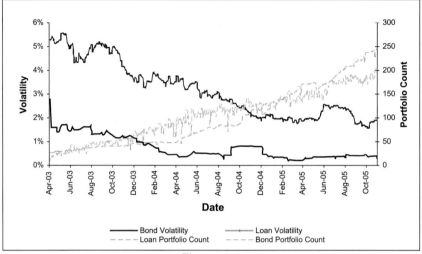

*Data and chart courtesy of **markit**™

both the loan and the bond are trading at a premium, increases in bond prices will be less and less likely to be accompanied by a corresponding loan price movement because of differences in call protection and the shorter average life of the loans. Second, as discussed earlier, when bond prices move as a result of movements in interest rates, loan prices may not move because of the floating-rate coupons and low interest-rate duration of the asset.

As an issue becomes distressed, however, the volatility in the loan price will increase. Over the period from 1987 to September 2005, the annualized standard deviation for defaulted bonds was 27.5 percent and 11.6 percent for loans.[1] In fact, in some cases, for deeply distressed issuers whose bonds are expected to have little to no recovery, the absolute (not percentage) price movements in the loan can actually be greater than in the bond. This is due to the fact that the major driver of distressed prices is the rate of return provided by the expected recovery of the loan or security, factoring in the embedded risks of the investment, rather than a yield to an expected maturity at par. The most common example of this occurred during

---

[1] Edward Altman, Max L. Heine Professor of Finance and Director of Credit and Debt Markets Research, NYU Salomon Center, Stern School of Business.

the heavy defaults in the telecom sector during 2001 and 2002. Following their bankruptcies, bonds for companies such as Global Crossing and McLeod USA were trading in the low single digits, effectively option value, as little to no recovery was expected to be available for unsecured holders. The loans, however, traded in much larger ranges on an absolute basis, as the Global Crossing bank debt traded in a range from the mid-20s to mid-teens and back to 25, and that of McLeod from the 40s to the 80s and eventually the 20s.[2]

Two more recent examples of recovery rates and risk to principal as drivers of trading levels in distressed situations are Delphi and Refco. In the case of Delphi (Sym. DPH), once a default became apparent, the 2006 bonds traded from 80 to the high 50s, while the 2029s moved from near 70 to the same levels as the market took a position on eventual recoveries. The term loan has remained within a three-point band, as the market has never really questioned the fact that the loans would enjoy par recovery at the end of the day (see Exhibit 6.10). In fact, rather than trading lower as the bonds did, the term loan traded up following the bankruptcy, moving from the 101s to trade as high as 104 as the loan began paying a default-rate coupon. Clearly, gauging loan trading levels simply from the movement in the bonds would have led to a poorly timed sale transaction. In the case of Refco (Sym. RFX), the bonds were trading well north of par when the original news of bad debts surfaced, traded as low as 20 when a liquidation looked likely, and moved all the way back to the high 70s as buyers for the company emerged and value for bond investors clearly became available. The bank debt traded from par to the high 50s and back into the mid to high 90s over the same period of time, as traders and loan investors digested the news flow, made assumptions about final recoveries (see Exhibit 6.11), and took into account that the waterfall of payments would go to the bank loan before it went to the bonds. Again, market views on eventual recovery levels had a large impact on trading levels for both bonds and bank loans, and gauging the overall loan price movements from changes in bond prices would have been difficult. However, as news flow for both instruments tended to be either positive or negative, the directional view would have served well, and buying or selling the bond or loan at an unchanged price based on a move in the other asset proved over time to have been a profitable trading strategy.

---

[2] Data from JPMorgan.

E X H I B I T   6 . 1 0

DPH Bonds and Term Loans

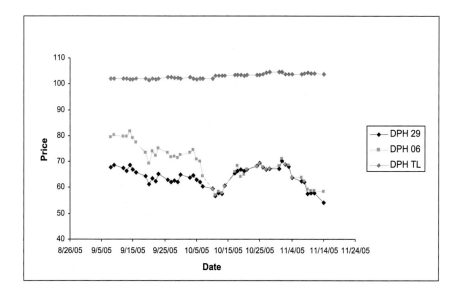

E X H I B I T   6 . 1 1

RFX 12 and RFX TL B Prices

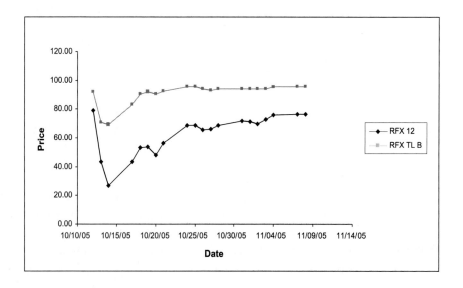

Overall, while volatility has dropped from 2003 into 2005 across the credit markets in general and loans in particular, in large part as a result of the combination of low defaults and generally high trading levels, round lot trading sizes have never returned to pre–2001 and 2002 levels. In fact, before the last default cycle, a round lot for a secondary trade was considered to be $5 million. Today, that amount has dropped to a size of $2 to $3 million. As the perception of price movement risk and volatility in the market has increased, dealers and buy-side participants both have tended to move away from making larger-sized, at-risk trades. Additionally, the number of market participants has increased, as has the number of individual subaccounts under management, which has led to both smaller-size primary allocations and small-er core holding size per subaccount in any particular deal. That being said, trading volumes overall continue to grow, and while average trading sizes may be smaller, total dollar volumes being traded and the numbers of transactions taking place has grown substantially.

A major difference between loans and other capital market instruments that is important for trading purposes is the recognition that not all investors have the same information. Traditionally, banks have required material nonpublic information, such as company projections of future earnings, from borrowers before making loans, will receive such information on an ongoing basis, and are bound by a confidentiality agreement that restricts them from sharing this information with public-side investors. Bank loan funds and CLOs investing in loans only are also typically on the private side, and are similarly restricted by confidentiality agreements. However, as the market has grown, insurance companies, high yield mutual funds, hedge funds, and collateralized debt obligation (CDO) managers, all of which may trade public securities, have started investing in loans from the public side, without the private information. The advantage to the private-side investors is access to the additional information that can be used to perform credit analysis and manage portfolios, while the advantage to public-side investors is the ability to trade and manage positions in other securities as well as the ability to hedge a loan position with a short sale of a bond or credit derivative. There are, however, many companies that are entirely private, with no publicly traded securities in their capital structure. In these cases, the entire bank group, including traditionally public participants, will generally be on the private side, again through the execution of a confidentiality agreement.

Another significant difference between loan and bond or credit derivative trading is that since loan investors can be positioned only on the long side, there is a finite amount of loans that can possibly trade. With no ability to be short, the only practical way for a market participant to sell a loan is if the market participant owns it. While attempts have been made to create a short-selling capability in the loan market in the past, there is currently no functional method of borrowing loans to deliver into a short-sale, as can be done in most bond markets or with equities. Technically, a loan market participant can short a loan simply by selling a loan that it does not own, but the net effect is similar to that of shorting a bond without a borrow, and the practice is generally frowned upon, as it leads to failed or unsettled trades, buy-ins, and other general inconveniences, especially from the perspective of the buyer.

In any case, the lack of shorting changes the personality of the way the loan market trades relative to the other asset classes. From a risk perspective, a loan market participant is either long or flat a loan. In particular, with no ability to short loans, what often happens in a down market is that bids drop but offerings may remain relatively unchanged, leading to a wider bid-offer spread and a lack of activity. Sellers who own the paper often wait for an uptick in price before selling, as they attempt to minimize their losses and often trade with their original cost basis in mind, whereas a short seller of a bond does not yet have a cost basis to be concerned with and might be more willing to set a position by making a sale at a lower level. Without the shorts, the loan market also avoids many of the technical-related trading events observed in bond markets, such as short squeezes, buy-ins, and, more recently, delivering bonds into triggered credit derivative contracts.

A common perception of the secondary loan market is that the technical indicators can make it seem as if all of the market participants are attempting to transact in the same direction at the same time—that the market has only buyers or only sellers at any given point. Of course, that is not an accurate statement, or loans would never trade, and generally speaking, the number of narrow bid-ask, two-sided markets that dealers will make is substantial, and liquidity can actually rival or exceed that of the high yield bond market on any given day. Nonetheless, the added liquidity for both the bid and the offer that is provided by the short seller or short-covering bid can help alleviate the perception of one-sidedness for the bond or equity markets and makes it easier for dealers to show two-sided markets. Additionally, there will always be certain borrowers whose loans will have more buyers than sellers, and other loans that rarely trade because of the lack of a bid for the loan. In these cases, it is also up to the market as a whole and the dealer community in particular to attempt to find the price where the marginal buyers and sellers meet to define the correct trading level. From a broader perspective, even at times when two-sided trading volumes have been high during recent years, the market has experienced periods where there is overwhelming cash to be invested and felt entirely "bid" with no real offers. The opposite has happened when offerings have swamped buy-side interest and subsequently forced trading levels lower. Both of these types of markets again lead to a generalization of one-sidedness in the technical indicators. In these cases, if the entire market appears to be characterized as either a buyer or seller, a prepared trader should have his or her analysis as complete as possible so that if the other side of the trade appears, the trader can quickly make a decision to buy or sell at the given price.

All things considered, the loan market has seen a huge growth in trading volumes and liquidity in recent years as a result of several factors. The overall size of the market, in terms of both the amount of cash to be invested and the number of market players buying or selling loans, has increased substantially. The number of loan market participants at a given time can be difficult to measure, but by some estimates the institutional investor community has as much as $250 to $300 billion to invest in loans. The number of market participants has expanded dramatically as well. JPMorgan, for example, traded loans with over 400 distinct counterparties in 2005. The growth in counterparties has come from many sources; new CLO managers, insurance companies, high yield fund managers, prop desks, and hedge funds have entered the loan space in record volumes. Not only have these new participants added cash to the market, but the growth in assets under management by existing players has also been substantial. In the past two to three years, bank loan funds have seen huge cash inflows and have also raised new funds after several years of outflows. Both existing and new

CLO managers have been able to raise billions of dollars for new vehicles, and even traditional commercial banks have come back into the market in large size. Borrowers have understood the growing institutional demand, and have met it with incredibly large leveraged transactions. For example, SunGard, one of the world's leading software and IT services companies serving financial services, higher education, and the public sector, issued $4 billion of institutional term loans in 2005, a leap from the old record, the $3 billion institutional term loan issued by Charter Communications in 2004, and a significant increase over the traditional $500 million term loan issued for a regular-way leveraged buyout. This record was topped again in early 2006 by Georgia Pacific, which placed an incredible $7.5 billion of institutional paper into the market across its 1st and 2nd lien tranches. Any of these jumbo loans might have over 200 participants, and the combination of the size and number of players usually leads to large amounts of trading, with significant depth on both the bid and offer sides. In these cases, buyers and sellers can trade in large sizes, sometimes upwards of $5 or $10 million per trade, with relative ease and in the context of a tight bid-offer spread, often as little as an eighth or quarter of a point.

Another item affecting trading volumes has been marking to market. The majority of bank loan funds started marking their portfolios to market in the late 1990s; during the massive defaults of 2001 and 2002, not only was the overall performance of the market weaker than expected, but the perceived performance of the bank loan funds was worse than it would have been had the funds not put daily market prices on their assets. Traditionally, bank loan fund accounting allowed fund managers to use accrual accounting and mark their positions at par, marking a loan at the market price only if the fund executed a trade. This scenario actually created a disincentive to make any trades at all, either purchases or sales, if the loan was trading below par, regardless of the manager's view of its future trading levels. Transacting below par generally forced the manager to mark the rest of the position to the same level as well, therefore recognizing a large loss. However, marking to market gives a better vantage point for observing the manager's true performance, and it also removes barriers to trading. The entire position is marked at the current trading level regardless of any transactions, and the portfolio manager is given an incentive to review the investment at its current price and take a view on its future levels in the context of the overall investment portfolio. If the portfolio manager thinks that the secondary loan price is too low, he may buy, and conversely, if he thinks that the price is too high or that it could go lower, he may sell the loan.

The advent of hedge funds has also had a tremendous impact on the trading characteristics of the loan market in recent years, even while causing some chagrin and concern among traditional loan market participants. Typical complaints include added competition for primary issuance and concern that the hedge funds will leave the loan space as quickly as they arrived when other markets provide more opportunities, dumping huge amounts of paper on the market in a hasty exit, and thereby driving down prices. While there is no doubt that the hedge fund community has soaked up paper in both the primary and secondary markets that other traditional bank loan fund managers may have been interested in owning, the hedge funds have also significantly deepened the secondary market liquidity in recent years, especially in the below par but not yet truly distressed space. Traditionally, if a deal became stressed or distressed, a bank loan fund investing primarily in par loans would have difficulty finding a bid until the asset reached the long-term internal rate of return sought by long-only distressed investors, which was sometimes upwards of 20 to 30 percent. In practical terms, that meant that there might be very little liquidity from prices in the mid-90s until the prices broke below 80. Hedge funds, which might not be investing from a long-only perspective, will often purchase loans as part of a strategy across the larger corporate capital structure, and they have become a major liquidity provider in the once very illiquid stressed trading space. Hedge funds have also been a large part of the rescue, and the second lien financings that have been done in recent years have, on many occasions, saved companies from bankruptcy by enabling them to pay out at par what could have become a distressed and discounted loan.

While overall trading volumes as well as the growth in the number and size of the traditional bank loan funds has been a huge driver for the syndicated loan market, the growth in the volume of hedge funds participating in this market has had even more of an impact. In 2000, hedge funds were just 10 percent of JPMorgan trading volume. In 2005, though, hedge funds accounted for nearly 30 percent of total trading volume, which means that hedge fund trading volume has grown an average of over 75 percent per year since 2000. These volumes are overweighted toward the stressed and distressed arenas as well as other "high-octane" situations such as second lien loans and rescue financings. Additionally, as more loan market participants join hedge funds in crossing over between the bond and loan markets, trading protocols and conventions from the public markets are seeping into the loan market as well.

More than ever, loan trading is taking place at a faster and faster pace, with dealers making two-sided markets, rapid trading happening after the allocations for new deals or news events, and prices immediately moving to reflect updated perceptions of risk and returns. The days of the secondary loan market as a sleepy backwater market with low trading volumes and even lower volatility are over.

Loan market participants invest in and trade loans using a large number of strategies, especially considering that there is no real ability to short the product. Loan market participants can employ loan-only trading strategies, including relative value between loans to different borrowers, between different tranches of the same borrower, or between the primary and secondary markets. They can use leverage to increase returns. They may also trade into various positions to get information or to control or have a voice in various corporate negotiations, such as amendments or workouts. (Loans can also be combined as the long side of capital structure relative value trades, such as buying loans versus buying protection, shorting bonds, or defending a position in bonds or the stock.)

From the long-only side, active portfolio managers use the secondary market in several ways to generate excess returns. The old trading adage of "buy low, sell high" aside, traders look to buy loans that will provide above-average returns based on fundamental credit analysis, are cheap relative to the return implied in the trading price of a loan to another borrower, or are cheap relative to another tranche of the same borrower. Of course, traders will sell loans that look likely to trade lower, either for technical reasons or because of fundamental credit analysis, or are expensive relative to other options. Some examples include buying a "risky" distressed loan for which credit analysis suggests an expected yield of 20 percent and selling a par loan that looks headed for trouble or a negative credit event. A bank loan fund may also look to sell a loan yielding L + 200 to buy another yielding L + 300 when the borrowers are in similar industries and are similarly rated, or to buy a term loan B and sell a term loan C to increase overall yield by 25 or 50 basis points. Additionally, a market participant might sell a loan to buy another if the dollar price of the loan purchased is significantly lower, even if the yield to maturity of each is the same, especially in cases where there is little or no call protection, since, as discussed earlier, loans are often refinanced early as well as having average lives that are much shorter than their stated maturities.

Another common trade is to look at value in the primary market versus the secondary. In times of strong demand for loans, often referred to as a "hot" market, secondary market prices may average well north of par, and in many cases north of 101. In these times, a popular strategy is to purchase almost every loan available in the primary market, which traditionally offers loans at par or a discount, and make room in the portfolio by selling older positions in the secondary market. This strategy may not work for investors that are heavy in cash, as the struggle to stay invested prevents giving up coupon-paying assets, regardless of price. In these cases, it's "buy, buy, buy" in both the primary and secondary markets, with little or no selling at all.

Loan market participants also use leverage to generate excess returns. Banks and prime brokers often offer total return swaps or similar financing vehicles, allowing a loan buyer to borrow money in an amount anywhere from 2.5 to 10 times the required collateral at a range of rates of LIBOR plus 35 to 75 bps. For example, a loan buyer might purchase a $5 million loan position with a coupon of L + 300 and finance it with five times leverage at a rate of L + 50. Effectively, the buyer posts $1 million to an interest-earning collateral account against the $5 million loan position, on which the buyer receives L + 300 minus L + 50, or 250 bps running. Net-net, the buyer is receiving 250 bps on the $5 million loan position plus the interest on the million dollars of collateral, which could be LIBOR or fed funds plus or minus a margin, for a levered coupon of approximately L + 1,250 on the million dollars invested. While this is appealing, using leverage has an accordingly higher risk profile. A 20 percent drop in the loan price, to 80 from 100, would result in a 100 percent loss on the original investment, and it is actually possible to lose more than the original investment if the price falls farther than that. Furthermore, additional collateral will usually be required if the price on the loan drops by a certain percentage during any given trading day, depending on the structure of the swap program, and passing voting rights to the beneficial owner of the loan can be difficult, and in some cases impossible. Of course, upside returns to the original principal are increased as well, since price gains as well as losses are for the benefit of the buyer, but, as discussed earlier, in the par and above par trading ranges, price risk is skewed to the downside. Nonetheless, the relatively low volatility of par loans makes them an attractive candidate for using leverage to generate returns, and this has become a common trading strategy.

When building a new position in a loan, a loan market participant might choose among a few strategies. The most conservative is to buy a very small position, $1 to $2 million notional, to "get in the information flow." A small position will encourage the participant to follow the markets in the name and allow access to information distributed to the bank group as well as the borrower's management team, both of which can be particularly important if the participant intends to trade the name from the private side. From there, a study of market technical indicators and the completion of credit analysis helps in determining additional entry points for more buys. For large deals, it is easy to be patient, since more paper is almost always available; it is a matter of measuring out events that will drive secondary pricing and trading accordingly. For small situations, the buyer will need to be more aggressive in terms of lifting offers in the desired price context, since only a limited amount of paper may be offered, and competition among buyers could become fierce.

Depending on the size of the deal and the capital available to the buyer, the buyer may ultimately seek to take a control position. For companies going through the Chapter 11 bankruptcy process, this will be two-thirds of a voting class for control or one-third for a blocking position. For performing loans undergoing an amendment, approvals usually require a 51 percent majority, but require 100 percent for changes in money terms that are unfavorable to lenders, such as a reduction in collateral or an extension of maturity. A control position allows the participant to drive negotiations with the borrower, and this strategy is particularly common during bankruptcies or restructurings. It is also one of the strategies at the core of traditional distressed loan investing. Buyers accumulate a majority stake in the bank loan in a fundamentally good but over-levered or soon-to-be-bankrupt company, convert all or a large portion of the loans to equity, possibly wiping out other stakehold-ers such as the prepetition equity or bonds, and allow the now delevered company to improve and grow its business. This allows the new equity to increase in value and the original distressed buyer to sell the equity or the entire company at a future date.

Loans are also used in a variety of capital structure trades. Hedge funds and proprietary trading desks commonly buy loans against a short in the equity, bond, or credit derivatives market, and some of the first credit derivative trades were done by banks as hedges against their loan portfolios. The longer-term view of the credit determines the weighting of the long and short ratios. For instance, an even notional amount of long loans versus short bonds or long credit protection is an implicitly bearish trade. As discussed earlier, bonds historically fall much further than loans in a negative credit event, so while the loan might fall a point, the bond might fall five; thus, the participant would be ahead four points on that particular trade (generically speaking, CDS spreads would be expected to move by an amount similar to bond spreads, so the economics will be similar). The loan will underperform on the upside as well, though, so the participant putting this trade on is taking the view that the borrower is going to have a negative cred-it event. Additionally, recall that bonds tend to have higher coupons than loans, so an even-dollar long/short is likely to have negative carry. This being the case, a trade could also be construct-ed as carry-neutral, which means that the hedge fund could weight the trade such that the carry generated by the long was roughly equivalent to that required to be paid on the short, allowing more patience, since there is no cost of carry in the trade. In both of these trades with a negative bias, the loan is effectively financing the short. In fact, more recently, pools of loans have been used to finance shorts across broader market-weighted baskets of unsecured debt, and single-name loans have been used to finance the premiums for equity puts on the same borrower.

For those looking to hedge a bond or loan position rather than to express a strong view, the historical bond versus loan volatility discussed earlier suggests that a relatively market-neutral hedge is a 4-to-1 ratio of loans to bonds for high yield borrowers, and closer to half that ratio for distressed borrowers, though fundamental credit analysis and predictions for potential trading levels will ultimately dictate the ideal ratios. Hedging loans against a potential default, rather than just against market moves, using credit derivatives can be complicated as well, since the trader needs to have a view on recovery rates for both loans and bonds, and weighting the trade properly can again be difficult. As a final strategy, traders may weight a trade overwhelmingly to the long side, so that the bond or CDS provides only a partial hedge against any downside scenario for the loan trading levels, for instance, using an 8- or 10-to-1 ratio of loans to bonds. In general, though, none of these trades should be put on without looking past the models and historical numbers and taking a view on future news and credit events that may affect the borrower and the related outcomes and impacts on trading levels.

The Secondary Loan Market: Settling Loan Transactions

Laura Torrado
Senior Managing Director
Bear, Stearns & Co. Inc

Michele B. Piorkowski
Associate Director
Bear, Stearns & Co. Inc

INTRODUCTION

Perhaps the greatest difference between loan trades and trades in virtually every other tradable asset is how loan trades settle. Whereas stocks, bonds, and most other tradable assets settle electronically over computerized systems, loans, because of their complexity, close on the basis of the exchange of negotiated documents. Distressed trades, in particular, present even greater challenges than loans that trade at par. While the LSTA has made great strides in shortening the settlement process and making loans more transparent, loan market participants still struggle to close many loan trades on a timely basis and in an efficient manner.

This article will describe the mechanics and nuances of settling loan trades. It will highlight important issues and identify certain pitfalls to be avoided when closing trades. The article will also review some of the documentation that is used to settle loan trades.

BACKGROUND

Before the organization of the LSTA in 1995, there was no standard documentation for purchasing, selling, or closing loans. Consequently, simple par trades could take weeks to close. The situation for distressed loans was far worse.

The LSTA's initial goal was to bring some standards to bear in the market, first by developing standard confirmations for both par and distressed trades, then by developing widely accepted market standards, and finally by developing and constantly improving additional standard trading documentation, a process that continues to this day. As a result of the efforts of the LSTA and interested market participants, the settlement of loan trades has indeed become more efficient and transparent. The trading and settlement structure described in this article is based almost entirely on the market standards developed over the years by the LSTA and its members.

PRETRADE ISSUES

While the confirmation is the first step in closing a trade, it is not the first step in making a trade. The trade is actually made orally between two loan market participants representing a seller and a buyer. Since October 2002, with an amendment to the New York State Statute of Frauds,[3] loan trades done orally are binding contracts, so long as the material terms of the contract have been agreed upon.

Since a trade is binding as soon as the parties agree to the material terms, it is crucial that traders be prepared and have a good handle on exactly what they are selling or purchasing. In addition, it is important that they make clear at the time of the trade whether a trade will be settling on par or distressed

---

[3] The LSTA published a market advisory pertaining to the Statute of Frauds in 2003. A copy may be obtained by contacting the LSTA at www.lsta.org.

documents. This issue will be discussed in detail later in this article. Because most loan agreements have numerous tranches and many borrowers have more than one credit agreement, this can be confusing, so it is important for traders to ensure that they are trading the same asset. In addition, there are many other important terms that can affect the economics of a loan trade. Understanding these issues is crucial to avoiding mistakes. In order to assist loan traders in avoiding mistakes or misunderstandings, the LSTA has developed a trade checklist that lists key issues that should be discussed and agreed upon prior to a loan trade (see Exhibit 6.12).

EXHIBIT 6.12

LSTA Trade Checklist as of May 5, 2005

Trade Checklist

Trade Date: _____

Name of Counterparty: _____

Type of Trade: ☐ Buy   ☐ Sell

Type of Documentation: ☐ Par   ☐ Distressed

Credit Agreement:_____

Name of Borrower:_____

Purchase Rate and Debt Description:

Purchase Rate: _____%	Purchase Amount:	$_____	
Facility/Tranche: _____	CUSIP Number:	_____	

Buyer Eligibility Considerations:

(a) Is Buyer an existing lender?	☐ Yes	☐ No
(b) Is Buyer an eligible buyer under the Credit Agreement?	☐ Yes	☐ No
(c) Does Purchase Amount meet the minimum transfer requirement, if any, under the Credit Agreement?	☐ Yes	☐ No
(d) Identify whether the counterparty is acting as a principal or agent.	☐ Principal	☐ Agent
(e) Are there any sub-accounts? If so, identify specific funds and sub-allocate within T+1.	☐ Yes	☐ No
(f) Is this an assignment only?	☐ Yes	☐ No
(g) Is this a participation only?	☐ Yes	☐ No
(h) Are there any netting arrangements?	☐ Yes	☐ No

Will Seller provide Credit Documentation?

☐ Yes (only if Buyer was not a lender on Trade Date and made its request on or prior to Trade Date)

☐ No

Are there any special fees or other unusual amounts? If so, consider how such amounts will be split or allocated.   ☐ Yes   ☐ No

Are there any amendments pending? Be mindful of public/private information issues, i.e., Seller and/or Buyer may be on the public side.   ☐ Yes   ☐ No

Is Seller or Buyer an Insider or Affiliate of any obligor or on any committee relating to the borrower or in connection with a bankruptcy case?   ☐ Yes   ☐ No

Does Seller or Buyer have "borrower confidential information" (as defined in the LSTA Code of Conduct)?   ☐ Yes   ☐ No

THE FOLLOWING APPLY TO DISTRESSED TRADES ONLY.

Accrued Interest: Consider adequate protection payment issues, if any.

☐ Trades Flat   ☐ Settled Without Accrued Interest

Are there any specific conditions or special representations? Flat representations will apply unless otherwise specified.

☐ Seller's sale is subject to Seller's buy-in   ☐ Buyer's purchase is subject to Buyer's on-sale

Flip representations: ☐ Yes   ☐ No

"Alternative" ERISA representation: ☐ Yes   ☐ No

Step-up provisions: ☐ Yes   ☐ No

The next step after a trade is orally agreed upon is the completion by each trader of a trade ticket that memorializes the economic terms of the trade. The trade ticket is then typically entered into the party's operational system.[4] Automated systems then generate a confirmation based on the information detailed in the trade ticket; manual systems require a mid-office professional to generate the confirmation. The trade confirmation is then sent to the counterparty for its review and signature. In trades between dealers and buy-side loan market participants, the confirmation is usually prepared by the dealer; in trades between dealers, the seller typically prepares the confirmation.

[4] Many traders still note their trades in a manual trade blotter and then generate a trade ticket.

THE CONFIRMATION: THE FIRST STEP IN CLOSING A TRADE

The confirmation is a two-page document that lists the deal-specific terms of a trade. Importantly, the standard LSTA confirmation incorporates by reference the detailed Standard Terms and Conditions (STCs) that set forth the market conventions and other terms that apply to all trades.[5]

The terms enumerated on the trade confirmation include the following[6]:

1. *Trade date:* The date on which the parties entered into the trade.
2. *Seller:* The legal name of the entity selling the loan and whether it is acting as agent or principal.
3. *Buyer:* The legal name of the entity purchasing the loan and whether it is acting as agent or principal.
4. *Credit agreement:* A legal description of the credit agreement to which the loans being traded relate.
5. *Form of purchase:* Whether the loans are being sold via assignment, participation, or otherwise.
6. *Purchase amount/type of debt:* The notional amount of debt being purchased, whether it is a term loan, revolver, litigation claim, letter of credit, or other; the relevant facility (tranche), and the CUSIP number.
7. *Purchase rate:* Stated as a percentage of par.
8. *Up-front fee (for par trades):* Whether and when an up-front fee is payable, and, if so, by whom.
9. *Accrued interest (for distressed trades):* Whether interest settles on a "trades flat" basis or with accrued interest.
10. *Credit documentation to be provided by seller:* Whether the seller is responsible for delivering the underlying credit documentation.[7]
11. *LSTA Standard Other Terms of Trade (for distressed trades):* These include whether the trade is subject to the buyer's or seller's first completing a third-party purchase or sale

---

[5] There are different STCs for par/near par confirmations and distressed confirmations.

[6] Many of these terms and the attendant issues will be discussed in more detail later in this article.

[7] This is applicable only if the buyer is not already a party to the credit agreement and made its request on or prior to the trade date.

of the underlying loan asset, or whether flip representations apply.

12. *Trade-specific other terms of trade:* This is a catchall designed to pick up any mutually agreed upon deviations from the standard confirmation or the STCs.

The confirmation ends with signature blocks for both the buyer and the seller.

COMMON SETTLEMENT ISSUES

The standard confirmation addresses a number of deal-specific issues. These issues are discussed here.

Principal/Agency Issue

The buyer and the seller indicate whether they are acting as principal, agent, or riskless principal.

- A principal is directly liable for the consummation of the transaction.
- An agent has arranged for another party to enter into the transaction but has no direct liability if the transaction is not completed and is usually paid a fee for arranging the transaction.
- A party acts as a riskless principal if on or prior to the trade date the parties have agreed that the other party's obligation to complete the trade is contingent on the successful completion of the purchase or sale of the underlying loan to a third party.

Allocation

Buyers and sellers who are asset managers also need to designate the funds on behalf of which they are acting, if applicable. The LSTA has set the standard that by trade date plus one day (T + 1) the parties should designate any specific funds or ERISA counterparties[8] involved in the transaction.

---

[8] A discussion of the issues concerning so-called ERISA counterparties is beyond the scope of this article. This topic is discussed in the LSTA publication "Alternative ERISA Representation" (May 2003) and is available online at www.lsta.org.

Forms of Purchase

Assignments

There are a number of different ways in which a transfer can be effected. The most common is through an assignment. Under an assignment, the seller transfers all of its legal, beneficial, and economic rights in the loan to the buyer. Legal title passes from the seller to the buyer, the buyer assumes the obligations of the seller, and, with certain limited exceptions, the seller is released from its obligations under the relevant credit agreement. In effect, the buyer replaces the seller.

Participations

Another form of purchase is a participation. Under a participation, the seller transfers to the buyer an undivided interest in its right, title, and interest in a loan. Effectively, the seller transfers to the buyer the beneficial and economic, but not the legal, rights under the loan.

Unlike assignments, most credit agreements limit the voting rights that can be passed on to participants. These rights typically include the right to vote on (1) an extension of the maturity date, (2) an increase in the commitment, (3) the release of collateral, and (4) a change in the rate of terms of repayment.

Notwithstanding the provisions of the credit agreements, some sellers prefer not to grant any voting rights to participants or prefer to limit their rights in other ways, generally by imposing a majority vote concept. Sellers seek to further limit the voting rights of participants in order to protect their own proprietary interests in the same loans or to protect important relationships with borrowers.[9]

Assignment or Participation?

For many reasons, assignments are generally preferred over participations. Nevertheless, buyers purchase participations rather than assignments for a number of reasons. A primary reason for purchasing a participation is that a buyer cannot meet certain thresholds set by the credit agreement. For example, many credit agreements have minimum size requirements, and the buyer could be purchasing an

---

[9] Since the voting rights of a member of a loan syndicate are not divisible, a seller of a loan participation that retains an interest in the loan cannot bifurcate its vote to accommodate its loan participant(s). Consequently, in order to protect its interests, it may refuse to grant any voting rights or, at a minimum, require a majority vote among all its participants. Conversely, even though credit agreements limit the voting rights of participants, sellers who have transferred their entire interest in a loan may consult with participants even on votes that are beyond the scope of the participants' rights.

interest that is below the threshold.[10] Alternatively, certain buyers might not meet the criteria necessary to become assignees under the credit agreement. These criteria include, for example, (1) an assignee must be a commercial bank, or (2) an assignee must have a minimum level of assets or credit rating. Another reason why a buyer might prefer to purchase a participation is to accumulate a significant position in a loan without the borrower (or other loan market participants) knowing.

Other Forms

When an assignment is not possible but a buyer has indicated on its confirmation that it will accept assignments only, a trade can *still* exist. This is a fundamental principle in the market and is often referred to as "a trade is a trade." The parties are entitled to the benefit of their bargain and must find a different way to obtain the economic terms of the original deal.[11]

Purchase Amount/Type of Debt

This section of the confirmation describes the amount of the loans and the tranches that are being traded. Parties need to be diligent in accurately describing the tranches to ensure that the confirmation reflects their original agreement. Since different tranches are likely to have different values, the economics of a transaction rely on the accuracy of the confirmation and the description of what is being purchased and sold.

Purchase Rate

This section describes the price being paid for the loan. All loan trade prices are expressed as a percentage of par.[12]

---

[10] Or, the buyer could be suballocating its interest among a number of funds, none of which is purchasing an interest large enough to make the threshold.

[11] One way to resolve the trade is to cash settle, where the parties determine the cash value of the loan and the "out of the money" party agrees to pay the economic benefit to the other.

[12] While calculating the price of a funded loan is simple (notional amount × purchase rate), calculating the price for an unfunded revolver is trickier, since the buyer will actually fund the loan at par no matter what the purchase rate under the trade may be. An example that illustrates this concept: assume that a buyer purchases a $5,000,000 loan commitment at 68 percent, and assume that $4,000,000 is funded and $1,000,000 is unfunded but available to the borrower. At closing, the buyer would pay the seller $2,720,000 ($4,000,000 × 68%) *minus* a credit on the unfunded portion equal to $320,000 [$1,000,000 × (100% − 68%)], for a total purchase price of $2,400,000. This protects the buyer in the event that any portion of the $1,000,000 is drawn by the borrower at a later time.

Interest Treatment

For any trade done on the LSTA par confirmation, any interest and accruing ordinary course fees (such as commitment, facility, and letter of credit fees) payable in connection with the loan under the credit agreement from and after the trade date [except for any paid in kind (PIK) interest] shall be treated in accordance with the "settled without accrued interest" convention described later (unless otherwise specified in trade-specific other terms of trade). Any amendment, consent waiver, and other similar nonrecurring fees payable from and after the trade date are for the benefit of the buyer.

All PIK interest is for the benefit of the buyer (at no cost) for any amount that has not been capitalized before the trade date. PIK interest is noncash interest that is "paid" as an increase to the principal amount of the loan that is owed to the lender.

Under the distressed confirmation, the parties choose the interest convention. "Trades flat" means that any interest or other amounts in connection therewith that accrue on or before the trade date but are paid after the trade date are for the account of the buyer. All payments made from and after the trade date are for the benefit of the buyer.

"Settled without accrued interest" means that any ordinary interest that has accrued but remains unpaid up to the settlement date (subject to any compensation for delayed settlement, which is discussed later in this article) shall be for the account of the seller, so long as such interest is received by the buyer (1) on or before the due date thereof or before the expiration of any grace period or, if no such grace period exists, the expiration of 30 days from such due date, and (2) before a default by the borrower or any obligor(s) in connection with any other payment obligations of the obligor(s) under the credit agreement. Otherwise, such interest and accruing fees (if and when paid) and any other accrued amounts due from and after the settlement date shall be for the account of the buyer, and the seller shall not be entitled to any part thereof. All interest payments include any adequate protection payments made by a borrower in bankruptcy.

If "paid on settlement date" is specified in a confirmation, the buyer agrees to pay the seller up front for any accrued interest owed to the seller up to the settlement date (subject also to the terms for delayed compensation). If the obligor ultimately fails to pay the interest, the seller does not have any obligation to repay the amount to the buyer.

Trade-Specific Other Terms of Trade

The two most common LSTA Trade-Specific Terms of Trade that are added to distressed confirmations are (1) that the seller's obligation to sell is subject to the successful completion of the purchase of the asset by the seller ("subject to buy-in") and (2) whether a seller can provide "flip" representation on its sale to the buyer. Flip representations are described later in this article.

Subject to the Buy-In
This condition is one of the most important for a sell-side broker, as well as the most negotiated. If this condition is agreed to, the selling broker does not have to deliver the loans to the buyer if it cannot purchase the loans from its counterparty.[13]

Flip Representations
"Flip representations" are chosen when the seller is a broker that is purchasing the loan on the same day on which it is selling it or on the previous day. Since the broker is making only a small commission, it is reluctant to assume the additional risks associated with distressed document representations. To qualify to make flip representations, the seller must indicate on the confirmation that it is acting as a riskless principal, and the seller must be prepared to settle the loan no later than one business day after the settlement of its purchase of the loans.

Under flip representations, the seller limits the scope of its representations with respect to title, outstanding principal amount/commitment, and proof of claim filing (if applicable) by

---

[13] Distressed loan transactions are highly negotiated, and usually the buyer knows that the broker is working to acquire the loans for the purpose of selling such loans to the buyer. The buyer knows that it will be paying a small spread or markup to the selling broker for its work in acquiring the loans. If this provision is not included in the trade confirmation from the broker to the buyer, and if the broker is not able to acquire the loans, the broker would be naked short the loans to the buyer. If the value of the loans were to increase, the broker could be at risk for a significant sum on a transaction for which it would be receiving minimal compensation. Buyers understand this risk and consider agreeing to the "subject to" provision on a transaction-by-transaction basis.

assuming the truth and accuracy of the representations and warranties on such matters made to the seller by the immediate prior
seller(s).[14] It is important to note that flip representations are not
available in trades between brokers.[15]

Reasonably Acceptable Documents

Finally, with respect to the confirmation and trading terms, each
distressed transaction is subject to the negotiation, execution, and
delivery of reasonably acceptable contracts and instruments of
transfer in accordance with the terms of the confirm. This section
means that the parties will agree to negotiate a document, usually
in the form of the LSTA Purchase and Sale Agreement, to complete
the transfer of the loan. This language is standard in very distressed loan transactions and binds the parties to work in good
faith to agree to an acceptable transfer agreement to transfer the
loans.

At this point, whether par or distressed, the transaction moves
into the closing phase, and the closing documentation is drafted.

LOAN CLOSING DOCUMENTATION
Par Loans

Par documents settle upon the execution of an assignment agreement (or a participation agreement) and a funding memo. There is
usually no involvement of counsel, and the attendant costs are
low. Agent transfer fees (often in the range of $3,500 per trade), to
the extent that they are not waived, are usually split between the
buyer and the seller. Settlements involving assignments are also
subject (in most cases) to consents by the borrower and/or the
agent, which consents typically are not to be unreasonably withheld. The standard period for settlement of a par trade is T + 7,
after which delayed compensation (to be discussed later) begins to
accrue.

---

[14] If the seller has met the conditions necessary to settle on the basis of flip representations,
the buyer cannot avoid receiving the flip representations merely by delaying the
closing.

[15] The market presumption for transactions between brokers is that the broker owns the
loans and it is the seller's risk with respect to these issues.

Distressed Loans

Distressed loan trades settle upon the execution of an assignment agreement (or, sometimes, a participation agreement), a purchase and sale agreement (PSA), a pricing letter, and sometimes a funding memo. Virtually all distressed loan trades are reviewed by lawyers at a cost of between $2,500 and $5,000 for each party. Agent transfer fees (often in the range of $3,500), to the extent that they are not waived, are usually split between the buyer and the seller. Settlements involving assignments are typically subject to the agent's consent (but, often, not the borrower's consent). The standard settlement period is 20 days, after which delayed compensation kicks in.

The PSA

The most important of the distressed settlement documents is the PSA. The PSA is divided into two sections, transaction-specific terms (TST) and standard terms and conditions (STC). The TST sets forth all the salient points that are specific to a particular trade and is the only part of the PSA that is completed by the parties to the trade. The TST identifies the asset being traded, the trade date, the agreement date, the names of the buyer and seller, the purchase amount, the name of the borrower, and whether credit documentation is to be provided. It is also the section that identifies any changes to the default provisions in the STC.

The major representations that are contained in a PSA pertain to the assigned rights and are not limited to the loans. The seller represents to the buyer that it is indeed transferring the entire bundle of rights, including claims and ancillary rights derived from ownership of the loans. The seller also represents the principal amount of the loans being transferred and that no other funding obligations related thereto exist (except as set forth in the TST). It also represents that it owns the assigned rights free and clear of any encumbrance, including any pledge, lien, security interest, charge, encumbrance, or other adverse claim. The seller also represents that it is not a party to any documents that could adversely affect the assigned rights, not just the loans. Perhaps most importantly, the seller represents that it has not engaged in any "bad acts" or conduct or made any omissions that would result in the buyer's receiving less favorable treatment than any other lender holding the same type of loans. This representation protects the buyer from anything the seller may have done that would not be detected by a review of the credit documentation.

Upstream Due Diligence

Another costly element of distressed loan trading is the buyer's practice of conducting due diligence on the seller's "upstream" chain of documentation. If the buyer finds a deficient document anywhere in the chain, the buyer is likely to demand "step-up" representations from the seller to the extent that the upstream documents are not "market standard." Step-up representations are discussed later in this article.

Par or Distressed Documents: How to Decide?

Market convention generally defines par loans as those trading at a price of 90 percent or above and distressed as those trading below that mark. The reality of the basis on which loans actually *trade* is actually more complex. While there are no hard and fast rules, there are a number of issues to consider:

- Loans of borrowers in bankruptcy almost always trade on distressed documents regardless of the price—indeed, even if the loan is trading well above par.[16] (Debtor in possession loans, however, almost always trade on par documentation.)
- What are the ratings of the borrower, its loans, and its other funded debt? What is the *trend* of its ratings?
- What is the *market* doing at the time the trade is done? If the market has shifted to distressed documents, a buyer will expect distressed documents.
- Is there significant litigation risk associated with the borrower? Does the borrower have public image problems?
- Are there negative prospects for the borrower and/or its industry?

These factors must be weighed against the increased cost and time necessary to close a loan trade on distressed documents. Are the protections that come with distressed documents worth the added cost?

---

[16] Many secured loans in bankruptcy trade above par, reflecting the expectation that unpaid accrued interest will be paid as part of a reorganization plan.

Step-Up Representations

It is also important to note that a loan market participant who purchased loans on par documents when the market convention was to sell on distressed documents will, upon its own sale of the loan, probably be required to "step up" its representations to cover any deficiencies in the documents of the "covered prior sellers." The LSTA has developed a "shift poll" mechanism to determine when the market has shifted to distressed documents. At the request of a member, the LSTA will poll about 12 dealers to determine the date on which each of them began trading the loan on distressed documents.[17] The results of the poll are distributed to the requesting member, who uses them as guidance to decide whether it must step up (or should expect its seller to step up).

Finishing the Closing: Pricing and Payment

After the relevant documentation is completed, the parties are ready to close. At this time, the actual purchase and the transfer of money for the asset are agreed upon. The seller prepares a funding memorandum with all of the underlying loan information as well as the pricing of the loan. If the seller is transacting with a broker, this responsibility may fall on the purchasing broker.

On the settlement date, the buyer pays the seller a purchase price for the amount of the loan being transferred (or, if the calculation produces a negative number, the seller pays the buyer). Purchase price calculations based on various trade scenarios are described step by step in the following pages. These calculations are based on the LSTA Standard Terms and Conditions (as of May 1, 2005). The sample scenarios contemplate both par and distressed trades, performing and nonperforming loans, unfunded commitments, and par and distressed settlement times of T + 7 and T + 20, respectively. The examples also include delayed settlement scenarios that describe cost of carry calculations, as well as interest and fee allocation. To simulate reality, additional variables such as paydowns and commitment reductions before settlement are added to the mix.

---

[17] If one of the polled dealers is involved in the dispute, it recuses itself from the poll. The results of shift date polls are available to all LSTA members (only) online at www.lsta.org.

There are several basic questions that need to be asked before beginning the calculation.

1. Is the trade a par trade or a distressed trade?
2. Is the loan a term loan, which is fully funded debt with no future funding obligation, or is it a revolving credit or letter of credit facility, which may have future funding obligations?
3. What was the loan amount on the trade date?
4. What was the loan amount on the delay date?
5. Is the loan denominated in U.S. dollars, or is it a multi-currency loan that is subject to one or more borrowings in one or more currencies other than the master currency?
6. What was the agreed-upon purchase rate for the loan?
7. Has the commitment amount of the loan changed since the trade date? Have there been any commitment reductions or principal repayments?
8. What was the agreed-upon treatment of interest?
   a. Trades flat
   b. Settled without accrued interest
   c. Paid on settlement date
9. Have any ordinary course fees (such as commitment, facility, and letter of credit fees) or nonrecurring fees (amendment, consent, waiver, and so on) been received by the seller since the trade date?
10. Is the settlement date a "delayed settlement date," occurring after the T + 7 date for par trades or after the T + 20 date for distressed trades?
11. Is there an agent fee?

PAR TRADES

Most loans trading on par documents are generally considered "healthy" loans, where the borrower is making regularly scheduled interest and fee payments, which further categorizes them as "performing loans." Par loans, unless otherwise specified in the trade confirmation, are usually traded using the settled without accrued interest treatment. This trading convention directs that all interest and recurring fees accrued up to but not including T + 7 or the settlement date, whichever is sooner, are for the account of the seller, i.e., the seller gets to keep these amounts. The only exception is for nonrecurring fees, which are for the buyer's account.

The following examples illustrate various purchase price and delayed settlement compensation calculations. To simplify matters, all examples will be based on the following repeating parameters, with a calendar provided for reference:

Sample Term Loan Trade Constants

Commitment amount:	$5,000,000
Trade date	April 12 (Wednesday)
T + 7	April 24 (Monday)*
Purchase price	98.00%

* April 14 is a holiday and not counted as a business day.

Term Loans

When calculating the purchase price for a term loan, you begin by multiplying the funded amount of the loan on the settlement date by the purchase rate. Assuming that the trade settles within T + 7, the purchase price for our sample trade would be the fully funded commitment amount multiplied by the purchase price, as shown in Example 1.

E X A M P L E 1

Basic Term Loan Trade, Settlement within T + 7

Term Loan Purchase Price:	$5,000,000 × 98.00%	$4,900,000.00

Now let's add a twist: assume that there is a commitment reduction between the trade date and the settlement date. Since the buyer "owns" the loan from the trade date, it is entitled to capture the 2.00 percent discount on the commitment reduction. This discount will be credited to the buyer at settlement. For example, using our sample trade, if the borrower repaid $500,000 on April 18 and the trade was settled on April 19, the buyer would pay 98.00 percent on the *settlement date* balance of $4,500,000 and receive a credit for the 2 percent discount on the $500,000 commitment reduction.

EXAMPLE 2

Term Loan Trade with Commitment Reduction before T + 7

Term loan purchase price:	$4,500,000 × 98.00%	= $4,410,000.00
Commitment reduction credit:	$500,000 × 2.00%	= ($10,000.00)
Net term loan purchase price:		$4,400,000.00

Settled without Accrued Interest Treatment

If the loan is a performing loan, the seller is entitled to keep all of the accrued but unpaid interest and fees up to the settlement date. These amounts are not reflected in the purchase price. If the buyer receives such amounts after the settlement date, the buyer shall pay them to the seller. Nonrecurring fees (e.g., amendment fees, consent fees, and waiver fees) are treated differently. If the seller receives any nonrecurring fees from and after the trade date, they are for the benefit of the buyer and are subtracted from the purchase price. For instance, if the borrower paid an amendment fee of 50 basis points (bps) after the trade date, the buyer would be entitled to a credit of $25,000.

EXAMPLE 3

Term Loan Trade within T + 7 with Nonrecurring Fee Allocation

Term loan purchase:	$5,000,000 × 98.00	= $4,900,000
Amendment fee credit:	$5,000,000 × 50 bps	= ($25,000)
Net term loan purchase price:		$4,875,000

Delayed Settlement Compensation Calculations: Performing Loans[18]

Par trades are expected to close on or before seven business days after the trade date. A business day is any day that is not a Saturday, a Sunday, or some other day on which the Federal Reserve Bank of New York *or* the New York Stock Exchange is

---

[18] At the time of writing this chapter, the LSTA is planning to revise its Standard Terms and Conditions for Distressed Trade Confirmations so that an average LIBOR for the delay period (ie, the sum of all the individual LIBOR for each day in such delay period divided by the total number of days in such delay period) is used to calculate delayed compensation rather than a locked in LIBOR on T + 18. A corresponding change will also be made to the LSTA's Standard Terms and Conditions for Par Trade Confirmations.

closed.[19] If a par trade closes past the T + 7 day, it is considered a "delayed settlement." In order to compensate for the delay, the seller pays the buyer the margin on the loan for every day from T + 7 up to but *not* including the settlement date, otherwise known as delayed compensation. The buyer is compensated only with the loan's margin because the hypothetical LIBOR[20] interest base that would have been earned on the asset is offset by the seller's actual LIBOR "cost of carry."

To calculate the delayed compensation for performing loans, you use either the applicable margin specified in the credit agreement or, if no applicable margin is specified, the all-in interest rate specified minus the LIBOR. This rate is then multiplied by the principal amount of the funded loans, as well as the actual number of days from T + 7 up to, but not including, the settlement date. The result is then divided by 360 for LIBOR-based draws. If the applicable base rate is prime, the result is divided by 365.

Using our sample trade, if you settle on May 1, delayed compensation will be due to the buyer. If the borrower has two outstanding interest contracts, each with an applicable margin of 2.00 percent, you would calculate the delayed compensation by multiplying the funded amount of the loan by the margin and then dividing that amount by 360 to determine the per diem interest amount. This amount is then multiplied by the number of days from and including T + 7, up to but not including the settlement date (April 24 through, not including, May 1 = 7 days). The delayed compensation amount is then subtracted from the purchase price as a credit for the buyer.

EXAMPLE 4

Performing Term Loan (TL) Trade with Delayed Compensation

Term loan purchase price:	$5,000,000 × 98.00%	= $4,900,000.00
Buyer's delayed compensation:	$5,000,000 × 2.00% × 7/360	= ($1,944.44)
Delayed settlement purchase price:		$4,898,055.56

If the borrower has two outstanding interest contracts with differing applicable margins, delayed compensation would be calculated on each contract separately. In the following example,

---

[19] In calendar year 2006, the NYSE observed one more holiday than the Federal Reserve Bank of New York: April 14 (Good Friday). Therefore, April 14 is *not* a business day.

[20] The LIBOR is the London Interbank Offered Rate and is the rate that creditworthy international banks dealing in Eurodollars charge each other for large loans.

we assume that one contract is for $2,000,000 at LIBOR + 2.50 percent and the other is for $3,000,000 at LIBOR + 2.00 percent and calculate the purchase price.

EXAMPLE 5

Performing TL with Multiple Interest Contracts and Delayed Compensation

Term loan purchase price:	$5,000,000 × 98.00%	= $4,900,000.00
Delayed compensation for contract 1:	$2,000,000 × 2.50% × 7/360	= ($972.22)
Delayed compensation for contract 2:	$3,000,000 × 2.00% × 7/360	= ($1,166.66)
Total delayed settlement purchase price:		$4,897,861.12

Delayed Settlement Compensation Calculations: Nonperforming Loans

If the loan is nonperforming and the trade settles past the T + 7 date, the seller is reimbursed for its financing cost, usually LIBOR, for the number of days delayed settlement. This is the seller's "cost of carry." In contrast to delayed compensation for performing loans, the buyer is *not* entitled to margin credit, since there are *no* hypothetical LIBOR + margin earnings. Without the LIBOR offset, if there is a delay, the buyer *pays* the seller's LIBOR cost of carry. To calculate the seller's cost of carry, (1) you take the purchase price amount on the T + 7 day; (2) multiply it by the one-month LIBOR two business days before the T + 7 day; (3) divide this amount by 360 to get the per diem amount; and then (4) multiply the per diem amount by the number of days from T + 7 up to but not including the settlement date. This cost of carry is then added to the T + 7 purchase price, resulting in the net purchase price. Following these steps and using our sample term loan, if the trade settles on May 1, the seller will be entitled to seven days of cost of carry. Assume that the one-month LIBOR two business days before T + 7 is 2.92 percent. This rate will be used throughout this article for all cost of carry calculations.

EXAMPLE 6

Nonperforming Loan Purchase Price Calculation with Cost of Carry

T + 7 purchase price:	$5,000,000 × 98.00%	= $4,900,000.00
Seller's cost of carry* (7 days):	$4,900,000 × 2.92% × 7/360	= $2,782.11
Total delayed settlement purchase price:		$4,902,782.11

*If the underlying interest contract is prime based, divide by 365.

Paid on Settlement Date Interest Treatment

In some cases the agent will pay the lender of record for the entire interest period, regardless of any transfers that have been made effective during the interest period. If the borrower is paying interest every six months and the seller does not want to wait until the buyer receives the interest payment from the agent, they may choose to settle the trade "paid on settlement date." If the trade is done on this basis, the buyer gives the seller a credit in the purchase price for any interest or fees that have accrued up to but excluding the settlement date, even though the buyer has not received such amount from the agent. As of this writing, the selection of this interest treatment is rare.

Using our sample trade, if the borrower is paying interest semiannually and the next payment is due on September 30, the seller would be entitled to interest accrued from March 31 up to the trade date of April 12, or 11 days. If the trade were done paid on settlement date, then the buyer would give the seller a credit in the purchase price for 11 days of interest.

Paid in Kind (PIK) Interest Treatment

When a loan is paying PIK interest, the buyer is entitled to keep all PIK amounts that are accrued but not yet capitalized or accreted by the trade date. This uncapitalized PIK essentially "travels for free" to the buyer. PIK interest is usually capitalized or accreted quarterly, on either a 360- or a 365-day basis, depending on what is stated in the credit agreement. If PIK interest is capitalized before the trade date, it is added to the principal amount of the loan, and the purchase rate is applied to the new principal amount. Using our sample trade, if the borrower is scheduled to make a 12 percent PIK payment on June 30 and the trade settles on May 1, the agent will apply the PIK amount ($5,000,000 × 12% × 90/360 = $150,000) to the buyer's balance as of June 30, increasing the buyer's commitment by $150,000. This treatment of PIK interest is the same for both par and distressed trades.

Proceeds Letters: Loan Is Paid in Full before Settlement Date

If the borrower repays the entire loan prior to the settlement date, the trade is generally closed on a proceeds letter. The proceeds letter is calculated by taking the purchase price on the day the seller received the proceeds and netting out the actual amount of

proceeds received by the seller. Using our sample trade, if on April
20 the borrower repays the entire loan, the seller will receive
$5,000,000 from the borrower. If the trade had closed on April 19,
the buyer would have paid the seller $4,900,000 ($5,000,000 ×
98.00%) and received the $5,000,000 directly from the borrower, for
a net balance of $100,000. Since the seller received the buyer's
$100,000 entitlement from the borrower, the seller will need to
credit the buyer at settlement.

If the borrower repays the loan after the T + 7 date and the
trade is on delayed settlement, the buyer owes the seller the cost of
carry on the T + 7 purchase price only up to but not including the
date on which the seller received the cash from the borrower. If the
trade settles after the date on which the seller receives the cash
from the borrower, the seller owes the buyer the cost of carry on
any excess cash proceeds received from the distribution date to settlement. The seller will have received excess proceeds whenever
the purchase price is less than par. Using our sample trade, if the
borrower paid the loan down on May 1, the seller is entitled to
seven days cost of carry. If the trade settles on May 5 (after the paydown), the buyer would be entitled to four days cost of carry from
and including May 1 up to but not including May 5 on the $100,000
balance, as calculated in the next example.

EXAMPLE 7

**Loan Paid in Full before Settlement with Delayed Settlement,
Purchase Price less than Par**

Term loan T + 7 purchase price:	$5,000,000 × 98.00%	= $4,900,000.00
Seller's cost of carry (7 days):	$4,900,000 × 2.92% × 7/360	= $2,782.11
May 1 purchase price owed to seller:		= $4,902,782.11
Loan repayment proceeds received by seller on May 1:		= $5,000,000.00
Owed to buyer on May 1:	$5,000,000.00 − $4,902,782.11	= $97,217.89
May 5 cost of carry to buyer:	$97,217.89 × 2.92% × 4/360	= $31.54
Total amount owed to buyer on May 5:		$97,249.43

When the purchase price is over par (at a premium), the economics change. If the buyer agreed to pay 102.50 percent for the
$5,000,000 term loan, the T + 7 purchase price would be $5,125,000.
If the borrower repaid the loan at par on May 1, the buyer would
owe the seller the difference of $125,000 as of that date. If the trade
doesn't close until May 5, the buyer would owe the seller additional
carry on the $125,000 (2.50% premium × $5,000,000) for four days.

EXAMPLE 8

Delayed Settlement of Loan Paid in Full before Settlement: Purchase Price over Par

T + 7 term loan purchase price:	$5,000,000 × 102.50%	= $5,125,000.00
Seller's cost of carry (7 days):	$5,125,000 × 2.92% × 7/360	= $2,909.86
May 1 purchase price:	Subtotal	= $5,127,909.86
Less cash paid down on May 1 by borrower:		($5,000,000.00)
Balance owed to seller on May 1:		$127,909.86
Cost of carry owed to *seller* (4 days):	$127,909.86 × 2.92% × 4/360	= $41.50
Total due to seller on May 5:		$127,951.36

Revolving Credit Commitments

When calculating the T + 7 purchase price for a revolving credit, you must first determine the funded and unfunded amounts as of the *settlement date*. Just as with a term loan, the funded portion is multiplied by the purchase price. As for a revolver's unfunded commitment, if the loan is purchased at a discount, the buyer is given a credit to simulate future draws being advanced at the same purchase rate. Conversely, the seller would get a credit if the loan were purchased at a premium. The credit for the discount on the undrawn amounts is calculated by subtracting the purchase price from 100.00 percent, then multiplying all unfunded commitments by that percentage. For example, the purchase price for a $5,000,000 revolving credit commitment consisting of $3,000,000 funded loans, $1,500,000 unfunded loans, and $500,000 of unfunded letters of credit (LC) would look like Example 9.

EXAMPLE 9

T + 7 Purchase Price of Revolving Credit Bought at a Discount to Par

Funded purchase price:	$3,000,000 × 98.00%	= $2,940,000.00
Buyer credit on unfunded:	$1,500,000 × 2.00%	= ($30,000.00)
Buyer credit on unfunded LC:	$500,000 × 2.00%	= ($10,000.00)
T + 7 revolving credit commitment purchase price:		$2,900,000.00

Revolving Credit Purchases with Delayed Compensation

If we use the same trade as in Example 9 and assume a settlement date of May 1, delayed compensation will need to be calculated for the settlement date purchase price. In addition to margin, the buyer is also entitled to a credit for any commitment fee or letter of credit fee as specified in the credit agreement accruing from the day the buyer was supposed to own the loan (T + 7). Commitment fees are generally 50 to 75 bps and are calculated on a 365/actual day basis. Letter of credit fees can range anywhere from 200 to 600 bps and are also calculated on a 365/actual day basis.

Letter of credit fees and commitment fees are recurring. The settled without accrued interest treatment protocol directs that these recurring fees be credited to the buyer when the trade is delayed. In Example 10, we assume a 50-bp commitment fee that is calculated based on all unfunded amounts, excluding LCs. We also assume 300 bps of LC fees. To obtain the commitment fee credit amount, take the product of the unfunded amount, 50 bps (the commitment fee), and the number of days delay (7) and divide that product by 365 ($1,500,000 × 50 bps × 7/365 = $143.84). For the LC fee credit, take the product of the amount of outstanding letters of credit, 300 bps (the LC fee), and the number of days delay (7) and divide that product by 365 ($500,000 × 300 bps × 7/365 = $287.67). Now subtract these two amounts from the purchase price. All of these components are added together in the pricing calculation in Example 10.

EXAMPLE 10

Performing Loan with Under Par Purchase Price and Delayed Compensation

Funded revolving credit (R/C):	$3,000,000 × 98.00%	= $2,940,000.00
Unfunded R/C credit:	$1,500,000 × 2.00%	= ($30,000.00)
Unfunded LC credit:	$500,000 × 2.00%	= ($10,000.00)
Delayed compensation:	$3,000,000 × 2.00% × 7/360	= ($1,166.67)
Commitment fee credit:	$1,500,000 × 50 bps × 7/365	= ($143.84)
LC fee credit:	$500,000 × 300 bps × 7/365	= ($287.67)
Subtotal credits:		= ($41,598.18)
Total delayed settlement purchase price:		$2,898,401.82

Revolving Credit Purchase Calculations: Nonperforming Loans

To calculate the cost of carry on a revolving credit commitment, you need to determine the T + 7 purchase price. For revolving credits, it is common to have a T + 7 purchase price that is different from the trade date price, since the funded and unfunded amounts of revolving credit commitments fluctuate regularly. So to change things, let's assume that our $5,000,000 revolving credit commitment now has $3,500,000 funded on the T + 7 day with

$1,000,000 unfunded and $500,000 letters of credit. Now, use these new figures to calculate the T + 7 purchase price. If the trade is settled on May 1, delayed compensation will be based on seven days cost of carry. The seller's cost of carry is the T + 7 purchase price multiplied by the LIBOR[21] multiplied by the number of days from T + 7 to the settlement date and divided by the day basis (360 days): $3,400,000 × 2.92% × 7/360 = $1,930.44. This amount is added to the settlement date purchase price as a credit for the seller.

EXAMPLE 11

R/C Purchase Price with Delayed Compensation and a Change in Funded Amount before T + 7

Settlement date funded:	$3,500,000 × 98.00%	= $3,430,000.00
Settlement date unfunded credit:	$1,000,000 × 2.00%	= ($20,000.00)
Settlement date LC credit:	$500,000 × 2.00%	= ($10,000.00)
T + 7 purchase price:		$3,400,000.00
Seller's cost of carry:	$3,400,000 × 2.9200% × 7/360	= $1,930.44
Delayed settlement R/C commitment purchase price:		$3,401,930.44

Revolving Credit Purchased at a Premium

If the purchase price for a revolving credit commitment trade is over par, the economics change. Instead of the buyer receiving a credit for any discount on the unfunded amounts, the buyer *pays* the premium over par multiplied by the unfunded commitment to the seller. Using a purchase price of 102.50 percent and holding all other sample trade details constant, we calculate the purchase price for a revolver bought at a premium.

EXAMPLE 12

Revolving Credit Purchased at Premium within T + 7

Funded purchase price:	$3,000,000 × 102.50%	= $3,075,000.00
Unfunded credit to seller:	$1,500,000 × 2.50%	= $37,500.00
Unfunded LC credit to seller:	$500,000 × 2.50%	= $12,500.00
Total purchase price:		$3,125,000.00

Multicurrency Revolving Credit Trades

If you are trading a multicurrency commitment, which is a commitment subject to draws (individual borrowings) in one or more currencies, the buyer pays the seller 100.00 percent (regardless of the purchase price) of the funded amount in the same currency as

---

[21] This is the one-month LIBOR published two London business days before T + 7.

the draws at the settlement date. The buyer also receives a credit of 100 percent minus the purchase price on the *entire* commitment amount in the designated master currency. For our example, assume that a $5,000,000 revolver commitment allows the borrower to draw in three different currencies, British pounds, euro, and U.S. dollars, with the master currency being U.S. dollars. To start the purchase price calculation, determine the funded amounts in each currency, as calculated by the agent in accordance with the credit agreement. Now multiply the entire commitment by 100 percent minus the purchase rate, which amount is credited to the buyer. Because the buyer receives a credit in the master currency on the full amount of the commitment, the buyer is better able to hedge its currency risk with respect to the facility.

For purposes of our example, assume that on the settlement date, the borrower has drawn down £2,000,000, €1,000,000, and U.S.$500,000. Using our purchase rate of 98.00 percent and the multi-currency draws just given, our purchase price would be calculated as shown in Example 13.

E X A M P L E   1 3

Multicurrency Revolving Credit Purchase Price Calculation

Pound draw amount:	£2,000,000 × 100%	= £2,000,000.00
Euro draw amount:	€1,000,000 × 100%	= €1,200,000.00
Plus:		
Dollar draw amount:	$500,000 × 100%	= $500,000.00
Credit on commitment amount:	$5,000,000 × (100% − 98%)	= ($100,000.00)
Net U.S.$ purchase price:	$500,000 − $100,000	$$400,000.00

If the buyer and the seller agree that the buyer will pay the entire purchase price in U.S. dollars, then the pound and euro purchase prices may be converted using a foreign exchange rate agreed upon by both parties no earlier than three business days prior to the settlement date, but this would require a modification of the standard terms and conditions. The purchase price calculation for a multicurrency commitment is the same for distressed trades as it is for par trades.

DISTRESSED TRADES

As in the previous section, "Par Trades," all trade examples in this section will be based on the following repeating parameters:

Commitment amount:	$5,000,000
Trade date:	April 12, 2006
T + 20 date:*	May 11, 2006
Purchase price:	72.00%
1-month LIBOR:†	3.66%

*April 14, 2006, is *not* a business day.

† Two London business days before T + 20 for seller's cost of carry calculations.

Term Loans

Unlike the treatment used for par trades, the interest treatment for distressed trades must *always* be specified in the trade confirmation. Since many of the borrowers are not making current interest payments, distressed trades are frequently done on a trades flat basis, meaning that the buyer is entitled to any interest and/or fees received by the seller after the trade date on a "when paid" basis. For example if the trade was done on April 12 and the borrower made a quarterly interest payment on April 15, the buyer would be given a credit for the entire payment in the purchase price, even though all but three days of the interest accrued prior to the trade date; thus, accrual periods are irrelevant in trades flat trades. However, this scenario is very unlikely because loans that are making current interest payments are not usually traded on a trades flat basis.

If the same trade were done settled without accrued interest, all interest and unpaid accrued fees would be for the account of the seller through the earlier of the settlement date or T + 20, regardless of when paid. These amounts are not reflected in the purchase price because the agent will typically pay the seller directly for the period up to the settlement date and the buyer for the period following the settlement date.

The only exception to this is for nonrecurring fees (amendment, consent, waiver, and so on), which are treated the same way as they are for par trades, i.e., the buyer receives the benefit of any nonrecurring fees received by the seller from and after the trade date as a purchase price deduction.

Sample Distressed Term Loan Purchase Price Calculation: Trades Flat

When calculating the purchase price for a distressed term loan traded trades flat, you begin by multiplying the funded amount of the loan on the settlement date by the purchase rate. So for our sample trade, the basic calculation is $5,000,000 × 72% = $3,600,000. In the following example, a $500,000 commitment reduction is assumed to be made on April 18, and the settlement date is April 19. Because the loan was purchased at a discount, the permanent commitment reduction would entitle the buyer to a credit on the purchase price equal to $500,000 multiplied by 100 percent minus the purchase rate, payable at settlement. This credit would also be calculated for a settled without accrued interest trade, since all nonrecurring fees are for the benefit of the buyer. Using our sample trade and the additional assumptions described earlier, the buyer's purchase price would be calculated as shown in Example 14.

EXAMPLE 14

Distressed Term Loan Price Calculation with Commitment Reduction before Settlement

Term loan purchase price:	$4,500,000 × 72.00%	= $3,240,000.00
Commitment reduction credit:	$500,000 × 28.00%	= ($140,000.00)
Total term loan purchase price:		$3,100,000.00

Delayed Settlement Calculations for Distressed Term Loans

If a trade settles past the T + 20 date, it is considered a delayed settlement date. If the trade is done trades flat and settlement is delayed, the buyer pays the seller's cost of carry. If the trade is done settled without accrued interest, the seller pays the buyer interest or delayed compensation, and the buyer pays the seller's cost of carry.

Cost of carry is calculated by determining what the purchase price would have been on the T + 20 date and then multiplying that purchase price amount by the one-month LIBOR (two London business days before the T + 20 date) for each day from the T + 20 date up to but not including the settlement date.[22] Using our sample trade and a trades flat basis, if settlement occurs on May 26, the buyer would owe the seller the cost of carry from May 11 up to but not including May 26, or 15 days, or (T + 20 purchase price × one-month LIBOR × 15/360). Using our sample trade, and assuming that the loan is nonperforming, i.e., not paying contractual interest and fees, the delayed settlement purchase price is calculated as shown in Example 15.

---

[22] This cost of carry calculation is subject to one exception known as the "25 percent rule," which is discussed later.

EXAMPLE 15

Trades Flat Distressed Nonperforming Loan with Delayed Settlement

T + 20 term loan purchase price:	$5,000,000 × 72.00%	= $3,600,000.00
Seller's cost of carry:	$3,600,000 × 3.66% × 15/360	= $5,490.00
Delayed settlement purchase price:		$3,605,490.00

Delayed Settlement Calculations for Distressed Term Loans: Settled without Accrued Interest

If settlement occurs past the T + 20 date and the loan is a performing loan that was traded settled without accrued interest, the seller receives the cost of carry as described previously, but the buyer is also entitled to a credit for any interest accrued from and including the T + 20 date up to but not including the settlement date. To determine the amount of interest owed to the buyer, you must look at the underlying loan contracts. Unlike in par trades, where the buyer is given a credit by multiplying the funded amount by the margin, in distressed trades the buyer is given a credit by multiplying the funded amount by the "all-in" rate.

If the borrower has outstanding interest contracts with different applicable rates, you would calculate the interest amount for each contract separately. Let's assume that one contract is for $2,000,000 at LIBOR (3.33 percent) + 2.50 percent, or all-in 5.83 percent, and the second contract is for $3,000,000 at LIBOR (3.74 percent) + 2.00 percent, or all-in 5.74 percent. The buyer's price is credited with the all-in rate multiplied by the funded amount divided by the day basis (360 days for LIBOR contracts and 365/actual for prime borrowings) and multiplied by the number of days delayed. Assume for the following example the same 15-day delay and settled without accrued interest treatment with the interest contracts described.

EXAMPLE 16

Distressed Term Loan with Two Interest Contracts on Delayed Settlement

Settlement date purchase price:	$5,000,000 × 72.00%	= $3,600,000.00
Seller's cost of carry:	$3,600,000 × 3.66% × 15/360	= $5,490.00
Buyer's all-in interest credit:	$2,000,000 × 5.83% × 15/360	= ($4,858.33)
Buyer's all-in interest credit:	$3,000,000 × 5.74% × 15/360	= ($7,175.00)
Total delayed settlement date purchase price:		$3,593,456.67

If the borrower subsequently defaults on payments credited by the seller to the buyer at closing, the buyer is required to refund such amounts to the seller.

Revolving Credit Commitments

Calculating the purchase price for a revolving credit commitment trading on distressed documents begins with determining how much of the commitment is funded and how much of the commitment is unfunded at the settlement date. Issued and undrawn letters of credit are treated as unfunded for pricing purposes. The funded amount is multiplied by the purchase rate, and the buyer is given a credit for the unfunded commitments by multiplying 100 percent minus the purchase rate times the unfunded commitments. For our examples, we'll use the following repeating parameters in our sample trades:

R/C commitment amount:	$5,000,000
Purchase rate:	72.00%
Funded R/C amount:	$3,000,000
Unfunded R/C:	$1,500,000
Issued and undrawn L/C:	$500,000
Trade date:	April 12, 2006
T + 20:	May 11, 2006
One-month LIBOR:*	3.66%

*Two London business days before T + 20 for seller cost of carry calculations.

Example 17 shows the purchase price calculation for a distressed revolving credit that settles within T + 20.

EXAMPLE 17

Trades Flat Revolving Credit Purchase Price Calculation, T + 20 Settlement

Funded R/C amount:	$3,000,000 × 72.00%	= $2,160,000.00
Unfunded R/C credit:	$1,500,000 × 28.00%	= ($420,000.00)
Issued and undrawn LC credit:	$500,000 × 28.00%	= ($140,000.00)
T + 20 revolving credit purchase price:		$1,600,000.00

Delayed Settlement for Distressed Revolving Credit Commitments

If the settlement occurs after T + 20 and the trade was done trades flat, the seller is entitled to the cost of carry. Since cost of carry is calculated using the purchase price on the T + 20 date, you have to determine what the funded and unfunded amounts were on the T + 20 date, as these amounts may have changed since the trade date. In our next example, assume a $500,000 increase in the funded amount before T + 20. The new unfunded amount is $1,000,000, and outstanding letters of credit are still $500,000. Using our sample trade, if the trade is settling on May 26, the seller is entitled to 15 days cost of carry. The carry amount is added to the T + 20 purchase price to obtain the settlement date price.

EXAMPLE 18

Trades Flat Delayed Settlement with Change in Funded Amount

T + 20 funded amount:	$3,500,000 × 72.00%	= $2,520,000.00
T + 20 unfunded credit:	$1,000,000 × 28.00%	= ($280,000.00)
T + 20 Issued and undrawn LC credit:	$500,000 × 28.00%	= ($140,000.00)
Total T + 20 purchase price:		= $2,100,000.00
Plus		
Seller's cost of carry:	2,100,000 × 3.660% × 15/360	= $3,202.50
Total trades flat delayed settlement purchase price:		= $2,103,202.50

Distressed Revolving Credit Delayed Compensation Calculation: Settled without Accrued Interest

Using the same trade, but switching to trading settled without accrued interest, the seller is still entitled to the cost of carry as calculated previously, but the buyer is now entitled to a credit for interest from the T + 20 date up to but not including the settlement date as well. The loan must be a performing loan in order for this credit to be due. The buyer's delayed compensation for interest is calculated by multiplying the $3,500,000 of funded commitments by 5.83 percent (the all-in rate) and by the number of days delayed (15) and then dividing by the day basis—360 days for LIBOR borrowings and 365/actual day basis for prime borrowings.

Buyer's delayed compensation: $3,500,000 × 5.83% × 15/360 = $8,502.08

Delayed Compensation Calculation: Funded Amount Changes between T + 20 and Settlement

If, however, the funded amount of the loan changes between the T + 20 date and the settlement date, you have to calculate the delayed compensation on the two amounts separately. For instance, if the funded portion of the loan was $3,500,000 on T + 20 (May 11), and then on May 15 the borrower repaid $500,000, decreasing your funded amount to $3,000,000, you would have to calculate the buyer's delayed compensation amounts using the actual funded amount for the period before the repayment and then using the adjusted funded amount for the period after the repayment. Remember that the buyer gets delayed compensation only if the trade is done settled without accrued interest.

Buyer's delayed compensation,
May 11–15: $3,500,000 × 5.83 × 4/360 = $2,267.22
Buyer's delayed compensation,
May 15–May 26: $3,000,000 × 5.83% × 11/360 = $5,344.16

Settled without Accrued Interest Recurring Fee Allocation

Just as in par trades, the buyer is also entitled to a credit for any commitment fees or any letter of credit fees specified in the credit agreement. These recurring fees constitute the second component of delayed compensation for settled without accrued interest trades. Returning to our sample trade's funded and unfunded amounts without a repayment between T + 20 and a May 26 settlement date, if the borrower is paying a commitment fee of 50 bps, you would multiply the amount of the unutilized commitment, $1,500,000 ($5,000,000 commitment – $3,000,000 funded loans – $500,000 outstanding letters of credit), by 50 bps by the number of days delayed (15) divided by 365. If the borrower is paying a 300-bp letter of credit (LC) fee, you would multiply the outstanding LC amount by the 300 bps by the number of days delayed (15) divided by 365 and subtract that amount from the purchase price.

Commitment fee credit: $1,500,000 × 50 bps ×
                         15/365 = $308.22
Letter of credit fee credit: $500,000 × 300 bps ×
                         15/365 = $616.44

The total of any delayed compensation amounts for interest and fees is subtracted from the settlement purchase price as a credit for the buyer.

In Example 19, we calculate a delayed settlement purchase of revolving credit commitment traded settled without accrued interest. The funded and unfunded amounts will be the same as in our sample trade and will remain constant from an April 12 trade date through a May 26 settlement date. The T + 20 date is May 11, and the number of days delayed is 15.

EXAMPLE 19

Settled without Accrued Interest Distressed Revolving Credit Purchase with Delayed Settlement

Settlement date funded price:	$3,000,000 × 72.00%	= $2,160,000.00
Settlement date unfunded credit:	$1,500,000 × 28.00%	= ($420,000.00)
Settlement date unfunded LC credit:	$500,000 × 28.00%	= ($140,000.00)
T + 20 purchase price (May 11):		= $1,600,000.00
Seller's cost of carry 15 days*:	$1,600,000 × 3.66% × 15/360	= $2,440.00
Trades flat May 26 purchase price:		$1,602,440.00
Buyer delayed compensation: Interest:	$3,000,000 × 5.83% × 15/360	= ($7,287.50)
Buyer delayed compensation: Commitment fee:	$1,500,000 × 50 bps × 15/365	= ($308.22)
Buyer delayed compensation: LC fees:	$500,000 × 300 bps × 15/365	= ($616.44)
Total settled without accrued interest delayed settlement purchase price:		= $1,594,227.84

*Based on T + 20 purchase price.

The next example is complicated and will combine a few of our previous scenarios. Assume a trade date of April 12 and a purchase price of 72.00 percent. The trade date and T + 20 funded amount is $3,500,000, followed by a $500,000 principal paydown on May 16, which is after T + 20 (May 11) and before the settlement date. Further assume a delayed settlement date of May 26 (15-day delay) on a settled without accrued interest basis. The settlement date purchase price would be calculated as shown in Example 20.

Distressed Trade with Permanent Reductions before the Settlement Date

If the commitment amount of the loan changes between the trade date and the settlement date because of a commitment reduction or a permanent repayment of principal, the buyer is entitled to a credit in the purchase price of 100 percent minus the purchase rate times the commitment reduction or permanent repayment. In the following example, assume a $750,000 permanent principal repayment before a T + 20 settlement date. The buyer would pay the purchase price on the new funded amount of $2,250,000 ($3,000,000 − $750,000) as well as receive a credit of 28.00 percent (100 percent − 72.00 percent) on the $750,000 repayment.

EXAMPLE 20

Distressed Revolving Credit Purchase with Delayed Compensation and Principal Reduction between T + 20 and the Settlement Date Traded Settled without Accrued Interest

Settlement date funded price:	$3,000,000 × 72.00%	= $2,160,000.00
Settlement date unfunded credit:	$1,500,000 × 28.00%	= ($420,000.00)
Settlement date unfunded L/C credit:	$500,000 × 28.00%	= ($140,000.00)
Seller's cost of carry,* 15 days:	$2,100,000 × 3.66% × 15/360	= $3,202.50
Delayed compensation (interest), 4 days:	$3,500,000 × 5.83% × 4/360	= ($2,267.22)
Delayed compensation (interest) 11 days	$3,000,000 × 5.83% × 11/360	= ($5,344.17)
Delayed compensation (commitment fee), 4 days:	$1,500,000 × 50 bps × 4/365	= ($82.19)
Delayed compensation (commitment fee), 11 days:	$2,000,000 × 50 bps × 11/365	= ($301.37)
Delayed compensation (LC fees), 15 days:	$500,000 × 300 bps × 15/365	= ($616.44)
Total delayed settlement date purchase price		= $1,594,591.11

*Based on T + 20 purchase price of $2,100,000 ($3,500,000 × 72% minus $1,500,000 × 0.28).

EXAMPLE 21

Distressed Revolving Credit Purchase with Principal Payment before Settlement

Settlement date funded amount:	$2,250,000 × 72.00%	= $1,620,000.00
Unfunded credit:	$1,500,000 × 28.00%	= ($420,000.00)
Unfunded LC credit:	$500,000 × 28.00%	= ($140,000.00)
Commitment reduction credit:	$750,000 × 28.00%	= ($210,000.00)
Total revolving credit commitment purchase price:		$850,000.00

Negative Funding

If the commitment was reduced by $2,000,000 before a settlement within T + 20, the purchase price calculation would produce a negative funding and result in the seller's *paying* the buyer on settlement date. For example, if your $5,000,000 revolving credit commitment was $3,000,000 funded on the April 12 trade date, the borrower paid down $2,000,000 on April 20, and you are settling on April 21 (within T + 20), your calculation would produce a negative number. The calculations are the same whether the trade was done on a trades flat or settled without accrued interest basis.

If the same trade settles on May 26 (15 days delayed compensation), the seller would additionally owe the buyer the cost of carry on $400,000 for every day from the T + 20 date up to but not

EXAMPLE 22

Negative Funding from Large Principal Paydown before Settlement

Settlement date funded amount:	$1,000,000 × 72.00%	= $720,000.00
Unfunded credit:	$1,500,000 × 28.00%	= ($420,000.00)
LC credit:	$500,000 × 28.00%	= ($140,000.00)
Commitment reduction credit:	= $2,000,000 × 28.00%	= ($560,000.00)
Purchase price owed to buyer:		= ($400,000.00)

including the settlement date. The cost of carry would be calculated on the T + 20 purchase price, which would be $400,000 × 3.660% LIBOR × 15/360 = $610. This amount would be added to the amount that the seller owes the buyer calculated previously, bringing the delayed settlement amount owed to the buyer to $400,610.

Trade Date and Settlement Date Purchase Prices greater than 25 Percent

If the purchase price on the settlement date has increased or decreased by more than 25 percent from the T + 20 purchase price, the cost of carry shall be calculated based on the purchase price calculated on each day from the T + 20 date up to the settlement date. For example, assume that the $5,000,000 revolving credit commitment was $3,500,000 funded on T + 20, but 11 days later, on May 22, the borrower paid down $3,000,000 as a permanent reduction. Using a settlement date of May 26, the settlement date purchase price would be 25 percent less than the T + 20 purchase price. A trades flat trade is also assumed, so there are no delayed compensation calculations.

EXAMPLE 23

Commitment Reduction with Negative Settlement Date Purchase Price

Settlement date funded amount:	$500,000 × 72.00%	= $360,000.00
Settlement date unfunded credit:	$1,000,000 × 28.00%	= ($280,000.00)
Settlement date LC credit:	$500,000 × 28.00%	= ($140,000.00)
Commitment reduction credit:	$3,000,000 × 28%	= ($840,000.00)
Settlement date (May 26) purchase price:		= ($900,000.00)

Since your purchase price of negative $900,000 is 25 percent less than the T + 20 settlement date price of $2,100,000 ($3,500,000 × 72.00% less $1,500,000 × 28.00%), you have to calculate the delayed compensation for every day from the T + 20 date up to the settlement date. In this case, the seller would receive cost of carry on the $2,100,000 T + 20 purchase price from May 11 through May 22, the day the borrower paid down the loan. The buyer, however, would receive cost of carry for 4 days on the ($900,000) purchase price from May 22 up to but not including May 26.

Seller's cost of carry: $2,100,000 \times 3.66\% \times 11/360 = \$2,348.50$

Buyer's cost of carry: ($900,000) \times 3.677\%$ as of $5/20 \times 4/360 = (\$367.70)$

These amounts are added into the purchase price calculation (trades flat).

EXAMPLE 24

Trade vs. Settlement Date Purchase Prices Differ by more than 25 Percent

May 26 settlement date purchase price:	(calculated in Example 23)	= ($900,000.00)
Seller's cost of carry (May 11–May 22):	$2,100,000 × 3.660% × 11/360	= $2,348.50
Buyer's cost of carry (May 22–May 26):	($900,000) × 3.677% × 4/360	= ($367.70)
Delayed settlement date purchase price owed to buyer:		= ($898,019.20)

Proceeds Letters

If a loan is trading on distressed documents, it is highly unlikely that a repayment in full would occur before the settlement date, but if that were in fact the case, the trade would settle on a "payoff letter" just like a par trade proceeds letter. Please refer to the proceeds letter discussion in the "Par Trades" section for purchase price calculations.

The more likely scenario for the use of a proceeds letter in a distressed situation generally occurs when a borrower emerges from bankruptcy between the trade date and the settlement date. Pursuant to a plan of reorganization, the debt is extinguished, and in satisfaction of the claim with respect to it, the lenders receive some form of distribution, which is called proceeds. Proceeds may take any form (e.g., debt or equity securities, new bank debt, or cash). The LSTA trade confirmation does not address proceeds. The market convention that has developed is that the seller will transfer the proceeds to the buyer pursuant to a proceeds letter. Although the debt specified in the trade confirmation no longer exists, the purchase price will still be paid based upon the preconfirmation principal amount of that debt. Because the debt no longer exists, any payments made after the receipt of the proceeds will not affect the principal amount of the debt on which the purchase price is based, i.e., principal payments made on any new debt would not reduce the principal amount of the old debt. Analogously, the buyer would receive the full amount of any such payments (not just the economic benefit). Compensation for delayed settlement applies to the same extent as it does in a nonproceeds situation, with the exception of the case where cash is part of the proceeds. In such a case, cost of carry will no longer be payable on the portion of the purchase price equal to any cash distribution. This is so because if it were, the seller would be getting both the actual benefit of the cash distribution (i.e., the seller may invest the funds and earn interest on it) and cost of carry on it, which is unfair to the buyer.

ASSIGNMENT FEES

Although not discussed previously, assignment fees have traditionally been an added cost in most loan trades. Assignment fees reimburse the agent for its administrative efforts and are due whether a loan is traded on par documents or distressed documents. These fees are usually in the area of $3,500. Under the most common practice, the seller remits the entire assignment fee to the agent and is reimbursed for half of the fee by the buyer as an increase in the purchase price. Recently, in an effort to enhance liquidity, many agent banks have discontinued charging assignment fees, which have been a substantial drag on par loan returns.

CONCLUSION

The loan trading business can be very lucrative. Like any lucrative business, it is fraught with risk. However, unlike the situation in the markets for most other tradable instruments, the process for settling loans, particularly in the market for distressed loans, can itself present risks. The analytics, trading, and settlement all work hand in hand in loan trading. These risks can largely be mitigated if care is taken prior to trading and in the settlement process.

CHAPTER 7

Secondary Market Pricing

Theodore Basta
Vice President, Market Data
The Loan Syndications and Trading Association

Tom Price
Director
Markit Group

Jean Cho
Analyst
Markit Group

Loan Valuation: The Origins of Secondary Market Pricing

Theodore Basta
Vice President, Market Data
The Loan Syndications and Trading Association

The U.S. syndicated loan market has become one of the most innovative and expanding sections of the U.S. capital markets over the past two decades. Today's syndicated loan market consists of an efficient primary market, where agent banks originate syndicated loans, and a liquid, transparent secondary trading market, where bank loan traders effectively buy and sell pieces of such syndicated credits. For the purposes of this chapter, this review of the origin and subsequent expansion of the U.S. secondary loan market and its investors will center on leveraged loans. Leveraged loans, those made to noninvestment grade borrowers, offer much higher returns for their increased level of risk. The term *leveraged* is normally defined by a bank loan rating of BB and below, or a loan's interest rate spread over LIBOR (London Interbank Offered Rate) above 125 basis points (bps). While investment grade loans, or nonleveraged loans, constitute quite a large portion of the primary syndicated loan market, leveraged loans constitute the overwhelming majority of secondary market trading activity, and hence are the cornerstone of discussion regarding secondary market pricing.

To simplify a complicated situation, banks began to realize the benefits of freeing up capital by selling portions of their loan holdings to both traditional (bank) and nontraditional (nonbank) institutions in a secondary market instead of holding such investments to maturity as they had done historically. Banks would now begin their metamorphosis from simply loan originators to loan traders, thereby engineering the flight to liquidity that investors demanded. As a result, investors began to look to the secondary market in order to better manage their loan exposures and credit risk, and thus active portfolio management through secondary trading was born. Historically, holders of loans would carry performing loans at par or face value, while valuations (expected sale prices) were internally assigned to defaulted loans. By the early 1990s, banks such as BT Alex Brown, Bear Stearns, Citibank, and Goldman

Sachs began to create loan trading desks that acted more as brokers than as traders, simply matching up buyers and sellers. In these early years, trade activity was relatively scarce, growing to roughly $40 billion by the mid–1990s, according to Reuters Loan Pricing Corporation (LPC). Most trades occurred on the distressed side of the market (defined for the purposes of this chapter as the body of loans priced below 90), as banks looked to clear their books of loans that had declined in value since their initial syndication. With the advent of this new and exciting secondary loan market, creating a process to properly value loans at where they would presumably trade became of the utmost importance.

In 1995, the Loan Syndications and Trading Association (LSTA) was formed, with a mandate to promote the orderly development of a fair, efficient, liquid, and professional trading market for commercial loans. At the same time, auditors and comptrollers of the many banks that were participating in secondary trading demanded an independent third-party provider of secondary market prices to validate the prices at which traders were marking their loan positions.

In early 1996, the LSTA established a dealer quote–based secondary mark-to-market process to value loans at a price indicative of where they would presumably trade, providing the broker/ dealer community with a standard benchmark pricing methodology. The LSTA began collecting dealer quotes (indicative bid and ask quotes reflective of where a facility would be expected to trade) on roughly 155 loan facilities from 12 broker/dealers on a monthly basis. By the late 1990s, the need to properly mark to market loan positions on a more frequent basis grew precipitously, as secondary trading volume reached $80 billion a year, according to LPC. With more than 20 banks involved in both brokering and trading bank loans, lenders were increasingly selling off pieces of loans to mutual funds and other institutional investors that were entering the marketplace.

Continuing its effort to facilitate liquidity and transparency, the LSTA, along with LPC, created the LSTA/LPC Secondary Mark-to-Market Pricing Service (SMPS) in 1999, an independent third-party provider of U.S. secondary market prices. This new service, which began as a weekly service but quickly moved to a daily service that same year at the request of buy-side investors, was to play a critical role in providing the marketplace with the necessary secondary market prices and information that it needed.

Also in 1999, at the request of the buy side, LPC created a loan pricing model to calculate a secondary market price for any illiquid loans not priced by the broker/dealer community. The Derived Pricing Model, as it is commonly referred to, produces an average yield for each rating category by accessing the SMPS database of loan prices and deal terms and conditions (coupon and maturity); these are updated daily. Using a standard discounted cash flow model, the loan's expected cash flows are discounted by the average yield of its rating. The model then adjusts (applies a premium or discount to) the subsequent yield-based price for factors such as coupon, industry, and short-term rating outlook. The Derived Pricing Model is still used today by a number of buy-side institutions in an effort to achieve 100 percent pricing coverage on their portfolios.

Another extremely important driver in the continued evolution of the secondary market was the widespread availability of bank loan ratings during the late 1990s, through companies such as Standard & Poor's, Moody's, and Fitch Ratings (formerly Fitch IBCA). According to Standard & Poor's, the agency rated 56 percent of the leveraged loan universe in 1998, and today that figure exceeds 75 percent. By the year 2000, the LSTA was having a profound influence on the development of secondary market liquidity through successful initiatives such as the creation of standardized documents and market practices, the partnership with LPC in forming the SMPS, and a partnership with Standard & Poor's in the creation of the S&P/LSTA Leveraged Loan Index (the standard benchmarking tool of the industry).

Despite the daily secondary market price fluctuations that were a product of increased trading volume and the new daily valuation process, many funds were still valuing most of their loans at face value until the Securities and Exchange Commission (SEC) issued an interpretive letter in the year 2000. The SEC ordered funds to change their valuation methodology, mandating that bank loan fund managers use a mark-to-market price (recording the market price or value of a security on a daily basis) rather than a fair value price (a rational and unbiased estimate of the potential market price) to determine the price of bank loans for net asset value calculations. Loans that traded or were available to trade in the secondary market now needed to be priced as they traded, or "marked to market," like stocks and corporate bonds. This policy increased not only day-to-day market volatility, but also liquidity, which historically had been an issue for bank loans, since they are not traded as widely as stocks or corporate bonds.

By the turn of the century, loan traders at more than 30 institutions were actively taking positions and trading loans on a daily basis. From 1999 to 2000, the SMPS increased its U.S. pricing coverage from 740 facilities to 1,514, while secondary trading volume soared to $102 billion, according to LPC. Just as the market's viability was on the rise, so was its visibility. The *Wall Street Journal* began weekly coverage of the syndicated loan market in 2000 by publishing LSTA/LPC secondary market prices on the most widely quoted and volatile loans, a true testament to how the secondary market had evolved over the preceding decade. The need for secondary market valuations on not only loans, but also other credit instruments, such as credit default swaps (CDS), led to new entrants into the secondary market pricing business. In response to this overwhelming demand, a new source for asset valuation data and services was born. Founded in 2001, Markit Group became only the second vendor to offer secondary market prices; it has since become a leading industry source for asset valuation data and services across the valuation spectrum, along with its predecessor LPC.

From 2000 to 2005, the secondary loan market continued to develop while attracting a new and diverse group of institutional investors that unwittingly have put a strain on supply, as demand for syndicated loans has become apparently unquenchable.

Exhibit 7.1 illustrates the supply and demand imbalance that has been in existence since 2003 by charting the percentage of loans priced in the secondary market above 100 or par (74 percent as of the first quarter of 2006). This statistic signifies that investors have increasingly needed to pay a premium in order to purchase bank loans in the secondary market as more and more institutions have entered the marketplace. Institutional investors, which now include the likes of CLOs/CDOs, prime funds, insurance companies, finance companies, and hedge funds, were quick to appreciate the high risk-adjusted returns of the asset class (loans have performed at the top end of the Sharpe ratio spectrum of various asset classes since 1997), while finding syndicated bank loans and their subsequent trading in the secondary market to be a very useful tool for managing credit risk and increasing portfolio diversification across the capital structure. As a result of this massive flood

EXHIBIT 7.1

Historical par-plus (> 100) market share.

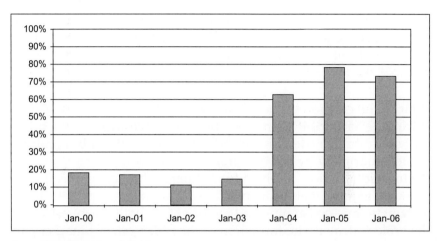

Source: LSTA/LPC mark-to-market pricing

of new investors into the asset class, the primary and secondary markets have grown in both depth and breadth. This growth has led to a much higher level of liquidity, a prerequisite for attracting the next phase of institutional investors, most notably pension funds. In closing, consider these statistics, which illustrate the development of not only the asset class, but also its level of liquidity:

- According to LPC, new-issue corporate loan volume hit $665 billion in 1995 and $1,196 billion in 2000, peaking in 2004 at $1,300 billion, while secondary trading volume, whose growth has clearly outpaced that of the new-issue market, reached $33.81 billion in 1995 and $101.97 billion in 2000, rising to an estimated $160 billion in 2005.

- According to Standard & Poor's LCD, there were 32 active loan investment vehicles in 1995; by the year 2000, there were 74 manager groups with 205 active loan investment vehicles; and by the end of 2005, those figures are estimated to be 192 and 489, respectively.

- Daily LSTA/LPC mark-to-market pricing coverage has grown from 155 U.S.–based facilities in 1995, to 1,820 in 2000, to more than 2,400 by the third quarter of 2005.

The LSTA/LPC Mark-to-Market Process: Then and Now

Theodore Basta
Vice President, Market Data
The Loan Syndications and Trading Association

Prior to the creation of the LSTA/LPC Secondary Mark-to-Market Pricing Service (SMPS) in 1999, buy-side investors would solicit individual broker/dealers for indicative prices (both bid and ask quotes), normally by fax transmission, and would then aggregate the individual prices received from different brokers in an effort to mark to market their loan positions. This process proved to be extremely time-consuming and inefficient for both the investor and the broker/dealer. The formation of the SMPS offered market participants two key benefits. First and foremost, the SMPS would deliver one "official" indicative price per loan facility per trading day to its customers and those broker/dealers who were a part of the submission process, instead of each institution determining the appropriate price internally. Second, by taking over the process, the SMPS would save both buy and sell sides time and energy, which was better used in assessing market prices than in collecting and distributing them.

Today's SMPS provides daily valuations (average bid and ask indicative prices) on more than 1,200 U.S.–based borrowers, representing more than 2,400 priced facilities (see Exhibit 7.2); these are derived from roughly 4,800 individual indicative bid and ask quotes from 30 broker/dealers (individual bid and ask quotes are collected, then aggregated prior to their release to the market). While times have certainly changed since the inception of the SMPS, its primary goals and objectives have stayed the same: to manage the efficient flow of pricing information between broker/dealers and investors, take part in extensive analyst review and audit procedures to ensure the highest-quality pricing, and deliver comprehensive, independent, unbiased, and confidential indicative pricing. The daily accomplishment of these goals and objectives has played an integral role in fostering price transparency, increased confidence on the part of market participants, and market liquidity. In short, SMPS analysts reach out to sell-side institutions each morning to collect, audit, and aggregate individual indicative bid

EXHIBIT 7.2

Historical LSTA/LPC U.S. mark-to-market price coverage.

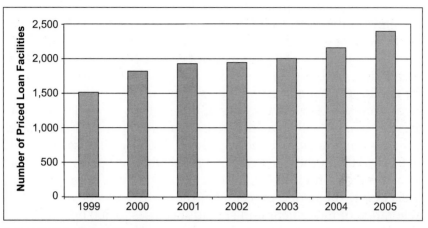

Source: LSTA/LPC mark-to-market pricing.

and ask quotes, in an effort to supply investors with an aggregated indicative price level that is reflective of where a particular loan facility would (or in fact did) trade. In today's market, most investors use the "mean of the mean" calculation (the simple average of the average bid and ask) to mark their loan positions to market.

Back in 1999, when the LSTA/LPC mark-to-market process was first created, the LSTA's board of directors, which had both buy- and sell-side representatives, created a detailed set of operational policies and procedures, governed by a series of price accuracy audits, that still govern the SMPS today. In each case where a particular audit has not been passed on a given price, an analyst will contact the appropriate broker/dealer in order to resolve the issue and complete the verification process prior to the release of the price in question. The first series of audits is directed toward identifying any human error on the broker/dealer side, such as, but not limited to, leaving a particular bid or ask null or mistakenly moving the bid price higher than the ask. The next series of audits is much more complex and centers on monitoring price volatility. Analysts first review the frequency of price changes and identify any individual broker/dealer quotes that have not changed over a three-week period. In many cases, a loan price, particularly one assigned to a smaller, less liquid facility, will not change over that period of time, but analysts will still confirm the level as being accurate and reflective of current market conditions.

Analysts then review all individual bid and ask quotes from each broker/dealer that have in fact changed from day to day, monitoring the magnitude of the change and any adjustments to the bid-ask spread (the difference between the indicative bid and ask prices) that have fallen outside of acceptable parameters. These parameters are based on the bid of the loan, as the audit will allow for greater price modification and wider bid-ask spreads as the bid level decreases. For the purpose of this section, we will be separating the market into two different segments, par and distressed, defining par as a bid at or above 90 and defining distressed as a bid of below 90. On the par side, analysts will verify price movement or a change in the bid-ask spread on any loan of more than 200 basis points (bps), or 2 percent. On the distressed side, the acceptable range of movement and spread increases to 500 bps, or 5 percent. As price falls below 90, bid-ask spreads will certainly widen as speculation on the borrower begins to rise, as does the risk of owning the loan. For example, the current average bid-ask spread on loans priced at 90 or above is 66 bps, while loans priced below 90 reported a figure of 292 bps.

Once each individual price change has been audited and confirmed, pricing analysts will then compare the individual bid quotes from each of the broker/dealers pricing the same facility, and will request verification on all quotes where the difference among the individual bids of the broker/dealers for the same facility is once again more than 200 bps for par loans and 500 bps for distressed loans. There is a definitive inverse relationship between where a particular loan facility is priced and the variances found in individual bid-ask quotes from different broker/dealers—as price decreases, the variance increases. As prices begin to dip below 98, variations among individual broker/dealer quotes on the same facility will begin to rise. Generally speaking, once prices fall below 90, speculation will begin to replace traditional pricing mechanisms, and as prices drop below 80, broker/dealers begin to assess the probability of default and expected recovery instead of concentrating on other factors, such as the yield of the loan. New entrants in the asset class, particularly hedge funds, have brought a substantial amount of newfound liquidity to this side of the market that did not exist in years past.

The mark-to-market process actually began as a weekly "pull" process, with broker/dealers providing their AXE sheets (a pricing sheet available to investors that contained the deals that the broker/dealer either was agent on and/or was currently making an active market in) each week via fax to the SMPS. At the request of the largest and most influential buy-side participants of that time, who needed to price their funds every day, the mark-to-market process shifted to daily in a matter of months from its inception. At the same time, the "pull" process (taking in the prices on those loans that a particular broker/dealer wanted to provide) was replaced by a "push" process, where the SMPS would solicit pricing from the appropriate broker/dealers on those loans held by their ever-increasing customer base, in an effort to provide 100 percent pricing coverage on all portfolios, which even today can sometimes be difficult to achieve. SMPS analysts would (1) ensure that the broker/dealer who had entered into the transaction with the buy-side customer was quoting the deal, and (2) review the credit agreement in an effort to obtain pricing from all sell-side banks that were a part of the original syndication process and were currently making a market in the name, most importantly the agent bank. This process still goes on today, as SMPS analysts are charged with not only ensuring the accuracy of the indicative price, but also making sure that all brokers who should be quoting the deal are in fact doing so. This is an extremely important process, as the level of an investor's confidence has historically increased as the number of quote providers included in the average price increased for illiquid loans—those loans that do not trade frequently.

It was also critical in making sure that a broker/dealer was quoting all facilities under a particular deal. Historically, deals usually consisted of two noninstitutional facilities (a revolving credit facility and a term loan A) and two institutional facilities (a term loan B and a term loan C). In today's institutional investor–heavy market, deals consist of less noninstitutional facilities (smaller spreads, shorter maturity dates, early amortizations) and more institutional facilities (larger spreads, longer maturity dates, back-weighted amortizations), and/or more money allocated to those institutional facilities to meet increased demand. In most cases, revolving credits are priced the lowest of all facilities within a deal, because of their illiquid and unfunded nature. Typically, a broker/dealer would price the revolver about 150 bps lower than the term loan A, and 250 bps lower than the term loan B/C, while the difference between the term loan A and the term loan B/C can range from 50 to 200 bps, depending on the structure of the facilities.

Once the prices of individual facilities within a deal fall below 90, it is typical that the broker/dealer will begin to price all facilities the same, as the credit issue will begin to trump all other pricing mechanisms, including supply and demand, which certainly has an effect on the varying prices of individual facilities within a deal. Most recently, arrangers have moved away from these traditional deal structures and have begun to structure deals to include first and second lien loans (discussed in detail in other sections of this handbook) in order to continue to attract a new and more diverse investor base. Given the varying structural differences between the first and second liens of a deal, one cannot accurately estimate the average difference in secondary market pricing between them.

Beginning each morning, SMPS analysts would create customized pricing sheets for each broker/dealer containing the prior day's bid-ask levels on all loans the broker/dealer was currently pricing, and then send these sheets to the appropriate institutions. Broker/dealers would then update their prices and send the pricing sheets back to the SMPS for entry into the database and the subsequent running of the audit procedures discussed earlier. Analysts were also charged with making the appropriate changes to their customers' portfolios, adding or deleting loans as per the customer's request, while soliciting prices on any new loans that were added to the portfolios that day. Once these steps were completed and all audit exemptions had been resolved, the SMPS would then manually send off the priced portfolios to its customers via a secured Internet delivery system by 4:00 p.m. each day.

Today's service is much more efficient and effective, as technology and information flow have certainly advanced since the "old days" of the late 1990s. For example, the audit procedures are now run intraday on a real-time basis following the receipt of each individual broker pricing sheet, which immediately alerts analysts of variations and price movements that necessitate follow-up with the broker/dealer community. Acting as a central hub for information gathering, the SMPS maintains strong relationships with broker/dealers and investors and is in continuous contact with market players throughout the day. Discussions include which names are trading and at what levels in order to better understand the day's activity. In 2003, the SMPS began incorporating trade levels into the audit verification processes.

Even now, however, while liquidity in the equity markets creates an active market in the vast majority of stocks, that is not the case in the secondary loan market. It is interesting to note that while the indicative levels have been proven to be extremely accurate when compared to actual trade prices (see the later article on the LSTA Trade Data Study), the reality is that not all loans trade. According to the LSTA, 52 percent of loans priced by the SMPS actually traded during the first quarter of 2005, up substantially from the 31 percent figure reported in 2002. Given this lack of major breadth in trade activity, it was paramount that the SMPS incorporate new systems that would monitor credit/market events affecting the indicative price level of loans as well as actual trades. Today, SMPS analysts continually scan the broader markets for news relating to specific credits, while monitoring daily rating changes via the three major rating agencies (a change in credit quality can most certainly lead to a change in the indicative price, given the subsequent change in the risk/reward profile of the company).

Also in 2003, the SMPS launched its transparency initiative, so that now investors can see the names of the institutions that are quoting a facility, if that facility has at least three quote providers. The SMPS also began monitoring nearby markets such as bonds and equities, where volatility is much more pronounced and is usually a good indication of possible price changes on the loan side. By 2004, the SMPS included cross-asset pricing capabilities in the audit verification processes, allowing it to monitor any substantial price movements in bond and equity prices on those borrowers that it was covering. Also in 2004, the SMPS revamped much of its operations, including the full automation of data entry and retrieval, which has led to reduced turnaround times, identification of follow-up items more rapidly, and the instantaneous auditing of information to ensure accuracy and efficient broker/dealer follow-up. The SMPS also created a new automated portfolio delivery system, which not only improved turnaround times, but also eliminated any possible human error during the delivery process. Finally, in 2004, the SMPS worked to improve the information included in the daily pricing sheets sent out to the broker/dealer community; it now includes the customization of particular fields, the incorporation of daily audit exceptions, and basic analytics such as the prior day's aggregate price change.

In total, these enhancements, coupled with an increase in the information and liquidity available to the market, have led to a much higher level of efficiency and effectiveness attributable to the daily operations of the SMPS, which in turn has led to the much higher level of quality associated with SMPS prices, as the next article in this chapter will surely illustrate.

The LSTA Trade Data Study: Measuring the Accuracy of Secondary Market Prices

Theodore Basta
Vice President, Market Data
The Loan Syndications and Trading Association

Over time, loan market participants began to ask, "What's the difference between a loan's indicative price and where it is actually trading?" In an effort to answer that question and to provide insight concerning the accuracy of the LSTA/LPC mark-to-market processes, the LSTA originated its annual Trade Data Study in 2002.

In order to quantify the accuracy and integrity of the LSTA/LPC mark-to-market (SMPS) process, this study compares the trade price for each facility traded with the SMPS mean of the mean indicative price (a simple average of the average of all bid and ask quotes). The study then looks to measure the average absolute difference (ignoring the direction of the difference, plus or minus) between the trade price and the SMPS mean of the mean, but will also look at the actual average difference in order to (1) illustrate the SMPS's tendency to over- or undervalue loan prices relative to their trade prices, and (2) analyze the accuracy of SMPS indicative levels from a process control perspective. The LSTA trade data analysis assumes that the comparable mark-to-market price for any trade event occurs on the trade date, as each day's mark-to-market levels are as of 3 p.m., theoretically capturing the day's market events through that time. The following text contains excerpts from this year's study.

Since its inception in 2002, the LSTA's trade data study has grown in breadth (see Exhibits 7.3 and 7.4) and depth (see Exhibit 7.5), keeping pace with the number of trade data providers, which has also grown steadily. There were 9 providers in 2002, 12 in 2003, and 16 in 2004. Despite losing two providers through bank consolidation, the 2005 trade study is made up of trade data from 18 of the largest and most influential buy-side (9) and sell-side (9) member institutions of the LSTA. As the number of data providers has grown, so has the volume of trade data collected. Trade data for the analysis, which covers only the first quarter of each year, consisted of $11.66 billion in 2002, $14.77 billion in 2003, $32.08 billion in 2004, and $40.97 billion in 2005 (see Exhibit 7.6).

In 2002, the study included 39 percent of Reuters Loan Pricing Corporation's (LPC's) estimated first-quarter secondary volume; in 2003, 46 percent; in 2004, 77 percent; and in 2005, a staggering 102 percent.

The first-quarter 2005 LSTA Trade Data Study included $40.97 billion in trade activity on 16,150 trades covering 748 borrowers and 1,133 facilities. At the end of the first quarter of 2005, the LSTA/LPC SMPS was quoting 2,210 facilities issued to 1,230 U.S. borrowers. Trade prices were obtained on 52 percent of all facilities

EXHIBIT 7.3

First quarter 2005 trade data facility coverage.

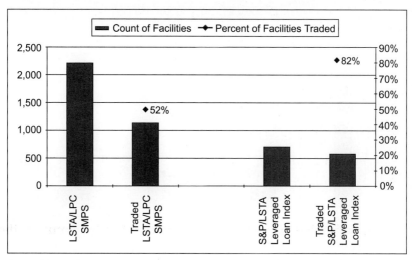

Source: LSTA Trade Data Study.

EXHIBIT 7.4

First quarter 2005 trade data borrower coverage.

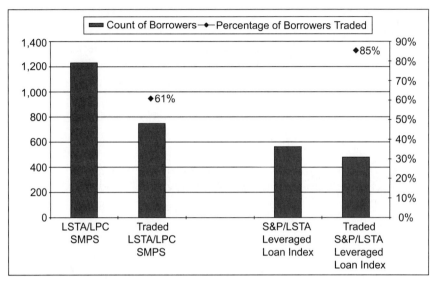

Source: LSTA Trade Data Study.

EXHIBIT 7.5

Historical trade frequency.

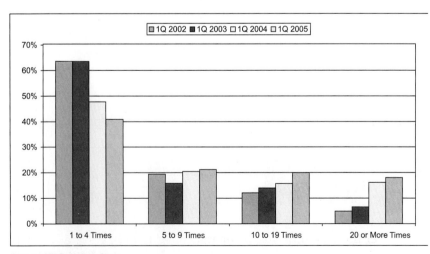

Source: LSTA Trade Data Study.

E X H I B I T   7 . 6

Historical trade volume.

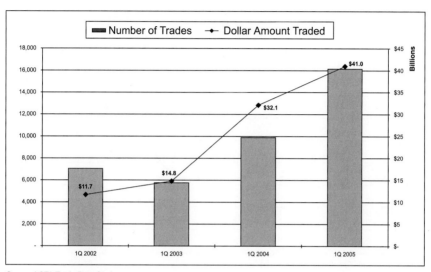

Source: LSTA Trade Data Study

that were marked to market (Exhibit 7.3), while coverage on the borrower level was reported at 61 percent (Exhibit 7.4). Within the S&P/LSTA Leveraged Loan Index, which uses SMPS indicative prices in calculating its returns, trade prices were collected on 580 facilities, or 82 percent of all facilities that reside in the index (Exhibit 7.3), while coverage on the borrower level was reported at 480, or 85 percent (Exhibit 7.4). Both figures illustrate the high correlation between loans that trade and loans that reside in the index, enabling the S&P/LSTA Leveraged Loan Index to be the standard benchmarking tool of our industry.

Over the past three years, the average SMPS mean of the mean and average trade prices have steadily increased (Exhibit 7.7), while average SMPS bid-ask spreads across both data sets have tightened (Exhibit 7.8). Secondary price performance has been dictated by the supply and demand imbalance, while an improving credit environment and strong technicals have truly overheated an already surging market.

Over the past four years, the relationship between trade prices and SMPS indicative prices has strengthened considerably, as the

EXHIBIT 7.7

Price history.

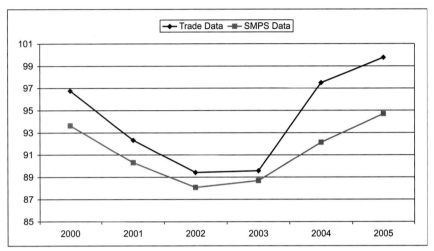

Source: LSTA Trade Data Study.

EXHIBIT 7.8

Bid-ask spread history.

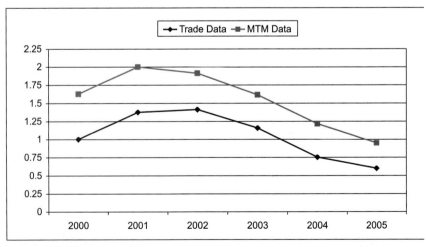

Source: LSTA Trade Data Study.

EXHIBIT 7.9

Historical statistical measures.

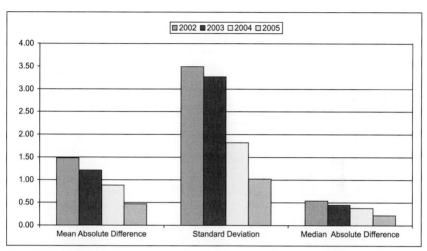

Source: LSTA Trade Data Study.

decreases in mean absolute difference, standard deviation, and median absolute difference in Exhibit 7.9 indicate. Year over year, the mean absolute difference fell 47 percent to 46 bps, the standard deviation fell 44 percent to 102 bps, and the median difference reported a decline of 42 percent to 22 bps (meaning that 50 percent of the population traded within 22 bps of the SMPS price today compared to 38 bps a year ago). Such dramatic improvements exemplify not only the increase in the efficiency and effectiveness of the secondary loan market, but also the mark-to-market process itself. Exhibit 7.10 illustrates the positive trends over time found by analyzing the percentage of loans that are trading within a particular range of their SMPS price. For example, in 2005, 79 percent of trades fell within 50 bps (including zero) of their SMPS price, up substantially from the 52 percent figure reported in 2004.

The inverse relationship between higher SMPS prices and lower mean absolute differences (trade price – SMPS price) is illustrated in Exhibit 7.11. Par credits (for the purposes of this study, those priced at or above 90) recorded a mean absolute difference of 36 bps, a standard deviation of 54 bps, and a median of 21 bps, while distressed credits (for the purposes of this study, those priced

EXHIBIT 7.10

Historical mean absolute difference distribution.

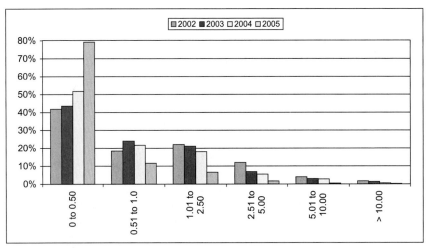

Source: LSTA Trade Data Study.

EXHIBIT 7.11

Statistical measures by price range.

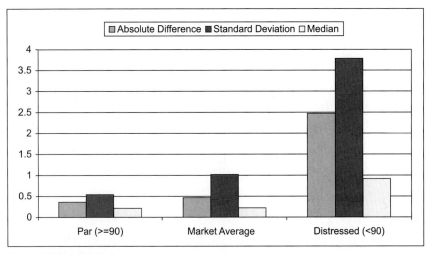

Source: LSTA Trade Data Study.

E X H I B I T   7 . 1 2

Absolute difference range by price range.

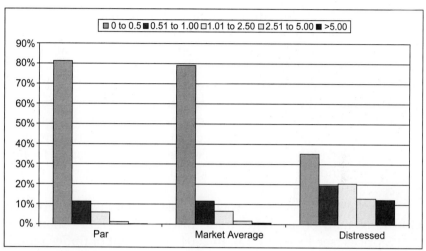

Source: LSTA Trade Data Study.

below 90), which accounted for a minimal 4 percent of total trade volume, showed figures of 247 bps, 378 bps, and 91 bps, respectively. Exemplifying the relationship further, Exhibit 7.12 illustrates the percentage of loans by price range (par and distressed) that reported a mean absolute difference within a particular range in order to determine at which price point(s) SMPS prices begin to exhibit a certain degree of imperfection.

As can be seen in Exhibit 7.12, 81 percent of par trades occurred within 50 bps of their SMPS price, and 92 percent within 100 bps. Once price falls below 90 and credits become "distressed," those figures drop substantially, to 35 percent and 54 percent, respectively. Even so, year over year, the market did an outstanding job of improving the quality of distressed SMPS prices. From 2004 to 2005, the percentage of loans that tallied an absolute difference of 50 bps or less grew from 19 percent to 35 percent;, those with a difference of 100 bps or less grew from 31 percent to 54 percent; and those with 250 bps or less, from 54 percent to 75 percent.

The study then went on to review the influence of both market liquidity and credit factors on the mean absolute difference between trade price and SMPS price. Besides the price-level analysis just discussed, market liquidity factors included bid-ask spread, quote count (the number of individual broker/dealers quoting a facility), and trade frequency. As a result of this analysis, the following conclusion was drawn: loans with higher prices, tighter bid-ask spreads, and more quote providers subsequently had higher ratings and liquidity, and exhibited the strongest relationships between trade price and SMPS price, as defined by lower mean absolute differences, median differences, and standard deviations.

Following the analysis of the mean absolute difference between trade price and SMPS price, the study went on to review first quarter 2005's mean difference in order to (1) determine if SMPS prices tend to over- or undervalue loans with respect to their trade price, and (2) analyze the accuracy of SMPS prices from a process control perspective.

For the second year in a row, the mean difference was positive; indicating that, on average, trade prices were higher than their SMPS prices (see Exhibit 7.13). In 2004, 83 percent of trades reported a positive mean difference; in 2005, that figure decreased to 56 percent. Conversely, the percentage of trades with a negative mean difference increased from 17 percent to 44 percent.

EXHIBIT 7.13

Mean difference distribution.

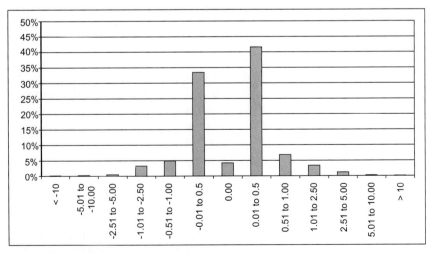

Source: LSTA Trade Data Study.

This year's analysis revealed a mean difference of 5 bps, substantially less than last year's figure of 27 bps. The standard deviation reported in the first quarter of 2005 revealed that 68 percent of trades occurred at +/−112.5 bps from the mean difference of 5 bps. From a process control perspective, basing control limits upon a multiple of the standard deviation is an acceptable practice. Usually this multiple is 3, and thus the limits are called 3-sigma limits, where an estimated 99 percent of differences (trade price – SMPS price) will be located between the upper and lower limits. The term *estimated* is used because the data do not follow a normal distribution, and thus are somewhat skewed. If the difference between trade price and SMPS price falls outside the control limits (upper sigma limit of 343 bps and lower sigma limit of negative 332 bps), the study has assumed that the SMPS process was probably "out of control." The results of this analysis showed that 230 of the 16,150 trades collected (or slightly more than 1 percent of activity) fell outside the upper and lower limits. These 230 trades involved 36 borrowers represented by 53 individual facilities, 83 percent of which were not a part of the S&P/LSTA Leveraged Loan Index. The study then went on to investigate such instances further to establish any common trends.

In conclusion, this year's analysis has illustrated that the secondary market continues to become more liquid and transparent, while the SMPS process continues to provide a higher level of accuracy year over year. The next article in this chapter, by Tom Price and Jean Cho from Markit, will describe that company's loan pricing model, which is used to produce a secondary market price for illiquid loans that are not priced by the broker/dealer community and presumably don't trade within the secondary market.

Introduction to Model Pricing

Tom Price
Director
Markit Group

Jean Cho
Analyst
Markit Group

Founded in 2001, Markit Group is an industry source for asset valuation data and services supporting independent price verification

EXHIBIT 7.14

Number of loans priced over time.

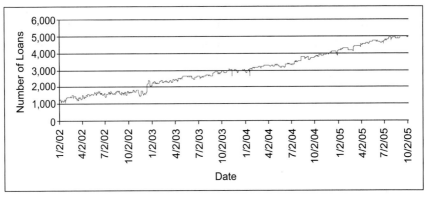

Source: Markit Group.

and risk management in global financial and energy markets. Working in conjunction with over 70 loan traders worldwide, Markit Group (Markit) has built an extensive database of historical loan prices. Growing by over 5,000 loan prices each trading day, (see Exhibit 7.14), the database now contains well over 2 million historical loan prices.

Drawing upon this database, Markit has developed a model loan price that is suitable for valuing illiquid facilities that are not priced by the dealer community. As part of its continuing development and improvement, the Markit model loan price has been subjected to rigorous independent comparisons to alternative models. As a demonstration of its accuracy, Markit compared the model loan price and dealer prices for an actual portfolio held by a large institutional portfolio. The difference in portfolio valuation between the model loan price and the dealer marks was just 62 bps.

MODEL METHODOLOGY

Each trading day, Markit calculates an industry/spread matrix using all available dealer loan prices. As the market at times disagrees with the rating agencies, there are occasions when higher-rated credits will have higher spreads than their lower-rated peers. In order to ensure that model prices do not decline with an improvement in risk rating, a smoothed industry/spread matrix (Exhibit 7.15) is calculated each day using a series of proprietary steps.

Based upon the parameters of a particular loan (e.g., risk rating, industry, and so on), a suitable spread to a two-year call is selected using the smoothed Industry/Spread matrix. This spread is then translated into a modeled loan price using the particular loan's amortization table and the spread currently paid by the issuer.

65 PERCENT OF MODEL PRICES ARE WITHIN 150 BASIS POINTS OF DEALER PRICE

In order to assess the accuracy of the model loan price, Markit compared over 40,000 model loan prices to the actual dealer prices for the identical facilities. Of these 40,000 model loan prices, 65 percent were within 150 basis points of actual dealer marks (see Exhibit 7.16).

As expected, the model loan price was most accurate for highly rated issuers. For example, 90 percent of the modeled loan prices for BBB-rated issuers are within 150 basis points of the actual dealer price.

As issuers deteriorate in credit quality and future cash flows become more suspect, the variance of dealer price opinions increases, and this variability in dealer price opinions is evident in the model as well. Like the greater variance between the average deal price and an individual dealer mark for stressed credits, the variance between the Markit model loan price and the dealer average price is more substantial for stressed credits. However, as a typical portfolio will have a relatively minor concentration in stressed credits, this variance has little impact on portfolio valuation.

ACTUAL PORTFOLIO IMPACT: MODEL VALUATION WITHIN 62 BPS OF DEALER VALUATION

The most critical assessment of a model loan price's accuracy is its impact on the valuation of an actual portfolio. As the majority of a typical loan portfolio's assets will be in the credits of performing issuers, the valuation of a portfolio would be heavily influenced by the BBB to B segments of the model (see Exhibit 7.17).

EXHIBIT 7.15

Smoothed industry spread matrix.

Industry	BBB	BBB-	BB+	BB	BB-	B+	B	B-	CCC+
Aerospace/Defense		L+130.2	L+157.0	L+192.5	L+194.5	L+196.4	L+252.3	L+308.2	L+323.0
Airlines		L+170.4	L+205.5	L+252.0	L+254.5	L+257.1	L+330.2	L+403.4	L+422.8
All Other		L+170.4	L+205.5	L+252.0	L+254.5	L+257.1	L+330.2	L+403.4	L+422.8
Automotive		L+185.6	L+223.8	L+274.4	L+277.1	L+279.9	L+359.6	L+439.2	L+460.3
Building Materials		L+192.4	L+232.0	L+284.4	L+287.3	L+290.2	L+372.7	L+455.3	L+477.2
Chemicals		L+194.1	L+234.0	L+286.9	L+289.9	L+292.8	L+376.1	L+459.4	L+481.5
Computers & Electronics		L+171.7	L+207.1	L+253.9	L+256.5	L+259.1	L+332.8	L+406.5	L+426.1
Construction		L+170.5	L+205.6	L+252.0	L+254.6	L+257.1	L+330.0	L+403.4	L+422.8
Consumer Nondurables		L+170.4	L+205.5	L+252.1	L+254.5	L+257.2	L+330.4	L+403.5	L+432.9
Educational Services		L+170.4	L+205.5	L+252.0	L+254.5	L+257.1	L+330.2	L+403.4	L+422.8
Entertainment and Leisure		L+127.8	L+154.1	L+189.0	L+190.9	L+192.8	L+247.7	L+302.5	L+317.1
Environmental Services		L+170.4	L+205.5	L+252.0	L+254.5	L+257.1	L+330.2	L+403.4	L+422.8
Financial Services		L+213.0	L+256.9	L+314.9	L+318.1	L+321.3	L+412.8	L+504.2	L+528.5
Food and Beverage		L+182.6	L+220.2	L+270.0	L+272.7	L+275.4	L+353.8	L+432.2	L+453.0
Forest Products		L+208.1	L+250.9	L+307.6	L+310.8	L+313.9	L+403.2	L+492.5	L+516.2
Gaming and Hotels		L+178.5	L+215.3	L+263.9	L+266.6	L+269.3	L+345.9	L+422.5	L+442.9
Government		L+170.4	L+205.5	L+252.0	L+254.5	L+257.1	L+330.2	L+403.4	L+422.8
Health care		L+161.9	L+195.2	L+239.4	L+241.8	L+244.3	L+313.8	L+383.3	L+401.7
Home Furnishings		L+187.9	L+226.6	L+277.8	L+280.7	L+283.5	L+364.1	L+444.8	L+466.2
Insurance		L+213.0	L+256.9	L+314.9	L+318.1	L+321.3	L+412.8	L+504.2	L+528.5
Leasing		L+170.4	L+205.5	L+252.0	L+254.5	L+257.1	L+330.2	L+403.4	L+403.4
Machinery		L+140.2	L+169.0	L+207.3	L+209.4	L+211.5	L+271.6	L+331.8	L+347.8
Manufacturing		L+170.4	L+205.5	L+252.0	L+254.5	L+257.1	L+330.2	L+403.4	L+422.8
Media		L+151.0	L+182.1	L+223.3	L+225.6	L+227.9	L+292.7	L+357.5	L+374.7
Metals and Mining		L+192.9	L+232.6	L+285.2	L+288.0	L+290.9	L+373.7	L+456.5	L+478.5
Not for Profit		L+170.4	L+205.5	L+252.0	L+254.5	L+257.1	L+330.2	L+403.4	L+422.8
Oil and Gas		L+213.0	L+256.9	L+314.9	L+318.1	L+321.3	L+412.8	L+504.2	L+528.5
Other Consumer Industries		L+170.4	L+205.5	L+252.0	L+254.5	L+257.1	L+330.2	L+403.4	L+422.8
Personal Loans		L+170.4	L+205.5	L+252.0	L+254.5	L+257.1	L+330.2	L+403.4	L+422.8
Personal Services		L+127.8	L+154.1	L+189.0	L+190.9	L+192.8	L+247.7	L+302.5	L+317.1
Printing and Publishing		L+138.2	L+166.7	L+204.4	L+206.5	L+208.5	L+267.9	L+327.2	L+343.0
Professional and Business Services		L+143.6	L+173.2	L+212.3	L+214.5	L+216.6	L+278.3	L+339.9	L+356.3
Railroads		L+127.8	L+154.1	L+189.0	L+190.9	L+192.8	L+247.7	L+302.5	L+317.1
Real Estate		L+173.5	L+209.2	L+256.5	L+259.1	L+261.7	L+336.1	L+410.6	L+430.3
Retail Food and Drug		L+142.9	L+172.3	L+211.3	L+213.4	L+215.6	L+276.9	L+338.2	L+354.5
Retailing		L+179.1	L+216.0	L+264.8	L+267.5	L+270.2	L+347.0	L+423.9	L+444.3
Securities and Trusts		L+170.4	L+205.5	L+252.0	L+254.5	L+257.1	L+330.2	L+403.4	L+403.4
Shipping and Ship Building		L+194.8	L+235.0	L+288.1	L+291.0	L+293.9	L+377.6	L+461.2	L+483.4
Steel		L+213.0	L+256.9	L+314.9	L+318.1	L+321.3	L+412.8	L+504.2	L+528.5
Telecommunications		L+164.2	L+197.9	L+242.7	L+245.2	L+247.6	L+318.1	L+388.6	L+407.3
Textile and Apparel Manufacturing		L+182.4	L+219.9	L+269.6	L+272.4	L+275.1	L+353.4	L+431.6	L+452.4
Tobacco		L+170.4	L+205.5	L+252.0	L+254.5	L+257.1	L+330.2	L+403.4	L+422.8
Transportation		L+170.4	L+205.5	L+252.0	L+254.5	L+257.1	L+330.2	L+403.4	L+422.8
Utilities		L+213.0	L+256.9	L+314.9	L+318.1	L+321.3	L+412.8	L+504.2	L+528.5
Wholesale Trade		L+170.4	L+205.5	L+252.0	L+254.5	L+257.1	L+330.2	L+403.4	L+422.8

Spreads are calculated using the weighted average of spreads for facilities within the specified industry and ratings class.

Source: Markit Group.

EXHIBIT 7.16

Overall model price/dealer price variance.

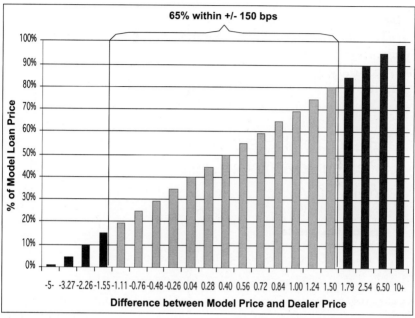

Source: Markit Group.

EXHIBIT 7.17

Model accuracy versus holding concentration.

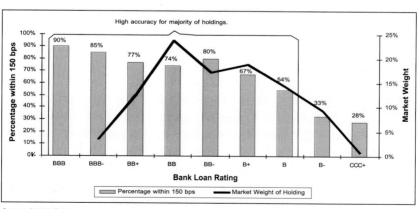

Source: Markit Group.

As would be expected, some of the loans in a portfolio have higher model prices than dealer marks, while others have lower. In total, the difference in portfolio valuation between dealer marks and Markit's model loan price for an actual large portfolio was 62 basis points.

The next article in this chapter, by Ted Basta of the Loan Syndication and Trading Association (LSTA), will analyze historical secondary price levels and quantify price distributions and volatility.

Historical Secondary Market Price Performance, Distributions, and Volatility

Theodore Basta
Vice President, Market Data
The Loan Syndications and Trading Association

As secondary trading and subsequent liquidity began to rise prior to the turn of the century, investors began to trade actively in the secondary market not only to manage portfolio concentrations and credit risk, but also to speculate on future upside price potential. Since that time, the study of secondary price behavior and volatility has become of great interest to current and potential investors in this asset class. This article will illustrate and briefly analyze historical secondary price levels for a six-year period (2000 to 2005), and will try to quantify price distributions and volatility during times of improving and declining credit quality, changes in supply and demand, and sudden shocks to the system such as September 11, 2001, and the WorldCom fraud of 2002. The analysis was drawn from the historical indicative secondary market price levels of the LSTA/LPC SMPS for the years 2000 through 2005. In an effort to look across the widely held and liquid side of the leveraged secondary loan market, the dataset used contained all term loans that were priced by at least three individual broker/dealers. As the coverage of the service expanded over the six-year period, the number of daily price points collected grew from a minimum of 375 in the early days, to a maximum of 500 at the end of 2005.

One of the more daunting realities of investing in the loan market is that, unlike other markets, where capital price appreciation is, to a certain extent, unlimited, there is little upside potential available on loans unless one is in the business of buying troubled debt—a practice that is commonly referred to as distressed investing and that many hedge funds actively participate in. In most cases, loans are purchased at or near par (100 cents on the dollar), and thus contain limited upside potential, given that a loan's price does not normally move above the 101 to 102 range.

The price component, or capital gain/loss portion, of the total return calculation offers investors an additional return above the loan's interest rate as price increases from purchase date though sale date, but can erode total return if price decreases below the purchase price over this period. While LIBOR and coupon rates, which represent the income portion of total returns, have certainly fluctuated over the years based on market factors such as supply and demand and changes in the credit environment, capital gains and losses have played a large and sometimes unexpected role in the level of total returns. Therefore, the study of price appreciation/depreciation and volatility becomes paramount in creating excess returns. This can be seen from the fact that the S&P/LSTA Leveraged Loan Index (LLI) reported the highest rate of return in 2003 since its inception in 1997, when average bid levels rebounded by more than 9 percent, the largest year-over-year gain on record (see Exhibits 7.18 and 7.19).

EXHIBIT 7.18

Historical S&P/LSTA Leveraged Loan Index (LLI) returns.

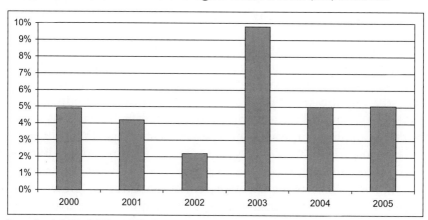

Source: Standard & Poor's LCD and S&P/LSTA Leveraged Loan Index.

EXHIBIT 7.19

Secondary market price history.

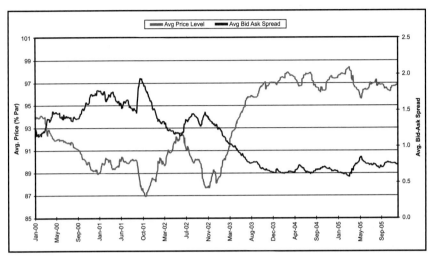

Source: LSTA/LPC Mark-to-Market Pricing.

While total return is in fact the measure of portfolio performance, it ignores the level of risk associated with achieving the return. The Sharpe ratio measures risk-adjusted performance by taking the rate of return for a portfolio less the risk-free rate and dividing the result by the standard deviation of the returns. Given that higher Sharpe ratios exemplify superior risk-adjusted performance, loans (as measured by the LLI) have performed at the top end of the Sharpe ratio spectrum of various asset classes since 1997 (see Exhibit 7.20). By the end of 2005, loans stood atop the spectrum with a 0.88 reading, finally surpassing the 0.77 reading produced by the Merrill Lynch High Grade Corporate Index (COAO).

Turning our attention back to Exhibit 7.19, we will begin to analyze historical secondary market price performance at the macro level. Average secondary levels reported a decline of 5.8 percent during the three-year span of deteriorating credit quality (2000–2002), but rebounded by 9.3 percent from 2003 through 2005 as credit quality improved and new investors, particularly those structuring CLOs/CDOs, began to create a supply and demand imbalance within the secondary market.

As reported, the year 2000 witnessed a rapid fall in credit quality, which had a dramatically negative effect on the performance of loans. According to Exhibit 7.21, the percentage of issuers

EXHIBIT 7.20

Sharpe ratio since 1997.

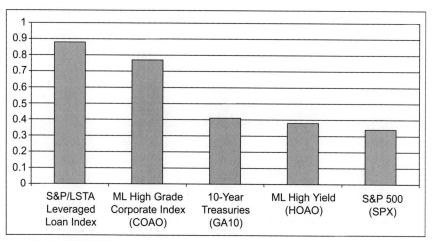

Source: Standard & Poor's LCD.

EXHIBIT 7.21

Historical percentage of issuers in payment default or bankruptcy.

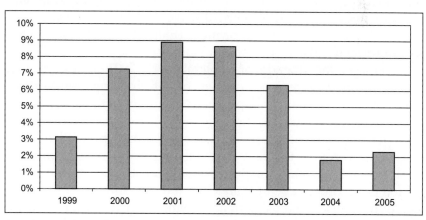

Source: Standard & Poor's LCD and S&P/LSTA Leveraged Loan Index.

in payment default or bankruptcy rocketed to 7.26 percent from 3.13 percent in 1999. From January to December of 2000, average bid levels fell by 469 bps, or 5 percent, while the average bid-ask spread widened by 48 bps, or 39 percent. During this time, the

E X H I B I T   7 . 2 2

Year 2000 price volatility distribution.

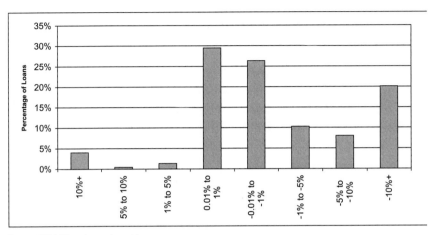

Source: LSTA/LPC mark-to-market pricing.

share representing the distressed market (the percentage of loans priced below 90) rose from 16 percent to 28 percent, while the percentage of deeply distressed loans (those priced below 80) rose from 11 percent to 20 percent. Over the 12-month span, 64 percent of loans declined in price, with 20 percent of the decliners reporting a price loss of 10 percent or more (Exhibit 7.22). Even so, bank loans churned out a 4.9 percent annual return, according to the LLI.

Prior to the tragedy of September 11, 2001, investors were already working in an environment of deteriorating credit quality (the percentage of issuers in payment default or bankruptcy rose to 8.9 percent) and earnings shortfalls, which continued to affect the market's ability to notch any sustainable gains, which it had done minimally through the first nine months of the year. Following September 11, the market experienced the most turbulent four-week period on record, as average bid levels fell by 311 bps, or 3.1 percent, while the average bid-ask spread expanded by 32 bps, or 3.5 percent. The distressed and deeply distressed share of the loan market rose from 26 percent to 32 percent and from 16 percent to 23 percent, respectively, as 96 percent of the market reported falling bid levels. Exhibit 7.23 looks at the distribution of price volatility for the four weeks following September 11, as well as for all of 2001.

EXHIBIT 7.23

Year 2001 price volatility distribution.

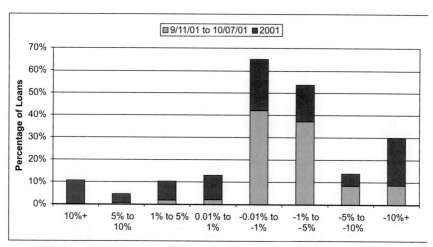

Source: LSTA/LPC mark-to-market pricing.

During the four-week period, 9 percent of loans plunged by more than 10 percent, while 45 percent fell by 1 to 10 percent. For the year, 21 percent of loans plunged by more than 10 percent, while 21 percent fell by 1 to 10 percent. The telecom sector was hit the hardest (average bid levels fell almost 10 percent from their highs in January to the end of the third quarter), and therefore impaired portfolio returns considerably given the large concentrations of telecom loans held at that time. Performance in 2001 could have been much worse, but the market was soon able to overcome the initial shock wave and in mid-October entered into a recovery period, aided by the CLO/CDO community, who unwittingly were helping the market's ascent by creating increased demand for existing loans in the secondary market. However, although more than 75 percent of loans reported strengthening bid levels after mid-October, recouping 110 bps on the market average, the secondary market was unable to salvage all losses by year end. In total, average bid levels reported a decline of only 1 percent, with 68 percent of all loans and 97 percent of all telecom loans tallying losses during one of the most volatile and sadly memorable years in our history. Even so, bank loans were able to once again deliver a positive return, 4.2 percent, according to the LLI.

E X H I B I T   7 . 2 4

Historical par and par-plus market share.

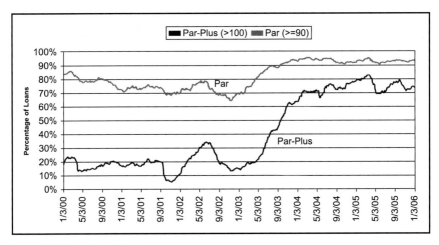

Source: LSTA/LPC mark-to-market pricing.

From January through the last week of June 2002, the secondary market was poised to continue its resurgence in the wake of increased demand for the loan asset. During this time, the percentage of par loans (> 90) increased from 70 percent to 79 percent, while the segment of the market priced above 100 grew to an unprecedented 34 percent as supply and demand economics began to clearly affect price performance within the secondary market (see Exhibit 7.24).

Average secondary prices improved marketwide, amassing more than 600 bps, or 2 percent, of price appreciation from the end of 2001, but the ride to recovery abruptly stopped there. The loan market's recovery period of the first six months was soon a distant memory as telecom bellwether WorldCom announced in late June that it had fraudulently increased profits by $3.8 billion over the previous five quarters. This is where the bank loan market flexed its senior secured muscle. Consider these statistics: during the second quarter of 2002, the Nasdaq composite dropped 16 percent, the S&P 500 fell almost 10 percent, but the LLI still delivered a positive return for the quarter, with advancers outnumbering decliners by a 1.5:1 ratio within the broader loan market.

Second-half performance in 2002 was characterized by the detection of fraudulent companies such as Adelphia Communications and WorldCom and the dramatic market downturn that this created. At the end of July, WorldCom announced that it would file for bankruptcy, sending shock waves through debt and equity markets alike. The third quarter was not so kind to investors, as the S&P 500 and Dow recorded the highest quarterly percentage losses since the late 1980s, while the LLI reported a negative quarterly return on its way to producing its lowest annual return on record, 2.2 percent.

From the time of WorldCom's announcement through mid-November, 65 percent of the secondary market declined in value, with 30 percent of loans reporting a price drop of more than 10 percent (see Exhibit 7.25). By the time 2002 finally had come to a close, the loan market's average bid level had improved by more than 100 bps from its November low, but was almost 300 bps short of its June high. All told, 58 percent of the market reported price losses by the end of the year, while tallying an average price loss of only 50 bps thanks to a much needed late-year rally (Exhibit 7.26). The rally featured 26 straight trading sessions in which the percentage of daily advancing prices was greater than those that declined. This late surge subsequently set the tone for a period of rampant recovery that redefined the landscape of the secondary market as we know it today.

EXHIBIT 7.25

Tale of three periods, 2002.

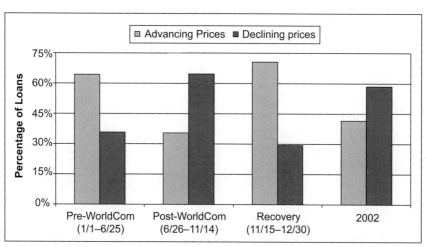

Source: LSTA/LPC mark-to-market pricing.

EXHIBIT 7.26

Price volatility distribution for 2002.

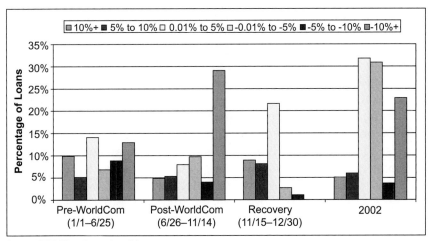

Source: LSTA/LPC mark-to-market pricing.

The year 2003 initiated a three-year period of strong secondary price performance backed by an improving credit environment. A flood of new investors continued to strain existing supply through increased demand, consequently elevating price levels and distribution percentages to heights that had been not only unattainable but also unimaginable in years past. From the beginning of 2003 to the end of 2005, the market's average bid level surged 821 bps, or 9.3 percent, to 97, while its average bid-ask spread tightened by 54 bps, or 43 percent, to 0.73 (see Exhibit 7.19).

The distribution of loan prices also changed dramatically, as excessive demand now truly overheated an already smoking secondary market. The percentage of par loans, those priced above 90, grew from 70 percent to 94 percent, while the percentage of loans priced above 100 ballooned from 15 percent to 74 percent (Exhibit 7.24).

Of the many conclusions that can be drawn from the study of historical loan performance over the past six years, one stands apart from the rest: the ability of the leveraged loan market to not only produce positive year-over-year returns, but also to provide high risk-adjusted returns through the most volatile and trying economic times. These high risk-adjusted returns, which are afforded to investors who look to invest at the top of the corporate capital structure, are no longer a secret. At this time, banks can no longer effectively produce enough supply to satisfy investor demand. This change in supply and demand has subsequently redefined the prices that investors are willing to pay in order to put their money to work in today's leveraged secondary loan market, at least until credit quality begins its inevitable descent.

The next article in this chapter, by Tom Price and Jean Cho from Markit, will further analyze secondary market price volatility from an empirical perspective, and introduce the concept of daily value at risk (DVaR).

Price Volatility and the Daily Value at Risk

Tom Price
Director, Markit Group

Jean Cho
Analyst, Markit Group

With nearly 2,000,000 loan dealer marks, the Markit database provides a unique opportunity to examine the characteristics of loan prices from an empirical perspective. Because of interest and demand from the dealer community and investors alike, this analysis will focus on assessing the daily value at risk (DVaR) of syndicated loans. For the purposes of this chapter, DVaR can be defined as a daily estimate of the probability of loss based on the statistical analysis of *historic loan price* volatilities and *trends*.

While theoretical and derived techniques exist for estimating daily value at risk for syndicated loans, none of these techniques are based directly on market prices. By examining the actual volatility of price changes over a 42-month period, this report adds another perspective to the calculation of daily value at risk and reserve requirements in the syndicated loan asset class. Specifically, this report addresses volatility within 15 distinct loan pricing bands, from above par (100+) to and 0 to 10. While the information is useful to a variety of market participants, it is most relevant in determining the value at risk of a portfolio of loans.

LOAN PRICE CHANGE VOLATILITY DISTRIBUTION

Understanding some of the fundamental characteristics of the loan price dataset is helpful in measuring the DVaR. An analysis of Markit's database with nearly 2,000,000 dealer loan prices showed the following:

- *Overall, loans are a stable asset class.* For loans priced at or near par, loan prices in the short term are nearly unwavering (see Exhibit 7.27). On average, loans priced above par move little more than one basis point in a typical trading day. As loans become more distressed and take on more equity characteristics, their price distribution becomes much wider. At the more extreme end of the scale, a small minority of loans priced well below 10 moved significantly.

- *Most loans are priced near par.* The height of the columns in Exhibit 7.28 indicates the number of bids within a particular pricing category in the Markit Loans historical pricing database. As expected, the chart indicates a significant decline in available pricing data for deeply distressed facilities. Because of their seniority in the capital structure, few leveraged loans trade below 50, even in default.

E X H I B I T   7 . 2 7

Average daily price change.

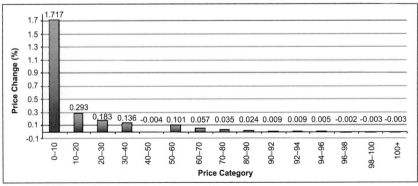

Source: Markit Group.

Loan distribution by pricing category.

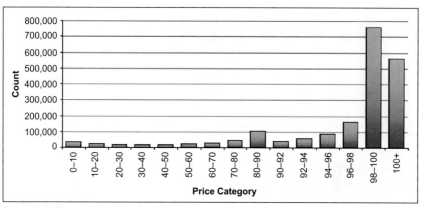

Source: Markit Group.

LOAN DAILY VALUE AT RISK: "WORST DAY IN 100" AND "WORST DAY IN 1,000"

Because of a lack of data, risk professionals measuring the DVaR of a leveraged loan portfolio have traditionally been forced to look to the high yield bond market for guidance. However, as high yield securities do not offer the seniority, covenants, or floating-rate basis of the leveraged loan market, DVaR has traditionally been overestimated in the loan market. While qualitative arguments for lower volatility estimates have existed for some time and loan indexes have shown the longer-term steadiness of the asset class, the daily stability of the loan market can now be empirically demonstrated.

Exhibits 7.29 and 7.30 illustrate the worst day in 100 and the worst day in 1,000 for 15 different loan pricing buckets, from above par (100+) to 0 to 10. Unsurprisingly, for both the worst day in 100 and the worst day in 1,000, par and near par loans are remarkably stable. As depicted in Exhibits 7.29 and 7.30, loans priced at 98 to par lose just 0.20 percent of their value on the worst day in 100 and 1.38 percent of their value on the worst day in 1,000.

As facilities become more distressed, they become increasingly volatile. Generally speaking, for both the worst day in 100 and the worst day in 1,000, each price category had less volatility than its lower-priced peers. In general, the most volatile category is loans

EXHIBIT 7.29

Worst loss in 100 days.

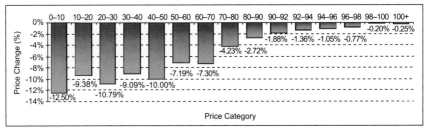

Source: Markit Group.

EXHIBIT 7.30

Worst loss in 1,000 days.

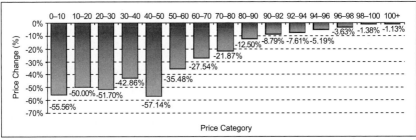

Source: Markit Group.

priced between 0 and 10. For the lower-priced loans in this category, even a minor basis-point swing in price has a considerable impact on volatility. For example, the bid of Winstar Communications' $475 million term loan B dropped 44 basis points during a single trading day. While this movement would entail a minor erosion of value for the vast majority of bank loans, it represented a 78 percent loss for Winstar term loan B holders, as the loan was previously bid at less than a penny on the dollar.

AVERAGE LOAN PRICE VOLATILITY BY PRICING CATEGORY

A survey of price movement across price categories shows that loan price volatility is not normally distributed. Exhibit 7.31 presents the average and standard deviation of price changes for loans with initial prices within 15 price ranges between above par and 0 to 10. As loan price volatility is not normally distributed, the average volatility plus and minus 2 standard deviations will not capture 97.7 percent of the results.

While the average volatility is presented in Exhibit 7.31, the daily value at risk charts presented in Exhibits 7.29 and 7.30 were created from the actual distributions of loan prices. The actual distribution tails used in identifying the worst day in 100 for daily value at risk are presented in Exhibit 7.32.

The average price change and the volatility of price change are calculated by sampling across both cross-section and time series. Within each price basket and time period, each sample represents a loan for which a price is available at both the beginning and the end of the period. In the Markit Loans database, most of the market is represented by near par and slightly distressed facilities. For example, loans with prices above par and at 98 to par represent 28.1 percent and 38.2 percent of the one-day samples, respectively. Loans priced above 90 represent 83.6 percent of the samples.

Loans with lower initial prices should have greater risk from both increased risk of default and uncertainty of expected recovery in the event of default. As expected, lower-priced loans demonstrate greater price volatility. Trends across price categories show that loans priced from 98 to par have the minimum standard deviation across all time periods. The exception to this trend is the basket of loans priced at par plus, which has slightly greater volatility than those loans priced at 98 to par. The most likely explanation for the increased volatility of par-plus loans is the increased likelihood of loan refinancing and a resulting drop in price to par.

LOAN PRICE VOLATILITY DISTRIBUTIONS BY PRICING CATEGORY

Because of the shape of the distributions of loan price changes, the daily value at risk cannot be accurately estimated using assumptions based on a normal distribution of price changes. However, Markit Loans' database allows the empirical examination of the actual price changes at a given percentile. The relevant negative price changes are summarized in Exhibit 7.32 over 1-day, 7-day, 30-day, and 90-day durations for 5, 1, and 0.1 percentile events.

EXHIBIT 7.31

Loan Price Volatility Over Time Grouped By Initial Price Category.

Initial Price Category	Average Percentage Bid Change / Standard Deviation of Percentage Bid Change / Sample Size											
	1-Day			7-Day			30-Day			90-Day		
Par Plus	−0.003%	0.35%	556,975	−0.008%	0.69%	109,957	−0.031%	1.33%	24,821	−0.107%	2.45%	7,157
98+ to Par	−0.003%	0.36%	757,521	−0.009%	0.62%	150,163	−0.030%	1.29%	34,498	−0.084%	2.22%	10,592
96+ to 98	−0.002%	0.66%	160,280	0.002%	1.07%	31,834	0.005%	2.19%	7,330	−0.088%	3.53%	2,270
94+ to 96	0.005%	0.80%	89,181	0.032%	1.45%	17,785	0.104%	2.90%	4,177	0.287%	4.84%	1,291
92+ to 94	0.009%	1.05%	55,075	0.079%	1.36%	10,964	0.266%	3.14%	2,573	0.771%	4.64%	823
90+ to 92	0.009%	1.37%	38,259	0.090%	2.17%	7,605	0.508%	3.64%	1,797	0.892%	7.47%	579
80+ to 90	0.024%	1.45%	103,138	0.123%	2.96%	20,638	0.518%	5.66%	4,884	1.501%	10.26%	1,634
70+ to 80	0.035%	2.15%	48,752	0.104%	4.51%	9,737	0.628%	8.66%	2,327	2.081%	15.13%	740
60+ to 70	0.057%	3.02%	30,818	0.320%	6.40%	6,175	1.022%	12.68%	1,456	2.928%	23.54%	472
50+ to 60	0.101%	3.94%	24,654	0.317%	7.46%	4,918	1.173%	15.04%	1,175	2.653%	24.45%	382
40+ to 50	−0.004%	5.03%	19,422	−0.105%	9.79%	3,854	−0.242%	16.39%	902	0.641%	32.87%	285
30+ to 40	0.136%	5.90%	19,447	0.408%	11.41%	3,876	1.332%	22.07%	909	7.626%	40.64%	282
20+ to 30	0.183%	8.47%	17,151	0.464%	15.17%	3,404	1.545%	30.22%	772	1.016%	47.56%	236
10+ to 20	0.293%	13.83%	24,399	0.859%	25.27%	4,835	2.923%	47.05%	1,102	10.464%	68.20%	325
0 to 10	1.717%	80.37%	36,754	2.206%	42.31%	7,287	5.682%	77.97%	1,680	8.782%	95.34%	514
North America	0.035%	11.82%	1,396,788	0.067%	6.82%	277,263	0.239%	13.72%	64,017	0.594%	19.09%	19,688
Europe		Not Applicable		0.044%	4.35%	72,956	0.171%	8.65%	16,688	0.373%	7.42%	5,048
Population	**0.039%**	**10.78%**	**1,981,826**	**0.074%**	**6.79%**	**393,032**	**0.237%**	**12.65%**	**90,403**	**0.590%**	**17.35%**	**27,582**

EXHIBIT 7.32

Percentile Price Changes Over Time By Initial Price Category.

0.1% Price Change 1% Price Change 5% Price Change / Sample Size

Initial Price Category	1-Day				7-Day				30-Day				90-Day			
	0.10%	1.00%	5.00%	Samples	0.10%	1.00%	5.00%	Samples	0.10%	1.00%	5.00%	Samples	0.10%	1.00%	5.00%	Samples
Par Plus	−1.13%	−0.25%	−0.02%	556,975	−3.01%	−0.66%	−0.20%	109,957	−7.02%	−1.50%	−0.56%	24,821	−19.88%	−3.73%	−0.99%	7,157
98+ to Par	−1.38%	−0.20%	0.00%	757,521	−3.95%	−0.76%	−0.13%	150,163	−9.34%	−2.04%	−0.44%	34,498	−19.60%	−4.76%	−1.01%	10,592
96+ to 98	−3.63%	−0.77%	0.00%	160,280	−7.75%	−2.27%	−0.51%	31,834	−17.53%	−5.33%	−1.54%	7,330	−30.42%	−13.40%	−3.63%	2,270
94+ to 96	−5.19%	−1.05%	0.00%	89,181	−11.99%	−3.16%	−0.71%	17,785	−40.93%	−7.37%	−2.40%	4,177	−55.17%	−16.32%	−5.21%	1,291
92+ to 94	−7.61%	−1.36%	0.00%	55,075	−13.98%	−3.79%	−1.08%	10,964	−23.91%	−8.28%	−3.23%	2,573		−18.48%	−7.46%	823
90+ to 92	−8.79%	−1.88%	−0.14%	38,259	−14.88%	−5.56%	−1.43%	7,605	−32.60%	−10.00%	−4.01%	1,797		−25.91%	−8.29%	579
80+ to 90	−12.50%	−2.72%	−0.29%	103,138	−29.41%	−7.85%	−2.35%	20,638	−44.54%	−17.71%	−6.83%	4,884	−86.60%	−35.04%	−11.77%	1,634
70+ to 80	−21.87%	−4.23%	−0.49%	48,752	−46.85%	−13.20%	−3.85%	9,737	−76.11%	−30.20%	−11.20%	2,327		−62.50%	−22.98%	740
60+ to 70	−27.54%	−7.30%	−0.90%	30,818	−43.36%	−17.00%	−6.25%	6,175	−83.33%	−39.25%	−16.67%	1,456		−85.29%	−41.67%	472
50+ to 60	−35.48%	−7.19%	−0.48%	24,654	−72.87%	−20.00%	−5.67%	4,918	−87.27%	−45.24%	−21.31%	1,175		−77.05%	−36.53%	382
40+ to 50	−57.14%	−10.00%	0.00%	19,422	−68.75%	−34.86%	−7.79%	3,854		−57.14%	−22.22%	902		−85.77%	−57.14%	285
30+ to 40	−42.86%	−9.09%	0.00%	19,447	−67.38%	−31.77%	−8.08%	3,876		−53.85%	−28.57%	909		−75.71%	−39.71%	282
20+ to 30	−51.70%	−10.79%	0.00%	17,151	−73.76%	−37.00%	−9.09%	3,404		−72.81%	−28.57%	772		−90.00%	−63.98%	236
10+ to 20	−50.00%	−9.38%	0.00%	24,399	−92.48%	−36.97%	−7.72%	4,835	−97.44%	−71.38%	−29.40%	1,102		−72.88%	−46.73%	325
0 to 10	−55.56%	−12.50%	0.00%	36,754	−94.59%	−33.33%	−4.16%	7,287	−100.00%	−62.99%	−29.41%	1,680		−97.60%	−53.95%	514
Population			/	1,981,826			/	393,032			/	90,403			/	27,582

These percentile price changes represent an estimate of the value at risk for a given loan within a given price category for the specified time frame. For example, the Markit Loans database has 757,521 daily price changes for loans priced between 98 and par. Of the loans priced between 98 and par, the 7,575th worst-performing loan (i.e., the worst 1 percent) lost 0.20 percent of its value, while the 757th worst-performing loan (i.e., the worst 0.1 percent) lost 1.38 percent of its value. These raw performance figures are used to estimate the daily value at risk for loans within the 98 to par pricing category. For a loan priced between 98 and par, the 100-day daily value at risk (DVaR) is estimated as 0.20 percent. That same loan is expected to decline 1.38 percent on the worst day in 1,000 days. Similarly, during the worst week in 100 weeks, a loan priced between 98 and par is expected to decline 0.76 percent (i.e., the worst 1 percent of the 150,163 seven-day performance figures).

As Exhibit 7.32 presents actual distributions, blank spaces indicate that no available data exist. For example, the worst 0.1 percent performance figure represents the worst performance in 1,000 days. Consequently, sample sizes of less than 1,000 cannot have a worst 0.1 percent performance figure.

Where the price change number for the exact percentile value did not exist, the number was interpolated directly from the adjacent values in the distribution. No values were extrapolated from the distribution.

Volatility of Loans Priced above Par

The logarithmic frequency distribution of 1-day and 90-day price changes for loans priced above par are presented in Exhibits 7.33 and 7.34.

While the charts address a variety of issues, the key characteristics of the charts are as follows:

1. *Relative scarcity of 90-day price volatilities.* The relative scarcity of 90-day price changes (Exhibit 7.34) compared to 1-day price changes (Exhibit 7.33) should be noted. It is the result of the nonoverlapping sample set. For example, a single loan priced all year long would produce 364 1-day price change samples. That same loan would produce only 4 90-day price change samples during the same period. Consequently, throughout this report, the 90-day sample size will be roughly 1/90th of its 1-day counterpart.

EXHIBIT 7.33

Loan price volatility, par+: 1–day.

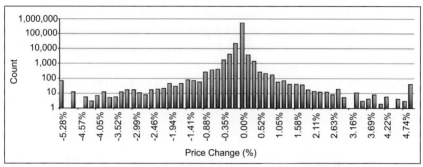

Source: Markit Group.

EXHIBIT 7.34

Loan price volatility, par+: 90–days.

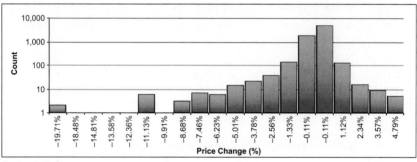

Source: Markit Group.

2. *Negative skew.* The distribution of both 1-day and 90-day price changes for loans priced above par is negatively skewed. The negative skew simply indicates that there are more negative price changes than positive price changes. This negative skew is primarily caused by refinancing risk and premium erosion.

   • *Refinancing risk.* Par-plus loans are often refinanced without penalty when an issuer's business prospects or overall loan market conditions improve and financing can be obtained with a reduced spread over LIBOR. The increased negative skew over the longer 90-day time period is expected, as the longer time frame entails more refinancing risk.

• *Premium erosion.* Loans with prices above par show
  negative average price changes as premium is eroded in
  exchange for greater coupon payments. Consequently,
  while above-par loans have a positive overall return
  because of interest payments, the average price change
  in this category must be negative. As this price erosion
  is greater over a longer time frame, there is a more pronounced negative skew in the distribution of 90-day
  price changes relative to the distribution of 1-day price
  changes.

Volatility of Loans Priced 98 to Par

The logarithmic frequency distributions of 1-day and 90-day price
changes of loans priced between 98 and par are presented in
Exhibits 7.35 and 7.36.

    As with Exhibits 7.33 and 7.34, Exhibit 7.35 depicts 1-day price
changes, while Exhibit 7.36 depicts 90-day price changes. While
the distribution is similar to the above-par distribution, there are
several key differences:

EXHIBIT 7.35

Loan price volatility, 98–100: 1-day.

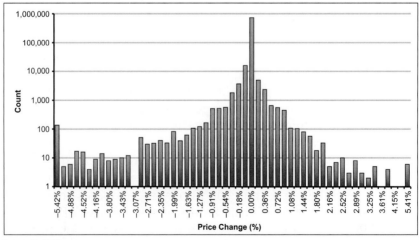

Source: Markit Group.

EXHIBIT 7.36

Loan price volatility, 98–100: 90-days.

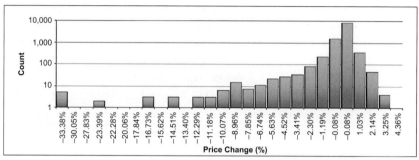

Source: Markit Group.

1. *More moderate negative 1-day skew.* Although the distribution of price changes for loans priced between 98 and par has a negative skew, its 1-day price change distribution is more normal than the distributions for loans above par. That is, there is a more even balance between positive and negative 1-day price changes in this price category.

2. *More pronounced negative 90-day skew.* For loans priced between 98 and par, the 90-day price change distribution skew is more negative than that for loans priced above par. A movement in loan price even slightly below par may foretell a more ominous future.

3. *Positive price change "ceiling" of 2 percent.* The distribution of price changes for loans priced between 98 and par has a pronounced curtailment of the positive price changes at just above 2 percent, corresponding to a loan trading at 98 moving to par pricing. The relatively fewer loans showing a more positive price movement presumably have call protection, allowing the price movement above par for a temporary period.

Volatility of Moderately Distressed Loans

The logarithmic frequency distributions of 1-day and 90-day price changes of loans priced between 80 and 90 are presented in Exhibits 7.37 and 7.38. One-day price changes are depicted in Exhibit 7.37,

EXHIBIT 7.37

Loan price volatility, 80–90: 1-day.

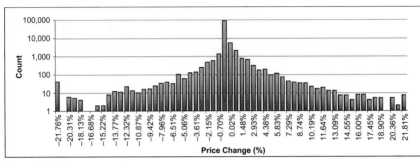

Source: Markit Group.

EXHIBIT 7.38

Loan price volatility, 80–90: 90-days.

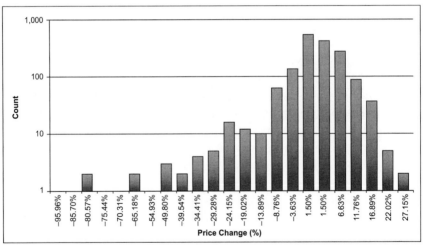

Source: Markit Group.

while 90-day price changes are presented in Exhibit 7.38. The distribution of price change volatility for even moderately distressed loans differs fundamentally from that of their par counterparts.

1. *More normal distribution.* Moderately distressed loans have a more symmetrical distribution of price changes. In short, the increased upside is made possible because the loans have room for the prices to increase to par.

2. *Positive price change to par "ceiling."* Like loans priced
   slightly below par, moderately distressed loans also evidence a par price ceiling. Given the stability of the asset
   class, this ceiling is less evident in the 1-day volatility
   than in the 90-day price change volatility. As the duration
   increases to 90 days, moderately distressed loans begin to
   show more negative skew. For example, a loan trading at
   80 could move up only 25 percent to par, while in the
   event of a bankruptcy, the same loan could fall to zero,
   for a negative price change of 100 percent.

Volatility of Severely Distressed Loans

The distribution of price volatility for severely distressed loans
differs significantly from that of their par counterparts. Unlike
loans priced between 80 and par, the distribution of price volatility for severely distressed loans demonstrates a strong positive
skew.

1. *Positively skewed distributions.* As demonstrated in the previous pages, par loans have negatively skewed distributions of price changes, and moderately distressed loans
   have relatively symmetrical distributions. However, as
   loans become more distressed, the distributions of price
   changes become positively skewed. This increased bias
   toward positive price changes is caused by both the lack
   of cash interest and the magnitude of the price drop
   from par.
   - *No cash interest compensation.* While par loan market
     participants are compensated through cash interest
     payments, distressed loan market participants receive
     returns primarily through price appreciation.
     Consequently, the returns to distressed loan market
     participants will be captured in a loan price volatility
     analysis, while the returns to a par loan market
     participant will not.
   - *Significant upside potential.* While par loans have only a
     few points of upside, the opposite is true of severely
     distressed loans. Consequently, the "par ceiling" that is
     visible in the distributions of performing loans is not
     as restricting in severely distressed loans.

EXHIBIT 7.39

Maximum and minimum 1-day percentage price change.

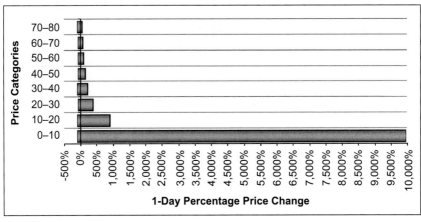

Source: Markit Group.

Exhibit 7.39 depicts the maximum and minimum 1-day percentage price changes for different distressed pricing categories. By focusing on the extremes, the chart ignores the breadth of distributions contained in previous graphs; however, it conveys the skew of price volatilities within the distressed categories more easily.

Analytics and Performance

Sean Kelley
Tall Tree Investment Management, LLC

Meredith Coffey
Senior Vice President
Reuters Loan Pricing Corp

William Deitrick
Vice President
Citigroup Global Market Inc.

Steven Bavaria
Vice President and Head, Syndicated Loan &
Recovery Ratings
Standard & Poor's

Neal Schweitzer
Moody's Investors Service

David Keisman
Moody's Investor Service

Steve Miller
Managing Director
Standard & Poor's Leveraged Commentary & Data

Sam DeRosa-Farag
Managing Director, Global Leveraged Finance Strategy
Credit Suisse

Analytics and Performance Overview

Sean Kelley
Tall Tree Investment Management, LLC

OVERVIEW

Since the beginning of time, it seems, humanity has derided lenders. Prophets and politicians, capitalists and communists, and individuals from any number of other dichotomous classes have found a common scapegoat in the banker. Aristotle, for one, believed that money "was intended to be used in exchange, but not to increase at interest." Income from lending, he thought, was "unnatural, and a mode by which men gain from one another." From Dickens's Scrooge to Tom Wolfe's Sherman McCoy, bankers in the English literary canon display callous disinterest in the human condition. The English social critic R. H. Tawney perhaps best summarized the common critique of lending as "contrary to nature, for it is to live without labour; it is to sell time, which belongs to God, for the advantage of wicked men." According to these arguments, the impious lender commits the sin of idleness. He shackles desperate men with debt and then reaps the rewards of their toil from his fancy marble office.

To counter this, lenders should launch a public relations campaign that describes the complexity, substantial risks, and analytical demands of loan portfolio management. Far from being idle, lenders today must out-hustle both alternative funding sources and nontraditional participants in the loan market. With competition, of course, absolute portfolio returns decline, and lenders search for relative advantages by conducting even more careful performance analysis. The ambitious lender does not just know his borrowers in isolation, but also understands how external variables affect his entire portfolio and ultimately produce a return above or below that of his peers.

In this section, we debunk many myths. We show that lenders very definitely labor at their profession. Those who embrace the leisure mode do not survive in a competitive environment fraught with risks. The winners not only work hard, but also work smart by employing many sophisticated techniques and heeding history. Moreover, the notion that lenders exploit borrowers falls flat once we consider the loan default and recovery experience.

Despite the risks, interest in the loan asset class has expanded exponentially in recent years as more investors have come to appreciate the positive return and volatility characteristics. Moreover, the dramatic improvement in secondary market liquidity over the last decade has not wrung out all opportunity. A portfolio manager who is willing to spend the time and dedicate the resources to fully understand past market behavior and individual investment decisions can outperform market indexes. In summary, the corporate loan market has attracted and should continue to attract industrious investors, and the image of the leisurely banker should fade from our collective consciousness.

Measuring Loan Returns

Meredith Coffey
Reuters Loan Pricing Corporation

As is the norm in the high-yield bond market, leveraged loan values are quoted as a percentage of par (or face value) in the secondary market. Though the LSTA has a series of pricing norms, there are two main quotes that are utilized in the secondary market: the bid is the price that a counterparty is theoretically willing to pay for a loan, and the ask or offer is the price for which a counterparty is theoretically willing to sell a loan. In addition, in calculating the value of loans, nonbank lenders may also use the "mean of mean," which is the average of the average bid and offer from a group of dealers that mark the loan.

Historically, most loans were neither bid nor traded above par. However, that has changed markedly: at the end of 2005, nearly 80 percent of multimark term loans in LSTA/LPC Mark-to-Market Pricing were bid at or above 100 cents on the dollar. When loans are bid and trade above par, this means that the actual spread on these loans has fallen below their contractual spread. However, the characteristics of loans can make calculating their yield somewhat tricky. For instance, the fact that most loans are freely callable at par at any time makes the concept of "yield to worst" a difficult one. For loans that trade above par, the yield to worst is generally, well, tomorrow. Moreover, if a freely callable loan is trading at a significant premium to par, the theoretical yield to worst on the loan is quite negative.

Because of the freely callable nature of leveraged loans, there are two main approaches to calculating the yield of a loan. The first is to calculate the yield to maturity. This requires valuing each future principal payment as well as each interest payment. The scheduled principal payments are documented in the loan's amortization schedule. (For many institutional term loans, this is 0.25 percent of the face value per quarter until the last year, when the quarterly amortization payment jumps to 25 percent of the outstanding amount.)

The interest payment is calculated by multiplying that period's "coupon" by the outstanding loan amount in the previous period. A period's coupon is that period's expected LIBOR plus the contractual spread on the loan. Once each period's payment is calculated, the yield is calculated using a discounted cash flow model that equates the secondary market price of the loan to the series of future cash flows. At that point, the inquirer solves for the discount rate and, then subtracts the appropriate LIBOR to calculate the secondary market loan spread.

However, there is a minor problem with this approach: it's simply not realistic. Almost no leveraged loans remain outstanding until maturity. For this reason, most market players take a more back-of-the-envelope approach and assume a maturity. (Favorite lengths for this exercise range from 18 months in a bullish market to as much as three years or more in a bearish one.) The yield calculated using an assumed tenor can be very different from a yield to maturity.

Consider the case of DirecTV, which closed a $1.5 billion, LIBOR + 150 term loan B in April 2005. The facility had a typical amortization schedule of 0.25 percent of face value for 30 quarters, and then a final bullet payment of $1.3875 billion at maturity in April 2013. At the end of 2005, DirecTV's term loan B enjoyed an average bid of 100.94 from a group of eight dealers.

If one used the yield to maturity calculation, the premium of 94 bps would be amortized over the course of more than seven years. In turn, the secondary market spread on the loan would be a tolerable (but not particularly lucrative) LIBOR + 135. However, the odds of DirecTV's loan remaining outstanding until 2013 are not high. If one assumed that the loan would be repaid at par in three years, the yield would fall to LIBOR + 117 bps. An expectation of a two-year maturity would pull the yield down to LIBOR + 101 bps. A one-year maturity would bring the yield down to LIBOR + 55 bps. So obviously, the assumed tenor plays a large role in what the analyst calculates the loan yield to be.

While the yield on a loan can be calculated in the straightforward fashion just described, the total return on a loan in a portfolio requires further work. For each measurement period, a manager needs to assess:

- *Realized gains or losses.* For instance, if a loan was bought above par and had an amortization payment at par, there would be a realized loss; conversely, if a loan was bought below par and repaid (or sold) at par, there would be a realized gain.
- *Unrealized gains or losses.* For instance, if a loan was bought above par and the price declined over the measurement period, there would be an unrealized loss; conversely, if a loan was bought below par and the price climbed over the measurement period, there would be an unrealized gain.
- *Scheduled interest payments.* These are simply the coupon payment described previously.
- *Fee payments.* These include amendment fees and other miscellaneous fees.

Consider the following situation: loan XYZ was purchased at the beginning of a month at 101.05; the face value was $9.939 million, and the price was $10.043 million. By the end of the month, the price of the loan had climbed to 101.34, creating an unrealized gain of $8,600, or 0.09 percent.

In addition, the loan paid interest of $46,000 and a fee of $2,450 during the month. The combined interest and fee payment totaled 0.51 percent. Furthermore, the manager—seeing a quick profit opportunity—sold $1.517 million of the loan mid-month at 101.225 and received $1.535 million, which translates to a realized gain of 0.20 percent.

Between the interest and fee payments and the realized and unrealized gains, the monthly return for the loan totaled 0.8 percent.

As this exercise illustrates, there are a number of ways to skin a cat (e.g., calculate the secondary market yield of a loan), as well as a number of factors to keep in mind when calculating the return on a loan.

Relative Value Analysis

William Deitrick
Vice President, Citigroup Global Market Inc.

A POWERFUL INVESTMENT TOOL

Comparing relative value between loans and bonds can be accomplished by adjusting for some differences between the two asset classes.

Relative value analysis is a powerful tool for investors in the leveraged loan and high-yield bond markets that is useful for identifying, evaluating, and executing spread arbitrage opportunities between loans and/or bonds of the same or comparable credits. Because leveraged loans and high-yield bonds are similar instruments in many ways, investors should consider them both and choose the one that provides the greatest potential benefit when contemplating taking on credit exposure to a company issuing debt.

While relative value analysis is as much of an art as a science, investors can make some quantifiable determinations about whether a loan or a bond offers a better value by evaluating some differences between the two from different perspectives. For general purposes, a good estimate of relative value can be determined by adjusting for the main difference between loans and bonds: the interest rate (see the next section of this article, "Fixed versus Floating Interest Rate").

Assessing the relative value of loans versus bonds requires adjustment for at least seven variables:

- Fixed rate versus floating rate
- Term
- Risk/return

- Recovery rates
- Interest-rate optionality
- Credit spread optionality
- Liquidity

FIXED VERSUS FLOATING INTEREST RATE

Interest rates on bonds are generally fixed, while those on loans are generally floating.

Loan and bond spreads are quoted using different interest-rate benchmarks. Bonds generally have a fixed interest rate with a spread quoted over a benchmark Treasury, while loans generally have a floating interest rate with a spread quoted over the benchmark LIBOR interest rate. To compare loans and bonds on the same interest-rate basis, the bond spread must be swapped from fixed to floating or vice versa. To swap a bond from fixed to floating rate, it is necessary to determine the appropriate swap rate for the bond's maturity and subtract that rate from the bond's fixed spread to get the floating-rate equivalent spread. For example, assume a ten-year bond yielding Treasuries + 400 bps. Assuming a ten-year swap spread of 80 bps, the bond can be converted to its floating-rate equivalent by subtracting 400 − 80 = a floating-rate spread of LIBOR + 320 bps.

TERM

Maturity differences affect the relative value of comparable securities.

The term of a loan or bond is the length of time until it matures and must be repaid. Often the maturity of a loan differs from that of the bond to which it is being compared. After adjusting the bond spread from a fixed rate to a floating rate, no further adjustment for the term structure of interest rates is necessary; however, an adjustment for the term structure of credit spreads remains. This adjustment is really a subjective assessment of credit risk over a longer duration. For example, in comparing a ten-year bond to a seven-year loan, an assumption could be made that extending the credit curve an extra three years is worth 25 bps of spread. The greater the credit risk of the issuer, the larger the adjustment might be.

Industry peculiarities may influence relative value spreads, so investors considering credits should take into account their respective industries. Interpolating the difference between maturities on this credit curve produces a more accurate estimation.

RISK/RETURN

Volatility affects investment returns and can be quantified.

Leveraged loans have historically demonstrated lower price volatility and higher risk-adjusted returns (using Sharpe ratios, recovery rates, or price volatility) than high-yield bonds, stocks, or Treasuries. Exhibit 8.1 shows bid price levels for leveraged loans and high-yield bonds during the period from 2001 to April 2005. As shown in this exhibit, average bond prices fluctuated from 82 to 102 during the selected period, while loans remained within a couple of points of par. Given that this graph captures a period of high default rates, which reached over 10 percent on a rolling 12-month basis at their worst, we believe that it is an important example of the relative stability of loans versus bonds (see the default rate chart in Exhibit 8.2). A factor contributing to the low price volatility of loans is superior recovery rates resulting from senior secured claims on issuers' assets as shown in Exhibit 8.3, which outlines recovery rates.

EXHIBIT 8.1

High Yield Bonds and Double B Rates Institutional Loans – Average Bid Prices.

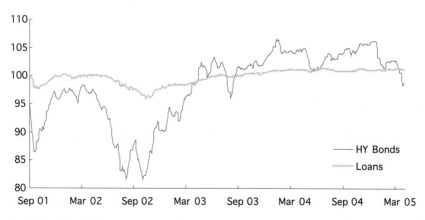

Source: Standard & Poor's.

EXHIBIT 8.2

Historical Recovery Rates, 1988–2003 vs. 1998–2002.

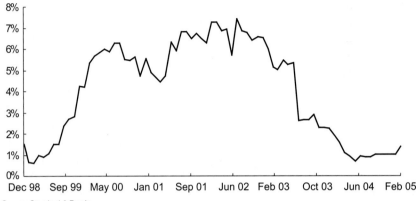

Source: Standard & Poor's

EXHIBIT 8.3

Updated Loan Recovery.

	1982–2004	1998–2003	2004
Loans	77.5	74.1	95.4
Senior Secured Notes	57.4	48.6	80.8
Senior Unsecured Notes	44.9	32.9	50.1
Senior Subordinated Notes	39.1	29.9	44.4
Subordinated Notes	32.0	22.4	NA
Junior Subordinated Notes	28.9	20.8	NA

NA Not available.
Note: 2,256 defaulted loans and bond issues that defaulted between 1987 and 2003.
746 defaulted loans and bond issues that defaulted between 1998 and 1992.
Recoveries are discounted at each instrument's predefault interest rate.
Source: S&P/PMD LossStats(TM) Database.

RECOVERY RATES

Loans have higher recovery rates, which improve their value and can be quantified.

The recovery rate shown in Exhibit 8.3, defined as the percentage of par value returned to the bondholder or loan investor in a default situation, is a function of several variables: the overall state of the economy, the market for corporate assets, the seniority of the issue within the issuer's capital structure, and the quality of the collateral. While the likelihood of default for various debt obligations of the same issuer is roughly the same, these obligations are readily differentiated by the severity of the loss from default, which depends heavily on seniority and collateral. In comparison to bonds, loans have superior recovery rates when the probability of default is the same (e.g., for the same issuer). The higher recovery rate for bank loans is primarily the result of seniority, collateral, covenants, and the provisions of credit agreements.

A recent (November 2003) study of bank loans in bankruptcy by Moody's Investors Service indicated an average bank loan recovery rate of 77.5 percent, versus an average of 64.7 percent for senior secured bonds, 41.5 percent for senior unsecured bonds, and 30.7 percent for subordinated bonds. In addition, collateral also plays an important role in determining the postdefault recovery that bank loan investors may realize. The most liquid collateral (accounts receivable, cash, and inventory) produces the highest average recovery rate, about 90 percent.

To recognize the significant difference between the recovery rates for bondholders and bank loan investors, it is necessary to make an adjustment to the spread for relative value analysis. If the loan is secured, there is an additional adjustment for the type of supporting collateral, allowing an estimation of recovery rates segmented by collateral type. In general, collateral is broadly classified into four categories: property, plant and equipment; accounts receivable/inventory; stock of subsidiaries; and all assets.

Expected loss calculations can be used to quantify the impact of default and recovery on the value of a security.

Combining the default rate assumption with the recovery rate assumption produces an expected loss assumption. For example, suppose the recovery rate analysis suggests that the loan would recover 80 percent, whereas the bond would recover 45 percent. If the default rate assumption from the historical transition matrix were 2 percent per annum, the expected loss on the loan would be 40 bps per annum versus an expected loss of 110 bps per annum for the bond. Consequently, an investor might ascribe a value of 70 bps per annum to the seniority and security of a loan.

The limitation of this approach, in our opinion, lies in the assumption that the default probability for different debt obligations is the same. In fact, the nature of the debt obligation conveyed in covenants may affect the likelihood of default. For example, a bank loan may have a more restrictive set of covenants that allows lenders to intervene in the company's affairs at an earlier stage of developing credit risk than the indenture of a public bond issue would allow. This early warning may allow the lenders enough flexibility to take mitigating actions, such as shoring up the collateral position or reducing exposure. From this perspective, the bank loan with tighter covenants can produce higher recovery rates than the average numbers.

INTEREST-RATE OPTIONALITY

Bonds are exposed to changes in market interest rates because of their fixed-rate nature, which can affect their value either positively or negatively.

Bonds are typically noncallable by the issuer for an initial period after a deal is done, usually five years. After the noncallable period expires, the issuer has the option to pay a call premium, which usually declines over time. Because most bonds earn a fixed rate of interest, the bond investor is exposed to an interest-rate option. In other words, if rates have tightened sufficiently because of market activity, the issuer has the ability to call the bonds and issue others at a lower rate; investors in floating-rate loans do not bear this interest-rate risk. The value of this interest-rate option can be estimated by pricing a cancelable swap with the same term and call structure as the bond. For example, assume a 10NC5 interest-rate swap, with a call premium that starts at half of the coupon in year 5 and steps down to zero in equal installments by the end of year 8.

This interest-rate optionality can also be valued by calculating the value of the call premium on the bond. This premium is then stripped out of the actual spread to compute the option-adjusted spread. To most accurately reflect the value of this premium, an American call option can be used to account for the fact that the holder is exposed to interest-rate risk for the entire life of the call period (see Exhibit 8.4).

EXHIBIT 8.4

Call period.

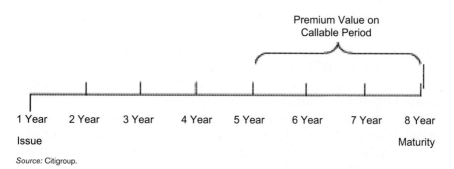

Source: Citigroup.

This process involves constructing a zero curve to be used for benchmarking, as well as assuming some levels for base volatilities. Taking into account the available strike dates and prices, the value of this option can be estimated fairly accurately. If the bond is not callable, then the bondholder is not exposed to the interest-rate risk, and no adjustment is needed.

CREDIT SPREAD OPTIONALITY

The callable feature of loans means that issuers can repay or refinance them when they choose.

Because loans are usually callable immediately, the investor is exposed to a credit spread call option for a longer period of time on a loan than on a bond. The company's decision to call will be based on an assessment of whether the company can access loan funds more cheaply because of improved market conditions, an improvement in the company's creditworthiness, and/or the availability of excess cash to pay down loans. The available cheaper market loan spread must be sufficient to compensate the issuer for bank syndication fees, legal and accounting costs, and management time dedicated to structuring and syndicating the new facility.

Such refinancing costs largely depend on the complexity of the deal transaction, the purpose of refinancing (whether it is acquisition-related or not), and the associated risks. While some fees, such as up-front fees, can be tracked, underwriting fees are never disclosed in the industry and are basically set by negotiation among agent banks. To our knowledge, the best estimate is a wide range from 175 to 250 bps for BBB- or below. Some loans have embedded pricing grids, allowing spread tightening or widening in certain circumstances without issuing new loans. Often, these grids are tied to leverage measures or credit ratings from the rating agencies. Roughly speaking, the refinancing cost to an issuer can range from 100 to 300 bps in the high-yield loan market.

Reasons for refinancing a loan include mergers and acquisitions, improved credit and/or market conditions, recapitalizations, and so on. Some call situations are virtually unforeseeable and must be examined on an individual basis. In some cases, companies may seek refinancing even if they will incur a loss. For these reasons, we would use a simple option pricing model to calculate the call value, assuming that the current spread and spread volatility should fairly reflect market perceptions and thus produce a fair value.

The embedded call option of a loan resembles an American call option, with the expiration date equal to the maturity date of the loan. The strike price is equal to the spread minus the amortized amount of the aforementioned refinancing cost over the call period (the loan period). For example, assume that the spread on a five-year loan is LIBOR + 250 bps, and further assume that the refinancing cost is 200 bps. Also assume that the annual amortization cost is 40 bps, and the strike price is 210 bps. If the spread tightens to 205 bps, the option will be in the money. Once the company calls the loan, the annual savings is 5 bps.

Because there is no secondary market for loan options, we derive the volatility from the historical daily volatility for corporate bonds. An illustration of our approach is as follows: spread is a function of the default rate and the recovery rate. Symbolically,

$$\text{Spread} = \text{default rate} \times (1 - \text{recovery rate})$$

Further assume that loans and bonds issued by the same issuer are subject to roughly the same default rate. Therefore,

$$\text{Volatility of loans} = \text{volatility of bonds} \times (1 - \text{recovery rate of loans})/(1 - \text{recovery rate of bonds})$$

The lower volatility of loans relative to bonds is consistent with our intuition that the extra protection provided by the seniority and collateral, as well as the loan covenants, indicates more predictable payments relative to bonds.

"Windfalls" Resulting from Imperfect Correlation

Because interest rates and credit spreads do not necessarily rise or fall in tandem, under certain circumstances bond investors may receive a "windfall" relative to loan investors. For example, if rates fall as credit spreads widen, the bond is likely to be called at par or better, whereas the loan will remain in place. If we assume that the call option on the bond was fairly priced, and thus that the investor received a fair price for interest-rate risk, the bond investor will have enjoyed a windfall by avoiding the consequences of spread widening suffered by the loan investor. If interest rates rise and credit spreads tighten, the loan is likely to be called, while the bond will remain in place. Again, the bond investor has a windfall gain, this time by enjoying the benefits of credit spread tightening while the loan investor does not.

Introduction: Rating Agencies in the Loan Market

Steven Bavaria
Standard & Poor's

BACKGROUND

Until recently, credit ratings and rating agencies played little role in the loan market. By providing transparency, credit ratings allow a broad audience of potential investors to understand a credit and become comfortable with the risk, regardless of whether the investor has direct knowledge of, or a relationship with, the borrower. In the bond market (or any *efficient* public debt market), ratings are necessary if large numbers of investors are to make credit, pricing, and buy-sell decisions about thousands of different debt instruments in both primary and secondary markets.

It was precisely because ratings provide this transparency that, until recently; banks had no interest in having their loans rated. Traditional "buy-and-hold" banking was (and still is) a classic *inefficient* debt market. Bank lenders did their own credit analysis and developed close relationships with their borrowers. They originated loans and held those loans on their own books until maturity, playing the role of both intermediary and investor. They benefited from the fact that other potential lenders did not have their exclusive knowledge about the credit of the borrower or the details of the deal itself. A rating that enabled others to understand the credit and therefore compete for the deal would only have undermined the bank's own competitive advantage with respect to that credit. The lack of a rating also kept the borrower at a competitive disadvantage. Without a clear idea of its own creditworthiness, which a rating provides, a borrower had no way to judge whether it was getting the best deal it was entitled to from its bank. First, it could not compare itself to other credits. But even if it could, with no transparency (i.e., outside research) available on other loans in the marketplace, the borrower would not be able to compare the terms it was receiving from its bank with the terms being offered to similarly rated borrowers by that bank or by other banks in the market.

TRANSPARENCY COMES TO THE LOAN MARKET

Bankers' motivations (along with their attitudes toward credit ratings and outside third-party research) changed once the loan market began to resemble a "real" market. As institutional investors [e.g., bank loan funds and securitized loan pools like collateralized loan obligations (CLOs) and collateralized debt obligations (CDOs)] became significant loan market participants, the role of the major syndicating banks changed from that of "buy-and-hold" lenders to that of true underwriters and intermediaries. Instead of being motivated to maximize the interest-rate spread on the loan, the lead banks' primary incentive became maximizing the fees earned for securing and executing mandates. That meant making sure that the loans were widely and successfully distributed at whatever interest-rate spread cleared the market.

In this new environment, syndicating banks have a different attitude toward credit ratings and outside research in general. They now view them positively as a means of encouraging additional investor groups to enter the loan market and become comfortable with credits that they would not otherwise be familiar with. Other types of outside research that provide information about deal terms and spreads have also been welcomed, since they—in conjunction with credit ratings—have allowed syndicators and loan market participants to benchmark new deals and price them in the context of other loans with similar terms and credit parameters.

The rise of the secondary market in loan trading, often by the same institutions that actively underwrite and syndicate loans in the primary market, has also contributed to the demand for loan ratings. If a loan is rated initially, and the rating is actively monitored and updated throughout the life of the loan, this means that there will be more potential loan market participants who are ready and able to consider buying into the loan than there would be if such coverage were lacking. This additional liquidity can be valuable to the initial buyers in primary syndication. Some early data have shown that loans that are rated have been more likely to "flex" in the borrower's favor than unrated loans, probably because of the greater certainty of potential secondary market resale of rated versus unrated loans.[1]

This evolution in the loan market, like any fundamental paradigm shift in market behavior, has resulted in both winners and losers. The winners have clearly been the large banks that have made the leap to being underwriters and traders, thus shifting their focus from earning spreads on holding loans to earning fees for trading and underwriting them. Other beneficiaries have been (1) the borrowers themselves, who now have many more potential loan syndicators and investors competing for their loans, (2) nonrelationship loan market participants (e.g., bank loan funds, CDOs, and so on), which now have access to credits that they previously never could have bought as well as secondary liquidity if they need

---

[1] More studies over a longer time period are needed to fully validate this. In the hyperliquidity of the recent loan market (2005), unrated and/or poorly rated credits have been made to pay less of a penalty than they probably would have in the past and will again when the credit cycle turns to a less forgiving one.

an exit, and, of course, (3) the providers of transparency (the credit rating agencies, loan research shops of all types, the trade press, and so on). Losers include (1) primarily the smaller or more traditional buy-and-hold banks, which have not been able to position themselves as underwriters/syndicators and are now competing for loans (in many cases at lower spreads) with a much wider set of other potential lenders, and (2) those borrowers that enjoyed the intimacy with, and control over, their lenders that the traditional buy-and-hold loan market provided to them.

Another major driver in the demand for loan ratings has been the growth in securitized loan vehicles, like CDOs. The debt issued by these vehicles is generally rated and sold into the institutional private placement market. The ratings on CDO debt are generally a function of the ratings on the individual loans that make up that CDO's portfolio, along with other factors, such as diversification by borrower and by industry. As the number of CDOs has increased and the consequent demand by CDO managers for loans to fill their CDO portfolios has grown, almost every new syndicated loan can count on ending up in the portfolio of a number of CDOs. This has driven the demand for ratings on the underlying loans, since CDO managers considering a new loan to include in their portfolio need to know the rating on the new loan in order to gauge the overall impact of that loan on the rating of the entire CDO.

LOAN RATING SCALES

By the end of 2005, about 75 percent of all new leveraged loans were being rated prior to syndication, generally by both of the major rating companies: Moody's and Standard & Poor's. Ten years ago virtually no loans were being rated, so this has been a major shift that has essentially mirrored the evolution in the loan market chronicled elsewhere in this book.

Loan ratings are different from traditional bond ratings in that they go beyond the risk of default on timely payment that is the focus of most bond ratings.[2] Most leveraged loans are

---

[2] Moody's has a more nuanced definition of its traditional bond rating than does Standard & Poor's, whose traditional rating is a "pure" default rating. Please refer to the following articles covering each rating company for more detail.

secured, and the credit rating attempts to capture not only the risk of the borrower's failing to make payment (i.e., the default risk), but also the likelihood of recovery in the event of default. In order to do that, the loan rating analysis includes an evaluation of the collateral, covenants, and any other protective features that may exist. Bankers traditionally referred to these features as the "second way out," and the goal of the loan rating is to evaluate how effective they may be in the event that the borrower defaults and lenders have to actually rely upon them for payment.

Rating agencies express the result of their loan rating analysis in several ways. For many years, both Moody's and Standard & Poor's have utilized their traditional letter-based rating scales,[3] but have also engaged in a practice often referred to as "notching" to adjust the rating of a secured loan higher than the rating of an unsecured or less secured bond or note. As a result, the various debt instruments within a borrower's capital structure may have different ratings that reflect the differing expectations that the rating agencies have about their likely potential recoveries in the event of default.

RECOVERY RATINGS

In order to separate the risk of a borrower's defaulting from the expected loss and/or recovery in the event of default more clearly, there has been interest in recent years in ratings that would express the likely loss and/or recovery by itself in a totally separate and transparent manner. As a result, Standard & Poor's introduced a separate and distinct recovery rating two years ago (December 2003), as a companion to its existing Bank Loan Rating, and has assigned such a rating to over 1,000 loans. Fitch, a smaller rating company that also rates some loans, introduced its own recovery rating in the third quarter of 2005.[4] Moody's has announced its intention to launch a competing product in 2006.

---

[3] Standard & Poor's scale utilizes AAA, AA+, AA, AA-, A+, A, and so on; Moody's scale uses Aaa, Aa1, Aa2, Aa3, A1, A2, and so on.

[4] Standard & Poor's recovery rating uses a numerical scale (1+, 1, 2, 3, 4, 5). Fitch's recovery rating scale is somewhat similar (1, 2, 3, 4, 5, 6).

Standard & Poor's Loan Recovery Ratings

Steven Bavaria
Vice President and Head, Syndicated Loan & Recovery Ratings
Standard & Poor's

Standard & Poor's rates the loans of over 1,300 companies, of which the total outstanding loan amount exceeds $1 trillion. Many of the rated loans are secured by collateral, which provides an additional source of repayment in case the borrower's primary source—cash flow from its business operations—proves insufficient and it defaults on loan payments. As Exhibit 8.5 shows, most secured loans experience complete or substantial recovery of principal and interest following a workout or bankruptcy, whereas with others (fortunately a distinct minority), secured lenders fare little better than unsecured lenders. Standard & Poor's introduced its bank loan and recovery ratings primarily to assist bankers and investors in differentiating the more effectively secured loans from those that are less well secured or, indeed, may be "secured" in name only.

E X H I B I T   8 . 5

Identifying better secured loans

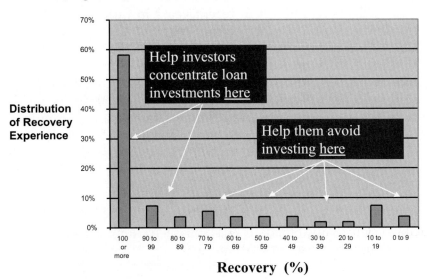

Recovery (%)

Loan ratings help investors evaluate likely loss and recovery in the event of default.

TWO TYPES OF LOAN RATINGS

Standard & Poor's provides two types of ratings on secured loans:

- *Loan ratings*, which focus on *both* the risk of default *and* the likelihood of ultimate recovery in the event of default. These ratings are assigned on the traditional rating scale (i.e., AAA to D) and can be notched up from the borrower's corporate credit rating, if the collateral security is expected to provide lenders with a full (i.e., 100 percent) recovery of principal.
- *Recovery ratings*, which focus *solely* on the likelihood of loss and recovery in the event of default. These ratings are assigned on a numerical scale, with 1+ indicating the highest expected likelihood of recovery and 5 representing the lowest.

The *pure* risk of default is captured in the traditional corporate credit rating (CCR), which focuses solely on the overall creditworthiness of the issuer. In assigning a loan rating, Standard & Poor's credit analysts look to see whether there is collateral security or some other enhancement that would enable investors to achieve ultimate recovery even if the loan defaults. If they determine that 100 percent of the principal is likely to ultimately be repaid, then they will notch up the loan (i.e., rate it higher than the issuer's corporate credit rating) by one or more notches. The greater the likelihood of recovery, the more Standard & Poor's may notch up the loan, with three (or, rarely, more) notches denoting a loan whose collateral security coverage is considered to be extremely protective.

The majority (about two-thirds) of the secured loans that Standard & Poor's rates are not notched up, and therefore receive a loan rating that is the same as the borrower's corporate credit rating. To provide additional transparency to the recovery prospects of these unnotched loans, Standard & Poor's introduced its recovery rating in December 2003 as a companion rating to its loan rating, and has, to date, assigned this rating to over 1,300 loan facilities. Currently, Standard & Poor's assigns *both* a loan rating (which may or may not be notched up from the corporate credit rating) and a recovery rating to secured loans that it rates.

E X H I B I T   8 . 6

Bank Loan & Recovery Ratings versus Traditional Corporate Ratings.

Standard & Poor's Recovery Ratings	Recovery Expectation	Relationship with Existing Bank Loan Rating Notching
1+ Highest expectation of *full* recovery of principal	100% of principal	CCR + 3 notches
1 High expectation of *full* recovery of principal	100% of principal	CCR + 1 or 2 notches
2 *Substantial* recovery of principal	80–100% of principal	BLR = CCR (Unnotched)
3 *Meaningful* recovery of principal	50–80% of principal	BLR = CCR (Unnotched)
4 *Marginal* recovery of principal	25–50% of principal	BLR = CCR (Unnotched)
5 *Negligible* recovery of principal	0–25% of principal	BLR = CCR (Unnotched)

Exhibit 8.6 shows the relationship between Standard & Poor's recovery ratings and the existing notched or unnotched loan rating.

DEFINITION OF RECOVERY

Standard & Poor's loan rating analysis uses the concept of *nominal recovery*, that is, it does not discount the repayment received at the end of the workout period or bankruptcy to calculate a present value at the time of default or some other point in the past. "Full recovery of principal" means that 100 percent of the par amount of principal outstanding is received after a typical workout or bankruptcy period of no more than 24 months maximum. Standard & Poor's believes that basing its loan ratings on a nominal recovery calculation makes the ratings more transparent and more easily validated against later empirical experience. Because the users of loan ratings include many different constituencies (banks, institutional investors, regulators, specialized vehicles, vulture funds, and so on) with different accounting and reporting policies for distressed loans, Standard & Poor's believes that it is simpler and less potentially confusing to provide ratings based on nominal recovery expectations and let the users apply whatever discounting or statistical adjustments are appropriate to their needs, rather than try to adopt a particular adjustment or discounting methodology that may not be appropriate for all. That would require some users to reverse-engineer Standard & Poor's methodology to get back to a nominal recovery base to then apply their own statistical adjustments.

BANK LOAN RATINGS: THE ANALYTICS[5]

There are several distinct factors that determine the bank loan and recovery ratings that are assigned to a particular secured loan. These are

- The value of the collateral security
- The amount of the loan being secured in relation to the value of the collateral security ("loan to value")
- The degree of access to and control over the collateral security that the lender exercises

Most of the analytical "heavy lifting" goes into the determination of the collateral valuation. Analysts first determine what a specific borrower's likely "path to default" would be, based on an analysis of its cash flow projections and the key operating factors that could most likely lead to default. The analysis does not suggest that the borrower necessarily *will* default (since it is the corporate credit rating that determines the *likelihood* of default), but only poses the question: "If this borrower were to default, what would the most likely scenario be?" Default scenarios may vary widely from borrower to borrower, reflecting different industry characteristics as well as individual issuer credit characteristics. Obviously, the higher the borrower's corporate credit rating, and therefore the more remote its prospects of default, the more challenging it is to define a realistic default scenario.[6]

---

[5] Please refer to Standard & Poor's publication "A Guide to the Loan Market" for a more detailed description of S&P's bank loan and recovery rating methodology.

[6] This leads to the ironic, but totally logical, result that many highly rated borrowers may end up receiving lower recovery ratings on their loans than borrowers with lower corporate credit ratings. This reflects the fact that highly rated companies are, by definition, less likely to default and would therefore have to undergo more serious or even catastrophic business reversals in order to arrive on bankruptcy's doorstep than would lower-rated companies. The latter's ratings may reflect their shaky financial structure and therefore might require only a modest change of fortune to induce default, in which case secured creditors would still have a healthy business to salvage.

Once the default scenario is established, then the analyst esti-mates the cash flow of the company at that time in order to deter-mine what the likely value of the company would be, based on a discounted cash flow, market multiples, or other appropriate valu-ation methodology. In cases where secured creditors hold collateral in the form of discrete assets, as opposed to the entire business enterprise, then specific valuation techniques more appropriate to the particular assets would be used.

The type and quality of the collateral (i.e., receivables; current assets; all assets; property, plant, and equipment; stock in sub-sidiaries; intangibles; and so on) are critical because they determine how much stress the secured assets can absorb and still hold their value. In general, the more liquid or predictable the value of a given collateral package is, the less it needs to be analytically "haircut" (i.e., stressed) to arrive at its simulated value in a default scenario. The amount of the collateral, as opposed to its type and quality, is equally critical. Standard & Poor's LossStats data demonstrate that all types of collateral security, even if of lower quality and less liq-uid, can be effective in protecting creditors if there is enough of the collateral in relation to the loan to provide a substantial cushion to absorb shrinkage in value. Other things being equal, lower-quality collateral would have to be stressed more than higher-quality collateral to achieve the same level of expected recovery.

The third factor focuses on the issue of access to and control over the collateral by the secured lender. The tighter the monitor-ing and control of the collateral by the lender, the greater the like-lihood that, in the event of default, the loan investors will actually benefit from the protection against loss that they were counting on when the loan was first made. Two loans with similar collateral security, but where one was an asset-based loan with tight moni-toring and control over the collateral and the cash cycle generated thereby, and the other was a more traditional secured leveraged loan with less rigid monitoring, would be likely to be rated differ-ently, even though in theory they had the same collateral protec-tion. The first might be rated three or (rarely) more notches above the borrower's corporate credit rating, reflecting a very strong likelihood of full recovery. The second might be rated one or two notches above the corporate credit rating, which still indicates a likelihood of full recovery, but not as strong a likelihood as for the first loan. The difference between the two does not reflect doubt about the second loan's collateral value, but rather reflects the concern that with fewer controls over the collateral, there was more chance of its "leakage" into cash that might accrue to the benefit of other creditors, especially in the weeks or months just prior to default, when a company is typically scrambling for cash.

Bank loan ratings that are notched higher than the corporate credit rating, regardless of how many notches, suggest an expected 100 percent recovery of principal. The difference is in the degree of confidence that Standard & Poor's has in that outcome, with three notches denoting "highest expectation" of full recovery and one and two notches denoting "high expectation" of full recovery.

Likewise, recovery ratings of 1+ and 1 both indicate expected recovery of 100 percent of principal, with the 1+ rating indicating the "highest expectation" and the 1 indicating "high expectation."

As noted previously, bank loan ratings that are unnotched and therefore the same as the corporate credit rating reflect Standard & Poor's opinion that lenders will not experience a full recovery in the event of default. For loans that are unnotched, investors must look to the recovery rating for a more explicit opinion of the expected recovery in the event of default.

EMPIRICAL DATA AND MARKET PRACTICE

Standard & Poor's bank loan and recovery rating methodology has been developed around what we believe to be market practice in secured lending, and is supported by the loss and recovery research of Standard & Poor's LossStats Database group. At present, Standard & Poor's believes that its recovery rating categories (with 1+ and 1 denoting different degrees of confidence regarding full recovery expectations, and 2, 3, 4, and 5 denoting various levels of partial recovery) provide sufficient latitude to differentiate among the various quality levels in the secured lending market. Over time, as more data are collected and the state of the credit art improves to the point where analysts (at Standard & Poor's and elsewhere) have tools to project losses and recoveries more precisely, we may redefine and expand the loan rating categories and/or add additional rating nomenclature (most likely through the use of additional pluses and minuses in the recovery rating scale). Typically, the spectrum of secured loans contains a number of different levels of security:

- Asset-based loans, which combine strong collateral with tight monitoring and control of the assets and the cash they generate
- Loans secured by strong collateral (all assets, current assets, and so on) and having conservative loan-to-value coverage, often with subordinated debt helping to provide an additional cushion for secured lenders
- Loans secured by strong collateral (all assets, current assets, and so on), but with more aggressive loan-to-value ratios, often reflecting the lack of subordinated or other significant junior debt to provide a cushion for collateral shrinkage
- Loans secured by assets that, while tangible, present less likelihood of retaining significant value independent of the issuer's business itself
- Loans that are secured with marginal or less tangible assets, stock in operating subsidiaries, and other assets that are expected to represent minimal value as a "second way out" in the event of default or bankruptcy
- "Second lien" loans, where the lender, while secured by collateral, has a junior position with respect to that collateral and may find its security position to be severely eroded or even eliminated in a default scenario

Standard & Poor's LossStats Database substantiates distinct ultimate recovery expectations for these different loan structure profiles. Loans that have traditionally enjoyed the benefits of the "virtuous circle" of high-quality assets as security and a significant cushion of unsecured or subordinated debt beneath the secured debt have experienced high rates of recovery and greater consistency of return, as measured by a relatively low standard deviation. In contrast, loans with undistinguished collateral combined with less cushion for secured creditors have fared significantly worse in terms of average level of recovery value and the consistency of the outcome.

The latter issue—the consistency of recovery—has implications for bank loan and recovery ratings and what they mean. Empirical data suggest that some of the loans that are not notched, and indeed, many that fall into the middle or bottom of the recovery rating categories, will actually experience higher recoveries than the descriptions of those rating categories suggest. But the quality of those loans' collateral security and/or their aggressive loan-to-value ratio make the predictability and dependability of such an outcome highly speculative.

USE IN THE MARKETPLACE

Standard & Poor's Bank Loan Ratings and Recovery Ratings, when used in conjunction with its Corporate Credit Ratings, are designed to provide bankers and loan investors with an opinion as to the likelihood of the issuer's defaulting in timely payment, and a further opinion of the likelihood of ultimate repayment in the event of default. This allows lenders to evaluate the two dimensions of a loan's credit risk—the risk of default in making timely payment, and the amount of loss to be suffered if such default occurs—independent of each other. This is important to most banks and institutional investors, as their risk capital allocation systems explicitly isolate the two dimensions ("default frequency" and "loss in event of default") in their calculation of required reserves and capital adequacy.

Loan Loss Given Default: Trends to Consider

Neal Schweitzer
Moody's Investors Service

David Keisman
Moody's Investor Service

Considering the sea change that has occurred in the syndicated leveraged loan marketplace over the past decade, institutional investors believe it valuable to identify and analyze new factors that will affect bank loan recovery rates. It is similarly useful to expose those factors that we believe will not affect loan ultimate recovery rates over the near term.

WHAT WE ARE SEEING NOW: PART 1

"Toto, I've a feeling we're not in 2000–2001 anymore."

The aphorism that generals train to fight the last war may apply equally to today's loan investors, because distressed investors are behaving as though they are reliving the last binge/bust loan cycle. The downside of that cycle started in late 1998 with an escalation of loan default rates, and accelerated in early 2001 (according to National Bureau of Economic Research) when the economy entered a recession. The current macroeconomic environment is fairly benign, combining a low default rate with healthy economic indicators. Even though a growing number of market commentators are anticipating an increase in loan defaults sooner rather than later, buyers of both performing and distressed paper seem to believe that the next default cycle will result in loan recoveries mirroring those of the last cycle.

The uncoupling of default cycles from economic recession cycles (in the last downturn, the recession started a couple of years after the default cycle) indicates the limited utility of linking loan loss given defaults (LGD) with a macroeconomic cycle. In fact, to date, analysis from a variety of sources has failed to demonstrate any robust linkage between macroeconomic variables and ultimate LGD for bank loans.

What *has* been demonstrated is that ultimate LGD for loans is best determined by evaluating the quality of a loan's structure. This has three main components:

1. Quality of collateral is not the estimated market value of distressed companies' assets, but the much more easily ascertained category of collateral supporting a loan. These categories range fro533m "highest" (encompassing all assets or loans legally secured by current assets) through loans supported by noncurrent assets, second liens, capital stock of operating entities, and, at the "lowest" level, unsecured bank facilities.

2. Debt cushion is defined as the amount of bank and bond debt contractually subordinated to an instrument as a percentage of an obligor's total debt. For example, if a company has a $300 million fully secured term loan outstanding and has issued $200 million in senior unsecured bonds and $500 million in subordinated bonds, the bank

debt would have a 70 percent debt cushion, the senior
bond debt would have a 50 percent debt cushion, and the
subordinated debt would have no debt cushion.

3. Active bank management is a proxy phrase for the consistently higher recovery rates earned by bank loans compared to similarly structured public bonds. Banks can, and do, monitor obligors more closely than do trustees of public debt. And, with the inclusion of certain covenants in loan documentation, banks have the ability to force a default more quickly, with the aim of securing greater value from a distressed borrower.

We reviewed loans rated by Moody's Investors Service to determine if these structuring issues had changed significantly over the last couple of years and observed the following.

Quality of Collateral

The emergence of second lien loans as a significant financing tool has been frequently discussed. This increase has indeed been robust: from under $100 million in volume rated by Moody's in 2001 and under $250 in 2002 to an estimated $12 billion in volume rated by Moody's in 2005. Nonetheless, the 2005 volume still accounts for just slightly more than 5 percent of the volume of all leveraged loans rated last year. Given the large volume of second lien loans and their importance to participating investors, we will continue to monitor these loans' behavior in distress and default.

However, a much greater influence on total LGD rates will be exerted by the percentage of rated loan volume secured by all of the assets of the borrower.

Debt Cushion

A strong influx of all-bank-debt deals may turn out to be as important to LGD rates as, if not more important than, the substantial increase in second liens. Analysis by Moody's Investors Service has shown these deals have increased from 26 percent in 2003 and 46 percent in 2004 to 60 percent in 2005. Prior analysis has shown debt cushion to be the single most important explanatory variable for ultimate LGD; therefore, it can be expected that this would have a negative impact on overall loan recovery rates.

Active Bank Management

An important theme of the October 2005 LSTA conference's investor panel was discussion of "low covenant" and "no covenant" deals originated over the last two years. To supplement the anecdotal evidence presented by panel members, Moody's Investors Service conducted a review of covenant changes in amendments to 72 credit agreements in 2005, dividing the changes based on how they would affect LGD or credit quality. Not surprisingly, 76 percent of the amendments reviewed had loosening of covenants that could serve to reduce recoveries for those loans.

In summary, in contrast to the 2000–2001 default cycle, which featured mostly well-structured loans recovering at historical average rates in a very challenging macroeconomic environment, we are now witnessing substantially fewer well-structured loans in a benign environment.

ULTIMATE LGD VERSUS TRADING PRICE AFTER DEFAULT

Like with macroeconomic and loan structure trends, trends in the trading prices of loans 30 days after the instrument defaults are also opposite to those in the last cycle. The trading prices of distressed loans analyzed by Moody's 30 days after instrument default averaged in the mid–60s through 2000. This average trading price declined to the mid–50s during 2000–2001 and then steadily increased from the mid–60s in 2002 to the mid–70s in 2003 and to 88.5 for the period 2004–2005. This recent systemic increase in trading prices after default has occurred without a corresponding increase in ultimate recovery rates. A database of historical ultimate recovery data compiled by Moody's Investors Service lists 2005 bank debt ultimate discounted LGD at slightly over 81 percent with a median of 100 percent, both consistent with historical average ranges.

This upward trend in average trading prices may be explained by two important variables: overall market sentiment and supply and demand.

1. Sentiment quickly moved negative in the 2001 cycle as defaults rose (providing an ample supply of distressed loans), the yield curve was inverted, and many investors

were preparing for the recession to hit. An environment had been created in which trading prices trended down to levels so low in terms of expected ultimate recovery that they allowed investors to realize above-average returns by holding distressed debt through ultimate recovery.

2. More recently, loan supply has decreased as default rates have dropped and liquidity has increased substantially with the continued entry of vulture funds and hedge funds into the market. How influential are these new players in the market? A published report by Greenwich Associates estimated that hedge funds accounted for over 80 percent of all distressed debt trades in 2005.

WHAT WE ARE SEEING NOW: PART 2

"Attention Kmart Buyers...": Are distressed loans the new Blue-light Specials?

Over the last three years, increasing use has been made of distressed exchanges (a.k.a. equitization of loans—loans receiving equity in settlement of the default as opposed to receiving cash or new bank debt in settlement). Historically, banks have tried to roll over defaulted loans or to get someone else (such as a different bank group or investor group) to cash them out. During the period 1986–2000, defaulted loans received new loans and/or cash almost 90 percent of the time. Recently, bank debt has received equity in settlement more than half the time. While this may sometimes be associated with distressed companies that are in such bad shape that equity is the only thing available in settlement, we believe that this trend is much more associated with a new trend in ownership of distressed debt by vulture firms and hedge funds, which are interested in buying distressed firms by purchasing the debt and having that debt converted into a majority equity position.

While this strategy has been around for years, its use has accelerated substantially recently. A "poster child" for this trend is Kmart. Kmart's bank debt traded at around 40 just prior to the firm's emergence from bankruptcy in May 2003. Investors who waited for the equity to trade, starting at $15 per share, received value of $48 quickly; those who waited longer saw the share price increase to $30 after six months, $44.30 after one year, and $144.70 after two years. The respective returns for an investor purchasing the debt at 40 (that debt traded as low as the mid–20s) would be 20 percent, 87.5 percent, 150.11 percent, and 235.4 percent.

It is not surprising that other investors would try to replicate this strategy. The results of a rush of new entrants into distressed debt include substantially increased liquidity, leading to higher trading prices after default coupled with mostly lower ultimate recoveries when holders of distressed loans are attempting to equitize. When banks were attempting to roll over or cash out, a major motivator was to achieve a recovery viewed as whole so as to keep the banks from having to take a charge against capital. The motivation for equity players is to minimize the stated recovery value so as to receive the maximum amount of equity. When this is done correctly, as it was with Kmart, then the ultimate recovery rate will increase substantially and relatively quickly. If it is not done correctly, then the combination of high trading prices and lower ultimate recovery rates will lead to low, or even negative, returns to investors.

SUMMARY

Much of the information and strategies learned in the last default and LGD cycle from 1998 to 2002 may very well be changing, if they are not already obsolete. This shift may be attributed to several factors, including the cyclicality of investor behavior and its corresponding "all pile in" mentality, substantially increased liquidity in the distressed market, decrease in the supply of distressed debt, and the continued shift in ownership of distressed loans away from banks and CDO funds and toward distressed funds and hedge funds. In the past, we believed that the overall market was overly pessimistic about loan recovery rates and returns from distressed debt. We now believe that several new trends may influence the market toward a slightly overoptimistic bent. These include

- A belief that all loans will do well in default based on how well loans and CLOs did in the last downturn.
  Documented research has shown that *well-structured loans* do well, while loosely structured loans do substantially worse. The all-bank-debt syndications and many second lien loans are expected to have recovery rates well below the average should they default. And the alarming trend toward less active bank management is similarly expected to lead to lower recovery rates.

- Debt cushion, quality of collateral, and active bank management are the three most important aspects associated with strong recoveries in default. It appears that all three of these variables are declining in the current market.
- Views that distressed loans will remain an excellent investment and that loan trading prices at default will systemically be much lower than ultimate recovery rates are looking increasingly risky as distressed loan trading prices increase substantially without corresponding increases in loan ultimate recovery.
- The shift in ownership of distressed loans away from banks and CLOs and toward distressed funds and hedge funds has led to lower recovery rates, as these funds accept equity instead of cash or new secured debt, lowering immediate ultimate recoveries while increasing distressed trading prices. If the equity markets don't continue to deliver Kmart-like returns or to allow for quick relisting on major exchanges, then these investments may lead to subsequent bankruptcies with even lower ultimate recoveries.

Given all of the potential confusion associated with the new trends, Moody's plans to supplement its current expected-loss-based (EL) security ratings and corporate family ratings (CFRs) with loss given default (LGD) ratings on speculative-grade loans, bonds, and preferred stocks and corporate family probability of default ratings (PDRs). The proposed methodology further develops our existing expected-loss approach to rating corporate obligations with varying levels of seniority and security. Our historical notching guidelines for investment grade credits remain unchanged; however, the current proposal provides greater rigor in rating the obligations of speculative grade issuers.

S&P/LSTA Leveraged Loan Index: Overview

Steve Miller
Managing Director, Standard & Poor's Leveraged
Commentary & Data

The S&P/LSTA Leveraged Loan Index (LLI) reflects the market-weighted performance of U.S. dollar–denominated institutional leveraged loan portfolios. The LLI is calculated weekly and has an inception date of January 1, 1997. There are eight subindexes published weekly in addition to the base index:

- *BB Index:* facilities with a rating of BB+ to BB- from Standard & Poor's
- *Single B Index:* facilities with a rating of B+ to B- from Standard & Poor's
- *Original-Issue BB Index:* facilities with an initial rating of BB+ to BB- from Standard & Poor's
- *Original-Issue B Index:* facilities with an initial rating of B+ to B- from Standard & Poor's
- *Performing Loan Index:* all loans excluding those in payment default
- *Industry Sector Indexes:* performance of loans by the industry sector of the issuer
- *Middle Market Index:* performance of loans to issuers with EBITDA of $50 million or less
- *Second-lien Loan Index:* facilities secured by a second lien on collateral

The LLI and all of its subindexes are designed to (1) illustrate the performance of the loan asset class and (2) give loan portfolio managers a robust set of benchmarking tools.

In addition to straight return information, S&P also publishes information on

- Principal returns from market value changes
- Loan market volatility
- Sharpe ratios comparing loans to other asset classes

DATA SOURCING AND MANAGEMENT

Standard & Poor's strives to use accurate market weightings and spreads for the facilities constituting the index. To do so, S&P acquires reference data each week from roughly ten buy-side firms that are active in the loan market.

To calculate index returns, S&P uses mark-to-market data from the LSTA/LPC Mark-to-Market Pricing service. Additionally, S&P LCD's comprehensive and detailed database of credits supports the index, allowing for the provision of an array of detailed analysis and comparables. JPMorgan FCS's Wall Street Office is the data management platform.

S&P's Index Services group, which supports all of S&P's indexes, created a calculation platform specifically tailored to the nuances of the syndicated loan market. The LLI calculation platform runs according to the rigorous standards and methodologies applied to all of Standard & Poor's indexes.

CRITERIA FOR INCLUSION AND DELETION

Facilities are eligible for inclusion in the index if they are U.S. dollar–denominated term loans from syndicated credits and meet the following criteria at issuance:

- Minimum initial term of one year
- Minimum initial spread of LIBOR + 125
- Minimum initial size of $50 million

The index consists primarily of senior secured and second lien loan facilities; however, it does include unsecured loans if they are broadly held by CLOs and other traditional loan accounts. Loans are retired when there is no bid posted on the facility for at least 12 successive weeks or when the loan is repaid.

PERFORMANCE CALCULATION FORMULAS

Like all S&P indexes, the LLI and its subindexes are all market-weighted. The return for each index is the composite of each component facility's return times the market value outstanding from the prior time period.

Description and Inclusion Rules of the Credit Suisse Leveraged Loan Index

Sam DeRosa-Farag
Managing Director, Global Leveraged Finance Strategy
Credit Suisse

This article includes descriptions of the

- Credit Suisse Distressed Loan Index
- Credit Suisse Institutional Leveraged Loan Index

INCLUSION RULES

The Credit Suisse Leveraged Loan Index is designed to mirror the investable universe of the U.S. dollar–denominated leveraged loan market. The index inception is January 1992. The index frequency is monthly.

New loans are added to the index on their issuance date if they qualify according to the following criteria:

- Loans must be rated "5B" or lower. That is, the highest Moody's/S&P ratings are Baa1/BB+ or Ba1/BBB+. See the section "Ratings" later in this article for more information. If loans are unrated, the initial spread level must be LIBOR plus 125 basis points or higher.
- Only funded term loans are included.
- The tenor must be at least one year.
- Borrowers must be domiciled in developed countries; borrowers from developing countries are excluded.

"Fallen angels" are added to the index subject to the new loan criteria.

Loans are removed from the index according to the following criteria:

- "Rising stars" are removed from the index when they are upgraded to investment grade.
- Loans are taken out of the index when they exit the market (for example, at maturity, refinancing, or workout).

Credit Suisse Distressed Loan Index

We maintain a subindex, the Credit Suisse Distressed Loan Index, that is designed to mirror the distressed sector of the U.S. dollar–denominated leveraged loan market. Starting with the Credit Suisse Leveraged Loan Index, we form the Credit Suisse Distressed Loan Index by including only those loan facilities that are priced at 90 or lower at the beginning of the month.

Credit Suisse Institutional Leveraged Loan Index

We maintain a subindex, the Credit Suisse Institutional Leveraged Loan Index, that is designed to more closely reflect the investment criteria of institutional leveraged loan market participants. The Credit Suisse Institutional Leveraged Loan Index is formed by excluding the following facilities from the Credit Suisse Leveraged Loan Index:

- Facility types TL and TLa
- Facilities priced at 90 or lower at the beginning of the month
- Facilities rated CC, C, or Default

ANALYTICS

We assume that coupons are paid quarterly on quarterly anniversary dates counting forward from the effective date. The coupon rate is the spread plus the value of the three-month LIBOR rate three months prior to the coupon payment date.

Average values are computed over the index for coupon, current yield, spread, and price. The average coupon, current yield, and spread are weighted by market value (amount outstanding × price) at the end of the measurement period for each loan in the index that is currently paying interest. (Some defaulted borrowers remain current on their scheduled leveraged loan interest payments.) The average price is weighted by market value at the end of the measurement period for *every* loan in the index.

Total return is computed for each loan; this is the percent change in the value of each loan during the measurement period. The *total return* is

$$\frac{[(\text{Current price} + \text{accrued interest} + \text{coupon paid (if any)} + \text{reinvestment interest on coupon paid}) - (\text{previous price} + \text{accrued interest})]}{(\text{previous price} + \text{accrued interest})}$$

Total return is the sum of three components: principal return, interest return, and reinvestment return. The *principal return* is

$$\frac{\text{Current price} - \text{previous price}}{\text{Previous price} + \text{accrued interest}}$$

The *interest return* is

$$\frac{[\text{Current accrued interest} + \text{coupon paid (if any)}] - \text{previous accrued interest}}{\text{Previous price} + \text{accrued interest}}$$

The *reinvestment return* is:

$$\frac{\text{Reinvestment interest on coupon paid (if any)}}{\text{Previous price} + \text{accrued interest}}$$

The reinvestment interest on the coupon is the amount of interest earned at short-term rates (using three-month LIBOR) on the coupon for the period from the coupon payment date to the end of the measurement period.

The average principal return, interest return, reinvestment return, and total return are computed over the index. The averages for each return component and for total return are weighted by market value (amount outstanding × price) at the *beginning* of the measurement period for every loan in the index.

All averages are based on market value, either at the beginning or at the end of a period. Since the leveraged loan market is a private market, the amount outstanding for each loan is not always known. In these cases, initial amount is used as a substitute for amount outstanding in the market value calculation.

The *cumulative return* over several periods is computed as

$$\left(\prod_i (\text{total return}_i + 1)\right) - 1$$

This computation assumes that coupon payments are reinvested in the index at the beginning of each period, which approximates the behavior of a portfolio. (Alternatively, the total return formula could be used to compute a single return from the beginning of the first period to the end of the last period, but this assumes that coupons are reinvested at short-term rates, which does not reflect the behavior of a portfolio.)

Averages on sectors of the index, such as industry, rating, or facility type, are also computed. The averages for each sector are computed in the same way as that for the entire index.

RATINGS

The Credit Suisse Leveraged Loan Index uses a single "blended" Moody's/S&P rating to compute averages sorted by rating. There are nine blended ratings: Investment Grade (which, of course, is excluded from the index), Split BBB, BB, Split BB, B, Split B, CCC/Split CCC, Distressed/Default, and Not Rated. We developed the blended ratings because Moody's and S&P do not always agree on equivalent ratings for a loan. The number of unique Moody's/S&P pairings in the index is large, with many groupings containing only a few loans.

We created the blended ratings by looking at the Moody's and S&P ratings by major ratings category, ignoring the 1, 2, and 3 Moody's subcategories and the + and − S&P subcategories. If both agencies rate a loan in the same major category, we assign that rating. If the agencies disagree on the rating by one major step, we assign a split rating. If the agencies disagree by two or more major steps, we make the conservative assumption and pick the lower rating.

There are some special cases that we must handle. If one agency does not rate the loan, the other agency's rating determines our rating. If either agency assigns the loan an A major rating or better, we classify the loan as investment grade regardless of the other agency's rating. Similarly, if the borrower is in bankruptcy or has missed a coupon payment and the grace period has expired, we classify the loan as Distressed/Default regardless of the agency ratings. If the S&P rating is D, we classify the loan as Distressed/ Default regardless of the Moody's rating.

The motivation for creating the blended rating is derived from the fact that there are about 50 unique Moody's/S&P pairings in the index; the exact number varies, as individual ratings on loans change over time. This is too many groupings to use to draw conclusions about the market's behavior. Further, about half of these groups contain three or fewer loans and thus lack distinct drivers, making aggregate calculations statistically meaningless.

Theoretically, there are 247 possible Moody's/S&P pairings for leveraged loans. A loan can have a Moody's rating as high as Baa1 when the loan is rated BB+ or below by S&P; similarly, a loan can have an S&P rating as high as BBB+ when the loan is rated Ba1 or below by Moody's. There are 16 Moody's ratings Baa1 or below and 16 S&P ratings BBB+ or below, including "not rated" by each agency. This gives $16 \times 16 = 256$ pairings, less 9 BBB-only pairings, resulting in 247 ratings.

The precise rating definitions are listed here.

Investment Grade

1. Moody's rating is Baa3 or higher and S&P rating is BBB− or higher.
2. Moody's rating is Baa3 or higher and S&P rating is NR.
3. Moody's rating is NR and S&P rating is BBB− or higher.
4. Moody's rating is A3 or higher (S&P rating is ignored).
5. S&P rating is A− or higher (Moody's rating is ignored).

N.B.: When loans are upgraded to Investment Grade, they are removed from the index.

Split BBB

1. Moody's rating is Baa1, Baa2, or Baa3 and S&P rating is BB+, BB, or BB−.
2. Moody's rating is Ba1, Ba2, or Ba3 and S&P rating is BBB+, BBB, or BBB−.

BB

1. Moody's rating is Ba1, Ba2, or Ba3 and S&P rating is BB+, BB, or BB−.
2. Moody's rating is Ba1, Ba2, or Ba3 and S&P rating is NR.
3. Moody's rating is NR and S&P rating is BB+, BB, or BB−.

Split BB

1. Moody's rating is Ba1, Ba2, or Ba3 and S&P rating is B+, B, or B−.
2. Moody's rating is B1, B2, or B3 and S&P rating is BB+, BB, or BB−.

B

1. Moody's rating is B1, B2, or B3 and S&P rating is B+, B, or B−.
2. Moody's rating is B1, B2, or B3 and S&P rating is NR.
3. Moody's rating is NR and S&P rating is B+, B, or B−.
4. Moody's rating is B1, B2, or B3 and S&P rating is BBB+, BBB, or BBB−.
5. Moody's rating is Baa1, Baa2, or Baa3 and S&P rating is B+, B, or B−.

Split B

1. Moody's rating is B1, B2, or B3 and S&P rating is CCC+, CCC, or CCC−.
2. Moody's rating is Caa, Caa1, Caa2, or Caa3 and S&P rating is B+, B, or B−.

CCC/Split CCC

1. Moody's rating is Caa, Caa1, Caa2, or Caa3 and S&P rating is CCC+, CCC, CCC−, CC, or C.
2. Moody's rating is Caa, Caa1, Caa2, Caa3, Ca, or C and S&P rating is CCC+, CCC, or CCC−.
3. Moody's rating is Caa, Caa1, Caa2, or Caa3 and S&P rating is NR.
4. Moody's rating is NR and S&P rating is CCC+, CCC, or CCC−.
5. Moody's rating is Caa, Caa1, Caa2, or Caa3 and S&P rating is BBB+, BBB, BBB−, BB+, BB, or BB−.
6. Moody's rating is Baa1, Baa2, Baa3, Ba1, Ba2, or Ba3 and S&P rating is CCC+, CCC, or CCC−.

Distressed/Default

1. Default flag is set, indicating that the borrower has filed for bankruptcy protection or missed a coupon payment and the grace period has expired (Moody's and S&P ratings are ignored).

2. S&P rating is D (Moody's rating is ignored).
3. Moody's rating is Ca or C and S&P rating is CC or C.
4. Moody's rating is Ca or C and S&P rating is NR.
5. Moody's rating is NR and S&P rating is CC or C.
6. Moody's rating is Ca or C and S&P rating is BBB+, BBB, BBB−, BB+, BB, BB−, B+, B, or B−.
7. Moody's rating is Baa1, Baa2, Baa3, Ba1, Ba2, Ba3, B1, B2, or B3 and S&P rating is CC or C.

Not Rated

1. Moody's rating is NR and S&P rating is NR.

Credit Suisse Institutional Leveraged Loan Index

Sam DeRosa-Farag
Managing Director, Global Leveraged Finance Strategy
Credit Suisse

The Credit Suisse Institutional Leveraged Loan Index, a subindex of the Credit Suisse Leveraged Loan Index, is designed to reflect the investment criteria of institutional leveraged loan market participants more closely, and thus to serve as a more applicable benchmark for institutional fund managers. By excluding pro rata and distressed facilities, the index provides institutional managers with a benchmark with more predictable returns and lower volatility than the overall leveraged loan market.

Starting with the Credit Suisse Leveraged Loan Index, we created the Credit Suisse Institutional Leveraged Loan Index by excluding the following facilities:

- Facilities of types TL and TLa
- Facilities priced 90 or lower at the beginning of the month
- Facilities rated CC, C, or in default

This article reviews the analytical basis for our criteria for the Credit Suisse Institutional Leveraged Loan Index and shows the resulting performance, risk, and profile of the new index.

EXHIBIT 8.7

Risk versus return of various asset classes: 1992–1Q04.

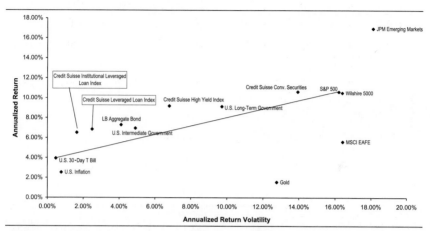

Source: Credit Suisse.

The Credit Suisse Institutional Leveraged Loan Index, from its inception in 1992 through the present, shows a slightly lower absolute return with less volatility than the Credit Suisse Leveraged Loan Index (see Exhibit 8.7). Eliminating the riskier facilities in the overall index helps to limit the downside risk, which is typically greater in facilities trading at lower prices. This becomes increasingly apparent in a bear-market period, as the institutional index outperformed the overall leveraged loan index for the periods 1995–1Q04 and 3Q98–2002 (see Exhibits 8.8 and 8.9).

As a preliminary step in creating the criteria that would limit the eligible universe for an institutional index, we selected only institutional loans, thereby eliminating all amortizing term loan facilities (TL and TLa) that are typically held by traditional banks. This was intuitive, as the remaining facilities are the tranches with which institutional loan market participants are most concerned.

- *Amortizing term loans (A term loans).* These are traditional bank installment loans. A term loans typically run for five to seven years, are coterminous with revolving credits, and require progressive repayments throughout the term.
- *Institutional term loans (B, C, and D term loans).* These loans were introduced on a broad scale in 1992 with reverse LBO transactions (IPO-related recapitalizations). They are

EXHIBIT 8.8

Risk versus return of various asset classes: 1995–1Q04.

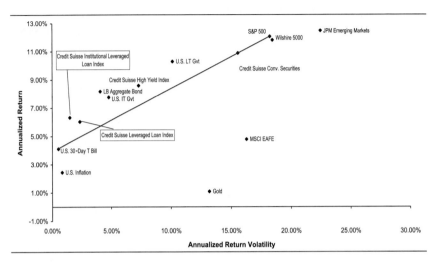

Source: Credit Suisse.

EXHIBIT 8.9

Risk versus return of various asset classes: 3Q98–2002.

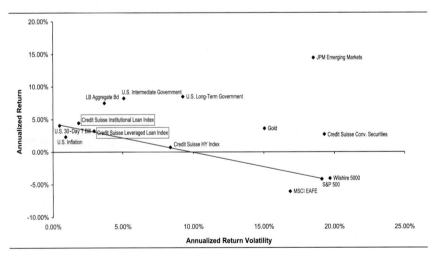

Source: Credit Suisse.

carved out specifically for institutional loan market participants and feature longer maturities, more back-end-loaded repayment schedules, and incrementally higher spreads than revolving credit and A term loans. Institutional term loans typically run from six to ten years, or six months to three years longer than revolving credit and A term loans of the same borrower.

The price criteria for the index were determined based on studies that we conducted regarding the relationship between price and risk. We examined the volatility of the Credit Suisse Leveraged Loan Index at various price points. When examining leveraged loans during an economic downturn, such as the 2001–2002 period, we found that the incremental volatility nearly doubled when we moved from a price break of 60 percent of par to a price break of 50 percent of par. Because all price points beginning below the 90 level show a high probability of migrating to a lower level after a one-year period, we selected the price level of 90 as the threshold for institutional loan market participants (see Exhibit 8.10).

Analyzing the risk/reward characteristics of institutional loans by price breaks further supports the exclusion of facilities priced less than 90. We examined sets of loans priced above 90, above 80, above 70, and above 60 (see Exhibits 8.11 and 8.12). When

EXHIBIT 8.10

Distressed leveraged loan price migration study one year after price break (<90).

Price Level Change One Year After Price Break	90%–80%	80%–70%	70%–60%	60%–50%	50% and Lower
	% of Par—Price Break Levels				
Above Starting Level	39.75%	39.15%	37.14%	44.00%	31.0%
Remain at Starting Level	21.43%	18.52%	28.57%	32.67%	69.0%
Below Starting Level	38.82%	42.33%	34.29%	23.33%	—
% Defaulted*	8.48%	20.83%	27.78%	26.67%	58.33%

*1993–First half 2000

Source: Credit Suisse.

EXHIBIT 8.11

Risk versus return of various leveraged loan price breaks:
1995–1Q04.

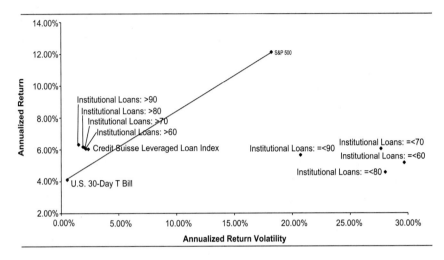

Source: Credit Suisse.

EXHIBIT 8.12

Risk versus return of various leveraged loan price breaks:
1995–1Q04.

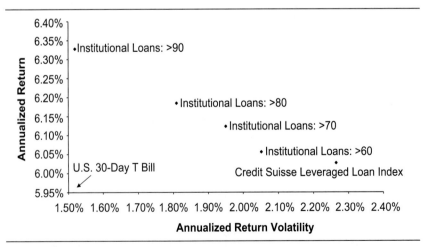

Source: Credit Suisse.

the return and volatility profile of facilities above 90 is observed over the long period 1995–1Q04, this set demonstrates greater efficiency on a risk/reward basis compared with the other price breaks.

Looking at the same price breaks during the bear-market period of 3Q98 to 2002, the facilities priced above 90 also showed the greatest efficiency (see Exhibit 8.13).

Because institutional loan market participants are focused on capturing the par portion of the market and are averse to holding distressed issues, we further examined loans by rating. Facilities rated BB and B appear optimal, as they lie above the capital market line for the long period, displaying greater efficiency than other ratings categories (Exhibit 8.14), and show greater resiliency during the bear-market period (Exhibit 8.15). It did not seem reasonable to eliminate facilities rated CCC/Split CCC despite their suboptimal efficiency from 1995 to 1Q04, as institutional loan market participants would not have zero exposure to this ratings class. These

EXHIBIT 8.13

Risk versus return of various leveraged loan price breaks: 3Q98–2002.

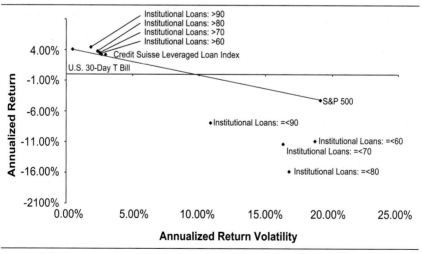

Source: Credit Suisse.

EXHIBIT 8.14

Risk versus return of various leveraged loan ratings breaks: 1995–1Q04.

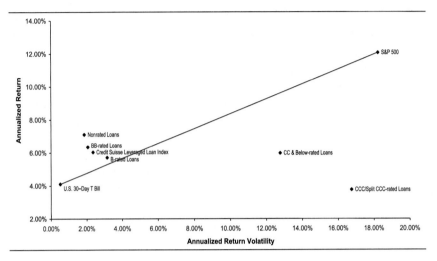

Source: Credit Suisse.

EXHIBIT 8.15

Risk versus return of various leveraged loan ratings breaks: 3Q98–2002.

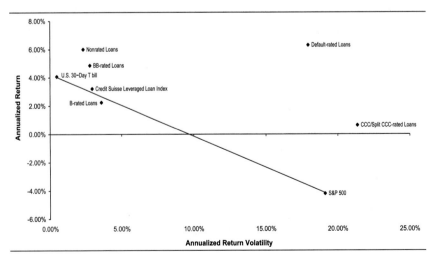

Source: Credit Suisse.

findings led us to exclude those facilities rated CC and lower in our selection criteria for the institutional index. Furthermore, the risk/reward profile for CC and below issues may be a bit skewed, especially during the long period, as pricing for these issues remains opaque.

We considered adding a minimum size criterion, but after further examination, it seems that unlike price breaks, size buckets are clustered very closely and show little dispersion in returns and volatilities (see Exhibit 8.16). This led us to eliminate the idea of selecting facilities by size because it did not seem a significant determinant in the goal of establishing a stable and efficient benchmark.

As institutional loan market participants own roughly two-thirds of the leveraged finance market (Exhibits 8.17 and 8.18), we considered it necessary to design benchmarks that more fairly reflected their investable universe. Therefore, we have introduced the Credit Suisse Institutional High Yield Index as well as the Credit Suisse Institutional Leveraged Loan Index.

E X H I B I T   8 . 1 6

Risk versus return of various leveraged loan size buckets: 1995–1Q04.

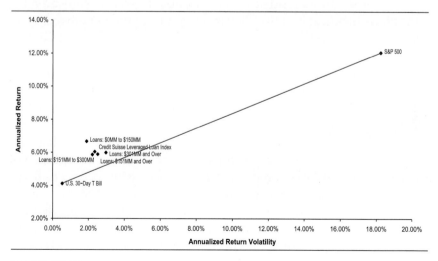

Source: Credit Suisse.

EXHIBIT 8.17

Who Owns High Yield: 2004.

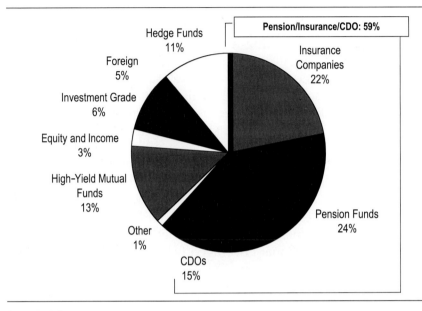

Source: Credit Suisse.

The institutional index was better able to weather the adverse conditions heading into the 2000 recession than the Leveraged Loan Index. It exhibited lower volatility and equivalent, if not higher, returns. However, the institutional index had a slightly reduced upside in the subsequent recovery, as the overall index outperformed the institutional index during the 2003 time period. See Exhibits 8.19 to 8.27 for performance of the indexes over segments of the larger period.

The Credit Suisse Institutional Leveraged Loan Index displays profile characteristics that are substantially different from those of the Credit Suisse Leveraged Loan Index (see Exhibits 8.28 to 8.31). This is not surprising because the selection criteria for the institutional index eliminate all deals priced less than 90 and/or rated CC or lower, effectively underweighting the riskier sectors. For example, the institutional index showed −2.20 percent less exposure in Media/Telecom and −2.53 percent less exposure in Utilities than the Credit Suisse Leveraged Loan Index.

EXHIBIT 8.18

Who owns leveraged loans?

United States	1994	1995	1996	1997	1998	1999	2000	2001	2002	2003	2004	Inc/(Dec) 04 vs. '95
Domestic Banks	29.37%	32.72%	29.30%	28.70%	27.74%	28.13%	25.24%	23.63%	17.48%	13.04%	11.95%	−17.42%
Finance Companies	3.85%	3.39%	2.40%	3.73%	4.28%	6.32%	4.32%	9.25%	7.64%	10.25%	6.39%	2.54%
Foreign Banks	41.26%	37.94%	34.38%	30.37%	35.46%	23.36%	19.34%	12.52%	13.02%	10.08%	16.69%	−24.57%
Institutional Investors	**24.48%**	**24.54%**	**31.08%**	**32.68%**	**30.73%**	**41.70%**	**49.52%**	**52.41%**	**59.87%**	**65.67%**	**63.59%**	**39.11%**
Securities Firms	1.05%	1.41%	2.85%	3.80%	1.79%	0.49%	1.58%	2.19%	1.98%	0.96%	1.38%	0.33%

Source: Credit Suisse; Standard & Poor's Leveraged Commentary and Data.

EXHIBIT 8.19

Risk versus return of various asset classes: 1992–1993.

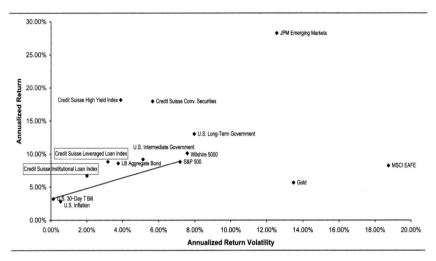

Source: Credit Suisse.

EXHIBIT 8.20

Risk versus return of various asset classes: 1994–1995.

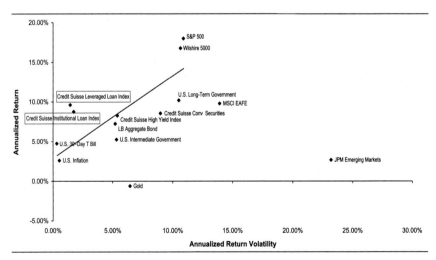

Source: Credit Suisse.

EXHIBIT 8.21

Risk versus return of various asset classes: 1996–1997.

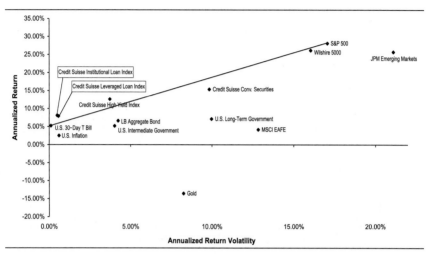

Source: Credit Suisse.

EXHIBIT 8.22

Risk versus return of various asset classes: 1998–1999.

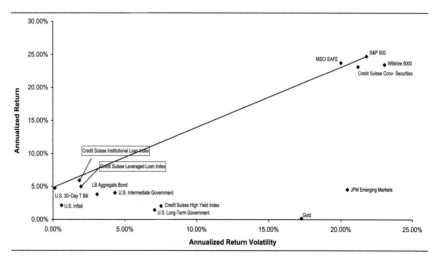

Source: Credit Suisse.

EXHIBIT 8.23

Risk versus return of various asset classes: 2000.

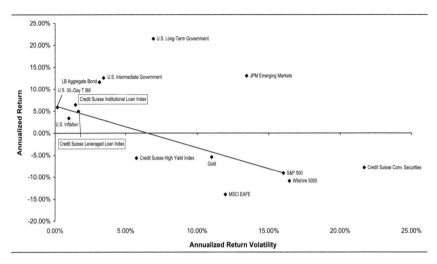

Source: Credit Suisse.

EXHIBIT 8.24

Risk versus return of various asset classes: 2001.

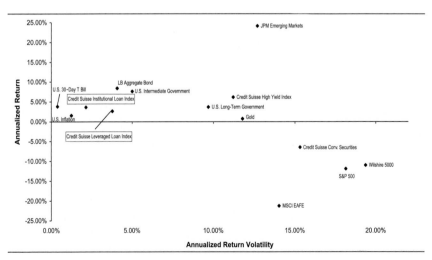

Source: Credit Suisse.

EXHIBIT 8.25

Risk versus return of various asset classes: 2002.

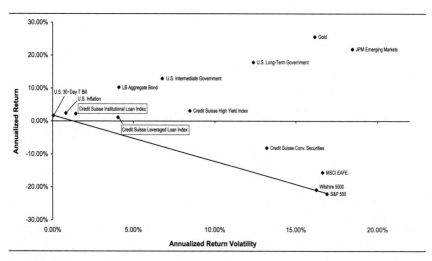

Source: Credit Suisse.

EXHIBIT 8.26

Risk versus return of various asset classes: 2003.

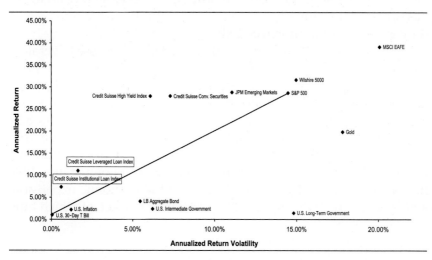

Source: Credit Suisse.

EXHIBIT 8.27

Risk versus return of various asset classes: 2004.

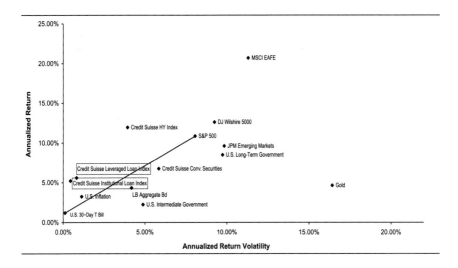

Source: Credit Suisse.

Through lower volatility and less exposure to riskier portions of the market, the Credit Suisse Institutional Leveraged Loan Index has shown substantially greater price stability and avoidance of downside risk over time (see Exhibits 8.32 and 8.33).

We compared the returns on the broad Credit Suisse Leveraged Loan Index and the Credit Suisse Institutional Leveraged Loan Index. The institutional index underperforms the broad index during recovery periods, outperforms during bear markets, and performs comparably during economic expansions (see Exhibits 8.34 and 8.35). This is best illustrated by the cumulative return differential between the indices. Exhibit 8.34 shows that the institutional index underperformed in the recovery years following the 1990 recession, performed comparably during the economic expansion, and outperformed during the 2000–2002 bear market, at which time the cycle repeated.

EXHIBIT 8.28

Profile of the Credit Suisse Institutional Leveraged Loan Index and Credit Suisse Leveraged Index.

Industry	Credit Suisse Institutional Leveraged Loan Index		Credit Suisse Leveraged Loan Index		Credit Suisse Institutional Leveraged Loan Index Less Credit Suisse Leveraged Loan Index	
	Market Weight as of 3/31/2004	Total Return LTM 1Q04	Market Weight as of 3/31/2004	Total Return LTM 1Q04	Market Weight as of 3/31/2004	Total Return LTM 1Q04
Aerospace	2.66%	5.57%	1.93%	6.65%	0.74%	−108bp
Chemicals	5.27%	5.44%	4.85%	8.40%	0.42%	−296bp
Consumer Durables	1.18%	4.50%	0.87%	6.23%	0.32%	−173bp
Consumer Nondurables	3.70%	5.77%	3.38%	4.66%	0.32%	112bp
Energy	2.08%	8.13%	1.67%	8.56%	0.41%	−43bp
Financial	0.41%	9.09%	0.90%	22.88%	−0.49%	−1379bp
Food and Drug	1.25%	5.43%	1.78%	6.92%	−0.54%	−149bp
Food/Tobacco	7.54%	5.78%	6.28%	6.41%	1.26%	−62bp
Forest Products	6.79%	6.45%	5.56%	7.31%	1.24%	−86bp
Gaming/Leisure	5.47%	7.13%	4.87%	11.41%	0.60%	−428bp
Health Care	6.58%	5.40%	6.99%	5.60%	−0.41%	−20bp
Housing	2.31%	5.64%	1.80%	6.68%	0.51%	−105bp
Information Technology	2.45%	7.06%	1.98%	13.18%	0.46%	−612bp
Manufacturing	5.12%	5.64%	4.54%	7.95%	0.58%	−231bp
Media/Telecom	27.52%	8.71%	29.72%	13.96%	−2.20%	−525bp
Metals/Minerals	0.73%	4.87%	1.51%	15.33%	−0.78%	−1046bp
Retail	1.94%	6.08%	1.77%	6.02%	0.17%	6bp
Service	5.20%	5.61%	4.34%	6.83%	0.87%	−123bp
Transportation	4.52%	8.14%	5.46%	10.37%	−0.94%	−223bp
Utility	7.26%	9.41%	9.79%	12.69%	−2.53%	−328bp

E X H I B I T   8 . 2 8   *(Continued)*

Rating	Credit Suisse Institutional Leveraged Loan Index		Credit Suisse Leveraged Loan Index		Credit Suisse Institutional Leveraged Loan Index Less Credit Suisse Leveraged Loan Index	
	Market Weight as of 3/31/2004	Total Return LTM 1Q04	Market Weight as of 3/31/2004	Total Return LTM 1Q04	Market Weight as of 3/31/2004	Total Return LTM 1Q04
Industry Type						
Cyclical	42.56%	6.35%	39.43%	9.58%	3.13%	−322bp
Defensive	55.36%	7.47%	58.91%	11.20%	−3.55%	−373bp
Energy	2.08%	8.13%	1.67%	8.56%	0.41%	−43bp
Split BBB	3.49%	6.01%	3.99%	5.70%	−0.50%	30bp
BB	36.76%	5.98%	33.30%	6.36%	3.46%	−37bp
Split BB	19.00%	7.13%	16.21%	8.41%	2.79%	−128bp
B	34.27%	9.46%	30.11%	13.20%	4.17%	−374bp
Split B	1.15%	7.08%	2.00%	16.73%	−0.84%	−965bp
CCC	0.86%	11.63%	0.90%	27.91%	−0.04%	−1627bp
Not Rated	4.46%	5.41%	7.98%	7.79%	−3.52%	−238bp
Distressed (CC, C, Default)	NA	NA	5.52%	29.00%	−5.52%	NA
Rating Tier						
Upper Tier	40.25%	6.00%	37.29%	6.30%	2.96%	−30bp
Middle Tier	54.43%	8.32%	48.31%	11.60%	6.12%	−328bp
Lower Tier	0.86%	11.63%	6.42%	29.23%	−5.56%	−1760bp
Size						
$0MM to $100 MM	4.71%	7.09%	5.06%	10.19%	−0.35%	−311bp
$101MM to $299MM	32.79%	6.26%	30.07%	8.58%	2.72%	−232bp
$300MM & Greater	62.50%	7.41%	64.87%	11.49%	−2.36%	−408bp

Source: Credit Suisse.

EXHIBIT 8.29

Profile of the Credit Suisse Institutional Leveraged Loan Index
and Credit Suisse Leveraged Loan Index.

	Credit Suisse Institutional Leveraged Loan Index		Credit Suisse Leveraged Loan Index		Credit Suisse Institutional Leveraged Loan Index Less Credit Suisse Leveraged Loan Index	
Volatility	Market Weight as of 3/31/2004	Total Return LTM 1Q04	Market Weight as of 3/31/2004	Total Return LTM 1Q04	Market Weight as of 3/31/2004	Total Return LTM 1Q04
Less than 2.50%	95.00%	6.14%	88.74%	6.37%	6.26%	−23bp
2.50% to 4.99%	3.06%	11.61%	7.58%	18.66%	−4.52%	−705bp
5.00% to 9.99%	1.87%	17.93%	3.14%	32.88%	−1.27%	−1495bp
10.00% to 14.99%	0.08%	2.74%	0.30%	30.02%	−0.21%	−2729bp
Percent of Par						
Less than 60%	NA	NA	0.65%	42.22%	−0.65%	NA
60%–80%	NA	NA	1.01%	35.89%	−1.01%	NA
80%–90%	NA	NA	1.57%	43.63%	−1.57%	NA
Greater than 90%	92.86%	7.23%	87.35%	7.23%	5.51%	0bp
Facility						
TL	NA	NA	9.37%	11.55%	−9.37%	NA
TLa	NA	NA	17.20%	13.61%	−17.20%	NA
TLb	82.20%	6.95%	60.41%	9.37%	21.80%	−242bp
TLc	10.00%	7.52%	7.55%	10.70%	2.45%	−319bp
TLd	3.53%	9.65%	2.64%	9.60%	0.89%	5bp
TLe	2.25%	5.39%	1.93%	5.93%	0.32%	−54bp
TLf	0.27%	3.18%	0.00%	3.50%	0.27%	−32bp
TLg	NA	NA	NA	NA	0.00%	NA

Source: Credit Suisse.

EXHIBIT 8.30

Market-weighted profile of the Credit Suisse Institutional
Leveraged Loan Index by industry.

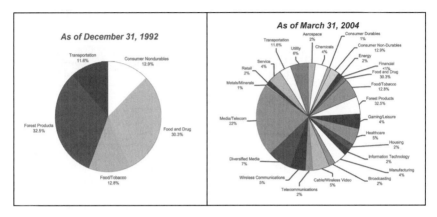

Source: Credit Suisse.

EXHIBIT 8.31

Market-weighted profile of the Credit Suisse Institutional
Leveraged Loan Index by rating.

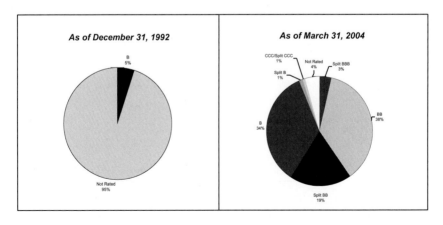

Source: Credit Suisse.

EXHIBIT 8.32

Average price of the Credit Suisse Institutional Leveraged
Loan Index compared with the Credit Suisse Leveraged
Loan Index.

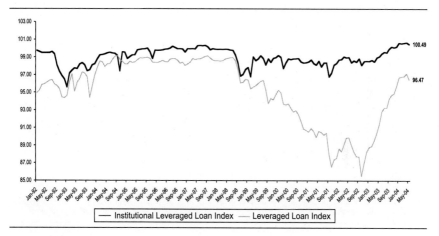

Source: Credit Suisse.

EXHIBIT 8.33

Current yield of the Credit Suisse Institutional Leveraged
Loan Index compared with the Credit Suisse Leveraged
Loan Index.

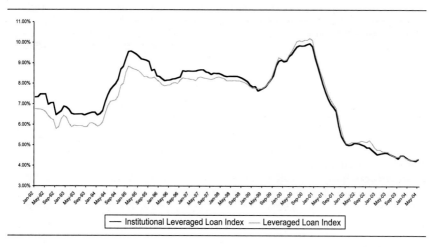

Source: Credit Suisse.

EXHIBIT 8.34

Cumulative return differential of the Credit Suisse Institutional
Leveraged Loan Index and the Credit Suisse Leveraged Loan
Index.

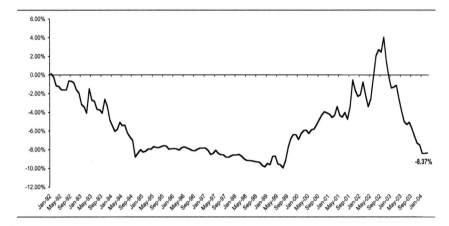

Source: Credit Suisse.

EXHIBIT 8.35

Total Returns of the Credit Suisse Institutional Leveraged Loan
Index and Leveraged Loan Index.

	1992	1993	1994	1995	1996	1997	1998
Credit Suisse Institutional Leveraged Loan Index	4.83%	8.60%	7.95%	9.58%	7.96%	8.25%	4.79%
Credit Suisse Leveraged Loan Index	6.75%	11.17%	10.32%	8.91%	7.48%	8.30%	5.31%
Institutional-Leveraged Loan Index	−1.92%	−2.56%	−2.37%	0.67%	0.48%	−0.05%	−0.52%

	1999	2000	2001	2002	2003	2004	Annualized 1992–2004
Credit Suisse Institutional Leveraged Loan Index	7.06%	6.44%	3.64%	2.22%	7.36%	5.21%	6.43%
Credit Suisse Leveraged Loan Index	4.69%	4.94%	2.65%	1.12%	11.01%	5.60%	6.75%
Institutional-Leveraged Loan Index	2.37%	1.50%	1.00%	1.10%	−3.66%	−0.39%	−0.31%

Source: Credit Suisse.

Leveraged Senior Loan Performance Attribution

Sean Kelley
Tall Tree Investment Management, LLC

Investment measurement and attribution have improved remarkably since industrialist J. Paul Getty exclaimed, "If you can actually count your money, then you're not a rich man." Investors today take a less cavalier approach toward the assets that they place with money managers; they expect not only detailed return statements, but also a description of how the manager achieved those returns. Traditional equity and fixed income managers often provide this reporting to accounts as standard fare. In more exotic asset classes, such as leveraged senior loans, a manager might struggle to describe his performance because of problems with data, benchmarks, and asset class characteristics that match neither the equity nor the fixed income model.

Indeed, leveraged senior loans encompass a diverse segment of the capital markets large enough to command attention, but quirky enough to frustrate even a performance attribution expert. In this section, we review standard equity and fixed income attribution approaches and then propose a leveraged senior loan attribution framework that incorporates both traditional techniques and calculations that price the qualities that are unique to loans.

WHY AND HOW

Through performance attribution, a manager describes his excess returns, defined as how his portfolios have performed relative to a benchmark. The process involves dissecting the difference through standard calculations, developing an output that allows both investors and the manager to understand the specifics of the return composition in a way that isolates the strategies used and the risks taken. With this information in hand, the investor can judge whether the manager's decisions fit a given mandate and can describe to an investment committee why the mandate did or did not achieve the envisioned returns. For the manager, performance attribution promotes accountability in an increasingly competitive environment. He can determine whether excess return occurred as a result of portfolio positioning decisions or individual security selection, with the obvious goal of continuing the positive processes and correcting negative trends.

This additional refinement matters during periods of low returns. Many public mutual fund managers receive accolades or even monetary compensation for performing in the top half of their peer group, and some receive even more for top-quartile performance. During periods of higher variance, when returns diverge, a good manager can readily differentiate himself from his competition. When returns are more stable, however, the manager has fewer opportunities to demonstrate his expertise. We can measure the divergence and contraction during the last credit cycle by tracking the size of the critical second Lipper quartile, defined as the difference between the monthly returns of the last fund in the first quartile and those of the first fund in the third quartile. At the low in secondary market prices, November 2002, the second Lipper quartile was worth 24 basis points. After the markets recovered and credit spreads narrowed to near all-time lows during September 2005, the difference amounted to only 10 basis points.[7]

Once a manager recognizes the benefits of performance attribution, he must decide upon a consistent analytical method. In his synopsis of the discipline, David Spaulding describes two laws of performance attribution: first, "the attribution model should represent the active investment decisions of the portfolio manager," and, second, "the sum of all the attribution effects must equal the excess return."[8] Accordingly, our performance attribution model must measure the decisions over which the portfolio manager has control, and the effect of these variables must completely describe the divergence from an index. A review of the literature, however, provides few insights into exactly how to construct such a model. Instead, we must take inventory of the best thinking on approaches in the fixed-income and equity markets.

Traditional equity and fixed income attribution models segment returns according to the fundamental qualities of each asset class. For equity attribution, many managers do not make the distinction between income and price appreciation returns, but, rather, analyze the allocation and selection effects on total returns.

---

[7] Lipper.
[8] David Spaulding, *Investment Performance Attribution: A Guide to What It Is, How to Calculate It, and How to Use It* (New York: McGraw-Hill, 2003), pp. 9–13.

Investment grade bond managers, in contrast, definitely consider income returns, but also decompose the price return into components that more typically reflect changes in the yield curve and those that are specific to the company that issued the bond. Since leveraged senior loans share certain qualities with these two mainstream asset classes, we review the performance attribution strategies of both and note the variables that we should incorporate into a leveraged loan framework.

FIXED INCOME PERFORMANCE ATTRIBUTION

While a fixed-income performance attribution framework would seem the obvious choice to describe the income component of leveraged senior loans, we soon realized that this approach cannot account for the entirety of leveraged loan returns. The fixed income approach, in fact, disregards credit risk and indexes portfolio performance to the Treasury yield curve and parallel sector shifts. An investment grade portfolio manager concerns himself more with movements in the yield curve than with credit quality migration. The fixed income performance attribution process, notes practitioner Stephen Campisi, is "driven by promised income, and by the effect that changes in yields have on bond prices. The small, unexplained residual is the selection effect."[9] Depending upon the debt instrument, of course, we might include or exclude variables. To advance the discussion, therefore, we review the components of a fairly inclusive attribution framework to highlight those that affect leveraged senior loan returns and consider others not proposed in the current literature.

For this comprehensive framework, we borrow the chart shown in Exhibit 8.36 from a presentation delivered by Louis Gehring of CMS BondEdge.[10] On the critical Price Return branch, the Term Structure Effect indicates how much each portfolio holding should have moved in price relative to changes in the yield curve. The Sector Spread Effect accounts for price adjustment in each risk category. In a given industry, for example, the bond index

---

[9] Stephen Campisi, "Primer on Fixed Income Performance Attribution," *Journal of Performance Measurement,* Summer 2000, p. 15.

[10] Louis Gehring, "Effective Approaches to Fixed Income Performance Attribution," presentation delivered at the Second Annual Performance Attribution Forum (New York, Doubletree Times Square), January 27, 2004. Presentation slides on file with the author.

E X H I B I T   8 . 3 6

Fixed Income Performance Attribution Model

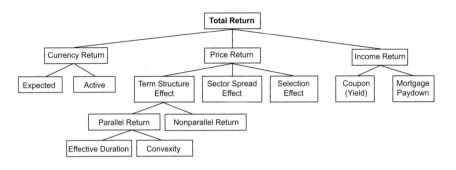

E X H I B I T   8 . 3 7

Pruned Fixed Income Performance Attribution Model

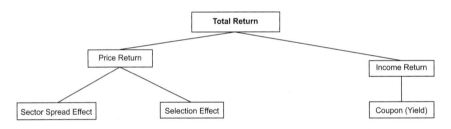

has a price return that serves as the baseline for the portfolio in that same industry. Finally, the Selection Effect is the residual of the portfolio performance on each category adjusted for the Term Structure Effect and Sector Spread Effect. A portfolio over- or underperforms because the manager either makes a yield curve or a sector bet or weights individual securities differently from the index.

While this framework provides us with some insight, we also note that much of it does not apply. Portfolio managers of loans denominated in U.S. dollars, of course, disregard the currency return. Since virtually all leveraged senior loans pay interest on a floating-rate basis, we should also ignore the term structure effect. Finally, mortgage paydown returns do not fit the leveraged senior loan framework.

Once we prune the excess branches from the tree, we are left with a pretty sparse, trivial framework (Exhibit 8.37).

EXHIBIT 8.38

Fixed Income Performance Attribution Model Adapted for Leverage Loans.

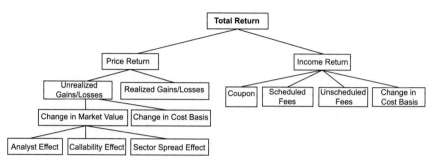

Clearly, this tree hardly captures the manager's decision set, and thus it fails to satisfy the first rule of performance attribution.

Once we take inventory of the categories that concern a leveraged loan portfolio manager, we can adequately complete the tree, as shown in Exhibit 8.38. We definitely consider income, and we propose subcategories in this area of (1) coupon, (2) scheduled fees (commitment fee and letter of credit fees), (3) unscheduled fees (amendment and forbearance fees), and (4) change in cost basis. The Price Return branch first divides into (1) realized gains and losses and (2) unrealized gains and losses, which equals the change in market value minus the change in cost basis. We can think about the change in market value, in turn, as being made up of (1) the sector spread effect, the amount that the portfolio should have returned for the category given the return of that category in the index; (2) the callability effect, the amount that the portfolio could not participate in the sector movement because of the short call option typically embedded in loans; and (3) the analyst effect, the residual. We use the term *analyst effect* rather than *selection effect* to avoid confusion with the selection effect in the equity model.

The additional branches on this tree, which we will call the adapted fixed income model, provide us with a substantial amount of information on how we achieved our return. However, when we contrast our approach to the traditional fixed income model, we realize that we have lost our benchmark. In the traditional approach, we consider returns mostly in the context of the term structure. To the extent that the term structure shifts and the portfolio has a different position, the manager either over- or underperforms. In our adapted fixed income model, we do not enjoy such a clear context; we describe neither our relative performance nor who was responsible for performance different from a benchmark.

EQUITY PERFORMANCE ATTRIBUTION

The adapted fixed income model fails to describe the asset class adequately simply because principal price changes can make up a significant portion of leveraged senior loan returns. Indeed, Robert Merton suggests that leveraged equity resembles a call option on the company assets with a strike price that corresponds to the face value of debt, or bankruptcy.[11] The price of an investment grade bond hardly responds to most company news, since, by definition, the company assets would have to decline substantially before the call approaches the strike. Leveraged debt prices, in contrast, ebb and flow with company fortunes, since the call option is closer to the strike price and the debtholders have a greater chance of relying upon the company assets for repayment.[12] This suggests that we should classify leveraged loans as a risky asset class and borrow the equity principal-return framework for our leveraged loan attribution.

Equity attribution most often follows one of two standard models, both of which consider the portfolio total return versus the benchmark.[13] The Brinson, Hood, and Beebower model divides the return into (1) an asset allocation effect, defined as the sum of the portfolio weight and the benchmark return minus the sum of the benchmark weight and the benchmark return, (2) a stock selection effect, defined as the sum of the benchmark weight and the portfolio return minus the sum of the benchmark weight and the benchmark return, and (3) a residual "other" effect. From the perspective of a leveraged loan portfolio manager, this asset allocation effect does not adequately credit a manager for avoiding underperforming industries. The Brinson-Fachler model corrects this shortcoming by defining the allocation effect as the difference between the sector benchmark return and the benchmark return multiplied by the difference between the portfolio weight and the

---

[11] Robert Merton, "On the Pricing of Corporate Debt: The Risk Structure of Interest Rates," *Journal of Finance*, May 1974.

[12] Martin S. Friedson, "Do High Yield Bonds Have an Equity Component?" *Financial Management*, Summer 1994.

[13] Spaulding, pp. 29–51, is the basis for all detail on equity allocation models.

benchmark weight. Since avoiding certain industries can produce as much excess return as selecting good credits, the Brinson-Fachler model provides us with the better core methodology for leveraged loan performance attribution.

COMBINING THE MODELS

The Brinson-Fachler equity model and the adapted fixed income model both provide the leveraged loan portfolio manager and his investors with valuable performance information. The adapted fixed income model describes how the manager achieved the returns through various income and principal return streams, but cannot readily answer who was responsible for the result. The Brinson-Fachler equity model, in contrast, assigns responsibility for the return among the portfolio manager and analysts, but does not provide sufficient detail on how the manager achieved the return. Clearly, both models should have a role in leveraged senior loan performance attribution.

To thoroughly analyze returns, a manager should perform the detailed analysis of the adapted fixed income model, roll up the results into the desired portfolio categories, and then compare the portfolio to a leveraged loan index using the Brinson-Fachler model. Examples most clearly illustrate this process (see Exhibit 8.39). First, we apply the adapted fixed income model to the most basic building block of our analysis, an individual loan position.[14]

In this instance, the loan performed close to expectations given the market. Had the adapted fixed income model not included the callability effect, the analyst would have underperformed expectations by −0.5748 percent. Such an analysis would not distinguish between true underperformance on the selection effect and price appreciation constrained by a more valuable call option. In other words, a similar noncallable loan might actually rally by more than the market would suggest; when the call option is

---

14 Readers who are proficient at mathematics, specifically pricing theory, may scoff at the imprecision of these return calculations. Many market participants do, in fact, approach the pricing exercise through an even rougher approximation by assuming that the coupon differential persists for an "average life" of two or three years. The calculations, as presented, hopefully improve upon the market practice without departing completely from the general convention.

EXHIBIT 8.39

Leverage Loan Performance Attribution Calculation Example

	A	B	C	D	E
	Beginning Balance	Prepayment	Ending Balance	Price	Cost Basis
1 Last Day of Period 1	$1,000,000.00			100.50%	99.40%
2 Last Day of Period 2		$500,000.00	$500,000.00	101.25%	99.41%
3 Coupon	2.50%				
4 LIBOR	4.30%				
5 Days in Period	30				
6 Industry Coupon, Period 1	2.25%				
7 Industry Coupon, Period 2	2.00%				
8 Years to Maturity, Period 1	5.0000				
9 Years to Maturity, Period 2	4.9167				
10					
11 Coupon Income	$5,666.67	= [A1×(A3+A4)]×(A5/360)			
12 Change in Cost Basis (Income)	$50.00	= C2×(E2−E1)			
13 Total Income Return	$5,041.67	= A11+A12		0.5042%	= A13/A1
14					
15 Realized Gain	$2,950.00	= B2×(1−E2)		0.2950%	= A15/A1
16 Change in Cost Basis (Income)	($50.00)	= −C2×(E2−E1)		−0.0050%	= A16/A1
17 Sector Spread Effect	$6,145.83	= C2×[(A6−A7)×A9]		0.6146%	= A17/A1
18 Callability Effect	($3,352.00)			−0.6704%	= A18/A1
19 Analyst Effect	$956.17	= [C2×(D2−D1)]−A17−A18		0.0956%	= A19/A1
20 Change in Market Value	$3,750.00	= A17+A18+A19		0.3750%	= A20/A1
21 Unrealized Gain	$3,700.00	= A16+A20		0.3700%	= A21/A1
22 Total Price Return	$6,650.00	= A15+A21		0.6650%	= A22/A1
23					
24 Total Return	$11,691.67	= A13+A22		1.1692%	= A24/A1

attached to the noncallable loan, however, it mutes the rally for reasons unrelated to the analyst's credit recommendation.[15]

Next, we perform a similar analysis for each loan held in the portfolio, roll each loan return into an appropriate category, such as industry or rating, that matches the manager's view on risk, and then compare those category returns to the same category returns in the index through the Brinson-Fachler equity model. An example, from the Reuters Loan Pricing Corporation Performance Attribution and Analytics Service, is shown in Exhibit 8.40.

The distinctions between the selection and allocation effects can be seen most clearly by examining an industry return for which the portfolio performed dramatically different from the index. The Ecological Services and Equipment industry portfolio return, for example, outperformed the index by 0.6308 percent during this particular month. Moreover, the portfolio manager weighted the industry 0.3844 percent more than the index. The performance attribution analysis suggests that the portfolio team made excellent picks within the industry, contributing 0.0180 percent of the 0.2822 percent selection effect. The allocation effect for the industry, however, was −0.0010 percent. By tracing through the formulas, we note that this negative result occurs because the manager elected to overweight an industry that underperformed the index. In other words, the excellent absolute performance was even more impressive given that the industry returns were below average. Through the Brinson-Fachler equity model, we properly credit the selection effect for this excess return.

Many loan managers organize their portfolio construction and credit processes by expressing general macroeconomic views through target industry weightings and then selecting individual credits according to the recommendations of their analyst staff. In this framework, we can interpret the selection effect as the general responsibility of the analysts and the allocation effect as the responsibility of the portfolio manager. The Brinson-Fachler equity model, then, tells us who achieved the given return. For industries that require additional return analysis, we can disaggregate the respective industry portfolio return into the components of the

[15] We calculate the value of this call option by pricing a callable and a noncallable loan on a binomial expansion tree and defining the value of the call option as the difference in the prices of the two bonds. The callability effect then equals the change in the value of the call option during the period. Such calculations involve considerable discussion and thus exceed the scope of this analysis.

EXHIBIT 8.40

Leverage Loan Performance Attribution Analysis Example

Industry	Portfolio Return	Index Return	Difference	Sector Weightings Portfolio	Sector Weightings Index	Sector Weightings Difference	Weighted Returns Portfolio	Weighted Returns Index	Weighted Returns Difference	Perf. Attr. Selection	Perf. Attr. Allocation	Perf. Attr. Total
Aerospace and Defense	0.6225%	0.3705%	0.2520%	3.0075%	2.9117%	0.0958%	0.0187%	0.0108%	0.0079%	0.0076%	-0.0001%	0.0075%
Air Transport	1.0000%	0.9773%	0.0227%	0.0000%	1.5059%	-1.5059%	0.0000%	0.0147%	-0.0147%	0.0000%	-0.0080%	-0.0080%
Automotive	1.0649%	0.2892%	0.7756%	5.1543%	4.9868%	0.1675%	0.0549%	0.0144%	0.0405%	0.0400%	-0.0003%	0.0397%
Beverage & Tobacco	3.2086%	1.1811%	2.0275%	1.3723%	2.1731%	-0.8008%	0.0440%	0.0257%	0.0184%	0.0278%	-0.0059%	0.0219%
Building and Development	0.6434%	0.5143%	0.1291%	5.2149%	6.6783%	-1.4813%	0.0338%	0.0343%	-0.0006%	0.0067%	-0.0010%	0.0057%
Business Equipment and Services	0.8320%	0.4221%	0.4100%	4.3090%	2.3138%	1.9952%	0.0359%	0.0098%	0.0261%	0.0177%	-0.0005%	0.0172%
Cable and Satellite TV	0.4660%	0.5476%	-0.0808%	3.3022%	6.1006%	-2.7984%	0.0154%	0.0334%	-0.0180%	-0.0027%	-0.0029%	-0.0055%
Chemicals and Plastics	0.6802%	0.6784%	0.0018%	9.0271%	5.9252%	3.1019%	0.0614%	0.0401%	0.0213%	0.0003%	0.0072%	0.0075%
Clothing - Textiles	0.0000%	0.7535%	-0.7535%	0.0000%	0.6221%	-0.6221%	0.0000%	0.0047%	-0.0047%	0.0000%	-0.0019%	-0.0019%
Conglomerates	0.6097%	0.4617%	0.1480%	0.6605%	1.7858%	-1.1253%	0.0040%	0.0082%	-0.0042%	0.0010%	-0.0002%	0.0008%
Containers and Glass Products	0.6953%	0.5863%	0.1091%	6.5110%	4.9389%	1.5721%	0.0453%	0.0290%	0.0163%	0.0071%	0.0022%	0.0093%
Cosmetics/Toiletries	1.5415%	0.4219%	1.1197%	0.5421%	0.5324%	0.0097%	0.0238%	0.0085%	0.0173%	0.0173%	-0.0015%	0.0173%
Drugs	0.8363%	0.6866%	0.1437%	0.6179%	1.2438%	-0.6259%	0.0052%	0.0085%	-0.0034%	0.0009%	-0.0015%	-0.0006%
Ecological Services and Equipment	0.8178%	0.1870%	0.6308%	2.8475%	2.4630%	0.3844%	0.0233%	0.0046%	0.0187%	0.0180%	-0.0010%	0.0170%
Electronics - Electrical	1.2898%	0.5492%	0.7406%	3.4254%	3.5763%	-0.1508%	0.0442%	0.0196%	0.0245%	0.0254%	-0.0002%	0.0252%
Equipment Leasing	0.3591%	0.5371%	-0.1780%	0.6880%	0.4099%	0.2788%	0.0025%	0.0022%	0.0003%	-0.0012%	-0.0004%	-0.0017%
Farming/Agriculture	0.8264%	0.5316%	0.0948%	0.6886%	0.4099%	0.2788%	0.0043%	0.0022%	0.0021%	0.0007%	0.0002%	0.0009%
Financial Intermediaries	0.2809%	0.1102%	0.1705%	1.3811%	1.8865%	-0.5054%	0.0039%	0.0021%	0.0018%	0.0024%	0.0017%	0.0041%
Food and Drug Retailers	0.4139%	0.6029%	-0.1890%	2.3811%	1.6724%	0.6887%	0.0098%	0.0101%	-0.0003%	-0.0045%	0.0011%	-0.0034%
Food Products	0.8589%	-1.3607%	-2.0196%	8.0353%	3.2364%	2.7999%	0.0389%	-0.0440%	0.0838%	0.1219%	-0.0506%	0.0713%
Food Service	0.5382%	0.5535%	-0.0153%	1.1031%	1.9420%	-0.8459%	0.0059%	0.0107%	-0.0049%	-0.0002%	-0.0009%	-0.0011%
Forest Products	1.1536%	0.4766%	0.6770%	1.1922%	1.1939%	-0.0017%	0.0138%	0.0057%	0.0081%	0.0081%	0.0000%	0.0081%
Healthcare	0.4430%	0.4535%	-0.0105%	8.2667%	5.2772%	2.9895%	0.0366%	0.0239%	0.0127%	-0.0009%	0.0002%	-0.0006%
Home Furnishings	0.8356%	0.6538%	0.1818%	2.1119%	1.1492%	0.9626%	0.0176%	0.0075%	0.0101%	0.0038%	0.0020%	0.0058%
Industrial Equipment	0.4598%	0.9371%	-0.4773%	1.5231%	1.9433%	-0.4202%	0.0070%	0.0182%	-0.0112%	-0.0073%	-0.0021%	-0.0093%
Insurance	0.5012%	0.5626%	-0.0613%	2.2521%	1.1275%	1.1246%	0.0113%	0.0063%	0.0049%	-0.0014%	0.0013%	-0.0001%
Leisure Goods-Activities -Movies	0.3307%	0.4551%	-0.1184%	4.4654%	3.2236%	1.2418%	0.0150%	0.0147%	0.0004%	-0.0053%	0.0001%	0.0052%
Lodging and Casinos	0.6230%	0.6087%	0.0143%	6.2703%	4.8825%	1.3878%	0.0391%	0.0297%	0.0093%	0.0009%	0.0023%	0.0032%
Nonferrous Metals - Minerals	0.4335%	0.5914%	-0.1579%	1.3508%	2.3598%	-1.0092%	0.0059%	0.0140%	-0.0081%	-0.0021%	-0.0015%	-0.0038%
Oil & Gas	0.3467%	0.4890%	-0.1423%	0.3466%	2.0703%	-1.7237%	0.0012%	0.0101%	-0.0089%	-0.0005%	-0.0008%	-0.0012%
Publishing	0.3892%	0.4062%	-0.0170%	5.1094%	3.3809%	1.7285%	0.0199%	0.0137%	0.0062%	-0.0009%	-0.0007%	-0.0015%
Radio and Television	0.1624%	0.5232%	-0.3608%	1.4099%	2.2889%	-0.8771%	0.0023%	0.0120%	-0.0097%	-0.0051%	-0.0007%	-0.0058%
Rail Industries	0.3765%	0.5079%	-0.1314%	0.0289%	0.2991%	-0.2702%	0.0001%	0.0015%	-0.0014%	0.0016%	-0.0012%	-0.0002%
Retailers (Not Food and Drug)	0.6716%	0.5323%	0.1393%	1.1244%	2.4912%	-1.3668%	0.0076%	0.0133%	-0.0057%	-0.0017%	0.0009%	0.0004%
Steel	0.3209%	0.6167%	-0.2958%	0.5645%	0.0527%	0.5118%	0.0018%	0.0003%	0.0015%	-0.0009%	-0.0003%	-0.0008%
Surface Transport	0.3841%	0.5568%	-0.1726%	0.5490%	0.8383%	-0.2893%	0.0021%	0.0047%	-0.0026%	-0.0009%	0.0009%	-0.0013%
Telecom	0.5756%	0.1937%	0.3818%	0.3814%	4.1997%	-3.8183%	0.0022%	0.0081%	-0.0059%	0.0015%	0.0096%	0.0111%
Utilities	0.1160%	0.2401%	-0.1241%	1.6091%	4.1519%	-2.5428%	0.0019%	0.0100%	-0.0081%	-0.0020%	0.0052%	0.0032%
Equities	0.7190%	0.0000%	0.7190%	1.0283%	0.0000%	1.0263%	0.0074%	0.0000%	0.0074%	0.0074%	-0.0046%	0.0028%
Cash	0.0754%	0.0000%	0.0754%	1.1794%	0.0000%	1.1794%	0.0009%	0.0000%	0.0009%	0.0009%	-0.0053%	-0.0044%
				100.0000%	100.0000%	0.0000%	0.6692%	0.4454%	0.2238%	0.2822%	-0.0584%	0.2238%

adapted fixed income model and, finally, even examine how each individual loan position in that industry affected each component. Using both the Brinson-Fachler equity model and the adapted fixed income model, a portfolio manager can identify the individuals responsible for the return and, in extraordinary detail, how they achieved the results.

CONCLUSION

The manager of a leveraged senior loan portfolio must negotiate numerous peculiarities that distinguish the asset class from mainstream equities and bonds. Since he makes decisions every day based upon how he believes these unique features will affect his returns, any useful performance attribution framework must also consider their effects. In this section, we propose a method for leveraged senior loan attribution that incorporates certain methods from equity and traditional fixed income models. While the final model involves substantial estimation and theory, it accounts for all investment considerations and, by that measure, disaggregates performance more thoroughly than simple adaptations of traditional models.

REFERENCES

Campisi, Stephen. "Primer on Fixed Income Performance Attribution." *Journal of Performance Measurement,* Summer 2000.

Friedson, Martin S. "Do High Yield Bonds Have an Equity Component?" *Financial Management,* Summer 1994.

Gehring, Louis. "Effective Approaches to Fixed Income Performance Attribution." Presentation delivered at the Second Annual Performance Attribution Forum (New York, Doubletree Times Square), January 27, 2004. Presentation slides on file with the author.

Merton, Robert. "On the Pricing of Corporate Debt: The Risk Structure of Interest Rates." *Journal of Finance,* May 1974.

Spaulding, David. *Investment Performance Attribution: A Guide to What It Is, How to Calculate It, and How to Use It.* New York: McGraw-Hill, 2003.

CHAPTER 9

Distressed Loan Investing

Peter T. Santry
Managing Director
Banc of America Securities LLC

Joeseph Lamport
Counsel and Senior Advisor
Sandelman Partners

David Isenberg, Esq.
Of Counsel
Milbank, Tweed, Hadley & McCloy LLP

Gregory A. Bray, Esq.
Partner
Milbank, Tweed, Hadley & McCloy LLP

William R. Wagner
Kaye Scholer LLP

Introduction to Distressed Loan Investing

Peter T. Santry
Managing Director
Banc of America Securities LLC

OVERVIEW

Distressed corporate loans have become a widely held asset in the portfolios of credit investors. Once found only in bank workout groups and traded by a small group of banks, brokers, and value investors, the distressed loan market has grown to encompass a broad spectrum of credit managers, including banks, loan funds, hedge funds, value investors, traders, and workout professionals. Their attraction to distressed loans is based on the same attributes that endear senior secured loans to par investors. The seniority and security in the capital structure, which loans enjoy, enhances their safety and increases recovery rates in the event of default. Investors are also attracted to distressed loans' floating rate of interest and the control that bank lenders can exert in the workout process. While the returns on a portfolio of distressed loans do not compare on an absolute basis with those of equities, they do provide a fairly predictable high-yield return that has made them a staple of most distressed investors. It is not only distressed investors that need to understand the distressed loan market. Since distressed loans have represented as much as 7 or 8 percent of a leveraged loan portfolio during recent high-default-rate periods, par loan managers operating in a bank, managers of collateralized loan obligations (CLOs), and prime rate funds must also comprehend the workings of this market. How a portfolio manager handles problem credits can affect returns and determine relative performance among funds.

This article will try to address the issues involved in investing in distressed, mainly corporate, loans. It will start by tracing the evolution and growth of the market, from its inception during the excesses of the leveraged buyout (LBO) market of the late 1980s to its current state in today's low-default-rate environment. It will review the market's peaks and troughs and the factors that most influence it, namely changes in speculative-grade new issuance and the economic and credit cycles. Not only will we look at the high recovery rates enjoyed by loans relative to other credit instruments, but we will also try to figure out why recovery rates fluctuate. Lastly, to help explain how distressed loans trade, we will delve into the types of investors attracted to the market and the general strategies they deploy. We will also look at factors affecting recovery rates and return variations through the market cycle.

BACKGROUND AND HISTORY

The distressed loan market had its origins in the aftermath of the LBO boom of the 1980s and the vast amount of leveraged loans that were created to finance them. Its seeds were found in the creation of a high-yield market for loans, which had not previously existed. For the first time, agent banks were able to underwrite and then sell the risks of their leveraged loan clients. As the loan syndication market developed, large, mainly money center banks originated and then distributed leveraged loans to regional banks, foreign banks (mainly Japanese and European), and, to a lesser extent, prime rate funds that were searching for high-yielding, floating-rate loans. This new origination/distribution model, combined with the emergence of the high-yield bond market, fueled the LBO boom of the mid to late 1980s. It also spawned the distressed loan market that followed (see Exhibit 9.1).

As bankers and borrowers pushed leverage multiples higher and earnings coverage lower, the United States was hit with a

E X H I B I T 9 . 1

Total U.S. syndicated loan issuance.

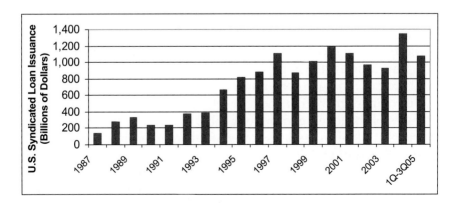

EXHIBIT 9.2

Total adversely rated credits (broken down between
special mention and classified) as a percentage of total
commitments, 1991–2002.

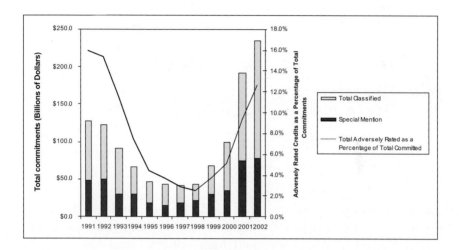

recession that crimped corporate cash flows and exposed the over-leveraged state of many high-yield companies. As many of the loans were downgraded by regulators and moved into workout areas (see Exhibit 9.2), banks were forced to report higher amounts of nonperforming loans on their balance sheets, which in turn raised credit concerns among the equity analysts following their stocks. Banks' share prices suffered.

In response to this decline, bank managements looked for ways to improve their nonperforming loan ratios, exploring liquidity options for this part of their portfolios. Although many structures were used to help alleviate this problem, including "good bank/bad bank" structures (which are beyond the scope of this article), many banks began to ask investment bankers and agent banks to provide them with liquidity to reduce these exposures. In response for this demand for liquidity, a small number of brokers, investment banks, and banks formed distressed trading groups resulting in the emergence of a broker/dealer market catering to a small number of investors: The distressed loan market was born (see Exhibit 9.3).

Since the distressed loan market's inception in the early 1990s, the supply of distressed loans has tracked (with a lag)

EXHIBIT 9.3

U.S. secondary loan market trading volume.

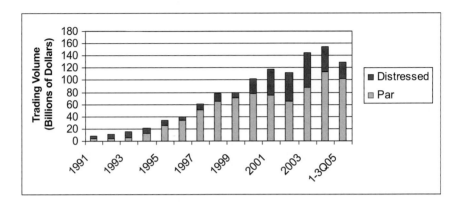

speculative-grade new issuance and the economic cycle. After default rates peaked in 1992, the loan market enjoyed a period of relative stability, with leveraged loan volumes and LBO activity below the previous peak. Default rates were similarly benign because of the strong economy of the period. That picture began to change with the financing of the capital expenditure boom of the telecom, energy and Internet industries, and the need to finance their capital expenditures.

The volume of lending to telecom/technology ventures was colossal. Banks and institutional investors doled out large sums of money to numerous companies, many of which had shaky business plans founded upon overly optimistic growth projection. Credit ratings were apparently not an issue (many companies rated CCC or below found funding from both banks and institutional investors easily available). But like everything else, the fascination with the technology sector came to an end, and in the late 1990s, it's unwinding resulted in another major spike in U.S. corporate defaults, leading to a host of fresh credits in the distressed market. U.S. institutional default rates started rising in early 1999 and spiked in late 2000 and through the third quarter of 2001 as the highly visible defaults of Enron, Owens Corning, Adelphia Communications, and WorldCom headlined a parade of large corporate Chapter 11 filers (see Exhibit 9.4).

The bursting of this credit bubble created record dollar volume of distressed loans, dwarfing the prior high set in 1991.

E X H I B I T   9 . 4

Default rate spike, 2000–2002.

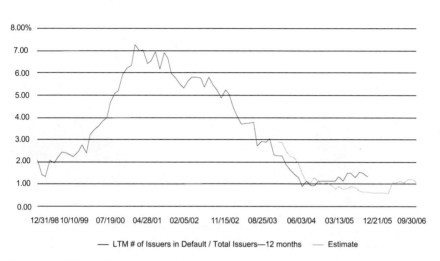

── LTM # of Issuers in Default / Total Issuers—12 months   ── Estimate

Source: Standard & Poor's LCD.

Once again the default spike was preceded by heavy issuance at the lower end of the noninvestment grade spectrum. New issuance of bonds rated CCC or below increased dramatically in late 1997 and mid–1998 with the financings for Global Crossing, McLeod USA, Inc., Nextlink Communications, PSI Net, RCN, Regal Cinemas, and Winstar (see Exhibit 9.5). In many cases the proceeds were utilized for massive capital expenditures to build out the expansions in the telecom and Internet, cable, theater, and other industries.

As Exhibit 9.5 shows, periods of easier credit standards followed by contractions in the economy, declines in corporate valuations, and lower earnings led to the two highest periods of distressed loan supply over the past 20 years.

FACTORS AFFECTING RECOVERY RATES

Now that we have discussed the factors that drive changes in corporate default rates, we need to look at loan recovery rates (loss given default) to understand how a portfolio of leveraged loans will fare over time. As we mentioned at the outset, most leveraged loans benefit from their position at the top of the capital structure

EXHIBIT 9.5

CCC or lower-rated issuance use of proceeds.

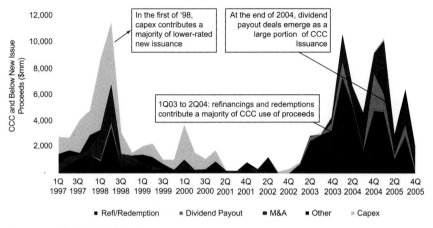

Source: Banc of America Securities LLC.

and from the collateral that is usually pledged as security for the loans. As a result, corporate loans enjoy the highest recovery rates among corporate debt obligations.

While loans perform well relative to other forms of corporate debt, loan recovery rates do vary over the business cycle. This variation is due to the supply of distressed loans in the market as well as to macro factors such as corporate valuation and the credit market's appetite for risk.

The supply of defaulted loans generated during periods of high default rates has an important effect on prices fetched in the period 30 days after the default, the common measure used by the credit rating agencies to define the recovery rate. As Exhibit 9.6 highlights, first lien recovery rates decline during periods of high supply of distressed loans, as was seen during the high default periods of 1990–1992 and 1999–2002. As default rates eased and returned to more normal levels, the supply of new distressed loans ebbed and recovery rates pushed higher (1995–1996 and 2004–2005). Obviously the dramatic increases in corporate earnings and creditworthiness as the economy rebounded from recession also influenced recovery rates (see Exhibit 9.7).

In addition to these factors, corporate valuations also increased as the stock market snapped back strongly in the postrecession

EXHIBIT 9.6

Recovery rates for all asset classes have improved with corporate earnings and higher stock valuations.

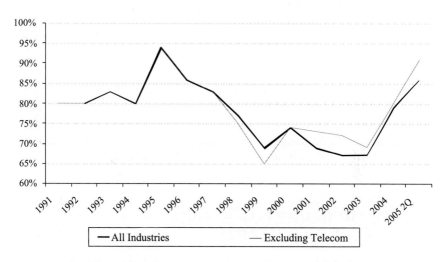

Source: Standard & Poor's LossStats Database.

EXHIBIT 9.7

Corporate earnings growth corresponds with higher recovery rates.

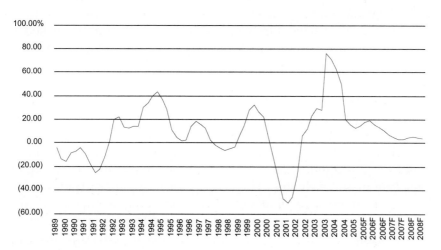

Source: Standard & Poor's LCD.

years of 1992 and 2003, which increased loan coverages. Lastly, the swelling demand for distressed assets coming from the new hedge funds dedicated to the distressed area was certainly a factor in the upswing in loan recovery rates in 2004 and 2005.

How a defaulted loan trades in the distressed market depends on the economic and credit cycles as well as on technical factors such as the supply of distressed debt and the flows of funds into the distressed market. In periods of weak earnings and recession and/or low corporate valuation, bids are scarcer and recovery rates are lower than when both earnings and the economy are healthy and inflows are plentiful. Despite this variability, distressed loan recovery rates have ranged between a low of 70 percent and a high of 94 percent, which underscores the high level of safety that loans provide.

TYPES OF INVESTORS AND STRATEGIES UTILIZED

We have discussed the conditions that influence the supply of distressed loans and the recovery rates; now we will address the demand side of the market. Who are the players, how do distressed loans trade in the market and why, and what should a buyer or seller expect upon entering the market to transact?

In order to answer these questions, it is useful to know the various strategies deployed by market participants. In the early years of the market, most distressed investors fell into two camps: fundamental investors who purchased a distressed loan and worked it out in a buy-and-hold strategy, and investors who waited until the details of the reorganization were released and then jumped in to try to take advantage of any endgame arbitrage opportunities.

With the explosion in the number of hedge funds devoted to distressed debt investing, the number of strategies deployed in the market has multiplied. Now, prices of bank debt are increasingly linked to movements in other debt instruments, as investors have positions throughout the capital structure that influence whether they buy or sell a distressed loan and for how much. Trading also occurs much more frequently over the life of a bankruptcy, with participants deploying short-term trades around less significant events. Many funds face quarterly redemptions and are forced to sell distressed loans in order to meet them, regardless of anything that may be happening in the credit. The advent of credit derivatives as a way to get long and short a credit has also added a technical layer of complexity to a product that has historically traded on credit and valuation fundamentals. All these factors make the loan market of today quite different from that of 15 years ago.

The major strategies used to trade distressed loans are outlined here. Hedge funds—a huge player in the distressed area—employ most of these strategies.

Fundamental/Value Strategy

As mentioned previously, fundamental value investors are the traditional players in the market. They generally buy distressed loans prior to or just after a company files for bankruptcy, with an eye toward becoming an active participant in the restructuring process. Because they buy early, during the most uncertain period, these investors purchase at the deepest discounts. Usually investors of this type have a long-term view and have access to long-term capital (i.e., they have money locked up for two years or more). They can afford to be patient and are able to weather illiquidity and mark-to-market price fluctuations.. The value investor will usually sit on creditors' committees, much like a workout officer at a bank, and will look to maximize the return by influencing the structure, the timing, and the form of consideration distributed to the creditors when the company is restructured.

Often these investors will seek control of the bankruptcy process by purchasing a majority or blocking position in the class. As a result of their entry during the riskiest point in a bankruptcy and their activist role in the process, value investors demand the most compensation for the liquidity that they provide.

Endgame Strategy

Another classic hedge fund strategy is the endgame arbitrage, in which an investor will purchase a distressed loan upon the announcement of a restructuring or the filing of a disclosure statement. This type of investment was first practiced by hedge funds with backgrounds in the risk arbitrage business; many of the early distressed investors viewed distressed investing as a countercyclical business to their core deal-driven risk arbitrage efforts. The skills and analysis are transferable.

In its simplest form, the investor buys the loan at a discount to the value of the consideration he or she will receive upon exiting bankruptcy. The discount exists because the investor is getting paid to deal with all the issues and complexities surrounding a company's emergence from Chapter 11. Potential delays and last-minute changes to the plan and complex operational issues involved in the distribution out of the bankruptcy create the arbitrage opportunity. Also, there are fewer buyers of bankrupt loans than investors that can hold postreorganization loans or securities, which helps the arbitrage. Usually the consideration received once the company exits from bankruptcy (cash, new bank loans and/or notes, and sometimes equity or equitylike instruments) will-exceed the value of the prepetition debt.

Returns on this type of investment are usually lower than what a fundamental investor gets, reflecting the higher certainty concerning the borrower's prospects and the well-defined value of the exit package the investor will receive.

Capital Structure Arbitrage Strategies

Increasingly, hedge funds are hedging their long distressed loan positions with junior securities of the same borrower or in the credit default swap (CDS) market. Opportunities for this strategy arise when there is a perceived mispricing of risk between two classes of debt in a capital structure. Sometimes the arbitrage may be between securities of two different companies in the same industry, such as between a supplier and an end user, for example. Investors will attempt to profit from this by arbitraging the price inefficiency; in the loan market, this is usually manifested by the manager's buying the loan and selling a more junior security. As a credit deteriorates and migrates toward bankruptcy, the senior secured bank debt will outperform most unsecured obligations of a borrower. As we discussed earlier, absolute recovery rates for senior secured loans are much higher than for other more junior asset classes. This strategy can affect loan prices to the upside as well, if the sold junior security rallies, the distressed loan will often appreciate in tandem. Changes in the equity and the bond price of a borrower are being imported into the price of distressed loans as a result of the activity of these players.

Loan managers who are accustomed to low price volatility now need to be aware of price changes in a given borrower's capital structure. Movements in price that are not explained by changes in a borrower's fundamentals can be attributable to this type of market activity.

Multistrategy Loan Investors

The newest participant in the distressed loan market is the traditional CLO fund manager who has expanded his horizons beyond the par market. Using his credit knowledge of the many borrowers in his par portfolio, the par manager can respond to a borrower's deteriorating prospects and purchase distressed loans—often before traditional hedge funds are up to speed on a credit. These managers will often create flexible vehicles that are able to house nonperforming and lower-rated credits that are unsuitable for the par structures. Often a hedge fund vehicle is used.

Because these managers have preexisting positions in their par funds, they can leverage off their existing knowledge base and personnel, spreading it over the distressed position and creating tremendous synergies. By combining the distressed and par positions, this type of investor has the size to control the process much like the value investor mentioned earlier.

Private Equity Investors

It is worth mentioning that a number of distressed loan investors are migrating toward using bankruptcy to gain control of the borrower's equity upon exit. They are achieving the same end result as a private equity fund that purchases a company in a more traditional manner. Many private equity firms are recognizing this and have raised money to enter the distressed arena, leveraging their considerable industry and corporate knowledge base to invest in distressed loans and bonds. Within the last year, several marquee private equity firms have opened up distressed hedge funds.

It is too early to tell whether these funds will deploy different strategies from those previously outlined, but with their substantial resources in fund-raising and human capital, they bear watching and could become a significant presence.

SUMMARY

Distressed loans have become an inevitable by-product of the corporate syndicated market for leveraged loans, especially during recessions following prolonged periods of relaxed credit standards. Even during times of economic downturn, distressed loans have performed well compared to other corporate debt instruments. As a result, hedge fund and par managers alike have accessed the distressed loan market to adjust their portfolios, resulting in dramatic growth in traded volume and number of participants. Distressed loans have become an accepted asset class and a core holding for most distressed managers.

We have attempted to trace the history of the distressed loan class and to measure its performance over time by looking at the default rate history and recovery rate information through a business cycle. We have tried to look at who the players in the market are and explored some of their basic strategies in order to better understand how distressed loans trade. Comprehending this asset class and its market is a necessity for all credit managers, as distressed loans will make up a significant portion of their holdings at some point during an economic cycle.

Securities Law Concerns Related to a Borrower's Bankruptcy

Joeseph Lamport
Counsel and Senior Advisor
Sandelman Partners

THE STATUS OF INTERESTS IN LOANS UNDER THE SECURITIES LAWS

Over the last two decades, as the syndicated loan market has grown and flourished, an important factor contributing to the market's health has been the fundamental assumption that an interest in a loan under a credit agreement (at least under ordinary circumstances) does not constitute a "security" for purposes of application of federal securities laws. This assumption is based on the definitions of a security in the Securities Act of 1933 (the Securities Act) and the Securities Exchange Act of 1934 (the Exchange Act), as interpreted by a long line of cases, which have consistently excluded traditional commercial bank lending relationships from being subject to the requirements of the securities laws. One leading case is *Reves v. Ernst & Young*,[1] where the Supreme Court set forth a "family-resemblance" test to determine when a note should be considered a security.[2] In addition to itemizing seven specific types of notes that should always be excluded from the statutory definition (including notes evidencing loans of commercial banks for current operations), the family-resemblance test supports an even broader exclusion for interests in loans by looking at such factors as the motivation of the buyer and seller, the common public understanding of whether a particular instrument is intended to be a security, and the availability of alternative regulatory protection for market participants. Even where some criteria indicate a basis for characterization as a security, the family-resemblance test establishes a bias against treating notes or similar interests created by commercial bank lenders as securities, inasmuch as the extensive bank regulatory scheme arguably obviates the need to impose additional controls on loan market participants under the securities laws.[3]

But the fundamental understanding that loans are not securities has nonetheless been subject to some qualification and uncertainty at the margins because of the way interests in loans are packaged and remarketed. Indeed, a separate analysis is necessary to determine whether derivative products based on a commercial loan (such as loan participations or syndications) should be classified as securities as a result of the originator's packaging and marketing activity. Although the Supreme Court has not yet directly addressed this question, the lower federal courts have consistently ruled that loan participations and syndications in the ordinary course should not be characterized as securities. In a number of cases, these decisions have been based on the fundamental *commercial* nature of the loan syndication or participation, in contrast to the investment expectations associated with securities offerings.

---

[1] *Reves v. Ernst & Young*, 494 U.S. 56, 110 S. Ct. 945 (1990).

[2] In spite of the inclusion of "notes" in the statutory definition under the Exchange Act, the *Reves* Court concluded that the statute merely established a rebuttable presumption that a note is a security, to be overcome based upon the analysis of the family-resemblance test. Ibid.

[3] Moreover, under the *Reves* test, the traditional assumptions of market participants that loans are not securities further reinforces the legal analysis.

For example, in *Banco Espanol de Credito v. Security Pacific Nat'l Bank*,[4] the Second Circuit analyzed a loan participation program established by Security Pacific for commercial borrowers as an alternative to a commercial paper arrangement.[5] Even though the Security Pacific program involved active remarketing of loan participation interests to institutional investors, the court applied the family-resemblance test in concluding that these loan participation interests were not securities.[6]

When a borrower is distressed, there may be an additional ground on which a loan or an interest in a loan to such a borrower could be characterized as a security. Under another line of cases, starting from the Supreme Court's decision in *SEC v. W.J. Howey Co.*,[7] an interest may be characterized as a security if it involves an investment "in a common enterprise and [the investor] is led to expect profits solely from the efforts of the promoter or a third party."[8] Earning interest on a commercial loan is generally not viewed as an expectation of profit within the meaning of the *Howey* decision. However, with a distressed borrower, the traditional commercial lending assumptions no longer apply, and a market participant in distressed loans will be much more likely to expect profit in the form of appreciation in the value of the loan, not just the contract rate of interest. Although there is no instance in which a court has actually concluded that a distressed loan should therefore be treated as a security, there are certainly grounds to support such an argument in the dicta of various decisions considering these issues.

If a borrower moves from the category of distressed and becomes the subject of bankruptcy proceedings, the status of an interest in a loan to such a borrower will undergo a further transformation. Once the borrower is in bankruptcy, the classification of

---

[4] *Banco Espanol de Credito v. Security Pacific Nat'l Bank*, 973 F.2d 51 (2d Cir. 1992), cert denied, 509 U.S. 903 (1993).

[5] In contrast to traditional syndicated loans, commercial paper is well recognized as a security under the Securities Act.

[6] The *Banco Espanol* court nonetheless noted that "even if an underlying instrument is not a security, the manner in which participations in that instrument are used, pooled, or marketed might establish that such participations are securities." Ibid. at 56, citing *Gary Plastic Packaging Corp. v. Merrill Lynch, Pierce, Fenner & Smith, Inc.*, 756 F.2d 230 (2d Cir. 1985).

[7] *SEC v. W.J. Howey Co.*, 328 U.S. 293 (1946). The *Howey* case concerned an investment contract relating to service contracts for citrus groves, facts very distinguishable from the typical commercial lending relationship. However, courts have tended to use the investment contract analysis as a catchall category.

[8] Ibid. at 298–299.

an interest in a loan as a security is no longer merely a theoretical possibility. Indeed, a successful reorganization of a debtor under Chapter 11 of the Bankruptcy Code will typically entail implementation of a plan of reorganization, pursuant to which the debtor's prepetition obligations will be exchanged for new types of interests in the reorganized entity. Very frequently, in order for a company to deleverage (i.e., reduce its debt burden), the plan of reorganization will distribute newly issued equity interests in exchange for prepetition debt, including loans, thereby potentially transforming an investor's interest into something that is unmistakably a security under the federal securities laws.

The transformation of an interest in a loan into ownership of a security through bankruptcy reorganization presents some unique legal concerns and risks for loan market participants. The special rules and risks relating to distributions of securities to pre-existing creditors by debtors in bankruptcy are discussed more fully in the remainder of this article.

ISSUANCE OF SECURITIES BY DEBTORS IN BANKRUPTCY

As mentioned previously, debtors in bankruptcy will frequently distribute new securities to creditors as part of a plan of reorganization. Section 1145 of the Bankruptcy Code provides an exemption from the registration requirements of Section 5 of the Securities Act for the express purpose of enabling the issuance of new securities pursuant to a reorganization plan in certain circumstances.[9] The general purpose of this exemption is to make it much less costly and burdensome for a debtor to issue new securities in connection with a plan of reorganization, thereby advancing the goal of the Bankruptcy Code by facilitating successful reorganization. At the same time, the holders of prepetition claims (including claims arising under prepetition loan agreements) benefit from the Section 1145 exemption because it enables the resale of newly issued reorganization plan securities without restriction.[10] Conversely, the unavailability of the exemption under Section 1145 will potentially impair the liquidity and value of newly issued plan securities,

---

[9] 11 U.S.C. §1145.

[10] The offer or sale of securities that are covered by the exemption under Section 1145(a) is deemed to be a public offering pursuant to Section 1145(c), thereby enabling resale without restriction.

which can place a creditor at a relative disadvantage in terms of recovery.[11]

The exemption under Section 1145 is available specifically with respect to the issuance of a security in the debtor or an affiliate of the debtor participating in a joint plan or a successor to the debtor under the plan where such security is being offered pursuant to a plan of reorganization. Additionally, in order to qualify for the Section 1145 exemption, the issuance must be either (1) in exchange for a claim against, an interest in, or a claim for an administrative expense in a debtor's bankruptcy case; or (2) principally in respect of any such exchange and partly for cash or other property.[12] Thus, the Section 1145 exemption will not be available for issuances of new securities by a debtor that are primarily or exclusively in exchange for new value, and any such issuance for new value must otherwise be pursuant to a registered offering or some other exemption from the securities laws. In contrast, the issuance of new securities to prepetition creditors (including those with claims arising under a prepetition loan agreement) under or in connection with a reorganization plan would typically satisfy the basic requirements of Section 1145(a), as a result of which such securities could be resold without restriction.

However, there are several important limitations on the availability of the Section 1145 exemption. As noted earlier, the Section 1145 exemption is a transaction exemption,[13] but it also provides protection for ordinary creditors who receive new plan securities and immediately resell them. However, the transaction exemption under Section 1145(a) is not available for any entity that is an underwriter as that term is defined in Section 1145(b). Thus, the key to understanding the scope of the Section 1145(a) exemption is the definition of underwriter set forth in Section 1145(b).

---

[11] There are generally two types of exemptions from registration recognized under the securities laws: securities exemptions established under Section 3 of the Securities Act and transaction exemptions under Section 5 of the Act. The major difference between the basic types of exemption is that securities exemptions cover both the original offer and sale and all subsequent resales, whereas transaction exemptions cover only the original offer and sale. The Section 1145 exemption is a type of transaction exemption, but it also provides protection for ordinary creditors (not including affiliates or underwriters) who receive new plan securities and immediately resell them.

[12] The statute further provides that the exemption will apply to the offer of a security through a warrant, option, or subscription right if it satisfies the other conditions set forth in Section 1145(a)(1). The exemption under Section 1145 also extends to so-called portfolio securities.

[13] See note 11.

Consequently, the key legal issue for holders of prepetition claims that are being exchanged for newly issued securities under a plan of reorganization is to avoid being classified as an underwriter under Section 1145(b) in order to preserve the validity of the Section 1145(a) exemption.

BANKRUPTCY CODE DEFINITION OF UNDERWRITER

Bankruptcy Code Section 1145(b)(1) identifies four circumstances in which an entity will be considered an underwriter, thus jeopardizing the validity of the Section 1145(a) exemption. Three of these cases involve factors unique to the bankruptcy/reorganization context and may pose a particular concern for entities that actively trade claims in the distressed market, including claims arising under prepetition loan agreements. The fourth ground for classification as an underwriter under Section 1145(b) is based on incorporation by reference of the definition of underwriter from Section 2(11) of the Securities Act.

For the three bankruptcy-specific elements of the underwriter test, Section 1145(b)(1) provides that an entity is an underwriter for purposes of the Bankruptcy Code if (1) it purchases a claim against, an interest in, or an administrative claim *with a view to distribution* of any security received or to be received in exchange therefore,[14] (2) it offers to sell securities offered or sold under a reorganization plan for the holders of such securities,[15] or (3) it offers to buy securities offered or sold under a plan from the holders if such offer to buy is made (a) *with a view to distribution* and (b) under an agreement made in connection with the plan, with consummation of the plan, or with the offer or sale of securities under the plan.[16]

Parties that actively trade in the distressed market will typically do so with a view to quickly reselling any new security that they receive in exchange for such claims under the plan of reorganization. Thus, the question raised by the plain language of Section 1145(b)(1) is the extent to which the mere acquisition of a prepetition claim (such as a claim based on a prepetition loan agreement) with a view to selling newly issued equity that will be received in exchange therefor would render the Section 1145(a) exemption unavailable.

---

[14] 11 U.S.C. §1145(b)(1)(A).
[15] U.S.C. §1145(b)(1)(B).
[16] 11 U.S.C. §1145(b)(1)(C).

The original legislative history of Section 1145 provides some guidance on how Congress intended the exemption to be interpreted. Specifically, the legislative history indicates that Congress wanted to limit the activities of "real underwriters" involved in a "classical underwriting,"[17] but did not intend to limit the activities of creditors who might fall into the definition on some technical ground. Congress provided further clarification on this issue when it amended Section 1145 in 1984 to preserve the Section 1145(a) exemption for any entity that is engaged in "ordinary trading transactions," even when that entity otherwise falls under the Section 1145(b) definition. Consequently, an entity that buys prepetition claims (such as claims arising under a loan agreement) with a view to distribution will not be an underwriter so long as it is engaged in ordinary trading transactions.

Given the nature of the distressed trading market, it may be difficult to determine when a particular trade qualifies as an ordinary trading transaction. The SEC has provided some insight into its view of the meaning of "ordinary trading transactions" for entities that are or may be underwriters under Section 1145(b)(1).[18] No-action letters have recognized that accumulators and distributors[19] of substantial amounts of claims may engage in ordinary trading transactions, but only subject to certain qualifications. Specifically, the no-action letters have provided that accumulators and distributors may be deemed to have engaged in ordinary trading transactions if such transactions are conducted on a national exchange or over the counter and satisfy each of the following three conditions:

- Not involving concerted action by the original recipients of new securities (or distributors on their behalf) in connection with any such resale
- Not involving the use of informational documents other than the plan and the disclosure statement
- Not involving payment of special compensation to a broker/dealer in connection with any such resale, other than routine compensation for a similar transaction

---

[17] H. Rep. No. 95–575 at 420–421 (1977).

[18] See, e.g., *In re Manville Corp.*, SEC No-Action Letter, 1986 WL 68341 (August 28, 1986); *UNR Indus., Inc.*, SEC No-Action Letter, 1989 WL 246122 (July 11, 1989).

[19] Under these no-action letters, accumulators are defined as entities that purchase claims prior to confirmation with a view to the distribution of plan securities received in exchange therefor, whereas distributors are defined as entities that offer to sell plan securities on behalf of claim holders.

In the event that an entity's market activities fall outside the scope of ordinary trading transactions, that entity will have to consider more carefully whether it may be subject to classification as an underwriter under Section 1145(b) and consequently be subject to restrictions on resale of any plan securities.

As noted previously, in addition to the three bankruptcy-specific definitions of underwriter in Section 1145(b), an entity will also be considered an underwriter for purposes of Section 1145(b) to the extent that it meets the definition of an underwriter under Section 2(11) of the Securities Act. This fourth test is generally understood to incorporate only the control person portion of the 1933 Act definition of issuer into the Section 1145(b) definition of underwriter.[20]

The test for control person is another area of uncertainty that may give rise to risk for creditors that have accumulated large holdings against a debtor in bankruptcy. Prior to the enactment of the Bankruptcy Code, the SEC had consistently expressed the view that any creditor that held in excess of 1 percent of a class of new securities issued by a reorganizing debtor should be considered a control person.[21] However, Section 1145 was clearly intended to liberalize this pre-Code approach. Moreover, the legislative history suggests that Congress considered a bright line test that only someone with 10 percent of new equity securities would be subject to underwriter status under Section 1145(b)(1)(D).[22] However, the control person test under Section 2(11) of the Securities Act, which was ultimately incorporated into the Bankruptcy Code, is a facts and circumstances test, based on a number of factors that demonstrate the general power to direct management. Consequently, a prepetition creditor that ends up holding 5 percent of a debtor's postreorganization equity may be a control person based on having board representation or other indicia of control.

---

[20] 11 U.S.C. § 1145(b)(1)(D). This clause of Section 1145(b) initially gave rise to considerable confusion because by the plain language, an issuer would seem to be an underwriter and therefore unable to benefit from the Section 1145(a) exemption, which would effectively render the exemption meaningless. However, courts that have considered the issue have concluded that Congress did not intend this result and have interpreted §1145(b)(1)(D) as applying only to the underwriter or control person portion of the Securities Act definition of underwriter. See *In re Frontier Airlines*, 93 B.R. 1014 (Bankr. D. Colo. 1988).

[21] See Sen. Rep. No. 989, 95th Cong., 2d Sess. 131–132 (1978), summarizing the SEC's position under pre-Code law regarding the status of holders of 1 percent of a class of outstanding securities as a presumptive underwriter.

[22] Ibid.

In sum, bankruptcy represents an exception to the general analysis regarding the characterization of an interest in a loan agreement as a security. In particular, a creditor that accumulates a substantial position in claims (including claims arising under a loan agreement) against a company in bankruptcy must pay close attention to the legal risks associated with the potential transformation of those claims into newly issued securities pursuant to a plan of reorganization. In the majority of cases, a creditor should be able to rely on the transaction exemption provided in Section 1145(a) of the Bankruptcy Code, which permits unrestricted resale of those newly issued plan securities. However, resale will be subject to restriction in the event that the creditor/claim holder may be classified as an underwriter pursuant to Section 1145(b), either as a result of bankruptcy-specific considerations (such as whether the creditor accumulated claims with a view to distribution of plan securities) or by virtue of being a control person.

Distressed Debt Investing—Risk Considerations

Gregory A. Bray, Esq.
Partner
Milbank, Tweed, Hadley & McCloy LLP

David Isenberg, Esq.
Of Counsel
Milbank, Tweed, Hadley & McCloy LLP[23]

AN OVERVIEW

The relatively higher returns commanded by distressed loans reflect the greater risks that loan market participants investing in

---

[23] Gregory A. Bray is a partner in the Financial Restructuring Group and David Isenberg is Of Counsel in the Global Corporate Group, respectively, in the Los Angeles Office of Milbank, Tweed, Hadley & McCloy LLC. The authors both specialize in the representation of secured and unsecured lenders and noteholders seeking to work out the obligations of distressed businesses, both in and out of court. The authors wish to thank all of those inside and outside of Milbank whose efforts are reflected in this chapter. In particular, the authors thank Eva Swayzee of Milbank's Global Corporate Group for her assistance in editing this chapter. Any errors of fact or analysis are strictly the authors'.

the distressed loan sector are exposed to. Indeed, the risks associated with investing in distressed loans are not only more likely to come to pass, but also more exotic than the risks posed by other forms of investment, including investment in performing loans. In distressed loan investing, the principal investment risk, poor economic performance by the borrower, is assumed. Any material discount from par reflects a level of concern in the market that the distressed loan will not be performing according to its terms. In this article, we explore the sources of legal risk to performance of the loan by the borrower that flow from the borrower's financial distress.

SETTLEMENT OF LOAN OBLIGATIONS

One of the most prevalent risks to a par recovery on distressed loans is the risk that loan market participants will be called upon to accept less than full payment of the amount due on a distressed loan in full satisfaction of the borrower's obligations under the credit agreement. This may occur prior to a bankruptcy filing in connection with a negotiated discounted payoff as part of a recapitalization of the borrower, a refinancing of the loan, or a liquidation of assets by the borrower. If the borrower's capital structure includes several tiers of loans, the subordination terms of the distressed loan held by the loan market participant will affect enforcement options and may contractually restrict the junior lenders' ability to receive a repayment of the distressed loan under certain circumstances.

Other risks to par recovery arise in connection with the bankruptcy process. If a borrower does commence a bankruptcy case, then full repayment of the distressed loan will be subject to a number of bankruptcy law provisions concerning, among other things, the sufficiency of collateral coverage, the ability to make interest payments on unsecured loans, and the terms of any plan of reorganization. Indeed, even if a plan of reorganization is proposed by a borrower in bankruptcy, it is possible that the borrower will offer longer terms of repayment at a lower rate of interest than the term or rate of interest provided for under the credit agreement. A bankruptcy court may split a loan secured by collateral that is worth less than the loan into secured and unsecured portions that receive very different treatment. Finally, a bankruptcy court may require the loan market participant to accept equity in the reorganized borrower in exchange for its claim with respect to the unsecured portion of the distressed loan.

Litigation Risk—Lender Liability

Lenders agree to voluntarily accept less than payment in full for a variety of reasons. Infrequently, less than the full payment will be agreed to by the parties to avoid litigation. Although "lender liability" does not now receive the sympathetic ear that it once did, new theories of lender liability arise from time to time and are asserted by borrowers in distress in order to gain negotiating leverage with the lenders. Recently, the theory of deepening insolvency has gained some currency, and the factual scenario most commonly asserted in deepening insolvency claims arises in the distressed loan context.

Deepening insolvency was first evaluated as a valid cause of action by the Third Circuit in the *Lafferty* case.[24] The *Lafferty* decision arose out of the bankruptcy of two lease financing corporations. The companies allegedly operated through the issuance of fraudulent debt certificates that were sold to individual investors. The *Lafferty* court recognized the validity of the "deepening insolvency" claim on three separate grounds: (1) logical soundness, (2) judicial acceptance, and (3) public policy in favor of compensating injury. Because this theory is somewhat new, the exact elements of a "deepening insolvency" action have tended to vary from court to court. However, the elements generally include some configuration of the following: (1) causing a company to become more insolvent by incurring additional liabilities or dissipating its assets, (2) fraudulent prolongation of an insolvent company's life by hiding the company's true financial condition, (3) damages to the company because value is lost that would have been realized but for the prolongation of its life, and (4) harm suffered by the company separate and distinct from the loss suffered by the creditors.[25] The *Lafferty* court also emphasized that debt that is alleged to "deepen insolvency" must be incurred in a fraudulent and concealed manner.

---

[24] See *Official Comm. of Unsecured Creditors v. R.F. Lafferty & Co.*, 267 F.3d 340 (3d Cir. 2001).

[25] See *Kittay v. Atl. Bank of New York (In re Global Service Group, LL)*, 316 B.R. 451 (Bankr. S.D.N.Y. 2004). Absent an allegation of fraud or other wrongful conduct, a lender does not incur liability simply for having extended credit to a financially troubled borrower.

Deepening insolvency actions may be brought by representatives of the debtor, including the trustee or the creditors' committee, and defendants in these actions may include the following: (1) directors and officers who make informed decisions to enter into additional lending arrangements, (2) secured lenders who have restructured loans or made new loans and obtained collateral while driving the company deeper into insolvency, and (3) professionals, including accountants, attorneys, and other financial advisors, who knew about the debtor's financial status and advised the company to enter into additional secured lending opportunities.[26]

To avoid the expense, time commitment, and uncertainty of litigation, creditors from time to time agree to leave sufficient assets in a distressed borrower to make ratable payments to other creditors and to cover the anticipated winding-down expenses of the borrower after liquidation. Settling asserted claims avoids litigation risk, accelerates resolution of the credit facility, and minimizes collection expenses.

Inadequacy of Collateral or Cash Flow

Lenders are also asked to accept less than full payoffs when collateral coverage and enterprise value are simply insufficient to repay a credit facility as agreed. Especially in high-technology-related credits, the business success or failure of the borrower is just a trend or innovation away. Particularly with high-technology credits, but common to most service-oriented borrowers, repayment of the credit facility is supported by both the promise of future cash flow and the enterprise value derived from a combination of intellectual property and the ability of highly skilled employees to perform a service that is in demand with customers. There are often few or no assets that can be liquidated to repay a loan to a service or technology company. Borrowers that correctly position themselves for the next wave of innovation will thrive. However, a distressed borrower has typically guessed incorrectly and made an investment in a dead-end technology or service.

---

[26] See *Schact v. Brown*, 711 F.2d 1343 (7th Cir. 1983).

Once the lenders identify that a borrower will not be able to carry out its business plan because of a bad business bet, salvage of the remaining enterprise value of the borrower in a consensual sale or refinancing transaction will usually produce a maximized recovery, albeit one that is insufficient to repay the lenders in full. Acceptance of a less than full payoff in these circumstances will almost always provide the lenders with a maximized recovery.

Intercreditor Agreement Risk

Lien priority in a multitiered credit structure will also come into play in the sale or refinancing of a distressed buyer when there is insufficient equity or enterprise value to pay all outstanding loans in full. Pursuant to an intercreditor agreement, lenders in the second lien position (those with claims on collateral second to those of first or senior lien lenders) may be contractually prohibited from accepting any payment and will have no ability to direct or object to a monetization of a company that is satisfactory to the senior lien creditors. In this scenario, the risk is that the senior lien creditors, who often have near complete, if not complete, control over the asset monetization process, will be satisfied to produce enough value to repay themselves, without maximizing value or preserving collateral. Junior creditors must accept what is left over for them. This intercreditor risk is sometimes mitigated by negotiating for certain sale parameters and processes, to give some assurance of maximization of recovery. However, these protections are not universally accepted by the senior lender community and are often not present in the final intercreditor agreement.

Cram-Down Risk and *In Re Till*

Once a borrower files a bankruptcy case, other factors come into play to prevent a loan facility from being repaid in full. Secured claims will generally be paid in full if they are fully secured and the collateral is not included in the borrower's reorganization plans. In those cases, the collateral is often sold during the course of the bankruptcy case, to permit the borrower to recover any surplus proceeds. Where there is little equity for the borrower to recover, such collateral is made available through a motion to modify the bankruptcy stay made pursuant to Bankruptcy Code Section

362(d)[27] or by agreement, so as to permit the lenders to enforce their liens under applicable state law.

In those cases where the collateral is necessary to the borrower's reorganization, the fully secured lender will in all likelihood receive a note under the plan of reorganization that is secured by the same collateral. This note will typically provide for payment of the secured claim in full over a period of time, which may be longer than the term of the original prepetition note. The plan of reorganization may also alter the nature of the note, such as changing the rate of amortization or providing for a balloon payment at maturity. Finally, there is no assurance that the rate of interest attached to the new note will be the same as that set forth in the prepetition credit, or will otherwise match the lender's view as to appropriate compensation for risk. If a distressed borrower had agreed to so-called subprime terms prior to the commencement of a bankruptcy case, it is likely that the secured note offered to the lenders under the borrower's plan of reorganization will be at a rate of interest that is less than the prepetition contract rate.

In the recent U.S. Supreme Court case of *In re Till*,[28] Justice Stevens, writing for a four-vote plurality and joined by Justice Thomas, held that in a Chapter 13 cram-down plan, the appropriate

---

[27] Bankruptcy Code Section 362(d) [11 U.S.C. §362(d)] states as follows:

On request of a party in interest and after notice and a hearing, the court shall grant relief from the stay provided under subsection (a) of this section, such as by terminating, annulling, modifying, or conditioning such stay—

(1) for cause, including the lack of adequate protection of an interest in property of such party in interest;

(2) with respect to a stay of an act against property under subsection (a) of this section, if—

(A) the debtor does not have an equity in such property; and

(B) such property is not necessary to an effective reorganization; or

(3) with respect to a stay of an act against single asset real estate under subsection (a), by a creditor whose claim is secured by an interest in such real estate, unless, not later than the date that is 90 days after the entry of the order for relief (or such later date as the court may determine for cause by order entered within that 90-day period)—

(A) the debtor has filed a plan of reorganization that has a reasonable possibility of being confirmed within a reasonable time; or

(B) the debtor has commenced monthly payments to each creditor whose claim is secured by such real estate (other than a claim secured by a judgment lien or by an unmatured statutory lien), which payments are in an amount equal to interest at a current fair market rate on the value of the creditor's interest in the real estate.

[28] See *Till v. SCS Corp. (In re Till)*, 124 S. Ct. 1951 (2004).

discount rate for any secured claim being paid out over time is not
the "coerced loan" rate, as the Seventh Circuit had found,[29] but
instead is the national prime rate, with a small risk adjustment
permitted based upon a judicial review of the debtor's particular
circumstances. Although *Till* was decided in a Chapter 13 context,
the plurality's commentary makes clear its expectation that the
principles enunciated in the *Till* decision will apply broadly to
Chapter 11 plans of reorganization. The plurality noted that similar
provisions exist in Chapter 11, and commented that it was likely
that Congress intended bankruptcy judges and trustees to follow
essentially the same approach when choosing an appropriate
discount rate under any of these provisions (i.e., Chapter 11 cram-
down plans). Lower courts will feel constrained to apply the principles set forth in *Till* when determining the applicable discount rate
for the cram-down of a secured creditor under a Chapter 11 plan.

Undersecured and Unsecured
Claims in Bankruptcy

If a loan is unsecured or undersecured as a result of collateral
inadequacy, lenders will not be able to recover interest, fees, or
reimbursable expenses that become due after the date that the
bankruptcy case was commenced, pursuant to Bankruptcy Code
Section 506.[30] Rather, the claim of an unsecured or undersecured
creditor is fixed as of the date that the case was commenced. The
secured portion of an undersecured claim is administered as
discussed previously. The unsecured claim, however, is subject to

[29] See *In re Till*, 301 F.3d 583 (7th Cir. 2002).
[30] Bankruptcy Code Section 506 (11 U.S.C. §506) states as follows:

    (a) An allowed claim of a creditor secured by a lien on property in which the estate
has an interest, or that is subject to setoff under section 553 of this title, is a secured
claim to the extent of the value of such creditor's interest in the estate's interest in
such property, or to the extent of the amount subject to setoff, as the case may be,
and is an unsecured claim to the extent that the value of such creditor's interest
or the amount so subject to setoff is less than the amount of such allowed claim.
Such value shall be determined in light of the purpose of the valuation and of the
proposed disposition or use of such property, and in conjunction with any hearing
on such disposition or use or on a plan affecting such creditor's interest.

    (b) To the extent that an allowed secured claim is secured by property the value of
which, after any recovery under subsection (c) of this section, is greater than the
amount of such claim, there shall be allowed to the holder of such claim, interest
on such claim, and any reasonable fees, costs, or charges provided for under the
agreement under which such claim arose.

further reduction by reason of ratable distribution to unsecured creditors of the unencumbered assets of the borrower, either under a plan of reorganization[31] or upon liquidation by a bankruptcy trustee.[32] Under the principle of ratable distribution, the unsecured bankruptcy claim of a lender, though allowed in its full amount, may nevertheless receive less than the full amount in actual dollars if the unencumbered assets of the borrower are inadequate to pay all claims in full. Instead, such unsecured lenders will receive only their ratable share of such assets.

Equity Dividends in Bankruptcy

Finally, plans of reorganization do not need to provide for a cash dividend to unsecured creditors, who may be paid in newly issued unsecured debt obligations or equity of the reorganized debtor if the court finds that, based upon the evidence, the new securities provide value equal to the allowed amount of the unsecured claim.[33] Loan market participants are thus at risk that a bankruptcy plan of reorganization may result in the unsecured portion of a loan being repaid with securities that are valued by the court at a certain amount, which may be less than 100 percent of the allowed claim amount. Indeed, there is additional risk because there is no certainty as to what the ultimate market value of such reorganization securities will be or the liquidity of any market for them.

LITIGATION RISK: AN UNKNOWN FOR ALL CONCERNED

Where a consensual resolution with the borrower is not available on acceptable terms, loan market participants may elect to initiate

---

[31] 11 U.S.C. §726(b).

[32] 11 U.S.C. §1123(a)(4).

[33] Bankruptcy Code Section 1123(a)(5)(J) [11 U.S.C. §1123(a)(5)(J)] authorizes plans of reorganization to provide for issuance of securities of the reorganized debtor to be distributed in exchange for unsecured claims.

Bankruptcy Code Section 1129(a)(7)(ii) [11 U.S.C. §1129(a)(7)(ii)] states as follows:

each holder of a claim or interest of such class ... will receive or retain under the plan on account of such claim or interest property of a value, as of the effective date of the plan, that is not less than the amount that such holder would so receive or retain if the debtor were liquidated under Chapter 7 of this title [11 USCS §§701 *et seq.*] on such date. As used in Chapter 11, "property" includes debt or equity securities of the reorganized debtor.

legal proceedings to collect the amounts due to them under the distressed loan. Litigation is inherently risky because it introduces into the process a third party, the judge, and perhaps a jury, that has no economic stake in the outcome of the litigation and that brings unknown experiences and biases into court. These factors insert uncertainty in the result of a judicial proceeding even when the facts and law support a decision in favor of the loan market participant. Litigation risk also arises as a result of differences in legal tradition and statutory schemes from state to state. For instance, California has a legal tradition of protecting borrowers that is deeply engrained in its statutes and case law. New York, on the other hand, has a legal tradition of enforcing the bargain struck by commercially sophisticated persons who enter into contracts. These differences in law and judicial tradition are mitigated, but cannot be entirely avoided, by having credit agreements contain provisions determining (1) the jurisdiction where such litigation may be initiated and (2) the substantive law to be applied in any such action. Finally, the human factor cannot be ignored. In the enforcement of any given distressed loan, a judge or jury that is not personally familiar with financing transactions may simply make an incorrect decision.

Bankruptcy court presents its own institutional risks, notwithstanding the use of uniform national statutes and rules. First and foremost, bankruptcy judges are products of their environment and local legal tradition. Furthermore, the very nature of the Bankruptcy Code is geared toward supporting the policy in favor of reorganization. Thus, bankruptcy courts generally are predisposed to err in favor of the debtor in order to maximize the opportunity for reorganization.

AVOIDING POWER CLAIMS AND ENFORCING RATABLE DISTRIBUTION

Bankruptcy policy favors ratable distribution of assets to creditors. To support this policy, transfers that permit nonratable distribution may be recovered by the debtor's estate for redistribution to creditors ratably under a variety of theories laid out in the Bankruptcy Code. We have already seen the impact of this policy in connection with the limitations on the amount of interest and reimbursable expenses that a loan market participant may be able to recover as a dividend with both secured and unsecured claims.

Such limitations on recovery are not the only risk presented by the policy of ratable distribution. There are several statutory scenarios under which a loan market participant can be legally compelled to return previously received payments or release previously granted collateral.

Bankruptcy Preferences

Set forth in the Bankruptcy Code as Section 547, the preference recovery action recovers for ratable distribution to unsecured creditors cash payments or collateral received from the borrower to satisfy existing obligations shortly prior to the commencement of a bankruptcy case. The underlying reason that preferential payments are recovered is to maintain a level playing field for those creditors that try to work with a troubled borrower instead of insisting on payment. As discussed in detail later in this section, there are a number of statutory defenses to the preference action that are intended to protect transfers made under a variety of circumstances. The hallmark of a preferential payment is a completely appropriate transfer that occurs proximate in time to the commencement of a borrower's bankruptcy case.[34]

Bankruptcy Code Section 547(b) provides in essence as follows: a bankruptcy trustee or debtor in possession may void any transfer by the debtor (1) of an interest of the debtor in property to or for the benefit of a creditor, (2) for or on account of an antecedent debt owed by the debtor before such transfer was made, (3) made while the debtor was insolvent, (4) made on or within 90 days, or within one year in certain cases, before the date of the filing of a petition commencing a case with respect to such debtor under the Bankruptcy Code, (5) if the transfer would enable the creditor to receive more than such creditor would receive if the debtor were liquidated under Chapter 7 of the Bankruptcy Code and the transfer had not been made.

Although not specified in the statute, the creditor to whom or for whose benefit the transfer is made must also be the person who holds the debt on account of which the transfer was made.[35] Preferential transfers to a third party for the benefit of the creditor

---

[34] However, transfers made to an insider of the debtor up to one year prior to the commencement of the bankruptcy case may be recovered as preferences.

[35] See *Ray v. City Bank (In re C-L Cartage Co.)*, 899 F.2d 1490, 1493 (Bankr. 6th Cir. 1990).

are recoverable from such third party as the "initial transferee" of the transfer.[36] The initial transferee is strictly liable to return a transfer that is indefensible as to the creditor for whose benefit it was made.[37] Upon recovery from such third-party creditor, that creditor holds an allowed unsecured claim in the bankruptcy case and will receive a ratable distribution on account of that allowed claim.[38]

Subject to rebuttal, the debtor's insolvency during the last 90 days prior to filing for bankruptcy is presumed by statute.[39] Unless the creditor to whom or for whose benefit the transfer was made is an insider, no transfer made more than 90 days prior to the transferor's bankruptcy (or within one year in certain cases) can be recovered as a preference.[40] Furthermore, a transfer to a fully secured creditor can never be a preference, because the transfer does not allow the fully secured creditor to receive more than it would have received upon liquidation in a Chapter 7 case.[41]

Bankruptcy Code Section 547(c) provides several statutory defenses to preference claims that are also relevant. Pursuant to Bankruptcy Code Section 547(c)(1), transfers given by the creditor to the debtor that are substantially contemporaneous exchanges for value are defensible. This defense generally gives credit for contemporaneous value received by the debtor, preserves state law relation back statutes, and otherwise imposes a rule of reason so that a perfection of a lien substantially contemporaneously with the extension of secured credit will not be subject to attack as a preference when perfection occurs a few days after the lien was granted.[42] Bankruptcy Code Section 547(c)(2) protects ordinary course payments made on account of existing extensions of credit. The policy in favor of recovering preferential transfers is to prevent aggressive action by creditors, not to recover every payment made by the debtor in the ordinary course of its business.[43] Finally Bankruptcy Code Section 547(c)(4) permits creditors to shelter payments that would otherwise be preferential to the extent that such

---

[36] See 11 U.S.C. §550(a).

[37] See *In re Video Depot*, 127 F. 3d 1195 (9th Cir. 1997).

[38] See 11 U.S.C. §502(h).

[39] See 11 U.S.C. §547(f).

[40] See *In re Greene*, 223 F.3d 1064 (9th Cir. 2000).

[41] See *In re Powerline Oil Co.*, 59 F.3d 969 (9th Cir. 1995).

[42] See *In re Dorholt, Inc.*, 224 F.3d 871 (8th Cir. 2000).

[43] See *Matter of Tolona Pizza Prods. Corp.*, 3 F.3d 1029 (7th Cir. 1993).

creditors thereafter extend additional unsecured credit to the debtor that is not repaid prior to bankruptcy.[44]

Potential preferential transfers can usually be identified through appropriate diligence on recent borrower transfers. Once such transfers are identified, the risk that they present can be compensated by appropriate representations, warranties, and pricing.

Fraudulent Transfers

A less common but not unusual voiding power claim, the fraudulent transfer recovery action, is set forth in Bankruptcy Code Section 548 and under state law as the Uniform Fraudulent Transfer Act. The function of the fraudulent conveyance claim is twofold. In the less usual situation, a transferee is sued by a bankruptcy trustee or debtor in possession to recover payments or collateral grants made by a borrower for the intended purpose of hindering or delaying collection of debts by other creditors or defrauding other creditors. The more common fraudulent transfer claim is referred to as "constructive fraudulent transfer" because no party need have any actual intent to damage other creditors. In constructive fraudulent transfer cases, the borrower is alleged to have made transfers (1) without receiving equivalent value in return and (2) under certain enumerated circumstances that leave the borrower unreasonably financially weak.

Pursuant to Bankruptcy Code Section 548(a)(1), any transfer made with actual intent to "hinder, delay or defraud" a current or future creditor is voidable regardless of any value that may have been received in exchange thereof.[45] Under Bankruptcy Code Section 548(a)(2), a transfer is constructively fraudulent and voidable when the debtor (1) receives less than "reasonably equivalent value" in exchange for its transfer of property and (2) either (a) the debtor was "insolvent" on the date of the transfer or became "insolvent" as a result of the transfer, (b) the debtor had an "unreasonably small capital" for current or anticipated operations, or (3) the debtor intended to, or believed that it would, incur debts beyond its ability to pay. Under this "constructive fraud" formulation, no intent to harm is required.

---

[44] See *In re Micro Innovations Corp.*, 185 F.3d 329 (5th Cir. 1999).
[45] See *In re Model Imperial, Inc.*, 250 B.R. 776, 793–795 (Bankr. S.D. Fla. 2000).

Bankruptcy Code Section 548(a)(2) states in essence as follows: the trustee may void any transfer of an interest of the debtor in property, or any obligation incurred by the debtor, (1) that was made or incurred by the debtor on or within two years before the date of the filing of the petition, (2) if the debtor voluntarily or involuntarily received less than a reasonably equivalent value in exchange for such transfer or obligation, and (3) either (a) the debtor was insolvent on the date that such transfer was made or such obligation was incurred, or became insolvent as a result of such transfer or obligation, or (b) was engaged in business or a transaction, or was about to engage in business or a transaction, for which any property remaining with the debtor was an unreasonably small capital, or (c) intended to incur, or believed that the debtor would incur, debts that would be beyond the debtor's ability to pay as such debts matured.

Under Section 548(d), a transfer occurs either (1) when the transfer is perfected, such that a bona fide purchaser or judicial lien creditor of the debtor cannot acquire a superior right in the property transferred, or (2) if the transfer is not perfected, immediately before the filing of the bankruptcy case. The determination of the date of a transfer under Section 548 is exclusively a matter of federal law, although state law must be consulted to determine the time of perfection.[46]

When determining the equivalence of the value given in exchange for an allegedly fraudulent transfer, courts analyze the relative value transferred by each party to the other as of the date of the transfer. Thus, reasonable equivalent value is determined with reference to value at the time of the transaction, not value enhanced or diminished by passage of time. Indeed, when the original investment is the purchase of a chance for a return with a risk of loss, the value of the chance at the time taken is the critical inquiry. It matters not whether the hoped-for value was ultimately realized so long as the opportunity to realize value was fairly priced when it was taken.[47]

Bankruptcy Code Section 548(c) contains a safe harbor provision that protects recipients of fraudulent transfers. Under Section 548(c), the recipient of a fraudulent transfer is entitled to retain

---

[46] See *In re Madrid*, 725 F.2d 1197, 1200 (9th Cir. 1984).
[47] See *Chomakos v. Flamingo Hilton (In re Chomakos)*, 69 F.3d 769, 770–771 (6th Cir. 1995).

property transferred to it and to enforce the obligations incurred in its favor to the extent that the recipient (1) gave value (2) in good faith. Once the trustee has established the elements of a fraudulent transfer, the burden of proof shifts to the defendant to establish good faith and value. Whether a transferee acts in good faith depends on whether the "transaction carries the earmarks of an arms-length bargain."[48] Knowledge by the transferee of the insolvency of the debtor at the time of the transfer may refute a claim of good faith on the part of the transferee.[49] Many courts have held that in order to qualify for the good faith safe harbor contained in the statute, a transferee must show not only that its actions were not intentionally fraudulent, but also that it was not the case that "the circumstances would place a reasonable person on inquiry of a debtor's fraudulent purpose, and a diligent inquiry would have discovered the fraudulent purpose."[50]

Bankruptcy Code Section 548 defines "value" as "property, or satisfaction or securing of a present or antecedent debt of the debtor, but does not include an unperformed promise to furnish support to the debtor or to a relative of the debtor." "Reasonably equivalent value" requires that a debtor receive sufficient consideration for the transfer of its assets. However, "reasonably equivalent value" does not require a penny-for-penny exchange.[51] Business intangibles, such as preservation of market share and opportunities, have been found to be sufficiently valuable to support a nominal third-party transfer as reasonable equivalent value. The satisfaction of a valid antecedent debt of the debtor constitutes value and can constitute reasonably equivalent value. As a general rule, however, a debtor does not receive reasonably equivalent value when the debtor transfers property in exchange for consideration if that consideration passes entirely to a third party. Neither does the payment of third-party debt usually constitute sufficient value absent some equivalent benefit in return.[52]

---

[48] See *Bullard v. Aluminum Co. of Am.*, 468 F.2d 11, 13 (7th Cir. 1972) (citation omitted).
[49] See *Murphy v. Nunes (In re Terrific Seafoods)*, 197 B.R. 724, 733 (Bankr. D. Mass 1996): "knowledge of [the debtor's] insolvency will deprive [the transferee] of the benefit of the § 548(c) defense" [citing *Dean v. Davis*, 242 U.S. 438 (1917)].
[50] See *Jobin v. McKay (In re M & L Bus. Mach. Co.)*, 84 F.3d 1330, 1335–1338 (10th Cir. 1996).
[51] See *Butler Aviation Int'l v. Whyte (Matter of Fairchild Aircraft Corp.)*, 6 F.3d 1119, 1125–1127 (Bankr. 5th Cir. 1993).
[52] See *Heritage Bank Tinley Park v. Steinberg (In re Grabill Corp.)*, 121 B.R. 983, 995 (Bankr. N.D. Ill. 1990); *accord In re B F Bld'g. Corp.*, 312 F.2d 691, 694 (6th Cir. 1963).

Equitable Subordination

The claim of a secured or unsecured creditor may be involuntarily
subordinated in a bankruptcy case if the court determines that the
creditor acted inequitably toward the borrower or other creditors
either prior to the commencement of the bankruptcy case or during
the course of the bankruptcy case. Set forth in Bankruptcy Code
Section 510(c), equitable subordination is a broad remedy available
to the bankruptcy court any time that a creditor is found to have
engaged in inequitable conduct. State contract law contains a
similar principle, commonly referred to as the implied covenant of
good faith and fair dealing.

Under principles of equitable subordination, secured claims
can be subordinated to other secured claims, otherwise valid liens
can be stripped by the estate for the benefit of creditors, and both
secured and unsecured claims can be subordinated to other unsecured claims. In the past, this harsh remedy has been sparingly
employed, and courts have focused on actions, rather than their
impact. Thus, enforcement by a creditor of its collateral or its legal
right to collect a debt according to legally enforceable agreements
generally will not expose a creditor to equitable subordination, no
matter how devastating to the borrower's business such collection
efforts may be. Equitable subordination risk generally arises when
a creditor exerts influence to control a borrower's management and
operations so as to favor the positions of the influence-exerting
creditor in a manner that harms other creditors. In recent years,
equitable subordination risk appears to be on the increase as institutional investors acquire both debt and controlling equity positions in their borrowers. The actions of such institutional investors
may be closely scrutinized by other creditors or a bankruptcy
trustee to determine whether the business decisions of a creditor-
dominated board of directors favored those creditors to the detriment of unrepresented creditors.

The fundamental guidelines for equitable subordination were
laid out by the Fifth Circuit in a three-pronged test announced in
the landmark 1977 case *In re Mobile*:[53] (1) the claimant must have
engaged in some type of inequitable conduct, (2) the misconduct
must have resulted in injury to the creditors of the bankrupt entity
or individual or conferred an unfair advantage on the claimant,

---

[53] See *Benjamin v. Diamond (In re Mobile Steel Co.)*, 563 F.2d 692 (5th Cir. 1977).

and (3) equitable subordination of the claim must not be inconsistent with the provisions of the Bankruptcy Code.

Mobile also details three principles to keep in mind when analyzing the above prongs: (1) the inequitable conduct need not be related to the claim; inequitable conduct directed at the debtor or its creditors may suffice; (2) the bankruptcy court's subordination power is remedial, not punitive; and (3) insiders are subject to heightened levels of scrutiny (more on this principle follows).

In addition, most courts now look to the same three subcategories of misconduct that qualify as "inequitable conduct": (1) fraud, illegality, or breach of fiduciary duties; (2) undercapitalization; and (3) claimant's use of the debtor as a mere instrumentality or alter ego.[54] First Circuit courts have looked to three different indicia of misconduct: (1) when a fiduciary of the debtor misuses its position to the disadvantage of other creditors, (2) when a third party dominates or controls the debtor to the disadvantage of others, and (3) when a third party defrauds other creditors.[55] Circuit courts and jurisdictions within circuits that have adopted *Mobile* have also allowed equitable subordination without a showing of inequitable conduct as required in the first prong, but these instances have generally been limited to subordination of tax penalty claims by a government entity.[56]

A final factor that affects an equitable subordination analysis is the status of the claimant: insider or noninsider. When the claimant is an insider, the opponent need prove only that the insider either breached a fiduciary duty or engaged in conduct that is somehow unfair in order to shift the burden back to the claimant (whereas for a noninsider, egregious misconduct must be proven with particularity). Following the opponent's presentation of unfair conduct, the claimant has the burden of demonstrating the good faith and fairness of the disputed transactions (all the earmarks of an arm's-length transaction). In addition to the shifted

---

[54] See *Fabricators, Inc. v. Technical Fabricators, Inc. (In re Fabricators, Inc.)*, 926 F.2d 1458 (5th Cir. 1999); *In re Lifschultz Fast Freight*, 132 F.3d 339 (7th Cir. 1997); *Le Café Crème, Ltd. v. Le Roux (In re Le Café Crème, Ltd.)*, 244 B.R. 221 (Bankr. S.D.N.Y. 2000).

[55] See *In re 604 Columbus Ave. Realty Trust*, 968 F.2d 1353, 1359 (1st Cir. 1992); *In re AtlanticRancher, Inc.*, 279 B.R. 411, 439 (Bankr. D. Mass. 2002).

[56] See *Burden v. United States*, 917 F.2d 115, 120 (3d Cir. 1990); *In re Airlift Intern., Inc.*, 97 B.R. 664, 670 (S.D. Fla. 1989); *Schultz Broadway Inn, Ltd.*, 912 F.2d 230, 234 (8th Cir. 1990); *Virtual Network Servs. Corp.*, 902 F.2d 1246, 1249 (7th Cir. 1990).

burden, the court must give "special scrutiny" to the claimants' transactions with the debtor.

Reclassification of Payments

Punitive Default Interest Rates and Default-Related Fees

Payments received as interest, fees, or reimbursement of expenses may be reclassified as payments of principal under both state law and the Bankruptcy Code. Under state law, usury statutes may restrict the amount of interest that can be charged on loans. These laws vary from state to state and must be reviewed on a case-by-case basis to determine whether usury restrictions apply and what the penalty for a violation may be.

A contract rate of interest that is not usurious will generally not be subject to attack under state law. However, the same cannot be said of default rates of interest or fees tied to defaults or waivers. Under typical state law, default rates of interest and default-related fees are permissible to the extent that they bear a reasonable relationship to the actual increase in risk and administrative expense experienced by the lender. Default interest or default-related fees that are deemed by a reviewing court to exceed the amount that is reasonably related to the increased cost and risk of the lender are often found to be punitive rather than compensatory. Default interest and default-related fees that are punitive will generally be unenforceable as illegal forfeitures.

Recharacterization of Adequate Protection Payments from Interest to Principal

Secured creditors in bankruptcy cases are generally entitled to protection from diminution in the value of their collateral, as determined by the bankruptcy court at the commencement of the bankruptcy case, pursuant to Bankruptcy Code Sections 361, 362, and 363. In order to maintain collateral coverage when collateral is thought to be diminishing in value, secured creditors are sometimes awarded cash payments to maintain or decrease the amount of the secured creditors' claim. With the amount of the claim controlled, the secured creditor's collateral coverage is adequately protected against contraction. If a creditor is believed to be oversecured at the commencement of a bankruptcy case, these payments will generally be applied by such oversecured creditor to interest, fees, and expenses recoverable under the applicable credit agreement. The Bankruptcy Code, at Section 506(b), provides that interest, fees, and expenses may be recovered only to the extent of available collateral.

The value of collateral accepted by a bankruptcy court early in a case will generally not be binding and may later be challenged in the claims allowance process. If, in connection with claims allowance, a collateral cushion that was provisionally determined to exist early in a bankruptcy case is found to be either smaller or nonexistent, then adequate protection payments received by the secured creditor and applied to interest, fees, and expenses will be reclassified as payments of principal to the extent that such adequate protection payments exceed the difference between the value of collateral at commencement and the amount of the secured claim as of the commencement of the case.

Recharacterization of Debt to Equity Based upon the Economics of the Underlying Transaction: The Triumph of Substance over Form

When an investment is nominally designated as debt but has the economic characteristics of equity, a bankruptcy court may ignore the form of the investment and, based upon the court's perception of the substance, recharacterize the investment as equity. The effect of such recharacterization is twofold. First, any interest and principal paid out may be reexamined as a dividend, and on that basis be recovered as an improper dividend under applicable state law.[57] The elements of a recharacterization action were recently set forth in the case of *Exide Technologies, Inc.*, in which the bankruptcy court, surveying prior decisions, enunciated the factors to be considered in any reclassification effort as follows: (1) the names given to the instruments, if any, evidencing the indebtedness, (2) the presence or absence of a fixed maturity date and schedule of payments, (3) the presence or absence of a fixed rate of interest and interest payments, (4) the source of repayments, (5) the adequacy or inadequacy of capitalization, (6) the identity of interest between the creditor and the stockholder, (7) the security, if any, for the advances,

---

[57] See, for example, California Corporations Code Sections 500, et seq., which set financial tests for the issuance of dividends and create a cause of action for corporations and their creditors to recover from shareholders dividends given in violation thereof.

(8) the corporation's ability to obtain financing from outside lending institutions, (9) the extent to which the advances were subordinated to the claims of outside creditors, (10) the extent to which the advances were used to acquire capital assets, and (11) the presence or absence of a sinking fund to provide repayments.[58]

ACCESS TO NONPUBLIC INFORMATION

Nonpublic Credit Agreement Disclosure by Public Companies

It is fitting that, in the information age, risk is associated with access to information. Investors in publicly traded debt and equity securities will typically have access only to information about the issuer that is also available to all other investors through public statements, analyst reports, and SEC filings. This is not the case for loan market participants, who will be eligible to receive information required under the applicable credit agreement. Typical credit agreements, including those entered into by companies that have issued publicly traded securities, will require the borrower to provide to the lenders detailed nonpublic information, including new product information, budgets, projections, and business plans. This information, which is not generally available to the public, will often constitute insider information under the securities laws and will impede the ability of loan market participants to invest in or divest publicly traded securities.

To avoid being tainted by nonpublic information that is routinely provided to lenders under credit agreements, loan market participants may engage in two strategies. First, an ethical wall can be established between the loan market trading desk and the public securities trading desk, so that public securities trading personnel have no access to information received by the loan market trading personnel pursuant to credit agreements. Second, a loan market participant may achieve an additional layer of separation by recusing itself from access to nonpublic information provided under a credit agreement. It is not unusual for lending groups to establish separate information distribution channels, often including restricted access to electronic sites, to permit loan market participants to elect to receive only public information from the borrower.

---

[58] See *Exide Techs., Inc.*, 299 B.R. 732 (Bankr. D. Del. 2003).

Nonpublic Disclosure to Members of Creditors' Committees in Bankruptcy

Similar information issues arise for loan market participants that serve on creditors' committees of bankrupt borrowers. Like loan syndicates, creditors' committees receive a substantial amount of nonpublic information, again including new product information, budgets, projections, and business plans. In addition, creditors' committees have access to information regarding litigation strategies, plan of reorganization negotiations, and other critical information regarding the bankruptcy case before such information is available to other creditors.

In bankruptcy cases, trading markets exist both for public securities issued by the debtor and for secured and unsecured claims with respect to operational obligations of the borrower. Loan market participants that have access to creditors' committee information have risk, including equitable subordination risk, if their trading desks are not insulated from information they receive while serving on a creditors' committee. Recently, members of creditors' committees have begun filing motions describing the protective measures they have installed to maintain a wall between personnel serving on creditors' committees and the trading desks of such institutions. By adhering to the court-approved walls internally established by such loan market participants, trading in both bankruptcy claims and publicly issued securities can continue without repercussion.

Trading orders were first introduced in the early 1990s in connection with the participation of mutual fund companies on the creditors' committees of public company debtors. In an unpublished decision, the bankruptcy court in *In re Federated Department Stores*[59] entered an order that Fidelity Management and Research Company would not be subjected to liability for trading in debt and equity of Federated, so long as a "fire wall" was maintained between the Fidelity personnel serving on the creditors' committee and the information that was received in that capacity, and the Fidelity trading desks, which would have access only to publicly available information. The Securities and Exchange Commission supported Fidelity's application for a trading order based upon an ethical wall being established, arguing that large institutional creditors, such as investment advisors and broker/dealers, have

---

[59] See *In re Federated Dep't Stores, Inc.*, No. 1–90–00130, 1991 WL79143 at *1 (Bankr. S.D. Ohio Mar. 7, 1991).

skills and expertise that are likely to be extremely valuable to the committee, and concluding that there is no legal impediment to permitting the service of such entities on official committees.[60]

The need for investors participating on creditors' committees to be vigilant in establishing court-approved shielding provisions was brought into stark focus in 2002, when a major investment bank was accused, first by the creditors' committee and later by the U.S. Trustee, of violating its fiduciary duty to creditors by trading securities of the debtor while serving on the creditors' committee for that debtor. In the bankruptcy case in question, the U.S. Trustee for the Southern District of New York formed a creditors' committee about ten days after the debtors had filed their cases. An investment bank was appointed to the committee and agreed to a "no-trade" prohibition as a condition for sitting on the committee.

The investment bank resigned from the committee the following year. The creditors' committee filed suit against the investment bank, alleging that while it was on the committee, the investment bank had violated its no-trade agreement and its agreement to keep confidential information that the committee obtained from its advisors or from the debtors and their advisors by using inside information to purchase secured bank debt claims against the debtor. The committee further alleged that contemporaneously with the investment bank's resignation from the committee, it became a member of an unofficial committee of secured claimants. The committee sought equitable subordination of all of the investment bank's claims and various other relief. The U.S. Trustee joined the committee's complaint by intervention. The U.S. Trustee filed a motion (which was granted) to intervene in the action against the investment bank, asserting the same facts as those alleged by the committee.

Less than a month later, the dispute was settled, with the investment bank essentially agreeing to create a seven-figure fund for distribution to the unsecured creditors and also agreeing to injunctive relief in favor of the U.S. Trustee (among other things) essentially as follows: (1) the investment bank agreed not to seek

---

[60] As quoted in a motion for a trading order recently granted in the *Winn Dixie* bankruptcy case, the Securities and Exchange Commission, in its memorandum filed in the *Federated* case, stated as follows: "Consistent with the requirements of the federal securities laws and the bankruptcy laws, an entity which is engaged in the trading of securities as a regular part of its business and which has established procedures reasonably designed to prevent the transmission to its trading personnel of information obtained through service on an official committee is not precluded from serving on the committee and, at the same time, trading in the debtor's securities." SEC Memorandum at 6.

membership on an official bankruptcy committee for six months, and (2) thereafter, the investment bank agreed that it would not, while serving as a member of an official committee, trade in any security or obligation of the relevant debtor if such trading was inconsistent with its fiduciary duties as a committee member, or to the extent prohibited by or inconsistent with any applicable law, court order, or rules or guidelines of the U.S. Trustee.

This case reinforced and expanded the practice of obtaining trading orders. Although there is no specific statutory basis for and no reported cases on this issue, trading orders have become commonplace when a creditors' committee includes investment banks or hedge funds that may want to trade in debt or equity of the Chapter 11 debtor. Recent cases in which such orders have been issued include *In re Winn Dixie, In re Adelphia Communications Corp., In re WorldCom, Inc., In re Global Crossing,* and *In re Enron.*[61] Based upon guidance from *Federated* and the memorandum filed by the Securities and Exchange Commission therein, trading orders now typically contain the following provisions: (1) written acknowledgment by personnel performing creditors' committee work that they could receive nonpublic information and are aware of the ethical wall procedures in effect; (2) a prohibition on the sharing of nonpublic creditors' committee information with other employees; (3) separate file space for creditors' committee work that is inaccessible to other employees; (4) restrictions on creditors' committee personnel's access to trading information; and (5) a compliance review process.

---

[61] See *In re Adelphia Comm's Corp.*, No. 02–41729 (Bankr. S.D.N.Y. Aug. 19, 2002), permitting members of the official creditors' committee to trade in the debtor's securities in certain circumstances provided that the committee members have established and implemented screening wall procedures; *In re WorldCom, Inc.*, No. 02–13533 (Bankr. S.D.N.Y. Aug. 6, 2002), permitting the same; *In re Global Crossing Ltd.*, No. 02–40187 (Bankr. S.D.N.Y. Mar. 25, 2002), permitting the same; *In re Enron Corp.*, No. 01–16034 (Bankr. S.D.N.Y. Feb. 27, 2002), permitting the same; *In re Dairy Mart Convenience Stores. Inc.*, No. 01–42400 (Bankr. S.D.N.Y. Dec. 20, 2001), permitting the same; *In re Iridium Operating LLC*, No. 99–45005 (Bankr. S.D.N.Y. Nov. 3, 1999), permitting the same; *In re Favorite Brands Int'l Holding Corp.*, No. 99–726 (Bankr. D. Del. May 28, 1999), permitting members of the official creditors' committee to trade in the debtor's securities provided the committee members established and implemented fire wall procedures; *In re Mid Am. Waste Sys., Inc.*, No. 97–104 (Bankr. D. Del. Feb. 21, 1997), permitting the same; *In re Ace-Texas, Inc.*, No. 96–166 (Bankr. D. Del. July 17, 1996), permitting the same; *In re Wherehouse Entm't, Inc. & WEI Holdings, Inc.*, No. 95–911 (Bankr. D. Del. Sept. 8, 1995), permitting the same; *In re Columbia Gas Sys., Inc.*, Case No. 91–803 (Bankr. D. Del. Sept. 10, 1991), permitting the same; and *In re Harvard Indus., Inc.*, No. 91–404 (Bankr. D. Del. July 15, 1991), permitting the same.

VOTING IN SYNDICATED CREDITS: THE TYRANNY OF THE MAJORITY

Loan market participants will find that investments in loans of distressed borrowers typically require active management, as covenants are more restrictive than those found in most indentures and the relationship between borrower and lender is closer and more communicative than the relationship between issuer and noteholder. As a result of these differences, transactions that are permitted under an indenture without a vote (upon satisfaction by the borrower of a financial test) typically will require a vote under a credit agreement. In addition, credit agreements generally require unanimous consent on more issues than do indentures.

Class Voting under Credit Agreements

While loan market participants will be called upon to vote more often on more issues, their votes may not be equal. Credit agreements may contain several classes, or tranches, of loans, some of which are too small to prevent certain actions not requiring a unanimous vote. In this situation, lenders holding the smaller loan tranche may be discriminated against by lenders holding the proportionately larger tranche, unless the credit agreement provides that those loan market participants who bear the burden of a modification must approve the modification as a class.

Intercreditor Agreements and Voting Rights

In addition to voting risk under a single credit agreement, the advent of multiple layers of secured credit provided to one borrower, the so-called second lien market, has given rise to an additional level of risk related to the relative voting and enforcement rights of each layer of secured debt. These voting and enforcement rights are determined by an intercreditor agreement between the two (or more) lending groups, one having first-priority liens and the other having second-priority liens. Intercreditor agreements are complex documents that address, among other things, the right to receive payments, drag-along provisions, lien priority, release of collateral, enforcement of liens, and ability to participate in the bankruptcy of a distressed borrower.

The Role of Intercreditor Agreements in Bankruptcy

Intercreditor agreements also play a role in restricting the ability of junior lenders to take positions in bankruptcy court that are contrary to the positions of the senior lenders. Although there continues to be some flexibility in the negotiation of intercreditor terms, intercreditor agreements will commonly provide that the junior creditor cannot attack the claim or lien of the senior creditor; oppose any debtor-in-possession financing, use of cash collateral, or sale of assets supported by the senior lender; or fail to vote as the senior creditor votes on any plan of reorganization. The risk to a loan market participant investing in distressed debt is that it will be unable to influence the course of the borrower's reorganization.

CONCLUSION

It is inherent in the nature of distressed loans that risks that are often considered theoretical by loan market participants investing in performing loans are suddenly real and require meaningful analysis by loan market participants investing in distressed loans. By undertaking diligence on these risks, loan market participants can make determinations as to the level of risk inherent in the borrower's current financial condition, as well as the risk of loss related to the external legal factors that we have highlighted in this article, and price their bids for loans in the distressed market accordingly.

Distressed to Recovery: A Look at the Restructuring Process

William R. Wagner
Kaye Scholer LLP

INTRODUCTION

Financial distress may overtake a borrower rather suddenly or as a result of protracted financial, operational, or competitive deterioration. Troubled companies often face a host of issues ranging from market developments well beyond their control to institutional flaws resulting from bad managerial decisions. As a result, loan market participants—whether original lenders or secondary purchasers—continually find themselves in the midst of the restructuring process as they analyze value, manage uncertainty, and ultimately seek to maximize the recovery of loans and other extensions of credit made to financially troubled companies.

So what is a restructuring, and what is the process? As used in this article, the term *restructuring* is intended to convey the broadest possible meaning and includes transactions ranging from out-of-court workouts that are implemented by consensus to comprehensive financial restructurings that are effected through formal Chapter 11 proceedings.

This article, therefore, takes a general look at selected restructuring issues and discusses (1) substantive considerations that shape the form and direction of the overall restructuring process, (2) initial steps for lenders who are about to engage in a restructuring, (3) some of the alternative paths that may lead to a restructuring, and finally, (4) an overview of selected Chapter 11 topics.

SUBSTANTIVE CONSIDERATIONS

Decisions

At the beginning of a workout, lenders (and borrowers) often do not have a clear indication as to whether their recovery goals are best served by one restructuring path or another. Just as the cause and severity of any default—and the underlying financial crisis of an individual borrower—vary greatly from case to case, the critical path of the restructuring process also varies greatly from case to case. Nonetheless, decisions must be made as borrowers and lenders carefully measure and balance the dual objectives of preserving value and maximizing recovery. Many factors affect the course of a financial restructuring and the strategic decisions to be made by borrowers and lenders during the process as they evaluate short-term priorities and long-term objectives. Some of the most prevalent factors that influence the course of the process include the overall cost to be incurred, the size and composition of the lender group, and the cause and severity of the borrower's financial distress.

Restructuring Costs

The costs incurred by borrowers and lenders during the restructuring process are a primary factor to be considered at the outset. Restructuring costs may be both tangible and intangible. Generally, the most recognizable tangible costs are those associated with the services provided by legal and financial professionals, as well as by consultants and other expert advisors who may be engaged to assist with the process. Intangible costs, by comparison, are not directly and immediately recognizable, but may have a substantial impact on a borrower's operations as well as on the efforts of lenders. Intangible costs include, for example, the time, energy, and commitment invested by management in coordinating the restructuring process and the time, energy, and commitment invested by the lenders' internal workout professionals in the same effort. Intangible costs also include the negative impact of the "stigma" attached to the financial distress experienced by a borrower, which may result in a lack of customer confidence, less favorable relationships with trade vendors, retention issues with key senior managers, and a generally reduced ability to focus on the long-term needs of the company, because the company is required to devote its energy and resources to the crisis at hand. Finally, restructuring costs are generally proportionate to the length of time required to complete the process. Lenders and borrowers, therefore, are keenly aware that a swift resolution of issues will almost certainly result in fewer and lower tangible and intangible costs.

The Lender Group

Another factor that shapes the restructuring process is the size and composition of the lender group. The requirements of managing the process increase dramatically as the size of the lender group expands. A small and cohesive lender group, for example, might be able to move through the restructuring process with a borrower in a more flexible manner than would a large and disparate syndicate of lenders.

The Severity of the Borrower's Distress

A lender's approach to the restructuring process will almost certainly be tempered by the actual extent of a borrower's financial distress. In many instances, the root cause of a borrower's financial difficulties may not be readily apparent. In some cases, the borrower's difficulties may stem from a temporary and identifiable liquidity issue. In other cases, the problems are more systemic and may result from a dramatic shift in the marketplace or a fundamentally flawed business plan.

Other Factors to Be Considered

Other factors that shape the restructuring process and the approach to recovery by lenders include the discovery of fraud or malfeasance on the part of the borrower or its management, the onset or threat of significant litigation against the borrower by third parties, and changes in law that adversely affect the borrower's operations. Lenders will also evaluate the circumstances differently depending upon the outstanding amount of the loan and whether the loan obligations are secured or unsecured, junior or senior, or vulnerable to the demands of competing creditors.

STARTING THE PROCESS

The Landscape

Lenders and other restructuring professionals must acquire a thorough understanding of the borrower and its business in order to manage the restructuring process successfully. In many cases, lenders become aware of a borrower's financial distress only after the borrower fails to make a scheduled payment of principal or interest on its loan or breaches one or more of the financial covenants in its loan documentation. At that moment, however, the lenders should take swift action to determine what, if any, measures should be undertaken in the near term in order to ensure that long-term recovery objectives remain achievable.

Loan Documents

One of the most important first steps to be taken by lenders and their counsel at the beginning of a restructuring is a diligent review of all of the borrower's loan and security documents. This review should first focus on the terms and structure of the borrower's obligations under the credit agreements, any guarantees, pledges, or security agreements and any other loan documents in order to understand the exact nature of the obligations of the borrower and the rights of the lenders. The review should also evaluate the adequacy and completeness of each of the documents in order to avoid surprise defects and to address the corresponding risks in a timely manner. If fundamental provisions are defective, or if the documentation is incomplete or ineffective, the rights and remedies of the lenders may be severely affected.

As part of the comprehensive review, particular attention should be paid to provisions in the loan documents that specify events of default and provisions that specify the lenders' remedies in each case. Defaults, such as the failure by the borrower to make a regularly scheduled payment of principal or interest or the breach of a financial covenant, will generally prompt more immediate action by the lenders than a breach of other affirmative or negative covenants. The nature and severity of existing or prospective defaults will shape the scope and immediacy of the lenders' actions.

Collateral Review

If the loan is a secured loan, it is also very important to verify the status of all matters relating to the lenders' rights with respect to any collateral that secures the obligations of the borrower under the loan documents. A thorough review of all collateral matters should enable the lenders to determine the existence of any defects in the original collateral structure and the existence of any unencumbered assets that could provide additional security as part of a restructuring plan.

The collateral review process requires verification that the liens and security interests of the lenders in the specified collateral have been properly granted, documented, and perfected. The review process should also determine whether any competing liens or adverse security interests in the same collateral have arisen since the making of the loans by searching and examining filings in each of the relevant public registries. These searches typically examine financing statements filed under the Uniform Commercial Code, filings with the Office of Patents and Trademarks, mortgages, and other real property filings. Title searches and updates may also be necessary with respect to real property interests. Additional searches should be conducted to identify any judgments, tax liens, or pending litigation.

Borrower's Business

The diligence process should also include a thorough examination of the borrower's business and operations. The borrower's organizational structure should be analyzed closely in order to identify intercompany relationships or obligations with a parent entity, subsidiary, or affiliate that may affect the course of a restructuring.

Similarly, the borrower's existing business model should be studied. This portion of the analysis would include, for example, third-party relationships, material contracts, management structure, and trends and competition in the marketplace. An examination of the borrower's business should also include an examination of the borrower's obligations to competing creditors.

Advisors

Depending upon the scope and complexity of a particular restructuring, lenders (and borrowers) may need to engage professional advisors and consultants in addition to existing legal counsel. Restructuring advisors can provide industry expertise and can assist greatly in the analysis of the borrower's current business plan and financial distress as well as in the evaluation of strategic alternatives and the development of a restructured business plan.

Remedies

Lenders also need to assess their ability to exercise any remedies that may be immediately available to them and the utility of doing so. Loan documents customarily specify remedies that are available to lenders in addition to any remedies that may already exist at law or in equity. Revolving credit agreements, for example, generally permit lenders to freeze further borrowing upon the occurrence and continuation of an event of default. Other legal and equitable remedies include setoff rights, recoupment, judgment proceedings, and foreclosure actions.

In each case, the exercise of remedies should be carefully evaluated in light of the particular circumstances.

Interim Documentation

The restructuring process generally seeks to promote long-term solutions. In the out-of-court scenario, these solutions may result in an amendment and restatement of all of the borrower's loan obligations or a similarly comprehensive workout agreement. In the initial and interim phases of the restructuring, however, several other forms of documentation are customarily employed by borrowers and lenders.

Following the occurrence of one or more events of default, the lenders usually deliver a "reservation of rights letter" to the borrower. The reservation of rights letter serves two fundamental purposes. Although the borrower and the lenders may collectively be aware of, and may have discussed, existing defaults, the letter provides a formal written notice to the borrower. Also, and as the name implies, the reservation of rights letter advises the borrower that the lenders can and may exercise remedies.

Other forms of interim documentation might include limited waivers (which may be temporary) and amendments that are designed to maintain the status quo or otherwise remove (if only temporarily) the borrower's defaulted status.

Forbearance agreements also embody waivers and amendments, but do so for a longer period of time to allow the borrower and its lenders to attempt to find a workable solution to the existing crisis. The forbearance agreement may be used to address a temporary condition, such as a seasonal liquidity condition. On the other hand, the borrower and its lenders may agree to a temporary forbearance arrangement in order to allow the borrower adequate time to consummate a refinancing of the existing loan obligations or find another long-term solution.

Under a forbearance agreement, the lenders agree to forbear from exercising remedies related to existing defaults for a specified period of time. In addition, the lenders may agree to loosen certain financial covenants during the forbearance period to address specific and presumably temporary conditions experienced by the borrower. The lenders, in accordance with the requirements of the credit agreement, may also consent to certain transactions, such as asset sales, the proceeds of which could be used to provide a cash payment to the lenders or additional liquidity for the borrower.

In exchange, the forbearance agreement may require, among other things, that the borrower pay interest on a more frequent basis (monthly, for example) than is currently specified in the credit agreement and at the applicable default rate. The forbearance agreement may also reduce or suspend the borrower's ability, if any, to draw additional loans under the credit agreement during the forbearance period. The forbearance agreement may also be used to increase the borrower's financial reporting requirements under the credit agreement, obtain additional collateral (if any exists) to secure the loan obligations, and reaffirm the borrower's obligations under all of the loan and security documents.

Forming a Strategy

Although each restructuring situation is unique and will have its own set of issues to be resolved, there are some typical strategies for dealing with a financially distressed borrower. One is to find and provide additional liquidity for the borrower. The borrower may need additional money to fund its business plan or to weather a temporary crisis. New money can be provided through a refinancing by another syndicate, although this may be difficult if the borrower is in severe financial distress. New money can also be provided by the existing lender group or by certain members of the existing lender group. The priority of this new money loan would certainly be the subject of negotiation in each instance. The new money might come from an outside source, perhaps as a second lien financing, or through a loan from a major equity holder (in which case it would most likely be deeply subordinated). The new money could also be in the form of an equity infusion.

Another strategy is to sell assets. The borrower may need to consolidate its operations in order to return to financial health, or it may be that a noncore business is putting a strain on an otherwise stable core business. The borrower could also agree in an out-of-court restructuring (or within a Chapter 11 proceeding, with the approval of the Bankruptcy Court) to sell certain assets or to raise a certain amount of cash proceeds from asset sales.

Yet another alternative would be a debt-for-equity exchange. If a company is simply overleveraged, this could provide a workable solution. The exchange could apply to a certain class of debt or a certain amount of debt. Again, this type of solution could be implemented in an out-of-court restructuring or through a bankruptcy proceeding.

ALTERNATIVE PATHS

In general, the most attractive restructuring alternative available to borrowers and lenders alike in a "perfect" restructuring world would be the collective negotiation and implementation of a consensual restructuring scheme without the need to resort to court supervision. The fundamental reasons are clear: out-of-court workouts provide an opportunity to restructure more rapidly and at far less expense than would typically be expected in a traditional Chapter 11 proceeding.

Unfortunately, not all borrowers and creditor groups can avail themselves of the opportunity to restructure without a formal proceeding. For example, if amendments to a credit agreement contemplate an extension of the maturity date, a postponement of regularly scheduled payments, or a sale of assets representing substantial collateral, a creditor group may not be able to muster the unanimous consent that is generally required to give effect to such amendments and their underlying strategic and financial objectives. Additionally, participants in a consensual restructuring process may not be able to carry out their plans without the assistance of the Bankruptcy Court. A company that is in financial distress, for example, may wish to sell certain of its assets on a selective basis in order to pay down debt, generate working capital, or eliminate the costs associated with maintaining or operating the assets to be sold. At the same time, an otherwise willing buyer may be reluctant to proceed in the absence of a court order declaring that the sale is final and is free and clear of any liens or claims of other creditors.

Prearranged and prepackaged plans help to overcome these issues while still avoiding some of the costs associated with a traditional Chapter 11 proceeding. The need for unanimous consent is also avoided, as the Bankruptcy Code requires the approval of only "two thirds in amount and one half in number" of each class of creditors. (See "Voting and Confirmation" later in this article for a further discussion of voting on plan confirmation.) In each case, the plan is negotiated prior to the borrower's filing a petition with the Bankruptcy Court and becoming subject to the protections of the Bankruptcy Code. Prearranged plans are negotiated and agreed to by the borrower—as a prospective debtor—and the requisite creditors, and the terms are set forth in an agreement that is often referred to as a "lock-up" agreement. Under the lock-up arrangement, the creditors agree to vote in favor of a plan of reorganization that conforms to the agreed-upon terms when such a plan is filed with the Bankruptcy Court in a formal Chapter 11 proceeding. A prepackaged plan is not only negotiated prior to the filing, but also approved by a vote of the requisite creditors. As a result, a prepackaged plan approved by the requisite creditors may be presented to the Bankruptcy Court at the time of the filing.

Finally, many cases simply require the supervision of the Bankruptcy Court and the structure of a traditional Chapter 11 proceeding in order to restructure the debtor's business and financial affairs. The Bankruptcy Court can provide a central forum for the settlement of outstanding litigation issues or disputes among creditors. In addition, the certainty of a Bankruptcy Court order will underscore restructuring efforts with far greater finality than would be enjoyed by the parties to a consensual agreement in an out-of-court restructuring.

At the same time, a traditional Chapter 11 proceeding has certain drawbacks. The first and perhaps most obvious is cost. A restructuring process that is conducted from start to finish under the supervision of the Bankruptcy Court can be far more costly than out-of-court alternatives and can take considerably longer to complete. In an out-of-court restructuring, control of the process is generally concentrated in the borrower and the lender group. In a formal Chapter 11 proceeding, that control is significantly diluted, as the restructuring process falls under the supervision of the Bankruptcy Court, and third parties (including the U.S. trustee and creditors' committees) join in the negotiation and development of a plan of reorganization.

CHAPTER 11 OVERVIEW

The Bankruptcy Code

Article I, Section 8 of the U.S. Constitution grants to Congress the authority to enact "uniform laws on the subject of Bankruptcies," and pursuant to this authority, Congress enacted the Bankruptcy Reform Act of 1978, thereby establishing the "Bankruptcy Code," a body of uniform federal laws that governs the federal bankruptcy process. The Bankruptcy Code, which is codified under Title 11 of the United States Code, draws heavily upon prior bankruptcy principles, statutes, and case laws, but supersedes all prior bankruptcy enactments and has been the focus of significant reforms and amendments. The most recent amendment, the Bankruptcy Abuse Prevention and Consumer Protection Act of 2005 (BAPCA), went into effect on October 17, 2006, for all cases filed on or after that date.

The Bankruptcy Code is divided into chapters that govern different types of bankruptcies and the procedural standards relevant to each. Administrative and procedural matters are covered in Chapters 1, 3, and 5. Chapters 1 and 3 contain general provisions and the applicable guidelines for case administration, while Chapter 5 addresses the rights and claims of debtors and creditors. Chapters 7, 9, 11, 12, and 13 address different types of bankruptcy cases and fall into two categories: liquidation (Chapter 7) and rehabilitation (Chapters 11, 12, and 13). Finally, Chapter 15, which was enacted as part of BAPCA, covers cross-border insolvencies.

Goals of Chapter 11

Chapter 11 codifies a policy designed to facilitate the efforts of a debtor to reorganize existing business and financial affairs and emerge from the Bankruptcy Court process with a "fresh start." The Chapter 11 process seeks to promote equality among creditors who are similarly situated while providing a "breathing spell" that allows the debtor to operate its business while negotiating a resolution—a plan of reorganization—with its creditors.

Commencement, First-Day Orders, and the Automatic Stay

All bankruptcy cases commence with the filing of a petition for relief with the Bankruptcy Court. The petition may be voluntarily filed by the debtor or involuntarily filed against the debtor by three or more of its creditors if they meet certain minimal criteria.

The impact of the filing is felt by the debtor and its creditors immediately. On the "first day," the Bankruptcy Court hears a series of motions to facilitate the transition into the bankruptcy process. These so-called "first day" motions are necessary because, once a debtor files for bankruptcy relief, it cannot act without the Bankruptcy Court's consent. First day motions are generally not controversial and are intended to assist the debtor in the ongoing management and operation of its business. Some of the matters addressed by first day orders include the retention of counsel and other professional advisors, the use of cash collateral the payment of certain prepetition obligations to employees (i.e., salary) and critical vendors, the preservation of existing bank accounts, the payment of taxes and utilities, and the extension of certain deadlines.

The most significant impact of the filing, however, is that *all* parties are automatically and immediately prohibited from taking any action against the debtor or its property to enforce or collect on the debtor's prepetition obligations. The automatic stay enjoins any and all judicial or administrative proceedings or any other enforcement actions available to creditors, whether or not such proceedings or actions were initiated prepetition. For the debtor, the automatic stay, in essence, provides a breathing spell during which it can manage its operations and begin the bankruptcy process in an orderly manner. Although the automatic stay may be lifted in certain circumstances, it generally prevents creditors from foreclosing upon or otherwise seizing assets that may be employed by the debtor in the restructuring process or distributed among the creditors according to an equitable scheme.

The Estate and the Debtor in Possession

The filing of a bankruptcy petition also creates an estate that consists of substantially all of the assets that were owned by the debtor at the time of the filing. With a few limited exceptions, the Bankruptcy Code takes a very broad and inclusive view of what constitutes assets of the estate. Although a trustee may be appointed in certain cases, the debtor remains in possession of its assets and manages its affairs subject to the oversight of the bankruptcy court.

U.S. Trustee and Creditors' Committee

The U.S. trustee is vested with primary responsibility for monitoring and supervising the administration of a Chapter 11 proceeding. The U.S. trustee, among other things, monitors the debtor's ongoing business operations; reviews the retention and reimbursement of legal and financial professionals by the debtor; reviews reports, plans, and disclosure statements filed in the Chapter 11 proceeding; and appoints the creditors' committee.

The creditors' committee generally consists of unsecured creditors holding the seven largest unsecured claims against the debtor, but may also include a representative cross-section of other significant groups of unsecured creditors. During the course of the proceeding, the creditors' committee also monitors the debtor's ongoing business operations and ordinarily participates in the process leading to the development of a plan of reorganization.

Avoidance Powers

Chapter 11 provides the debtor in possession (or the trustee, as the case may be) with effective tools to void certain transactions and to recover assets that were transferred by the debtor during specified periods prior to the filing of the bankruptcy petition. Among the most significant of these tools is the ability to void certain transfers that are deemed to be "preferential" or "fraudulent." Within the meaning of the Bankruptcy Code the subject of a "transfer" may include virtually any interest in the property of the debtor. In effect, transactions meeting the criteria prescribed by the Bankruptcy Code may be nullified and the underlying assets returned to the debtor. Any assets that are recovered in this manner automatically become part of the bankruptcy estate.

Under Section 547, of the Bankruptcy Code defines a preferential transfer to be one: (1) made "to or for the benefit of a creditor," (2) made for or on account of an "antecedent debt," (3) made while the debtor was insolvent, (4) the transfer was made on or within 90 days prior to the petition date, or between 90 days and a year prior to the petition date if the transferee was an "insider" of the debtor, and (5) that enables the transferee to receive a greater distribution than if the debtor's estate were liquidated in a Chapter 7 proceeding.

Note, however, that the Bankruptcy Code also identifies certain transactions that may not be voided as preferential. For example, the debtor may not void transfers that are made in the ordinary course of its business, such as customary payments that are made to creditors according to ordinary business terms. Similarly, a transfer that is made by the debtor for a contemporaneous exchange of "new value" from the transferee may not be voided by the debtor.

Section 548 of the Bankruptcy Code empowers the debtor or the trustee to void a "fraudulent transfer"—a transfer (including an incurrence of obligations) that occurs during a specified period prior to the petition date and that actually or constructively defrauds other creditors. The look-back period for fraudulent transfer actions is the one-year period prior to the petition for all cases filed prior to April 20, 2006. Following the enactment of the BAPCA, the look-back period has been extended to two years prior to the petition date for all cases filed after April 20, 2006.

Under Section 548(a)(1)(A) of the Bankruptcy Code, a transfer made or an obligation incurred within the applicable look-back period may be voided if it was made or incurred with "actual intent to hinder, delay or defraud" creditors. In the alternative, Section 548(a)(1)(B) permits the nullification of transfers made or obligations incurred if the debtor received "less than equivalent value in exchange for such transfer or obligation" and (1) the debtor was insolvent on the date of the transfer or rendered insolvent as a result, (2) the debtor was left with an unreasonably small capital base with which to conduct its business, (3) the debtor incurred debts that would be beyond its ability to pay as they came due, or (4) the transfer was made to or for the benefit of an insider under an employment contract and not in the ordinary course of business.

In addition to its ability to void preferential and fraudulent transfers, the debtor may also void transactions that would be voidable under state law or other applicable nonbankruptcy law. Section 544 of the Bankruptcy Code permits the debtor to void certain transfers made or obligations incurred by it to the extent that such transactions are voidable under state law. Note, for example, that similar state laws guarding against fraudulent transfers look back substantially longer than the period prescribed under Section 548. As a result, the limitations period for fraudulent transfers may be considerably longer than the periods prescribed by the Bankruptcy Code.

Assumption and Rejection of Executory Contracts and Unexpired Leases

Section 365 of the Bankruptcy Code governs "executory contracts and unexpired leases." This section of the Bankruptcy Code permits the debtor, with the approval of the Bankruptcy Court, to assume or reject certain leases and other agreements that are in effect on the date of the filing. As a result, the debtor is able to free itself from certain economically undesirable contractual obligations or agreements that would otherwise impair its ability to implement a restructured business model.

More specifically, a debtor may assume or reject any of its executory contracts. An executory contract is an agreement under which the debtor and its counterparty both have material performance obligations. Similarly, the debtor may reject unexpired leases of real or personal property. In each case, the debtor must make its election within specified periods dating from the filing of the petition.

Use of Cash Collateral

As the debtor in possession moves through each phase of a Chapter 11 proceeding, it also continues with the day-to-day operation of its enterprise. In the course of managing its business, the debtor may seek the consent of its creditors and an order of the Bankruptcy Court for the use of "cash collateral" in order to fund its liquidity needs. Section 363 of the Bankruptcy Code governs the use, sale, or lease of property that is within the debtor's bankruptcy estate and provides special provisions that restrict the use of cash collateral. Under Section 363 cash collateral includes "cash, negotiable instruments, documents of title, securities, deposit accounts, or other cash equivalents, whenever acquired, in which the estate and an entity other than the estate have an interest" and includes the proceeds, products, or offspring, rents, or profits of property. A debtor, therefore, may seek to use available cash collateral, if any, or cash collateral resulting from a sale of property of the estate.

In addition to Bankruptcy Court approval, however, the debtor must provide "adequate protection" to each creditor having an interest in the cash collateral to be used. In this way, Section 361 of the Bankruptcy Code attempts to protect creditors with an interest in the cash collateral to be used from a partial or total loss of the value of their interest. Under Section 361, the debtor may provide adequate protection to its creditors in one of several ways. The debtor, in order to restore the creditors' loss in value, may (1) make periodic cash payments ("adequate protection payments") to its creditors, (2) provide its creditors additional liens ("replacement liens") on other property of the estate, or (3) enter into such other arrangements as will result in the creditors receiving the "indubitable equivalent" of the loss in value of their interest.

Plan of Reorganization and Disclosure

Chapter 11 gives the debtor an exclusive right to propose and file a plan of reorganization during the 120-day period immediately following the petition date. During this "exclusivity period," no other creditor or party in interest may propose and file a plan. Chapter 11 also gives the debtor a 180-day period (a "solicitation period") during which it may solicit and obtain the acceptance of its plan. Upon the expiration of the exclusivity period, however, a creditor may file and seek the approval of its own plan, which may compete with any plan previously proposed by the debtor.

Note that for cases filed prior to October 17, 2005, the effective date of the BAPCA, successive extensions of the exclusivity period (and the corresponding solicitation period) could be, and have been, granted by the Bankruptcy Court upon a showing of cause. As a result, the exclusivity period in pre-BAPCA cases could be extended for years. Following the enactment of the BAPCA, the 120-day exclusivity period may not be extended beyond 18 months after the petition date, and the solicitation period may not be extended beyond 20 months after the petition date.

In tandem with the plan proposal, the debtor must also file a written disclosure statement with the Bankruptcy Court. The goal of the disclosure statement is to provide to creditors sufficiently detailed information ("adequate information") about the debtor and its business to enable the creditors to make an informed decision as to whether to accept or reject the proposed plan. As a general rule, Bankruptcy Court approval of the disclosure statement is a prerequisite to plan approval.

Voting and Confirmation

Sections 1129(a) and 1129(b) of the Bankruptcy Code set forth the elements required for the confirmation of a plan of reorganization depending upon the level of "acceptance" by all creditors who are entitled to vote.

Pursuant to Section 1123(a) of the Bankruptcy Code, a plan of reorganization must classify creditors according to their separate claims and interests and specify whether each class is "impaired" or "unimpaired." The designation of classes may be based, for example, on whether the creditor and its interest is secured or unsecured, priority or nonpriority, or otherwise distinguishable based upon its claim. A class of creditors is impaired if the plan offers less than payment in full to that class or otherwise modifies or limits the rights of that class.

The voting process to obtain plan approval is conducted by class. If at least two-thirds in amount and one-half in number of the holders of allowed claims or interest within a class vote to accept the plan, the plan is binding upon and is deemed to have been accepted by the entire class. Note, however, that only impaired classes are entitled to vote, because the unimpaired classes expect to be paid in full and, under Section 1126 of the Bankruptcy Code, are presumed to have accepted the plan.

A hearing must be held before the Bankruptcy Court in order to confirm a plan of reorganization. If the proposed plan satisfies all of the elements set forth in Section 1129(a) and the requisite lenders in each impaired class have voted to accept the plan, the plan can be confirmed by the Bankruptcy Court. In the event that an impaired class rejects the proposed plan of reorganization, Section 1129(b) of the Bankruptcy Code provides that the plan may still be confirmed if the plan (1) satisfies all of the elements of Section 1129(a), other than the requirement that each unimpaired class of claims or interests shall have accepted the plan, (2) has been accepted by at least one other impaired class, and (3) does not "discriminate unfairly" and is "fair and equitable" to the impaired class that has rejected the plan.

CONCLUSION

Most companies that are in financial crisis, if given the opportunity, would prefer to undertake a consensual restructuring process with their creditors. Restructuring without court supervision is generally less expensive and less time consuming. Not all workouts, however, can be effectively implemented without the tools and safeguards afforded by Chapter 11. Prearranged and prepackaged plans mitigate some of the difficulties encountered by companies trying to effect a consensual restructuring, such as avoiding the need for unanimous consent. If, however, a company is not able to reach an agreement with its creditors in a consensual environment, a formal Chapter 11 proceeding may provide the only avenue for an effective financial restructuring of a borrower in distress.

CHAPTER 10

Vehicles and Products Derived from the Asset Class

Philip Nisbet
Director
Barclays Capital

Richard W. Stewart
Managing Director and Senior Portfolio Manager
Nomura Corporate Research and Asset Management Inc.

Sam DeRosa-Farag
Managing Director, Global Leveraged Finance Strategy,
Credit Suisse

Mark Herzinger
Director
Barclays Capital

Introduction

Philip Nisbet
Director, Barclays Capital

A variety of structured products and derivatives based on bank loans that allow the risk and reward of this asset class to be divided up and traded in customized forms have evolved over the last 15 years. The three main structured products that have evolved are total return swaps (TRS) in the early 1990s, then collateralized loan obligations (CLOs) in 1996, and finally loan-only credit default swaps (CDS), developed in the late 1990s, but with no real volume until recently. All three products were adapted from similar products already in use for other asset classes.

Total return swaps on bank loans began trading when institutional investors made inroads into the bank loan market. Whereas banks had internal sources of funding and leverage, institutional investors, including hedge funds, often needed to arrange asset-specific financing. The absence of a repurchase market to leverage bank loans was filled by total return swaps, which were already in use for equities.

While TRS are effective at providing leverage, because of lack of guidance from regulators at the time, they did not offer regulatory capital relief for banks, and their derivative format made them inappropriate for syndication to groups of investors. Thus, the CLO market was born, first as a means for banks to reduce their exposure to bank loans that they owned, improving returns on equity and reducing capital usage. Cash flows on diversified pools of fixed income assets were already being carved up in other markets, most notably the mortgage market with collateralized mortgage obligations (CMOs). These types of securitization structures allowed banks to transfer risk while obtaining funding and regulatory capital relief, in a format (notes and shares) that was marketable to investors.

The initial CLOs (NatWest's Rose Funding in 1996 and NationsBank's first CLO in 1997) were termed balance sheet CLOs, as the motivation was to move assets off of the sponsoring banks' books. Soon thereafter, arbitrage CLOs, where the bank loans are assembled from the primary and secondary markets, outgrew the balance sheet CLO market, and now the CLO market is almost entirely composed of arbitrage transactions. With TRS providing basic leverage on bank loans, and CLOs offering more specific tranches of risk in securitized form, various structured alternatives for "long" positions in bank loans trade in the amount of tens of billions of dollars per year.

However, until recently, there was still no product that provided the ability to take short positions in bank loans. TRS do not work well for short positions because they exactly mimic the loan cash flows, which can be irregular and complex, thus requiring ownership of at least a piece of the loan to track these cash flows. Default swaps on corporate credits started to be transacted in the mid–1990s, and even though there have been some loan-only trades for years, the loan-only CDS has only recently begun to show promise as the product that will allow investors and hedgers to go short bank loans or the bank loan market. As loan-only CDS become more liquid, the bank loan market will have in place practical, usable tools to leverage individual loans and loan indices, to divide up the risk of pools of loans into tranches and rated securities, to take short positions on individual loans and loan indices, and to create synthetic tranches of pools of loans that can be transacted from both the long and the short side. TRS, CLOs, and loan-only CDS, the three primary types of structured transactions that accommodate the aforementioned positions, are discussed in more detail in this chapter.

Collateralized Loan Obligations: A Primer

Richard W. Stewart
Managing Director and Senior Portfolio Manager,
Nomura Corporate Research and
Asset Management Inc.

The textbook definition of a collateralized loan obligation (CLO) is a security backed by or collateralized by a diversified pool of corporate loans. The practical definition adopted by the capital markets is more expansive. According to practitioners, a CLO is a special-purpose investment vehicle (SPV) established to accumulate a diversified pool of loans (collateral). The accumulation of the collateral is funded by the issuance of a series of rated notes plus equity. The rated notes are usually sequentially tranched, with the higher-rated tranches having a priority claim on the cash flows generated by the collateral pool and increasingly higher levels of subordinated capital support to protect against collateral losses. Effectively, CLOs are created by applying traditional asset-based structuring technology to a pool of loans.

The CLO market is a subset of the broader collateralized debt obligation (CDO) market, which includes a variety of different collateral pools, among them asset-backed securities, residential and commercial mortgage-backed securities, high-yield bonds, investment grade bonds, trust preferred securities, and various types of synthetic instruments. The CLO market itself includes different structures and investment objectives. The primary focus of this article will be on cash flow arbitrage CLOs, the most commonly issued type of CLO. Brief descriptions of other types of CLOs are included at the end of the article, but the general concepts discussed apply across all types of CLOs.

The investment objective of a cash flow CLO, from the perspective of an equity investor, is to create an arbitrage, or generate excess spread from the current return on the collateral pool less the cost of the underlying liabilities. CLOs utilize a high amount of investment leverage to achieve this objective. The rated-note investors receive a coupon, typically at a spread over LIBOR. Investors in the equity tranche of a CLO receive the excess spread, which is equal to the collateral yield less the coupon paid on the rated notes, management fees, and administrative expenses. Cash flow CLOs are not net asset value (NAV) (i.e. not mark-to-market based) investment vehicles, and the rated notes are nonrecourse to the equity investor and the collateral manager. The investment strategy is to maximize cash flow after credit losses over a six- to ten-year investment horizon. The strategy is not primarily total return– or trading-oriented. Given the investment leverage in the CLO structure, portfolio strategy emphasis is on loss avoidance and maintenance of portfolio income. The typical CLO is between $300 and $800 million in size (the average in 2005 was approximately $500 million) and accumulates a diversified collateral pool consisting of 125 to 175 issuers in 25 to 30 industry groups.

WHY DO CLOs EXIST?

CLOs have taken the loan market one step further in its development. They have opened the loan market to a broader spectrum of investors with different risk/return profiles. These investors might otherwise have been precluded from participating in noninvestment grade or less liquid markets, or been hesitant to participate in the loan market because of the cost of creating the credit analysis platform that is critical for effective decision making. Prior to the creation of CLOs, the options available to investors were limited to managed accounts, bank loan funds, and direct participation in the loan market. These options left investors with "first loss" credit exposure and with interest-rate and prepayment risk.

CLOs enable investors to participate in the loan asset class according to their own tolerance for risk and return. The rated notes increase or decrease the degree of leverage applied to the sector. Senior tranches deleverage the asset class, whereas junior tranches and the equity tranche leverage both the credit risk and return embedded in the asset class. Investors can take a view on the underlying fundamentals of the loan asset class and participate in the CLO tranches consistent with that view. Segmenting the credit risk in the loan market and rating that segmented exposure expands the loan market to a larger, more diverse investor base beyond traditional noninvestment grade debt buyers. In turn, by broadening the pool of investors, CLOs increase market demand for the loan asset class and help to improve the efficiency of the loan market.

The loan asset class is ideally suited for securitization for several reasons:

- Loans exhibit high and relatively consistent mean principal recoveries in the event of default, limiting the par value erosion of the collateral pool.
- Stable prices enable prepayments to be reinvested at or near par, minimizing the par value spent on premium-priced collateral.
- Interest-rate risk is limited, given the matching of floating-rate assets with primarily floating-rate liabilities.
- The low correlation of returns on the loan asset class with returns on virtually any other asset class provides significant diversity to aggregate investment portfolios.

- Liquidity in the loan market has improved significantly over the last five years.
- Loans as an asset class have a performance history, which can be analyzed to calibrate the risks in a securitization.
- Loans, the underlying collateral, have individual, independent credit assessment from the rating agencies, again assisting with the calibration of the risks in a securitization.
- Experienced asset managers with developed credit organizations can utilize CLOs as an asset-gathering vehicle.

CLOs enable investors to diversify into the loan asset class through an investment grade security if desired, using professional management expertise. Today CLOs attract a global investor base, ranging from multi-national banks to high net worth individuals. In the senior tranches, banks, insurance companies, structured investment vehicles, and conduits, among others, are the major investors. Some of these investors also participate in the junior tranches or equity tier, where institutional investors, hedge funds, alternative investment groups, and high net worth individuals, among others, become more active. Several CDO equity fund of funds have also been created which target CLO equity as their primary asset class.

BASIC CLO STRUCTURE AND MECHANICS

The starting point for a CLO is the formation of an SPV, an entity created for the sole purpose of investing in a pool of loans (collateral), the purchase of which is funded by the issuance of notes and equity. A collateral manager engages an investment bank to assist with (1) the formation of the SPV, (2) the structuring of the capitalization and rating of the notes, (3) the offering and distribution of the debt and equity securities, and (4) the accumulation of the collateral by providing a warehouse facility. Conceptually, a CLO seems like a simple transaction; however, the details are quite complex (see Exhibit 10.1).

The cash flow generated by the collateral portfolio is distributed to the note and equity holders. This distribution is governed by a priority of payments or "waterfall," which dictates that payments are made first to the debtholders in order of priority. Any residual cash flow is distributed to the equity investors. The notes are assigned credit ratings by the major ratings agencies based upon the credit quality of the collateral investments, portfolio

EXHIBIT 10.1

Basic CLO structure.

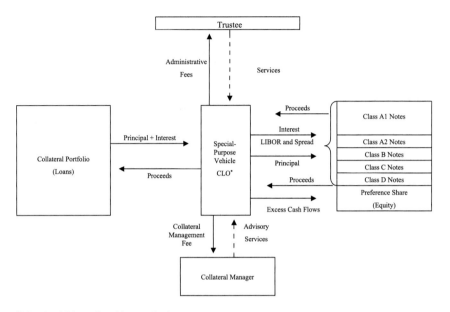

*Collateral portfolio is owned by and the notes and equity are
obligations of the CLO Special-Purpose Vehicle.

diversification, excess spread, and priority of payment in the
waterfall. The terms and conditions of the note obligations are documented in an indenture. This indenture provides noteholders
with protections and maintains the integrity of the ratings through
several types of covenants, including asset and interest coverage
tests, collateral eligibility criteria, and collateral quality maintenance tests. These tests are intended to maintain a certain portfolio
risk profile during the term of the CLO and, in certain situations,
restrict cash distributions to lower-rated debt tranches and equity
shares in favor of the holders of senior debt. Collateral managers
select credits for the portfolio, monitor the credit quality and other
characteristics of the portfolio and trade when appropriate. The
collateral manager is paid a collateral management fee based on
the size of the collateral pool. This fee is typically split between
senior and subordinate tranches, which have different priority levels in the waterfall. Collateral managers typically can also earn an
incentive fee after distributions to equity holders have achieved a
designated internal rate of return (IRR) threshold.

Capital Structure

Outlined in Exhibit 10.2 is a sample capital structure for a generic CLO. In practice, however, the capitalization of each CLO is uniquely constructed based upon a number of considerations, which include, among others, (1) the composition of the target collateral pool, (2) investment flexibility, (3) current market conditions for collateral spreads and liability spreads, (4) the weighted average cost of the debt capital, and (5) the desired ratings of the notes in the capital structure. Ultimately, the objective is to create the most efficient capital structure, given the collateral manager's investment style, to maximize the risk-adjusted return on the equity. The trade-off is between an effort to allocate as much of the debt up the capital structure to the lowest cost debt tranches, thereby reducing the weighted average cost of debt capital, without unduly restricting the collateral manager's investment flexibility to generate attractive returns on the collateral pool.

The equity content in this capital structure for a generic CLO is approximately 8 percent or approximately 12 times leverage to the equity. The typical CLO is leveraged 10 to 12 times. The largest component of the capital structure is the AAA/Aaa-rated notes class, which typically constitute 70 to 80 percent of the capital structure.

Ratings are assigned to each debt tranche based upon a number of considerations. One principal consideration is the construction of the collateral pool. What is the probability of default, and what is the expected principal recovery in the event of default? How diversified is the collateral pool by issuer? By industry? By

EXHIBIT 10.2

Capital structure for a generic CLO.

	Ratings	Amount/ % of Capitalization
Class A1 Note	Aaa/AAA	$370.0 MM / 74.0%
Class A2 Notes	Aa2/AA	30.0 MM / 6.0%
Class B Notes	A2 /A	280. MM / 5.6%
Class C Notes	Baa2 /BBB	20.0 MM / 4.0%
Class D Notes	Ba2 /BB	12.0 MM / 2.4%
Equity	Not Rated	40.0 MM / 8.0%
		$500.00 MM / 100%

rating? What types of obligations are in the pool, senior secured, second lien, subordinated debt? Another consideration is the capital structure of the CLO. What is the level of subordination beneath the debt tranche to protect against credit losses in the collateral pool? A third consideration is the cash flow from the collateral pool and the debt service requirements of the more senior debt tranches. How much cash flow cushion exists before the debt service payments would be impaired? Each rating agency has a proprietary model that incorporates its analysis of these considerations, plus others. In order for the debt tranche to achieve a certain rating, it must meet the minimum credit standards for that rating level.

The notes are typically structured with a 12- to 15-year final maturity; however, their expected life is shorter, starting at 7 to 9 years for the AAA/Aaa-rated notes. A typical CLO has a 5- or 6-year reinvestment or "revolving" period during which the manager is permitted to reinvest prepayments or proceeds from collateral sales into new eligible collateral. After the reinvestment period expires, proceeds from principal repayments on collateral investments are applied to prepayment of the notes' principal balances, starting with the most senior class and working down the capital structure. Only after all the notes have been repaid will any principal proceeds be distributed to the equity investors. Nonetheless, while principal proceeds are being dedicated to reduce the note balances, the equity investors may continue to receive excess interest distributions. (Please refer to the section "Payment Waterfall" for further descriptions of principal proceeds and interest proceeds.)

The majority of the rated notes are usually issued as floating-rate obligations of the CLO. The coupon is set at a fixed spread over three-month LIBOR. This spread increases as the investor moves down the capital structure, reflective of the higher risks and lower ratings of the more junior notes. Distribution of CLO liabilities is targeted primarily to floating-rate investors. Some portion of the notes may be structured with a fixed-rate coupon, depending on investor demand and/or to help match fund fixed-rate assets included in the collateral pool. The notes are typically noncallable for three to five years. After the noncall period, the floating-rate notes are usually callable at par. Fixed-rate notes generally have a call premium structured as a make-whole provision or declining fixed premium.

Collateral

The notes are secured by the CLO's investment portfolio, known as the collateral. The collateral portfolio will consist primarily of floating-rate assets, although some portion might be invested in fixed-rate obligations. Otherwise, the composition of the collateral varies among CLOs, based upon the investment strategy of the collateral manager. A basic CLO would invest primarily in the par institutional loan market. Other CLOs could, for example, focus on middle market loans, mezzanine loans, or distressed investments. Basic CLOs may have baskets for high-yield bonds, second lien loans, structured finance assets, or synthetic investments. As noted earlier, the rating agencies evaluate the default and recovery statistics of the collateral pool. The higher the risk profile of the collateral, the more subordination, or protection against credit losses, will be required for the debt tranches at each level of the capital structure. The required equity content will also be greater.

CLOs typically incorporate a three- to six-year reinvestment period. During the reinvestment period, principal repayments on investments are reinvested in additional collateral. After the expiration of the reinvestment period, principal repayments on investments are not reinvested, but instead are applied to amortize the CLO note obligations, starting with the most senior tranches, effectively delevering the capital structure.

The Arbitrage

The difference between the weighted average cost of debt capital, the management fees and ongoing administrative expenses, and the return on the collateral pool creates the arbitrage that generates the excess spread for the equity. An example, using an overly simplistic set of assumptions demonstrates this concept.

Collateral return (LIBOR + 250 bps):   250 bps

Weighted average cost of debt capital (50 bps on 92% of the capital structure):   46 bps

Collateral management fees: 50 bps

Fees and expenses: 5 bps

Credit losses (2% defaults, 75% recoveries):   50 bps

Excess spread (the arbitrage):   99 bps

If the CLO were leveraged 12 times, the nominal one-year return would be approximately 12 percent after adjusting for credit losses. The actual return on the CLO equity investment should be higher than 12 percent if credit losses are realized later in the life of the investment. Initial cash-on-cash distributions would not suffer from the deduction for credit losses.

The arbitrage occurs with a matching of higher spread floating-rate assets with lower spread floating-rate liabilities. As noted earlier, some portion of the assets could be invested in fixed-rate investments, and some portion of the liabilities could be fixed-rate obligations. If an asset/liability mismatch occurs, an interest-rate hedge may be required to protect the arbitrage against changes in interest rates during the life of the CLO. The investment objective of the CLO is to segment the credit risk in a loan portfolio, not to assume duration and/or interest-rate risk. An interest-rate hedge, if necessary, is intended to minimize the duration risk in the CLO structure. The rating agencies evaluate the adequacy of the interest-rate hedges when assigning ratings to the notes.

Payment Waterfall

The cash flow generated by the collateral pool is distributed among the various layers of the capital structure according to the payment waterfall specified in the CLO indenture. There are two components to the cash flows: interest proceeds and principal proceeds. The payment waterfall addresses both. A typical waterfall is outlined in Exhibit 10.3.

The payment waterfall dictates the priority of payments. At the top of the waterfall are any taxes and senior fees and expenses, such as trustee fees and the senior collateral management fee. Then the cash flows are directed to debt service payments, starting with the most senior notes. At several points in the waterfall, coverage tests are inserted. If the cash flows or collateral value are insufficient to pass these tests at any of these points, distributions to points further down the waterfall are cut off and are diverted to redeem the most senior class of notes still outstanding. Cash flows are diverted to delever the structure until the tests are passed again, a self-correcting mechanism. At the bottom of the waterfall are the subordinated management fee and equity distributions. Thus the payment waterfall ensures that any deterioration in the credit quality of the collateral or the cash flows generated from the

EXHIBIT 10.3

Typical CLO payments waterfall.

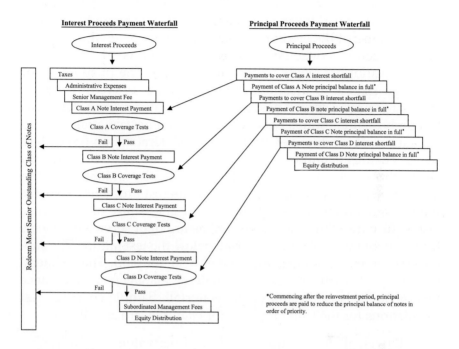

collateral affects the investors at the bottom of the capital structure first.

Indenture Covenants

Incorporated into the indenture are two types of covenants to protect the noteholders and maintain the integrity of the credit ratings on the notes, portfolio quality tests and collateral coverage tests. Quality tests are effectively investment restrictions designed to maintain the portfolio profile assumed in the initial note credit ratings. Some of the quality tests protect against deterioration in the credit quality of the portfolio, such as minimum levels of portfolio diversification, the maximum weighted average credit rating, maximum amount of CCC-rated investments, and minimum estimated recovery values. Quality tests such as the minimum weighted average spread ensure the sufficiency of cash flows to make the debt service payments. The quality tests merely restrict trading, and are described as "maintain or improve tests." If the CLO fails any quality test, all subsequent portfolio trades must maintain or improve the failed test level. They do not affect the priority of payments under the waterfall, including the payment of the collateral management fees. However, failure of quality tests could lead to a downgrading of the credit ratings on the notes.

Failures of coverage tests, on the other hand, do disrupt the priority of payments under the waterfall. The purpose of the coverage tests is to maintain minimum levels of credit enhancements and excess spread to support the assigned ratings. There is a test for both minimum asset coverage and interest coverage. Credit enhancement is addressed by the overcollateralization (O/C) test, which ensures a minimum level of par value asset coverage for each debt tranche. Excess spread is protected by an interest coverage test, which ensures the adequacy of interest proceeds to pay the interest due on the notes. In the event of the failure of a coverage test, equity distributions are cut off, as are debt service payments for any debt tranche in the waterfall below the test failure. The subordinate collateral management fee is also not paid. The collateral manager still earns the senior collateral management fee, since this payment is at the top of the waterfall. Sample coverage test calculations for the Class B notes, for example, are as follows:

Class B overcollateralization = collateral par value/par value of
Class A & B notes

Class B interest coverage = (collateral coupon – senior fees and
expenses)/Class A & B coupons

It is important to note that these overcollateralization tests are based on asset par value and not market value which is a key characteristic of the cash flow CLO structure. As described below, many traditional portfolio-financing structures rely on collateral market value for coverage tests and ultimate debt repayment.

Warehouse Facility

A CLO investment portfolio is accumulated over an extended period of time, typically six to nine months or longer. In an effort to minimize the negative drag on the CLO liabilities caused by the funding costs, a collateral manager generally targets the portfolio to be 70 to 75 percent ramped up at closing. The remaining 25 to 30 percent would be accumulated 90 to 180 days postclosing.

A warehouse facility is required to finance and hold the preclosing accumulation. The investment bank engaged by the collateral manager typically provides this facility. At closing, investments are typically contributed to the CLO at the original purchase price.

OTHER TYPES OF CLO

Market Value CLOs

The market value CLO structure is similar to the cash flow structure in that it provides a vehicle the ability to leverage the returns of the underlying portfolio assets. These structures typically include one or more classes of debt financing, but, unlike cash flow CLOs, they rely primarily on the market value of the portfolio as protection for the debtholders. The portfolio management style and objectives for these CLOs tends to be more total return– and trading-oriented, and the collateral pool utilizes a broader range of asset types. Typically the market value of the underlying assets is "haircut" by assigning an advance rate to different types of collateral in the portfolio (e.g., based on rating, seniority, and/or liquidity). This haircut collateral value must be equal to or greater than the amount of debt; if it is less, the debt must be partially repaid to cure the deficiency. These funds tend to be less leveraged than a cash flow CLO at 5 to 6 times. They also generally allow for more flexibility in the portfolio quality tests because of the added credit protection provided by the mark-to-market maintenance requirements. Often these funds include a variety of asset classes in addition to bank loans, including high-yield bonds, distressed debt, and special situation assets.

Balance Sheet CLO

Cash flow CLOs are typically of one of two types, depending on the motivation for the deal: arbitrage or balance sheet. Arbitrage transactions are typically motivated by the desire to acquire collateral with a yield higher than that of the liabilities to create arbitrage investment opportunities for equity investors. Balance sheet transactions, in contrast, may be motivated primarily by an issuing institution's desire to reduce or remove the credit risk of assets on its balance sheet by transferring those assets into a cash flow CLO or to use a CLO vehicle as an alternative source of financing.

Accordingly, in arbitrage transactions, the collateral manager will usually select the assets that will be in the CLO during the warehousing period, in a balance sheet transaction, however, the pool of assets is typically predetermined by the credit risk that the issuing institution desires to remove from its balance sheet. The cash flow mechanics of the two types of CLOs are the same, but the investment objective of a balance sheet structure may not be to maximize the return to the equity holders.

Synthetic CDOs

The economics behind synthetic CDOs are similar to those of cash flow CDOs; however, the collateral in these transactions is typically credit derivatives, including credit-linked notes and credit default swaps. With the credit default swap technology, the performance of transactions is primarily a function of credit events, and this reduces some of the risks associated with cash flow CDOs, including interest-rate risk. The synthetic CDOs enter into contracts selling default protection against assets and, in return, receive a spread for the risk of a credit event. The capital structure of synthetic CDOs is similar to that of cash flow CDOs, where the risk of loss to the notes is segmented into tranches and each tranche is paid a coupon that reflects the risks of that tranche. The most junior tranches would bear first-loss positions on credit events on the contracts, and each subsequent tranche would bear any additional losses, if any. In addition, since the synthetic CDO enters into contracts rather than purchasing the actual underlying collateral, some of the liabilities may be either funded or unfunded. Typically, the super senior tranche (the most senior tranche) is unfunded and would be required to fund the transaction only upon significant losses, whereas the more junior tranches would fund their notes. Cash proceeds from these notes are held in a reserve account and applied as needed to fund losses in the underlying synthetic contracts upon the occurrence of specified credit events.

HISTORY OF THE CLO MARKET

CLOs evolved from the technology developed in the early 1980s with the creation of collateralized mortgage obligations (CMOs), or structured vehicles with mortgages as collateral, by structuring tranches of risk in the mortgage market. This same technology was

EXHIBIT 10.4

Annual CDO Issuance

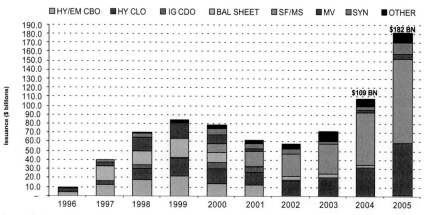

Source: Credit Suisse.

applied to tranches of credit risk in the second half of the 1980s. Initially the application of tranches of credit risk was more prevalent in the high-yield bond market, although the earliest forms of structured investment vehicles securitized by loans were established at the same time. The modern era of the CLO market originated in the mid–1990s, concurrent with the evolution of the loan asset class into a financial instrument with a market unto itself. Since 1997, loans have been a large part of the CDO market, even as other asset classes have moved in and out of favor with investors.

The resiliency of loan collateral was clearly demonstrated during the weak credit market with high default rates from 2000 to 2002. A good indicator of relative performance among various types of CDOs is the number of ratings downgrades. As shown in Exhibit 10.5, CLOs have dramatically outperformed other types of collateral pools.

Initially, multi-billion-dollar balance sheet CLOs drove new-issue loan volume. In the past few years, however, cash flow arbitrage CLOs have driven new-issue volume (see Exhibit 10.6). This growth in cash flow CLOs has been exponential. In 2005, new-issue cash flow CLOs almost doubled.

Certainly increased investor awareness of CLOs has contributed to their unprecedented popularity, but several general market trends have also encouraged their growth in the past years.

EXHIBIT 10.5

Rating Agency Downgrades

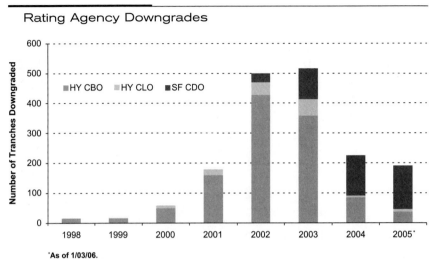

'As of 1/03/06.

Source: Credit Suisse, Moody's Investors Service, Standard & Poor's, Fitch.

EXHIBIT 10.6

Annual CLO Issuance

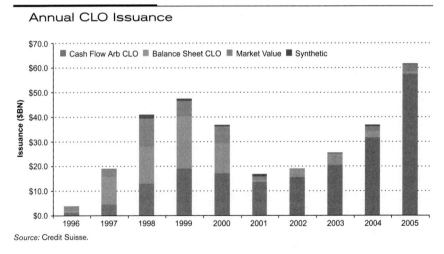

Source: Credit Suisse.

First, some large, sophisticated investors have been unenthusiastic about the outlook for returns in the traditional equity markets and have pursued alternative investment ideas. Some of these investors discovered that CLO equity could generate 12 to 15 percent IRRs, with the further benefit of enhanced portfolio diversification through participation in the credit markets. CLO equity is particularly appealing, since it generates a high amount of current cash income. If investors project a benign credit environment for several years, the equity distributions will materially reduce the principal balance of the investment prior to the start of the next adverse credit cycle.

Second, investors did perceive a benign credit market after the weak credit markets during the 2000–2002 default peak. Indeed, credit losses diminished dramatically from 2003 through 2005.

Third, a significant portion of the demand for CLO floating-rate liabilities can be linked to investor expectations for rising interest rates. Floating-rate liabilities virtually eliminate mark-to-market principal losses caused by duration risk. Generally, interest rates in the United States have been rising since mid-year 2004.

Fourth, CLO liability spreads are wider than comparably rated corporate spreads. This gap can be attributed to less liquidity, less transparency, and more complexity in the CLO market. Investors have become more willingly to devote the time and resources needed to evaluate CLO investments, particularly during low-yield, tight-spread capital markets. The spread premium available has been dissipating with time as the CLO market moves down the path of improved market efficiency, and increased investor sophistication. Exhibit 10.7 demonstrates the significant tightening in CLO liability spreads, driven by the second and third market trends.

EXHIBIT 10.7

CLO Liability Spreads

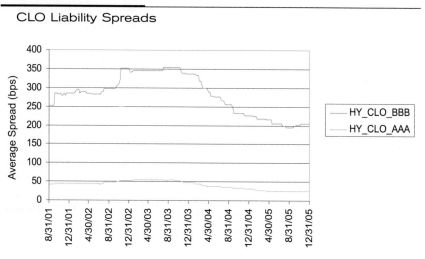

CURRENT MARKET CONDITIONS

Tighter liability spreads create a greater arbitrage for excess cash flow distributions to CLO equity investors, which, in theory, should increase marginal demand for CLO equity. Demand for CLO equity has increased dramatically, as noted earlier in this article. This demand, in turn, has created substantial demand for loan assets to ramp up collateral portfolios. Indeed, Standard & Poor's Leveraged Commentary & Data (LCD) estimates that CLOs accounted for 63 percent of the primary market demand for institutional loans in 2005. The demand from CLOs thus has likely had a significant impact on the spread tightening witnessed in the loan market since 2003. When collateral spreads tighten, the excess spread arbitrage contracts, consequently reducing the potential returns on CLO equity. Throughout the past two years, the contraction in CLO liability spreads kept pace with the contraction in asset spreads, so demand for CLO equity remained strong. If liability spreads widen, the excess spread arbitrage will contract. Given the interaction between the two markets, however, changes in CLO liability spreads would be expected to have a major influence on loan market spreads.

In a spread-tightening environment, turnover in a loan portfolio increases. If credit quality is held constant, proceeds from loan prepayments are reinvested in loans with lower spreads. This environment may affect the CLO market in several ways. For example, the weighted average spread (WAS) covenant levels have been declining in new-issue CLOs. In existing CLOs, which have higher covenant levels, CLO managers have been challenged to maintain the required WAS covenant. This challenge has been addressed in several ways. One strategy is for the manager to increase the risk profile of the collateral portfolio. This strategy, for example, created demand for second lien term loans from CLOs. But this solution could create complications for the weighted average rating factor covenant. Alternatively, managers can recommend an amendment to the WAS covenant. This amendment is typically subject to the approval of the majority of each class of note and equity holders. The amendment can also be subject to reconfirmation of the existing note ratings by the respective rating agencies. Amendments to WAS covenants in existing CLOs increased dramatically in 2005. Generally, noteholders have responded favorably to these amendments, perceiving them as a more attractive solution than increasing the risk profile of the collateral portfolio.

Tightening spreads, strong secondary bid prices for loan collateral, high prepayment rates, and low default rates all have contributed to an increase in early redemptions of existing CLOs. After the noncall period on the notes, a CLO can typically be redeemed with the vote of a supermajority of the equity holders, even before the expiration of the reinvestment period. Conditions in the loan market in 2005 encouraged many early redemptions for several reasons. First, cash positions in CLOs were accumulating, representing a drag on generating excess spread. Cash balances accumulated because older-vintage CLOs had higher WAS covenants. If a CLO fails a WAS covenant, then each subsequent trade must maintain or improve the covenant level, a difficult thing to do in a tightening-spread environment. Second, liability spreads on older-vintage CLOs were higher than those on new-issue CLOs. The excess spread had been squeezed in the tight-spread environment, so equity distributions declined dramatically. Third, mark-to-market portfolio values increased as a result of the strong demand for loans in the secondary market and the favorable credit environment that minimized par value erosion from credit losses. Collateral portfolios could be liquidated and the proceeds applied to prepaying the notes, while still making a significant residual distribution to the equity holders. This distribution could then be reinvested in a new CLO that had a more favorable excess spread arbitrage given a lower weighted average cost of CLO liabilities. In addition, after the expiration of the reinvestment period, the CLO notes will begin to amortize starting with the most senior and lowest cost notes. As the senior notes begin to amortize, the cost of financing of the CLO will increase and thereby compress the net excess spread available to the equity. This effect can also increase the incentive for equity holders to call the structure.

Recent developments in the CLO market also include enhanced protections for noteholders. Two examples are interest deflection tests and purchase price– or ratings-based haircuts to collateral values used for calculating overcollateralization (O/C) ratios. Many indentures now require that assets purchased at a discount be carried at that discount price rather than at par value when calculating collateral value. In addition, investments rated CCC+/Caa1 or below beyond a certain percentage of the collateral may also be carried at market value. The effect of this protection is to reduce the par value in the numerator of the O/C test for riskier

investments, thereby lowering the ratio and increasing the likelihood that the test will be tripped and excess cash flows will be
diverted to reduce the principal balance of the senior notes. An
interest deflection test diverts excess spread from equity distributions to purchase additional collateral. This test is calculated like the
overcollateralization ratio, but it is set at a higher level than the O/C
test. An interest deflection test postpones the delevering of a CLO
by purchasing additional collateral before a violation of an O/C
ratio requires excess spread to be diverted to prepay the most senior
class of notes.

DEVELOPMENT OF THE SECONDARY MARKET

Development of an active secondary market has also been a major
contributor to the growth in the CLO market. Secondary market
participants point to one major catalyst for this development: in
late spring 2003, a large European financial institution liquidated
a large CDO portfolio. Prior to this large liquidation, CLO paper
primarily traded by appointment in the secondary market, dealers
focused almost exclusively on transactions that they had underwritten. As such, the investment analysis was very time-consuming and cumbersome, since no robust or standardized analytical
tools had been developed for secondary trading. A portfolio
liquidation this large attracted significant buyer interest, spurring
dealers to dedicate the time and resources needed to participate in
the auction, and a true secondary market for CLO paper evolved.

　　While this large liquidation may have been the catalyst, three
other factors have been critical contributors to the development of
the secondary market. First, analytical tools were created to ease
the burden of the analysis of these complicated investments. Intex,
in particular, has been a key contributor. Intex is a third-party cash
flow projection model that provides data on the underlying collateral investments and constructs the cash flow waterfall. The user
then inputs basic assumptions on how the collateral will perform
in the future. Second, dealer desks have built the IT and personnel
infrastructure necessary to support the secondary trading business.
Third, the volume of paper distributed in the primary market,
combined with the recent positive performance of CLOs, has
markedly expanded the investor base. Three years ago, the limited

secondary market activity was sell-motivated, driven by investors' desire to exit from a problem credit. Today trading activity is purchase-driven, with investors striving to ramp up a portfolio for a new structured investment fund or looking to improve yield on an existing portfolio.

Total annual volume in today's secondary CLO market is estimated to be in excess of $10 billion, counting only one side of a trade, more than a tenfold increase from three years ago. Trading activity occurs at every level of the capital structure, and bid-ask spreads are tightening, starting with as little as 3 bps at the AAA/Aaa tranche. The highest dollar volume of trading activity is at the AAA/Aaa-rated note tranche, since this tranche typically represents 70 percent or more of the capital structure of a basic CLO. Dealers have committed capital to building trading books and will make markets. As recently as 18 to 24 months ago, trading desks were primarily just brokering trades. The number of secondary buyers has also increased dramatically, totaling as many as 100 active participants.

Secondary trading activity in the CLO market has increased dramatically. Market efficiency and transparency have improved tremendously. But the secondary CLO market has not achieved the level of liquidity, efficiency, or transparency that exists in other mainstream structured products markets—for example, the market for mortgage-backed securities. These liquidity, efficiency, and transparency gaps are likely to remain for several reasons. First, the CLO market is primarily a private market; the notes and equity are distributed in private placement transactions under Rule 144A or other exemptions from registration. Other structured products are distributed primarily through registered public offerings. Second, the collateral portfolio is much less homogeneous or actuarial than other types of collateral and more exposed to single credit risks. The analysis of a CLO investment can be much more complex, given the nature of the collateral pool and specific structural terms and investment criteria which can vary from deal to deal. The work involved in developing a bid for a secondary offering can be time-consuming. Third, a critical assessment of the collateral manager's ability and investment style is more important and requires due diligence and performance record review. Given these liquidity, complexity, and efficiency gaps, CLO paper trades at spreads wider than more traditional structured product markets.

RISK CONSIDERATIONS

When contemplating an investment in a CLO, whether debt or equity, there are a number of risks to evaluate, some more obvious than others. The following are the key risk considerations.

Leverage

The most obvious risk is that a CLO utilizes a high degree of leverage. The use of leverage enhances the returns to equity holders, but it also compounds the volatility of performance of the underlying collateral, thereby increasing the risk of principal loss, particularly for the equity investors and the junior debt tranches. The loan asset has exhibited a relatively stable historical performance. Nonetheless, CLO investors should remember that the collateral is investments in the loans of noninvestment grade borrowers. Leverage of up to 12 times is applied to a structure that invests in loans of borrowers with leveraged balance sheets.

Credit Risk

The other most obvious risk consideration is the credit quality of the underlying collateral portfolio. Any deterioration in the par value is difficult to regain in the loan asset class. In the event of default on a collateral position, CLO equity bears the first-loss risk. CLO debt investors will experience a loss of principal only to the extent that the credit losses consume the subordination underneath their particular note tranche. The timing of any credit losses is a less obvious, but equally important, consideration. The loss of par value early in the life of a CLO will affect the structure's ability to generate cash flow for the entire life of the CLO. The equivalent par value erosion later in the life of the CLO will have a dramatically smaller impact on the IRR to the equity investors. Cash flow distributions to equity investors are typically front-loaded and should generate substantial positive arbitrage in the early years of the CLO, assuming no deterioration in the par value and no spread tightening on the collateral.

Reinvestment Risk

The historical average turnover rate in the loan market is approximately 20 percent per year. The turnover rate on a high-quality loan portfolio in a spread-tightening environment can be as high as 50 percent per year. A high turnover rate in the collateral pool of a CLO means reinvestment risk to the CLO investors. When an investor makes the initial decision to commit capital to a CLO, that decision can be reasonably insightful based upon a studied view of the credit quality of the accumulated collateral portfolio and a judgment on the near-term outlook for conditions in the loan market during the final stages of the collateral accumulation period. During the reinvestment period, however, the characteristics of the collateral pool are subject to change and will be dependent on market conditions during the reinvestment period and the credit selection ability of the collateral manager. Have spreads widened or tightened? Has the credit environment improved or deteriorated? What is the availability of attractive investment ideas and their purchase price? A high turnover rate during the reinvestment period implies more risks related to changes in the portfolio. Cash positions can build if attractive investment ideas are limited, reducing the excess spread arbitrage and thereby reducing distributions to equity investors. Tighter spread environments can cause challenges with maintaining the required weighted average spread covenant, or weaker credit conditions can cause deterioration in the quality of the collateral portfolio.

After the reinvestment period, the turnover rate determines how quickly the CLO will delever. Principal proceeds from prepayments are applied first to the most senior tranches in the capital structure. CLO note investors are therefore exposed to early prepayment risk based on the seniority of the note class. Equity investors are exposed to a contraction of the excess spread distribution. The cheapest layer of financing is prepaid first. Therefore, the weighted average cost of financing increases, resulting in less arbitrage between asset spreads and the weighted average liability spread. Eventually the arbitrage will become unattractive, and the equity holders will seek to redeem the CLO, liquidate the collateral, repay the notes, and receive any residual principal proceeds distribution.

Collateral Manager Selection

The ability of the collateral manager is critical to the performance of a CLO. As noted previously, during the reinvestment period, CLO investors rely on the collateral manager to reinvest prepayments wisely. Credit selection drives the performance of CLOs. Thoughtful collateral managers are very protective of maintaining par value, since it is difficult to recover once it is lost. The primary consideration is the manager's track record with the asset class. An evaluation of the manager's track record should include a history of credit losses, not only from defaults but also from distressed sales. In addition, what is the manager's recovery rate on credit problems? Did the manager's decision to hold or sell maximize the principal recovery on the investment? Does the collateral manager have experience managing loans as collateral within the context of a CLO? Portfolio management tactics differ depending on the structure, covenants, and limitations of the investment vehicle. A collateral manager's total return track record may not be a good indication of that manager's ability to manage an investment vehicle that is oriented toward preservation of par value and generation of cash flow, like a CLO.

Collateral manager due diligence should also include an assessment of

- The quality and depth of the research team to support the credit selection process
- The IT and administrative personnel infrastructure to monitor and control the complex operational aspects of managing CLOs
- The manager's ability to access attractive investment ideas to keep the CLO fully invested without paying a premium for assets, which erodes present value at the margin
- The importance of CLOs to the manager's business and whether the manager has made a capital commitment to the CLO
- The manager's commitment to investor communications
- How the manager will address the potential conflicts between the interests of equity holders, which are to maximize equity distributions, and the interests of noteholders, which are primarily the preservation of par value

Redemption

At the end of the noncall period on the notes, the equity investors typically have the sole option to redeem the CLO. A redemption would require the liquidation of the collateral, the proceeds of which would prepay the notes prior to the stated maturity, and even earlier than contemplated given the expected repayments from collateral prepayment proceeds after the reinvestment period expires. The equity investors are motivated to redeem the CLO at the point in time that will maximize their return on investment, regardless of the impact on the noteholders. The optimum time for the equity investors to redeem the CLO will depend on a number of factors, including, among others, the collateral prepayment rate and available reinvestment opportunities for the collateral prepayments, the projected level of future excess cash flow distributions from the arbitrage, the net equity value derived from the market value of the collateral portfolio less the face value of all CLO liabilities, and reinvestment alternatives for the residual equity distribution from the redemption of the CLO.

Liquidity

CLO notes and equity shares are not widely distributed through a public offering. CLO securities are designed for long-term, buy-and-hold investors. Typically these securities are offered in a private placement. A secondary market for CLO notes and equity has developed over the last three years; however, this market is not as liquid, efficient, or transparent as other fixed income or asset-backed markets. As a result, CLO securities trade in the secondary market, but at a discount to securities in these other markets.

Interest-Rate Risk

CLOs are typically structured to mitigate the risks associated with volatility in interest rates or a mismatch between the duration of the collateral portfolio and the CLO liability structure. If an interest-rate gap exists between the assets and liabilities of the CLO, then this gap is hedged with an interest-rate swap or an interest-rate cap. However, not all of the risks associated with volatility in interest rates can be eliminated, however. For example, CLO liabilities are typically priced off three-month LIBOR contracts, whereas LIBOR contracts on assets are typically one, two, or three months in length. Furthermore, the equity component of the capital structure is not priced off LIBOR. A rise in interest rates will increase the excess spread generated by a CLO, because the LIBOR component of the return on the portion of the collateral funded by equity is not netted against a LIBOR-based funding cost. The reverse is also true; a decline in interest rates will reduce the excess spread generated by a CLO. In addition, LIBOR reset dates for CLO liabilities and the underlying loan collateral may not occur at the same time, resulting in a basis mismatch in LIBOR settings.

Note: The author would like to acknowledge contributions by Jerry DeVito, Mike Kurinets, and Cary Ho of Credit Suisse to this article.

Using Loan-Only CDS in the Leveraged Finance Markets: Implications in an Increasing Volatility Environment

Sam DeRosa-Farag
Managing Director, Global Leveraged Finance Strategy, Credit Suisse

While leveraged loans are trading within a historically tight range, we believe that loan market participants can position themselves for an increase in volatility at a fairly cheap cost. One way in which loan market participants can do so is through credit derivatives, specifically by buying protection via credit default swaps.

Credit default swap indices are widely traded in the high-yield bond universe via the CDX and iTraxx. Single-name high-yield CDS are very active as well. However, loan-only CDS have been slower to develop. In October 2003, Credit Suisse introduced the SAMI (Secured) Index to provide a convenient method for buying or selling protection on a basket of 50 credit default swaps, where the reference obligations are all senior secured loans. With the increase in asymmetric credit risk, however, loan market participants have been eager to hedge their risk on individual reference obligations.

In this article, we will discuss

- Loan credit default swaps as a convenient vehicle for gaining long or short exposure to a specific issue or market segment.
- Trade mechanics for entering into a loan-only CDS.

- Weightings by sector and industry. Because of the impact of negative catalysts in the form of higher commodity prices and obsolescence in specific industries (e.g., automotive, supermarkets, and cable), we believe that capital market access and liquidity should decrease in 2006 and later years.

TURN OF THE CYCLE

Over the past few decades, GDP growth cycles have been longer, and there has been less volatility in the economy—indeed, volatility has been substantially lower in the past 20 years than it was in the 1970s and earlier (see Exhibit 10.8). Because of the Federal Reserve Bank's transparent policies, the risk-free rate has become more predictable, and thus less risky. However, in the financial markets, as asset-liability gaps have grown, the appetite for risk has intensified.

As economic cycles have become milder, financial markets have actually increased the levels of risk in the system (see Exhibit 10.9). Because of the excess liquidity in the financial markets, however, the effects of this net increase in risk are back-loaded toward the end of the credit cycle. As riskier borrowers enter the market, this would imply a deeper financial recession when the economic slowdown hits.

EXHIBIT 10.8

Real GDP volatility, 1955–2Q05.

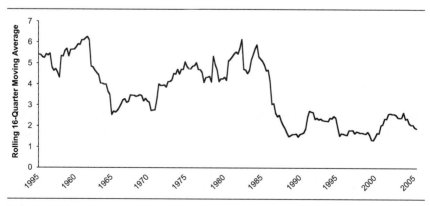

Source: Credit Suisse.

EXHIBIT 10.9

Rolling 20-month return volatility of the U.S. intermediate
Treasury and the S&P 500.

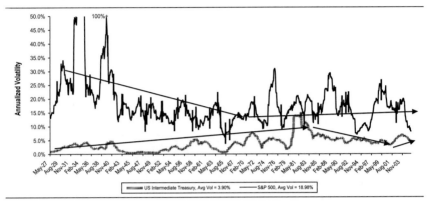

Source: Credit Suisse.

EXHIBIT 10.10

Annualized quarterly high yield default rates, 1Q80–3Q05.

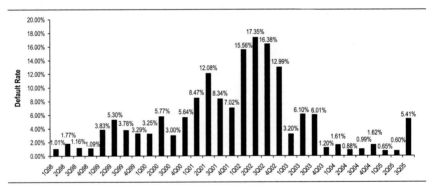

Source: Credit Suisse.

Although we do not expect a full recession for a few years, we
do expect more volatility in the near future (in support of this, we
note the recent increase in high-yield defaults and equity volatility
in the latter half of 2005).

In the third quarter of 2005, we had an uptick in default rates,
mostly from the airline and automotive industries (see Exhibit
10.10). We view the increase in defaults (to an annualized rate of 5.4
percent) as a signal that, while the average default rate for 2005

EXHIBIT 10.11

VIX versus S&P 500 return volatility: 1986–October 20, 2005.

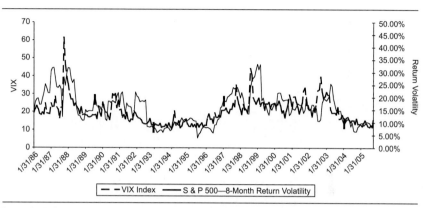

Source: Credit Suisse.

remains low, there are likely to be more spikes to mid-single-digit quarterly defaults in the next few years.

While volatility in the broader equity market has also been muted, in October 2005 we saw an uptick in the VIX (see Exhibit 10.11).

As event risk in the leveraged finance markets has increased, the largest driver of high-yield events has shifted to transition probabilities. Overall, positive event risk, such as M&A and tenders, overwhelms negative event risk, such as defaults (see Exhibit 10.12). While the ratio of upgrades to downgrades is above 1 for high yield, there has been significant credit deterioration in investment grade credits (see Exhibit 10.13). Loan market participants who had previously been long only should consider protecting their portfolios from this downside risk as they recognize the true asymmetry of fixed income assets.

Leveraged loan spreads have tightened during 2005, tightening 30 bps during the year (see Exhibit 10.14). With spreads having come down to an eight-year low, we believe that this is currently an opportunistic time for those who wish to hedge their credit risk to buy loan-only CDS, as the market has priced protection so inexpensively.

Although high-yield bond CDS is often employed as an overlay strategy for leveraged loan investments, correlations between the two assets are actually decreasing (see Exhibit 10.15). After

EXHIBIT 10.12

Annual impact of high yield events as a percentage of the bonds outstanding, 1995–2004.

	M&A Target	M&A Acquirer	Default	Upgrade	Downgrade	Redemptions	Tenders	Equity
1995	1.19%	3.42	1.97	17.61%	13.71%	1.16%	1.51%	4.42%
1996	2.05%	1.91	0.75	15.01%	14.59%	1.14%	2.08%	3.77%
1997	3.07%	7.28	0.84	22.16%	12.11%	1.18%	2.45%	5.66%
1998	7.23%	16.29	1.00	16.23%	19.47%	1.33%	3.27%	4.61%
1999	13.97%	24.70	3.83	18.49%	28.33%	1.35%	2.35%	11.65%
2000	10.13%	33.87	4.42	15.19%	35.92%	1.33%	1.81%	7.67%
2001	11.79%	29.09	8.65	12.54%	64.33%	1.27%	1.16%	8.30%
2002	8.20%	10.96	13.99	7.85%	82.06%	1.81%	1.03%	6.13%
2003	3.79%	9.82	4.07	15.45%	40.67%	4.69%	2.89%	10.16%
2004	4.33%	17.55	1.30	21.96%	31.42%	9.07%	6.00%	13.38%
Average 1995–2004	6.57%	15.49%	4.08%	16.25%	34.26%	2.43%	2.46%	7.57%

Source: Credit Suisse.

EXHIBIT 10.13

Ratio of upgrades to downgrades, 1987–1H05.

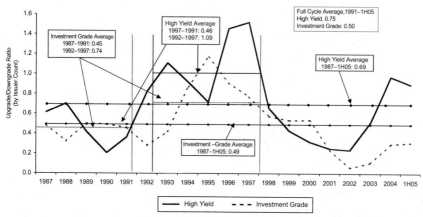

Source: Credit Suisse, Moody's Investors Service.

EXHIBIT 10.14

Credit Suisse Leveraged Loan Index spread,
1992–September 2005.

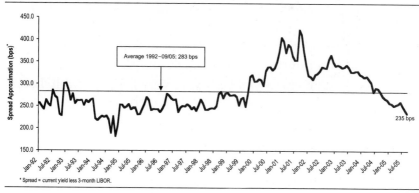

Source: Credit Suisse.

peaking at around 80 percent in mid–2003, the correlation between high yield bonds and leveraged loans has declined and is just 24 percent at the end of 2005. Given the option, loan market participants should consider directly hedging the leveraged loan market with loan-only CDS, as opposed to using bond CDS, which is a less efficient strategy.

EXHIBIT 10.15

Twenty-month rolling return correlations of leveraged loans versus high yield bonds, Treasuries, and LIBOR returns, 1992–September 2005.

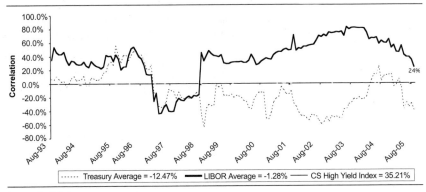

Source: Credit Suisse.

LEVERAGED LOAN CREDIT DERIVATIVES

General Information

- Credit default swaps give loan market participants a liquid vehicle through which to gain long or short exposure to a specific issue or market segment.
- Credit default swap indices are widely traded in the high-yield bond universe via the CDX and iTraxx.
- Single-name high-yield CDS are very active as well. Loan-only CDS have been slower to develop.

As in a traditional CDS contract, the buyer of protection pays a running fixed spread per year, paid quarterly on a notional amount (see Exhibit 10.16). If a credit event occurs, the seller of protection receives the deliverable obligation and pays the notional par amount.

Typical Terms for Loan-Only CDS

- The reference obligation is either a term loan facility or a revolver specified in the borrower's credit agreement.
- If the reference obligation ceases to be outstanding, a substitute reference obligation that is pari passu with the original

EXHIBIT 10.16

Summary of trade mechanics.

If no credit event occurs:	
Long the credit–seller of protection	
Receive:	Running fixed spread of X bps $\times$ notional amount (per annum, paid quarterly)
Short the credit–buyer of protection	
Pay:	Running fixed spread of X bps $\times$ notional amount (per annum, paid quarterly)
If a credit event occurs:	
Long the credit–seller of protection	
Pay:	Notional amount
Receive:	Notional face value amount of deliverable obligation or market value equivalent in cash
Short the credit–buyer of protection	
Receive:	Notional amount
Deliver/pay:	Notional face value amount of deliverable obligation or market value equivalent in cash

Source: Credit Suisse.

reference obligation is selected. If there are no pari passu facilities outstanding, the trade is terminated.

- A credit event is triggered by bankruptcy or failure to pay on any borrowed money of the borrower.

The tenor of the most liquid bond CDS has been five years. However, loan-only CDS have traded with tenors of five years and shorter, and we expect short-dated loan-only CDS to be popular as the market develops.

Credit Events

- The loan-only CDS contract is physically settled. If physical settlement is not possible, participation agreements or cash settlement can be used.
- Only the specified secured priority (e.g., first or second lien) loan facility, pari passu with the reference obligation, may be delivered.
- Revolvers (undrawn, partially drawn, or fully drawn) may be deliverable, but the liability of the seller of protection is capped at the notional amount of the trade.

Loan Market Participants

Loan-only CDS are appealing to both buyers and sellers of protection (see Exhibit 10.17). These trades allow protection buyers to hedge portions of their loan portfolio in an efficient manner and with less volatility compared to unsecured credit default swaps. Typical buyers of protection in the loan-only CDS market would include banks, retail and institutional mutual fund managers, hedge funds, and corporate treasuries (see Exhibit 10.18). For sellers of protection, loan-only CDS offer a convenient way to gain immediate leveraged exposure to loans. Typical sellers of protection would include hedge funds, insurance companies, and CLO managers in the process of ramping up their portfolios (see Exhibit 10.19).

EXHIBIT 10.17

Net sellers and buyers of credit default swaps.

Net Sellers of Protection	Net Buyers of Protection
Insurance Companies/Reinsurers:	Banks:
Looking to write corporate insurance for additional fixed-rate income	Hedge portions of loans on balance sheet or capital relier
	Hedge Funds:
	Convenient overlay for relative value trade strategies
	Securities Houses:
	Hedge portions of loans on balance sheet for capital relief

Source: 2003/2004 BBA Credit Derivatives Report, Credit Suisse.

EXHIBIT 10.18

Institutional buyers of credit protection.

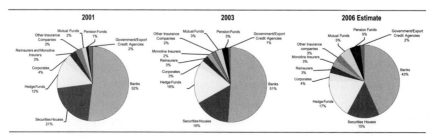

Source: 2003/2004 BAA Credit Derivatives Report, Credit Suisse.

Exhibit 10.20 gives a sample of the indicative spreads on the most-liquid single-name loan-only CDS issues as of October 2005.

Loan-only CDS are most often settled with physical delivery (see Exhibit 10.21).

EXHIBIT 10.19

Institutional sellers of credit protection.

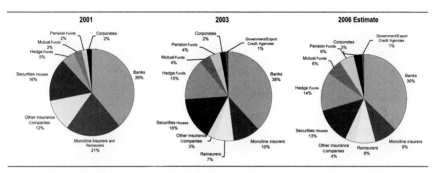

Source: 2003/2004 BAA Credit Derivatives Report, Credit Suisse.

EXHIBIT 10.20

Single-name loan CDS traded: recent indicative spreads as of October 2005.

Reference Entity	Bid	Ask	Reference Entity	Bid	Ask
AES	120	140	Goodyear (Third Lien)	350	400
Affinion	285	305	Graham Packaging (Second Lien)	320	360
Allied Waste	185	205	Hayes Lemmerz (Second Lien)	575	650
American Tower	80	100	Metaldyne	440	490
AYE Supply	80	100	MGM Mirage	125	145
Boyd Gaming	100	120	MGM Studios	155	175
Carrizo (Second Lien)	420	450	Neiman Marcus	200	225
Charter	280	300	NRG	145	165
Cheniere	245	270	Penn Natl Gaming	130	150
Cincinnati Bell	100	120	Regal Cinema	150	170
Coffeyville (Second Lien)	470	500	Reliant	165	185
Davita	120	140	Rockwood	125	150
DirecTV	85	105	Sunguard	185	205
Dynegy	210	240	TRW	110	130
Eastman Kodak (2-year)	100	130	United Rentals	185	210
Eastman Kodak (5-year)	190	215	Venetian	125	145
El Paso	145	165	Visteon	300	330
F&W Publications	145	165	Warner Chilcott	225	250
Fidelity Natl	135	160	Warner Music	140	165
GGP	135	155	Wiltel (Second lien)	460	510
Goodyear (Second Lien)	235	265	Average:	207	233

Source: Credit Suisse.

What types of settlement are used for credit derivatives?

Physical settlement	86%
Cash settlement	11%
Fixed amount	3%

Source: 2003/2004 BAA Credit Derivatives Report, Credit Suisse.

Bank Loan Total Return Swap Primer

Philip Nisbet
Director, Barclays Capital

With editorial assistance on the tax section from

Mark Herzinger
Director, Barclays Capital

INTRODUCTION

Bank loan total return swaps (TRS) are an important catalyst for the growing bank loan market. They enable hedge funds, leveraged loan funds, and other institutional investors to acquire bank loans using leverage. This puts these investors on a more even footing with banks and collateralized loan obligations, users of different sources of leverage to acquire bank loans.

The product, which is transacted in derivative form and offered by several commercial banks, has existed for at least a decade. As the bank loan market has broadened and become more liquid, bank loan total return swaps have also grown to allow bank loan market participants to finance most types of bank loans, including revolving loans, stressed and distressed loans, second lien and unsecured loans, and European loans. Total return swaps can be transacted on single loans or can be arranged to finance a portfolio of loans up to $1 billion in size or larger.

Because total return swaps are over-the-counter derivatives, transactions are not reported in league tables, and thus the size of the market is not known with any confidence. Anecdotal evidence indicates that there are as many as one dozen commercial banks offering the product, that as many as 200 different bank loan investment vehicles or 100 manager groups are currently using the product, and that the aggregate market size is approximately $75 billion, making the TRS market nearly as large as the CLO market.

Bank loan market participants use total return swaps to obtain leverage, which is available up to 10 times the initial cash amount invested, and to outsource some of the administration of the bank loans to the bank providing the swap or its trustee. This is particularly important to smaller hedge funds that do not have a large loan administration staff. Using leverage, bank loan market participants can achieve a yield of up to 15 percent per annum or greater on the cash invested, before fees and certain expenses and before any losses from defaults and gains or losses from trading. Returns vary greatly depending on the type of trading strategy and the amount of leverage employed. One thing that is certain, however, is that the availability of flexible financing through total return swaps has put bank loans on the radar of hedge funds, whose return targets simply would not allow them to consider investing in par or other low-yielding bank loans otherwise. While high target returns using little or no leverage may be available on distressed and second lien loans, typical rated, syndicated first lien par loans would not be attractive investments for loan market participants seeking double-digit returns if they were not able to leverage these investments.

Because most total return swaps are full recourse to the bank loan market participant using them, if the bank loans decline in value on the secondary market, the bank loan market participant will be responsible for contributing additional capital to support the total return swap, in much the same way that it would in a margin lending account for other assets, such as common stocks. Therefore, as the use of total return swaps continues to grow, the possible capital calls on loan market participants will grow in a declining market. As with other forms of leverage, this could exacerbate the next eventual downturn in the bank loan market, but it can also create opportunities for long-term investors with available capital.

The following sections of this article discuss the following questions related to bank loan total return swaps:

- What is a bank loan total return swap?
- Which loan market participants use bank loan total return swaps?
- Who are the dealers providing this product?
- Why do loan market participants use bank loan total return swaps?
- How are total return swaps documented?
- How do the operational aspects work?

WHAT IS A BANK LOAN TOTAL RETURN SWAP?

Description

A bank loan total return swap is a derivative contract between two parties to exchange the return on one or more bank loans. The swaps were first traded in the early 1990s and grew to prominence as a result of the desire for leverage and the lack of the existence of a repurchase market where institutional loan market participants could leverage their investment in bank loans. The repurchase, or "repo," market never took hold for bank loans for two reasons: (1) bank loans are complex, and (2) since they settle physically (rather than through an electronic clearing system such as the Depository Trust Company, or DTC), they are more difficult to rehypothecate, or relend to another party. Rehypothecation is important to the financial institutions providing the leverage, as it enables the institutions to obtain liquidity for assets that they fund. Assets that are difficult to rehypothecate will tend to be funded internally, thus creating a much larger claim on the institution's funding capacity. Since repo desks tend to focus on assets that use liquidity and resources most efficiently, bank loans were largely ignored.

Derivatives and bank loan trading desks responded to the need for a flexible means of financing and applied the generic total return swap that was already in use for other assets to bank loans. Institutional loan market participants (in this capacity, "swap counterparties") use TRS to obtain leverage and to outsource much of the operational aspects of investing in bank loans. As rules for bank capital usage evolved, banks were able to avail themselves of the favorable capital treatment applied to derivatives and trading assets generally, giving a further boost to the product.

The cash flows that are exchanged in a bank loan TRS are shown in Exhibits 10.22 to 10.26.

At the inception of a TRS, the bank that is providing the total return swap (the "funding bank") will pay the purchase price for the bank loan (the "reference bank loan") to the primary or secondary market seller, shown in Exhibit 10.22 as a secondary trade from a bank loan trading desk. Some funding banks will hold the asset directly on their own balance sheet, whereas others will set up special-purpose entities (SPEs) to hold the loans for operational, accounting, and control reasons. The swap counterparty will deliver a fraction of the bank loan purchase price (the "swap collateral") to the funding bank. The funding bank holds the swap collateral, which can be cash or a safe and liquid alternative such as U.S. Treasury securities, as security for the future payments owed by the swap counterparty under the TRS. The initial swap collateral is known as the "haircut" or the "independent amount" in swap parlance. If the swap counterparty fails to make any required payments under the TRS, the funding bank can terminate all of the swaps between the two parties and use the swap collateral to satisfy any amounts owed to the funding bank, including the cost incurred to unwind the transactions. In this sample transaction, the $1,500,000 swap collateral represents 15 percent of the purchase price of the $10,000,000 principal amount of the bank loan, which

EXHIBIT 10.22

Initial cash flows for a $10,000,000 total return swap with a 15 percent independent amount.

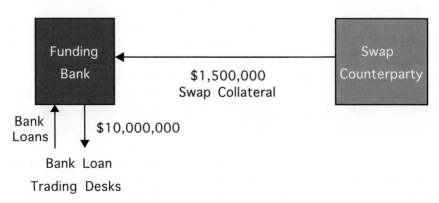

Ongoing swap cash flows for a $10,000,000 total return
swap with a 15 percent independent amount.

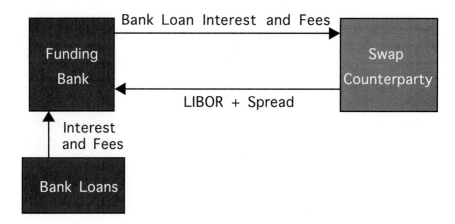

is assumed to be purchased at par. A 15 percent haircut equates to
6.67 times initial leverage (assets/equity).

Parties to a bank loan TRS agree to exchange certain cash
flows (Exhibit 10.23) periodically, typically monthly. The funding
bank pays the swap counterparty the interest and fees that it
receives as a holder of the $10,000,000 bank loan. The swap coun-
terparty pays a funding cost, LIBOR plus a spread, calculated on
the purchase cost of the bank loan. The difference between this
swap funding cost and the funding bank's own cost of funding is
the main source of the funding bank's profit. As long as the bank
loan is currently paying interest, the swap counterparty will have
positive net interest under the swap, since the bank loan spread
will exceed the swap financing spread.

Periodically the funding Bank will credit interest on the swap
collateral that it holds as security for the TRS (Exhibit 10.24). This
interest is generally reinvested for the swap counterparty unless
the swap counterparty requests that it be distributed. If the swap
counterparty posted U.S. cash, the typical rate of interest paid is the
federal funds effective rate. If the swap counterparty posted U.S.
Treasury securities, it will earn the rate of interest on those specific
securities.

When a loan or portion thereof is sold or repaid, the parties to
the TRS will exchange a realized capital gain or loss payment.
When there is a realized gain, the funding bank pays this amount

EXHIBIT 10.24

Ongoing collateral cash flows for a $10,000,000 total return swap with a 15 percent independent amount.

EXHIBIT 10.25

Final cash flows for a $10,000,000 total return swap with a 15 percent independent amount.

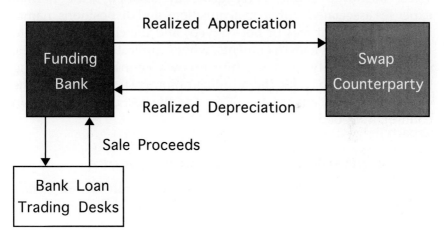

("realized appreciation" in Exhibit 10.25) to the swap counterparty. When there is a realized loss, the swap counterparty pays this amount ("realized depreciation" in Exhibit 10.25) to the funding bank. By passing through all interest and fees paid on the bank loans and exchanging realized gains and losses, the funding bank simply earns a net spread over its cost of funding, and the swap counterparty earns the "total return" of the bank loan net of the cost of the swap funding.

Upon the termination of the swap, which occurs when both parties have satisfied all of their obligations under the TRS, the

EXHIBIT 10.26

Final collateral cash flows for a $10,000,000 total return swap with a 15 percent independent amount.

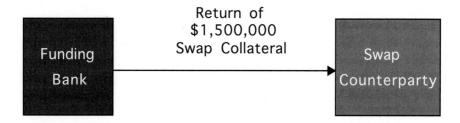

funding bank returns the swap collateral to the swap counterparty (Exhibit 10.26).

In addition to the cash flows shown in Exhibits 10.22 through 10.26, the swap counterparty generally also pays the normal expenses associated with loan acquisitions and dispositions, namely, the assignment fees (if not waived) and the cost of counsel to review distressed loan documents, where applicable and when the swap counterparty does not hire its own counsel. The funding bank will often pay for the administration cost of the loans, the cost of setting up any related SPEs, and the cost of hiring its own counsel, if needed.

Bank Loan Acquisition Process

Bank loan total return swaps are self-directed transactions in that the swap counterparty arranges the acquisition of the bank loans, including selecting the dealer and negotiating the purchase price. The loan syndications and trading desks of funding banks may also offer loans that can be financed through the TRS, but the swap counterparty is not obligated to transact with the funding bank on the underlying loans. Once the swap counterparty has arranged for the purchase of the bank loan, the swap counterparty notifies the seller where it should deliver the loan: to the funding bank itself, or to an SPE that the funding bank uses to hold loans that have been put into a TRS. Managing a TRS is similar to managing a fund or CLO in that the swap counterparty acts in a similar capacity to an investment advisor, acquiring loans and notifying the trustee (the funding bank) so that it can settle and administer the loans.

DIFFERENT TYPES OF BANK LOAN TOTAL RETURN SWAPS

This section explains how certain types of bank loan total return swaps work, including TRS on non-U.S. dollar bank loans, TRS on revolving loans, TRS on single loans, and TRS on actively managed portfolios of loans. We also discuss the types of assets that can be financed using total return swaps and indicate market haircuts for each.

TRS on Non-U.S. Dollar Loans

Investing in non-U.S. dollar bank loans poses a currency risk to a U.S. dollar–based loan market participant. Because most bank loans are prepayable and allow the borrower to change the interest-rate contracts, it is too expensive to execute a perfect currency hedge in the foreign exchange markets. Approximate hedges, such as a "short" spot or futures foreign exchange position (to offset the "long" foreign exchange position of holding a non-U.S. dollar loan) or a dollar-nondollar basis swap create basis risk and require the loan market participant to mark the various positions to market to determine the hedge's efficacy and to adjust the hedges periodically based on loan paydowns, coupon payments, and so on. Often the execution of separate foreign exchange hedges is conducted by different departments at the funding bank and requires the loan market participant to take the risk of market movements between the timing of the loan paydown or sale and the timing of the hedge execution in the foreign exchange market.

Total return swaps on non-U.S. dollar loans can have an automatic currency hedge as part of the contract terms, reducing or alleviating the need to execute and track separate currency hedges. The embedded hedge is accomplished by denominating the TRS funding in the local currency. For example, a euro-denominated bank loan would have a euro-denominated swap funding cost. This matching of the assets and liabilities in the same currency in the same contract results in a hedge of all currency risk except for the net profit or loss to the swap counterparty. The residual currency risk is due to the fact that the swap counterparty will be receiving or paying a net swap payment in the local currency. For example, if the underlying bank loan is yielding EURIBOR plus 275 basis points, and the TRS financing charge is EURIBOR plus 75

basis points, the net carry of 200 basis points will be paid to the
swap counterparty in euro. If the euro depreciates, the U.S. dollar
equivalent value of the euro payment is reduced. Likewise, if there
is a capital appreciation or depreciation payment, that payment
will also be denominated in the local currency of the loan, and
would create foreign exchange exposure for the U.S.–dollar loan
market participant. If the net profit and loss can be estimated in
advance, foreign exchange hedges can be executed to immunize
this. Unexpected repayments and credit deterioration resulting in
sales are more difficult to predict and thus to hedge. However, the
net currency exposure on a local currency TRS is materially less
than that on buying a non-U.S. dollar loan outright, and so the
need for external hedging is greatly reduced.

TRS on Revolving Loans

Revolving and delay draw loans are eligible assets for bank loan
TRS. The general market practice is to calculate the haircut based
on the commitment amount rather than the funded amount, since
the price change of a revolving loan in the secondary market, and
therefore the funding bank's exposure, is based on the commitment
amount. However, the funding spread would be charged only on
the funded amount, although there may be a sharing of the commitment fee on the revolving loan between the funding bank and
the swap counterparty. Because haircuts are required even on the
unfunded portion of a bank loan in a TRS, the TRS provides lower
effective leverage for these loans than for fully funded term loans.

Single-Name TRS versus Portfolio TRS

Total return swaps can be executed on one loan at a time ("single-
name TRS"), or a facility can be arranged to finance a portfolio of
loans ("portfolio TRS"). By dollar volume, loan market participants
finance one-half to two-thirds as portfolio TRS and one-third to
one-half as single-name TRS. Descriptions of each type of transaction follow, with a focus on the differences between the two types
of transactions.

Single-Name TRS
The single-name TRS is economically the most similar to a typical
"repo" transaction. A loan market participant will contact a funding

bank and request TRS financing on a single loan. If the haircut percentage and funding rate are acceptable, the loan market participant will execute the trade at that time, and a swap confirmation (and often an interim term sheet) will be sent by the funding bank after the trade. The trade size of a single-name TRS is typically $5,000,000 to $10,000,000 but could be $1,000,000 to $50,000,000 or larger.

All single-name TRS are full recourse to the swap counterparty. This means that the swap counterparty has the full risk of loss on the reference bank loan, above and beyond the initial swap collateral that was posted with the funding bank. If the reference loan falls in price, the swap counterparty will generally be required to fully collateralize the unrealized loss exposure by posting additional swap collateral with the funding bank. If the price on the reference loan subsequently recovers, the swap counterparty can request that the additional swap collateral be returned. Recourse is generally limited to the specific legal counterparty that the loan market participant is using (e.g., a specific loan fund or a specific hedge fund). The funding bank would generally not have recourse to other affiliates of the swap counterparty, such as the swap counterparty's investment advisor or parent company.

The trade depicted in Exhibits 10.22 through 10.26 is a single-name TRS.

Single-name TRS are preferred by loan market participants that want the most flexibility and the least restrictions. While market practice varies, in general, single-name TRS do not impose any minimum holding period restrictions or early termination penalties on the swap counterparty. Nor do funding banks impose specific obligor or industry concentration restrictions on single-name TRS counterparties, although each funding bank will carefully monitor the TRS positions for each swap counterparty for excess exposure to a single borrower or industry.

While single-name TRS are very flexible, loan market participants must look elsewhere for term financing, as most single-name TRS mature in one year. While they can be rolled over, this requires the approval of the funding bank, and the pricing and haircut are subject to change. Single-name TRS also do not provide a committed funding source for additional purchases, as each new single-name TRS must be approved by the funding bank and is subject to available credit lines that the funding bank has established for the swap counterparty. Finally, the leverage available through single-name TRS is lower than that available through portfolio TRS.

Portfolio TRS

Whereas a single-name TRS is economically similar to a repo, a portfolio TRS is a synthetic market value version of a collateralized loan obligation (CLO). In both products, the first-loss investor earns the yield on the entire portfolio of bank loans minus the interest cost of the liabilities to finance the portfolio. Portfolio TRS are used by loan market participants that want to arrange a committed financing line for bank loans meeting certain characteristics. The portfolio would be actively managed by the swap counterparty or its investment advisor. The advisor would not normally be limited to trading only credit-impaired or credit-improved loans, as is common in collateralized loan obligations, nor would there be a minimum spread test. However, the swap counterparty is required to maintain other portfolio criteria, such as maximum obligor and industry limitations and ratings requirements. Haircuts can be agreed upon at the time the portfolio TRS is established or can be established on a case-by-case basis, with diversified portfolios of par loans being more likely to use fixed haircuts and less diversified portfolios that include distressed loans being more likely to have case-by-case haircuts.

Unlike single-name TRS, which are always full recourse to the swap counterparty, portfolio TRS can be full recourse or nonrecourse. Under a nonrecourse trade, the funding bank would bear second-loss risk on the portfolio, and the swap counterparty would be exposed only to loss of the initial swap collateral that was posted with the funding bank. Trade sizes for portfolio TRS are typically $250,000,000 to $750,000,000, but they can be $75,000,000 to $1,000,000,000 or larger. Portfolio TRS trades can be one to five years in length and are often extended beyond the original maturity date, and thus can represent a semipermanent source of financing.

Portfolio TRS offer certain advantages over single-name TRS, including longer-term financing, the existence of a committed line of credit that will be available even during weaker market conditions, higher leverage, and more flexibility to finance less-liquid loans. These favorable terms result from the fact that diversified portfolios are less volatile than single-name loan positions, and thus the funding bank needs a smaller amount of collateral to protect itself against the future obligations of the swap counterparty.

To obtain the benefits just described, the swap counterparty agrees to maintain certain portfolio criteria and to use a minimum amount of the line at all times. These requirements are not present in single-name TRS.

Portfolio TRS are customized transactions with three main variables: portfolio criteria, haircuts, and financing spread. Loan market participants that buy only high-quality, liquid par loans and diversify widely can obtain higher leverage and better pricing than those that buy distressed, unrated loans in larger position sizes. Exhibits 10.27 and 10.28 show criteria for two different sample portfolios. Funding banks may provide haircuts averaging 10 to 20 percent (5 to 10 times leverage) for the diversified par bank loan portfolio, whereas the less diversified stressed/distressed bank loan portfolio is likely to require higher haircuts, on the order of 25 to 35 percent (approximately 3 to 4 times leverage).

EXHIBIT 10.27

Sample criteria for a diversified par bank loan portfolio.

Criteria	Requirement
Senior Secured First Lien Loans	At least 85%
Senior Secured Second Lien Loans	Up to 15%
Maximum Obligor Exposure	3% to 5%
Maximum Industry Exposure	7% to 10%
Minimum Rating at Inception	B3/B-
Average Portfolio Rating Factor	2300 (Moodys)

EXHIBIT 10.28

Sample criteria for a less diversified stressed/distressed bank loan portfolio.

Criteria	Requirement
Senior Secured Loans	At least 50%
Unsecured High Yield Bonds	Up to 50%
Maximum Obligor Exposure	5% to 10%
Maximum Industry Exposure	10% to 20%
Minimium Rating at Inception	None
Average Portfolio Rating Factor	None

Eligible Assets for TRS

Most types of noninvestment grade bank loans can be financed through a TRS, although each funding bank will have its own requirements and limitations. Rated, syndicated par loans of large companies where secondary market pricing is widely available are the easiest loans to finance through a TRS. Middle market, microcap, and bilateral loans are the most difficult loans to finance through a TRS. Because TRS are a mark-to-market product, as opposed to a cash flow product like conventional CLOs, the ability to obtain daily market prices for the bank loans is an important requirement. Middle market, microcap, and bilateral loans are less likely to be quoted by bank loan traders, but may be able to be financed as a discretionary bucket in a larger portfolio TRS containing mostly liquid loans.

Haircuts for Various Eligible Assets

Haircuts are security for the potential future obligations of the swap counterparty under the TRS contract. The size of the haircuts is based on the credit quality of the swap counterparty and the size of the potential future obligation for a specific TRS, whether portfolio or single-name (see Exhibit 10.29). The determination of the potential future obligation takes into account not only the periodic swap financing payments but, more importantly, the potential decline in value of the reference bank loans during the estimated liquidation period, assuming that the swap counterparty fails to make a margin call and the funding bank terminates the trade. The two factors that affect the potential future obligation calculation are

EXHIBIT 10.29

Market haircuts for selected assets.

Asset	Typical Haircut
Par Term and Revolving Loans	10%–20%
Second Lien Loans	15%–30%
Stressed Loans	15%–35%
Distressed Loans	15%–50%
Middle Market and Direct-Financed Loans	35%–80%
High-Yield Bonds	20%–35%
European Loans	10%–50%

the volatility and liquidity of the assets. Less volatile, liquid assets require small haircuts, and risky, less liquid assets require large haircuts. Volatility directly affects the size of the potential future obligation, whereas liquidity affects it indirectly by increasing or decreasing the period required to liquidate (less liquid assets will take longer to sell than liquid assets, during which period of time there could be additional price declines). Because portfolios of bank loans are less volatile than individual bank loans, portfolios deserve lower haircuts, averaging 5 to 10 points of collateral lower.

WHO USES BANK LOAN TOTAL RETURN SWAPS?

Market Size

Most bank loan market participants use leverage when buying bank loans. Banks and insurance companies use internal leverage, whereas CLOs mostly issue liabilities. Hedge funds and nonpublic leveraged loan funds use a variety of financing sources, including leverage from other assets, medium-term note issuances, conduit programs, and TRS. The North American bank loan TRS market size is estimated to be $75 billion. Unlike other products that provide leverage on bank loans, like CLOs, TRS transactions are not reported, and thus there is little hard evidence concerning the specific size of the market or the number of actual users. Out of 230 institutional manager groups that purchased primary bank loans in 2005, 85 (37 percent of all accounts tracked) are known directly by Barclays or indirectly from reliable sources to have used bank loan TRS. Most accounts listed as TRS users continue to participate in the market and grow their usage of the product.

Based on this information, it is estimated that there are approximately 200 different bank loan investment vehicles and 100 manager groups that are currently using TRS. Some of these participants use multiple funding banks, with a few using as many as six or more funding banks.

Users of TRS are described here in order of cumulative volume (largest to smallest).

Hedge Funds

Hedge funds dominate the bank loan TRS market, accounting for more than half of the volume. "Hedge fund" is a broad category of funds that includes multistrategy funds, arbitrage funds, distressed debt funds, and credit opportunity funds. Just as their strategies are varied, so are their target returns and the degree of leverage employed. Hedge funds use both single-name TRS and portfolio TRS.

Leveraged Loan Funds

These funds are often set up by CLO managers to respond to investor demand for less leveraged alternatives to CLOs that have more flexible investment criteria. Most leveraged loan funds do not obtain credit ratings from a ratings agency. Because of their focus on a single asset class, they often use TRS to obtain leverage, since they have few nonloan assets to leverage in the form of repo or prime brokerage lending. Because these funds are not rated, there are fewer investment restrictions, and thus they often allocate some capital to unrated loans, second lien loans, and stressed or distressed loans. Leveraged loan funds would typically use portfolio TRS that provide a term funding commitment, since their access to funding is less certain than that of a broader hedge fund.

Market Value CLOs

Many market value CLOs use TRS to obtain some of their leverage. The TRS would replace the top part of the capital structure, typically represented by AAA-rated tranches. Historically, the reason that TRS have been used in these structures is that many market value CLOs obtain ratings from only one ratings agency, which reduces the marketability of the highest-rated tranches. The holders of the lower classes of many market value CLOs are insurance companies, which may require only a single rating to obtain the National Association of Insurance Commissioners (NAIC) investment grade capital charge that they seek.

Only a subset of cash flow CLO AAA investors are familiar and comfortable with market value covenants, so it is often more economical for the funding bank to retain the top risk of a market value CLO structure through a TRS than it is to distribute it in the capital markets. Market value CLOs use nonrecourse portfolio TRS.

Separate Accounts/Asset Managers

When a single investor (high net worth or institutional) wants a specific investment strategy and cannot find it in a commingled leveraged loan fund, a separate account can be set up for that investor. Most often this investor will not be a loan market participant and will hire a bank loan asset manager to manage the account. The use of leverage in the form of a TRS allows the account to potentially achieve a higher return and also control a larger pool of loans, which makes it easier to diversify. Typically a separate account using leverage would require a minimum equity investment of $50,000,000 and a minimum asset size of $200,000,000. Separate accounts use recourse and nonrecourse TRS. The nonrecourse version would be used if the investor was unwilling to have additional capital calls.

Loan Market Participants That Do Not Use TRS

Banks are unlikely to use TRS, since their internal funding rates are much lower than TRS funding rates. This is also true for insurance companies. Publicly traded and open-ended bank loan mutual funds do not use TRS, since most of them do not use leverage. Those that do, use very little leverage and find an alternative source for it, such as a revolving bank line, since they may not be permitted to use derivatives, and the cost for a very low leverage TRS is not attractive relative to that of bank lines. Most CLOs do not use TRS, since they obtain leverage through issuing notes, although there is a growing list of CLO transactions that are using TRS or other derivative contracts to place the most senior risk with the bank underwriter.

WHO ARE THE FUNDING BANKS?

Funding banks are mostly commercial banks. Only a small portion of the North American TRS volume is transacted by funding banks that are securities firms. There are several reasons for this:

- Commercial banks have lower average funding costs and more diversified sources of funding than securities firms.
- Because of the sheer size of the commercial banks, they are more willing to use their GAAP balance sheet for funding products such as TRS.

- Commercial banks control a majority of the loan market, holding the top six underwriter rankings for U.S. leveraged loans for the year 2004 and year to date 2005.[1]

The leading TRS funding banks include Bank of America, Barclays, Citigroup, Deutsche Bank, UBS, and Wachovia. Other funding banks may compete in limited segments of the bank loan TRS market, e.g., they will finance rated par loans only.

The economics of TRS for funding banks are as follows:

- The funding bank's profit is the swap funding charge less the funding bank's internal funding cost less program operational costs (legal and trustee). The net spread is usually at least 50 basis points per annum on the funded balance.
- The risks of operating a TRS program include counterparty risk, price risk on nonrecourse trades, liquidity/funding risk, and typical operational risks associated with derivatives trading, such as collection of collateral, proper marking of positions, and so on.

WHY USE BANK LOAN TOTAL RETURN SWAPS?

The two main reasons that loan market participants use TRS are to obtain leverage and to partially outsource their loan operations to the funding bank or its trustee. Leverage is the dominant reason. The operational aspects are discussed in the following section. In this section we illustrate how leverage affects the returns on an investment in bank loans and discuss four popular trading strategies that loan market participants use with TRS.

TRS Return Example

The following are assumptions for a sample yield calculation for a total return swap. Note that actual inputs will vary depending on the portfolio criteria, the swap counterparty, and market conditions:

---

[1] Bloomberg, as of November 3, 2005.

- Loan portfolio size: $100,000,000
- Three-month LIBOR: 4.25%
- Average par loan coupon: LIBOR + 2.50%
- Swap financing cost: LIBOR + 0.70%
- Swap collateral yield: LIBOR – 0.25%
- Leverage factor (assets/cash employed): 6.67 times (equals 15% haircut)
- Collateral posted: $15,000,000 ($100,000,000/6.67)
- No trading gains and no credit losses (or, trading gains offset credit losses)
- Returns shown exclude management fees, manager incentive fees, and expenses

Exhibit 10.30 shows the cash flows for this example, and Exhibit 10.31 shows the sensitivity of yield to leverage.

EXHIBIT 10.30

Diagram of cash flows for sample TRS.

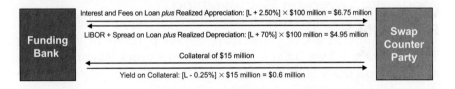

Annual yield = ($6.75 million – $4.95 million + $0.6 million)/ $15 million = 16.0%

EXHIBIT 10.31

Leverage sensitivity analysis: illustrative cash-on-cash yields

Leverage	Annual Yield
10×	22.0%
8×	18.4%
6×	14.8%
4×	11.2%

Popular Bank Loan Trading/Investment Strategies That Use TRS

Hedge funds and leveraged loan funds use a variety of strategies that utilize TRS. Four popular strategies are discussed here. Note that each of these can lean toward a carry (hold) strategy or a total return (carry plus trading gains) strategy, and also that some managers blend these strategies or use more than one, depending on market conditions and other factors.

Capital Structure Arbitrage

This strategy involves going long one part of the capital structure of a company and shorting another part of the same company. A common trade would be to buy a senior bank loan on leverage using a TRS and selling the unsecured debt short, in the bond market or by using credit default swaps. The loan market participant may buy a greater notional amount of bank loans than the notional amount of unsecured debt sold, depending in part on its assessment of the respective recovery values. Profit from the strategy can be from carry and/or from capital gain upon divergence.

Moderate-Leverage Par Investing

This strategy is a lower-risk, lower-return investment alternative to buying equity in a CLO. The loan market participant will buy a senior par bank loan using a TRS with 4 to 5 times leverage, which is lower than the 8 to 10 times leverage that can be available for this type of loan in a TRS and the 10 to 13 times leverage that is available to CLO equity investors. The target returns are commensurately lower, usually 0.75 to 1 percent per month, consistently.

High-Leverage Par Investing

This strategy relies on using leverage rather than buying weaker credits to obtain a 15 to 20 percent target annual return. The loan market participant buys the highest-quality first lien credits using a TRS and diversifies widely. While these loans provide lower yields than the average leveraged loan, the use of maximum TRS leverage (8 to 10 times) allows the loan market participant to achieve a high current yield, which can be supplemented with an active trading strategy depending on market conditions. It is possible that this high-leverage strategy could have a higher Sharpe ratio, or return per unit of risk, than the other lower-leverage strategies because of the higher quality of the loans being leveraged.

Low-Leverage Distressed Investing
This strategy is the opposite of the high-leverage par investing strategy. The loan market participant buys stressed and distressed loans and applies low leverage using a TRS. Target returns may equal or greatly exceed those for the high-leverage par investing strategy.

HOW ARE BANK LOAN TOTAL RETURN SWAPS DOCUMENTED?
Documentation

Bank loan TRS are documented using standard derivative documentation produced by the International Swaps and Derivatives Association, Inc., the global trade association representing participants in the over-the-counter derivatives markets (www.isda.org). There are three basic sets of documents that are required for a bank loan TRS: (1) ISDA Master Agreement and Schedule, (2) Credit Support Annex, and (3) swap confirmation. In addition, a fourth document transferring the right to vote on loan consents and prepayments to the swap counterparty may also exist (known as an investment management agreement or voting rights agreement). The ISDA Master Agreement and Schedule and the Credit Support Annex are executed only once and apply to all derivative transactions between the two parties. A swap confirmation would be executed for each TRS. The benefit of using a master agreement structure is that it reduces the counterparty risk to both parties, in that all cross-obligations are netted, with only a single net amount being owed if one of the counterparties defaults.

ISDA Master Agreement and Schedule

All counterparties in the derivatives markets put in place bilateral agreements called the ISDA Master Agreement and Schedule governing their trading with one another. This agreement permits all types of derivatives transactions, including interest-rate and currency swaps, credit derivatives, and equity derivatives. The agreement covers a variety of general topics, including netting of swap payments, responsibility for withholding taxes, events of default, events that could cause termination of the agreement and all swaps done thereunder, notice provisions, and contact information.

Credit Support Annex

A Credit Support Annex (CSA) is often executed at the same time as the ISDA Master Agreement and Schedule. The CSA governs the posting of collateral for derivatives transactions. The CSA is beneficial to both parties, as it reduces the credit risk of each counterparty. While a CSA is not required in order to engage in derivatives transactions, virtually all participants in the TRS market operate under a CSA. The CSA covers the following topics:

- The types of assets that are *eligible collateral,* such as cash or U.S. Treasuries.
- The *independent amount,* or the initial collateral required to be posted for each transaction under the CSA. Independent amounts vary by transaction and may even be zero for some non-TRS transactions.
- The *exposure,* or the current net mark-to-market value of all the derivatives under the CSA. Variation margin must be posted to cover this amount, subject to certain exceptions and limitations.
- The *credit support amount,* or the total amount of collateral that is required; it equals the sum of the independent amount and the exposure.
- *Thresholds* for posting collateral. If the amount owed is below the threshold, it is not required to be posted. The threshold is the amount of unsecured exposure that one counterparty is willing to take to the other.
- *Minimum transfer amount* (MTA) for posting collateral. Only payments greater than the minimum transfer amount are required to be made. The MTA exists to avoid small nuisance transfers.
- *Delivery and return amounts,* or the amounts to be paid or returned as collateral under the CSA, after considering thresholds and minimum transfer amounts.
- Where the collateral is held.

- The interest rate paid on the collateral (generally the effective federal funds rate).
- Notices.
- *Setoff*, which is whether amounts owed under other obligations can be set off against amounts owed under the ISDA.
- Dispute resolution procedures.

Swap Confirmation

The swap confirmation represents the agreement on all terms between the funding bank and the swap counterparty for a specific TRS transaction. The swap confirmation for a TRS would address the following topics:

- *Legal names* of the funding bank and the swap counterparty.
- *Term of the TRS.*
- *Ramp-up/ramp-down periods.* These are the periods during which the swap counterparty has to get the portfolio in compliance with the portfolio criteria. They do not apply to single-name TRS.
- *The notional amount.* This is the funded amount of the TRS and represents the principal amount multiplied by the purchase price for term loans. It is reduced by the discount amount for the unfunded portion of a revolver trading below par.
- *Minimum/maximum notional.* This applies to portfolios and sets limits that the swap counterparty must keep the portfolio size within.
- *Swap calculation period and payment dates.* Typically, a TRS will distribute all earnings on the bank loans, less the swap financing cost, on a monthly basis (the "swap calculation period") on a set day each month (the "swap payment date").
- *Swap payments.* These are the sum of the following amounts for the swap calculation period:
  - Interest and fees paid to the funding bank on the reference bank loans.

- The swap financing amount charged by the funding bank on the funded amount of the bank loans plus any fee charged on the unfunded portions of revolving loans.
- Certain expenses passed through by the funding bank to the swap counterparty, principally the assignment fees (if any) and the cost for legal counsel on distressed loans.
- Capital appreciation, or the realized gain on sales or repayments of bank loans.
- Capital depreciation, or the realized loss on sales or repayments of bank loans.
- *Termination rights.*
  - The swap counterparty will generally have the right to terminate the TRS at any time with a few days' prior notice to the funding bank.
  - The funding bank may have the right to terminate the TRS under the following scenarios:
    - A credit event occurring with respect to a reference bank loan.
    - Portfolio criteria noncompliance (applies to portfolio TRS only).
    - Price-based termination events.
  - A fee may be due if a TRS is terminated early. Generally single-name TRS do not have early termination fees, whereas portfolio TRS do, because the funding bank has made a long-term commitment to the swap counterparty and would expect to be compensated if the swap counterparty did not use that commitment.
- *Determination of final price.* This can be done by a negotiated sale or a market auction of the reference bank loan.
- *Representations and warranties.*
- Credit support. Usually the independent amount (haircut) will be detailed in the swap confirmation.
- *Preapproval.* The swap counterparty may be required to obtain the consent of the funding bank prior to adding a bank loan into the TRS.

- *Obligation criteria.* For portfolio TRS, the swap confirmation will delineate the acceptable characteristics for eligible assets, including
  - Asset types, including the types of loans and bonds that are permitted.
  - Currency limitations.
  - Security/priority limitations.
  - Par/distressed limitations.
  - Minimum initial price requirements.
  - Minimum ratings requirements.
- *Portfolio criteria.* For portfolio TRS, the swap confirmation will delineate the acceptable characteristics for the portfolio in much the same way that a CLO has portfolio criteria, although restrictions in a portfolio TRS are much less than those in a CLO. The portfolio criteria are negotiated between the two counterparties and are customized for each transaction. The typical criteria include

  - Obligor exposure limit, typically 2.5 to 10 percent per obligor, as a percent of the total portfolio.
  - Industry exposure limit, typically 8 to 15 percent per obligor, as a percent of the total portfolio.
  - Portfolio ratings requirements.
  - Buckets for certain types of assets:
    - Revolvers.
    - Second lien loans.
    - High-yield bonds.
    - Debtor in possession loans (DIPs).
    - Limited distribution and middle market loans.

Investment Management Agreement or Voting Rights Agreement

A TRS is a synthetic transaction, as it does not confer ownership rights to the swap counterparty. Generally, funding banks may reserve the right to sell the physical bank loan or not to buy it at all when the reference bank loan is added to the TRS. If the funding bank takes either of these actions, that would make it "short" the risk of the bank loan, since it would be obligated to pay the total return of that bank loan to the swap counterparty, but it would not be earning that total return from ownership of the loan. It is rare that a funding bank would do this, but as the TRS and loan markets continue to develop, it is inevitable that TRS will be used to facilitate short positions, just as repo transactions are used similarly for bonds.

While the TRS does not confer ownership of the reference bank loans, it may be possible for the swap counterparty to control voting rights on the bank loans that are held by the funding bank or its SPE through an investment management agreement or voting rights agreement. One of these agreements would give the swap counterparty the right to accept or reject optional prepayments and the right to vote on amendments, covenant waivers, and other issues. Because voting rights cannot be split between multiple counterparties, the funding bank would have to either segregate each swap counterparty's bank loans in a separate legal entity or give the vote to the largest holder.

HOW DO BANK LOAN TOTAL RETURN SWAPS WORK?

In this final section, we discuss the operations, taxation, and accounting for bank loan TRS.

Operations

The funding bank will either act as the bank loan administrator or hire a third-party trustee to do so. Since funding banks are usually commercial banks with large loan holdings of their own in addition to those held in their TRS books, most funding banks use their own staff to administer the bank loans held for TRS. However, the operations required for a bank loan TRS differ from the administration of a commercial bank's own portfolio or trading positions in several respects, and thus some funding banks use third-party trustees to administer the bank loans. Bank loan TRS administration requires more customer service, reporting, tracking, and forwarding of information on the loans than internal bank administration groups may normally provide (banks that own full-service trustees are excepted). Swap counterparties require the full amount of payment information that they would receive as owner of the loan so that they can confirm that the swap payments are calculated correctly. Nevertheless, the operational requirements for bank loan

TRS are significant no matter which method of administration is used. These requirements include the following:

- *Loan settlements.* Once the swap counterparty notifies the funding bank that it is adding a bank loan to the TRS, the funding bank or its trustee will contact the seller or underwriter of the bank loan to arrange for the transfer of that loan to the funding bank or one of its SPEs. It will arrange for the funding memorandum detailing the cash payment amount and the assignment agreement and will make the funding payment on the closing date. Information regarding the loan settlement is provided to the swap counterparty.

- *Interest, fee, and principal collection.* As owner of the bank loan, the funding bank or its trustee will collect the payments made to the lenders and will provide this information to the swap counterparty.

- *Swap payment calculation.* Each swap calculation period, generally monthly, the funding bank or its trustee will tally up all of the receipts and payment obligations according to the terms of the TRS and will report this to the swap counterparty. The swap counterparty will confirm the amounts and direct the funding bank as to where the swap payment should be made.

- *Consent requests.* The funding bank or its trustee may contact the swap counterparty if a consent request exists on any of the bank loans in the TRS. If the swap counterparty has a voting rights agreement or similar document in place, the swap counterparty may direct the funding bank as to how to vote on the consent request and will be entitled to any economic consideration as a result.

- *Reporting and tracking.* In addition to providing the information just listed to the swap counterparty, the funding bank or its trustee will generally provide periodic reports.

- A swap positions report will show the reference bank loan positions, compliance with any obligation criteria and portfolio criteria, unsettled positions, and current valuations of the reference bank loans, including accrued interest.

- A swap collateral report will show the swap collateral held, its current value, interest accrued thereon, and calculations of the collateral requirements, including collateral excesses or deficiencies from other derivatives contracts between the funding bank and the swap counterparty that are netted with the TRS collateral requirements.
- *Forwarding of financial information with respect to the reference bank loans.* The funding bank or its trustee may agree to forward certain financial information regarding the borrowers for the reference bank loans. This information may be confidential information that is not allowed to be freely distributed. Funding banks that distribute this information may rely on confidentiality provisions in their swap confirmation or investment management agreement, which would limit how the swap counterparty could redistribute or use the confidential information, or may rely on general market practice, which allows for distribution of confidential information to prospective purchasers of bank loans (which may or may not require a confidentiality agreement, depending on the terms of the credit agreement).

Taxation

Several tax issues exist with respect to TRS, including the tax treatment of the swap itself, whether withholding taxes apply, and whether the swap counterparty is considered to be conducting a U.S. trade or business for tax purposes.

- *Tax treatment of swaps.* Possible tax treatments include (1) as a "notional principal contract," where taxation would be based on the net swap income, in a manner similar to the taxation of an interest-rate swap. The tax issue turns on whether the reference bank loan can be characterized as an "index based on objective financial information" for U.S. tax purposes—in particular, whether the bank loan is under the control of the lender/counterparty, i.e., unique to the lender's circumstances. (2) Alternatively, from a technical tax perspective, the swap could be integrated with the reference and the swap counterparty could be deemed to own the reference bank loan for U.S. federal income tax purposes.

- *U.S. trade or business.* If the TRS is not characterized as a notional principal contract, the U.S. tax question raised is whether an offshore swap counterparty is deemed the beneficial owner of the reference bank loan and, as a result, is underwriting loans to U.S. borrowers and receiving interest and commitment fees on such obligations. This recharacterization could raise the issue of whether the swap counterparty is considered to be engaged in a U.S. trade or business for U.S. tax purposes. Generally, if an offshore swap counterparty entity is deemed to be engaged in banking or other similar financing-type activities by virtue of the TRS, it could potentially be liable for U.S. tax on its net income and have annual U.S. tax reporting compliance obligations. However, the TRS on loan product is generally structured by tax advsiors to decrease the chance that the counterparty would be subject to U.S. taxation. Furthermore, this technical U.S. tax risk is disclosed in the TRS swap confirmation (especially when the swap counterparty is an offshore hedge fund that does not otherwise have any U.S. taxation nexus or other permanent establishment in the United States and in particular, where certain types of loans are the basis of the reference obligation). For example, those reference obligations originated by an affiliate of either the reference lender or the swap counterparty.

- *Documentation of intended tax treatment.* Generally, each party will agree in the swap confirmation to treat the TRS on loan transaction for U.S. federal income tax purposes as a "notional principal contract" within the meaning of U.S. Treasury Regulations Section 1.446–3(c) and to take all actions consistent with such treatment unless there is a change in law or interpretation thereof that is inconsistent with such treatment or any action is taken by a taxing authority against such party in which the taxing authority has asserted a different treatment.

- *Withholding tax.* The basic objective is to structure the TRS to avoid withholding taxes. The issue turns on the domicile of the tax owner of the reference bank loan and requires analysis of whether that domicile has a tax treaty with the domicile of the borrower. The potential tax owners are (1) the funding bank, (2) the funding bank's SPE if the loan is held therein, or (3) the swap counterparty. As these three entities may each have a different domicile, with different tax treaties, the liability for withholding tax could vary depending on who is determined to be the tax owner of such reference bank loan.

Accounting

Accounting treatment for swap counterparties is rarely an issue because most TRS counterparties are hedge funds or special-purpose entities, neither of which is usually required to make reports under generally accepted accounting principles. In practice, most swap counterparties make summary reports to their investors that detail the full exposure to the loans that are in the TRS and explain that the economic exposure to the loans is being acquired with leverage.

CHAPTER 11

CDOs: A Primer

The Bond Market Association

WHAT ARE CDOs?

CDOs Defined

A CDO, or collateralized debt obligation, is a structured repackaging vehicle that issues multiple classes of liabilities created from a pool of assets (the collateral pool). Typically, a bankruptcy-remote special-purpose vehicle (SPV) is created to hold the collateral and issue liabilities, which will comprise both debt and equity components (Exhibit 11.1). The collateral pool can be static or revolving. A revolving deal often employs an asset manager to reinvest the collateral proceeds and to conduct limited trading. Besides the underwriter and the asset manager, other key participants involved in CDOs typically include rating agencies, a trustee, and a hedge counterparty.

The difference between a CDO and other pooled investments, such as mutual funds, is the partitioning of risk among the investors. Unlike a mutual fund, in which investors have rights and risks in proportion to the size of their investment, some CDO investors have more rights and greater security than other CDO investors in the same transaction have based on the priority level of repayment for each tranche of securities, which is based on the

EXHIBIT 11.1

Basic CDO Building Blocks.

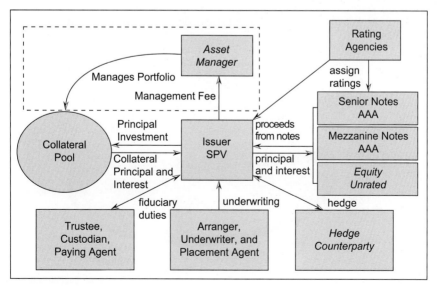

Source: Credit Suisse.

risks associated with each of the investments. The specific rights and security of each investor are outlined in the transaction's indenture. Investors with higher risk tolerance may choose to invest in higher-yielding and riskier CDO debt or equity, while risk-averse investors are likely to choose more senior, but lower-yielding, CDO debt. In fact, one benefit of CDO technology is that it allows investors to choose securities that are suitable to their risk/reward profile.

The relationships among the parties and a general overview of a typical CDO structure are shown in Exhibit 11.1

Market Growth and the CDO Family Tree

Underpinning the growth of the CDO market is innovation, and CDOs' structural versatility has afforded plenty. The CDO market, which began in 1989, now represents 14.4 percent of the $1.8 trillion U.S. asset-backed securities (ABS) market, a significant component of the securitization market (see Exhibit 11.2).

The utility of CDOs as a capital market tool is underscored by their diversity of collateral and range of purposes. CDOs are usually defined by three characteristics: structure, purpose, and collateral (see Exhibit 11.3). Each of these characteristics is discussed here.

EXHIBIT 11.2

ABS outstanding by major types of credit as of June 30, 2004.

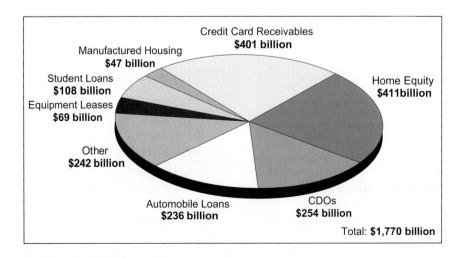

Credit Card Receivables
$401 billion

Manufactured Housing
$47 billion

Student Loans
$108 billion

Equipment Leases
$69 billion

Home Equity
$411billion

Other
$242 billion

Automobile Loans
$236 billion

CDOs
$254 billion

Total: **$1,770 billion**

EXHIBIT 11.3

CDO Family Tree.

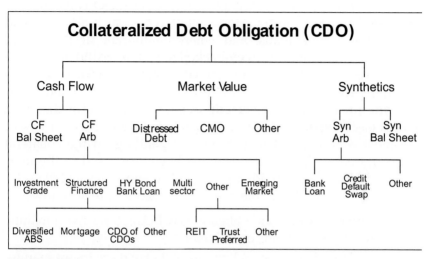

Source: Credit Suisse.

Structuring Mechanisms

There are three broad structural categories of CDOs: cash flow, market value, and synthetic. The performance of *cash flow* deals is mainly tied to the credit performance of the underlying portfolio; market price fluctuations are of secondary importance. The principal risk to collateral cash flows is credit risk, i.e., the possibility that the expected stream of cash flows will not be collected as a result of collateral default.

In contrast to cash flow CDOs, *market value* CDOs are rated based on market value overcollateralization, where collateral market price and price fluctuations are key performance drivers.

Synthetic CDOs behave like cash flow structures economically, but they typically employ credit derivatives, such as credit default swaps, and have simple structures with few cash diversion mechanisms.

Purpose

There are two basic drivers of CDO issuance: spread arbitrage and balance sheet management. Arbitrage CDOs seek to capture the excess spreads of higher-yielding assets over liabilities. In contrast, the primary purposes of balance sheet transactions are to reduce regulatory capital requirements, hedge risk, or enhance balance sheet flexibility.

Collateral Types

A testament to CDOs' versatility is the breadth of asset types included in their collateral pools. Over time, CDO collateral has expanded beyond the traditional asset types, such as high-yield (HY) bonds, bank loans, and emerging market (EM) debt, to include products such as asset-backed securities (ABS), mortgage-backed securities (MBS), commercial mortgage-backed securities (CMBS), private equity, trust preferred securities, small and medium enterprise (SME) loans, credit default swaps, and hedge fund shares (see "Types of Assets" for a detailed description of five of the most common collateral types). Depending on the collateral type, alternative CDO classifications have been used in the marketplace. However, individually and collectively, they all fall under the umbrella of CDOs. Some common categories are as follows:

- Collateralized bond obligations (CBOs); these invest mainly in corporate bonds or EM debt.
- Collateralized loan obligations (CLOs); these invest mainly in bank loans.
- Structured finance CDOs; these invest mainly in CMBSs, ABSs, REIT debt, and other CDOs.
- Collateralized synthetic obligations; this mainly refers to credit default swaps.
- Collateralized fund obligations; these invest mainly in hedge funds.
- Collateralized equity obligations; these invest mainly in private equities.

CDOs versus Other Structured Finance Products

Fundamentally, CDOs apply technologies similar to those used in other structured finance markets. These include priority of payments and credit enhancement triggers to distinguish between senior and junior liabilities. For example, cash flow CDOs use the interest and principal payments from collateral to pay CDO liabilities based on a prespecified priority of payments.

However, there are also some structural aspects that are unique to CDOs. For example:

- CDO collateral is often rated, whereas the collateral for other structured finance products is usually unrated.

- With the exception of some balance sheet CLOs and SME deals, CDO collateral pools are often lumpy (more akin to aircraft lease ABSs and CMBSs), whereas most ABS collateral pools consist of large numbers (i.e., more than 1,000) of loan/receivables that are more homogenous, with similar size and credit quality.
- Currently, CDOs are Rule 144a or private placement transactions, which are not publicly registered.

THE BENEFITS OF INVESTING IN CDOs

CDOs provide a number of unique benefits that make them attractive to investors for a variety of reasons.

Investment Diversification

CDOs offer investors exposure to a wide array of assets. Because CDO structures strictly limit the collateral concentration within any one issuer, industry, or geographic region, investors are able to diversify among a large number of credits via a single investment. In addition to achieving greater diversity within specific asset types through exposure to a pool of perhaps 100 investment grade credits, CDO investors can also diversify across asset types within the same transaction. For example, a typical multisector ABS pool may consist of home equity loans, CMBS, and residential mortgage-backed securities (RMBS). Hence, via their collateral pools, CDOs enable traditional fixed income investors to participate in varied underlying collateral markets while relying on the investment managers' resources and expertise in those markets.

Customized Risk/Reward

CDO structures allow investors to choose securities suitable to their specific risk/reward profile by separating the cash flows of the underlying collateral into tranches of investment grade and non-investment grade securities. Risk tranching also enables issuers to offer CDOs across the entire risk/reward spectrum, ranging from the least risky, AAA-rated securities to the high-risk, unrated equity investment, within a single transaction. A risk-averse investor, for example, can choose to invest in the higher-rated senior notes, while investors with higher risk tolerances can select from the subordinated notes and equity asset classes.

Attractive Yields

CDOs often offer higher yields when compared to other ABS sectors and investment grade corporate bonds. The yield pickup increases as investors move toward the riskier end of the credit spectrum.

Leveraged Returns

As a leveraged investment, the equity in cash flow CDOs represents a unique investment opportunity, as it is part of a diversified portfolio of financial assets without mark-to-market or margin call unwinding risk. The financial leverage provided by a CDO can be fixed for as long as 12 years, although the equity owner has the right to exercise an optional redemption feature and call the deal sooner. The optional redemption feature provides additional flexibility to an equity investor in a CDO, offering potentially greater upside if the collateral performs well and appreciates in price.

Transparency

In contrast to other alternative investments, CDOs offer a high degree of transparency. Monthly trustee reports provide information such as portfolio composition, trading activity, and deal performance in the form of a balance sheet of assets and liabilities and an income statement detailing sources and uses of cash. In addition, rating agencies closely monitor the CDO market and publish regular reports containing deal-level, asset-level, and vintage-level data.

TYPES OF ASSETS

Over time, the types of assets that can be secured in a CDO have greatly expanded. Beyond the traditional asset types, such as high-yield bonds, bank loans, and EM debt, products such as ABS, MBS, CMBS, private equity, trust preferred securities, SME loans, credit default swaps, and hedge fund shares are also securitized. Several of the most common asset types are discussed here.

Leveraged Loans

A corporate leveraged loan generally has multiple tranches, including a revolving credit facility (RC) and a term loan A (TLA), along with single or multiple institutional term loans. While any of these subclasses of leveraged loans can be, and has been, securitized, the largest subclass is the institutional term loan tranche.

Revolving Credit Facility
The revolving credit facility is an unfunded or partially funded commitment by lenders that can be drawn on and repaid at the issuer's discretion until maturity. The borrower pays a nominal commitment fee on the undrawn amount and a coupon on the drawn amount. Maturities are usually either one year or in the three- to five-year range.

Term Loan A
A term loan A is a fully funded term loan that usually amortizes throughout the life of the loan. It is unlike the RC facility in that once the borrowed amount is paid back to the lenders, the borrower cannot reborrow the money under the TLA facility. In virtually every case, the spread and term of the RC and the TLA are the same.

Institutional Term Loan Tranches
In contrast to the payments on the TLA, amortization payments on institutional term loans are usually more heavily backloaded or come as a bullet payment at final maturity. Institutional tranches are usually named in alphabetical order (term loan B, C, D, and so on, depending on the number of tranches). For example, TLA might be five years, TLB might be six years, TLC might be seven years, and so on.

Together, the revolving credit facility and the term loan A are traditionally referred to as a "pro rata" tranche, because banks that take part in the syndication must commit to an equivalent proportion of both the RC and the TLA. Coupons (shown as LIBOR plus a spread) on pro rata tranches are often lower than comparable coupons on institutional tranches because of the higher up-front fees and accelerated payments associated with pro rata tranches.

The leveraged loan new-issue market reached $139 billion in 2002, with the pro rata and institutional term loan markets accounting for $81 billion and $58 billion, respectively.

Asset-Backed Securities

Asset-backed securities (ABS) are bonds or notes backed by financial assets. Typically these assets consist of receivables other than mortgage loans, such as credit card receivables, auto loans, manufactured-housing contracts, and home-equity loans. ABS differ from most other kinds of bonds in that their creditworthiness, which is at the AAA level for more than 90 percent of outstanding issues, derives from sources other than the paying ability of the originator of the underlying assets. This is much the same as the paying ability of a CDO, which does not depend on the collateral manager or the investment bank, but rather depends on the performance of the collateral.

Commercial Mortgage-Backed Securities

Commercial mortgage-backed securities (CMBS) are notes backed by a pool of loans secured with commercial rather than residential property. Commercial real estate includes multifamily properties, retail establishments, office properties, and so on.

Both ABS and CMBS are characterized by high ratings, high liquidity, low rating volatility, and separation from originator/servicer bankruptcy. However, since these securities are not standardized, numerous details associated with their structure, credit enhancement, diversification, and so on must be analyzed when valuing these investments.

At the end of the second quarter of 2004, mortgage-backed securities accounted for a total of $4.5 trillion, and asset-backed securities totaled $1.8 trillion.

Corporate Bonds

Corporate bonds are debt obligations issued by corporations. The bonds can be characterized as either high-yield (HY) or investment grade (IG) securities, based on their current ratings. HY bonds have ratings below BBB (or Baa3); IG bonds have higher ratings, reflecting their relatively lower credit risk. Bond coupons are usually fixed for the life of the bond. In lieu of cash bonds, synthetic CDOs use credit default swaps linked to the cash bonds.

Since the majority of CDOs have at least one floating-rate tranche, interest-rate hedging is a particular concern with CDOs backed by corporate bonds. Generally, the resulting interest-rate mismatch (fixed-coupon collateral versus floating-rate liabilities) is mitigated through interest-rate hedging in the CDO structure.

Corporate bonds are probably the best-known debt instruments in the CDO market, with extensive historical data being readily available for research and due diligence purposes. The U.S. corporate bond market totaled $4.6 trillion at the end of the second quarter of 2004.

Capital Trust Pass-Through Securities

Capital trust pass-through securities (TRUPS) are credit-linked notes issued by a bank holding company (BHC) through a pass-through grantor trust. TRUPS are a low-cost, tax-deductible form of tier 1 regulatory capital for U.S. BHCs. TRUPS are subordinated to all other senior and subordinated debt of the BHC. The notes are delinked from the common shares of the BHC; therefore, the issuance of TRUPS does not increase the number of common shares outstanding. The notes usually have a maturity of 30 years, but are callable at par after 5 years. Floating-rate, fixed-rate, and fixed/floating-rate variations are available. The BHC must also comply with a number of additional restrictions in order to participate in the TRUPS program.

Since the October 1996 Federal Reserve Board announcement permitting BHCs to include TRUPS in tier 1 capital, approximately $107.0 billion of TRUPS-like securities have been issued by BHCs to provide low-cost core capital. Approximately $39.0 billion of the securities were issued in the retail market, and $68.0 billion of the securities were issued in the institutional market.

TYPES OF STRUCTURES—CASH FLOW, SYNTHETIC, AND MARKET VALUE
Basic CDO Structure

Although no two CDO structures are alike, they do fall neatly into three categories: cash flow, synthetic, and market value CDOs. We will focus our discussion primarily on the first two, as very few market value structures—used to securitize relatively more volatile, equitylike assets and funds—have been used in the past few years.

What all CDO structures have in common is the basic asset-
liability structure: the assets of the CDO trust are funded by a capital structure consisting of some combination of debt and equity.
For purposes of this chapter, our focus is on the right-hand side of
the CDO balance sheet (i.e., the debt and equity).

In a CDO, a trust issues multiple classes of debt and equity
that are tranched with respect to credit losses and timing of cash
flows. The equity tranche receives all residual cash flows after payments to the noteholders. Therefore, the equity investors absorb
any of the first losses and are subordinate to the debtholders'
claims. The amount of equity that deal requires is primarily a function of the riskiness of the underlying collateral and ranges from
approximately 3 to 5 percent for a deal involving IG assets to 8 to
12 percent for HY asset portfolios. The debt tranches are structured
to balance the constraints of investor requirements with the CDO's
objective in a way that minimizes funding costs. Subordinated
CDO tranches (e.g., B and BB) absorb losses before the mezzanine
(e.g., BBB and A) and senior tranches (e.g., AA and AAA) and
therefore carry commensurately higher yields.

Structural Distinctions

In distinguishing between cash and synthetic structures, the major
difference is the former's strict senior funding reliance on triple-A
bond investors and the latter's ability to access the more cheaply
priced super-senior swap market. The funding advantage for
synthetics is so great that over the past six years they have accounted for all of the growth in the global CDO market. However, the
securitization of most assets other than IG corporate credits
still requires the cash structure, which can be applied to all debt
collateral types.

Multisector CDOs—where the collateral is primarily structured
products, including other CDOs in some cases—have the greatest
overlap of cash and synthetic structures. However, even here, the
synthetic structure is usually more beneficial for securitizing senior-
rated, low-spread asset pools to achieve commensurately lower
senior financing costs in the swap market.

Another important distinction in CDO structure is managed
versus static. Managed deals are typically, but not always, cash
flow structures and "rule-based," ensuring that the manager balances the interests of both the equity investors and the debtholders.

By contrast, static deals, which increasingly are giving investors limited substitution rights, are typically synthetic structures that either arbitrage the spread between the assets and the trust's funding costs or use on-balance sheet credits for regulatory and/or economic capital relief.

Cash Structure

The assets of a cash flow CDO are funded by a capital structure consisting of some combination of debt and equity (see Exhibit 11.4). As the first-loss holder, the equity has the highest expected return and volatility. Like a CMO's debt, the debt of the CDO trust consists of tranched notes rated as low as B and as high as AAA. The lower-rated tranches absorb losses before the higher-rated tranches and enjoy a commensurately higher coupon in return for this additional risk. Principal cash flows are paid to the tranches sequentially. Hence, the percentage of each note's subordination increases, as its principal is amortized later in the CDO's life in accordance with maturing assets. The number of tranches varies greatly from deal to deal, with some CDOs having only one tranche and others having

EXHIBIT 11.4

Example of a Cash Flow CDO Structure.

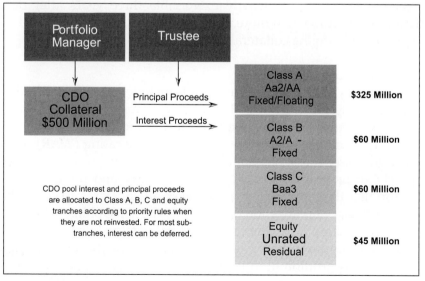

Source: Banc of America Securities LLC.

more than 10. Furthermore, the expected average life of each tranche varies based on the structure's prioritization of cash flows under a base-case assumption for the expected timing and amount of future losses. However, depending on these assumptions, the actual collateral, and the structure, senior tranches typically have average lives of six to eight years, whereas junior tranche average lives typically extend from eight to eleven years.

Coverage Tests

In managed cash flow CDOs, debtholders are protected primarily by asset quality and cash flow coverage tests. The portfolio of a managed cash flow CDO is restricted by asset quality tests involving the collateral's minimum ratings, industry/obligor limits, minimum coupon or spread, and maturity profile. The asset quality tests are particularly relevant during the deal's reinvestment period, which consists of a preset time frame within which the manager may use principal proceeds to purchase additional assets and to effect asset substitutions.

Whereas a breach of the asset quality test(s) can result in the downgrading of CDO notes, cash flow coverage test failures can actually accelerate cash flows to the higher-rated tranches. Specifically, when either the principal or the interest coverage test is not met, principal is paid to the most senior outstanding tranches until the tests are corrected (mandatory redemption). Finally, an optional redemption—usually exercisable three years after deal issuance—occurs when more than two-thirds of the equity holders vote to liquidate the collateral portfolio.

Asset Quality Tests

Asset quality tests for cash flow CDOs include a list of criteria that the aggregate portfolio of collateral assets must meet on an ongoing basis. One type of asset quality test is the minimum average rating test, under which the weighted average rating (WAR) of all collateral assets must be at or above a specific level (for example, B for HY deals or BBB- for IG deals). Industry and obligor limits ensure that the outstanding principal of all collateral assets in the same industry classification or issued by the same obligor does not exceed a maximum percentage of the total outstanding principal. A typical maximum industry concentration is 8 percent, whereas the obligor concentration limit is generally 2.5 percent. The minimum weighted average coupon (WAC) test requires that the WAC of all collateral assets be above a minimum level. Finally, the cumulative maturity distribution test ensures a predictable amortization profile for the rated debt after the end of the reinvestment period.

Cash Flow Coverage Tests

There are two types of cash flow coverage tests: a par amount over-collateralization (OC) test and an interest coverage (IC) test. The OC test ensures that a minimum amount of collateral par amount secures the rated debt, and the IC test ensures that the cash coupon payments generated from the collateral will be adequate to pay the fees and interest due on the rated notes. In most transactions, the OC test would typically be failed before the IC test, so the market's focus is placed on the performance of the former test. An OC test is set for each tranche to accelerate cash flows to the most senior notes and subsequently to amortize more subordinated notes if the deal continues to perform poorly.

Synthetic Structure

Synthetic CDOs utilize technology from the credit default swap (CDS) market to synthetically replicate a cash flow CDO. As credit derivatives separate credit risk from the other risks associated with fixed income instruments, such as interest-rate risk, synthetic CDOs represent a pure play on credit for investors and issuers. Synthetic CDO notes are essentially tranched exposures to a portfolio of single-name CDS. In a single-name CDS contract, the "protection seller" receives a periodic premium payment—or a spread roughly comparable to an asset swap spread—for its obligation to compensate the "protection buyer" for credit losses upon the occurrence of a credit event. In a synthetic CDO, a similar contract is simply extended to a portfolio of credits tranched with respect to credit losses. For example, the most subordinate tranche above equity receives a periodic premium as compensation for its second-loss position in the capital structure. The subordinate noteholder's coupon would be much greater than that of the mezzanine and senior noteholders, who bear exposure only to the subsequent losses, if any.

Whereas cash flow CDO liabilities are always funded notes yielding a spread over a benchmark such as LIBOR or Treasuries, in synthetic CDOs the liabilities can be either funded, unfunded, or both. Similarly, on the asset side of a synthetic CDO, the collateral can be either cash bonds (funded), credit default swaps (unfunded),

EXHIBIT 11.5

Example of Synthetic CDO Structure.

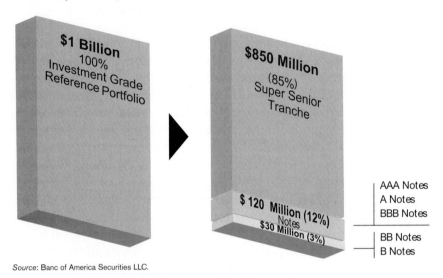

Source: Banc of America Securities LLC.

or both. The synthetic CDO trust issues credit-linked notes (funded) and/or swaps (unfunded) with various degrees of exposure to losses incurred as a result of credit events in the portfolio. The remaining super-senior risk is typically swapped out to investors in an unfunded format (see Exhibit 11.5). Single-tranche CDOs (ST CDOs) represent the newest evolution of synthetic CDOs; they forgo the requirement that the CDO trust include the entire capital structure. Instead, ST CDOs allow for investment in part of the capital structure of an underlying reference portfolio. The ST CDO investor determines this reference portfolio, and is then given flexibility to choose the desired level of subordination and the tranche size of the investment.

Synthetics versus Cash

It is possible to obtain structured exposure to a portfolio of credits in a number of ways. The major distinction arises between the cash and synthetic structures. In the cash structure, the collateral is usually actively managed, and the liabilities are fully funded without using derivatives. In the various synthetic structures, the collateral is typically static (although progressively managed), and the liabilities are normally only partially funded, with the senior risk being swapped out to a counterparty or retained by the sponsor. The major characteristics of synthetics and how they differ from cash flow CDOs are discussed here.

Investor Perspective

- *Isolated credit risk.* Synthetics typically isolate credit risk from other risks, such as interest-rate, prepayment, and currency risk, assumed by cash CDO noteholders. Therefore, investors in synthetic structures can focus on selecting the optimal asset classes, desired leverage, investment criteria, and style of portfolio management.
- *Short maturity.* Corporate-backed synthetics typically have an average life of six years (versus eight to twelve years for cash CDOs), yet they offer comparable or better spreads.
- *Low funding cost.* First, super-senior funding in the default swap market—which constitutes 75 to 90 percent of total funding—is much cheaper than the relatively higher spreads demanded by AAA cash investors. Second, synthetic CDOs usually require lower equity deposits because of their enhanced structural flexibility. For both of these reasons, synthetic CDOs typically require lower collateral spreads. However, lower equity deposits translates into less subordination protection for noteholders.
- *Low sourcing risk.* There is generally little sourcing risk in synthetic CDOs for three main reasons. First, CDS can be created based on almost any corporate credit and can be sourced within a matter of days, compared with months for cash CDOs. Second, synthetic CDOs do not require the physical transfer of assets into a trust. Therefore, a wider universe of assets can be used in the synthetic structure (e.g., syndicated loans with restrictions on selling without the borrowers' consent). Third, the lower funding gap resulting from the cheaper senior funding expands the universe of investable assets to relatively higher-rated collateral, which is easier to source.
- *Hybrid note/equity tranching.* In synthetic CDOs, the lower-rated notes and equity certificates are often a hybrid of debt and equity, something that is a rarity in cash CDOs. For example, the BBBs may have a stated coupon plus

participation in the residual returns. Similarly, the equity certificates of synthetic CDOs may have a stated coupon close to that of a BB cash CDO tranche, plus residual cash flows.

- *Simplicity of waterfall rules.* Cash CDOs can be difficult to analyze, in part because of their intricate waterfall rules, which divert principal payments to higher-rated tranches when collateral tests are tripped. These rules also vary from deal to deal. In contrast, such waterfall or priority of payment rules are either nonexistent or negligible in most synthetic CDOs, because senior risk is often swapped out to a counterparty or retained by the manager or dealer. In synthetics, waterfall rules are usually designed to protect the mezzanine investors, who in cash deals get only second priority, after the AAA and AA senior investors. Another difference is that in synthetics, cash flow coverage tests, when tripped, usually divert excess spread into a cash reserve account or restrict the manager's trading, thereby stopping the leakage of cash to the equity investors and/or subordinate noteholders.

- *Single-tranche technology.* Whereas cash CDOs require the issuance of an entire capital structure, synthetic CDOs based on liquid CDS names may sell only a portion of the capital structure thanks to delta-hedging technology (analogous to that used to manage residual interest-rate risk in a swap book).

Issuer Perspective

- *Ease of execution.* As fewer rated notes need to be placed (most of the funding is often a super-senior swap) and lower equity deposits are required, the marketing process for a synthetic CDO can be more efficient than that for a cash CDO; thus, there is a higher probability of the deal's closing. Furthermore, the documentation process for synthetics is more streamlined than that for cash CDOs.

- *Ability to securitize nontransferable assets.* Balance sheet CLOs—the first synthetic subsector—came into being in 1997 because credit derivatives allow financial institutions to achieve capital relief for loans that they either want or need to leave on their balance sheet.

- *Lower funding cost.* Since synthetics typically have lower funding costs than cash deals, the manager is able to concentrate investments in higher-quality collateral, and thus faces less sourcing risk. Particularly in balance sheet deals where the issuer is a highly rated bank, the CDO's funding cost may exceed that of the sponsor. Therefore, the lower funding costs of the synthetic structure are often a necessity in order to achieve the requisite economics in a balance sheet deal.

- *Passive versus active management.* Since most synthetics in the market are passively managed, much of the issuer's decision on whether to select the cash or synthetic structure hinges on passive versus active management. The passive structure has enjoyed tremendous growth because of the proliferation of credit-savvy investors who prefer to do their own analysis on a known static portfolio of IG corporate credits. Furthermore, there is a cost associated with independent management that needs to be taken into account. Many "static" synthetics actually allow limited substitution rights subject to a trading account and/or WAR test, industry limits, and other tests.

Market Value Structure

Similar to hedge fund managers, the market value CDO manager purchases a financed pool of assets that carries, in the manager's estimation, a high total return probability with relatively low risk. That said, the assets of market value CDOs are much more volatile than those of cash flow or synthetic CDOs. Therefore, equity deposits for market value CDOs range from 18 to 22 percent for HY deals and 28 to 33 percent for hedge fund deals. High-yield market value CDOs include a variety of assets across the risk/return spectrum, including cash, Treasuries, commercial paper, bonds, loans, mezzanine debt, distressed debt, equity, and emerging market debt. The market value structure has more recently been applied to hedge funds and private equity funds.

Features that characterize market value CDOs include a structure in which collateral assets are marketable, cash-paying instruments for which price volatility rather than cash flow is assumed to be predictable. Marking to market is usually performed daily for market value CDOs. Trading flexibility within this structure allows portfolio managers to periodically adjust the collateral pool by shifting the market value weight of each asset type that makes up the pool. Trading restrictions are nonexistent as long as asset test requirements are met. The mandatory liquidation of bonds is activated when the minimum net worth and/or market value overcollateralization tests are not met and have not been remedied within a cure period.

PRINCIPAL RISKS AND ANALYSIS OF CDOs

CDO Risks

Proper evaluation of a CDO requires a thorough identification and evaluation of the risks that investors are being compensated for. The primary risks that investors must analyze include the following.

Systemic or Modeling Risk

This is the potential rating agency modeling risk assumed by investors, and it stems from (1) the appropriateness of the statistical methods employed by the agencies when assigning ratings and (2) the accuracy and predictive power of the proprietary default and recovery data used in the models. The rating agency algorithms determine the level of credit enhancement for a given tranche's risk level (i.e., rating). These methods drive about 80 to 90 percent of CDO deal structures.

Collateral Credit Risk

This is the credit risk of the collateral at the portfolio level (diversification requirements within the structure limit bond-specific risk). This risk is a function of the performance of each underlying collateral sector as affected by the domestic/global credit cycle or secular events such as high-yield market performance, the impact of 9/11 on aircraft leases, and so on. Senior CDO investors are insulated against collateral credit risk because of the significant amount of credit enhancement that exists at the top of the CDO capital structure. However, subordinated and equity investors are not. Rather, their investment is a leveraged view of the collateral performance, and they are compensated for their higher exposure to collateral credit risk.

Structural Risk

Structural risk relates to the adequacy of the structural tests to (1) preserve collateral quality and (2) redirect excess spread and interest cash flows of subordinate investors to pay down senior noteholders if the collateral performs worse than expected. The stringency of the tests determines the timing and amount of cash flows to be diverted away from junior notes.

Servicer/Manager Risk

This risk is a function of the adequacy of the asset manager's infrastructure, credit, and portfolio management skills. The asset manager makes asset allocation decisions and selects the underlying bonds within a sector that will make up the collateral pool. To the extent that the ABS CDO collateral manager has strong credit resources and a solid infrastructure, he or she can buffer investors from collateral risk through better buy/sell decisions at the asset allocation and bond level, both initially and during the reinvestment period. However, CDOs do have built-in criteria to keep wayward managers in check. Such portfolio quality covenants include

- Limits on the amount of CCC investments
- Restrictions that prohibit the collateral manager from excessive trading
- Limits on collateral concentration
- Revocation of trading privileges if the initial risk profile of the collateral pool is not maintained

Call Risk

In most transactions, CDO debt investors are exposed to call risk. Generally, CDO deals are callable, in their entirety, after three years. Fixed-rate tranches are callable at make-whole prices, while floating-rate tranches are callable at par. Deals will be called if there is significant appreciation in the collateral or, more typically, once the reinvestment period ends and the transactions begin to delever.

Credit Analysis and Management of the Major Investment Risks

Credit analysis of CDOs is intended to address the previously identified risks, as described here.

Systemic or Modeling Risk

Investors should complete a thorough review of each rating agency modeling algorithm, particularly with respect to the main drivers of deal cash flows: default and recovery rates. The primary factor determining tranche performance is the adequacy of the expected loss assumptions for the collateral pools. The end point of an investor's analysis of the rating agency algorithm should

- Provide a conclusion with respect to the reasonableness and predictive power of the default and recovery rates used in the model for the collateral pool. Although an analysis of historical default and recovery rates, particularly during a downturn in the sector, is a good starting point, past performance may not always be the best predictor of future performance if sector or collateral dynamics have changed.
- Determine whether the "cushion" around the average or breakeven level is reasonable for the ratings level.
- Investors can get information on and an orientation to rating agency modeling approaches through
- Data published by rating agencies.
- Discussions with specific rating agency analysts.
- Research published by underwriters of CDO deals.
- Investment bankers who structure CDO deals. Bankers can provide information concerning the modeling framework used by a particular agency, as well as specific deal information, i.e., expected default and recovery rates for a given portfolio or collateral pool.
- The use of market tools such as Intex (a vendor of CDO analytical software that can be used, among other things, to run breakevens).

To the extent the investor concludes that the modeling assumptions are conservative, it may want to consider going down in the structure and purchasing the deal's lower-rated securities, in order to benefit from the "overenhancement." Conversely, to the extent that an investor has concerns about the adequacy of the model assumptions, the investor can move up in the structure in order to gain more protection against this risk. As with collateral risk, the more senior the tranche, the more insulated an investor is from the modeling risk.

Collateral Credit Risk

Investors should assess the collateral risk of the pool at the asset allocation level. For example, investors should look at the following with respect to the sectors of the portfolio:

- Current spreads for the sector (at the relevant ratings level)
- Current default data and downgrade/upgrade/watch list activity for the sector as published by the rating agencies
- CDO portfolio spread and dollar price

The goal of this analysis is to obtain a sense of how investment sectors included in the portfolio are performing. Sector risk cannot be diversified away; however, an asset manager can diversify against individual bond risk, potentially enhancing deal performance through individual bond selection.

Structural Risk

Investors should perform breakeven analysis to determine the amount of collateral net losses that can occur before a tranche becomes cash flow impaired. Generally, bankers can provide investors with custom scenarios containing specific default and recovery assumptions. Investors should derive a scenario that is conservative—i.e., worst case—and then determine how the tranche performs. This would be the "money good" scenario. Also, investors should assess how many times their tranche is covered relative to historical losses; this is the "relative value" assessment.

In addition to looking at what the structure can absorb in terms of breakeven and average loss coverage multiples, investors also should evaluate the following:

1. Level of amortization triggers and the trade-off between credit enhancement from excess spread and subordination
2. Portfolio constraints and their effectiveness in protecting the investors during the reinvestment period

Asset Manager

As mentioned previously, the asset manager makes the asset allocation decision and picks the underlying bonds within a sector. To the extent that the CDO portfolio manager has strong credit resources, he or she can protect all investors from collateral risk.

Also, the asset manager must monitor the portfolio, and is expected to serve as a loss mitigator by exiting from positions where the potential for cash flow impairment has increased or is likely to increase in the future.

Due diligence on the asset manager should include a review of the following:

1. Number of analysts per name and years of average experience.
2. Total rate of return (TROR) track record in the asset class or CDO management history.
3. When a TROR record is lacking or not relevant because of the absence of a market benchmark for comparative purposes, investors can review the manager's record with respect to (a) the number of defaults and distressed sales made within a sector, the dollar price of sales, and the ultimate recovery value on assets and (b) the manager's ratio of upgrades to downgrades.
4. Review of the rationale behind the manager's asset allocation decision.
5. The manager's credit approval process for bond selection.
6. The manager's approach to monitoring the portfolio and the genesis of sell decisions.

Call Risk

Call risk is generally mitigated for fixed-income investors through a make-whole provision. Also, deals are generally noncallable for at least three years.

As detailed previously, a comprehensive analysis will include an examination of the parties involved in the transaction as well as any factors that may affect cash flows to investors. Collateral quality, structure, credit enhancement, and management expertise should provide investors with a sufficient foundation to allow for attractive investment returns.

A SURVEY OF CDO VALUATION METHODOLOGIES

CDOs are complex structures backed by diverse pools of collateral; because they are complex, there is no standard method of valuation for them.

This section summarizes the most common valuation techniques with the intention of providing market participants with better tools for approaching and understanding the valuation of CDO securities.

CDO Valuation

Cash flow CDOs rely primarily on the cash flows generated by the underlying portfolio to repay debt and provide returns to equity holders. Like other, more traditional securitization transactions, cash flow CDOs rely on the cash flow from a pool of financial assets to service debt. A common approach to the valuation of asset-backed securities, based on the value of projected cash flows, may be applied to CDOs. This approach is commonly referred to as the discounted cash flow (DCF) valuation technique, and it attempts to simulate the future payment characteristics of the security. Other approaches may also be applied to CDO valuation. In situations where liquidation is a possibility—where an optional call is expected, or where the collateral may be liquidated as a result of a triggering event set out in the indentures—the net asset value (NAV) approach may be more appropriate. In these cases, the current net liquidation value of the assets will determine the proceeds to the investors. In still other situations, investors may want to separate the principal and interest components of a CDO and value them on an interest-only (IO) and principal-only (PO) basis. Market participants will often use more than one approach to make sure that their assessment of value stands up to different ways of analyzing a CDO.

The basic analysis of a cash flow CDO structure involves the evaluation of a particular asset portfolio and related reinvestment as well as the specific transaction structure. Maintenance tests and assumptions as to future expected default and realized loss rates must also be considered. The level of expected losses will vary depending on a number of factors, such as the types of assets in the portfolio and the credit quality and diversity of the assets.

Methodologies

Discounted Cash Flow Analysis

A technique that is commonly used to value CDO securities is the discounted cash flow method. As with any traditional DCF analysis, a stream of cash flows is projected and then discounted at an appropriate discount rate to arrive at a value for the cash flow stream. With respect to cash flow CDOs, the primary variable in any projection is the future performance of the asset portfolio. Since many CDOs are actively managed, the actions taken by the collateral manager in trading the portfolio in the future will also be an important consideration.

Before a DCF analysis can be performed, the transaction must be accurately modeled. Then a series of inputs and assumptions must be applied to the model. See the later section "Assumptions Used in Valuation Analysis" for a list of the assumptions typically used in performing DCF analysis. The cash flows are then discounted at an appropriate rate to arrive at a valuation. The discount rate is generally based on the then-current market rate for a similar security.

The discount rate used depends on a number of factors. These include the performance of the transaction to date, the credit quality and other characteristics of the portfolio, the track record and expertise of the collateral manager, how the security is projected to perform under different scenarios, and other factors. A higher discount rate may be appropriate if the transaction is perceived to have more risk than a newly issued CDO because of poor asset performance, a higher concentration of lower-quality credits, or a less experienced asset manager.

Valuations are usually created for a range of assumptions regarding portfolio performance—such as different default and recovery scenarios—and market discount rates. These scenarios may also be stressed to determine the sensitivity of the valuation to changes in assumptions. An implied valuation can then be determined, taking into consideration all the relevant factors and the evaluator's views on the fairness of the assumptions.

Interest-Only and Principal-Only Valuation

CDOs can also be decomposed into separate interest- and principal-only components. Thinking of the IO and PO parts as separate securities can make the CDO price thus determined a more accurate assessment of the value of the security. The IO and PO components are treated as having two distinct credit ratings based on their payment priority in the waterfall. Certain bonds may continue to receive interest payments, though principal repayment is less likely. Typically, this will occur with back-pay senior notes or mezzanine bonds.

As is the case with all CDO securities, IO investors need to analyze the priority of payment and the language defining the "events of default" in a transaction. They must also determine whether the IO is categorized as current pay or payable-in-kind (PIK), or PIKable. In current-pay tranches in some structures, the coupon payment is senior to the principal payments in all other classes. For PIKable tranches, the coupon may be subordinate to the principal on senior classes.

IO Valuation

Because the cash flows of a current-pay IO are relatively secure, this portion of the bond can be priced at a tighter spread than the bond's rating implies. Pricing PIKable IOs is more complex. Generally, they are either performing or distressed. The IO on a distressed bond is deeply discounted, as the coupon will be paid only after the coverage tests are satisfied, and a bond backed by distressed collateral may be failing or close to failing those tests.

PIKable IOs backed by performing collateral require further analysis. Investors need to quantify the loss rate that the deal can experience before all excess cash is diverted from the IO. They must also assess the IO's long-term credit risk by looking at where in the capital structure deferred interest is repaid. Once this is known, investors must assume a level of expected loss on the underlying collateral. A price is derived by comparing the cumulative expected loss rate with the total credit enhancement available to make the coupon payments. Armed with this information, investors can judge whether the expected return is fairly priced in relation to the level of credit risk in the IO.

CDOs have not yet been stripped into separate IO and PO securities. Therefore, an IO investor does not face any real threat from amortization risk, which would truncate interest payments earlier than expected. While amortization could curtail interest payments, it would also increase the value of the PO. The PO, then, is a natural hedge to the IO.

PO Valuation

When valuing POs, it is useful to divide them into three distinct groups: those with little or no likelihood of receiving principal payments, those with little to no credit enhancement, and those with a significant level of credit enhancement.

POs with no principal value can be thought of as out-of-the-money options. Depending on the volatility of projected default rates, however, the PO may have some value.

For POs with little to no credit enhancement, investors should, again, look to assign different probabilities to potential loss rates. Using this information, they can calculate a probability-weighted return of principal to the PO. The value can be thought of as the premium on an option. POs with limited credit enhancement are typically a relatively small portion of the CDO's capital, a ratio that affects their volatility. Smaller classes are the most volatile, as they are the most frequently in or out of the money.

A PO with significant credit enhancement can be valued in much in the same way that a PIKable IO is viewed. The precise level of credit enhancement—which typically takes the form of excess spread and the bond's subordination level—should be determined. Investors should then focus on the expected loss from the portfolio's underlying collateral.

Assumptions Used in Valuation Analysis

The value of DCF analysis as a tool for arriving at appropriate valuations is the fact that the DCF analysis attempts to model the actual expected payment pattern of the CDO security. If the assumptions employed are reasonable based on available information and market conditions, the DCF analysis can provide a realistic expectation of actual performance and fair value.

DCF pricing models must take a range of factors into consideration. These include, among others in the following list, anticipated collateral default rates, recoveries on defaulted assets, the interest-rate environment, and collateral prepayment rates. While the model itself renders an objective analysis, the factors influencing the results require investors to make several assumptions.

Key Assumptions for Cash Flow Projections

1. Current capitalization of the CDO issuer
2. Priority of payments (allocations of cash received)
   - Allocation of principal proceeds and interest proceeds
   - Allocation of trading gains and premiums
   - Operation of collateral coverage tests

3. Assumed level of interest rates (e.g., LIBOR), to the extent that the assets and/or liabilities are floating rate
   - Use of a forward LIBOR curve or other rate scenarios
   - Evaluation of interest-rate risk in the structure
4. Structure of any interest-rate hedge agreements
5. Current portfolio characteristics
   - Use of actual collateral portfolio versus "weighted average" collateral metrics
   - Evaluation of distressed assets
6. Future characteristics of the portfolio based on reinvestment
   - Reinvestment assumptions
   - Change of average spread or coupon
   - Assumptions as to future asset prices
7. Average cash balance expected
   - Portion of the asset portfolio (on average) that may be uninvested
8. Ongoing administration fees and expenses
9. Structure of fees to the collateral manager, including any incentive or performance-based fees
10. Default and loss rates
    - Level and frequency of defaults
    - Realized trading losses and distressed sales
    - Recovery levels and timing of proceeds received on defaulted/distressed assets
11. Prepayment rates
    - Prepayment characteristics and expectations of the underlying assets
12. Call options
    - Likelihood of optional call by equity holders
13. Other items
    - Bond insurance fees
    - Contingent interest or step-up coupon tranches in capital structure
    - Reserve funds
    - Other cash diversion tests in addition to standard coverage tests
    - Other collateral valuation requirements (e.g., "CCC" haircut tests)

CHAPTER 11

Net Asset Value

The NAV technique approaches the valuation of CDOs by estimating the value that could be distributed to noteholders and equity holders in a termination scenario. It assumes that the asset portfolio is liquidated at current market value and the resulting proceeds are distributed to noteholders and equity holders in accordance with the priority of payments. Thus, the NAV valuation is complementary to the discounted cash flow valuation, which assumes that the deal remains outstanding to final maturity, and that the collateral continues to generate cash flows that are distributed to noteholders and equity holders according to the priority of payments.

The calculation is straightforward and looks at all sources of value in the asset portfolio, including the following:

- Current market value of collateral debt securities, including accrued interest
- Hedge agreements (swaps, caps, floors, and so on) at current market value or breakage cost (e.g., swap market values may be positive or negative to the CDO)
- Current cash balances of principal and interest collections

Once the realizable value of the asset portfolio has been determined, this value is compared to all outstanding classes of liabilities and equity (including accrued interest). The NAV of each class is computed by determining how much of the asset value can be distributed to such class in accordance with the priority of payments as specified in the indenture. Generally this means that any realized value from the asset portfolio is first distributed to the senior notes, then the remaining proceeds are distributed to the mezzanine notes, and, finally, any residual proceeds are distributed to the equity classes. The NAV (in percentage terms) is equal to the ratio of the distribution proceeds received to the par amount outstanding of the class being evaluated.

The NAV is a useful valuation method that is often used in conjunction with the discounted cash flow valuation, particularly in the following situations:

- Valuation of market value deals (which may be difficult, if not impossible, to analyze in a discounted cash flow framework that requires estimating future cash flows and trading gains).

- Deals in which an optional call scenario should be assessed as part of the valuation (here, any applicable call premiums for the liabilities should be included in the calculation).
- Distressed deals in which an event of default/liquidation scenario should be assessed as part of the valuation.
- Relative value of a deal versus comparable deals or versus "re-creation value." NAV can be a useful measure of the relative quality and extent of collateralization for a CDO security, particularly in the context of the relative value of secondary offerings and new issues.

While it is a widely used and informative valuation indicative, the NAV approach has certain limitations, including the following:

- Because it assumes an immediate liquidation of the collateral pool, the NAV ignores the considerable excess spread (the difference between asset yields and funding spreads) that is generated over time in a cash flow CDO, which is the primary economic basis for investing in a cash flow CDO.
- The NAV does not equate to the economic value that an investor may realize over time. Cash flow CDOs typically have limited trading flexibilities (e.g., annual turnover on the order of 20 percent) and are generally never required to liquidate (except in extreme event of default scenarios). As a result, the NAV does not necessarily equal the distributions that are likely to be paid to an investor over time.

The NAV is subject to mark-to-market volatility of the underlying assets, which may not be reflective of the intrinsic value of the CDO security (since CDOs are generally not required to liquidate positions). In other words, non-credit-related price volatility of the underlying portfolio may have a significant impact on the CDO NAV.

PARTIES TO THE CDO TRANSACTION
Collateral Manager

The primary function of the collateral manager, sometimes referred to as the portfolio or asset manager, is to sell investments in the collateral pool that may lose value, default, or become impaired, and to purchase investments with attractive yields and a favorable investment outlook. Therefore, the manager must possess a fundamental knowledge of the collateral as well as broad market trading abilities. Collateral managers are not given free rein to invest in any security, however; they are subject to certain rating agency and investment criteria as set forth in the deal's indenture. Of course, this responsibility applies only to actively managed structures and is not relevant to CDOs with unmanaged or static portfolios, where trading in the underlying assets is prohibited.

Investment Bank (Arranger, Underwriter, and Placement Agent)

The role of an investment bank is multidimensional and is crucial to the creation, but not the ongoing operation, of a CDO. Often, the same bank will serve as deal arranger, underwriter, and placement agent. Although these roles are related, each could be, but rarely is, performed by a separate firm. As the arranger, the investment bank facilitates conversations between parties that are interested in a CDO transaction. For example, the arranger will organize meetings between investors and a collateral manager in order to discuss a potential transaction, or the investment bank may advise the collateral manager concerning rating agency requirements or apprise the manager of the specific nuances of certain investors. As underwriter and placement agent, the investment bank is responsible for the orderly execution and delivery of the promised bonds. Usually the bank underwrites CDOs on a best efforts basis.

Trustee (Trustee, Custodian, Paying Agent)

Like the trustees of other securitized products, the trustee for a CDO transaction is custodian of the collateral and protects investors' security interests by ensuring that transaction covenants are honored. These responsibilities include an evaluation of the trade recommendations of the collateral manager in order to ensure compliance with deal covenants, the release or receipt of cash or securities (from trading activities, for example), the distribution of cash to investors, and the creation and distribution of deal surveillance reports, as well as other general administrative duties for the trust.

Rating Agencies

Moody's Investors Service, Standard & Poor's, and Fitch Ratings Ltd. assign credit ratings to different parts of the CDO capital structure based on their perception of the levels of risk. Factors considered include the riskiness of the underlying collateral, collateral manager trading restrictions, structural features governing the allocation of cash to investors, and credit enhancements such as those provided by monoline insurers. Qualitative aspects of the CDO transaction, such as the experience of the collateral manager and the manager's trading record, also influence rating assignments.

Investors

CDO investors are typically sophisticated institutional investors, such as insurance companies, money managers, banks, pension funds, hedge funds, and asset-backed commercial paper conduits. These investors are attracted to the diverse collateral pool supporting CDO transactions, as well as the relatively high yields and wider spreads compared to similarly rated corporate or ABS paper. Thus, these investors are generally already familiar with asset-backed and investment grade corporate securities, but they want exposure to these assets in a leveraged format. Some investors prefer CDOs that are managed by a collateral manager with specific product expertise, while others prefer a static but diverse ABS or corporate debt pool. CDO equity investors, who buy the most subordinate part of the CDO transaction, are typically seeking high yields and are comfortable with the risk profile associated with a highly levered investment. These investors tend to be insurance companies, high net worth individuals, and hedge funds.

Hedge Counterparty

The hedge counterparty is generally a highly rated investment or commercial bank that enters into an interest-rate swap, currency swap, liquidity swap, or some other type of basis swap for the purpose of removing non-credit-related risk from the CDO transaction.

Credit Enhancer

The credit enhancer is generally a monoline bond insurer that is paid an up-front and/or ongoing fee to insure a class of CDO securities against losses. Typically, any senior debt that ends up with credit enhancement would have an underlying rating of AAA, AA, or A; the credit enhancement wrap ensures a AAA rating on the security.

Special-Purpose Vehicle (Issuer)

The issuer of a CDO transaction is a bankruptcy-remote special-purpose vehicle (SPV) located in a tax-friendly jurisdiction. The SPV purchases the securities that will make up the collateral pool and issues CDO securities. Because the operation of the SPV is precisely defined in the indenture, there is no need for employees, and therefore it has none. Its function—to facilitate the transfer of cash from the assets to the investors—is purely mechanical.

WHAT ARE SYNTHETIC CDOs?

Synthetic CDOs are the result of an innovative combination of two technologies—the securitization techniques used by cash CDOs to transfer credit risk and credit derivatives—that enables the isolation of credit risk from other components of risk. Effectively, synthetic CDOs are CDOs using credit default swaps (CDS). Within that broad description, there is a wide variation in the underlying credit-risky assets, whether or not they are managed, the extent of associated funded issuance, and the motivation behind the risk transfer, each of which defines a particular type of synthetic CDO.

Single-Name CDS

As the basis for a discussion of how synthetic CDOs work, we revisit the basic mechanics of a credit default swap (Exhibit 11.6). A CDS is akin to an insurance policy that protects the buyer of protection against the loss of principal in an underlying asset when a credit event occurs. The protection buyer pays a premium, typically on a quarterly basis, to the protection seller until a credit event occurs or the contract matures, whichever is earlier. The underlying asset is defined by a reference obligation, which indicates the scope of the protection. When a credit event occurs, depending upon the settlement mechanism specified in the CDS contract, the buyer of protection delivers a reference obligation to the seller and either receives par in return (physical delivery) or receives the difference between the par amount of the reference obligation and

EXHIBIT 11.6

How a Typical CDS Works

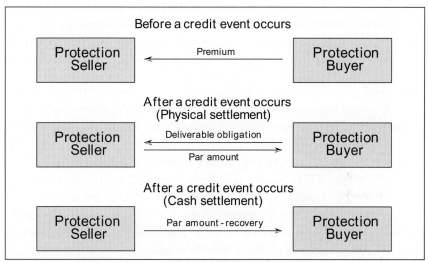

its recovery from the seller (cash settle). Standard credit events include bankruptcy, failure to pay, and restructuring of the debt.

Basket CDS

The next product in logical progression is the basket CDS. A basket CDS is a product through which the investor gains either long or short exposure to a relatively small basket of credits. The typical size of a basket ranges from four to ten credits. The investor is either selling or buying protection on the Nth credit in the basket to default, as with a plain vanilla credit default swap, except that the reference credit is a basket instead of a single name. Five-name baskets are most common, and protection is typically bought or sold on either a first-to-default (FTD) or a second-through-fifth default basis.

Suppose an investor sells FTD protection on a five-name basket of reference credits. The investor will receive a periodic payment (the "premium") in exchange for taking on the credit risk of the basket. If no credit events occur during the term of the basket default swap, the swap expires. If a credit event occurs during the term of the basket, the swap is terminated and the buyer of protection delivers the reference credit that experienced the credit event to the seller of protection in exchange for a par payment (equal to the notional amount of the swap). This process is analogous to a single-name credit default swap.

Settlement in case of default is done either through cash settlement or physical delivery, if the security qualifies for delivery under the terms of the underlying default swap on the credit. A credit event is defined the same way as it is in the single-name market, with investors having the option of choosing the restructuring definition. When a credit event occurs, the seller of protection for the basket is effectively losing par minus the recovery value of the defaulted asset.

A second-through-fifth default basket (assuming five credits) is analogous to a senior CDO tranche; any credit event after the first default triggers the contract. Unlike the situation with FTD baskets, the swap remains in effect until maturity or until all the covered credits default. The risk/return profile is similar to that of a CDO senior tranche in that a protection seller is protected from idiosyncratic risk, but is exposed to the risk of multiple credit defaults (also known as "tail risk"). However, a key difference is that the return profile of the protection seller in a second-through-fifth default basket is independent of the severity of the first loss.

From CDS to CDOs

A synthetic CDO may be thought of as a more complicated variation of a basket CDS, with exposure to a larger set of issuers, a more comprehensive capital structure, and more complex waterfall mechanisms. Much like cash CDOs, synthetic CDOs typically involve a special-purpose vehicle that acquires exposure to a collateral pool of credit-risky assets distributed to investors in a tranched form, with different tranches having varying levels of credit risk and correspondingly varying levels of return (Exhibit 11.7). Unlike cash CDOs, in which the SPV purchases the assets from the market or a sponsoring financial institution, in synthetic CDOs the SPV acquires the risk exposure through credit default swaps.

The SPV sells protection on the reference pool of assets to the sponsoring financial institution or other market participants and receives a premium for the risk being assumed. The credit risk so acquired is distributed to investors in different tranches, who receive a portion of the premium that depends upon the amount of credit risk assumed by each tranche. When a credit event occurs with respect to any asset in the collateral pool, the SPV pays the protection buyer an amount linked to the loss incurred on the asset. The loss is then passed on to investors in reverse order of seniority

EXHIBIT 11.7

How a Typical Synthetic CDO Works.

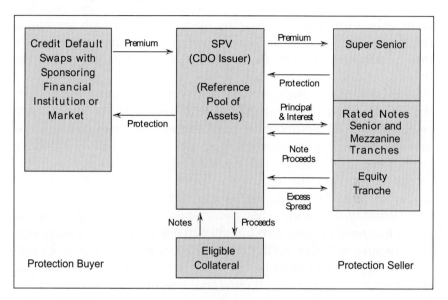

(i.e., the most junior tranche bears the first loss). Often, some of these tranches are funded tranches, which are analogous to credit-linked notes, with the only difference being that the risk and return are linked to a portfolio of assets as opposed to a single asset. The proceeds of the funded note issuance are invested in low-risk "eligible collateral."[1]

Thus, in a synthetic CDO, investors act as the sellers of protection on a pool of underlying assets, the sponsoring financial institution or the market participants are the buyers of protection, and the SPV is the intermediate vehicle that effectively distributes the cash flows involved. As a result, synthetic CDOs are the derivative counterparts of cash CDOs.

It is important to understand the terminology of attachment and detachment points[2] to follow the mechanics of synthetic CDOs. An attachment point, expressed either as a percentage or as an absolute value, defines the amount of losses in the reference pool of assets that need to occur before a particular tranche starts

---

[1] Eligible collateral consists mainly of investments in cash or government bonds or guaranteed investment contracts (GICs) issued by highly rated insurance companies.

[2] Also called the exhaustion point.

to experience losses. A detachment point, also expressed either as a percentage or as an absolute value, defines the amount of losses in the reference pool of assets that needs to occur for a complete loss of principal for that tranche. The size (width) of each tranche is the difference between the attachment and detachment points for that tranche and defines the maximum amount of losses that the tranche will experience.

Exhibit 11.8 illustrates a possible capital structure for a hypothetical synthetic CDO with high-yield unsecured corporate credit risk exposure. The numbers in parentheses are tranche widths. The equity tranche has an attachment point of 0 percent and a detachment point of 10 percent. This means that the first 10 percent of the credit losses from the underlying portfolio are absorbed by the equity tranche. Similarly, the super-senior tranche has an attachment point of 30 percent and a detachment point of 100 percent. All portfolio credit losses exceeding 30 percent are borne by the super-senior tranche. If the portfolio experiences losses equal to 15 percent, the equity and BB tranches would be wiped out, and the BBB tranche would lose half of its notional amount.

E X H I B I T   1 1 . 8

Capital Structure of a Hypothetical Synthetic CDO.

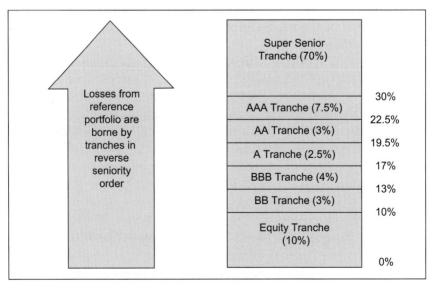

Note: The ratings and the capital structure shown above are merely for illustration purposes and do not represent an actual transaction.

Note: The ratings and the capital structure shown in Exhibit 11.8 are merely for illustration purposes and do not represent an actual transaction.

Funded versus Unfunded[3]

Unfunded portfolio credit default swaps are the most basic of all synthetic CDOs (see Exhibit 11.9). The protection buyer enters into a CDS on a specific portfolio of reference entities with the SPV, which in turn obtains protection by entering into CDS on a tranched basis with the investors, who are the ultimate sellers of protection. The CDS with investor(s) in each tranche defines the attachment and detachment points and the credit events. As sellers of protection, each tranche receives a fixed spread that is applied to the tranche size. As losses occur, the sellers of protection make loss payments to the SPV in the reverse order of seniority, and these are passed on to the protection buyer.

The structure of the funded synthetic CDO is more complicated (Exhibit 11.10). In funded tranches, the CDO investor pays the notional amount of the tranche at deal inception, and losses caused

EXHIBIT 11.9

Structure of a Typical Unfunded Synthetic CDO.

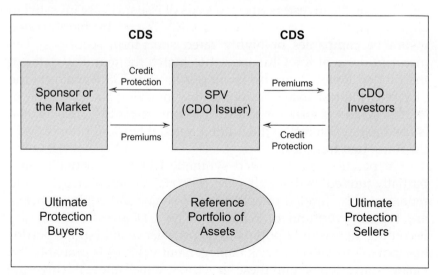

---

[3] The diagrammatic representations used in this section have been adapted from "Moody's Approach to Rating Synthetic CDOs," Moody's Investors Service, July 29, 2003.

EXHIBIT 11.10

Structure of a Typical Funded Synthetic CDO.

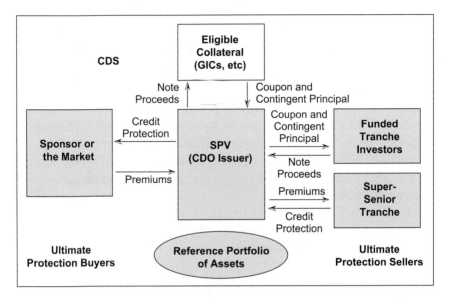

by any credit events result in a principal writedown. Throughout the life of the transaction, the investor receives LIBOR/EURIBOR plus a spread that reflects the riskiness of the tranche. The amounts paid by tranche investors (the proceeds of issuance) are invested in eligible collateral—typically, either GICs issued by highly rated insurance companies or highly rated short-term securities. The maturity dates of the GICs are set to match the maturity dates of the funded notes. Premium income from the CDS written by the SPV and interest income received by investing the proceeds in eligible collateral form the source of income to the SPV; this income is used to pay interest to the funded noteholders and premiums to the unfunded tranches.

In practice, most funded synthetic CDOs are actually only partially funded, in that only parts of the CDO capital structure are represented by funded tranches. Super-senior and equity tranches are typically unfunded. Single-tranche CDOs (ST CDOs) are becoming increasingly popular. The prevalence of bespoke portfolios looking for effective risk management vehicles is probably the major motivation behind these structures, which allow the investor to customize the amount of credit risk exposure to assume or lay off by picking the reference pool as well as the attachment and detachment points.

CDS INDICES AND TRANCHES OF CDS INDICES

What Is a CDS Index?

A CDS index is simply a standard portfolio of equally weighted single-name CDS. Just as single-name credit default swaps provide default protection on the underlying asset, CDS indices provide default protection on each single-name obligor in the underlying portfolio (see Exhibit 11.11).

The protection buyer makes fixed quarterly payments to the protection seller for the duration of the contract, or until a credit event (as described later in this section) occurs. A buyer of protection on a CDS index is implicitly paying the same premium on all the names that constitute the index.

Whenever there is a credit event on any of the names in the index, the protection buyer has the right to sell the defaulted bond to the protection seller at its par value. The defaulted entity is removed from the index, and the contract continues with a reduced notional amount for its remaining term.

The first set of CDS indices (Trac-X and iBoxx) was launched in 2003. These coexisted as competing families of indices until 2004, when they were merged to form one new set of indices called DJ

EXHIBIT 11.11

CDS Index Economics.

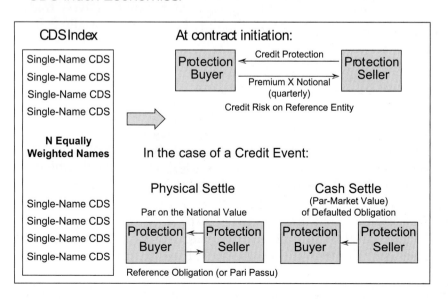

CDX [North America and Emerging Markets (EM)] and DJ iTraxx (Europe, Australia, and Asia). Since then, these CDS indices have become one of the most liquid trading instruments in the credit derivatives world and have been mainly responsible for the increase in liquidity and depth of the tranched credit risk market. The standardized nature of these CDS indices makes them easy to trade, and they have attracted a diverse investor base to this market. Investors in these indices can implement directional and relative value trades, diversify their portfolios with specific credit exposures, and also utilize the indices for hedging and rebalancing correlation portfolios.

CDS Index Characteristics

Composition
Indices or subindices in the CDS market have been grouped based on various attributes, such as geographical regions (North America, Europe, EM, and so on), ratings (investment grade, high-yield, B, BB, and so on), and industry groups (financials, industrials, and so on). These classifications have given investors a myriad of options in terms of their preferred credit exposure, and are one of the underlying reasons for the increased liquidity in these instruments.

Static Portfolio
When a particular CDS index is initiated, the most actively traded CDS names in the universe of qualified entities are usually included. The index then remains static until maturity (unless an entity defaults). Importantly, all names are equally weighted in the index rather than being weighted by market capitalization.

Standardized Tenors and Payment Dates
The CDS index market trades based on standard payment dates (the 20th of March, June, September, and December of every year) and standard maturities (5 years and 10 years are usually the most liquid, although contract maturities from 1 to 10 years exist).

Rollover
A new "on-the-run" index of benchmark maturity is launched every six months. The on-the-run index typically contains the

latest, most liquid names in the required subset of single-name CDS. The market continues to trade the previous series of indices but, as with off-the-run Treasuries, with reduced liquidity.

Premiums

Premiums are paid every quarter on the given payment dates. However, an accrued premium is paid by the protection buyer in the event of default if the default does not happen on one of the standard payment dates. Moreover, if the contract is initiated between payment dates, the protection buyer makes only a pro rata payment of premium for the remaining period until the next payment date.

Fixed Coupon

CDS indices are launched with a fixed premium or spread [this gives the index a zero net present value (NPV) at issuance]. This is the premium paid by the protection buyer every quarter on a running basis until the maturity of the index. Any subsequent change in the NPV of the index (due to changes in valuations of the underlying single-name CDS) is accounted for by the requirement of an up-front payment when the contract is initiated.

Funded and Unfunded

CDS indices trade in both funded and unfunded forms. While the unfunded version is just a multiname CDS, in the funded version, the protection seller pays an up-front notional amount that is invested in a pool of appropriate securities. This pool is used as collateral by the protection buyer, thereby eliminating any exposure to counterparty risk in the contract.

Committed Market Making

A global group of broker/dealers makes markets in standardized CDS indices, and bid-offer spreads are fairly tight, especially on the most actively traded contracts. For example, bid-offer spreads on the five-year CDX.NA.IG have been in the range of 0.5 to 5 basis points (bps) for an index level around 60 bps.

Credit Events

The definition of credit events differs between U.S. and European CDS indices. U.S. indices consider only bankruptcy and failure to pay as credit events that trigger default on any underlying single-name obligor in an index. Restructuring is not included as a credit event, even though most of the underlying single-name CDS contracts in the U.S. indices trade with modified restructuring as a credit event. On the other hand, European indices trade with the same credit events as the underlying CDS contracts, which include bankruptcy, failure-to-pay, and modified restructuring.

Benchmark CDS Indices

At a high level, CDS indices are set up geographically, with at least one index for each continent. These indices, in turn, have various subindices based on industry subsectors and ratings. The names making up each index are identified through a polling process administered by Dow Jones or iTraxx, in which names are polled from participating dealers. Once the list of single-name obligors is chosen, the fixed spread on the index is calculated by obtaining quotes from participating dealers, leaving out the outliers, and taking an average of the rest.

CDX.NA.IG (North American Investment Grade Index)

This index is made up of the 125 equally weighted North American investment grade names with the highest volumes in the single-name CDS market. The first series of this index was launched on October 21, 2003 (CDX.NA.IG 1), and since then it has been rolled into a new series every six months. The current "on-the-run" series—CDX.NA.IG 5—was launched on September 20, 2005. The most liquid maturities in this index are the five-year (maturing June 20, 2010) and the ten-year (maturing June 20, 2015). The rules of the index specify that each series will be launched on September 20 and March 20 (or on the next business day if that day is a holiday) of each year. The broad index is further segmented into various subindices:

HVOL (High Volatility Index). This consists of the 30 names from the broader index that have the widest five-year CDS spreads. This is the most liquid subindex in the investment grade sector and gives investors exposure to the "high beta" portion of the investment grade index.

Industry sector indices. The broad index also has subindices based on the industry sector classification of the single-

name obligors in the broader index. There are five such
subindices:
Financials: 24 financial-sector names.
Consumer: 34 consumer-sector names.
Energy: 15 energy-sector names.
Industrial: 30 major industrial names.
TMT: 22 names in technology, media, and telecom.

CDX.NA.HY (North American High Yield Index)

This index comprises 100 equally weighted North American
subinvestment grade obligors. The first series of this index was
launched along with the investment grade index on October 21,
2003, and since then it too has rolled into a new series every six
months. The current "on-the-run" series—CDX.NA.HY 4—was
launched on March 21, 2005. The most liquid maturities traded are
again the five-year (maturing June 20, 2010) and the ten-year
(maturing June 20, 2015). The broad index is further segmented into
various subindices, all of which are quoted in dollar price terms.

1. B: 44 names rated single-B.
2. BB: 43 names rated double-B.
3. HB: 30 high-beta names in the high-yield index.

The one major difference between the HY and IG indices is that
the HY index is quoted in dollar price terms, not in spread terms.
For example, a high-yield CDS index with an NPV of zero will be
quoted at par, while an index with a negative NPV will be quoted
at a discount.

CDX.NA.XO (North American Crossover Index)

This consists of the 35 equally weighted U.S. entities with the highest
CDS volumes and with credit ratings that are either

1. A crossover 5B rating (i.e., a BBB/Baa rating by one of
   S&P/Moody's and a BB/Ba rating by the other)
2. A 4B rating (i.e., a BB/Ba rating by both S&P and Moody's)
3. A BB/Ba rating by one of S&P/Moody's and no rating by
   the other

iTraxx Europe (European Investment Grade Index)

This index consists of the 125 equally weighted European
investment grade names with the highest CDS volumes in the

single-name CDS market. This replaced the previous DJ TRAC-X Europe 100 and the iBoxx Diversified indices with a standard trading platform. The broad index is further segmented into various subindices.

1. *iTraxx HiVOL (high-volatility index)*. This consists of the 30 nonfinancial names in the broad index with the widest five-year CDS spreads. It gives exposure to the "high beta" portion of the investment grade index.

2. *Sector indices*. The broad index also has subindices based on the industry sector classification of the underlying single-name obligors in the broad index. There are seven such subindices:

   (i) Financials: 25 financial-sector names.
   (ii) Consumer cyclicals: 15 cyclical consumer-sector names.
   (iii) Consumer noncyclicals: 15 noncyclical consumer-sector names.
   (iv) Autos: 10 auto-sector names.
   (v) Energy: 20 energy-sector names.
   (vi) ndustrial: 20 major industrial-sector names.
   (vii) TMT: 20 names in technology, media, and telecom.

iTraxx Corporate

This consists of 52 of the largest, most liquid nonfinancial names from the iBoxx EUR corporate bond index. The constituents of this index are not equally weighted but weighted by duration and market value. The names with the highest multiples of duration and market value in the corporate bond index are included in the iTraxx Corporate, thus giving exposure to the high-beta investment grade nonfinancial names in Europe.

iTraxx Crossover

This consists of 40 of the most liquid nonfinancial names with at least $100 million of publicly traded debt and rated BBB-/Baa3 or lower with a negative outlook. Entities eligible for this index also have a spread at least twice the average spread of the 100 nonfinancial constituents of iTraxx Europe (as of the next rollover date), subject to a maximum of 1,250 bps or 35 percent up front. This gives an investor exposure to the high-yield nonfinancial sector of European names.

iTraxx CJ (Japanese Corporates)

This index consists of 50 equally weighted names selected from among the most liquid CDS names in Japan, with a maximum of 10 names for each market sector.

iTraxx Asia (Asia ex-Japan Corporates)

This index consists of 50 equally weighted names from the rest of Asia (excluding Japan), again selected on the basis of the highest volumes in single-name CDS. It includes both investment grade and noninvestment grade names. It includes regional subindices that allow investors to achieve credit exposure on names from a particular region of the continent:

1. Korea: 10 Korean corporates.
2. Greater China: 16 names with at least two each from China, Hong Kong, and Taiwan.
3. Rest of Asia: 23 names, including names from India, Malaysia, Philippines, Indonesia, Singapore, and Thailand.

iTraxx Australia (Australian Corporates)

This is a portfolio of 25 equally weighted credit default swaps on Australian entities, again based on the most liquid names from that region in the CDS market.

CDX.EM (Emerging Market Sovereigns)

This is composed of 15 sovereign issuers from three regions: (1) Latin America, (2) Asia, and (3) Eastern Europe, the Middle East, and Africa. It provides investors with credit exposure to sovereign risk from these regions.

CDX.EM.Diversified (Sovereign and Corporate)

This index is composed of sovereign and corporate issuers from three regions: (1) Latin America, (2) Asia, and (3) Eastern Europe, the Middle East, and Africa (EEMEA). It comprises 40 names. Initial compositions have consisted of 8 to 12 corporate issuers and 28 to 32 sovereign issuers, with the following regional breakdown:

1. Latin America: between 10 and 15 initially, then between 10 and 20 at each roll.
2. EEMEA: between 10 and 15 initially, then between 10 and 20 at each roll.
3. Asia: between 10 and 15 initially, then between 10 and 20 at each roll.

Over the past few months, the market has witnessed a growing interest in a GLOBOXX portfolio (an equally weighted combination of the CDX.NA.IG and the iTraxx Europe portfolios), although no standard portfolio has emerged as yet.

Tranches of Standard CDS Indices

A CDS index tranche involves a bilateral contract that transfers a portion of the credit risk of the index portfolio from the protection buyer to the protection seller. The main advantage of CDS index tranches is that they are on standardized index pools and have standard attachment and detachment points (Exhibit 11.12).

The risk transference is limited to losses in a specified band, which is defined in terms of a percentage of the reference portfolio notional amount, that is, by its attachment and exhaustion[4] points. The attachment point determines the credit enhancement or subordination of the tranche. The exhaustion point determines the point beyond which the tranche gets exhausted, i.e., loses all its notional amount. The difference between these two points gives the thickness of the tranche.

The protection buyer pays for credit protection in the form of either a running spread or a combination of an up-front payment

E X H I B I T 1 1 . 1 2

Index Tranche Mechanics.

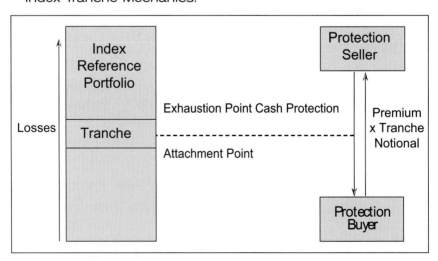

[4] Also called the detachment point.

and a running spread. An up-front payment plus a running spread is common for tranches that are most likely to incur default losses, such as first-loss pieces. Other tranche characteristics, such as maturity, payment dates, credit events, and accrual of premium, mirror those of the underlying standardized CDS index.

The protection seller compensates the buyer for any losses in the index portfolio that breach the tranche's attachment point. Defaults exceeding the tranche's attachment point decrease the notional amount of the tranche on which the running spread is paid. Protection payments end either when the contract matures or when portfolio losses exceed the exhaustion point of the tranche, whichever comes first.

Tranches have been issued on several CDS indices, but the more liquid ones are those on the Dow Jones CDX.NA.IG index in the United States and on the iBoxx in Europe. Over the last year, standard tranches on the CDX.NA.HY and iTraxx Asia and Japan have started improving in liquidity as well. Exhibit 11.13 presents a list of standard tranches on these indices. Although these are the standard tranches quoted by dealers on a daily basis, tranches with nonstandard attachment points like 8 to 10 percent are also traded in the market.

In all the investment grade indices, the first-loss 0 to 3 percent tranche is structured with an up-front payment in addition to a running spread. The first two tranches on the high yield index (0 to 10 percent and 10 to 15 percent) trade with only an up-front payment and no running spread. After the initial transaction, as in the case of standard CDS indices, a tranche can be traded either by unwinding the contract or by assigning it to a new counterparty.

EXHIBIT 11.13

Standard CDS Index Tranches.

North America Investment Grade	Europe Investment Grade	Asia (ex. Japan) Investment Grade	Japan Investment Grade	North America High Yield
0–3%	0–3%	0–3%	0–3%	0–10%
3–7%	3–6%	3–6%	3–6%	10–15%
7–10%	6–9%	6–9%	6–9%	15–25%
10–15%	9–12%	9–12%	9–12%	25–35%
15–30%	12–22%	12–22%	12–22%	35–100%
3–100%	3–100%	3–100%	3–100%	

For example, the 3 to 7 percent CDX.IG tranche has an attachment point of 3 percent, an exhaustion point of 7 percent, and a tranche width of 4 percent. Assuming an index notional amount of $1 billion, the tranche will start sustaining losses when losses in the underlying index portfolio exceed $30 million, and its notional amount would be reduced to zero at $70 million of losses. This clearly implies that the closer the tranche attachment point is to 0 percent (first loss), the higher the probability of the tranche sustaining losses is. To compensate for this risk, spreads tend to be higher on tranches that are lower in the capital structure. In addition, the thinner the tranche width, the higher the probability of the tranche being exhausted once it starts getting written down. So, all else being equal, a thinner tranche would tend to have a higher spread to compensate an investor for the higher risk. Premiums on standard tranches are also determined by the forces of market supply and demand.

It is important to note that tranche attachment points signify a percentage of *losses* on the portfolio notional amount and not the percentage of *defaults* in the portfolio. Taking the same example, the 3 to 7 percent tranche can withstand defaults up to 5 percent of the portfolio (the 3 percent attachment point divided by an assumed loss rate given default of 60 percent) or defaults in 6 names out of the 125.

SYNTHETIC STRUCTURED FINANCE CBOs

During 2005, the market began applying many of the same tools used in corporate synthetic CDOs to the resecuritization of structured finance (SF) bonds.[5] The standardization of ISDA documentation for SF bonds[6] is facilitating this growth, despite their more complicated credit event profile compared to corporates. From a collateral standpoint, synthetic SF CBOs look just like their cash flow cousins, which reference HELABS (Home Equity Loan ABS), CMBS, CDOs, and other ABS. By mid–2005, most cash flow SF CBOs were utilizing 20 to 35 percent buckets for synthetics; this section focuses on the 100 percent synthetic deals.

[5] When we refer to "structured finance CBOs," we exclude the 300+ outstanding synthetic ST CDOs, which have as reference a basket of "risky" corporate synthetic CDOs and low-risk, senior-rated SF bonds.
[6] On June 21, 2005, after 18 months of work, the ISDA published its "Dealer Form" for CDS based on HEL ABS and CMBS.

Investors can expect significant growth in the synthetic SF CBO market primarily as a result of cheaper super-senior funding and ease of collateral sourcing:

- *Cheaper funding.* Whereas super-senior cash funding costs 27 bps, as of mid–2005, reinsurers and monolines typically charge, on average, 12 bps for this off-balance sheet risk. In effect, the participation of derivative investors saves the structure money by delinking the funding from the credit risk. The synthetic format has an excess spread advantage of approximately 10 bps in mezzanine deals and 13 bps in senior deals.[7]

- *Ease of sourcing collateral.* As any SF bond can be used as a reference synthetically, no matter where the physical bonds may be parked, there is virtually no limit on the availability of collateral. Furthermore, synthetic ramp-up can be completed in a matter of weeks instead of months.

This article covers the following issues:

- Synthetic technology applies to all SF CBO sectors.
- Synthetics benefit from efficiencies, including cheaper funding and ease of collateral sourcing.
- A sizable synthetic-cash pickup is largely due to a complexity and liquidity premium.
- The major risk in synthetics is the potential mismatch between credit event definitions and more standard measures of default.

Synthetic Technology Applies to All SF CBO Sectors

The following three sectors are the areas where synthetic technology is likely to have the largest impact.

Mezzanine SF CBOs

Mezzanine deals, which use as reference BBB-average pools of SF bonds, are the largest beneficiaries of standardizing documentation and ease of collateral sourcing:

---

[7] This calculation assumes a super-senior size of 90 percent in senior deals and 70 percent in mezzanine deals.

- Mezzanine deals benefit the most from the new ISDA standards. It was the lack of any documentation standard that had impeded the development of this market in the first place. Defining credit events is a far more delicate matter for lower-rated reference obligations than for higher-rated bonds.
- Availability of collateral (which is largely limited in cash deals to the amount of BBB-rated HELABS new-issue supply) is not a constraint. Synthetics can concentrate on any vintage; whereas cash deals are forced to concentrate on whatever deals happen to be in the primary market because of the limited secondary trading of SF bonds. Some arrangers or managers use the bid list process to accumulate numerous single-name CDS positions at one time.

Senior SF CBOs (High-Grade)

Senior deals, which use AA-average SF bond pools as reference, benefit the most from cheaper super-senior funding. In senior deals, up to 90 percent of the capital structure is super-AAA (versus about 70 percent in mezzanine deals). The estimated 13-bp pickup in excess spread can potentially double the senior SF CBO equity internal rate of return (IRR), assuming the average 67 times leverage factor and no other changes to the capital structure.

Hybrid Cash/Synthetic Mezzanine

Hybrid cash-synthetic SF CBOs enjoy the same benefits as pure synthetics—greatly expanded collateral supply and even potentially cheaper funding—but on a slightly smaller scale. Hybrid deals are distinguished from cash deals with large synthetic buckets as follows:

- Cash deals with 20 to 30 percent synthetic buckets mostly focus on the structure's ability to easily source premium HEL ABS at par using CDS.
- Hybrids with, say, 60 percent synthetic allocations additionally achieve cheaper funding by issuing a 60 percent unfunded super-senior swap, as opposed to 70 to 90 percent in a pure synthetic.

Hybrids are a newer development borrowing from an idea used years ago in the corporate space to marry the benefits of synthetics and cash.

Synthetics Offer More Efficiency than Cash

Synthetic SF CBOs have a lot in common with their cash cousins in that they both use structured finance bonds as reference. However, the synthetic format differs from cash largely in its improved structural and collateral sourcing efficiency:

Structural Efficiency

- The CDO uses the assets as reference synthetically instead of owning the actual physical bonds.
- Super-senior funding is about 15 bps cheaper in synthetics. With the synthetic structure, the cost to buy *unfunded* protection on super-senior risk directly from reinsurers is 10 to 12 bps, compared to the 27-bp *funded* spread demanded by AAA cash investors.
- Synthetic SF CBOs have mostly been static, with initial allocations arranged by dealers and subsequently negotiated by investors (e.g., bespoke). However, substantial growth is expected in independently managed, rule-based synthetics in the near term.
- Synthetics can be issued on a single-tranche basis, allowing investors to time their entry into the market more easily. Any investor along the capital structure can invest without waiting for multiple investors to agree on a full capital structure.

Collateral Sourcing Efficiency

- Synthetics allow instantaneous ramp-up. Therefore, investors know the entire portfolio composition and pool spread at pricing.
- Synthetics enable the CDO to maximize risk-adjusted pool returns by opening up security selection to the entire investable universe:
  - Buy risk in the secondary market that it is not possible to source physically.
  - Obtain desired allocations in the primary market.
  - Have a dependable source of risk when collateral volume slows.

Other

- Synthetics allow buckets for capital structure arbitrage
  and shorting (in case the credit cycle turns).

The Synthetic-Cash Basis Is Positive and Volatile

Over the second half of 2004 and the first half of 2005, the synthetic-cash basis[8] averaged 17 bps in junior AAAs and approximately 30 bps in the AA, A, and BBB tranches. The synthetic-cash basis has had somewhat of a roller-coaster ride, having risen in the second half of 2004, fallen in the first half of 2005, and risen again as we entered the second half of 2005.

The synthetic pickup to cash is largely due to a complexity and liquidity premium, since every deal has slightly different documentation:

- *Complexity premium.* The investor is paid to understand divergent credit event language and to size how any mismatch between synthetic and cash definitions of default is reconciled with any additional credit enhancement.
- *Liquidity premium.* The variation in documentation from deal to deal makes this a less homogeneous sector and therefore more time-consuming to trade. Therefore, investors demand extra spread for this incremental liquidity risk. Such intrasector heterogeneity is likely to persist because of the wide variety of underlying SF bond structures.

On average, the rating agencies are doing a reasonable job of accounting for any risk of loss greater than the actual bond's risk. However, agencies are likely to be doing a better job of accounting for these differences in some deals than in others. If the agencies do not account for any additional risks, the market should command an offsetting return.

Relative to cash deals, there is value in synthetics depending on the risk/return trade-off:

---

[8] The synthetic-cash basis is simply the synthetic spread minus the generic new-issue cash spread. Synthetic spreads were calculated based on the 14 visibly priced dealer-arranged nonmanaged transactions issued between July 2004 and July 2005.

- *Return:* The synthetic-cash basis.
- *Risk:* To what extent does any additional credit enhancement offset any incremental default risk?

Credit Event Definitions May Vary from Cash

The major risk that is unique to the synthetic CDO structure is credit event definitions, which can be more liberal than those in the cash structure:

- While credit event language is evolving, documentation varies from one synthetic SF CBO to another.
- While some definitions introduce new risks that may make SF bond defaults appear less back-ended than they are known to be, others reduce risk by capping the amount that a bond may PIK at the CDS premium.[9]

Some synthetic mezzanine SF CBOs introduce new credit events that are not part of the pay-as-you-go (PAYGO) framework established in the single-name SF synthetic market. (PAYGO was designed to allow the synthetic to virtually mimic cash flows on the underlying SF bond, much like a total return swap.)

As of July 2005, material credit events that introduced risks into synthetic mezzanine SF CBOs that would not necessarily exist if the bond was owned outright included the following:

- *Distressed rating trigger.* If the collateral security is downgraded to CCC or CC (depending on the document), the contract is cash settled using a specified dealer-poll valuation process. However, this language is typical in the PAYGO single-name market. According to Moody's,[10] only 8 percent of CDOs have been downgraded to Ca or below and not suffered a PIK event. Therefore, there is a 92 percent probability that a rating event set at the Ca level would be triggered only in cases where the CDO has PIKed one period at a minimum.

---

[9] To avoid negative carry, where investors pay an interest shortfall amount ("payment in kind" or "PIK") greater than the CDS premium that they receive, some contracts cap the PIK amount at the CDS premium.

[10] See "Default & Loss Rates of U.S. CDOs: 1993–2003," Moody's Investors Service, March 9, 2005.

- *Undercollateralization ("implied writedown").* Writedown credit events are typically settled in the PAYGO format by the protection seller simply paying the buyer the amount of the writedown in each relevant period. The implied writedown is the amount, if any, by which the reference bond's principal plus any pari passu notes plus all the senior notes exceed the collateral pool balance. Whereas writedowns for HEL ABS are explicitly defined in the bond's own documents, CDO writedowns typically are not. Therefore, by putting CDOs on an equal footing with HEL ABS, the synthetic language introduces an event of default that does not exist in the CDO itself.

- *Material PIK event.* Many contracts include a requirement whereby PIKing for a period of two or three years requires cash settlement via the valuation process. This event, of course, introduces the risk that investors will suffer a valuation loss in addition to lost cash flows from prior PAYGO payments to the protection buyer. However, the cure rate for CDOs that PIKed for any amount of time is only 5 percent, according to the same Moody's report cited earlier. Therefore, it is extremely unlikely that a CDO would ever survive a material PIK event anyway.

Following the June 2005 release of ISDA standardized documentation, the synthetic SF CBO market is poised to grow enormously. The efficiencies that synthetic technology brought to the corporate CDO market are just as relevant for SF CBOs. Tradable synthetic ABS and CMBS indices are likely to be launched in the second half of 2005, and standardized tranches thereafter. The major difference between corporate synthetics and the synthetic SF CBO market is that in the latter, managers will play a larger role, as far fewer investors are familiar with SF bonds than with corporates.

Investors that do the necessary homework regarding the differences between cash and synthetic structures stand to gain the most. Their relative value analysis should largely consider whether or not the additional spread compensates for any marginal default risks after taking into consideration credit enhancement differences between cash and synthetic structures.

SYNTHETIC CDOs, MARKET PARTICIPANTS, AND INVESTMENT STRATEGIES

Synthetic CDOs are one of the key products in the structured credit world. In the past several years, synthetic CDOs have evolved through different stages, from full-capital-structure deals to single tranches. Their issuance has exceeded the issuance of cash CDOs. Today, synthetic CDOs are firmly established as a credit investment and hedging tool. In this section, we discuss the factors driving the growth of the synthetic CDO market and the main differences between synthetic CDOs and cash products. We also describe the participants in the market and the main investment strategies followed by hedge funds and real-money investors in the synthetic CDO market.

Motivation behind Synthetic CDO Products

Synthetic CDOs gained their popularity because of the variety of advantages that they offer over cash CDOs and other related credit investments. We discuss these differences in greater detail later in this section, but the advantages of synthetics are primarily their ease of structuring, their ability to separate funding (interest-rate component) and risk transfer (credit risk component), and the versatility that they offer to investors to express different views on the market.

No Need to Place a Full Capital Structure

Instead of structuring a full-capital-structure CDO, many synthetic CDOs are issued in single-tranche form, in which each transaction is a transfer between the seller and the buyer of protection of the credit risk on a specific part of the capital structure.

Flexibility of Bespokes

The synthetic CDO market is separated into flow tranche products, such as index-linked tranches, and bespoke (customized) tranches, which are privately or publicly placed synthetic CDOs with structures that are designed to fit individual investors' needs. The bespoke tranche market has developed at a rapid pace. Buy-and-hold investors, who focus on senior bespoke tranches, use these products not just as leveraged investments, but also to diversify their positions.

Liquidity of Index Tranches

Dealers use index-linked tranches to hedge their positions in bespoke products. The liquidity of index-linked tranches has recently improved significantly across the term structure. Credit investors, especially hedge funds, make relative value plays by taking on long or short leveraged positions or express directional view strategies.

Comparison to Cash CDOs

Synthetic and cash CDOs have many similarities, as they both offer leveraged exposure to a diversified basket of credits. Synthetic CDOs use as reference credit default swaps that are standardized bilateral contracts, whereas cash CDOs are more akin to miniature banks, financing real assets and distributing cash flows. The following are some of the main differences between the two types of products.

Separation of Credit Risk from Other Types of Risk

Synthetic structures are not exposed to interest-rate risk, prepayment risk, and other types of risk that are common to cash CDOs. In particular, synthetic CDOs allow investors to disconnect their choice of interest-rate duration from their choice of credit duration.

Sourcing Collateral: Asset Diversity and Speed of Ramp-Up

With synthetic credit risk transfer technology, originators are not limited by the ability to physically acquire the collateral assets. Moreover, synthetic CDOs can be structured quickly, as they do not require a ramp-up period. Yet, the need of dealers to hedge single tranches typically restricts the names that can be included in synthetic deals to credits traded in the single-name CDS market.

Single-Tranche versus Full-Capital-Structure Deals

Unlike cash CDOs, in which the entire capital structure is sold, synthetic CDOs are usually structured as single-tranche deals, in which the risk of only a limited part of the capital structure is sold to investors. Dealers hold the residual risks (e.g., spreads, defaults, and correlation), which are aggregated and hedged in their correlation book. Full-capital-structure synthetic CDOs are rare, but they are attractive for dealers, as they prevent imbalances in the dealers' correlation books.

Simplified CDO Structures

Standard synthetic CDOs are much simpler than cash CDOs, as they involve only the distribution of default losses. Cash CDOs rely on complex cash flow waterfalls and various technical features, such as interest coverage and overcollateralization tests, prepayments, and so on. The simplicity of synthetics has enabled structurers and investors to use simple models with only a limited number of inputs (CDS spreads, correlations, and tranching details) for pricing and risk management. Proper modeling of cash CDOs requires a detailed knowledge of the underlying pool of assets and of the cash flow distribution rules.

CUSTOMIZATION AND EASY EXECUTION

The simplicity of synthetic CDOs allows them to be customized in terms of size and attachment points for each individual tranche. Investors can select their reference portfolios and choose the credit exposure that best fits into their strategy.

Static versus Managed Structures

Index-linked tranches are static in nature, but bespoke tranches can be managed. In private transactions, investors can play the role of the manager if the structure includes credit substitution rights. Publicly placed synthetic deals usually have an external manager.

Liquid and Transparent Market for Standard Index-Linked Tranches

Index-linked tranches are among the most liquid products in the credit space. With the growth of CDS indices, use of new asset classes as references, and the increasing number of liquid tenors, the expectation is that the index-linked tranche market will continue to expand. Derivatives using index-linked tranches as references are also likely to be introduced in coming years. No such benchmark exists for cash CDOs.

Shorting the Credit Risk in a Leveraged Form

Unlike cash CDOs, which are primarily buy-and-hold investments, investors can take long or short positions in synthetic tranches. The synthetic CDO market provides a variety of different directional and hedging investment opportunities. Short buckets can also be included in bespoke synthetic CDOs to mitigate the effect of a credit market sell-off.

Market Volatility

The accounting treatment of derivatives and their perceived mark-to-market volatility can be major obstacles for certain types of investors. As synthetic tranches are marked to market and largely held by leveraged accounts, the tranche market can experience strong technical periods leading to significant repricings, as witnessed in May 2005.

Market Participants

One of the main attractions of CDOs (cash or synthetic) is that they enable investors to split the choice of credit risk for the actual investment (the tranche) from that of the underlying assets. For example, an investor may want to buy triple-A paper, but based on double-B collateral. This property of CDOs makes them accessible to a very large section of the investment community, from risk-averse pension funds to yield-hungry hedge funds (see Exhibit 11.14).

Hedge Funds and Proprietary Desks

Investors at the bottom end of the capital structure (equity and very junior mezzanine tranches) are primarily hedge funds and

EXHIBIT 11.14

Schematic Distribution of Synthetic CDO Tranche Investors

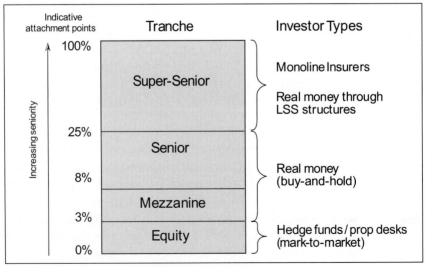

Source: Citigroup.

bank proprietary desks. These investors are willing to take first-loss risk against the expectation of high returns, in some cases in excess of 10 percent per annum. These investors mark their positions to market and tend to delta-hedge them, either by buying single-name protection or by shorting an index or a mezzanine tranche.

Real-Money Investors

"Real-money" investors (asset managers, banks, insurance companies, and pension funds) primarily focus on mezzanine and senior tranches, which are safer than equity tranches, but offer lower returns. These investors tend to buy and hold and are often rating-sensitive, and so are attracted by the higher spreads typically offered by synthetic CDOs compared with cash products with identical ratings.

Dealers and Other Market Participants

One of the key differences between cash and synthetic CDOs is that synthetics most often are not full-capital-structure deals, but rather single-tranche CDOs. This means that structurers do not sell all the risk of the underlying portfolio of CDS, but only a portion, for example, the 3 to 9 percent tranche. Strong demand for mezzanine tranche risk from real-money investors can lead dealers to hold significant positions. Exhibit 11.15 illustrates schematically the left-over position of a dealer that has sold a mezzanine tranche to an investor in two extreme scenarios.

In the first scenario, the dealer sells the mezzanine tranche risk to the investor and does not hedge its position, resulting in a net short mezzanine position. In the second scenario, the mezzanine position is hedged with the full underlying portfolio of the CDS, resulting in long equity and super-senior positions. These positions (long equity, long super-senior, and short mezzanine) are typical of the dealer community.

Therefore, dealers hold significant positions in synthetic CDOs in their correlation books and are not mere arrangers of deals, as is often the case for cash CDO. Equity risk is either retained by dealers or passed on to hedge funds. Super-senior tranches can also be retained by the bank or sold to monoline insurers ("wrappers"). The risk on these tranches can also be transferred to real-money investors through leveraged super-senior (LSSs) structures. LSSs consist of recourse leverage notes using the super-senior tranche as reference and levered several times to enhance return. They are usually

EXHIBIT 1 1 . 1 5

Dealer's Residual Position after selling Mezzanine Tranche Risk.

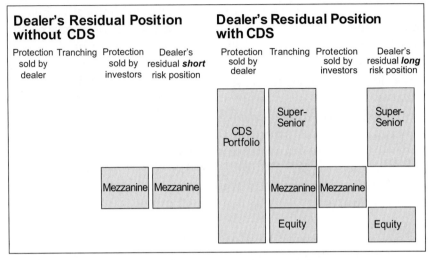

Source: Citigroup.

designed to have a low probability of recourse (justifying a triple-A rating), but their leverage makes them quite sensitive to mark-to-market fluctuations. Hence, they are better suited for buy-and-hold investors.

Investment Strategies

Investment strategies in synthetic CDOs are as diverse as investors in tranches. Broadly speaking, strategies can be split into leverage trades, relative value trades, and directional trades. Tranches can also be used to hedge portfolios.

Taking Leverage

The tranching of CDS portfolios distributes the risk to the various tranches and introduces leverage. The delta of a tranche is the sensitivity of that tranche's spread to a 1-basis-point change in the underlying portfolio. By definition, the delta of the portfolio itself (which can be seen as the 0 to 100 percent tranche) is equal to 1. The deltas of junior tranches are significantly higher than 1, and the deltas of very senior tranches are below 1. Thus, the junior tranches are levered in spread terms, while very senior tranches are delevered. Tranching concentrates most spread and default risk into the equity and junior mezzanine pieces, but although both sources of risk are greater at the bottom of the capital structure, the relative balance between default risk and spread risk is very different for senior tranches. Thanks to their high degree of subordination, senior tranches bear very little default risk, but they still suffer from some spread risk. Equity tranches are subject to relatively more default risk than spread risk, and the opposite is true for senior tranches. At this stage, it is useful to distinguish between idiosyncratic (single-name) spread risk and marketwide spread risk. What is referred to as spread risk, unless clearly stated otherwise, is the widening of the spread on the entire market or underlying portfolio, not on a single credit or group of credits.

Exhibit 11.16 (right panel) illustrates a tranche combination that relies on these differences in default and spread risks. Assuming that the equity tranche has a delta 20 times higher than that of the senior, one can build a delta-neutral position by buying one unit of the equity tranche and selling 20 units of the senior. The resulting position has a positive carry to compensate investors for default risk, but does not have exposure (ignoring convexity) to marketwide spread risk. This "bull-bear" trade (long default risk but spread hedged) is popular with hedge funds, but is very sensitive to single-name shocks and changes in correlations. In particular, falls in correlations hurt the trade both on its long leg and on its short leg.

EXHIBIT 11.16

Indicative Risks and Returns of Tranches and Bull-Bear Combination.

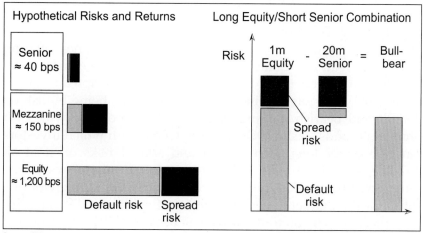

Source: Citigroup.

In summary, tranching distributes spread and default risks unequally across tranches. Investors can choose the type of risk that they want to assume and their degree of exposure by investing in more or less senior tranches. The spreads paid on the tranches are compensation for both sources of risk. Through tranche combinations, risk can be separated into a spread component and a default component. It is important to remember that market-neutral strategies are not immune from all spread risk. Market-spread (delta) hedging protects against small moves in the average spread of the portfolio, but not against large swings. Also, tranches exhibit convexity (second-order spread sensitivities) that can be significant.

Relative Value Trades

Arguably, for real-money investors, the main motivation for investing in tranches is the search for relative value. Value is present at two levels in synthetic CDOs. First, market segmentation, the lower liquidity of bespoke synthetic tranches compared with cash instruments, and their higher mark-to-market sensitivity make them trade cheaper (offer higher spreads) than cash products with identical ratings. Thus, rating-sensitive investors who are able to hold their positions to maturity and can withstand mark-to-market fluctuations can find tranches attractive on a risk/reward basis. Second, as mentioned, tranches enable investors to target underlying assets that they consider as offering good relative value, irrespective of their ratings. Thus, they can extract the value from these underlying assets in levered form and benefit from the additional value afforded by synthetic structures.

Directional Trades

There are countless possible combinations of tranches offering different spread and default risk sensitivities. These enable savvy investors to express their views on the direction of spreads and of default risk, possibly in different directions (e.g., being bullish on default and bearish on spreads). This is not possible with cash products (bonds, cash CDOs, or even CDS), with which investors must be either long both default and spread risks or, if at all possible, short both risks. Other trades do not take views on the direction of the market, but rather take views on the behavior of a subset of the market (a sector, a group of credits, and so on). For example, a dispersion trade consists of buying a senior tranche and delta-hedging the position by selling a more junior tranche on the same portfolio. If all spreads move by an equal small amount, the trade should be unaffected (it does suffer from negative convexity for large moves), but if a given subset suffers from a large spread widening while the overall market remains unchanged, the trade should benefit. This is due to the greater sensitivity of more junior tranches to idiosyncratic (single-name) risk.

Tranches as Hedging Vehicles

Although the majority of single-tranche CDOs are issued to satisfy customer needs to take risk and receive premiums, some investors also use them as hedging devices. Exhibit 11.16 (left panel) makes apparent the advantage of hedging a portfolio with senior mezzanine tranches. Investors who are comfortable with the default risk on their portfolios can hedge their spread risk (delta-hedging) by buying protection on a mezzanine or senior tranche of a synthetic CDO that uses the same or similar names as references. This hedge will offer little protection against default risk but should be significantly cheaper than single-name CDS protection or even index protection. Thus, protection buyers pay only for the risk that they want to hedge, spread risk in this example. The leverage of CDO tranches often requires hedgers to buy protection on a tranche of a smaller notional amount than that of the hedged portfolio, unless they use a very senior tranche (with a delta lower than 1).

Bank loan managers and insurance companies can also use tranche hedges to optimize their returns on regulatory capital. The cost of hedging some parts of their portfolios can be offset by a significant reduction in capital requirements. The proposed new banking regulatory framework of Basel II recognizes tranches as hedging tools, subject to their providing a "significant risk transfer." Under the current capital treatment (Basel I), which does not allocate regulatory capital based on the riskiness of corporate exposures, the incentive has been for banks to buy protection on low-risk and low-yield exposures. These are cheaper to hedge and offer the same capital relief as more risky exposures. The new framework takes a risk-based approach to capital allocation and removes a lot of incentive to securitize or buy protection on low-risk exposures. Tranche protection buying will take place in the position of the capital structure where capital relief is sufficient to offset the cost of hedging. This is likely to be in the junior mezzanine area.

VALUATION OF SYNTHETIC CDOs: CORRELATION

Investors often hear the word *correlation* when looking at tranches. Default correlation is the likelihood that defaults will occur close together. If correlation is high, then if there is one default, investors can expect other defaults to occur within a relatively short period of time. High correlation may be thought of as "contagion," where there are either many defaults or very few defaults. If correlation is low, then defaults are relatively independent: just because one credit defaults does not mean that investors expect to see additional defaults within a short period of time.

Correlation has nothing to do with the probability of default. Instead, correlation simply describes the likelihood that, given one default, other defaults are likely to occur (high correlation) or not likely to occur (low correlation). It is entirely possible to have a low default rate and high correlation; this means that should there actually be a default, investors should expect to see more defaults. Similarly, there may be a high default rate and low correlation; this means that many defaults are likely, but—in the extreme case of zero correlation—investors may be just as likely to see five defaults occur once per year over five years as to see all five in one month.

An Options Framework

To understand how correlation affects tranche pricing, it is useful to look at tranches from an options perspective. Exhibit 11.17 illustrates losses on the underlying credit index versus the percentage of the tranche notional amount remaining at each loss rate.

The seller of equity tranche protection is long a put option on the loss rate of the underlying index, with a strike at the exhaustion point. As expected losses rise, the put option moves further out of the money, decreasing the value of the equity tranche (spreads widen). And, as with put option pricing, as volatility rises, the value of the option increases (spreads tighten).

Higher Default Correlation Means Higher Volatility

An investor may think of high correlation as high volatility in the number of defaults. To understand why, consider a simple example of perfect (100 percent) correlation. Assume 100 underlying credits and a 10 percent probability of default per credit each year. With

EXHIBIT 11.17

Viewing Tranches Within an Options Framework Losses on Underlying Index versus Percent of Tranche Notional Remaining.

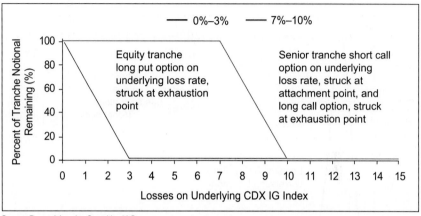

Source: Banc of America Securities LLC.

perfect correlation, there are only two possibilities: no credits default, or all credits default. In this case, the probability of 100 defaults over one year is 10 percent, and the probability of no defaults over one year is 90 percent. This is a high-volatility scenario, because the only two possible outcomes are extremes. The expected number of defaults is 10 ($100 \times 10\% + 0 \times 90\%$).

By contrast, low correlation means low volatility in the number of defaults. Consider the same example with no (0 percent) correlation. Since each credit now defaults independently, there are many possibilities. The probability of 100 defaults in one year is $10\%^{100}$ (a very small number), and the probability of no defaults in one year is $90\%^{100}$ (also a very small number). Most possibilities lie in between zero and 100 defaults, creating a relatively low-volatility scenario. Even though volatility has declined, note that the expected number of defaults remains unchanged at 10. Exhibit 11.18 illustrates this graphically.

In reality, correlation lies somewhere between zero and 100 percent, but the general principle still holds: the volatility of the number of defaults increases with correlation.

Since higher volatility comes from higher correlation, the seller of equity-tranche protection wants correlation to increase. This is because the investor is long a put option, which increases in value as volatility rises. That is, equity-tranche spreads compress as correlation rises.

EXHIBIT 11.18

Volatility in the number of defaults increases with correlation distribution of number of defaults over one year assumes 100 underlying credits, each with a 10 percent default rate.

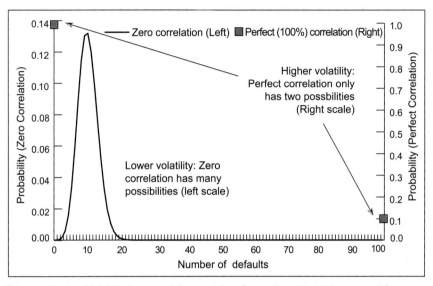

The expected number of defaults in the zero correlation scenario is ten (100 credits × 10% default rate per credit.)

Source: Banc of America Securities LLC.

The seller of more senior tranche protection is short a call spread on the loss rate of the underlying index, with a lower strike at the attachment point and an upper strike at the exhaustion point. (Equivalently, the investor is short a call option with a strike at the attachment point, and simultaneously long a call option with a strike at the exhaustion point.) As expected losses approach the attachment point, the call option moves further in-the-money. The value of the senior tranche decreases (spreads widen), because the senior-tranche holder is short the call option. Similarly, as volatility falls, the value of the senior tranche increases (spreads tighten). Since lower volatility comes from lower correlation, the seller of senior-tranche protection wants correlation to decline. That is, senior-tranche spreads compress as correlation declines.

The mezzanine tranche is often referred to as "correlation independent." This means that mezzanine tranche spreads stay unchanged for small moves in correlation. This is because the mezzanine tranche is between an equity tranche and a senior tranche. For bigger moves in correlation, the mezzanine tranche adopts the behavior of a new spread environment. That is, if market spreads became significantly wider, the mezzanine tranche would behave more like an equity tranche because overall risk would increase, causing the mezzanine tranche to become long correlation. If instead, market spreads became significantly tighter, the mezzanine tranche would behave more like a senior tranche because overall risk would decrease, causing the mezzanine tranche to become short correlation. It is usually reasonable to think of a large change in correlation as being accompanied by a change in the overall spread environment, because some external factor that also affects credit spreads, such as a marked change in macroeconomic conditions, is likely to cause the move in correlation.

Overall, Exhibit 11.19 compares tranche terminology with terms used in an options pricing model.

For readers who would like a more basic introduction to correlation, please see Appendix A, "Using a Coin Toss to Understand How Correlation Affects Tranche Spreads."

Implied Volatility in the Context of ST CDOs

In option valuation, an investor does not estimate equity volatility over the horizon of an option to determine the price. Instead, the price of the option determines volatility; hence the term *implied volatility*. In ST CDO pricing, default correlation functions in a similar way. Rather than defining each default correlation pairwise (meaning that there is a different default correlation for each set of credits), in practice the market assumes an average default correlation across all credits. The price of the tranche implies this average correlation.

EXHIBIT 11.19

How tranche value changes with various risk factors: equity tranche is long a put option and senior tranche is short a call spread, on the underlying loss rate.

Risk Factor		Tranche Value		
Tranches	Options Model	Equity	Mezzanine	Senior
Loss rate increases	Stock price increases	↓	↓	↓
Correlation increases	Volatility increases	↑	↔	↓
Time decay	Time decay	↓	↔	↑
Interest rate increases	Interest rate increases	↓	↓	↓

Mezzanine tranche value assumes a small change in volatility or correlation. Spreads move inversely with tranche value.
Source: Banc of America Securities LLC estimates.

However, there is an important distinction between tranche valuation and option valuation. In both cases, volatility is the key input to valuation. But in equity options, volatility is generally observable and hedgeable. In ST CDOs, default correlation is neither observable nor hedgeable. This means that correlation risk can be significant, as it cannot be hedged. We now turn to a measure to quantify this risk.

Correlation01 for Investment Grade Tranches

To get a basic idea of how much a 1 percentage point move in correlation affects CDX IG index tranche pricing, or "Correlation01," consider Exhibit 11.20.

A 1 percentage point increase in correlation decreases the equity tranche premium by 0.78 point up front (for example, from 31 points up front to 30.22 points up front), making the equity tranche look far more sensitive to correlation than other tranches. However, Exhibit 11.21 shows that this is due to the high premium for the equity tranche. Relative to its initial tranche premium,

EXHIBIT 11.20

Correlation01 is largest for equity tranche change in tranche premium due to correlation rising 1 percentage point as of December 13, 2004.

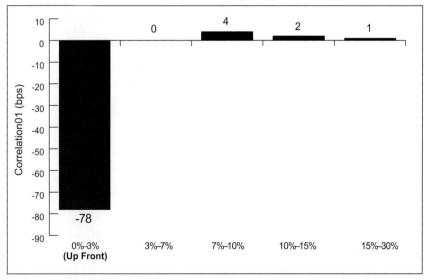

Underlying index is IG3 March 2010.

Source: Banc of America Securities LLC estimates.

EXHIBIT 11.21

Because of its high premium, Correlation01 relative to
tranche premium as of December 13, 2004.

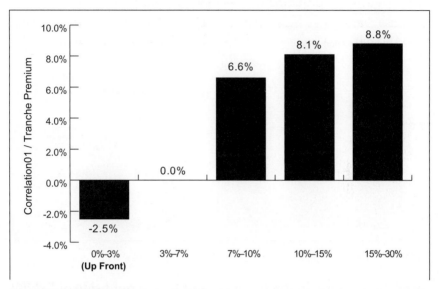

Underlying index is IG3 March 2010.
Source: Banc of America Securities LLC estimates.

senior tranches are more sensitive to correlation than junior tranches.
This is because even though the equity tranche investor cares
about correlation, he or she is more concerned with the default
rate and recovery values. On the other hand, more senior tranche
investors do not particularly expect a loss of notional value. They
are far less concerned with the default rate and more concerned
with correlation.

For more details on how correlation affects investment grade
tranches, please see Appendix B, "Base Correlation Models."

APPENDIX A: USING A COIN TOSS TO UNDERSTAND HOW CORRELATION AFFECTS TRANCHE SPREADS

To make it more clear that equity tranche spreads tighten when
correlation increases, and senior tranche spreads tighten when
correlation decreases, consider a coin toss.

In one example (the left side of Exhibit 11.22**)**, two coins are
tossed, and each lands on either heads or tails. The outcome for
one coin is independent of the outcome for the other coin, so that

EXHIBIT 11.22

Flipping two coins, either separately or glued together at one edge. Payoff is $1 for each heads, $0 for each tails. Investor will pay $1 to participate in either game.

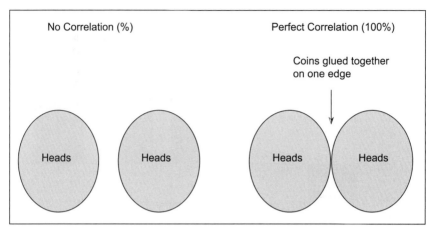

No Correlation (%)   Perfect Correlation (100%)

Coins glued together on one edge

Heads   Heads   Heads   Heads

Source: Banc of America Securities LLC.

correlation is zero. In the second example (the right side of Exhibit 11.22), the two coins are glued together on one edge, so that both coins always land on heads or both coins always land on tails. That is, the two coins are perfectly (100 percent) correlated. The payoff in both examples is $1 for each heads and zero for each tails.

As shown in Exhibit 11.23, an investor is willing to pay $1 to participate in either game.

Now consider a first-loss tranche of the coin toss example, in which the investor receives $1 for the second heads, but zero for the first heads and zero for each tails. This is analogous to an equity tranche. Exhibit 11.24 shows the payoffs. The "Heads, Tails" and "Tails, Heads" combinations now pay zero because there is just one heads, decreasing the expected payoff for the zero-correlation case to just 25 cents. By contrast, these two possibilities never existed for the perfect correlation case, and so that payoff falls only to 50 cents. That is, higher correlation is good for the investor who is long risk in the first tranche, or sells equity tranche protection.

Alternatively, consider a second-loss tranche of the coin toss example, in which the investor receives $1 for the first heads, but zero for the second heads and zero for each tails. This is analogous to a senior tranche. Exhibit 11.25 shows the payoffs. The "Heads, Tails" and "Tails, Heads" combinations again pay $1 each, raising

EXHIBIT 11.23

Payoffs from coin toss example. The payoff is $1 for each heads and $0 for each tails. The investor will pay $1 to participate in either game.

Outcome		Two Separate Coins No Correlation (0%)			Two Coins, Glued Together at the Edge Perfect Correlation (100%)		
				Expected Payoff			Expected Payoff
		Probability	Payoff	Payoff	Probability	Payoff	Payoff
Coin 1	Coin 2	(%)	($)	($)	(%)	($)	($)
Heads	Heads	25	2	0.50	50	2	1.00
Heads	Tails	25	1	0.25	0	–	–
Tails	Heads	25	1	0.25	0	–	–
Tails	Tails	25	0	0.00	50	0	0.00
Total Expected Payoff				**1.00**			**1.00**

Source: Banc of America Securities LLC.

EXHIBIT 11.24

First-loss position in coin toss example, analogous to equity tranche. The payoff is $1 for the second heads, $0 for the first heads, and $0 for each tails. Correlation is good for an investor who is long risk (sells equity tranche protection).

Outcome		Two Separate Coins No Correlation (0%)			Two Coins, Glued Together at the Edge Perfect Correlation (100%)		
				Expected Payoff			Expected Payoff
		Probability	Payoff	Payoff	Probability	Payoff	Payoff
Coin 1	Coin 2	(%)	($)	($)	(%)	($)	($)
Heads	Heads	25	1	0.25	50	1	0.50
Heads	Tails	25	0	0.00	0	–	–
Tails	Heads	25	0	0.00	0	–	–
Tails	Tails	25	0	0.00	50	0	0.00
Total Expected Payoff				**0.25**			**0.50**

Source: Banc of America Securities LLC.

the expected payoff for the zero-correlation case to 75 cents. By contrast, these two possibilities do not exist for the perfect-correlation case, and that payoff stays at 50 cents. That is, higher correlation is

EXHIBIT 11.25

Second-loss position in coin toss example, analogous to senior tranche. The payoff is $1 for the first heads, $0 for the second heads, and $0 for each tails. Correlation is bad for an investor who is long risk (sells senior tranche protection).

Outcome		Two Separate Coins No Correlation (0%)			Two Coins, Glued Together at the Edge Perfect Correlation (100%)		
		Probability	Payoff	Expected Payoff	Probability	Payoff	Expected Payoff
Coin 1	Coin 2	(%)	($)	($)	(%)	($)	($)
Heads	Heads	25	1	0.25	50	1	0.50
Heads	Tails	25	1	0.25	0	–	–
Tails	Heads	25	1	0.25	0	–	–
Tails	Tails	25	0	0.00	50	0	0.00
Total Expected Payoff				0.75			0.50

Source: Banc of America Securities LLC.

bad for the investor who is long risk in the second tranche, or sells senior tranche protection.

Expanded to the credit universe, the fact that higher correlation is good for the equity tranche and bad for the senior tranche means that there is a tranche somewhere in between for which correlation is neither good nor bad. That is, the mezzanine-tranche payoff would not change based on small moves in correlation, and therefore is said to be "correlation independent."

APPENDIX B: BASE CORRELATION MODELS

Since mezzanine-tranche pricing does not change with a small move in correlation, the market is moving in the direction of base correlation pricing. In this framework, tranches are treated as a combination of equity tranches. Exhibit 11.26 illustrates base correlation pricing for the 3 to 7 percent mezzanine tranche. This tranche is simply the difference between a 0 to 7 percent equity tranche and the 0 to 3 percent equity tranche. In turn, there are two implied correlations—one at the lower attachment point (3 percent), and one at the upper exhaustion (or detachment) point (7 percent).

To see how pricing works in a base correlation framework, consider Exhibit 11.27.

EXHIBIT 11.26

Base Correlation Model for the 3 percent–7 percent Mezzanine Tranche.

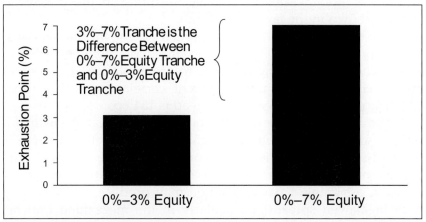

EXHIBIT 11.27

Using base correlation to price CDX IG five-year tranches. As of December 15, 2004. The underlying index is IG3 March 2010 (46 bps).

Attachment Point (%)	Exhaustion Point (%)	Correlation Lower (%)	Correlation Upper (%)	Breakeven Spread (bps)
Equity Tranche Pricing				
0	3	0	20.4	1,345
0	7	0	31.1	614
0	10	0	36.3	436
0	15	0	46.4	291
0	30	0	65.6	146
Implied Standardized Tranche Pricing				
0	3	0	20.4	1,345
3	7	20.4	31.1	184
7	10	31.1	36.3	63
10	15	36.3	46.4	24
15	30	46.4	65.6	8

The top panel shows pricing for all equity tranches of the CDX IG index. Since these are equity tranches, the correlation at the lower attachment point is always zero. The correlation at the upper attachment point varies by tranche, resulting in the breakeven spreads shown in the far right column.

The bottom panel shows the implied pricing for the standardized tranches of the CDX IG. For example, on the 3 to 7 percent mezzanine tranche, using a 20.4 percent correlation at the lower attachment point and a 31.1 percent correlation at the upper exhaustion point, the breakeven spread is 184 bps.

The benefit of base correlation pricing is that it ensures a unique solution to tranche pricing. Since the correlation curve is upward-sloping—that is, base correlation increases with the exhaustion point—there always is a well-defined price point. By contrast, assigning a flat correlation may produce unrealistically high breakeven spreads, particularly in the mezzanine tranche, which is correlation independent.[11]

---

[11] More precisely, a flat (Gaussian) correlation model produces a smile, in which the implied correlation for the mezzanine tranche is below the implied correlation for both the equity and the senior tranches. This may allow an investor to arbitrage the position by replicating the tranche at different pricing levels.

CHAPTER 12

Loan Portfolio Management

Michael P. McAdams
President and CEO
Four Corners Capital Management, LLC

Jack Yang
Partner
Highland Capital Management, LP

Howard Tiffen
Managing Director
Van Kampen Investment Advisors

Geoffrey A. Gold LLC
Partner
Strategic Value Partners

Introduction

Michael P. McAdams
President and CEO, Four Corners Capital Management, LLC

Despite the growth of the corporate loan market, loan portfolio management has received less than its full share of attention for its role in the development and maturation of corporate loans as an asset class.

Yet, managing a portfolio of loans in a proper way requires managers to track market growth over time, particularly in light of the fact that the investor base for syndicated loans is so broad and diversified. If this is true, shouldn't analytical depth by bankers and nonbankers alike have increased? So, what is the status of loan portfolio management analysis today? What do market participants of all types do differently, and why do differences persist? Do the tried and true rules still apply, and what are the current "cutting-edge" techniques?

To answer these questions, it is important to look briefly at the organizational and oversight realities of major current loan market participants. In Exhibits 12.1 to 12.3, you will note the well-documented change in the types of organizations (and funding sources thereof) that participate in today's loan market. One might expect that each type of firm would have its own loan philosophy and strategies. However, despite their differences, by reviewing Exhibit 12.4, one can also see the large number of common issues that participants share. Exhibit 12.5 highlights the regulatory and other oversight considerations that are both contributing to current procedures and driving changes in the industry. Despite all the differences, not surprisingly, it seems there are common themes and realities associated with caring for other people's money.

The premise of the articles in this chapter underscores the combinations of structural reasons why people manage loans both differently and consistently throughout the industry. Enlarging the participant base for syndicated loans has made credit analysis more integrated and universal, as some have embraced new techniques from outside the world of loans and corporate bonds. However, as shown in this chapter, there continue to be subtle differences between market participants, despite the growing similarities,

E X H I B I T   1 2 . 1

Primary market for highly leveraged loans: banks versus nonbanks.

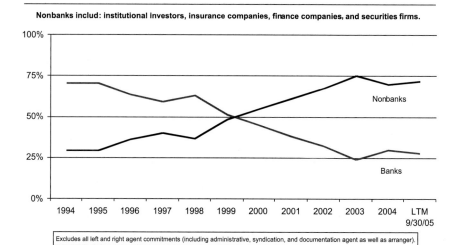

Nonbanks includ: institutional investors, insurance companies, finance companies, and securities firms.

Excludes all left and right agent commitments (including administrative, syndication, and documentation agent as well as arranger).

Source: Standard & Poor's Leveraged Lending Review, 3Q05.

E X H I B I T   1 2 . 2

Primary market for highly leveraged loans by broad investor type.

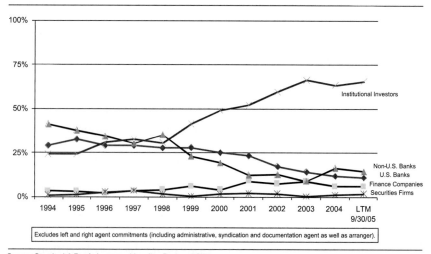

Excludes left and right agent commitments (including administrative, syndication and documentation agent as well as arranger).

Source: Standard & Poor's Leveraged Lending Review, 3Q05.

E X H I B I T   1 2 . 3

Primary institutional market by investor type.

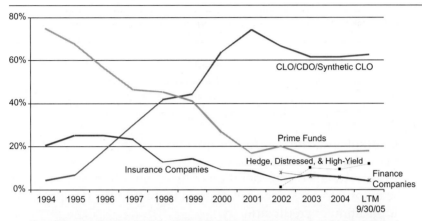

To provide a more realistic view of institutional buying habits in today's market, we add to the CLO tally the institutional commitments held by the arranger at close. For tax purposes, of course, CLOs tend to participate as primary assignees and therefore are often left off the "at close" allocation list. In addition, beginning in 2002, we have made a better effort to track hedge funds and other investors in this analysis. As a result, we can provide data for finance companies and hedge, distressed, and high-yield funds only starting in 2002.

Source: Standard & Poor's Leveraged Lending Review, 3Q05.

E X H I B I T   1 2 . 4

Common issues/shared challenges.

• Costs	• Tracking error
• Learning curve	• Benchmarking
• Volatility management	• Counterparty risks
• Relative value	• Liquidity management
• Risk-adjusted returns	• Sell discipline
• VAR	• Underwriting standards
• Commodities/energy prices	• Compensation of credit personnel
• Performance attribution	• Political risk
• Systems risk	• War/terrorism risk
• Validity of accounting information	• Regulatory realities
• Asset allocation	• Rating agencies
• Tax	• Momentum/technical analysis
• Alpha	• Quantitave research
• Delta	

E X H I B I T   1 2 . 5

Confluence of regulatory and oversight authorities.

• SEC	• State insurance boards
• Federal Reserve	• Attorneys general
• Comptroller	• CFTC
• BIS requirements	• NASD
• IRS	• Rating agencies
• NAIC	• Securities analysts

which might indicate the future direction of the practice of loan management and credit strategy.

Prior to detailed consideration of these and other issues, it may also be helpful to consider a few themes that affect the development and application of credit strategy.

The degree to which organizations embrace developments in credit instrument valuation has the greatest impact on credit practices. Of course, bonds are very often publicly traded and are normally daily-valued instruments. But many corporate loans now have similar liquidity. Nevertheless, the use of current market valuation information for loans is recent and, as a result, is not yet universal the way it is for bonds.

As background, in the late 1990s, members of the LSTA board of directors recognized that establishing an accurate, timely, objective, and transparent valuation methodology was critical to the development of the corporate loan market. Considerable time was required to reach a compromise among the different market participants (including insurance companies, retail funds, large originating banks, regional and foreign institutions, funds, and brokers), but by early 2000 the LSTA/Loan Pricing Corporation valuation methodology, which pooled information from major sell-side trading desks, became the first means by which private loan instruments could be frequently valued. However, this new technology increased focus on the loan market at an awkward time; coincidentally, marking to market became widely available just as the market experienced a substantial and cyclical rise in defaults caused by a broad economic slowdown that gave rise to increased problem credits and losses.

While many in the industry have struggled uncomfortably (often because of their unique regulatory or structural situations) to adapt to the existence of current loan valuation, other firms have willingly embraced this information because it has provided them with more feedback on credits in advance of downgrades, defaults, or losses. Market valuation adds a new layer of sophistication to credit analysis, not just in terms of analysis of the odds of ultimate loss or full repayment, but also by documenting the degree of relative stability or volatility of a loan over its life. Investors and their clients are able to see more clearly the attractive features and benefits of bank loans in reducing overall portfolio volatility (compared to other asset classes), and have gained ways of tracking and quantifying volatility over each loan's life. As this analysis progressed, issuers, originators, and investors alike were able to compare the short-term impact of structure, spread, and other loan features. As a result, stratification of strategies between risk, coupon, and total return has been facilitated, as has been the development of "covenant light," second lien, and other hybrid structures designed to fill the gaps between senior loans and other debt investment strategies.

Diversification strategies addressing risks from unanticipated events have also become more important to loan portfolio management. Clearly, as loans have minimal upside, diversity is an important cornerstone of risk management, and, as the saying goes, "diversification protects against ignorance and surprise." Accordingly, because of regulatory investment guidelines, capital allocation strategies, and value-at-risk common sense, manager-specific diversity strategies have been widely adopted.

However, strategies for dealing with intentionally less diversified portfolios (as part of a particular firm's differentiated business strategy) have resulted in new ways of defining credit diversity. That is, nondiversified portfolio management strategies are emerging from hedge funds that have chosen to be industry or "situation" specialized lenders, focusing their analysis to maximize results. Some have argued that such developments are not that different from managing large traditional bank portfolio exposures, either prior to successful syndication or as part of a borrower relationship. In this last area, traditional banks have pioneered means of hedging such "lumpy" exposures. And whether it be a covered hedge or an outright short used to hedge a position or increase total returns, much is presently developing in credit management theory and practice in this area. Thus the traditional "long only" bias of credit management for senior secured floating-rate corporate loans is changing. Despite the benefits of collateral and ultra-short duration, investor tolerance of loan product "surprises" is driving innovation.

An outgrowth of this increased focus on volatility management has been an increase in the importance of sell-disciplined credit management. Despite relationships with borrowers, more institutions consider each and every dollar of exposure to capital loss more critical. In the absence of deep and liquid hedges being available on all names, establishing sell disciplines has become more important.

Finally, "vendor-assisted" portfolio management has become an important part of the marketplace. Included in this category are, of course, the rating agencies, as well as several individual default-predictive and portfolio management models. Clearly, consideration of external ratings adds an objective aspect to traditional fundamental analysis (although few firms have yet adopted the approach of selecting noninvestment grade loans purely on the basis of ratings). We have also seen market-driven default models grow in acceptance; a combination of fundamental rating migration analysis tempered with current market value data has added incremental value in some circumstances. This has been more dramatically seen in investment grade loan management, where the presence of public securities in addition to a loan issue makes cross-market references easier.

Looking ahead, data collection and analysis will continue to improve, and asset allocation models between loans and bonds (as well as between different tranches of term loans, second lien loans, and high-yield securities) are also likely to become more sophisticated. Optimization of loan investment strategies by return, default likelihood, volatility, liquidity, capital treatment, and relationship profitability will also need to be more fully addressed on a more sophisticated level. Similarly, there will be an increased effort to expand analysis beyond loan-based return and volatility parameters in order to adjust for strategies between loans and virtually any other asset class. As a result, future credit management strategies may allow for variable leverage alternatives as well as differentiated investor return and volatility sensitivities.

As detailed in the following articles, the loan market's unique development path and the perspective and objectives of each institution and investor will continue to drive the dynamic nature of corporate loan investing.

Loan Investment Strategies: An Overview

Jack Yang
Partner, Highland Capital Management, LP

Modern portfolio management theory has demonstrated the ability to achieve both higher returns *and* lower risk by diversifying portfolio investments among holdings that have low or negative correlation to each other. As discussed in Chapter 1, senior secured loans have consistently demonstrated high risk–adjusted returns and low correlation with other asset classes on both a relative and an absolute basis.

The high risk–adjusted returns of the loan asset class are driven more by the extremely low volatility of the returns than by exceptionally high gross returns. While the historical returns on loans have been only in the single digits, the extremely consistent nature of those returns improves the quality of this asset class's returns compared to those on other assets, which may achieve higher returns in any given year, but with a wide range of possibilities and a high degree of uncertainty from year to year.

These fundamental attributes make senior secured loans a highly attractive allocation as part of an investment portfolio. Exhibit 12.6 illustrates the broad range of current investment strategies available to investors via senior secured loans.

A portfolio of senior secured loans is frequently used as an investment strategy by investors who are seeking preservation of capital and current income higher than that available from traditional money market investment opportunities. The portfolio's senior secured collateral and diversification reduce the potential loss of capital from market volatility and/or credit defaults, and the high-yield credit spread on the individual loans exceeds the total return associated with money market investments, given their investment grade credit rating, short investment maturity, and modest potential for capital gains.

The risk and return associated with this strategy can be customized to an investor's risk and return objectives. A higher portfolio yield can be achieved by incorporating term loans and/or lower rated loans as part of the portfolio, while concurrently

EXHIBIT 12.6

Investment Strategies via Secured Loans

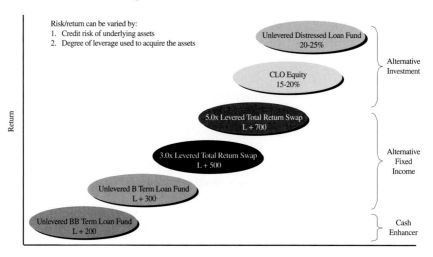

Risk/return can be varied by:
1. Credit risk of underlying assets
2. Degree of leverage used to acquire the assets

Unlevered Distressed Loan Fund
20-25%

CLO Equity
15-20%

5.0x Levered Total Return Swap
L + 700

3.0x Levered Total Return Swap
L + 500

Unlevered B Term Loan Fund
L + 300

Unlevered BB Term Loan Fund
L + 200

Return

Alternative Investment

Alternative Fixed Income

Cash Enhancer

overall portfolio risk can be managed by an increase in portfolio diversification.

While this strategy is potentially effective at any time, it is particularly popular in periods of rising interest rates. The floating-rate aspect of loans significantly mitigates the potential for capital losses due to rising interest rates compared to traditional fixed income securities. Furthermore, as interest rates rise, the coupon on the underlying loans is reset at higher levels, providing an income stream that increases in direct correlation to higher interest rates.

Both institutional and individual investors participate in this strategy. Institutional investors invest in commingled loan funds and separate accounts, and individual investors invest in mutual funds commonly referred to as "floating-rate" funds. Examples of institutional investors that invest in unleveraged senior loan funds include banks, insurance companies, foundations, endowments, and corporations. Investors in Europe and Asia also participate in such investments, both with and without utilizing foreign exchange hedging mechanisms.

ALTERNATIVE FIXED INCOME STRATEGIES

Given the ultra-low volatility of loan returns, analysis indicates that a significant amount of leverage can be employed compared to other asset classes, with the benefits of higher returns outweighing the risks associated with the correspondingly higher volatility. All other factors being held constant, applying leverage to a diversified portfolio of loans will not materially affect the correlation of the returns with those on other asset classes.

Over the past 20 years, both institutional and individual investors have increasingly invested a portion of their fixed income portfolios in high-yield bonds as a means of achieving higher returns. Because the returns on high-yield bonds are materially determined by credit migration, high-yield bonds have a relatively low correlation with the returns on investment grade bonds and money market securities.

A diversified portfolio of senior secured loans that employs leverage can provide returns comparable to those from a high-yield bond portfolio, but with less credit and interest-rate risk and even lower correlation with other fixed income investments. Adding an allocation of modestly leveraged senior secured loans to a portfolio of investment grade bonds can reduce the portfolio's duration, interest-rate risk, and overall volatility, with results superior to those of comparable high-yield bond allocations.

Exhibit 12.7 illustrates the impact of adding allocations of high-yield bonds and portfolios of loans leveraged 1.4 times and 3.0 times to a portfolio of investment grade bonds as represented by the

EXHIBIT 12.7

The impact of adding high-yield bonds and loans to investment grade bonds.

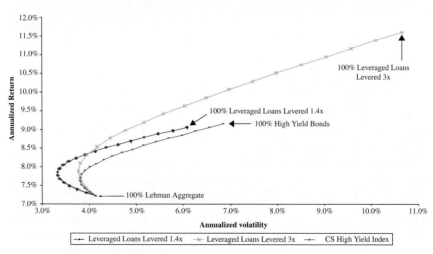

Source: CS, Ibbotson Associates, Bloomberg.

Lehman Aggregate, using the performance data of the asset classes from 1992 to 2003.

As indicated by the portion of the loan curves that are to the left of and above the high-yield curve, an investor could have achieved both higher returns *and* lower volatility by incorporating leveraged loans as an alternative fixed income investment rather than an unleveraged portfolio of high-yield bonds.

Institutional investors are investing in senior secured loan portfolios leveraged 3 to 6 times as a complement to traditional core fixed income portfolio strategies, with demonstrated success. While the number of institutional portfolio managers implementing this strategy is relatively low at this time, one can easily envision senior secured loan strategies increasing in prevalence, similar to the way in which, over the past 20 years, high-yield bonds have gone from an esoteric novelty to a widely accepted asset allocation among institutional investors of all types. Today, the senior secured loan market is already larger than the high-yield bond market, thereby offering a wealth of investment opportunities.

In a strategy such as this, an investor's capital is used to purchase loans that serve as collateral and first-loss capital ("equity") for the fund. The leverage for these low-leverage loan structures is usually provided in the form of a total rate of return swap (TRS). A significant number of commercial and investment banks provide TRS financing, looking to the diversified portfolio of loans as collateral to offset potential losses associated with defaults in the loans.

A structure such as this simplistically resembles a traditional collateralized loan obligation (CLO), but with lower leverage, and with debt financing coming from a swap instead of from multiple tranches of debt securities distributed into the capital markets. Like a CLO, a low-leverage structure normally involves parameters focusing on minimum industry and issuer diversification, minimum average credit quality, and minimum spread requirements. The investment portfolio parameters for the fund are mutually negotiated among the investor, the investment manager for the fund, and the swap provider.

However there are significant differences between these structures and traditional CLOs in addition to lower leverage and the associated lower expected return and volatility. These funds are established as private transactions, unlike CLOs, which involve the distribution of publicly registered securities. Consequently, low-leverage funds do not require any involvement with the Securities and Exchange Commission or ratings agencies, and thus are much faster and cheaper to close than CLOs. The maturity of the swap financing is generally in the range of three to five years and can be either terminated or extended with the consent of the swap provider. This represents significant flexibility, as compared to the longer, noncallable nature of CLO debt tranches.

In a situation in which the equity for the fund is coming from one investor, the initial structure and portfolio parameters for the fund can be customized to the investor's specific goals, as compared to the market determined, "one size fits all" nature of a multi-investor CLO. The small number of parties involved in a low-leverage fund creates the opportunity for much greater flexibility over the life of the fund, unlike a CLO, where all the terms are established at closing and any changes require a consent process involving the debt and/or equity investors and input from the ratings agencies.

TOTAL RETURN INVESTMENT STRATEGIES

Several loan strategies are achieving wide acceptance among portfolio managers who are focused on total return and traditional alternative investments such as private equity, hedge funds, and real estate. These loan strategies, such as CLO equity and distressed loans, have the potential for attractive absolute and risk adjusted returns, as well as low correlation with traditional alternative investment options.

An investment in the equity of a CLO provides the investor with exposure to the returns of a diversified portfolio of senior secured loans, typically leveraged 8 to 10 times. Research by CS indicates that CLO equity over the period from 1996 to 2003 delivered a gross return of 17.76 percent with a standard deviation of 5.60 percent. This compares highly favorably with the returns on the S&P 500, private equity, mezzanine debt, and hedge funds over the same period from both return and volatility perspectives.

Given that the returns on the underlying senior secured loans have low correlation with traditional alternative investments, the leveraged returns as represented by CLO equity have a similarly very low correlation. Research by CS indicates that from 1992 to the second quarter of 2004, CLO equity returns had a correlation of only 0.15 with private equity, 0.32 with the HFR Fund Weighted Composite index, and 0.46 with the NAREIT index.

The return profile of CLO equity is an attractive complement to the return profile of investments in private equity. CLO equity returns are determined by the amount and timing of cash flow distributions received from the loan portfolio that are in excess of the cash required to pay interest expense on the fund's debt securities. CLOs are typically structured with the expectation that the equity investors will receive quarterly distributions totaling their initial investment within the first five years. Alternatively, the returns on private equity funds are largely and generally driven by capital gains, with realizations only beginning to occur three to five years postinvestment.

Returns on private equity funds tend to be driven by investments that are concentrated and lumpy, with a typical fund consisting of no more than 10 to 25 investments. In contrast, a CLO has minimum requirements related to issuers, industries, and ratings that ensure broad investment diversification. At any given time, CLOs generally have over 100 investments, and over the life of a structure, equity returns will be determined by several hundred loans.

The transparency associated with portfolio holdings and management for a CLO is very high. Investors receive a quarterly trustee's report that details the CLO's collateral and calculates compliance with the fund's financial and portfolio management requirements. This is far more favorable than the essentially blind pool nature of investing in a new private equity fund and the limited, opaque information provided to investors by hedge fund managers.

In summary, similar to the way in which an allocation of modestly leveraged loans can enhance the returns and lower the risk of a fixed income portfolio, an allocation of CLO equity has been shown to increase the return and lower the risk of alternative investment portfolios.

Investments in portfolios of distressed loans have the potential to offer investors attractive absolute and risk-adjusted returns with low correlation with other investments.

This strategy involves buying the loans of companies that are experiencing operational and/or financial problems in the secondary market, with the view that they are undervalued relative to their trading or recovery value in the future. This activity has grown significantly as the size of the loan market has grown and is largely pursued by hedge funds and other types of investment managers who specialize in distressed investments. Many of the brokers and dealers who make secondary markets in par loans also do so for distressed loans. A detailed discussion of the distressed loan market is given in Chapter 9.

In conclusion, the low volatility and low correlation of senior secured loans make them an attractive complement to many types of investment portfolios. The use of leverage in varying forms allows the asset class to meet a wide range of return objectives. Advances in derivatives and securities technologies have addressed many of the structural and market issues that have historically inhibited institutional investors from participating in the asset class.

The generally favorable experience that investors have had from incorporating loan strategies into their portfolios bodes well for broader market penetration. These strategies are being helped by, and are receiving greater visibility because of, the current trend of rising interest rates. All signs indicate that the variety and acceptance of loan-related investment strategies will continue to grow.

A Retail Loan Fund Manager's Perspective

Howard Tiffen
Managing Director, Van Kampen Investment Advisors

The portfolio manager for a mutual fund has multiple functions. The manager's main objective will be to produce relatively strong, reliably predictable performance. This comes from being a good analyst of the individual investments in the portfolio. It also requires visionary industry selection, not so much in deciding which industries to buy, but in choosing which are to be avoided. The manager must be sure that his or her fund is given the opportunity to consider the broadest possible array of investment alternatives. Finally, the managers must be able to explain clearly and straightforwardly what a senior loan fund is and how it has or will behave in different conditions. Let's examine each component.

The goal of retail investors in senior loan mutual funds is to earn a relatively high yield with as little risk to capital as possible. In simple terms, this translates into high yield rather than large total returns. The relatively high yield will typically come from a portfolio of leveraged senior loans. The more return is derived from asset price appreciation, the higher the volatility will be. Volatility is not a quality that the typical retail senior loan fund investor is looking for. It may work for an investor in commodity funds or growth stocks, but it is not expected by coupon-clipping income seekers.

The most successful managers in this asset class have been able to maintain relatively stable net asset values (NAVs) by diversifying their portfolios extensively. It is really left to the institutional and hedge fund managers to take the kind of big bets that may produce outsized returns, but will bring comparable asset value volatility as well. The majority of loans purchased will not experience a default or even distress, but those that do become "stressed," or those that do not have covenants enabling the lenders to renegotiate below-market spreads in the event of a breach, will experience high degrees of volatility. The manager's goal will be to keep the impact of those events in a retail portfolio as low as possible.

The excess volatility comes from the inherent characteristics of the secondary market. Although the number of participants in the market generally has exploded in the last few years, most of them are not equipped to deal with distressed or stressed transactions. This may come from the underlying goals of the fund (for instance, looking at the two most important aspects of growth in the asset class over the last three years, most CLOs are not designed to hold material amounts of defaulted or very weak credits; it will be difficult for daily-access senior loan funds to become buyers of stressed transactions, as the asset price volatility will be unacceptably high). It may be the result of a shortage of the kinds of analysts who are accomplished investors in stressed or defaulted deals. Either way, there will inevitably be many more sellers than buyers of transactions below 95 percent. This phenomenon tends to drive prices inexorably lower in times of profound credit weakness, such as 1990 to 1992 or 1999 to 2002. Furthermore, price declines have tended to resemble a skier's fall near the top of an icy double black diamond downhill run rather than a controlled, thoughtful descent, with each step based on knowledge of where the next stair tread will be. A clear majority of CLO and mutual fund managers seek income-paying, performing credits for their portfolios.

That is why being an outstanding analyst is so important. Mutual fund investors do not have the cushion of excess capital to protect them against losses; they are the first and only absorber of losses in the portfolio. The mutual fund manager sees the outcome of his or her decisions daily when the fund's NAV is published at the close of business. The effect of those decisions gets passed on undiluted (or magnified if the fund in question uses leverage) to investors each day. For most managers, therefore, there is really no substitute for looking at credit and business metrics the old-fashioned way, and this requires excellent diligence, insightful analysis, a clear appreciation of management and of the goals of the owners, a review of the collateral, an understanding of the points at which protective covenants will bite, and some form of sensitivity or downside analysis just to show how badly the company can fare before a financial crisis appears. A good analyst's skills will improve over time. The ability to see how a fact pattern plays out and recognize similar patterns in other cases is tough to learn without having watched it or felt it happen. Observing a variety of management teams and equity sponsors negotiate a tough environment with a leveraged balance sheet is infinitely more valuable than a business school case study. The successful portfolio manager will have this perspective and will be able to detect flaws in proposals being made by other analysts. Successful avoidance of potential losses is the best way to produce strong relative performance and avoid volatility, which retail investors abhor.

The other key to avoiding volatility is not making adverse industry selections. Problem credits can emerge at a given point from any industry, but there are times when particular industries exhibit cyclical or secular weakness. Chemicals and health care are examples of the first type of dislocation, and autos and air transport have been going through the latter type for most of this decade. The structural rigidity of CLOs means that in order to stay fully invested, they sometimes have to be in industries that make poor credit bedfellows. Mutual funds are generally spared this pressure. The mutual fund manager has the advantage of being able to choose to avoid entire industries or sectors. Even stronger companies in weak sectors can exhibit relatively high price volatility (guilt by association) and are preferably avoided by managers of mutual funds as they seek to minimize price disruption.

The mutual fund portfolio manager is able to control the decision-making process only if he or she gets to see the broadest possible sampling of the investments available in the market. Portfolio managers need to be aware of as many investment opportunities as possible in every available industry. They may choose not to participate, but having the option is critical. Even in out-of-favor industries or sectors, excellent businesses or management teams will exist. The opportunity to make choices from the widest possible array of options will come through being accessible to lead lenders and equity sponsors and being relevant and important to them. Accessibility is being able to provide speedy, objective feedback to deal arrangers. Importance has something to do with size and with being able to make material, thoughtful investment decisions. The fine line here is maintaining relationships and access without losing objectivity.

The techniques and habits described in this section are the building blocks for excellent performance. Beyond that, though, mutual fund managers must communicate with end investors and shareholders in a senior loan mutual fund. Senior loans present a special dilemma for the financial advisor and portfolio manager, since the underlying investment is not something that individual investors are able to buy on their own. Loans, after all, are private instruments, and the disclosures made to the manager by a borrower are often not in the public domain. The information that is naturally available to end investors is unusually small. Of course, plenty is written about the small percentage of transactions that default during the cycle, so the image that the popular press will leave is one of a serially troubled asset class. This characteristic has to be overcome with excellent communication.

The emergence of daily pricing services at the end of the 1990s facilitated a much more transparent, arms-length recitation of net asset value. That has certainly helped to build trust in the asset class. Beyond that, portfolio managers have to maintain a steady drumbeat of education and information so that financial advisors can explain the asset class and its behavior to their clients, the end investors. This requires portfolio managers to conduct conference calls, write regular market updates, travel to brokers' offices, and participate in conferences with mutual fund analysts, as well as writing the familiar semiannual shareholder letters. It is no good having fabulous performance if the audience of existing and potential investors doesn't understand how it was derived.

Portfolio Management by Nonbank Loan Investors

Michael P. McAdams
President and CEO, Four Corners Capital Management, LLC

INTRODUCTION

In essence, managing a portfolio of loans for a nontraditional manager on behalf of either individual or institutional investors should not differ from managing loans within a large financial institution. But beyond the basic elements of risk and return achievement, there are numerous ways in which nonbank credit has evolved away from its roots in commercial bank lending.

The focus of this article is on (1) highlighting the critical similarities that persist, (2) offering possible explanations for the evolution of differences, (3) providing guidance in defining nonbank investment philosophies and strategies, (4) reviewing core credit strategies of nonbank managers, and (5) providing a view on the possible direction of credit management trends. This article is intended to focus on current developments and key issues; detailed and quantitative information underlying these comments is available in the rich body of research on fundamental accounting, finance, and credit management issues.

Lending remains a field that relies upon a significant amount of experience and subjective judgment. Accordingly, interpretation of credit principles results in the introduction of biases of individual practitioners and firms. Each practitioner has his or her own history of successful credit decisions and expensive lessons that contribute to these biases and differing views and approaches to the subject.

This chapter will also look mostly at liquid leveraged, or noninvestment grade, par corporate loans. Through this focus I hope to illustrate the essential aspects of loan management at nonbank managers (which have historically focused on such noninvestment grade loans), allowing the reader to adjust the application of these principles to investment grade, middle market, and other types of loan investing.

NONBANK MANAGERS AND LOAN MARKET INVESTORS

Some nonbank managers invest their own capital; most invest significantly on behalf of their clients, the ultimate loan market investors. Some participants who routinely originate and sell loans and even some buyers (who buy loans because that is what they were hired to do) may not fully appreciate the fundamental motivations of the ultimate investors seeking loan investment strategies.

Loan originators normally make or hold loans because loans provide the best asset-liability match as well as the best return given their risk preferences. On the other hand, ultimate or end investors buy investments for the specific balance of certain characteristics: liquidity, risk, and return. Compared to banks, investors, and therefore nonbank managers, are less constrained by narrow regulatory or historical conventions for the funds they construct. They are thus able to consider a greater number of alternative investments.

Indeed, mutual funds, as one type of nonbank fund, are a type of investor that is able to look at a very wide array of alternatives, from pooled government-guaranteed mortgages like GNMAs to junk bonds. However, market volatility has resulted in increased desire for the best risk-adjusted returns.

As a result, ultimate investors have turned to the advantages of commercial loans (e.g., their insulation from the impact of interest rates as a result of floating rates and their senior secured credit standing, which provides a cushioned downside to the investment outcome) to achieve their investment goals. Similarly, the structure of any retail or institutional product needs to be distinct from that of other investments. This is important for banks as loan sellers to understand when they evaluate the likelihood of a nonbank's purchase of any types of bank-originated loan paper (i.e., standard term loan B structures, second lien loans, synthetics, real estate loans, and so on).

Thus, as a prerequisite for understanding nonbank fund investment philosophy and strategy, it is critical that (1) each investment should provide a risk-adjusted return that is sufficient to justify the investment, and (2) the complexity of any investment concept must also be considered in evaluating the advisability of including it in a portfolio that is ultimately sold to broad categories of investors.

ESTABLISHING AN INVESTMENT PHILOSOPHY

Before purchasing any individual loan, much less venturing into building a portfolio of any type of credit instrument, a philosophy to guide investing activities at a particular firm needs to be defined. On one level, this is basic for any endeavor in life, as failure to clearly identify objectives and potential solutions puts any effort at risk of not being successful. But banks often have clear goals handed down by multiple internal and external constituencies. At a nonbank, though, several practitioner-level philosophical and organizational realities need to be considered. Some of these issues are merely a matter of deciding which way to accomplish a given task, and other issues are a matter of living within constraints that have little chance of variation because of an organization's history or budget constraints. A reader may find the checklist given in Exhibit 12.8 helpful in defining her or his own core philosophy. Note that the issues listed in Exhibit 12.8 are likely to be only a partial list of the reasons for a particular firm's way of doing things. But, at the end of the day, understanding the philosophy, sophistication, and risk tolerance of investors may be the most basic starting place for all investment activities.

An investment philosophy is neither a mere lofty goal nor an oblique and frothy mission statement written as an introduction to policy manuals that are read only by trainees. Rather, investment philosophies are guiding principles that every member of an investment management team should consider in every decision to staff, organize, and manage daily investment activity.

CREDIT STRATEGY OVERVIEW

Credit management is both a "bottom-up," or credit-by-credit, fundamental discipline and a "top-down," or economic, market, sector, and industry-weighted, portfolio management exercise.

The purpose of "bottom-up" analysis is to isolate unsystematic or company-specific risks, with a goal of minimizing individual credit defaults, losses, and unfavorable internal or external rating migrations. Top-down portfolio management, in short, seeks to

EXHIBIT 12.8

Inputs into establishing a nonbank investment credit philosophy.

- Risk tolerance of management and clients
- Organizational type and size
- Budget
- Existing organizational support
- Experience of team
- Return requirements
- Return time horizon
- Asset class bias
- Workout traditions: scope and extent
- Organization capability
- Legal support
- Trading competency
- Comfort with rating agency methodologies
- Information systems
- Portfolio data collection, retention, and accessibility realities
- Global verses regional outlook
- Performance attribution traditions
- Availability of industry specialists
- Competency of operational staff
- Training resources
- Staff compensation structure and incentives
- Regulatory position
- Access to economic research
- Public/private "Chinese wall" issues

avoid unintended correlations among individual borrower and industry exposures. The combination of both efforts seeks to generate superior portfolio performance. But in addition, an objective should be to do so within expected levels of volatility relative to the market. This can be referred to as endeavoring to generate a low portfolio beta relative to the market. In addition, managers may seek to generate returns through a variety of differentiated core market strategies (this is sometimes referred to as generating alpha). Excess returns may also be generated through the exploration of alternative markets or techniques (which may be known as the gamma of portfolio returns). Such modern portfolio theory and option market references have become an important part of developing loan market practices, if only because of the increasingly sophisticated nature of

EXHIBIT 12.9

Inputs into nonbank credit strategy implementation.

- CLOs – Cash flow or market value
- CLOs – Balance sheet or arbitrage
- Synthetic or cash investing
- Retail funds – open end or closed end
- Hedge fund – fixed income allocations, targeted originations, or special situation
- Middle market, investment grade, leveraged loan, or asset-based
- Par, stressed, or distressed; passive or control-oriented
- Liquid or illiquid strategy
- Long only, or long-short
- Head office, separate business unit, or hybrid
- Industry specialized/generalists
- Loans, bonds, mortgages, leases
- Public/private/hybrid
- Team, trader, and portfolio manager authorities
- Floating rate/fixed income
- Liquidity biased or buy-and-hold
- Individual loans/bonds/indices or composites
- Financing/structuring options

loan manager clients; those clients now ask the same questions of loan managers that they ask of managers of any other asset class.

There are other aspects of determining a credit strategy. Many of them are very basic but have as much importance as sophisticated investor-driven performance targets. For example, one needs to consider product design, market segment expertise, and organizational realities. Some examples of other factors affecting strategy selection in general are highlighted in Exhibit 12.9.

Prior to reviewing the basics of credit and portfolio management techniques or strategies, it may be helpful for the reader to revisit the introduction to this chapter for a review of the factors that have significantly influenced loan investment philosophy and strategy establishment.

CREDIT STRATEGY IMPLEMENTATION

While there are many ways to approach credit analysis, a basic methodology for individual loan credit analysis (to which many bank-trained analysts have been exposed) remains the easiest way

E X H I B I T   1 2 . 1 0

The "5 Ps of credit" updated for the nonbank loan manager.

Purpose	• Use of proceeds, capital structure, strategic purpose/justification for transaction
People	• Management, sponsor, accountant, and agent
	• Experience and reputation of firms and individuals
	• Fundamental review of business: its products, business strategies, customers, suppliers, cost structure, market leadership, patents, trademarks, facilities, controls, policies, and operations
Payment	• Cash flow modeling/sensitivities, synergetic cash flow generation, cost savings possibilities
	• Capital market needs and likelihood of access
Protection	• Collateral valuation, likelihood of valuation maintenance in bankruptcy or workout, claims on collateral, intercreditor arguments, setoffs, legal documentation and covenant review, swaps, and so on
Perspective	• Ratings and spread
	• Fees and price
	• Liquidity of the loan in the market
	• Relative value of loan, various loan tranches, and other debt
	• Top-down economic and industry concentrations
	• Value-at-risk considerations
	• Technical factors, including industry funds flows, familiarity with borrower by market
	• Prepayment risk analysis
	• Overall strengths and weaknesses

to present the material. Exhibit 12.10 outlines a method of organizing essential aspects of basic credit analysis in a format known as the "5 Ps of credit." Each "P" represents a broad topic of fundamental analysis for a specific borrower. Each subpoint is an aspect for detailed consideration by the analyst in reaching a credit decision.

Following the individual credit analysis basics, there are also some key factors that can be used to implement nonbank portfolio management. Augmenting the 5 Ps model, Exhibit 12.11 outlines the basics of portfolio management in a model referred to as the "5 Ds of nonbank portfolio management."

Rather than elaborate on every point or subpoint in Exhibits 12.10 and 12.11, it may be more helpful to review a process for applying the updated 5 Ps and the contemporary 5 Ds credit and portfolio management methodologies.

EXHIBIT 12.11

The "5 Ds of nonbank portfolio management."

Diversity	• Diversity by issue, issuer, industry, and sector • Exposure to common themes (commodity prices, common suppliers, and so on) • Exposure to market correlations
Defaults	• Rating by agencies • Analysts' confirmation of ratings • Portfolio WARF and recovery rate scores
Directives	• Portfolio guidelines and investor expectations • Regulatory considerations • Volatility/yield considerations • Portfolio liquidity needs
Delta	• Loan market correlations to other markets • Hedging/shorting strategies • Interrelationships between a hedged position and its hedges
Discipline	• Consistency with philosophy of manager • Adherence to sell/hedge triggers

Sourcing of Investment Opportunities

A critical element for implementing any loan investment strategy is maximizing the number of primary or secondary opportunities from which to select. Long-term loan market participants tend to receive reasonable attention from sales desks compared to "asset allocators," who invest in loans only during certain phases of the economic cycle. Likewise, there is a selective advantage for managers that are neither too small to offer a significant sell-side business opportunity (and thereby see fewer offerings) nor too large, so that as a practical matter, they must buy most of what is available.

Screening and In-depth Fundamental Analysis

At a nonbank manager, the more quickly unacceptable opportunities can be screened out, the more time there is available for other aspects of credit management. Typically, reasons for early credit turndown include excessive leverage, prior bad experience with the industry or borrower, off-market pricing, or poor relative value compared to other current market offerings. While application of 5 P– and 5 D–type guidelines is critical, it is typically done by experienced, industry-focused analysts who are empowered to decline any investment they do not favor; the classical process of "going to the credit committee" is typically minimized, as final approvals tend to be more about confirmation and/or strategy discussions, with more significant weight placed on the work of the analysts.

Given the relatively significant level of standardization of legal documentation, analysts tend to utilize legal counsel only for more unusual structures or where possible conflicts of interest between borrower, agent, and syndicate members may exist.

Covenants continue to be areas of considerable contention. The concept of "covenant light"[1] has continued to trouble the buy-side, and from time to time, ineffective covenant packages have been grounds for late-stage turndowns.

Monitoring and Management

With so many publicly rated loans available, and with so many borrowers that also issue public securities, monitoring of positions has become easier. However, better information also brings with it the need to sort and understand more information than can often be processed. Also, there may be situations in which analysts will need to deal with conflicting trends in the prices for an issuer's stocks, bonds, loans, and CDS. Fundamental financial information is critical, but with increased loan valuation efficiency, technical indicators and sentiment have greater impact than was previously the case. On an ongoing basis, managers that have alternative ways in which to redeploy assets do so. This is evidenced by the substantial rise in secondary loan volume. However, each firm has its own basis for selling, buying more, or moving responsibility for a name to a workout or distressed asset professional.

In addition to changes in the prospects for individual names, more nonbanks actively change allocations and position sizing based upon changes in the market, industry, or sector, as opposed to relying solely on original "money good" underwriting conclusions.

---

[1] Loans whose credit agreement contains minimal covenant requirements like those of some bond indentures.

Practical Nonbank Credit Lessons Learned

An expedited way of emphasizing the critical aspects of credit at nonbank firms is to provide some examples of lessons that typical nonbank investors have learned.

1. *Simplicity is good.* If a borrower's business is simple to understand and/or more narrowly focused, this typically means that there is a greater likelihood that the borrower will attain its business goals and there will be fewer credit surprises. And, paraphrasing ledgendary mutual fund manager Peter Lynch "It is better to finance a firm that is simple enough that even a fool could run, because at some point a fool will."

2. *Conglomerate diversification.* While having many different business units gives the company the option of raising cash by spinning some of them off, the complexity of actually running all of the separate units is usually daunting for company management. (See item 1.)

3. *Unsubstantiated synergy.* Not all "projected synergy" is bad, but projected synergy does have a bad name in credit circles, since one plus one often equals not two but 1/2. Simply put, cost savings that are unattainable may have resulted in more defaults than oil price rises, fraud, and competition put together.

4. *Equity and high yield are the "smart money."* Just because there is a large amount of public or private equity or high yield that is subordinate to a bank loan in a capital structure doesn't mean that the loan is protected from loss. It could also mean that the high-yield buyers are even more yield-hungry than the bank lenders. With that said, it is better to have the high yield and equity cushion than not to have it.

5. *Complexity isn't sophistication.* Transactions with elaborate capital structures, unusual intercreditor arrangements, and innovative collateral or cash flow sharing terms often become even more complex during workouts.

6. *Beware of price takers.* Companies whose products or services are not unique or in high enough demand to

allow them to set and maintain price advantages are more vulnerable to market, economic, or competitor challenges.

7. *Falling knives.* Buying a credit that suddenly becomes cheap can result in either a low-cost entry point or getting in at the top. In bank loan credit, the market sometimes processes information more slowly. When in doubt, buy patiently. Better to buy on a substantiated recovery than on "a dead cat bounce," (which is a temporary recovery from a prolonged decline or bear market, after which the market continues to fall.)

8. *The "money good" myth.* Analysts who write a ten-page analysis at syndication on why a credit is money good in all circumstances are typically slow to change that fundamental premise, even in the face of a dramatic change in outlook.

9. *Formula-based analyst compensation.* No analyst whose compensation is based on a formula (and who impressed management with his or her intelligence enough to be hired) will fail to find a way to beat the management bonus formula if allowed to do so. A subjective bonus scheme, consistently and fairly applied, will result in better portfolio performance.

10. *The value of covenants, legal and accountant opinions, or litigation rights.* There are very few instances in which any of these have ever qualified as a primary source of repayment. They are all advantageous, but if they are truly needed, the situation is already worse than was desired.

11. *Your first loss is your best loss.* While at times it seems that only "old school" credit people believe this, it is they who have seen every type of incomplete "Hail Mary pass" and unsuccessful turnaround story. In the modern, relatively liquid loan market, there is nothing to stop an early seller of a loan from repurchasing that loan once it has hit bottom and started to show tangible signs of recovery. (See item 7.) And while not selling may result in taking less of a loss, it doesn't seem to turn out that way very often.

12. *Fraud happens.* Despite Sarbanes-Oxley requirements, increased accountant scrutiny, and (litigation-inspired) improved investment bank due diligence, the possibility that fraud will occur has not markedly declined. Overly rapid growth, highly decentralized accounting, and loose management controls can create environments in which fraud can start and grow unnoticed. The prospective benefit of fraud in the mind of a truly "skilled practitioner" will always offset the ultimate costs of SafetyKleen/Enron/WorldCom/Parmalat and Refco-styled attempts at greed and obfuscation.

13. *It is not individual borrowers' defaults or market collapse that hurts performance the most.* Any experienced manager diversifies away the risk of an individual surprise blowing up a portfolio. And any portfolio that weathers a marketwide storm with less damage than market trends (because of the manager's credit selectivity) will see the manager live to "fight another day." However, being overextended in an industry that collapses even for unanticipated reasons can result in serious losses, as well as losses of client relationships and a decline in a manager's business prospects. It therefore can be helpful to be sure that analysts look at a diversified group of industries to help them maintain perspective and objectivity and to avoid overconcentration even in "sure thing" industries.

14. *Technical factors matter.* Portfolios and individual loan purchases do not exist in a vacuum. Current price and funds-flow data as well as forward calendar and market prepay experience all influence technical price moves.

15. *Beware of shifting deltas.* As hedging and shorting become more credible loan market activities, the difference in price movements (the delta) of individual loans and price movements of loans and other securities are critical. The problem is that for a considerable period, there will not be significant data to analyze delta changes optimally. In addition, loan prices rely on recovery rate assumptions, which are often a challenge to evaluate in the early phases of a developing situation.

FUTURE OUTLOOK FOR CORPORATE LOAN CREDIT MANAGEMENT OVER THE NEXT FIVE YEARS

Even the best credit management strategies should not be etched in stone. Just as the market is dynamic, so too are the credit investing strategies of most nonbanks. The following is a compilation of trends and concepts that may affect credit management in the loan market over the next few years.

1. *Liquidity will continue to increase.* Prospects for "main-streaming" of the loan asset class will continue to bring a broader ultimate investor base, including renewed and expanded retail investment and meaningful participation by endowments, family offices, foundations, and public and private pension funds. Developments in hedging techniques, reductions in assignment size, and transaction cost declines will continue. Mark-to-market accuracy and increases in the number of daily-quoted loans will all continue to reduce bid-ask spreads and increase the availability of real bids and real offers on a larger portion of the market.

2. *Hedging and shorting.* These techniques will become as routine for noninvestment grade loans as they are for investment grade loans today. The costs and ease of shorting and hedging will allow all types of managers to protect against the downside and generate higher returns.

3. *Performance attribution of loans will become more sophisticated.* Efforts by Standard & Poor's, Loan Pricing Corporation, and others to provide market data and analysis will expand to provide the same level of asset class performance analysis that exists in traditional bond and equity markets. Managers will learn to "slice and dice" their own performance more accurately, providing better feedback for future investment strategy.

4. *Counterparty issues will become real and significant.* With the growth of hedging, shorting, and derivative transactions, settlement risks and counterparty exposure will grow in importance. Several major bank and/or non-bank organizations will fail to settle on sizable CDS positions, causing significant short-term disruptions.

5. *Dispute resolutions and market practice adjudication.*
Disputes between participants will benefit from a meaningful and efficient mechanism for dispute resolution
without litigation. Market practices for trading, settlement, and syndication as well as amendment procedures
will be further standardized. A more formal code of
ethics may be established by the LSTA. Violation of
market practices will result in meaningful censure of the
offending party by the market.

6. *Loans will become a real market.* A "tape," or broker-
reported record of all significant trades, will be created.
A clearinghouse exchange or some other mechanism will
be established to substantially decrease settlement periods. The LSTA may choose to expand its role in market
regulation, standardization, and oversight. While these
trends may result in loans becoming true securities, the
benefits to all parties will outweigh the costs.

7. *Globalization.* Twenty-four-hour trading of larger credits
through coordinated brokerage in Europe, the United
States, and Asia will become routine. Currency differences between the denomination of debt and investor
capital will be efficiently managed through linked and/
or embedded hedges. Common-language documentation
and standardized settlement documents will be created
and adapted. There may well be a merging or joint venturing of all loan market trade associations in the United
States, Europe, and Asia.

8. *Increased breadth of the loan market.* The same trends that
have led to growth in larger liquid loans will influence
middle market loans and even smaller community
banking loans.

9. *Buy-side and sell-side designations will blur.* Selected buy-
side shops will participate more aggressively in functions
usually reserved for sell-side shops. Sell-side originators
and traders will buy, hold, and actively manage loans like
a buy-side nonbank manager.

10. *Credit management strategies will become newsworthy.* The
technologies, strategy, and philosophies of credit will be
as widely reported and discussed as trading volume,
pricing trends, and league tables.

CONCLUSION

Nontraditional loan investors, including a wide array of nonbanks, enjoy substantial advantages that make them logical holders of bank loan credit instruments. Nonbanks benefit from independence from customer relationship issues and capital market objectivity. Primarily floating-rate bank loans free managers and their clients from the management of duration and rate risks, which frequently obscure fundamental credit risk/return considerations. The senior collateralized status of bank loans provides investors with a proven mechanism to reduce credit volatility. The application of techniques from other markets is improving analytical methods and portfolio strategies to enhance returns and reduce volatility.

Nevertheless, nonbank loan investment management shares an undeniable common lineage with bank credit portfolio management. Developments in investment grade hedging techniques that have been pioneered by traditional commercial and investment banks are likely to become standard techniques with which nonbanks hedge their noninvestment grade portfolios. This can be considered either a full-circle return to bank credit strategies or an expression of the reality of the common issues facing all credit investment operations.

Just as this article was being completed, the International Association of Credit Portfolio Managers (the IACPM, which is a trade association comprising credit and risk managers at most major commercial and investment banks globally) completed a document entitled "Sound Practices in Credit Portfolio Management." This document is available to IACPM members and to the wider credit market at www.iacpm.org. While this organization's historical focus has been on bank credit management, its growing desire for nonbank membership and its recognition of the need for global sound practices in credit appear to represent the ultimate "feedback loop" in the evolving loan market. From the vantage point of a nonbank investor, it is apparent from reviewing the IACPM report that even among the largest commercial and investment banks, credit investment philosophy, strategy, and practice will, in the future, differ little between organizations. Market dynamics are likely to further reduce any remaining differences over time.

The author would like to express appreciation to Ed Freiermuth, Mort Glanz, and John Richter for their inspiration and selfless sharing of a lifetime of experience in credit. The assistance of Nancy Fabian is also acknowledged and greatly appreciated.

Distressed Loan Portfolios

Geoffrey A. Gold
Partner, Strategic Value Partners, LLC

The use of bank debt can add significant value in the construction of distressed debt portfolios. In certain portfolios, senior and secured loans are the predominant target for investment. In fact, there are certain managers in the distressed debt hedge fund universe, including Strategic Value Partners, that actively invest in bank debt for substantial percentages of their portfolios. The reasons for the use of bank debt include its risk/reward characteristics, exhibited in its resistance to market volatility and its significant upside potential, its ability to create a control position in restructuring and bankruptcy scenarios, and its ability to substantially enhance the due diligence process. Furthermore, the size of the global private debt universe of defaulted and stressed deals is enormous in absolute terms, much larger than the universe of public debt.

RISK/RETURN CHARACTERISTICS

It is common knowledge that one of the strongest attributes of bank loans is that they are senior in the capital structure and are often secured by specific collateral, which can include the real estate, accounts receivable, or inventory of a particular company. By virtue of this position within the capital structure, loans provide excellent risk/return characteristics. They are less affected by volatility in global markets, especially when compared to unsecured and subordinated debt. Exhibit 12.12 depicts the Loan B Index and the ML B bond index spreads and clearly shows the stability of loan spreads during periods of significant widening in bond-related credit spreads. Although the chart relates to par high yield rather than distressed debt, the point is the same. The underlying collateral and position within the capital structure provide protection from excessive volatility in periods of market dislocation (see Q3 2002 in Exhibit 12.12).

EXHIBIT 12.12

Loan B Spread versus ML Bond Index Spread

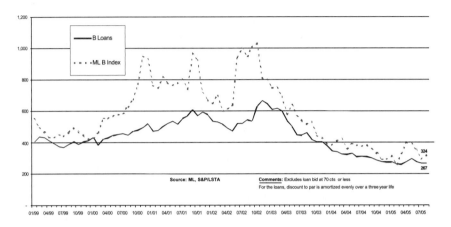

ACCESS TO INFORMATION

Under standard loan documentation, lenders have the right to receive private (nonpublic) information, provided that they have given an appropriate confidentiality undertaking. This information might include monthly financial reports, more detailed information about the business and the industry, various consultancy reports, and access to management. All of this information allows for a much deeper level of due diligence. The portfolio manager will have more and better information to use in the decision-making process, and hence will have a higher comfort level in making a particular investment. The downside of signing confidentiality agreements and becoming restricted is that the investment universe becomes limited to private instruments. The portfolio manager is giving up other potentially attractive investments in the subordinated levels of the capital structure in return for more precise information and ultimately a greater degree of certainty in the investment thesis.

INFLUENCING THE RESTRUCTURING PROCESS

Within a bankruptcy, loans provide the portfolio manager with the ability to control and/or influence the reorganization process. This influence may come through suggesting certain turnaround managers, including a chief restructuring officer (CRO), working with the company's legal and financial advisors in formulating a plan of reorganization (POR) that satisfies the requirements of the senior secured creditors first, and providing debtor in possession (DIP) financing if necessary. Each of these aspects of control and influence leads to position protection and value enhancement. In addition, lenders have protection through covenants in loan agreements. While this is not a major point within a bankruptcy, as covenants have already been breached, it can be very significant in the case of an out-of-court restructuring process. Covenants that are particularly important to distressed managers include those that involve leverage and capital expenditures. If the company does not meet these covenants, it will need to get waivers from the lending group. The covenant renegotiation process gives the holder of the loan critical influence.

SUPPLY AND DEMAND

Additional characteristics of loans that increase their attractiveness involve the market structure of the loan universe. First, on the supply side, sellers of private debt instruments, including banks, insurance companies, and various finance companies, are not necessarily economic sellers. Loans may be trading above a certain internal reserve, which would result in an accounting gain. Or, given scarce management resources, the institution may decide that selling in the market is preferable to proceeding through what will probably become a time-intensive workout process. This creates market inefficiency, which is attractive to distressed debt fund managers. Second, on the demand side (from the distressed hedge fund manager's perspective), the market is inefficient as well. Monetary capital alone is not significant for an invitation to participate in new and "undiscovered" private debt situations. "Intellectual capital," in addition to well-developed and long-standing relationships with firms that source private debt, is also necessary.

DISTRESSED DEBT UNIVERSE

The sheer size of the private distressed debt universe is an interesting attribute for fund managers. According to Professor Edward I. Altman of NYU's Stern School of Business, there is more than

EXHIBIT 12.13

Distressed and Defaulted Debt Outstanding

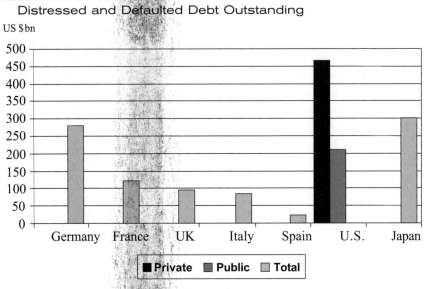

US $bn

Sources: Professor Edward I. Altman, Strategic Value
Partners, LLC, Ernst & Young, Mercer Oliver Wyman,
PriceWaterhouseCoopers

$530 billion face value of distressed and defaulted debt outstand-
ing in the United States alone. Adding estimates for Europe brings
this number to approximately $1.0 trillion (Professor Edward I.
Altman, Strategic Value Partners, LLC, Ernst & Young, Mercer
Oliver Syman, and PricewaterhouseCoopers; see Exhibit 12.13).
Moreover, according to Professor Altman's estimates, the ratio of
private to public distressed and defaulted debt outstanding is more
than 2.20:1 in the United States. In Europe, the ratio is even more
skewed. On the other hand, investment capital dedicated to this
area is estimated to be less than $100 billion. This dichotomy is
interesting from an opportunistic fund manager's perspective.

INEFFICIENT MARKET

Another aspect of the distressed loan market that makes it attractive relates to the structural inefficiency of the market. This has
been alluded to in previous sections that have discussed market
size and reasons that financial institutions may choose to sell in the
secondary market. The importance of these inefficiencies should be
emphasized, however. The first aspect revolves around the general

lack of transparency in this market and the importance of sourcing new deals. The lack of clarity or opaqueness of the market itself gives an edge to managers with the historical relationships that provide access to the product. In addition, there are important operational issues that must be taken into consideration. Specifically, the ability to deal with monthly interest rollovers, letter of credit facilities, or unfunded revolving lines of credit is an operationally intensive issue that many managers are unwilling or unable to deal with. Lack of transparency and operational intricacies create high barriers to entry into this loan universe and therefore make it very attractive to distressed managers with the experience and specialization to capitalize on it.

In conclusion, bank loans provide the distressed fund manager with a broad set of attractive investment characteristics. This results from a combination of the bank loan's seniority within the capital structure, the unique opportunities created by an inefficient market structure, and an inherent supply/demand imbalance. Seniority within the capital structure dampens the impact of market volatility, while still providing significant upside potential, and the inefficient market structure and supply/demand imbalance mean that only a limited number of managers can access investment opportunities within the distressed loan market. In order to take advantage of this, however, the manager must have an operational infrastructure in place that is capable of dealing with the complexities of distressed loans. Ultimately, fund managers who can bring together the experience, relationships, and operational capabilities necessary to access the distressed loan universe can add significant value in portfolio construction.

CHAPTER 13

Legal, Regulatory, and Accounting Issues

Bala Ayyar
Canadian Imperial Bank of Commerce

Wayne Lee
Canadian Imperial Bank of Commerce

Seth Grosshandler
Cleary Gottlieb Steen and Hamilton LLP

Kate A. Sawyer
Cleary Gottlieb Steen and Hamilton LLP

John C. Pattison
Canadian Imperial Bank of Commerce

Introduction to Accounting Standards Applicable to Loans: A Bank's Perspective

Bala Ayyar & Wayne Lee
Canadian Imperial Bank of Commerce

This article sets out the highlights of accounting for loans and loan products under U.S. GAAP. To apply these rules to any individual set of facts and circumstances will require due diligence and exercise of professional judgment.

Adequate loan accounting policies and procedures are essential to sound and effective overall risk management processes in a bank. The accounting treatment and classification of a loan are both largely dependent on and driven by management's holding intent. For example, loans that are designated as trading are carried at fair value, and loans that are classified as held-to-maturity are carried at amortized cost less allowance for credit losses. It is, therefore, important for a bank to have a clear set of policies and procedures in place to determine which positions should be included in, and which should be excluded from, each loan classification. Common loan classifications include the "trading book," the "banking book," and "held for sale."[1]

INITIAL RECOGNITION AND MEASUREMENT

In general, a bank should recognize a loan, whether originated or purchased, on its balance sheet when the bank becomes a party to the contractual provisions of the loan. Assuming that origination coupons are set to market yields, the loan should initially be measured at cost. Thus, for loans that are originated by the bank, the cost is the amount lent to the borrower adjusted for any net deferred loan fees or costs that are similar in nature to interest (e.g., fees or costs that are calculated on a time basis or by reference to

---

[1] For certain institutions (i.e., investment companies) that do not have a banking book, the trading intent is assumed at origination or purchase. Such institutions typically mark to market all their loan positions in inventory.

the amount of the loan). Where a loan has been acquired from a third party, the cost generally is the fair value of the consideration given to acquire the loan at the time of acquisition. Loans that are acquired for noncash consideration should be initially measured at estimated fair value.

TRADING BOOK

Loans that are originated or acquired either with a trading intent or to hedge other elements of the trading book can be designated as "trading" and recorded in the bank's trading book. Examples of loans that are typically recorded as trading loans include loans acquired in the secondary market, including any distressed loans that are acquired and held intentionally for short-term resale, and loans that are held to hedge total return swaps (TRSs) in the trading book.[2] Trading book loans are measured at fair value, i.e., they are marked to market through the income statement. Interest income is recognized on an accrual basis, and all transaction costs or other fees are recognized immediately in net income.

Fair value is determined based on market value, but when market prices are not readily available, fair value is estimated using pricing models that are based on current market data wherever possible (see the discussion of pricing models in Chapter 7). Valuation adjustments, where appropriate, are employed to value loans to cover market risk, model risk, and credit risk.

BANKING BOOK

Loans recorded in a banking book are measured at amortized cost, net of allowance for credit losses, and any interest income is recognized on an accrual basis.

Allowance for Credit Losses

An allowance for credit losses measured on a present value basis is recorded on impaired loans. A loan is impaired when, based on current information and events, it is probable that the bank will be unable to collect all amounts due according to the contractual

---

[2] Loans held to hedge TRSs may have a longer holding period than traditional trading book items.

terms of the loan agreement. Generally, loans on which repayment of principal or payment of interest is contractually over 90 days in arrears are considered impaired unless they are fully secured and in the process of collection.

Fees/Expenses

Fees associated with lending activities that represent compensation to the bank for activities that are integral to a specific lending arrangement are recognized as revenue over the expected term of the resulting loan as an adjustment of yield on the loan. However, fees that represent compensation to the bank for services that are not expected to result in specific lending arrangements are recognized as revenue over the period of the contractual obligation, according to the nature of their service (i.e., over the commitment period or as service is rendered).

Syndication Fees

Any syndication fees, also known as skim fees or syndication skim, paid to a bank upon syndication of a loan are recognized when the syndication is complete unless a portion of the syndicated loan is retained.

When a portion of the syndicated loan is retained by the syndicating bank, if the yield on the portion of the loan retained by the bank is less than the average yield to the other syndication participants after considering the fees passed through by the bank, then the bank should defer a portion of the syndication fee to produce a yield on the portion of the loan retained that is not less than the average yield on the loans held by the other syndication participants. The balance of fees can be recognized as income on completion of the syndication.

Participation Fees

Loan participation fees are amortized into earnings over the term of the loan. When part of a loan is subsequently sold off, a proportionate amount of unamortized loan participation fees should be recognized at the time of sale. The remaining unamortized fees related to the retained portion of the loan should be included in the net carrying amount of the loan and should be amortized into earnings over the remaining term of the loan.

Incremental direct costs incurred to originate or acquire a loan are netted against loan origination or acquisition fees and deferred and amortized over the life of the loan to which they apply, as a reduction of the loan's yield. These costs include costs to originate a loan that (1) result directly from and are essential to the lending transaction and (2) would not have been incurred by the lender had the lending transaction not occurred. Examples of these are third-party payments for appraisal and legal fees, commissions paid to loan brokers, and employees' compensation costs that are directly related to time spent performing origination activities.

All other lending-related costs, including costs pertaining to activities performed by the bank for advertising, soliciting potential borrowers, servicing existing loans, and other ancillary activities related to establishing and monitoring credit policies, supervision, and administration, are charged to expense as incurred. Employees' compensation and fringe benefits related to those activities, unsuccessful loan origination efforts, idle time, and other overhead costs are also charged to expense as incurred.

HELD FOR SALE

Some banks, such as mortgage banks, may classify loans in a "held for sale" portfolio. Loans classified in this way include mortgage loans or other loans that are held in order to be securitized or sold. These loans are measured at the lower of cost or market value.

TRANSFERS BETWEEN PORTFOLIOS

The transfer of a loan between trading and banking categories is accounted for at fair value; however, given the nature of a trading asset, transfers into or out of the trading category are rare. When a decision is made to sell a loan or portion thereof that was not originated or initially acquired with the intent to sell, the loan must be transferred from the banking book to the held for sale portfolio. Loans transferred into the held for sale portfolio are recorded at the lower of their carrying or fair value on a loan-by-loan basis. Losses on transfer that are determined to be credit-related are charged to the provision for credit losses. Losses that are determined to be other than credit-related are charged to other noninterest income.

OTHER LOAN-RELATED INVESTMENT PRODUCTS

Beside loans and traditional debt securities, it has become increasingly common for institutions to acquire credit risk/exposure through credit-related investment products like collateralized debt obligations (CDOs) and synthetic CDOs. In addition, many hedge funds are also utilizing derivative instruments like total return swaps to leverage and acquire credit exposure.[3]

A position in CDO paper (except for market value CDOs) is treated as a debt security by virtue of the rules set out in EITF 99–20. Accordingly, it is accounted for in accordance with *FAS 115* and can be classified as "trading," "available for –sale," or "held to –maturity."

The accounting treatments for debt securities that are held for trading and held to maturity are basically the same as the treatments for loans that are in the trading book and the banking book, respectively. However, a debt security can be classified as held to maturity only if the bank has the positive intent and ability to hold that security to maturity. A sale of an investment from the held-to-maturity portfolio will most likely bring into question the bank's intent and may taint the classification of the entire remaining portfolio.

Debt securities not classified as trading or held-to-maturity securities are classified as available-for-sale securities. Available-for-sale securities are measured at fair value on the balance sheet. Unrealized holding gains and losses are generally excluded from earnings and reported in other comprehensive income until realized.

Credit exposure acquired through synthetic CDOs, total return swaps, and other similar instruments is viewed as a derivative instrument and is subject to the provisions of *FAS 133*. Credit products that are considered derivative instruments are measured at fair value, with changes in fair value included in earnings.

ACCOUNTING FOR CREDIT-RISK HEDGING ACTIVITIES

There is an increasing range of methods available to manage or divest exposure to specific credit risk. It is quite common for banks

---

[3] We have excluded from this discussion conventional credit exposure acquired through instruments like bonds, convertibles, and commercial paper, to which the regular securities accounting rules would apply.

to hedge their credit-risk exposure by buying credit default swaps (single-name or basket) or to transfer their credit-risk exposure by selling credit-related investments such as credit-linked notes and synthetic CDOs. However, one common problem with hedging banking book items is that the hedging of the credit risk can often fail to qualify for hedge accounting under *FAS 133*, thereby resulting in asymmetric accounting treatment and consequent earnings volatility. In general, it is more difficult to qualify for hedge accounting for credit derivatives under the hedge effectiveness test.

A bank may also need to hedge its credit-risk exposure originating from products such as credit-linked notes and total return swaps. Such exposure may be economically hedged by purchasing loans or debt securities. These loans or debt securities are usually classified in a category that has accounting treatment similar to that of the underlying products, to minimize the accounting mismatch.

FASB SPE CONSOLIDATION RULES

A bank (or any institutional player) that has exposure to loan products is likely from time to time to encounter special-purpose entities (SPEs). The accounting rules concerning the consolidation of SPEs changed significantly in 2004, when the Financial Accounting Standards Board (FASB) issued *FASB Interpretation 46R*, "Consolidation of Variable Interest Entities" (*FIN 46R*). The old rule had been criticized for enabling companies to keep billions of dollars of assets off the balance sheet by moving them into SPEs or other entities that they did not "control." Furthermore, an independent third party had only to invest minimal equity in the SPE—typically 3 percent of the SPE's capitalization. The new rule attempts to address these deficiencies.

Institutions should ensure that their activities in the loan market do not inadvertently trip the consolidation requirements of *FIN 46R*. The following sections describe both the gist of the accounting rule and its applicability in certain generic situations.

Overview of *FIN 46R*

A variable interest entity (VIE), as defined under *FIN 46R*, is usually an entity with very small equity interest or one in which the equity owners' vote is not meaningful. The normal condition for consolidation (ownership of a majority voting equity interest) does not apply to a VIE. Instead, under *FIN 46R*, each holder of an interest in the VIE, including both equity and other interests that will either absorb losses or participate in profits (known as variable interests or VIs), evaluates its economic position to determine whether its variable interest will absorb a majority of the VIE's expected losses, receive a majority of the VIE's expected residual returns, or both. For purposes of analyzing its economic position, a holder should combine its holdings with the holdings of its related parties as defined in *Statement of Financial Accounting Standards No. 57*, "Related Party Disclosures," and its de facto agents.

A holder that will absorb a majority of the VIE's expected losses, receive a majority of the VIE's expected residual returns, or both is deemed to be the VIE's primary beneficiary and should consolidate the VIE. If one holder will absorb a majority of the expected losses and another holder will receive a majority of the expected residual returns, the holder absorbing a majority of losses is the primary beneficiary and should consolidate the VIE. A VIE can have only one primary beneficiary, but some VIEs have no primary beneficiary. If no holder will absorb a majority of the expected losses or receive a majority of the expected residual returns, the VIE is not consolidated.

A holder of a variable interest should determine whether it is the primary beneficiary of a VIE at the time the holder becomes involved with the entity (i.e., when ownership or a contractual or other financial relationship begins). The primary beneficiary should reconsider its initial decision to consolidate if the VIE's governing documents or the contractual arrangements change or the primary beneficiary sells all or part of its interest to unrelated parties. A holder of a variable interest that is not the primary beneficiary also should reconsider the need to consolidate if it acquires newly issued interests in the VIE or a portion of the primary beneficiary's interest in the VIE.

Excluded from the scope of that interpretation are certain not-for-profit organizations, government organizations, certain qualifying special-purpose entities (QSPEs) as defined under *Statement of Financial Accounting Standards No. 140*, "Accounting for Transfers and Servicing of Financial Assets and Extinguishments of Liabilities" (*FAS 140*), and certain qualified businesses.

Loans to a Variable Interest Entity

Generally, a loan is subject to consideration as a VI. For instance, if the loan is not expected to change in value (in this case the rate is fixed and the credit risk is determined not to be significant), then it would generally not have enough variability for the lender to be the primary beneficiary. In contrast, if the bank loan funds all or a substantial part of the VIE's assets, then the bank would probably be the primary beneficiary of the VIE.

Investments in CDOs and Other Similar Vehicles

From time to time, banks may purchase and sell investments in VIEs such as asset-backed papers or securities in the primary and secondary markets. Investors in the lowest tranche (i.e., subordinated debt or equity) usually absorb a majority of the expected losses and, therefore, are most likely to consolidate the entity. Each variable interest holder should determine the VIE's expected outcomes and allocate the expected losses and the expected residual returns pursuant to the contractual arrangements. The contractual arrangements will determine how the VIE's outcomes are to be distributed (both in amount and in priority) to its variable interest holders.

In cases where the VIE has experienced significant losses, holders of the more senior note/security may end up with the majority of the expected losses. In general, these investment vehicles are structured in such a way that there is no primary beneficiary, as no one party will absorb a majority of the expected losses and/or will receive a majority of the expected residual returns.

Loan Securitizations

Securitization provides companies with an alternative funding source, and it may also reduce risk exposure and provide regulatory capital relief. Many banks and finance companies securitize their mortgage loans, credit receivables, or other loans using SPEs.

FAS 140 sets forth U.S. GAAP accounting standards for transfers of financial assets. There are two common ways to achieve nonconsolidation treatment for a securitization transaction. The first is to transfer the loans to a QSPE. QSPEs are not required to be consolidated on the balance sheet of another entity under *FAS 140,* while SPEs enjoy no such exemption. The second is to sell the loans to a third-party-administered multiseller conduit. As long as the transfer meets the true sale criteria under *FAS 140*, the transferor does not hold other variable interests (i.e., commercial papers, debts, or equities) in the conduit, and the transferred assets represent less than 50 percent of the total assets in the conduit, the transaction is likely to achieve nonconsolidation treatment under *FIN 46R*.

In August 2005, FASB issued three exposure drafts on the proposed amendments to *FAS 140*. The proposed amendments would tighten existing criteria governing which types of SPEs can achieve QSPE status and would also introduce some new criteria for sale accounting treatment and derecognition of portions of financial assets when transferred as loan participations. Final guidance is expected to be issued in the second quarter of 2006.

REFERENCES

FAS 65, "Accounting for Certain Mortgage Banking Activities."

FAS 91, "Accounting for Nonrefundable Fees and Costs Associated with Originating or Acquiring Loans and Initial Direct Costs of Leases."

FAS 115, "Accounting for Certain Investments in Debt and Equity Securities."

FAS 133, "Accounting for Derivative Instruments and Hedging Activities."

FAS 140, "Accounting for Transfers and Servicing of Financial Assets and Extinguishments of Liabilities," a replacement for *FAS No. 125*.

FIN 46R, "Consolidation of Variable Interest Entities," an interpretation of *ARB No. 51*.

EITF 99–20, "Recognition of Interest Income and Impairment on Purchased and Retained Beneficial Interests in Securitized Financial Assets."

"Interagency Guidance on Certain Loans Held for Sale," March 26, 2001.

Basel Committee on Banking Supervision: *Trading Book Survey: A Summary of Responses*, April 2005.

Basel Committee on Banking Supervision: *Sound Practices for Loan Accounting and Disclosure*, July 1999.

FAS 140 as Applied to Assignments and Participations

Seth Grosshandler
Cleary Gottlieb Steen and Hamilton LLP

Kate A. Sawyer[4]
Cleary Gottlieb Steen and Hamilton LLP

Statement of Financial Accounting Standards No. 140, "Accounting for Transfers and Servicing of Financial Assets and Extinguishments of Liabilities" (*FAS 140*), issued by the Financial Accounting Standards Board (FASB) provides the accounting and reporting standards for transfers of financial assets, including transfers of loans via assignment and participation. *FAS 140* was issued in September 2000 and replaced the former *FAS 125*, which similarly provided the accounting and reporting standards for transfers of financial assets. The following discussion focuses exclusively on the provisions of *FAS 140* that address the accounting treatment for direct (one-step) transfers of interests in corporate loans pursuant to assignment or participation. This discussion does not address multiple-step transfers (whether by assignment, participation, or otherwise), the transfer of assets in securitizations, or transfers of other assets.

FAS 140 provides the standards for distinguishing for accounting purposes between a transfer of financial assets that constitutes a sale and a transfer of financial assets that constitutes a secured borrowing. When a transfer constitutes a sale under *FAS 140*, the transferor is required to derecognize the assets sold, recognize as proceeds of the sale the assets obtained and the liabilities incurred in consideration of the transferred assets (either by measuring such obtained assets and liabilities at fair value or by applying an alternative measurement), and recognize in earnings any gain or loss on the sale.[5] In contrast, when a transfer does not qualify as a sale under *FAS 140*, the transfer is characterized as a

---

[4] Seth Grosshandler is a partner at Cleary Gottlieb Steen and Hamilton LLP specializing in creditors' rights and related matters. Kate A. Sawyer is an associate at Cleary Gottlieb Steen and Hamilton LLP specializing in secured transactions and Articles 8 and 9 of the Uniform Commercial Code.

[5] Paragraph 11 of *FAS 140* sets forth the specific accounting requirements for transfers that meet the criteria of Paragraph 9 of *FAS 140*.

secured borrowing—the "proceeds of the sale" are instead the amount "loaned" by the transferee to the transferor secured by the assets "transferred." The transferor continues to recognize the assets on its books, and the proceeds received from the transfer are a liability to the transferee.

The *FAS 140* criterion for distinguishing between a sale and a secured borrowing focuses on control. Transfers in which the transferor surrenders control over the financial assets are accounted for as sales, and transfers in which the transferor retains control over the financial assets are accounted for as secured borrowings. The transferor is considered to have "surrendered control" over such transferred assets only if all of the following conditions are met: (1) the transferred assets have been isolated from the transferor (the "isolation requirement"), (2) each transferee has the right to freely pledge or exchange the assets that it received, and (3) the transferor does not maintain effective control over the transferred assets through either an agreement entitling or obligating the transferor to repurchase or redeem such transferred assets before their maturity or the ability to unilaterally cause the transferee to return specific transferred assets.[6] We discuss these conditions in reverse order in the following paragraphs.

The transferor has not surrendered control if the transferor—either through agreement or otherwise—is entitled or obligated to repurchase or redeem the assets before their maturity or has the ability to unilaterally cause the transferee to return specific

---

[6] These conditions are specified in Paragraph 9 of *FAS 140*, which provides:

> 9. A transfer of financial assets (or all or a portion of a financial asset) in which the transferor surrenders control over those financial assets shall be accounted for as a sale to the extent that consideration other than beneficial interests in the transferred assets is received in exchange. The transferor has surrendered control over transferred assets if and only if *all of the following conditions* are met:
>
> a. The transferred assets have been isolated from the transferor—put presumptively beyond the reach of the transferor and its creditors, even in bankruptcy or other receivership (paragraphs 27 and 28).
>
> b. Each transferee (or, if the transferee is a qualifying SPE (paragraph 35), each holder of its beneficial interests) has the right to pledge or exchange the assets (or beneficial interests) it received, and no condition both constrains the transferee (or holder) from taking advantage of its right to pledge or exchange and provides more than a trivial benefit to the transferor (paragraphs 29–34).
>
> c. The transferor does not maintain effective control over the transferred assets through either (1) an agreement that both entitles and obligates the transferor to repurchase or redeem them before their maturity (paragraphs 47–49) or (2) the ability to unilaterally cause the holder to return specific assets, other than through a cleanup call (paragraphs 50–54).

transferred assets. Paragraphs 47 to 54 of *FAS 140* provide implementation guidance to assist in the application of these criteria.
Direct (one-step) transfers between nonaffiliated entities of interests in corporate loans pursuant to assignment or participation
would not typically involve ongoing rights or obligations of the
transferor to reacquire the transferred assets.

Similarly, the transferor has not surrendered control if the
transferee does not have the right to freely pledge or exchange the
assets received. In the case of loan participations, the participation
agreement must give the participant the right to pledge or
exchange the participation interest transferred to the participant.
Paragraphs 104 to 106 of *FAS 140* provide additional implementation guidance for the application of this requirement in the context
of loan participations.[7] Specifically, the following limitations, by
themselves, will not cause the transfer to fail the "freely pledge or
exchange" limitation: (1) a transferor's right of first refusal on a
bona fide offer from a third party, (2) a requirement to obtain the
transferor's permission, which shall not be unreasonably withheld,
or (3) a prohibition on sale to the transferor's competitor if other
potential willing buyers exist.

Lastly, the transferor has not surrendered control over the
transferred assets unless the transferred assets have been "isolated"
from the transferor. It is this isolation requirement that prompts the

---

[7] Paragraphs 104 to 106 provide:

104. Groups of banks or other entities also may jointly fund large borrowings through
loan participations in which a single lender makes a large loan to a borrower and subsequently transfers interests in the loan to other entities.

105. Transfers by the originating lender may take the legal form of either assignments
or participations. The transfers are usually on a nonrecourse basis, and the transferor
("originating lender") continues to service the loan. The transferee ("participating
entity") may or may not have the right to sell or transfer its participation during the
term of the loan, depending upon the terms of the participation agreement.

106. If the loan participation agreement gives the transferee the right to pledge or
exchange those participations and the other criteria in paragraph 9 are met, the transfers to the transferee shall be accounted for by the transferor as sales of financial
assets. A transferor's right of first refusal on a bona fide offer from a third party, a
requirement to obtain the transferor's permission that shall not be unreasonably
withheld, or a prohibition on sale to the transferor's competitor if other potential willing buyers exist is a limitation on the transferee's rights but presumptively does not
constrain a transferee from exercising its right to pledge or exchange. However, if the
loan participation agreement constrains the transferees from pledging or exchanging
their participations, the transferor presumptively receives a more than trivial benefit,
has not relinquished control over the interests, and shall account for the transfers as
secured borrowings.

majority of the debates with respect to the application of *FAS 140* to direct (one-step) transfers of interests in corporate loans pursuant to assignment or participation. Paragraph 27 of *FAS 140* provides the primary implementation guidance to assist in the application of the isolation requirement.[8] In essence, in the context of direct one-step transfers, transferred assets are considered to be isolated only if the legal analysis would support a conclusion that the transferred assets would not be part of the estate of the transferor in the event of bankruptcy or receivership. This requirement is typically interpreted to require that the transfer constitute a "true sale" under U.S. law.[9]

The true sale analysis asks the fundamental question of whether, in an insolvency proceeding of the transferor, the transferred assets would be considered property of the transferor and would therefore be available to other creditors of the transferor. In the case of an assignment of a loan, the transferred asset is the underlying loan. In the case of a participation of a loan, the transferred asset is a beneficial interest in the underlying loan. Whether the assets could be considered property of the transferor's bankruptcy or receivership estate determines whether the transferee of those assets would be able to exercise ownership rights over the assets in the event of the transferor's insolvency. If the assets are pledged and not sold, the transferee's exercise of rights over the

---

[8] Paragraph 27 provides:

27. The nature and extent of supporting evidence required for an assertion in financial statements that transferred financial assets have been isolated—put presumptively beyond the reach of the transferor and its creditors, either by a single transaction or a series of transactions taken as a whole—depend on the facts and circumstances. All available evidence that either supports or questions an assertion shall be considered. That consideration includes making judgments about whether the contract or circumstances permit the transferor to revoke the transfer. It also may include making judgments about the kind of bankruptcy or other receivership into which a transferor or SPE might be placed, whether a transfer of financial assets would likely be deemed a true sale at law, whether the transferor is affiliated with the transferee, and other factors pertinent under applicable law. Derecognition of transferred assets is appropriate only if the available evidence provides reasonable assurance that the transferred assets would be beyond the reach of the powers of a bankruptcy trustee or other receiver for the transferor or any consolidated affiliate of the transferor that is not a special-purpose corporation or other entity designed to make remote the possibility that it would enter bankruptcy or other receivership (paragraphs 83(c)).

[9] *FAS 140* itself does not require an actual "true sale" legal opinion. However, AU Section 9336— which provides auditing standards with respect to the use of legal interpretations to support a conclusion as to the isolation of transferred financial assets—states that a "would-level" legal opinion is usually necessary for transfers that entail continuing involvement of the transferor.

assets is not only subject to the automatic stay (in the case of the Bankruptcy Code), but also limited to the value of the obligation secured. (If the assets are solely collateral for the transferee, the transferee as a secured party would not benefit from increases in the value of the assets beyond the amount of the obligations secured.) Furthermore, in general, for a secured party to have a priority claim in an asset, it has to have "perfected" its security interest.[10] Thus, the question of whether an asset has been legally sold, or instead pledged, can take on great significance.

Stated broadly, the primary factors that are considered relevant to the legal analysis in determining whether a transfer constitutes a sale or a pledge are (1) the objective manifestation of the parties' intent, (2) the legal characteristics of the transfer, and (3) the economic substance of the transaction. For a transaction to constitute a sale, the documentation used by the parties to characterize the transaction and the actions of the parties subsequent to the transfer (including the parties' practices, objectives, business activities, and relationships) must indicate that the parties intended that the transfer constitute a sale. For example, the ability of the transferor to substitute new property for the property transferred, an obligation of the transferor to transfer additional property to the transferee with no additional payments from the transferee, and a structure of level payments by the transferor to the transferee regardless of amounts collected on the transferred property have been cited by some courts as factors leading to the conclusion that a transaction constituted a secured loan by the transferee to the transferor.[11]

Many courts have gone beyond the conduct of the parties and the legal characteristics of the transfer, holding that an analysis of the economic substance of the transaction is an essential element of the characterization process. The major factors identified by courts in their analysis of the economic substance are the extent to which the benefits and risks associated with ownership of the property have been transferred to the transferee. The benefits associated with ownership consist primarily of the opportunity for gain

---

[10] Indeed, many true sale cases are brought because the transferee has not taken the steps necessary to perfect a security interest in the asset purportedly sold to it. See, Codification of Statement on Auditing Standards, Statement on Auditing Standards AU Section 9336 *"Using the Work of a Specialist: Auditing Interpretations of Section 336."*

[11] See, e.g., *In re Evergreen Valley Resort, Inc.*, 23 B.R. 659, 661 (Bankr. D. Me. 1982) and cases cited therein.

through an increase in the market value of the property or receipt of income or proceeds of such property. The risks of ownership are essentially that the property transferred will either decline in value or suffer payment defaults. When the transferor retains the risks associated with ownership of the property, courts have held that the economic substance of the transaction is that of a secured loan by the transferee to the transferor. In particular, when the transferee has recourse to the transferor to compensate it for losses, courts have concluded that the transferor has retained the related risk and that the economic substance of the transaction is that of a loan rather than a sale.[12]

However, some level of recourse against the transferor is not inconsistent with a sale transaction. In the context of transfers of corporate loans pursuant to assignment or participation, transferees often have recourse to the transferor for breaches of representations and warranties concerning the nature and status of the underlying asset (e.g., a loan has a certain unpaid balance; the borrower is of a certain type; the collateral for the loan is of a certain type). In such contexts, a transferee's recourse to the transferor with regard to such contractual breaches typically would not be sufficient by itself to deny a legal sale characterization. Similarly, *FAS 140* acknowledges that certain limited recourse is not inconsistent with sale accounting treatment.[13]

Applying the true sale criteria to the transfer of a loan via assignment is relatively straightforward—namely, assessing the recourse that the transferee has to the transferor with respect to the assigned loans and whether the transferee has acquired the risks and rewards of ownership of the underlying loan. In contrast, applying the true sale criteria to the transfer of an interest in a loan via participation raises more issues that require consideration. A transfer of a loan via assignment substitutes the transferee for the transferor as the lender of record. In contrast, a transfer of a participation in a loan maintains the relationship between the transferor and the underlying borrower intact. What is transferred in a

[12] See, e.g., *In re Corporate Fin., Inc.*, 221 B.R 671, 678 (Bankr. E.D.N.Y. 1998); *Serv. Institute*, 421 N.Y.S.2d at 327.
[13] Paragraph 113 of *FAS 140* states that "[i]n a transfer of receivables with recourse, the transferor provides the transferee with full or limited recourse.... The effect of a recourse provision on the application of paragraph 9 may vary by jurisdiction. In some jurisdictions, transfers with full recourse may not place transferred assets beyond the reach of the transferor and its creditors, but transfers with limited recourse may."

participation is not a complete interest in the loan, but rather a beneficial interest in the underlying loan. In a participation, the transferor will continue to be the record owner of the underlying loan and thus will service or control the servicing of the loan. To the extent that the participation constitutes a true sale in an insolvency proceeding of the transferor, the participant's share of the proceeds of the underlying loan is not considered property of the transferor.[14]

Typically, in the context of a loan participation, the following conditions would have to be present in order for the transfer of the participation to constitute a true sale under U.S. law and not be characterized as a secured borrowing:

- The transferor does not guarantee repayment to the participant or provide other recourse inconsistent with a sale.
- The participation has the same remaining duration as the underlying obligation.
- The participation requires that the transferor/servicer directly pass through any proceeds received from the financial asset to the interest holders, less any proceeds that represent servicing or other compensation to the transferor or an interest in the financial asset kept by the transferor.
- The participation purports to be a sale of a property interest.
- The transferor/servicer is not permitted to commingle for any significant period of time proceeds received on the underlying financial assets.
- The transferor/servicer agrees to act in a custodial capacity on behalf of or in trust for the participant with respect to its holding of any underlying instrument or collateral and in holding any proceeds received with respect to the underlying financial assets.

---

[14] Other distinguishing features of a participation include: the transferee cannot enforce the loan directly against the underlying borrower—it is dependent on the transferor for the collection of the proceeds of the loan; the transferee cannot offset amounts owed by it to the underlying borrower against amounts owed by the underlying borrower under the loan; and, in the absence of an enforceable waiver (and unlike in the case of a full assignment of a loan), the transferor may be able to offset amounts owed by it to the underlying borrower against the amounts owed under the participated loan.

- The transferor/servicer agrees to service the loans under a standard that does not give it unfettered discretion as to all matters.

PROPOSED REVISIONS OF *FAS 140*

Over the past few years, FASB has been involved in ongoing efforts to revise *FAS 140*. The LSTA has been involved in advising and commenting on the proposed revisions to *FAS 140* since January 2004, when FASB began to question, among other things, whether a loan participation should be accounted for as a sale.[15] In August 2005, FASB issued for public comment a revised Exposure Draft of *FAS 140*, "Accounting for Transfers of Financial Assets" (the Exposure Draft).

The Exposure Draft is a revision of the June 2003 Exposure Draft, "Qualifying Special-Purpose Entities and Isolation of Transferred Assets." In addition to the Exposure Draft, FASB issued two other proposed statements that would also amend *FAS 140*, namely, "Accounting for Servicing of Financial Assets" and "Accounting for Certain Hybrid Financial Instruments." The former relates to the accounting for servicing of financial assets. The latter relates to the accounting for hybrid financial instruments and would affect the accounting for beneficial interests in securitized financial assets issued by a qualifying special-purpose entity and also amend *FAS No. 133*, "Accounting for Derivative Instruments and Hedging Activities."

The Exposure Draft maintains the same basic framework for derecognition based on whether the transferor has "surrendered control" as outlined in paragraph 9 of *FAS 140*. However, the Exposure Draft has further narrowed the circumstances in which a transfer would constitute a sale under *FAS 140*—often making them narrower than the circumstances when a transfer would constitute a true sale under legal analysis.

The Exposure Draft includes a specific exception for direct (one-step) transfers of interests in corporate loans pursuant to participation agreements. This exception allows the derecognition criteria in Paragraph 9 of *FAS 140* to be applied to the transfer of a

---

[15] The authors, acting on behalf of the LSTA, prepared various memoranda and comment letters for FASB and participated in various roundtables and education sessions at FASB with respect to issues raised by the proposed revisions to *FAS 140*.

portion of a financial asset (such as a loan participation) if that portion represents a proportionate share of an original asset and there is no recourse to the transferor or subordination. Under this approach, those portions meeting this standard are called "participating interests." Participating interests retained by the transferor are not considered a new financial asset and are initially measured at allocated carryover basis. For portions that do not meet the criteria of a participating interest, the whole original asset is required to be transferred to a qualifying special-purpose entity (a QSPE) in order to achieve sales accounting. The resulting interests from a QSPE are called beneficial interests, and the derecognition criteria in Paragraph 9 are applied to the entire original asset. Beneficial interests held by the transferor are considered new financial assets that are initially measured at fair value.

In December 2005, FASB decided to follow the staff recommendation and delay—the issuance of the proposed revisions to *FAS 140* governing transfers of financial assets. The delay is prompted by the extensive comments that FASB received on the Exposure Draft, primarily relating to the application of the proposed changes to multiple-step transfers (whether by participation or otherwise) and transfers of other assets.

The Loan Market and Basel 2 Regulatory Capital Requirements

John C. Pattison
Canadian Imperial Bank of Commerce

INTRODUCTION

"Basel 2" is a short way of referring to the revised requirements for calculating regulatory capital for large, internationally active financial institutions, mainly but not exclusively banks. Investment banks in some countries and near-banks in others are also covered by these regulatory requirements, depending upon national regulatory structures. The basic reference document, *International Convergence of Capital Measurement and Capital Standards: A Revised Framework* (Basel Committee on Banking Supervision, 2004) (the Framework) was the product of international negotiations to create a common minimum standard; thus, implementation in individual countries may reflect higher standards in some cases. In addition, the Framework provides for specifically identified "national discretions." These permit each national supervisor to select from specific choices for the customization of the Basel Framework for reasons that may legitimately (in most cases) reflect local situations.

For reasons that are made clear in this article, Basel 2 represents a fundamental change in the way regulatory capital is calculated, and hence it is of importance to the financial industry in general and credit market participants in particular. The focus will be on the impact of Basel 2 on credit markets; however, other aspects of these regulatory changes, such as those dealing with operational risk, are of substantial importance. Indeed, it is important to properly categorize operational loss data relative to credit loss data. In many cases, credit losses can be created as a result of operational failures.

FROM THE BASEL ACCORD TO BASEL 2

The international financial system was increasingly unstable in the 1980s and 1990s. This was a result of international debt crises caused by failures of banks and near-banks in a number of countries, including the savings and loan sector in the United States, as well as bouts of problem loans in real estate. In addition, in the 1980s, the appetite for asset acquisition on the part of Japanese financial institutions, which were often more highly leveraged than banks in other developed countries, caused international supervisory attention to be focused on the importance of bank capital standards. This concern led to the 1988 Basel Capital Accord, initially agreed upon by the Group of Ten countries and later extended to approximately 100 countries.

This topic is important to participants in international and domestic credit markets for the following reasons:

1. Basel 2 is the new vocabulary of bank capital management and its operations and governance; hence, practitioners should be fluent in its basic principles.
2. This vocabulary extends to risk management data, metrics, and controls.

3. Financial market participants need to be knowledgeable of, and attuned to, supervisory directives and changes in the regulation of capital.

4. All financial market players should be able to assess the impact of Basel 2 in terms of transactions, asset and risk types, counterparties, and the incentives they face as a consequence of the impact of these variations on regulatory capital.

5. This process focuses supervisory, management, and board attention on both regulatory and economic capital, and the differences between them.

6. There are strategic implications in terms of mergers and acquisitions, the profitability of business lines, and the desirability of certain products and customer types over the business cycle, because of the impact of the new capital regime.

WHAT IS BASEL 2?

While facilitating broad international coordination of minimum capital requirements, Basel 2 offers a menu of approaches to measuring regulatory capital. This is a landmark in the history of financial regulation and supervision. Heretofore, fixed rules were applied to the calculation of capital. These rules did not reflect the vast variations in underlying risks for which the capital was attributed. Beyond the availability of these new choices, the most important change in Basel 2 is that banks' own internal data and estimates of risk parameters—probabilities of default, loss given default, and exposure at default—may be used in the calculation of capital.

Regulators have made it clear that they wish to maintain the level of capital in the financial services industry as a whole, despite the fact that the calculation of capital is intended to be much more risk sensitive. Their thinking is that riskier banks—banks with portfolios of higher-risk credit assets, trading room instruments, and operational risks—will face higher capital requirements, while banks with a lower risk profile will see a reduction. Nonetheless, there is concern over creating such a broad supervisory goal on an a priori basis without reference to the actual facts (i.e., information about a bank's risk-weighted assets). Moreover, international regulators have also contemplated adding a scaling factor to raise capital to higher levels should they not be satisfied with the outcome of the risk-based calculations. Having said that, the other major variable in the determination of regulatory capital by individual institutions is the individual and collective views of rating agencies. Not only are some rating agencies concerned that capital not fall unreasonably or in a manner that is inconsistent with their own methodologies, but financial institutions in general need to assure themselves that their major credit counterparties are satisfied with the outcomes. For example, it is sometimes noted that credit standings within the international swap markets are a key determinant of capital positions maintained by international banks that are active in these markets.

Basel 2 is, naturally enough, the successor to the original Basel Capital Accord. This international agreement was arrived at by the Basel Committee on Banking Supervision (the BCBS), which is a committee of the Bank for International Settlements (the BIS) in Basel, Switzerland. The BIS was originally set up to coordinate German reparations after the First World War. However, after the failure of the Bankhaus Herstatt in 1974, the central bank governors that meet regularly at the BIS set up a committee to deal with international banking regulation and supervision.

Since that time the BCBS has been a focal point for international cooperation and coordination of regulatory and supervisory policy (see Fratianni and Pattison, 2000 and 2001). The 1988 Basel Capital Accord was the first example of a significant multilateral regulatory agreement for the financial sector. Prior to that, cooperation was ad hoc and often bilateral at best. The 1988 Accord was controversial and remains so. Nonetheless, it was the best that could be achieved at that time through international negotiations among diverse national supervisors with different legal and regulatory systems. It was widely recognized that the details of the Accord were seriously flawed in a number of respects. For example:

- The 1988 Accord did not differentiate among the risks of corporate borrowers.
- Country risk was based upon membership in the Organization for Economic Cooperation and Development (the OECD), resulting in higher-risk member countries, such as Mexico, having lower capital requirements than lower-risk nonmembers, such as Singapore.

- Maturity was not factored in appropriately, so that incentives for uncommitted short-term debt facilities were created, thereby increasing risk rather than reducing it.
- Market risks were not treated until an amendment in the 1990s.
- Operational risks were not specifically treated.

The consequences of these weaknesses were serious and encouraged behavior that exacerbated risks rather than reducing them—for example, encouraging the securitization of low-risk assets, since with a standard risk-weighting system for corporate exposures, low-risk assets required excessive capital, whereas high-risk assets required less capital than their risks would have required on an economic basis.

Thus, the stage was set for a revision of this Accord. The public launching commenced in 1999. It is best to consider this regulatory initiative as an "evergreen" process rather than a one-time development, because the fundamental innovation of Basel 2 is to allow individual financial institutions to use internal methods and data to calculate capital. The eventual goal of such a process would be a convergence of economic and regulatory capital models, so that regulatory capital would accurately reflect the long-run risks of the portfolios of financial institutions.

BASEL 2 AND INCENTIVES

In designing Basel 2, it was important to bank supervisors, as well as the affected institutions themselves, that the capital framework be consistent with appropriate incentives. For example, if less sophisticated methods of calculating capital resulted in lower capital requirements than advanced methods, banks would not utilize the latter. Also, there must be some incentive, beyond the ongoing thrust of improving risk management data and technology generally, to invest in some elements of the Basel 2 program that are of a predominantly regulatory, rather than a risk management improvement, nature.

It is too early to make an assessment of the effectiveness in operation of the incentives contained in the Basel 2 Framework. While the gap between economic capital and regulatory capital will be narrowed, it will not be closed by Basel 2. Another reason why it is difficult to assess the impact of incentives on financial institutions is the differing dates of implementation in various jurisdictions: 2008 in most countries, 2009 in the United States, and beyond this date in other countries, particularly developing countries. There is also a need to assess the post-implementation impact of differences in implementation, including how local supervisors have utilized their national discretion and whether implementation is equitable across jurisdictions. A further reason is that there are temporary floors to some of the variables that could be relaxed by supervisors with greater experience over time. It is also the case that Basel 2 cannot be assessed until it has been through at least one full and significant credit or business cycle. Since Basel 2 will create a wealth of data that will be in the public domain, there will be great opportunities for academic and analytic research on this topic.

BASEL 2 AS "REGULATORY DIALECT"

As noted previously, Basel will become an evergreen process, constantly evolving under the tutelage of financial supervisors to reflect changes in products, risks, data, and ultimately portfolio effects. The latter are embedded in portfolio management analytics, including correlations between asset classes. However, the equations created by the Basel Committee on Banking Supervision for the calculation of regulatory capital currently include fixed, predetermined correlation factors.

The best way for practitioners to approach Basel 2 is as a new regulatory dialect. The key components of this dialect are as follows. It is based upon pillars, asset classes, and other regulatory descriptors.

PILLARS

Basel 2 is structured on three "pillars."

Pillar One

Pillar One covers how risk-weighted assets and minimum capital requirements are to be calculated. It contains the detailed regulatory rules and choices, including definitions of default, to which financial institutions must adhere. If different institutions utilized their own definitions of default or other key definitions, there would be both a lack of a level playing field and the possibility of undermining the regulatory objectives.

Pillar One includes minimum capital requirements for credit risk, operational risk, and market risk and includes related "trading book" issues; it also includes mathematical formulae with which financial institutions can calculate their minimum capital requirements. Market-risk issues are substantially unchanged from the 1996 amendments; however, there are "boundary" issues, so that what is in the trading book versus the banking book, and how such assets are valued, needs to be considered. In this regard, it should be noted that while financial institutions have choices under Basel 2, "cherry-picking" is recognized by supervisors as undesirable and a risk. The structure of these new regulations takes steps to discourage it.

Pillar Two

The chairman of the Basel Committee, Jaime Caruana (2005, page 2), noted that Pillar Two "reminds bank managers that ultimately they are responsible for the adequate capitalization of their institutions, and creates an incentive for banks to conduct their internal reviews carefully and responsibly, on the basis of a well-defined strategy." In practice, Pillar Two requires banks to conduct a self-assessment of risks matched against the capital applied against these risks. Banks are to assess all risks, including those not covered by the calculation of minimum capital under Pillar One. Examples would include, but not be limited to, credit concentration risks, interest-rate risk in the banking book, and political risks. Banks will have considerable scope to design and provide comprehensive risk analysis and metrics, linking risks to the balance sheet and capital resources. Work on "risk appetite" assessments has progressed in some institutions, and these assessments could be integrated and reviewed at board and senior management levels.

Supervisors would then review the bank's self-assessment and make appropriate recommendations to the bank or use their supervisory power to demand an increase in required capital under Pillar Two. Financial institutions have been concerned that Pillar Two could be applied in a somewhat automated or standardized method to require regulatory add-ons to capital. While international regulators have tried to provide comfort on this point, it remains to be seen how Pillar Two will work in practice. At a minimum, and as a practical matter, it is likely that it will not be applied consistently across countries. Post-implementation, this will be a development that will be closely observed.

Pillar Three

Pillar Three is the requirement for widespread public dissemination of risk management and capital metrics for financial institutions. The thinking is that broad disclosure will enhance market discipline by enlisting new armies of well-informed analysts, financial journalists, and depositors as well as supervisors who are able to look into the risk management practices of individual institutions and compare and contrast their effectiveness.

Institutions would have some latitude within the scope of the disclosure required by supervisors to determine the details of how they make their own disclosure. Also, individual institutions could use disclosures in annual reports, financial statements, supplementary financial reporting, and their Web sites to provide this information.

The proposal itself is fair. However, the difficulties include the following:

- Much of the disclosure will be complex and may involve a great deal of additional, institution-specific *qualitative* information that will have to be assessed accurately. There is concern about the required granularity of these disclosures. Thus, there is uncertainty in some quarters as to whether this could provide an overload of information, particularly for unsophisticated readers.
- There is also concern over the confidentiality of certain kinds of disclosure, where the information may reveal confidential information by providing data on small or identifiable segments, especially to knowledgeable readers familiar with these segments. This could be particularly relevant in the cases of distressed loan data.

At one time there was concern about how Pillar Three would work in the presence of international accounting standards and the differences among them. Provisioning and hedging were areas of concern. In general, experience will be necessary to evaluate Pillar Three. Since banks have not yet operated under this pillar and regulators have provided less guidance on it, there remains some anxiety as to how it will function in practice.

RISK TYPES

Basel 2 covers credit risk, market risk, and operational risk. The original thrust was improvements in identifying the sensitivity of capital to credit risk as well as providing a new framework for operational risk capitalization.

While this thrust has been maintained, in 2004 the Basel Committee on Banking Supervision began working with the International Organization of Securities Commissions (IOSCO) on trading book issues and "double default" in particular. This resulted in guidance from the Basel Committee in July 2005, which had been agreed to by IOSCO, entitled "The Application of Basel 2 to Trading Activities and the Treatment of Double Default Effects." This paper also dealt with (1) how counterparty credit exposures arising from over-the-counter derivatives, repurchase, and securities financing-type transactions should be treated, and arrangements for cross-product netting, (2) maturity adjustments, (3) improvements in the current trading book regime, in particular in relation to the treatment of specific risk, (4) a regime for failed and unsettled transactions, and (5) the treatment of double default effects for covered transactions. By breaking new ground well into the development of the new capital regime, there was less time for refinement of these trading book amendments and for the consideration of operational implications. Thus, there is a need for these trading book issues to be developed and refined further.

One of the important trading book issues was the definition of the trading book versus the banking book. Because there are transactions involving a wide spectrum of instruments of varying degrees of liquidity, and because financial institutions either have already moved or could move arguably less liquid instruments into the trading book, these are issues that are of broad interest to credit practitioners and their supervisors.

NATIONAL DISCRETION; HOME AND HOST SUPERVISORS

The basic Basel 2 rulebook is common to all countries that adopt Basel 2. While this agreement is essentially among the Group of Ten countries, many more countries will voluntarily adopt the standard, as they did for the original Basel Capital Accord. Ong (2004, p. xxiv) estimated that 100 countries were applying the original Accord. The language that is used to describe the roles and responsibilities of the individual supervisors divides these into *home* and *host* regulators. This distinction is important in order to ensure that their interdependent roles are coordinated. Coordination is required to prevent unfair competitive consequences arising from individual countries favoring domestic financial institutions. Also, the existence of international branches and subsidiaries requires regulators and supervisors to cooperate with one another for the benefit of consolidated supervision, as well as to ensure that stand-alone entities are prudently supervised.

Finally, there are efficiency gains from reducing or eliminating overlap and duplication of regulatory responsibilities.

- Home supervisors are those in the country where the head office of an international bank and its lead regulator are located. Host supervisors are those in countries where a subsidiary, branch, or other type of legal entity of an international bank is located.
- It is important for international financial institutions that home-host cooperation be effective and efficient. Otherwise, many regulatory functions could result in conflicts, e.g., where the home supervisor approves the use of a model that a host regulator rejects.

ONGOING GUIDANCE

The regulatory framework for Basel 2 will change on a regular basis as a result of learning from its initial implementation, as well as enhancements to make the risk sensitivity and calibration more precise. As discussed previously, a review of the implications for the trading book and boundary issues has already been conducted. A further example of expanded regulatory interpretations from the Basel Committee was "Guidance on Paragraph 468 of the

Framework Document," also published in July 2005. This addressed issues relating to loss given default in economic downturns.

In addition to the output of supervisory guidance from the BCBS, national regulators such as the Federal Reserve Board, the Office of the Comptroller of the Currency, or the Financial Services Authority in the United Kingdom must be monitored by internationally active institutions. While other regulators are likely to follow closely the perspectives of the United Kingdom's Financial Services Authority or the United States' regulators, it is vital for a firm to stay up-to-date on the requirements of national regulators in any nation where its subsidiaries are located, such as the Australian Prudential Regulatory Authority or the Canadian Office of the Superintendent of Financial Institutions. The Hong Kong Monetary Authority, for example, has announced that it will not allow the full range of operational risk methodologies at the outset. A further variation on this theme is that the regulators who are members of the European Union publish frequent guidance from the Committee of European Banking Supervisors (CEBS), which is necessary and helpful for international banks that have local subsidiaries.

RISK QUANTIFICATION

The quantification of credit risks at each bank will lead to the key Basel 2 parameters: probability of default (PD), loss given default (LGD), and exposure at default (EAD). However, there are numerous factors at play that will result in each bank's quantifying its estimates of default and loss in different ways. These are:

- The quality of internal data, given product changes, bank mergers, management changes, and data management regimes at each institution. There are many other data issues as well, such as whether bank systems adequately capture the boundaries between credit risk and operational risk and between market risk and operational risk. The definition of default is fundamental. Adherence to all definitions is vitally important.
- The length of time over which internal data are available, and hence whether they are sufficiently sensitive to economic cycles, is a central issue. Put another way, regardless of the minimum data requirements in the Framework, how many business cycles are embodied in each bank's data?

- Whether a bank's risk rating system works at a "point in time," "through the cycle," or some hybrid variation of these two.
- The operation of a bank's risk rating systems.

These risk quantification issues are technical and controversial in many respects. In the final analysis, risk quantification needs to be based upon empirical analysis and competing statistical methodologies. Judgment must be exercised by both financial institutions and supervisors. Basel 2 requires financial institutions to validate their risk rating systems, controls, and operations as well as their estimated parameters on a regular basis. There are many controversial risk quantification issues that bear on the calibration of the Basel 2 regime and on future modifications to the equations for the calculation of regulatory capital. These issues include the following:

- Are PDs correlated with LGDs? If they are correlated, the existing formula could underestimate capital through the business cycle.
- Does the estimate of the correlation among default estimates in the Basel 2 regulatory equations approximate the true correlation observed for particular asset classes?
- Could further improvements be made by allowing the use of internal models that calculate correlations unique to each bank's portfolio? How would supervisors provide adequate oversight of these variable, complex, and unique methodologies?

Thus, it can be seen that quantitative issues will remain on the table and thrive under Basel 2 and future variations of this regime. As time passes, correlations will change. Also, new products, customer behavior, and changes in insolvency laws will alter estimates of default and loss. The system is designed to accommodate such changes.

ASSESSING BASEL 2

It is always difficult to assess complex public policy issues in advance, particularly when the data to test alternative outcomes are not available. For example, it was widely viewed that the original Basel Accord was targeted at Japanese banks. Wagster (1996) examined the Basel Accord in terms of alternative theories of regulation. He noted (pp. 1321–1322) that "[i]ts ulterior goal was to eliminate the funding-cost advantage of Japanese banks that allowed them to capture more than one-third of international lending during the 1980s." Wagster also found (p. 1342) that "empirical results suggest that the Basel Accord failed to eliminate the pricing advantage of Japanese banks," and that (p. 1343) "during the course of the negotiations, the regulation was shaped in such a way as to benefit shareholders of Japanese banks."

Given the complexity of the Basel 2 amendments relative to the 1988 Basel Accord, empirical work will be required to shed light on Basel 2's impact on pricing various types of risks, its impact on different countries and risk categories, and the consequences for shareholders in financial institutions affected by Basel 2. Nonetheless, the following issues are already on the list for reviewing the success of Basel 2:

- First, it is appreciated that the calibration of this regulatory capital framework is fraught with difficulty. Calibration addresses both the amount of regulatory capital that must be held by individual institutions and the total for each financial system. Moreover, calibration must be accurate for macro-prudential reasons and also equitable, both among institutions within a country and between countries. Concerns with how regulators will actually achieve *their* goals of calibration arise from many sources, including the fact that earlier quantification exercises were carried out at times when there were deficiencies in credit data and the new analytics were still under development. Also, the possibility of regulators applying a scaling factor, effectively a multiplier, casts doubt on the overall efficacy and fairness of the program designed to use risk-based information to derive capital calculations. A multiplier would be inconsistent not only with the logic of a risk-based system, but also with the substantial investments made by the global financial industry in Basel 2. An internationally agreed-upon scaling factor is likely to create cross-border inequities, and it is difficult to see how regulators could have confidence in the results.
- A second issue concerns properly recognizing the portfolio characteristics of Basel 2 banks and the implications for

the capital calculation. There are a multitude of issues here; for example, as noted earlier, the Basel Framework embodied fixed correlation coefficients rather than coefficients derived from the portfolios of individual banks. Even at a more general level of analysis, the diversification of portfolios does not seem to have been adequately recognized, except under Pillar Two, where there is less chance for consistency of application domestically or internationally. The ultimate resolution of this complexity would be the recognition of internal risk models that contain their own asset correlations.

- A third issue concerns the properties of this new capital regime during an economic downturn. Although simulations can be carried out, because of the cumulative interaction of financial institutions and attempts to take mitigating steps in advance, how Basel 2 will behave in a deteriorating credit market or economic cycle generally is not clear. Because capital for credit risk is no longer a linear function, but is nonlinearly related to credit quality, there is uncertainty about the macroeconomic outcome and implications. It is untested whether bank, rating agency, and supervisory behavior will be highly interrelated or lagged, and what the cumulative impacts over the complete business or credit cycle might be. On the other hand, it is correctly pointed out by supervisors that all capital regimes are likely to be inherently pro-cyclical to some extent. They also note that there is likely to be greater clarity concerning the cyclical character of the Basel 2 regime as well as significant benefits in formalizing the review that must be carried out by each bank under Pillar Two. This review would inevitably require the board of directors as well as senior management to be informed and to pass judgment on this forward-looking issue.

- Fourth, conservatism is a required input to capital requirements for financial institutions, as dictated by numerous sections of Pillar One of the Framework. It is also a requirement for Pillar Two, where banks are required to demonstrate conservatism and regulators may require additional capital on top of the estimates made by financial institutions. It is not clear how the *cumulative* impact of conservatism will be managed by banks or by their supervisors. The risks are that excessive or uneven conservatism may be applied by financial institutions themselves and that the regulatory and supervisory processes will not ensure that this conservatism is consistent across domestic institutions—at least, not in terms of international competitive and prudential issues. Should this outcome prevail, and it is certainly likely, given the moving parts involved, it would undermine some of the initial goals of Basel 2.

CONCLUSION

The themes of this discussion are that Basel 2 is a new regulatory dialect that must be mastered by credit and other financial practitioners and that Basel 2 will be an evergreen process that is subject to periodic change as data and behavior shed light on how such a complex regime will operate in practice. Regulators will make periodic changes to this Framework in response to a regular flow of new information, as well as to institutional, legal, and behavioral changes in national economies that affect PDs, LGDs, and EADs. These will occur within the international network established by the BCBS.

While the birth of Basel 2 between 1999 and 2006 (prior to its implementation at different dates in different countries) was politically controversial, beneath the rhetoric is an agreed-upon longer-term goal among supervisors to make this system work, driven by the data and analytics of individual financial institutions. If economic and regulatory capital calculations can converge as a consequence, all parties will be better off.

BIBLIOGRAPHY

Basel Committee on Banking Supervision. *International Convergence of Capital Measurement and Capital Standards: A Revised Framework.* Basel: Bank for International Settlements, 2004.
Basel Committee on Banking Supervision. "The Application of Basel 2 to Trading Activities and the Treatment of Double Default Effects." Basel: Bank for International Settlements, 2005.

Caruana, Jaime. "Reform of the International Standard for Bank Capital," Notes for testimony before the Committee on Economic and Monetary Affairs, European Parliament, January 18, 2005.

Fratianni, Michele, and John Pattison. "An Assessment of the Bank for International Settlements," in International Financial Institution Advisory Commission, *Expert Papers.* Washington, DC: Department of Treasury, 2000.

Fratianni, Michele, and John Pattison. "The Bank for International Settlements: An Assessment of its Role in International Monetary and Financial Policy Coordination." *Open Economies Review,* vol. 12, no. 2, April 2001, pp. 197–222.

Ong, Michael K. (Ed.). *The Basel Handbook: A Guide for Financial Practitioners.* London: Risk Books, 2004.

Wagster, John D. "Impact of the 1988 Basel Accord on International Banks." *Journal of Finance,* vol. 51, no. 4, September 1996, pp. 1321–1346.

CHAPTER 14

The Globalization of the Loan Market

Meredith Coffey
Senior Vice President
Reuters Loan Pricing Corporation

Clare Dawson
Loan Market Association

Philip Cracknell
Standard Chartered

Suraj Bhatia
Senior Managing Director
The Sumitomo Trust & Banking Co. Ltd., New York Branch

Jennifer Ashe
Vice President and Head of Research
The Sumitomo Trust & Banking Co. Ltd., New York Branch

Mike Kerrigan
Partner
Hunton & Williams LLP

Steve Curtis
Partner
Clifford Chance LLP

Ian Sandler
Vice President
Morgan Stanley

Global Loan Market Review

Meredith Coffey
Senior Vice President, Reuters Loan Pricing Corporation

Over the past decade, the syndicated loan markets have taken on an increasingly global flavor. Trends around the world often work in tandem, and, while the regional markets have their own peculiarities, developments in one market often spread quickly into others.

This article will look at the global loan market and then break it down into its regional constituencies, discussing issuance and structural trends, purposes, and the growth (or lack thereof) of a secondary trading market. Several global trends, such as climbing loan issuance, falling loan spreads, and a boom in merger and acquisition activity, will be dissected in each market. In particular, the European and U.S. markets, which have grown closer in recent years, will be compared and contrasted.

Finally, the regional trends will be reunited to discuss where the global loan market may be heading in the second half of the 2000s.

A BRIEF HISTORY OF GLOBAL LENDING

As Exhibit 14.1 indicates, over the past several years, the global loan market has grown to immense proportions. Global lending (excluding Japan) exceeded $2.8 trillion in the 12 months ended September 30, 2005, up 16 percent from 2004 and up 67 percent from 2003. Add in Japan, which has slowly opened its syndications market, and global syndicated lending tops $3 trillion.

But as Exhibit 14.1 also indicates, the period between 1997 and 2005 saw several complete cycles in the loan market. Thus, 1997, which enjoyed global lending of $1.7 trillion, was an early cyclical peak. Liquidity was rampant, spreads were thinning (both in developed and in emerging areas), and issuance hit record highs. But 1997 was also when the Asian economies began to stumble. In 1998, the contagion spread to Russia, creating the Russian debt default, which then created a ripple effect through Europe and the United States. As lenders pulled back, leveraged spreads skyrocketed,

Global loan issuance follows credit cycles.

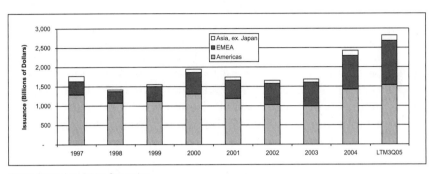

Source: Reuters Loan Pricing Corporation.

deals stalled, and structures became far more conservative. Little wonder, then, that loan issuance fell 20 percent globally in 1998, and by as much as two-thirds in Asia. Indeed, although lender appetite returned reasonably quickly, Asia-Pacific lending volumes would not return to 1997 levels for nearly a decade.

The downturn, however, was short-lived in the United States and Europe. In 1999, the Euromarket broke nearly every standing record on a surge of M&A activity. In the United States, 1999 brought a muted replay of 1998 when the high-yield bond market closed down in the second half of the year, stranding a number of leveraged loans. Still, the American markets recovered, posting solid investment grade volumes and record leveraged ones. In 2000, spreads were compressing in Asia as lender competition picked up, and volumes hit $90 billion, roughly double where they were in the immediate postcrisis years (though still far below 1997 levels). In the United States and Europe, the middle of 2000 marked the peak of the credit cycle, with nearly $2 trillion in global issuance. The year began with aggressive structures and strong volumes. But the slew of telecom debt and a flood of downgrades and defaults meant that a year that started out strongly ended with rumblings of a credit crunch.

After a tough end to 2000, lender appetite returned once again early in 2001, but the respite was brief: credit structures were weakening and default rates were climbing even before the events of September 11, 2001. Mergers were an early casualty of increasingly bearish sentiment: M&A lending fell more than 60 percent in Asia,

1Q05–3Q05 Global Top-Tier Full Credit Volume League Table

Rank	Lender Name	Full Credit Volume	Pro Rata Volume	# of Deals
1	JP Morgan	749,532,083,133	355,834,582,921	776
2	Citigroup	734,902,700,620	273,694,415,876	607
3	Bank of America	439,829,052,048	216,727,606,425	774
4	BNP Paribas	431,813,265,457	84,639,564,471	399
5	Royal Bank of Scotland Plc	358,993,137,907	69,446,114,419	293
6	Barclays Bank Plc	348,832,029,258	75,992,683,898	288
7	HSBC	336,391,878,177	50,956,000,599	286
8	Calyon Corporate & Investment Bank	312,035,647,560	48,281,044,207	308
9	Deutsche Bank	303,689,866,955	79,772,833,198	194
10	ABN AMRO Bank N.V.	300,131,351,216	54,770,112,358	293

1Q05–3Q05 Asia Pacific Mandated Arranger League Table

Rank	Lender Name	Volume (US$)	# of Deals
1	ANZ Investment Bank	9,745,327,730	57
2	National Australia Bank	7,151,125,228	42
3	Citigroup	6,815,126,158	64
4	Commonwealth Bank of Australia	5,120,706,704	46
5	Westpac Banking Corp	4,343,160,123	40
6	HSBC	4,300,114,460	67
7	Calyon Corporate & Investment Bank	4,136,968,453	73
8	Standard Chartered Bank	4,011,984,981	67
9	DBS Bank	3,596,821,785	73
10	ABN AMRO Bank	3,245,857,276	44

1Q05–3Q05 Japan Mandated Arranger League Table

Rank	Lender Name	Volume (US$)	# of Deals
1	Mizuho Bank/Mizuho Corporate Bank	54,390,525,600	442
2	Sumitomo Mitsui Banking Crop	49,731,632,108	420
3	BOT-Mitsubishi	19,237,668,649	339
4	Citigroup	5,308,645,342	11
5	UFJ Bank	1,807,431,642	23
6	BNP Paribas	1,417,367,476	1
7	Development Bank of Japan	690,935,720	3
8	Resona Bank	643,355,946	11
9	HSBC Tokyo	558,647,823	4
10	Sumitomo Trust & Banking	539,885,699	8

1Q05–3Q05 EMEA Mandated Lead Arranger League Table

Rank	Lender Name	Pro Rata (US$)	Full Credit (US$)	# of Deals
1	Citigroup	69,575,480,436	379,439,207,305	220
2	BNP Paribas	67,291,315,510	389,279,762,038	277
3	Royal Bank of Scotland	57,745,296,924	335,578,439,902	237
4	Barclays	56,796,743,897	306,502,759,545	231
5	Deutsche Bank	46,354,259,665	242,931,308,412	117
6	HSBC	45,385,146,694	311,481,517,300	202
7	SG CIB	42,486,128,143	276,587,356,419	170
8	JP Morgan	41,793,536,314	260,568,635,913	103
9	Calyon	40,176,158,800	279,649,822,040	193
10	ABN AMRO	38,261,814,744	266,868,539,404	145

1Q05–3Q05 Americas Lead Arranger League Table

Rank	Lender Name	Volume (US$)	# of Deals
1	JP Morgan	312,736,385,641	669
2	Bank of America	203,714,146,565	711
3	Citigroup	192,158,732,659	311
4	Wachovia Securities	61,082,424,000	248
5	Deutsche Bank	32,650,594,190	70
6	Credit Suisse First Boston	29,205,319,730	105
7	Wells Fargo & Company	19,596,197,500	133
8	Goldman Sachs & Company	19,501,112,500	40
9	Barclays Bank Plc	18,169,484,333	36
10	Lehman Brothers	16,610,624,999	46

50 percent in the Americas, and 30 percent in Europe, the Middle East, and Africa (EMEA). And while the U.S. and European markets recovered relatively quickly from September 11, the attacks nevertheless halted lending for one month and crippled it for the remainder of the year. European lending tumbled 15 percent as telecom, media, and technology (TMT) credits came home to roost; the United States suffered from recession, credit deterioration, and, of course, the fallout from the tragic event of September 11. Though less affected by these factors, Asia lending slipped 4 percent as borrowers opted to tap local currency bond markets, not loans. All told, in 2001, global lending fell 10 percent from 2000 levels.

But while 2001 was very difficult, resilient lender appetite picked up in December, and lenders hit 2002 quite hungry and quite ready to lend. For the first five months, 2002 was red-hot. And then, with the WorldCom default, the U.S. markets collapsed and issuance fell 14 percent. Europe bifurcated into a storied high-grade market and a slam-dunk leveraged one. Together, these markets pushed overall EMEA lending up 17 percent above the year-earlier levels. Although disconnected from the credit stories that were roiling the United States and Europe, Asia-Pacific volume nevertheless edged down as lenders chose not to refinance thinly priced loans. All told, global lending slipped another 5 percent in 2002. Meanwhile, global M&A activity—supported only by the European LBO market—fell another 20 percent (Exhibit 14.2).

If 2002 was bifurcated, 2003 was uniformly bullish. But while lenders were ready to lend, U.S. and Asian borrowers were less ready to borrow. As a result, issuance slipped 4 percent and 3 percent in the United States and Asia-Pacific, respectively. But borrowers were less reticent in EMEA, and lending there climbed a whopping 16 percent from 2002 levels. All told, global loan issuance edged up a bit less than 2 percent to $1.6 trillion, but positive sentiment far outstripped the statistics.

EXHIBIT 14.2

Global M&A lending swoons, recovers.

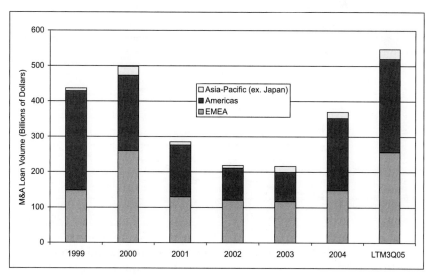

Source: Reuters Loan Pricing Corporation.

It wasn't until 2004 that improvements in sentiment were reflected in the statistics: global M&A lending soared more than 70 percent, mostly on the back of a resurgent U.S. market, where it more than doubled. Overall lending climbed more than 40 percent in each geographic area. In addition to growing M&A activity, excess lender demand in 2004 also facilitated the return of opportunistic refinancings, which further buoyed growth in lending. After such a rapid rebound in 2004, the rate of growth slowed in 2005. Still, the year has been quite strong, as of this writing. M&A lending will overtake its previous record, and global lending will top $3 trillion. EMEA lending is poised to break $1 trillion for the first time ever. And finally, in the 12 months ended September 30, 2005, Asia-Pacific (excluding Japan) lending topped $145 billion, surpassing the levels last seen in 1997, before the Asian crisis decimated that market.

Not only has the global loan market grown dramatically, but its regional constituents have also changed a great deal (Exhibit 14.3). In the late 1990s, EMEA syndicated lending accounted for less than 20 percent of global loans issued. By 2005, its share had climbed to 40 percent of the market. By the same token, the

EXHIBIT 14.3

EMEA market share soars, Americas slip.

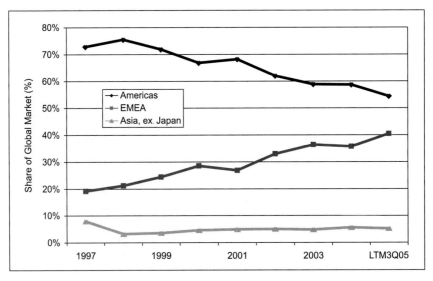

Source: Reuters Loan Pricing Corporation.

Americas market share tumbled from more than 70 percent to around 55 percent of the global loan market. Not only are EMEA and Americas volumes converging, but the markets are increasingly interacting, creating a quasi-arbitrageable transatlantic loan market as well.

THINK GLOBALLY, LEND LOCALLY

Transatlantic arbitrage notwithstanding, the reality is that while it may be helpful to look at loan volume on a global or regional basis, there is no monolithic global market. Each regional market comprises a series of national markets. In some cases, like Europe, the regional market is reasonably diversified. In other cases, like the Americas, there is one dominating country. As Exhibit 14.4 illustrates, U.S. lending makes up a remarkable 94 percent of all lending in the Americas. At 4 percent and 1 percent, respectively, in 2005, Canada and Mexico make up nearly all the remainder.

Asia is similarly imbalanced. The Japanese loan market (which historically has been closed to international banks, as many corporations have traditionally relied on their house banks) alone

EXHIBIT 14.4

U.S. lending dominates the Americas in 2005.

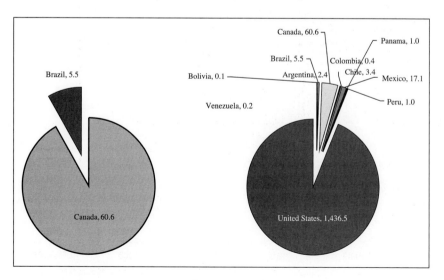

Source: Reuters Loan Pricing Corporation.

is larger than the rest of Asia-Pacific lending. (Exhibit 14.5 reflects annualized first through third quarter 2005 figures.) Even as the Japanese market opens further to non-Japanese banks, and many lenders inside Japan work to increase transparency and transactability, it remains distinct. The three big banks control the vast majority of the market, and offshore banks often do not get to participate in these deals. For this reason, Japanese volume statistics and league tables are seldom combined with the rest of AsiaPacific. Most lending in Japan is thinly priced plain vanilla financing, made up primarily of 364-day facilities, revolvers, and some term loans. Australasia, the second-largest region, has a bigger share of project financings and merger-related loans. Lending in Hong Kong, which has an 8 percent market share in the AsiaPacific region, often backs property developers and is usually made up of thinly priced relationship credits. Taiwan, with 6 percent of the Asia-Pacific market, offers a wide range of loans, but the bulk is local currency loans supported by domestic lenders. Finally, in South Korea, much of the lending backs local banks. Outside of Australasian project finance, in most jurisdictions, many of the loans

EXHIBIT 14.5

A resurgent Japan dominates the Asia-Pacific region.

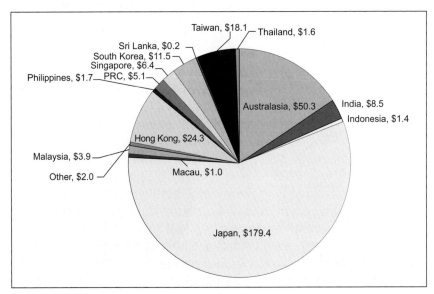

Source: Reuters Loan Pricing Corporation.

EXHIBIT 14.6

EMEA last 12 months ending with the third quarter of 2005 volume by country.

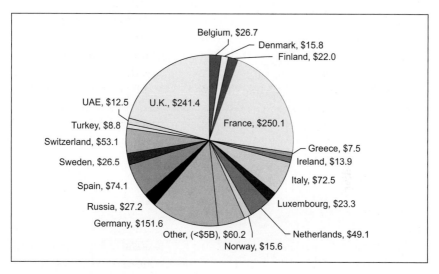

Source: Reuters Loan Pricing Corporation.

are structured as thinly priced, multiyear plain vanilla revolvers or term loans.

Europe, meanwhile, shows a refreshing diversity among the countries (Exhibit 14.6). For instance, in the last 12 months ending with the third quarter of 2005, France has proven to be dominant, thanks mostly to a flurry of large M&A transactions. With 22 percent of the market, it surpassed the United Kingdom (21 percent) and Germany (13 percent). However, France's dominance is more aberration than truism: in 2002–2004, U.K. loan volume was significantly higher than France's, and Germany played a larger role.

STRUCTURAL SIMILARITIES

Thanks to similar regulatory pressure, similar borrower needs, and cross-fertilization of ideas, loan structures are more similar than different around the globe, even if there are differences between individual markets. The United States and Europe have distinct investment grade and leveraged markets, which look remarkably alike on both continents. Lending in Asia tends toward plain vanilla, blue-chip revolvers or term loans; however, a small leveraged

EXHIBIT 14.7

Characteristics of regional markets.

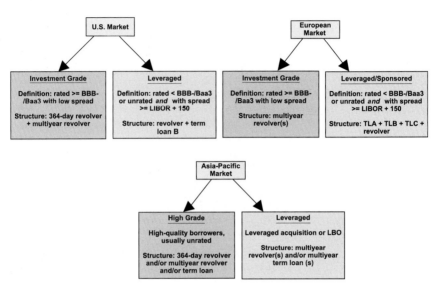

Source: Reuters Loan Pricing Corporation.

market does exist (Exhibit 14.7). Outside of Japan, high-grade loans
are often multiyear revolvers or term loans with relatively low
drawn spreads over the regional base rate. Within Japan, 364-day
facilities are prevalent, as well as multiyear revolvers and term
loans. The few leveraged loans in the region are usually multiyear
revolvers and term loans.

At more than $1.4 trillion, the U.S. loan market is by far the
largest domestic market in the world, and it is quite diverse. U.S.
investment grade lending is defined as loans to companies rated at
or above BBB-/Baa3 whose loans have relatively low drawn and
undrawn spreads. Investment grade lending comprises roughly
half of the overall U.S. loan market; it is a relationship market in
which loans are usually undrawn and backstop commercial paper.
Pricing comprises a LIBOR spread on the funded portion, an
annual/facility fee (which is paid regardless of whether the loan is
drawn), a utilization fee that is paid if more than a certain amount
(for instance, 50 percent) is drawn, and in some cases an upfront
fee. Historically, U.S. investment grade loans have been divided
into two tranches: a 364-day revolving facility and a multiyear

EXHIBIT 14.8

High-grade loan tenor varies around the globe (Asia vs. Europe vs. United States).

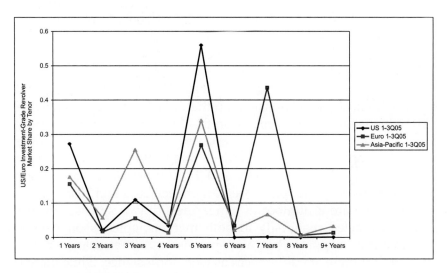

Source: Reuters Loan Pricing Corporation.

revolver. (There are very few investment grade term loans, as the commercial paper market is a cheaper source of funded debt.) In 2004 and 2005, the 364-day facility was increasingly being replaced with a five-year revolver. As Exhibit 14.8 illustrates, the modes for U.S. investment grade tenor are at 364 days and five years.

Though the nuances are different, the European investment grade loan market is broadly similar to that in the United States. The European investment grade market includes loans to borrowers rated at least BBB-/Baa3 with a relatively low margin. However, the European high-grade market is even more of a relationship market than the U.S. market, which means that loan spreads tend to be lower and tenors tend to be longer. European investment grade loan pricing usually comprises a LIBOR margin on the funded portion, a commitment fee on the unfunded portion (as opposed to the U.S. market's facility fee, which is paid on the entire commitment), a utilization fee, and occasionally an upfront fee. Like investment grade loans in the U.S. market, European investment grade loans are often unfunded and historically had a 364-day component and a multiyear component. However, investment grade European borrowers abandoned their 364-day facilities even earlier than U.S. borrowers did. As a result, in 2005, only 15 percent of European investment grade loans were 364-day facilities (as opposed to 27 percent in the United States). In addition, European loan tenors tend to be longer. In 2004 and 2005, European high-grade borrowers migrated toward seven-year loans, through issuing either loans with a straight seven-year tenor or five-year loans with two one-year extension options. By 2005, more than 40 percent of European investment grade loans enjoyed a seven-year tenor; practically no U.S. loans ran that long, and only 7 percent of Asian loans hit seven years (Exhibit 14.8).

Not only are European investment grade loan tenors longer, but European spreads—at least for A- and BBB-rated loans—tend to be lower as well. Exhibits 14.9 and 14.10 illustrate European and U.S. investment grade spread trends between 2001 and 2005, respectively. There are a number of similarities: drawn spreads on BBB loans contracted materially in both markets, spreads on A-rated loans contracted somewhat, and spreads on AA-rated loans barely moved. But there are differences as well; for instance, while there is little spread premium on European BBB loans, U.S. BBB loans offer a considerable risk premium over their A-rated counterparts.

E X H I B I T   1 4 . 9

European investment grade loan spreads.

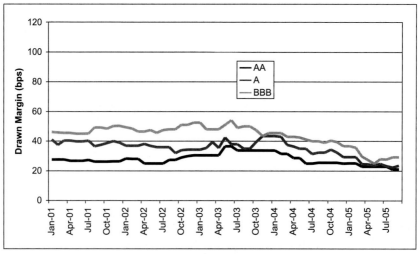

Source: Reuters Loan Pricing Corporation.

EXHIBIT 14.10

U.S. investment grade loan spreads.

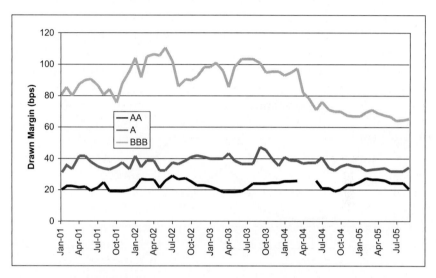

Source: Reuters Loan Pricing Corporation.

The growth pattern in the U.S. and European loan markets has diverged as well. As Exhibit 14.11 shows, in the 1990s, the U.S. investment grade loan market was significantly larger than that in Europe. Both markets retrenched in the early 2000s as low margins and a raft of fallen angels made lenders rethink their investment grade lending strategy. Since they started recovering, however, the markets have diverged, and since 2003, European high-grade issuance has outstripped U.S. issuance. With strong relationships in place, most European borrowers are refinancing (and reducing spreads) at least once a year. In contrast, once U.S. borrowers shifted to a multiyear loan strategy, many stopped coming back to market every year, reducing nominal loan issuance. In addition, European high-grade M&A lending has remained (relatively) robust at $126 billion in the year through September 30, 2005. U.S. investment grade M&A lending has lagged, with a mere $32 billion in the same period.

Ultimately, while the U.S. and European investment grade markets are following similar stars, the European market is more relationship-driven, more aggressive, and evolving more quickly—traits that are manifested in the longer tenors, lower spreads, and greater optionality embedded in European loans.

EXHIBIT 14.11

European investment grade loan issuance has climbed; U.S. issuance has fluctuated.

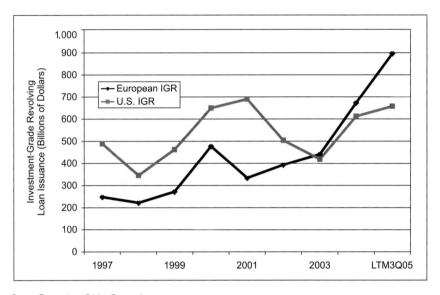

Source: Reuters Loan Pricing Corporation.

LEVERAGED LENDING AROUND THE GLOBE

Though the European high-grade market is more aggressive and faster moving than its U.S. counterpart, the reverse is true of the leveraged loan market. Meanwhile, the leveraged market in Asia is just beginning to emerge. There has been considerable talk of Asia developing a buyout market, and 2005 has put in a good start, with more than $3 billion of LBO financing. However, that pales in comparison to the whopping $50 billion emerging from both the United States and Europe. The leveraged loans that do emerge from Asia typically are structured with multiyear revolvers and multiyear term loans. The alphabet tranche phenomenon has yet to arrive, as nonbank lenders were not participating in syndicated loans in the Asia-Pacific region as of late 2005.

In both the U.S. and the Western European market, leveraged loan issuance is defined as loans to companies rated below BBB-/Baa3 (or unrated) and with a spread of at least LIBOR + 150. As

EXHIBIT 14.12

U.S. leveraged lending outstrips European.

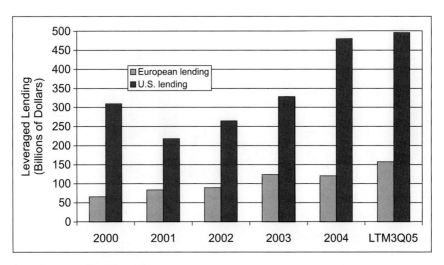

Source: Reuters Loan Pricing Corporation.

Exhibit 14.12 indicates, the U.S. leveraged loan market is a magnitude larger than the European market.

In the 12 months ended third quarter 2005, U.S. leveraged loan issuance approached $500 billion, while European leveraged loan issuance approached $160 billion. The reason for the discrepancy lies in the types of loans that are done. In Europe, there are relatively few leveraged corporate borrowers. Unlike U.S. entities, few European corporations are comfortable operating as leveraged entities for any length of time. This means that in a downturn, when there are fallen angels or companies facing liquidity crises, there will be a steady flow of leveraged corporate loans. In better times, leveraged corporate borrowing is more limited. In contrast, the U.S. market has a consistent supply of corporate borrowers that are comfortable operating for extended periods with a level of leverage that excludes them from the investment grade ranks. In turn, even though LBO lending in Europe was at roughly the same level as in the United States in 2004 and 2005, and much higher in 2001 to 2003 (Exhibit 14.13), the overall leveraged loan market is far larger in the United States.

EXHIBIT 14.13

LBO lending in the United States and Western Europe.

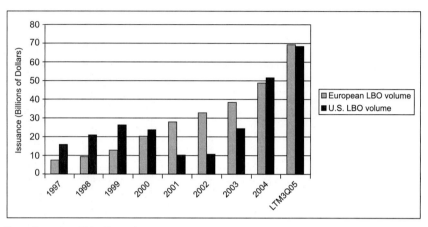

Source: Reuters Loan Pricing Corporation.

The U.S. leveraged loan market is dominated by nonbank lenders, such as collateralized loan obligations (CLOs), bank loan funds, hedge funds, and other asset managers. This dominion by nonbank lenders leads the U.S. market to be more flexible, more volatile, and generally more market-oriented than the European leveraged loan market. Supply and demand dynamics lead to more volatile secondary prices and more flexible primary spreads in the U.S. market. Prices and spreads in the European market are stickier, but are beginning to become more responsive to market pressures.

DIFFERENT LENDER CLASSES LEAD TO DIFFERENT OUTCOMES

The difference in who buys leveraged loans in the United States and Europe is illustrated in Exhibit 14.14. In the European market, banks continue to account for 80 percent of the buyers of leveraged loans, while nonbank buyers are picking up roughly 15 percent. In contrast, nonbank market share in the United States has sky-rocketed, climbing from less than 20 percent of the market in the early–2000s to half the leveraged loan market by 2005.

The fact that nonbank buyers dominate in the United States brings a more "market" kind of mentality to U.S. leveraged loans.

EXHIBIT 14.14

Nonbank lender market share (United States vs. Europe).

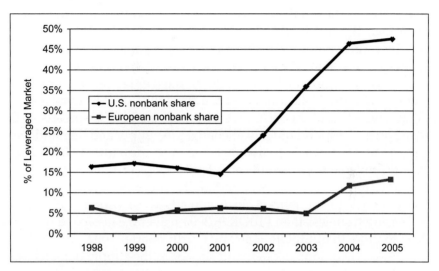

Source: Reuters Loan Pricing Corporation.

These lenders are not relationship lenders (so they make buy/sell/hold decisions based solely on the attractiveness of the loan), and they need loans that can trade in the secondary market (so that they can manage their portfolios). This nonrelationship mentality allows the market to adjust to changes in supply and demand far faster than it has historically—and far faster than what is observed in Europe.

For instance, the deal structure of leveraged loans has evolved considerably in the United States, whereas it has barely budged in Europe. In the late 1990s, the structure of U.S. and European leveraged loans was similar: a revolver, a six-year term loan A, a seven-year term loan B, and possibly an eight-year term loan C would be a typical structure. In the United States, the revolver and term loan A would be purchased by banks. The term loans B and C would be purchased by nonbank investors. In Europe, banks were more comfortable with longer tenors, and would purchase nearly all of the loan paper.

However, since the late 1990s, the structure of U.S. leveraged loans has changed. Instead of a series of alphabet tranches, U.S. leveraged loans now usually offer a small revolver (purchased by banks) and a large term loan B (purchased by banks and nonbank investors).

In Europe, leveraged loan structure has not changed as dramatically as it has in the United States: there is still the term loan A, term loan B, term loan C, and the revolver. Nonbank lenders are buying larger amounts of European loans, purchasing nearly half the term loans B and C now, but the banks still dominate.

This bank domination has led to stickier terms and prices in Europe. Exhibit 14.15 illustrates the flexibility of U.S. term loan B (TLB) spreads and the stickiness of European TLB/C spreads. U.S. loan spreads respond quickly to changes in supply and demand and can vary widely. For instance, in the downturn following WorldCom's sudden default and bankruptcy in mid–2002, lender demand for U.S. loans evaporated. In order to tempt nonbank lenders back to the market, loan spreads were widened abruptly, increasing from less than LIBOR + 300 on average in second quarter 2002 to more than LIBOR + 400 by fourth quarter 2002.

And when nonbank demand surpasses the supply of loans—as was the case between first quarter 2003 and first quarter 2005—U.S. leveraged loan spreads can contract as quickly as they rose. In fact, spreads fell more than 170 bps from peak to nadir. As Exhibit 14.15

EXHIBIT 14.15

European TLB/C spreads are more stable than U.S. spreads.

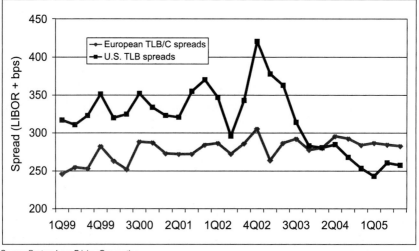

Source: Reuters Loan Pricing Corporation.

also illustrates, spreads on European TLB/TLC loans showed no such volatility, fluctuating less than 50 bps during the same period.

U.S. leveraged term loan spreads are driven almost entirely by supply and demand. The spread on the term loan B can be 100 bps wider than that on the revolver—or it can be 50 bps narrower than that on the revolver. The spread relationship is tied to little other than the whims of the market.

European loan spreads are less likely to fluctuate, primarily because of the stickiness of their pricing mechanics. Such uncertainty is unacceptable in Europe, where spreads seldom vary. In fact, European leveraged loan spreads tend to have a formulaic structure, and only the rare deal deviates from the norm. Take by way of example a typical LBO spread from early 2004, which ran as follows: a term loan A at LIBOR + 225, a term loan B at LIBOR + 275, a term loan C at LIBOR + 325, and a revolver at LIBOR + 225. Few dared to deviate from this structure until recently. Leverage on LBO loans might have fluctuated; spreads seldom did.

But the European leveraged loan market is now changing in several ways. Nonbank lenders have adopted a higher-profile role and are buying more paper, and U.S. nonbank lenders are also increasingly coming to Europe and setting up shop to buy loans. As more nonbank lenders—and consequently a market mentality— emerged, the European leveraged loan market began to evolve in a manner that resembles its U.S. counterpart.

In the past few years, several attributes of the U.S. loan market that were previously unheard of in Europe have become commonplace. Price flex, a mechanism that allows loan spreads to be increased or decreased to the market-clearing level, is a fixture of the U.S. loan market, allowing almost all loans to clear the market at the "right" spread. It has more recently found a home in the European market as well.

As Exhibits 14.16 and 14.17 show, however, both upward and reverse flex play a much larger role in U.S. syndications. For instance, in the 12 months ended September 30, 2005, U.S. borrowers enjoyed nearly $76 billion of reverse flex (whereby they reduced their loan spreads as a result of overwhelming demand). In contrast, European reverse flex totaled $11 billion. The U.S. market is also more likely to utilize upward flex to prod along a slow syndication: In the same 12-month period, the U.S. leveraged market saw $20 billion of upward flex, while European borrowers suffered only $1.3 billion.

EXHIBIT 14.16

U.S. flex activity, 2003–2005.

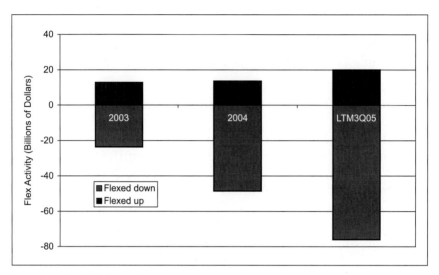

Source: Reuters Loan Pricing Corporation.

EXHIBIT 14.17

European flex activity, 2003–2005.

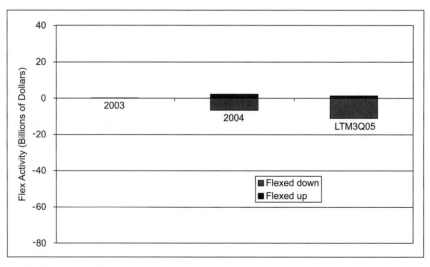

Source: Reuters Loan Pricing Corporation.

SECONDARY MARKETS

This pattern of a U.S. revolution followed by a slower European evolution has emerged in the secondary loan market as well. The U.S. secondary market developed in the early 1990s as banks looked to shed distressed assets. However, secondary market development accelerated in the mid–1990s with the rise of the non-bank lender class, which required a secondary market in which to manage portfolios, to trade—and simply to follow loans in the secondary market. The number of loans being marked in the secondary market can act as a rough proxy for the development stage of the market. As Exhibit 14.18 illustrates, in 1999, roughly 800 U.S. loan facilities were being marked by the LSTA/LPC Mark-to-Market Pricing on a daily basis. By 2005, more than 2,200 U.S. facilities were being marked.

While the U.S. secondary market got an earlier start, the European market is catching up quickly. Exhibit 14.19 illustrates the growth of price activity in the European market. At the beginning of 2002, fewer than 100 facilities were being marked actively (and a number of these were investment grade loans). By third quarter 2005, nearly 1,600 facilities were being marked daily.

EXHIBIT 14.18

U.S. secondary loan bids have tripled since the 1990s.

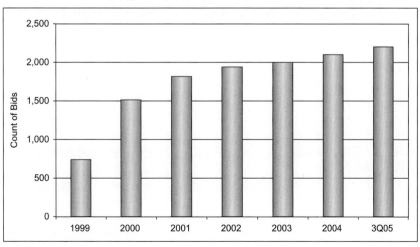

Source: LSTA/LPC Mark-to-Market Pricing.

EXHIBIT 14.19

European bid counts climb 15-fold since 2002.

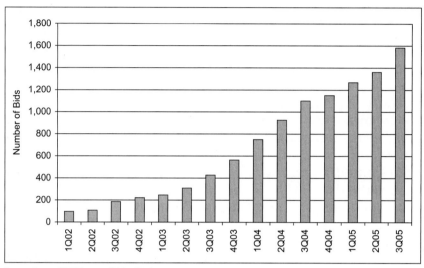

Source: Reuters LPC European Pricing Service.

Unsurprisingly, given their nonbank buying base, U.S. loans tend to be more volatile in the secondary market, dropping in downturns such as those following September 11, the WorldCom default, and the more recent (and less serious) second quarter 2005 bond meltdown. Similarly, in market upturns, U.S. loans tend to appreciate more than their European brethren. Exhibit 14.20 illustrates this phenomenon. In early 2003, U.S. and European TLB/Cs were still suffering from high default rates, the TMT fallout in Europe, and the WorldCom hangover in the United States. The average rated U.S. institutional term loan bid (excluding those loans rated CCC or lower) was less than 96 cents on the dollar. The far less volatile TLB/C bid in Europe had slipped below 98. But 2003 was the beginning of the upturn. U.S. bids rallied past par by early 2004, while European bids did not pass that bogey until early 2005.

But it was not all smooth sailing—at least, not for the U.S. market. As the U.S. secondary market has taken on more market characteristics, it also suffers more in tandem with other markets, such as high-yield bonds. For example, in second quarter 2005, the average high-yield bond bid slipped 700 bps. Meanwhile, bids on

EXHIBIT 14.20

U.S. secondary loan bids are more volatile than European bids.

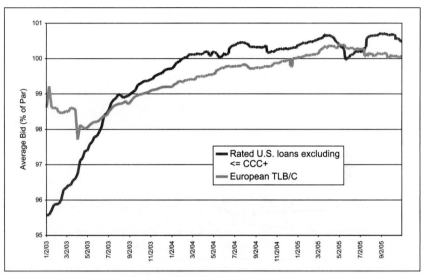

Source: Reuters LPC European Pricing Service; LSTA/LPC Mark-to-Market Pricing.

U.S. loans rated B3 and higher fell from more than 100.66 on average to slightly less than par. But as Exhibit 14.20 shows, the effect in the European market was far milder, and came with a considerable lag. This illustrates the lower responsiveness and lesser volatility in the European market. It might be an indication of lesser liquidity as well.

European secondary bids are not as volatile as their American cousins. However, as was seen in the primary market, the European secondary market is developing in a similar manner to the U.S. market. This is clearly illustrated in the evolution of the distribution of secondary market bids in the United States and Europe (Exhibits 14.21 and 14.22). As Exhibit 14.21 shows, at the end of 2003, the distribution of TLB bids in the United States and Europe differed dramatically. Reflecting nonbank appetite, more than 60 percent of U.S. TLBs were bid at or above 100 cents on the dollar. At that time, the concept of a loan being bought above par was abhorrent to most European lenders. In turn, less than 20 percent of European LBO TLBs and TLCs were bid at or above par. But by the end of 2004, this had changed. While the share of U.S. TLB

EXHIBIT 14.21

European and U.S. price distributions *diverge* in 2003.

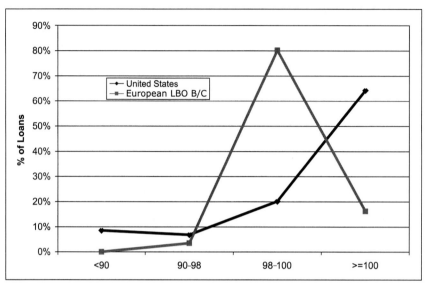

Source: Reuters LPC European Pricing Service; LSTA/LPC Mark-to-Market Pricing.

EXHIBIT 14.22

European and U.S. price distributions *converge* by 2004.

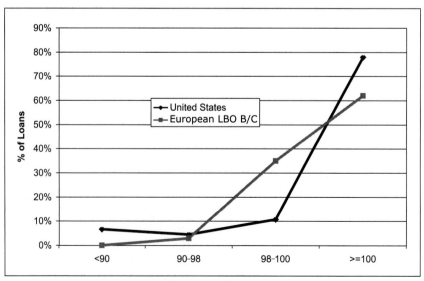

Source: Reuters LPC European Pricing Service; LSTA/LPC Mark-to-Market Pricing.

loans bid at 100 and higher had climbed toward 80 percent of the secondary market, the European market had undergone a revolution. From less than 20 percent of the market in 2003, the percentage of LBO TLBs and TLCs that were bid at or above par had gone to more than 60 percent by 2004.

And, in fact, the revolution didn't stop there. Bids in the secondary markets climbed even higher, led first by the U.S. market, but followed by the European market. In fact, an increasing share of loans was bid (and bought) at or above 101 cents on the dollar. Exhibit 14.23 illustrates the 101+ market share in the United States and Europe. As usual, the U.S. market moved first and has proved to be far more volatile. The share of very highly bid loans climbed from less than 20 percent of the U.S. market in early 2004 to more than half the market in April 2005. As the high-yield bond market slumped in the second quarter of 2005, it knocked the underpinnings out from the U.S. market, and the 101 market share tumbled to less than 15 percent. But like a phoenix, it rose again, approaching 50 percent of the market by late third quarter 2005.

EXHIBIT 14.23

101+ market share jumps as trends in the European secondary market converge to the U.S. model.

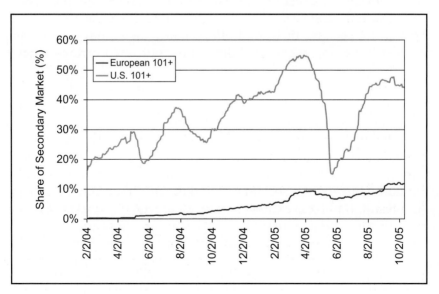

Source: Reuters LPC European Pricing Service; LSTA/LPC Mark-to-Market Pricing.

What's remarkable is not the volatility of the U.S. market—lenders have come to expect that—but that the European market echoed this trend, albeit quietly and with a slight lag. In early 2004, almost no European loans were bid at 101, but as nonbank lenders' appetite grew, so did the share of 101+ loans. By April 2005, 10 percent of European loans were bid at or above 101. While the average European bids barely moved when the high-yield bond markets softened in 2005, the share of highly bid loans slumped from nearly 10 percent of the market to well below 7 percent. And, as in the U.S. market, once the crisis had passed, the share of highly bid loans jumped again. In fact, by the end of third quarter 2005, 12 percent of European TLB/C loans were bid at 101 and above—the highest level ever seen.

In sum, while the development of the European leveraged loan market has lagged its American counterpart, it has begun to take on market-oriented characteristics such as price flex, more flexible loan structures, and a more reactive secondary market. It is, perhaps, all part of the inexorable march toward a transatlantic syndicated loan market.

But while a transatlantic leveraged market may be emerging, a global leveraged market has yet to emerge. The leveraged revolution in the United States and evolution in Europe have been met primarily with yawns in the Asia-Pacific region. Though there has been sporadic LBO activity in Asia—more than $3 billion of LBOs emerged in the last year—leveraged lending remains relatively rare. This is not because of lack of effort: many banks have expressed interest in buying higher-yielding loans, but few borrowers have emerged.

Meanwhile, the Asia-Pacific secondary loan market seems to have almost taken one step backward for every step forward. The dedication of regional trade associations—which are working toward creating greater transparency and liquidity—have been more than counteracted by technical imbalances in the loan market. Strong lender demand for loans has meant that there are plenty of would-be buyers in a secondary market, but practically no sellers. As a result, trading is extremely thin. However, the market may see evolution toward a more traded market in coming years. Lending—specifically, higher-margin acquisition finance—has increased. The combination of strong regional trade association support and a better supply-demand balance might allow stronger regional trading to emerge.

TOWARD A MORE GLOBAL LOAN MARKET?

A number of similar trends have emerged across the regional loan markets in the past several years: overall lending is up, and LBO loan issuance has climbed dramatically. But even as issuance has grown, there nevertheless has been a considerable supply-demand imbalance in nearly every region, leading to strong lender competition and slipping spreads. But these events might simply be regional trends that happen to be moving in the same direction, thanks to excess liquidity everywhere. They do not answer the question of whether there is a true *global* syndicated loan market emerging. For the answer to this, we turn to the wisdom of the market. Or, more specifically, a poll run by Reuters Loan Pricing Corporation that asked: How global will the loan market become? As Exhibit 14.24 shows, a strong majority of respondents said that the U.S. and European markets would continue to converge

EXHIBIT 14.24

How much will the loan markets converge?

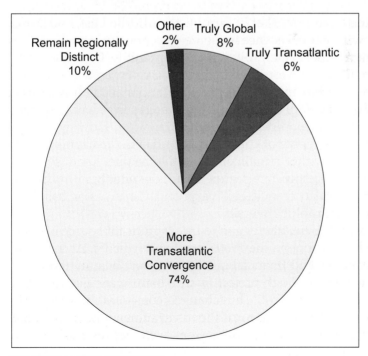

Source: Reuters Loan Pricing Corporation poll.

toward each other. But only 8 percent of respondents believed that syndicated lending would actually evolve into one global monolithic syndicated loan market. A truly global loan market may have to wait.

The next part of this chapter will discuss the European, Asian, and Japanese loan markets in detail, examining the historical development of the loan asset class in each, as well as the players operating in each. The section will help to give a better understanding of the differences and similarities that exist between regions, and the paths that each region has followed in developing its domestic syndicated lending markets.

The European Syndicated Loan Market

Clare Dawson
Loan Market Association

The syndicated loan market in Europe, the Middle East, and Africa (EMEA) has been in existence for some 40 years, during which time it has shown remarkable growth and adaptability. Over the years, numerous new borrowers and investors have entered the market, transaction size has increased markedly, and a secondary market for loans has developed. Many of the changes that have occurred have reflected developments in the U.S. market. However, while there has been a degree of convergence and standardization across the region, the market remains a very diverse one. Legal systems, market practice, insolvency regimes, and, despite the introduction of the euro, local currencies all vary, and the investor base also reflects this geographic diversity.

Syndicated loans first began to be a significant source of funding in the EMEA zone in the 1960s (see Exhibit 14.25). At that time, sovereign entities and financial institutions were heavily represented as borrowers, although project finance loans were also frequently seen. This borrower profile has changed considerably, and in 2004 corporate transactions made up 77 percent of new loan volumes in the region, while sovereign borrowers were represented almost exclusively by emerging market entities.

EXHIBIT 14.25

Euroloan Market Timeline

Late 1950s	Offshore U.S. dollar market develops
1958	Major European currencies become freely convertible to U.S. dollars
Early 1960s	Origins of syndicated loan market
Early 1980s	FRN market develops
1990	First investment grade corporate deal exceeding $10 billion U.S.
Early 1990s	Secondary loan market begins to develop
1996	LMA formed
	Secondary market annual volume exceeds $10 billion U.S.
1997	LMA secondary trading (par/near par) documents launched
1999	Launch of the euro
	LMA secondary trading (distressed) launched
2000	First investment grade corporate deal exceeding $20 billion U.S.
	First leveraged deal exceeding $5 billion U.S.
2001	LMA launches investment grade primary documents
2003	Secondary market annual volume exceeds $50 billion U.S.
2004	LMA launches leveraged primary documents
2005	First leveraged deal exceeds $10 billion U.S.

EXHIBIT 14.26

Euroloan volumes.

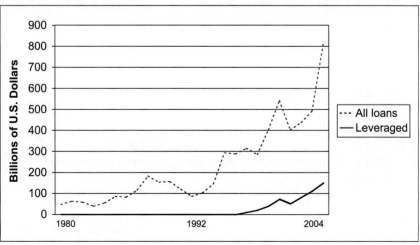

Source: Dealogic Loanware.

Although from its earliest days the market showed gradual steady growth, it was in the 1990s that volumes showed a really rapid rate of increase (see Exhibit 14.26). In 1999 new loan volume exceeded US$400 billion for the first time, and 2000 saw another record year, with US$543 billion in new deals. Despite the downturn in 2001, caused by a number of major corporate restructurings, compounded by the effects of September 11 and the fall from grace of the telecom sector, volumes have subsequently continued to grow, with transactions in 2004 totaling an unprecedented US$814 billion, although it should be recognized that a considerable proportion of this new funding was refinancing of existing transactions.

Moreover, during this period the market became capable of absorbing larger and larger deals. During the late 1990s and early 2000s, deals of over US$10 billion became fairly commonplace, with 15 deals over US$10 billion being finalized between 2000 and the autumn of 2005.

Another trend during this period was the rapid geographic diversification of major corporate borrowers (see Exhibit 14.27). Although from its outset the market has financed borrowers from throughout the region, in the corporate market, the United Kingdom was the predominant source of issuers for many years.

EXHIBIT 14.27

Borrower nationality—percentage of total volume.

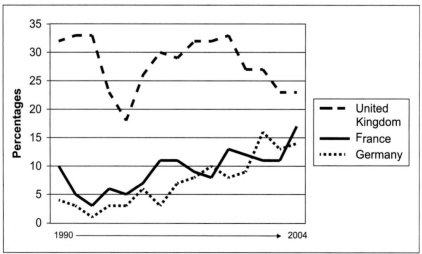

Source: Dealogic Loanware.

This began to change in the 1990s, driven largely by a number of major acquisition finance deals in continental Europe, such as US$27.3 billion for France Telecom and US$22 billion for Unilever, both in 2000.

Whereas in 1990, the United Kingdom represented 32 percent of total primary volume, by 2004 this was down to 23 percent, with France and Germany showing significant growth and becoming major sources of new deals.

Another important development of the late 1990s was the growth of a leveraged loan market in Europe. In 1995, European leveraged deals amounted to only US$0.1 billion out of a total volume of almost US$300 billion. By 2004, they had reached approximately US$150 billion out of a total of over US$800 billion, some 18 percent of the total market. Like the investment grade market, the leveraged market has become increasingly geographically diverse: in 2004, U.K. deals represented around 32 percent of the total, France 11 percent, Germany 17 percent, and Italy 5 percent (see Exhibit 14.28).

As with investment grade deals, the market soon became capable of absorbing larger and larger transactions. Whereas in 1999, the deals for Punch Taverns and Imetal, both US$2.3 billion, represented the largest amount ever raised in Europe, by 2005 deals of US$5 billion, or even US$10 billion, had become commonplace, and the deal for Wind Tel was over US$12 billion. An important factor in the capacity of the market to absorb these deals has

EXHIBIT 14.28

Borrower nationality—percentage of leveraged volume.

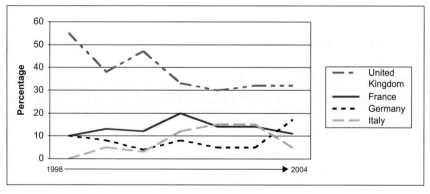

Source: Dealogic Loanware.

undoubtedly been the growing presence in Europe of institutional investors—both home-grown and U.S. entities—and arrangers have increasingly been structuring deals to attract these new investors.

While mezzanine finance has been used in the European leveraged market for quite some time, since the early 2000s, mezzanine tranches have increased in size, in line with the growth in average deal size. Second lien loans are a more recent development in Europe, but have lately become commonly used in capital structures, usually in conjunction with mezzanine finance. The process of pricing transactions has also begun to change, with much more price discovery during syndication, and subsequent use of market flex. Comparison of underlying credit and structural risk in a more diverse market has also led to more variation in pricing than had traditionally been seen in this sector of the market.

DEVELOPMENT OF THE SECONDARY MARKET

While the European syndicated loan market was growing steadily in size and sophistication throughout the 1980s, it was not until the early 1990s that a small number of banks began to trade corporate syndicated loans on the secondary market. By 1996, estimated volumes of secondary trades had reached US$12 billion,[1] and it was at the end of that year that the Loan Market Association (LMA) was founded. Initially established to help the development of the fledgling secondary market, the LMA's first major achievement was to produce standard form documentation for trading par/near par loans. These were followed by documentation for trading distressed debt, and the LMA has subsequently gone on to produce template documents for the primary loan market, both investment grade and leveraged (see Exhibit 14.25). After a relatively slow start, secondary trading in Europe began to increase rapidly in the second half of the 1990s, in part mirroring the growth in the primary market, especially the jumbo acquisition financings, which typically had fewer restrictions on transferability (see Exhibit 14.29). More banks also began to manage their loan portfolios actively, a trend that was encouraged by the wave of bank mergers seen in those years, which in turn added momentum to the growing secondary volumes in Europe.

---

[1] Source Barclays Capital.

EXHIBIT 14.29

European secondary loan trading volumes.

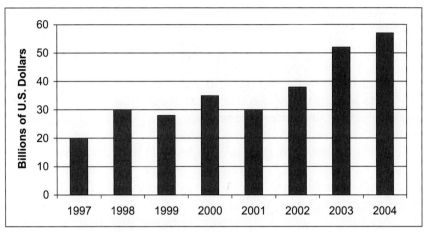

Source: LMA.

In line with activity in the primary market, secondary trading has seen a steady shift from investment grade toward leveraged, with 34 percent of trading in 2004 being in leveraged deals, compared to 18 percent in 2001.[2]

As a subset of the secondary market, distressed debt trading was for many years confined to a relatively small number of banks. In the last few years, however, more primary lenders have proved willing to sell distressed loans, and the market has received an influx of interest from U.S. investors who see attractive opportunities in the European market. This has led to a considerable increase in trading activity, as well as to a focus on the variation in both market practice and documentation between the U.S. and European markets. In response to this, the LMA and the LSTA worked together on a distressed debt documentation project, which resulted, in October 2005, in the publication of revised LMA distressed debt trading documents and a joint User Guide to facilitate cross-border trading between the two markets and help improve market participants' understanding of the differences between the two markets.

---

[2] LMA.

THE EUROPEAN VERSUS THE U.S. MARKET

The single most obvious difference between the Euroloan market and the U.S. market is the fact that, despite the introduction of the Euro, even within the EU different local markets continue to exist. While large syndicated loans will generally be syndicated across a wide range of lenders across the region, local banks retain a strong position as both arrangers and lenders in their home markets (see Exhibit 14.30). Conversely, looking at the region as a whole, this leads to a considerable degree of geographic diversity among arranger banks, by virtue of the strong position they hold in their domestic markets.

At the global level, the Euroloan market has had a strong influence on the Australasian market, particularly in terms of language and legal systems, and for historical reasons, several European banks are major players in that market.

Another important difference between the two markets is currency. Despite the introduction of the euro in 1999, several other currencies remain in use in the region, the most important being the

EXHIBIT 14.30

Top ten banks in selected European countries.

Country	Top 10 Provider Banks
United Kingdom	**Barclays Bank; Royal Bank of Scotland; HSBC Bank; Lloyds TSB Bank**; Citigroup; Deutsche Bank; **Bank of Scotland**; JP Morgan Chase; ABN AMRO Bank; Mizuho Financial Group
France	**Calyon; BNP Paribas; Natexis Banques Populaires; SG CIB; IXIS CIB**; HSBC Bank; **Banque Federative du Credit Mutuel**; Royal Bank of Scotland; ABN AMRO Bank; Banco Bilbao Vizcaya Argentaria
Germany	**Dresdner Kleinwort Wasserstein; HVB Group; Deutsche Bank**; JP Morgan Chase; ABN AMRO Bank; Citigroup; **WestLB; Commerzbank; BayernLB**; HSBC Bank
Italy	**UniCredit Banca Mobiliare; Banca Intesa; Capitalia; Mediobanca**; Calyon; Barclays Bank; **Banca Nazionale del Lavoro**; Goldman Sachs & Co.; Royal Bank of Scotland; **Sanpaolo IMI**
Spain	**Banco Santander; Banco Bilbao Vizcaya Argentaria; Caja Madrid**; Calyon; Barclays Bank; Citigroup; SG CIB; **La Caixa**; Royal Bank of Scotland; JP Morgan Chase
Nordic	**Nordea Bank; SEB Merchant Banking; Svenska Handelsbanken**; Barclays Bank; HSBC Bank; Citigroup; **Danske Bank; DnB NOR Bank**; Deutsche Bank; JP Morgan Chase

pound sterling. Multicurrency options are extremely common, with euro, U.S. dollars, and pounds sterling the likely base currencies.

While the Euroloan region is dominated by transactions coming out of the major EU jurisdictions, in particular the United Kingdom, France, Germany, and Italy, emerging market issuers represent a small but significant part of the primary market. In 2004, loans to sub-Saharan African, central and eastern European, north African, and Middle Eastern borrowers amounted to about 8 percent of the total.

This brings to lending in the region factors such as political risk, as well as the need to look across a very wide range of the credit spectrum. Also, in the Middle East in particular, project finance and transactions for financial institutions make up an important part of the market; see Exhibit 14.31 for a comparison of project finance loan volumes as a percentage of (1) the overall total loan volumes and (2) the ME/Africa region loan volumes.

In the leveraged market, the role of the institutional investor has grown rapidly in Europe, but is still some way from reaching U.S. levels. In the 12 months ending with the third quarter of 2005, institutional investors accounted for 37 percent of primary lending in the European leveraged market, compared with 66 percent in the United States.[3] While much has been done to facilitate the entry of nonbank investors into the market (for example, the changes in the

EXHIBIT 14.31

Project finance percentages.

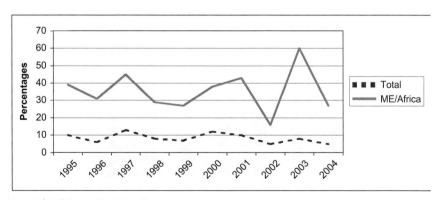

Source: Dealogic Loanware.

---

[3] Standard & Poor's.

withholding tax treatment of U.K. nonbank investors), restrictions on nonbank lending remain in a number of jurisdictions, and these continue to inhibit the growth of this investor base.

Despite progress having been made in a number of areas to create a single market for financial services within the EU, a number of barriers to cross-border activity remain, and this is also the case in the non-EU countries. Of these, one of the main issues is withholding tax, which affects transactions in a number of jurisdictions, including Italy, Portugal, Greece, and the Baltic states. This is an issue on which the LMA has done a considerable amount of lobbying, and it is an ongoing area of work for the association.

On the secondary side, the European market has grown more slowly than the U.S. market (see Exhibit 14.32) and, unlike the situation in the United States, until 2004–2005 was dominated by trading of investment grade loans, although secondary trading in leveraged loans has risen rapidly as a proportion of the total in recent years (see Exhibit 14.33) and is now approaching 50 percent.

This has reflected the increase in leveraged deals in the primary market, as well as the increase in institutional investor activity, which has boosted the amount of secondary activity in that area. The widespread acceptance of LMA documentation has undoubtedly been an important factor in facilitating loan trading across the Euroloan region, as a common set of documents that is accepted across the various jurisdictions has made cross-border trading easier and more efficient.

EXHIBIT 14.32

U.S. and European secondary market volumes.

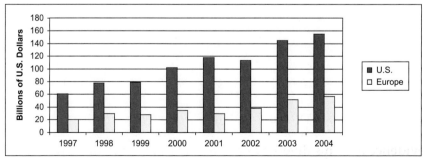

Source: LSTA/LMA.

EXHIBIT 14.33

Leveraged loans: percentage of total secondary activity in Europe

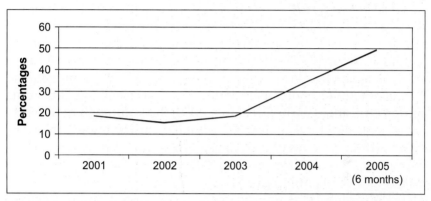

Source: LMA.

Despite progress on the documentation front to achieve more standardization in the region, even within the EU the financial markets remain relatively diverse. Although much of the legislation that governs the market now originates at the EU level, it is still the responsibility of the individual member states to implement it in their own jurisdictions. This can lead to distinct variations in the way in which the different national governments regulate their financial markets. Moreover, much of the general legal framework within which companies operate is still based on long-standing national legislation. Thus, insolvency regimes vary considerably across different jurisdictions, with some being significantly more creditor-friendly than others. Legal systems themselves also differ, with some, such as that in England, being based on a common law system and others, such as that in France, on a codified system.

It is clear, therefore, that, while the Euroloan region should certainly be seen as one market when put in a global context, from a practitioner's perspective, it retains a considerable degree of geographic, economic, and structural diversity. Nonetheless, the success and growth of the syndicated loan market in the region is evidence that this diversity need not be a barrier to the functioning of a highly effective and growing sector of the capital markets.

The Syndicated Loan Market in the Asia-Pacific Region

Philip Cracknell
Standard Chartered

The loan market in the Asia-Pacific region had a strong year in 2005, as measured both by the number of new loans arranged and by the dollar volume. This is depicted in Exhibit 14.34. At the date of this writing, in early December 2005, the volume of new syndicated lending stood at US$304 billion, already higher than last year's volume. A number of major deals are yet to close, and we expect total volume for the year to be at US$330 billion or more, which will be the highest level on record.

The countries in the region with the largest amount of borrowing are Japan and Australia (see Exhibit 14.35). Japan accounts for loans of US$154 billion, or just over 50 percent of the total market. Australia accounts for loans of US$48.5 billion, or 16 percent of the total market. Hong Kong is just a fraction ahead of Korea as the third largest Asian market.

The loan market in Japan is very much a domestic market, with the big four Japanese banks arranging loans, typically denom-

EXHIBIT 14.34

Asia loan market activity and volumes.

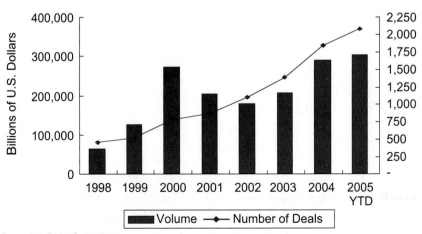

Source: Loan Pricing Corporation.

EXHIBIT 14.35

2005 year-to-date Asian volumes by region.

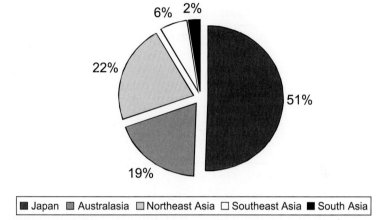

| ■ Japan ■ Australasia □ Northeast Asia □ Southeast Asia ■ South Asia |

Source: Loan Pricing Corporation.

inated in yen, and then syndicating them to the plethora of smaller Japanese regional banks. It is interesting to note that back in 1997, the year of the Asian financial crisis, the volume of syndicated lending in Japan was less than US$1.5 billion, and there were only 15 transactions. Contrast that with today's volume, which is in excess of US$150 billion with over 1,420 separate transactions (see Exhibit 14.36).

The growth in the Japanese syndicated loan market was caused by the Asian financial crisis and the impact it had on the Japanese banks, which needed to share risk rather than taking the whole risk on their balance sheet through bilateral lending. The switch from traditional bilateral lending to syndicated lending is driving the market.

We may see a similar development in China. In 2004, the volume of new lending in China (excluding Hong Kong) was US$6.33 billion. For 2005 to date, the volume stands at US$12.6 billion, an increase of 100 percent, but still low relative to Japan and Australia, especially given the size of the Chinese economy and the rate of economic growth. While in Japan a considerable amount of the lending is in yen, in China the local currency syndications market is still relatively nascent, and a lot of lending is provided on a bilateral basis. Recently there have been official recommendations that for deals over a certain size, banks should lend on a syndicated

EXHIBIT 14.36

Syndicated loan market volumes in the Asia-Pacific region.

	2001	2002	2003	2004	2005 YTD
Asia	203.9	177.1	205.4	288.0	304.2
Asia (ex. Japan)	109.6	86.5	90.6	145.0	150.4
Asia (ex. Japan/Australia)	85.6	66.4	61.9	98.3	101.9
Japan	94.3	90.4	114.9	143.0	153.8
Australia	23.9	20.1	28.7	46.7	48.5
Northeast Asia	61.4	44.0	42.4	65.4	67.0
Southeast Asia	17.8	14.0	15.0	21.0	16.7
South Asia	3.1	1.8	2.5	4.1	7.3

Source: Loan Pricing Corporation.

basis rather than a bilateral basis. As China switches from bilateral to multilateral lending, we can expect to see a significant increase in the volume of syndicated lending in China.

In addition to the switch from bilateral lending to syndicated lending, another theme of the market in recent years has been the development of local currency syndicated lending. The markets in Korean won and new Taiwan dollars are of considerable size, as are the longer-established markets in Hong Kong dollars, Singapore dollars, and Malaysian ringitt. In 2005 there was a significant increase in the number of Indian rupee syndications, and there are now local currency syndication markets in almost every country in Asia.

It can be seen in Exhibit 14.37 that the North American market is relatively stable in terms of volume. Over the period since 1999, it has grown from US$1.09 trillion to US$1.4 trillion, an increase of nearly 30 percent. The loan market in Western Europe has grown by over 100 percent, from US$430 billion in 1999 to an expected US$900 billion volume for 2005 over the same period. This has been helped by a significant increase in leveraged buyouts and acquisition financing.

In Asia, the loan market has grown at an even faster rate. In 1999 the Asian loan market recorded a volume of US$126 billion, and since then it has grown by over 160 percent; it is anticipated to reach a volume of US$330 billion in 2005.

The continuation of the seemingly inexorable downward trend in pricing has also been seen in 2005. The market continues

EXHIBIT 14.37

Global syndication volumes.

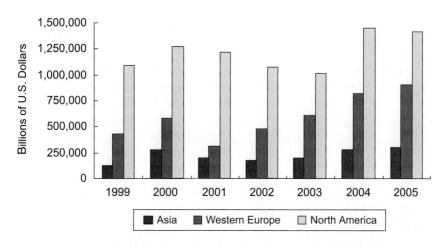

EXHIBIT 14.37A

The syndicated loan market in Asia, at US$300–330 billion, is still only a quarter of the size of the North American loan market, estimated at approximately US$1.42 trillion. It is also much smaller than the Western European market, with expected 2005 volume of approximately US$900 billion. The comparative size is illustrated in the diagram.

to be characterized by high levels of liquidity in the banking sector, which has contributed to a further reduction in margins across Asia's loan markets. Just one example is India's Reliance Industries, which tapped the market on three separate occasions for five-year loans in 2005: in March at 90 basis points (bps), in June at 80 bps, and again in November at 60 bps. Indeed, pricing in Asia is now probably below the levels seen in the United States for similarly rated credits. Energizer Asia recently tapped Singapore's loan market at a level inside that obtained by its U.S. parent.

As in other world markets, we have also seen a significant increase in acquisition finance in Asia. These deals have generally been financed in the syndicated loan market, although the bond markets are increasingly being used for the subsequent take-out financing. While there has been a relatively small number of syndicated loans financing leveraged buyouts in Asia (outside of Australia and Japan), those that have been completed have been large and to some extent groundbreaking. These have included the US$700 million syndicated loan to finance the leveraged buyout of Raffles Holdings, the hospitality arm of the CapitaLand Group, by Colony Investments. The transaction attracted significant media coverage, as it involved the sale of Raffles Hotel, one of Singapore's most iconic assets.

Indonesia saw its largest-ever leveraged buyout, in the form of the US$600 million five-year syndicated loan for Arindo Global, financing the purchase of an integrated coal mining group in Kalimantan, Indonesia. The target acquisition consisted of a coal mine (Indonesia's largest), storage, and port facilities. The equity was provided by a consortium of investors led by Farallon and was made up of both common equity and a US$350 million mezzanine financing. Within six months of signing, this loan had been refinanced by a high-yield bond issue and a syndicated loan for the balance.

Another major acquisition finance transaction was the Philippines' San Miguel Corporation's purchase of National Foods of Australia, in the face of competitive bidding. This was financed via a bridge loan that was initially underwritten as a US$1.85 billion syndicated loan, although it was subsequently reduced to US$1.15 billion. This was the largest syndicated loan ever arranged for a Philippine corporation. There were 29 banks participating in the US$1.15 billion bridge facility, which was later refinanced through a US$650 million syndicated loan in which 23 banks participated.

There are also a growing number of private equity firms operating out of Asia, and there is considerable liquidity in private equity funds looking for investment. However, there has been a dearth of opportunities in an environment in which many of the mid-cap firms are family-owned or family-controlled. Notwithstanding this, as we look ahead to 2006, it is probable that there will be an increase in the number of financial investor–sponsored leveraged buyout transactions similar to the Arindo and Raffles deals.

However, the main activity in acquisition finance is likely to continue to be corporate-driven, strategic acquisitions like San Miguel's acquisition of National Foods. Asian companies, particularly those in China and India, are increasingly looking to expand overseas. Chinese companies, for example, have been making acquisitions in the United States, Europe, and Africa in addition to Asia. Examples of this can be found in the attempts by CNOOC to acquire Unocal and Minmetal's attempt to buy Noranda, and, more successfully, in the acquisition of IBM's personal computer business by the Chinese computer company Legend. This acquisition was financed by a US$600 million syndicated loan.

Another likely trend in 2006 is a further step-up in loans relating to the financing of casinos. The second Wynn Resorts financing took place in 2005, and other casino financings for Venetian Macau and Crown Macau are currently in the market. Next year will see MGM Grand Macau tapping the loan market, as well as the expected financings for Singapore's much heralded "integrated resorts."

The loan markets in Asia are becoming more sophisticated, deals are getting bigger, and the prospects are looking very good as we enter 2006. The only thing that worries me is that next year happens to be the Chinese New Year of the Dog!

With Limited Options in the Domestic Loan Market, Japanese Investors Look to the United States for Investment Opportunities

Suraj Bhatia
Senior Managing Director, The Sumitomo Trust & Banking Co. Ltd., New York Branch

Jennifer Ashe
Vice President and Head of Research, The Sumitomo Trust & Banking Co. Ltd., New York Branch

INTRODUCTION

The Japanese Investment Environment

The Japanese investment environment has traditionally been characterized by low rates of return and a conservative investment mindset. Japanese individuals have a high propensity to keep careful control of their assets, and thus the Japanese post office has nearly $2 trillion in savings deposits.

Japanese institutional investors, with $4.5 trillion in investable assets, have also tended to be quite cautious since the Japanese economic bubble burst in early 1990 (the Japanese stock market index had reached almost 40,000 in December 1989 when the downward spiral began; in eight months, it plummeted to 23,000). Coupled with decreasing real estate values, losses of Japanese wealth have been estimated to be as much as $15 trillion, so institutional investors naturally became risk averse and were content with low absolute returns, so long as they were stable.

Japanese Investments in U.S. Bonds

Traditionally, Japan's insurance companies and the nation's corporate pension plans have invested in low-risk Japanese corporate and government bonds. Japanese investors have also been large buyers of U.S. Treasury bonds (Exhibit 14.38).

Rates around 4 percent on U.S. bonds are attractive to Japanese investors, whose domestic rates hover around zero. These investors have also bought Japanese government bonds heavily. Now, however, there is concern that bond prices will crash if, as the economy improves, interest rates rise. Moreover, given Japan's aging population, pension funds must earn more on their investments. Major Japanese institutional investors such as pension funds and securities trusts have been increasingly looking to over-

EXHIBIT 14.38

Japanese holdings of U.S. Treasuries.

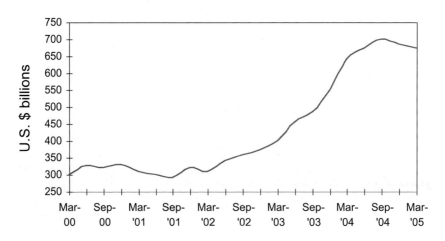

seas assets in recent years, as the domestic investment environment has been stagnant.

JAPANESE INVESTMENT STRATEGIES AND METHODS

Shift in Investments

In the late 1990s, Japanese assets started flowing into market-neutral strategies run by U.S.-based institutions, such as State Street Global Advisers, Goldman Sachs, and JP Morgan, as well as by Japanese asset managers. In recent years, potentially higher-returning products such as hedge funds, structured products, and managed accounts have been gaining popularity among institutions. Interest rates have been near 0 percent for almost ten years, making it hard to achieve positive yields in fixed income and cash. At the same time, there has been a shift to risk control and diversification.

DOMESTIC LOAN MARKET OPPORTUNITIES

Japanese Syndicated Loan Market

Japan's syndicated loan market effectively started in the late 1990s, but significant volume growth has really been seen only in the past few years (Exhibit 14.39).

Syndicated loans still account for only about 10 percent of overall Japanese commercial and industrial lending, compared with 35 percent in the United States. Still, based on the statistics compiled by the Bank of Japan, in Japan the origination value of syndicated loans climbed from 4.6 trillion yen in the third quarter of 2003 to 8.1 trillion yen in the third quarter of 2005, a 76.7 percent increase over the two-year period. More notably, origination of syndicated term loans more than doubled, from 1.9 trillion yen to 4.4 trillion yen, during the same period. The outstanding balance reached 32.9 trillion yen, consisting of 18.6 trillion yen of term loans and 14.3 trillion yen of commitment lines, at the end of September 2005.

Bankers and analysts believe that syndicated loans are going to play an even bigger role in corporate finance in Japan in the years ahead. The market has been expanding with the growth of large-scale deals involving corporate mergers and acquisitions, and more midsize companies are also choosing to syndicate loans.

EXHIBIT 14.39

Development of the Japanese syndicated term loan market (in trillions of yen).

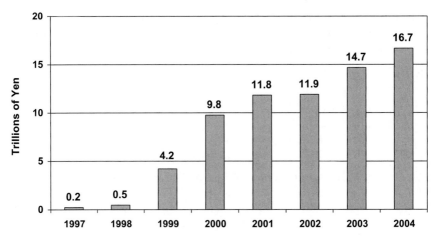

Source: Thompson Financial.

Notably, syndicated loans are growing at a time when overall lending by Japanese banks has fallen for over five years in a row. Recent high-profile deals suggest that syndicated loans are catching on as a financing option.

Although an established source for market share data does not exist yet, based on one market source, in 2004 almost 90 percent of Japan's syndicated loan business was done by so-called Japanese megabanks, which were consolidated into three with the merger of Bank of Tokyo Mitsubishi and UFJ. Even the top non-Japanese bank was a distant fourth, with only a handful of deals.

While syndicated loan markets in the United States and Europe have prospered for years, traditional banking practices have hindered the development of a similar market in Japan. Some U.S. observers claim that, under Japan's traditional "main bank" system, close ties between banks and their corporate clients were further strengthened by cross-shareholding. Typically, this meant that just one or a few large banks did business with and had access to financial information about a given company. These lending practices helped to create a significant amount of bad loans, which have weighed on the nation's financial system for over a decade.

During the late 1990s, however, a series of credit events with major financial institutions such as Yamaichi Securities, LTCB, and Hokkaido Takushoku Bank led to severe credit contraction. At this point, foreign banks successfully contracted with healthier Japanese corporate borrowers to provide a syndicated commitment line. Loan syndication received further momentum as the consolidation of major Japanese banks progressed. Newly born megabanks tried to reduce their lending portfolio while seeking additional fee income through syndication. Their deteriorating risk-asset ratio prompted this move. They started utilizing loan syndication as a means to achieve this objective.

The speed of expansion of syndicated loan origination, however, has now stalled, since syndicated loan originators such as megabanks now have less incentive to originate such loans. Having dealt with their problem loans, they are able to expand their loan portfolio by assuming additional risk. Thus, the banks' priority has shifted from asset reduction to growth.

Future expansion of the Japanese syndicated loan market will partially hinge upon the strategies pursued by major Japanese banks. At the same time, clear disclosure of the terms and conditions of the syndicated loans in the market and added liquidity in the secondary market will certainly help the market expansion.

Japanese Secondary Loan Market

Like the development of a primary market for syndicated loans, secondary trading in bank loans has also been slow to catch on in Japan. The secondary market for loans is still tiny, despite a recent increase in activity. According to the statistics compiled by Bank of Japan, 931 loans with a total amount of 1.5 trillion yen, exclusive of distressed debts, changed hands during the one-year period ending September 2005. Further growth in the secondary market seems to be a prerequisite for the continued growth of loan syndication in Japan.

Growth in loan trading would make Japan's banking system more flexible, allowing lenders to unload unwanted exposure or take on extra risk. It also would provide essential infrastructure for Japan's expanding syndicated loan market, making it easier for banks to adjust their portfolios after participating in group deals.

Although there is awareness in Japan of the benefits of having a developed syndicated loan market in place, hurdles still abound, especially in the mindsets and attitudes that continue to prevail. Although changes have been observed, borrowers tend to object to the idea of their banks' selling their debt. This mindset is a holdover from a time when selling loans to a third party was unthinkable. As for banks, as a result of the recent improvements in their asset quality, their need for portfolio adjustment is not as high as it was a few years ago. A renewed focus on portfolio management motivated by risk-adjusted returns on assets and equity would stimulate the market. Additionally, there is no centralized source for reliable loan pricing (such as Loan Pricing Corporation/ LSTA in the United States), and this makes it difficult for banks to trade loans. Furthermore, because most market players are banks that mostly have similar needs, the Japanese secondary loan market currently tends to be one-sided. Participation of nonbank investors such as pension funds and mutual funds would lead to more active trading.

Japanese CDO Market

Given the limited opportunities to invest in loans in the syndicated and secondary loan market, many Japanese investors have turned to the domestic collaterized debt obligation (CDO) market. In late 2002 and early 2003, Japan's major banks arranged a number of CDOs that removed a huge amount of assets and risks from their books. They preferred CDOs over loan syndication and participation because CDOs do not open up a window of opportunity for other banks to expand banking relationships with their clients.

By aggressively repackaging loan and debt exposures into CDOs, banks sought to remove credit risk from their portfolios, in an effort to maintain their capital adequacy ratios at levels that would allow them to continue to conduct international business. According to Moody's Investors Service, CDO issuances reached 3.14 trillion yen ($26.20 billion) in 28 transactions in 2002. In 2003, CDO issuance grew even more, to 4.24 trillion yen. (See Exhibit 14.40.)

Banks issued both cash CDOs and synthetic CDOs. The latter, which transfers only the credit risk associated with the loan or bond assets using credit default swaps, was more popular with Japanese banks.

While top banks stepped up their efforts to customize CDOs, cash-rich investors, who were seeking higher returns and more

EXHIBIT 14.40

Japanese CDO volume (billions of U.S. dollars).

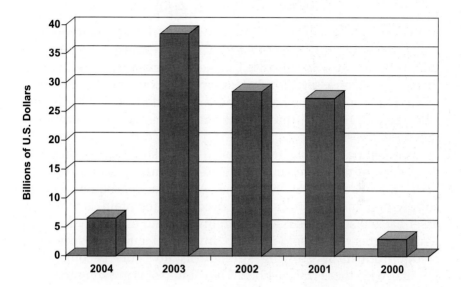

diversified portfolios, showed keen interest in increasing their holdings of CDOs. CDOs were appealing to investors because they contained a wide variety of industries.

But in 2004, Japan's major banks, helped by strong share prices, did not need to issue CDOs to remove risk from their balance sheet. The only growth now in the Japanese CDO market comes from deals that securitize loans to small businesses as a result of a push by both the government and the Bank of Japan to make financing more readily available to these firms. These deals, though, are not large in size and are certainly insufficient to satisfy demand for the product.

As noted, Moody's rated 24 CDO transactions worth 4.24 trillion yen in 2003, which was up 35 percent over 2002. But in a sign of a slowing market, the agency rated only four transactions worth just 150 billion yen in the final quarter of 2004. The sharp contraction in issuance goes some way to explain the excess of demand over supply in the primary market. Another factor is the lack of trading opportunities in the secondary market, as some deals are privately placed and have insufficient liquidity.

GLOBAL OPPORTUNITIES: MOVING BEYOND THE DOMESTIC MARKET

Investing in U.S. Assets

With overall Japanese CDO issuance likely to fall and volumes failing to satisfy investor demand, arrangers are encouraging Japanese investors to buy into global CDO deals backed by non-Japanese loans and other assets. Marketers have been successful in selling CDOs that are backed by assets that are mostly from countries outside Japan, primarily the United States, to a limited number of Japanese investors.

Global transactions have proved successful because they take advantage of the more generous credit spreads and a much larger pool of assets in the United States. A natural consequence of the supply-demand dynamics, many specialists maintain, is that more asset-backed securities issues from Europe and especially from the United States will be sold in Japan. Investor demand for structured credit products is growing strongly as investors become more familiar with these transactions. Thus, interest is growing in CDOs backed by non-Japanese assets, especially U.S. assets.

Thus, the first key trend for the foreseeable future is investors' shift from Japanese risk to global risk because Japanese credit spreads are so low. The other is investors' shift from debt to equity. As Japan's economic recovery gains momentum, investors are buying more tailored CDOs in which they can take on more risk lower down the capital structure to meet their return expectations. Exhibit 14.41 depicts the typical CDO structure. While they initially favored the less risky tranches, Japanese investors are becoming more comfortable with the product and with certain investment managers and are thus more open to investing in equity tranches.

Japanese Banks' Role

Japanese banks and institutional investors are both now looking to the U.S. market for investment opportunities.

For Japanese banks, this comes at a time when they are ready to invest again after years of contraction and a focus on cost savings and rationalization rather than business development. Banks, having written off nonperforming assets, are looking to build their balance sheets again. Japanese banks are seeing a turnaround in their fortunes.

EXHIBIT 14.41

Typical CDO structure.

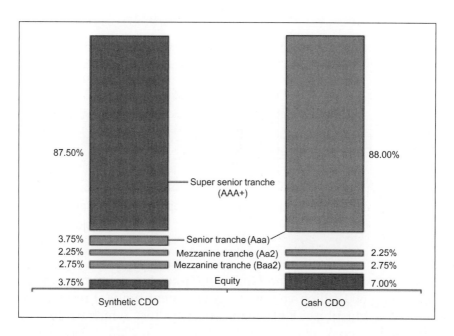

After many years of dealing with bad loans and inadequate capital, these institutions are finally regaining their financial health. This is a result of greatly improved earnings and the resolution of the bad debt problems that plagued them in the 1990s and early 2000s. In fact, as shown in Exhibit 14.42, by March 2006, they are expected to have repaid nearly 50 percent of the $95.1 billion that the government injected in the late 1990s to replenish their capital; as of March 2005, $15.9 billion had been repaid.

The industry's bad loans peaked at $325.7 billion in March 2002. The banks accelerated their write-offs of bad loans, leading to years of massive losses, and reduced bad debt to $166.5 billion by the end of March 2005, according to Japan's Financial Services Agency.

The industry as a whole booked four straight years of losses before reporting its first combined net profit in 2004. The Financial Services Agency has called on banks to repay the funds advanced by the government in the late 1990s ahead of schedule now that the banking crisis is over. Banks, seeking to eliminate any interference in their operations by the authorities, are eager to do so.

E X H I B I T   1 4 . 4 2

Japanese banks' outstanding public funds (in trillions of yen).

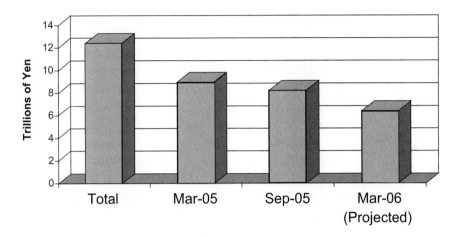

For example, Mizuho Financial Group Inc. aims to repay the remaining 600 billion yen of the government funds it received by July 2006. Mitsubishi UFJ Financial Group Inc., which earlier had intended to repay all public money by autumn 2007, is considering doing so more than one year earlier. Sumitomo Mitsui Financial Group also intends to move up its payment schedule. It previously had intended to repay the 1.1 trillion yen it still owes by the end of fiscal 2007. Sumitomo Trust actually completed its repayment of public funds in January 2004.

With the banking crisis over, banks are now free to focus more intently on business development and investing and are actively seeking investment opportunities not just at home, but also abroad.

In addition to the banks, other big investors such as insurance companies and pension funds are becoming more sophisticated and globalized, and these can be expected to return to the U.S. loan market through direct investments, managed investments, CDO debt investing, CDO/CLO equity investing, and loan fund management.

TYPES OF JAPANESE INVESTORS

The following major Japanese investors are now seeking more lucrative investments.

- Corporate pension funds
- Institutional investors
- High-net-worth individuals
- Banks and bank subsidiaries

Corporate Pension Funds

Corporate pension funds are increasingly looking for other avenues for deploying their capital, since returns on traditional Japanese investments are low.

Increasingly, corporate pension funds are being staffed by sophisticated financial professionals who are looking to maximize returns while diversifying risk. Working together with their advisors, such pension funds have been looking overseas. They are investing in the high-yield loan market through a variety of vehicles, including

- Managed accounts
- CLO/CDO debt
- CLO/CDO equity
- Hedge funds

Not all investments by corporate pension funds have been successful. Some of the earliest investments with hedge fund managers have proved to be poor performers, according to an investor. However, through enough diversification and intelligent asset allocation, overall returns have been optimized.

High-Net-Worth Individuals

Japanese high-net-worth individuals historically have kept relatively large portions of their assets with banks. However, because of the long-lasting low-interest-rate environment, they have started to allocate a larger portion of their assets to investment products, including those with non-Japanese risks, such as U.S. high-yield loans.

One structure that has been used in the past is principal protected investment vehicles (PPIVs). In this structure, investors provide money to a vehicle that hires a professional fund manager to manage monies invested in institutional loans. The principal is protected via a wrap-around letter of credit, typically provided by a bank that takes the credit risk of the portfolio.

PPIVs have provided a return to investors that is better than the return found on Japanese investments. Also, they are more cost-effective than traditional CLOs because rating agency fees are unnecessary and costs associated with issuance are minimized. However, it is quite difficult and cumbersome for the arrangers of such transactions to coordinate and provide reporting to a rather large number of individuals with small investments. Because of that, these structures have not remained as popular as they were during the trial phase.

Institutional Investors

Institutional investors in Japan are becoming increasingly savvy and aware of developments in the U.S. high-yield loan market. They are also staffed by sophisticated financial professionals who are looking to maximize return while diversifying risk. They make investments in the high-yield loan market through many vehicles, including

- CLO/CLO debt
- CLO/CLO equity
- Hedge funds
- Private equity firms that in turn invest in leveraged buyouts

Institutional investors have been going through a phase of learning through their investments. They have collected sufficient data to be able to go into the next phase, which might include investments in funds of funds and building relationships with specific advisors, arrangers, and fund managers.

Banks and Bank Subsidiaries

The major Japanese banks still continue to lend to pro rata facilities. However, as mentioned before, several banks have started investing in the loan market through a variety of vehicles, including

- Proprietary funds, i.e., funds that are entirely funded by the banks and are run by internal portfolio managers along the same lines as CLOs
- Bank subsidiaries that engage in an asset management business such as CLO management, using the bank's

money as partial equity, while placing the debt and remainder of the equity

- . Managed accounts, managed by outside professional managers
- Equity investments in CLOs

Banks and bank subsidiaries have used their traditional expertise in leveraged loan lending to enter the field of high-yield loan fund management. Such banks have changed the original model of relationship/pro rata lending, and are now poised to take more innovate approaches to leveraged loan investing on behalf of their customers.

WAYS IN WHICH JAPANESE INVESTORS ARE ACCESSING THE U.S. HIGH-YIELD LOAN MARKET

Like other institutional investors, the Japanese have found a myriad of opportunities to invest in the loan asset class. While banks started out by investing directly through the syndicated loan market, they and other players have now moved on to secondary loan markets, direct investments in CDOs/CLOs, managed accounts, private equity funds, and, increasingly, hedge funds. These investments are graphically represented in Exhibit 14.43.

CONCLUSION

The once very conservative Japanese investment mindset has now shifted. Institutional investors, once satisfied with getting the slimmest of returns in order to ensure minimal risk, are now taking bolder steps to obtain higher returns for their investments. Japanese banks, having weathered a serious crisis, are now focusing on new business opportunities to enhance profitability. Options for investing in the domestic market have proliferated in recent years, with hedge funds, loan markets and structured products helping Japanese investors move from traditional investments such as government bonds.

Still, the domestic Japanese market is limited in the offerings it can provide and there is by far greater demand for attractive investment vehicles than the domestic market can provide at this time. This is precisely the reason that Japanese investors have been

EXHIBIT 14.43

Various ways in which Japanese investors are accessing the U.S. high-yield loan market.

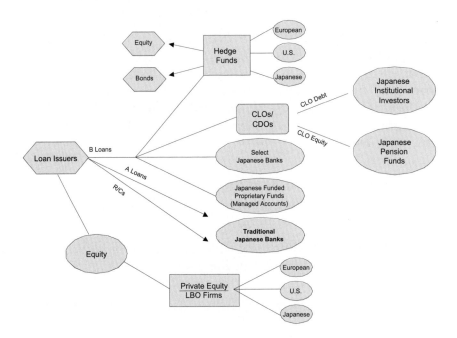

looking abroad, and specifically to the United States, for new investment alternatives. Structured products such as CDO debt and equity have been an exciting new area of investment for the Japanese. Having become more comfortable with these products, investors can be expected to gain exposure through direct loan market investments, CDO investments, and managed accounts.

The Japanese investor base has become increasingly sophisticated as investors rely on in-house professionals and advisors to gain knowledge in the area of high-yield loans. It represents a huge potential pool of investors, poised for growth as they seek better risk-return profiles. This presents unique opportunities for arrangers, advisors and fund managers. As the appetite for high-yield Loans grows, it is bound to fuel the growth of the loan market. This appetite is timed with the corresponding increase in the reach of the leveraged loan issuance market, and is a catalyst in enabling the high-yield loan market to become a solid foundation of the capital markets.

Research and contributions to this article by:
Yoshiaki Hirayama, Group Manager Syndicated Loans, The Sumitomo
Trust & Banking Co., Ltd., Tokyo
Linda Goggans, Business Information Coordinator, The Sumitomo Trust
& Banking Co., Ltd., NY Branch
Rohan Kerr, Research Associate, The Sumitomo Trust & Banking Co.,
Ltd., NY Branch

Toward a More Integrated World: The Future of the Global Distressed Loan Market

Mike Kerrigan
Partner, Hunton & Williams LLP

Steve Curtis
Partner, Clifford Chance LLP

Ian Sandler
Vice President, Morgan Stanley

INTRODUCTION: THE CALL TO CONVERGENCE

As the past few years in the loan market have shown, distressed investors' search for yield knows no borders. During that period, the actual or perceived lack of U.S.-originated distressed loans led many investors overseas in search of greater yield. Yet applicable laws, relevant trading protocols, and market customs are not as universal as the market forces driving this quest, and when increased transaction costs and settlement delays depress the prospective return that made the opportunity attractive in the first place, investors are invariably frustrated. Nevertheless, many fundamental issues (for example, security interest perfection and priority arrangements, regulated activity, insolvency laws and regulation, and withholding tax liability) vary depending on the domicile of the debtor, what law governs, and, in certain cases, what treaties apply. This is the main dilemma facing cross-border trading: the laws and market customs that need to be taken into consideration by the parties to the trade are as varied as the jurisdictions themselves.

There is no "Uniform Commercial Code" for global debt trading, but that does not mean that nothing can be done to enhance global liquidity in the loan market. To be sure, market participants can encourage relevant loan market associations in one jurisdiction to review their standardized trading documents in union with counterpart organizations elsewhere, with a goal of creating as much parity as applicable law and market custom will allow.

This was the challenge of the recently completed Cross-Border Project (the project), a joint initiative by the Loan Syndications and Trading Association (LSTA) and the Loan Market Association (LMA). The project operated in two stages, with an initial short-term goal and, as the project evolved, a longer-term contribution to the marketplace. At the outset, the project called for the production of a Users' Guide and Trading Glossary, which is now available on both the LSTA's and the LMA's Web sites. The users' guide explains the key terms of LSTA and LMA distressed trading documentation and summarizes the key differences in market practices, all to enable informed decision making by market participants at the time of trade. Toward that end, the glossary contains definitions of key LSTA and LMA distressed trade terms.

The short-term goal having been achieved, the project evolved into a forum to discuss the actual convergence of LSTA and LMA distressed trading documentation. Since the LSTA trading documents had been revised in May 2005 (with buy-in from many LMA market participants) and the LMA trading documents were then under revision, both organizations realized that a rare opportunity to apply the theory of convergence to practice was presenting itself. The LSTA and the LMA made the most of that opportunity, and the result is revised LMA distressed trading documentation published for use by members as of October 17, 2005 (the revision date), that contains as much documentary parity as applicable law and market custom would permit. It is the belief of the LSTA and the LMA that the project should greatly enhance liquidity in the global loan market by reducing transaction costs and settlement times.

HISTORICAL CHALLENGES TO ANSWERING THE CALL

There were many historical challenges to achieving the project's long-term convergence goal. First of all, there are fundamental differences in the role of the respective trading documents them-selves. In an LMA trade, the trade confirmation incorporates the LMA Standard Terms and Conditions (the LMA conditions) and, subject to election by the parties, the applicable Standard Representations and Warranties (the LMA representations), and indicates the form of additional transfer document called for to settle the trade. It is the core document setting forth the terms and conditions by which the seller and the buyer have agreed to be bound, and, together with the additional transfer document it contemplates, is meant to be read as an integrated whole. In an LSTA trade, the trade confirmation serves a slightly different function. Although it also sets forth the terms of a binding trade, it is superseded at settlement by the operative transfer document (usually the LSTA form of Purchase and Sale Agreement) contem-plated in the trade confirmation. The trade confirmation, while a binding and enforceable contract between the parties, is not included among the integrated whole of closing documents on the settlement date.

Because of their function, the standard terms and conditions governing a distressed LSTA trade contain provisions that are pri-marily relevant to the time of trade. Because the LMA trade confir-mation constitutes the sale and purchase agreement between the parties, the LMA conditions contain terms that are equally relevant to the time of trade and the time of settlement. In addition to this difference in function, the LMA trading documentation was devel-oped principally with the European syndicated corporate loan market in mind and is governed by English law. The LSTA trading documentation was developed principally with the U.S. syndicat-ed corporate loan market in mind and is governed by New York law. Of course, as much as anything, it was the fact that both documents are frequently used in cross-border trades that inspired the project.

Traditional assumptions with respect to the finality of due diligence differ between the regimes. Under both the LSTA and the LMA documents, the buyer is assumed to have done its due dili-gence on the borrower and the terms of the trade prior to the trade date. Historically, however, the LMA trade confirmation contained a provision entitling the buyer to make the trade conditional on the buyer's satisfactory legal review of the sufficiency of the credit doc-uments. The standard terms of the LSTA trade confirmation never permitted a trade's binding nature to be contingent on the buyer's satisfactory legal review of the credit documents. This fundamental difference in approach went to the essence of the proposition that "a trade is a trade," the accepted view that the parties were bound from the trade date through a telephone discussion agreeing to the material terms of the trade. While this was also the premise of an LMA trade, the historical ability to agree to conditions to the trade (such as the legal due diligence condition) that, if not satisfied, would allow the parties to cancel the trade without liability on either side demonstrated much greater reliance on a moral code and the desire to protect one's reputation in the market as a means of self-regulation.

The LSTA and LMA settlement mechanisms themselves historically were, and remain after the revision date, fundamentally different. Unless otherwise agreed, secondary LMA sales settle against receipt of predecessor-in-title representations. Rather than providing predecessor transfer agreements (often referred to as "upstreams") and assigning the seller's rights against such predecessors-in-title to the buyer, the seller gives predecessor-in-title representations. This means that the seller's representations speak not only to the seller's own status, action, and inaction, but also to the status, action, and inaction of all predecessors-in-title for their respective periods of ownership of the traded asset. By contrast, unless otherwise agreed, secondary LSTA sales settle not on predecessor-in-title representations, but on the delivery of upstreams and the assignment to the buyer of all of the seller's rights against predecessors-in-title thereunder. These settlement preferences are entrenched positions based on long-established market customs, typifying perhaps the most fundamental difference between English and American distressed debt trading.

The difference between these closing protocols can be seen most acutely in the enforcement of rights under the applicable transfer document between the seller and the buyer. In an LMA closing, a buyer with a claim has a claim only against the seller. This is because the seller "steps up" for its predecessors-in-title through the making of predecessor-in-title representations. Furthermore, a seller under the LMA acts as the guarantor of each predecessor-in-title: if the predecessor-in-title goes out of business or becomes insolvent, the seller remains liable, even though it may not be able to recover against the actual party in breach. Under the

LMA, the seller and each predecessor-in-title in the chain of title have contingent liability, as each of them can be sued by their respective buyers. Compare this to the standard LSTA settlement on the delivery of upstreams. In that situation, the seller conveys to the buyer in relevant part all of its rights against all predecessors-in-title under the upstreams to the extent related to the traded asset. Only the party in breach, whether the seller or any predecessor-in-title, retains liability. Settlement on the basis of upstreams is as much a hallmark of trading under the LSTA as settlement by predecessor-in-title representations is of LMA trading.

Delayed compensation has never been a convention adopted by the LMA in its distressed trading documentation. Under the LMA, the economics of the trade shift to the buyer only on the settlement date. In contrast, delayed compensation applies to and is a hallmark of LSTA trades. If the transfer of a distressed credit closes more than 20 business days after the trade (a date known as T + 20), the LSTA trade confirmation provides for delayed compensation. The theory behind delayed compensation is to put the parties in the position they would have been in had the trade closed by T + 20. Thus the buyer receives the benefit of the interest and fees paid with respect to the relevant distressed loan for the period from T + 20 onward. Conversely, the buyer pays the seller interest on the funded amount of the loan times the purchase rate at the LIBOR rate (or other relevant funding rate) in effect on the market quotation date for the relevant currency of the loan for the setting of LIBOR (or other relevant funding rate) for the period commencing on T + 20 and ending on the settlement date. The two payments are netted against each other as part of the purchase price calculation. In short, the economics of the trade shift on the actual settlement date under the LMA and on T + 20 under the LSTA. Like the differing settlement and enforcement protocols discussed previously, this is a fundamental difference between trading distressed debt under the LSTA and the LMA.

CONVERGENCE REALIZED: FOUR FOCUS AREAS

As the project began in earnest in the autumn of 2004, it became clear that market participants were eager for LSTA and LMA consensus—or, failing that, more clarity—on the treatment of four key components of distressed debt trading: (1) claims against third parties, (2) when is a trade a trade, (3) distributions, and (4) delayed compensation. When the users' guide and glossary were finished and consideration of deeper convergence steps began, the LSTA and LMA remembered this mandate and focused their energies in large part on these four critical areas.

Claims against Third Parties

Historically, in LMA trading, the assets that are the subject of the trade (the purchased assets) did not include any detailed reference to third-party claims beyond the reference to "advances, *claims* and other rights included in the Traded Portion of the Seller's participation under the Credit Documentation," which would pass only to the extent that these claims arose under (but not outside of) the credit documents. Furthermore, because LMA trades generally settle on predecessor-in-title representations from the seller, the buyer lacked the opportunity or the cause to review the upstreams and determine for itself the full nature and scope of the "bundle of rights" constituting the purchased assets. Given how entrenched the LMA predecessor-in-title representation settlement protocol is, any resolution that mandated a shift in LMA trading to settlement on the basis of upstreams would be no resolution at all, as market participants in Europe are typically unwilling to sanction the additional time and expense that an upstream review would in many cases require. However, such a mandate became unnecessary in light of the new LMA provisions.

Under the new LMA conditions, the seller agrees to sell and the buyer agrees to acquire the purchased assets, which now include those rights and claims of the seller that relate to the traded asset, over and above those rights of the seller that pass automatically on any legal transfer of the traded asset (the ancillary rights and claims). The rights and claims that pass automatically as purchased assets are the buyer's right to receive and to sue in its own name for the payment of interest and repayment of principal on the traded asset. In addition to these rights, the seller is now required to sell all claims beyond these automatic rights that it may have in relation to the traded asset. Such ancillary rights and claims may include claims against third-party professional advisors involved in the origination of the underlying debt, against whom a claim may lie in tort or contract. These rights against third parties are often referred to as "litigation rights" in LSTA parlance.

The philosophy behind the change in the definition of purchased assets is that the seller ought to sell all the rights that it has in relation to the traded asset, whether they are derived from the credit documents or beyond. This change brings the nature and scope of the rights sold by the buyer into line with the LSTA position on litigation rights. It is very important to note that under both the LMA and the LSTA, conveyance is subject to the important caveat that ancillary rights and claims are capable of being or are permitted to be assigned by the seller, whether by law or by contract. In the same spirit, for any trade (whether LMA or LSTA) where the buyer is attributing specific value to a specific ancillary right or claim, the buyer is recommended to take separate legal advice and to enter into a specific assignment agreement for that ancillary right or claim.

In view of the LMA practice for the sellers to trade on the basis of predecessor-in-title representations, the sellers are now required to "step up" for their predecessors-in-title for the ancillary rights and claims traded under any predecessor transfer agreements. Without this step-up, in the absence of a review of each upstream, the buyer would not be able to satisfy itself that the nature and scope of litigation rights assigned from the original seller to the buyer match substantially the nature and scope of the commonly defined ancillary rights and claims. The step-up for ancillary rights and claims is included in LMA Representation 2.11 (bank debt/secondary lender).

There are, however, two points to note in relation to the step-up. First, the step-up does not apply to a seller that is an original lender of record, as in this case there are no prior owners for which to step up. Second, the sellers are required to step up only for ancillary rights and claims sold under upstreams that were entered into in trades made since the revision date. This means that trades made with a secondary lender on or after the revision date should include the seller's ancillary rights and claims (which would automatically be the case if the new LMA Standard Terms and Conditions are adopted by the seller and the buyer) to avoid the risk of a breach of warranty by the seller. While the step-up from the revision date for assets that traded for some time prior to the revision date may mean that nothing of value will pass (on the basis that the original ancillary rights and claims will most likely have been retained by the original lender of record), the position will correct itself over time as new assets become distressed following the revision date. In the meantime, the parties will become accustomed to trading with ancillary rights and claims and demanding that the sellers step up for their predecessors-in-title for trades made since the revision date.

Conditionality: When Is a Trade a Trade?

Prior to the revision date, under standard LMA trade terms, if a condition to a trade remained unfulfilled on the proposed settlement date, it was not possible after reasonable endeavors to ensure its fulfillment, and the parties did not wish to adopt an alternative means by which the trade could be implemented, then the trade was cancelable without any liability on either side, regardless of any changes in the market price of the traded asset since the trade date. It is worth noting that the right to cancel a trade applied only when a condition remained unfulfilled. For trades in which there were no conditions or in which all conditions were satisfied, the parties were obliged to settle the trade. New LMA Condition 5 now obliges the parties to find a means of settling the trade, regardless of any failure to fulfill a condition. This is what is commonly known in LSTA parlance as "a trade is a trade." Typically, the parties would settle the trade through a funded participation unless the parties had elected in the trade confirmation for a "Legal Transfer only." In this case (and also for all other cases if a funded participation cannot for any reason be entered into), the seller must settle on the basis of a mutually acceptable alternative structure or arrangement that provides both parties to the trade with the economic equivalent of the original trade.

Similarly, a trade cannot be avoided on the basis that the trade confirmation provided for the purchased assets to include the rights of the seller under its predecessor transfer agreements (the retained rights). If the parties have elected an LSTA-style settlement in their LMA trade confirmation, and if any necessary third-party consents to the transfer of retained rights are not obtained by the proposed settlement date, then (with respect to only the portion of the retained rights for which consent to a transfer cannot be obtained) the transaction must be settled as a legal transfer, with the seller giving predecessor-in-title representations to the buyer on the basis of the LMA representations.

Finally, the notion that due diligence unequivocally will have been undertaken by the buyer prior to the trade date is consistent with the concept of "a trade is trade." The LMA conditions no longer include any conditionality regarding due diligence. The only condition to the fulfillment of the trade that the LMA trading documentation contemplates relates to the negotiation of mutually acceptable representations and warranties of the seller. This condition applies only if the parties do not wish to settle on the basis of the LMA representations and have elected in the trade confirmation to agree to a mutually acceptable bespoke set of representations and warranties. However, if the parties are unable to agree upon a mutually acceptable set of representations and warranties by the proposed settlement date, they are now obliged to settle the trade on the basis of a mutually acceptable alternative structure or arrangement that provides both parties to the trade with the economic equivalent of the original trade.

Read together, the LSTA and LMA distressed trading documents strongly and actively support the proposition that "a trade is a trade."

Distributions

If "settled without accrued interest" is the selected LMA interest convention, then broadly speaking all interest and ordinary course accruing fees (recurring fees) accrued up to but excluding the settlement date are for the seller's account. If "trades flat" is the selected interest convention, then all interest and recurring fees paid after the trade date will be for the account of the buyer. However, the seller's obligation to account for any interest paid is limited to the actual monies received by the seller. This contrasts with the LSTA trades flat protocol, which requires the seller to pay if the borrower pays, regardless of any shortfalls in receipt by the seller resulting from, for instance, the default or insolvency of any predecessor-in-title. As under the LMA protocol, the seller is not obliged to pay unless funds are received; it follows that, except for its own concerns about its reputation (which may nevertheless be significant), the seller has no incentive to enforce its rights to payment under the applicable predecessor transfer agreement, nor does the

EXHIBIT 14.44

Where's the convergence?

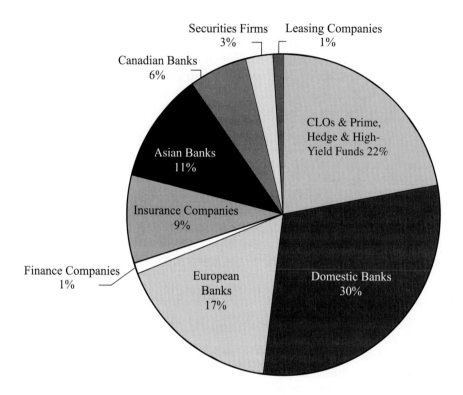

buyer have any recourse to the defaulting predecessor-in-title. Furthermore, the shortfall could have arisen not through the default of a predecessor-in-title but through a mismatch of the interest conventions under which the seller acquires the traded asset and sells the traded asset. Such a mismatch might arise, for instance, if on the same trade date the seller were to buy the traded asset on a settled without accrued interest basis and to sell the asset on a trades flat basis, as Exhibit 14.44 demonstrates.

New LMA Condition 13.6 addresses these specific issues. It requires the seller to enforce its rights against its predecessor-in-title and to take all steps reasonably available to it to recover any sums due to the seller and unpaid by its predecessor-in-title as if the seller had remained the sole legal and beneficial owner of any interest and recurring fees or other amounts payable or due with respect to the traded portion. Also, the seller now is obliged to pay the buyer any interest and recurring fees or other amounts payable or due on the traded portion, to the extent that such amounts have been paid or delivered by the underlying borrower, if the cause of any shortfall in receipt by the seller arises from a mismatch in terms involving the seller's entitlement to such sums under the terms of its predecessor transfer agreement and the buyer's entitlement to such sums under the terms of its trade confirmation with the seller.

Delayed Compensation

Over the course of the project, the application of delayed compensation to the LMA distressed trading documentation was considered. Ultimately the LMA, with the backing of its constituency, decided that the convention would not be adopted in the trading documents published for use by members on the revision date (although the LMA has recently published a delayed compensation option for its par trading documentation). The convention therefore remains that when trading distressed credits under the LMA, the economics of the trade shift to the buyer only on the settlement date. Of course, the parties are free to negotiate a form of delayed compensation when doing an LMA trade by agreeing to a target settlement date from which delayed compensation will begin to accrue.

Consider for a moment what was put on the project agenda and what was accomplished, all within one year. The LSTA and the LMA, two venerable organizations with differing constituencies and trading protocols but common goals, met and highlighted four areas in which their markets diverged in their treatment of trading terms considered material by global market participants: (1) claims against third parties, (2) conditionality/when is a trade a trade, (3) distributions, and (4) delayed compensation. Within one year, having used the project as a forum for active dialogue, the LSTA and the LMA have, in large measure, bridged the documentary gap that existed on each of these action items, except for delayed compensation. This is a significant accomplishment. With so many other examples of documentary convergence—the fruits of the project— to point to, it may well be that distressed LMA trades will settle more quickly now, notwithstanding the lack of delayed compensation, satisfying those in the marketplace who were most keen to include the convention in LMA distressed debt trading in the first place.

CONCLUSION

The bedrock market principles that drive the decisions of distressed loan investors know no borders. They are a universal language, and they direct those who would apply them to maximize the return accompanying investment risk wherever the opportunity presents itself. By their very nature, applicable laws and trading customs are not, and can never be, so seamless. However, the fact that law and economics do not necessarily move instantaneously in tandem does not mean that they do not work together, or that they should not be encouraged to do so. This was the conclusion drawn by the LSTA and the LMA in carrying out the project: that the challenge is great does not mean it should not be undertaken. Indeed, by being first movers in converging their distressed trading documents to the greatest extent that governing laws and market customs would allow, the LSTA and the LMA hope to lead by example, and to encourage counterpart organizations to look at their own documentation in conjunction with that of related organizations and jurisdictions that are sources of frequently traded debt. The goal of maximum documentary parity is an ambitious one, but the more it is undertaken by market participants, the more liquid the global loan market becomes, which inures to the benefit of the entire marketplace. From experience, the LSTA and LMA can confirm without reservation that it is time well spent.

GLOSSARY OF TERMS

364-Day Facility   A revolving credit facility that runs 364 days. These facilities have proliferated because loans with an original final maturity of less than one year are not subject to regulatory capital charges for undrawn amounts.

Acceleration   The mechanism pursuant to which the total outstanding principal amount of a loan becomes due and payable; a lender or group of lenders may accelerate a loan upon the occurrence of certain events described in a credit agreement (for example, the borrower's failure to make a scheduled payment, the borrower's filing for bankruptcy, or the borrower's nonperformance of certain covenants).

Accordion Feature   Increases under a credit agreement can be offered as an "accordion feature." An accordion feature is normally available only for increases to revolving credit facilities and will permit the amount of the revolving credit commitments to increase if the lenders are willing. The interest, maturity, and other terms of an increase will be identical to those applicable to the existing (and increased) revolving credit facility. The accordion mechanism will provide that, upon any increase, the borrower will adjust the loans (through appropriate borrowings and prepayments) so that the loans in the increased facility are held by the lenders ratably.

Accrued Interest   Interest that is owed to a lender but has not been paid by the borrower.

Acquisition   Purchase of a company by another company or group of companies.

Acquisition Loan   A specific type of loan that typically cannot be reborrowed. Funds can be drawn down from the line of credit only for a specific period of time and only to purchase specified assets.

Administrative Agent   The institution that performs the recordkeeping associated with a loan, handles the interest and principal payments to be made in connection with the loan, and generally monitors the ongoing administration of the loan.

Administrative Agent Fee   The annual fee paid to the administrative agent for its loan administration services.

Affiliate   With respect to any entity, another entity that directly or indirectly through one or more intermediaries, controls, is under common control with, or is controlled by the entity specified.

Agent   The title given to certain financial institutions that take on specific roles with respect to the administration or distribution of a credit agreement (i.e., administrative agent, syndication agent, and documentation agent). The term is frequently used to refer to the financial institution that is leading the transaction.

Allocation   The distribution of a facility among committed lenders by the arranger; it takes place when the sales process has been completed. The primary syndication is considered completed once the allocations have been announced, following which the loan may begin trading.

Amendment   A revision to the terms (financial or otherwise) of a credit agreement, typically requested by a borrower.

Amendment and Restatement   A revision to a credit agreement that reflects substantial modifications to the original credit agreement (either in one amendment or in a series of previous amendments).

Approved Fund   As used in the LSTA's Model Credit Agreement Provisions, any fund that is administered or managed by a lender, an affiliate of a lender or an entity or an affiliate of an entity that administers or manages a lender.

Arrangement Fee   The fee paid by a borrower to the arranger for structuring and syndicating the loan.

Arranger   The firm that leads the structuring and syndication of a loan. (See "Lead Arranger.")

Asset-Backed Security (ABS)   A security backed by an underlying asset, such as loans, bonds, or mortgages.

Asset-Based Loan (ABL)   A loan that is secured by specific assets (typically receivables or inventory) and made on the basis of a borrowing formula (borrowing base) that reflects a percentage of the value of such assets.

Assigning Lender   A lender that is selling and assigning its rights and obligations under, and any claims against any person arising in connection with, a credit agreement (and any other documents related to such credit agreement) to another party pursuant to an Assignment and Assumption Agreement.

Assignment   A transfer of a loan that has the effect of substituting the assignee/buyer for the assignor/seller such that the assignee/buyer comes into privity of contract with the borrower, obtaining the rights and assuming the obligations of the assignor/seller under a credit agreement.

Assignment and Assumption Agreement (also known as an Assignment Agreement)   The agreement that documents the sale and assignment of rights and obligations under a credit agreement by a lender to an assignee. This agreement is typically a form that is attached to each credit agreement.

Assignment Fee   The fee charged by an administrative agent and set forth in the applicable credit agreement for the costs associated with causing an assignment agreement to be effected. In recent years, many institutions have been waiving assignment fees on a reciprocal basis or eliminating them entirely.

Bankruptcy A judgment that a debtor is legally insolvent; it may be made upon petition filed by the debtor or invoked by the debtor's creditors.

Bankruptcy Code The Federal Bankruptcy Code of 1978, presently codified as Title 11 of the United States Code.

Bankruptcy Court The specialized federal court that hears matters arising under the Bankruptcy Code.

Bankruptcy Proceedings The proceedings in a specialized federal court relating to the bankruptcy of an entity.

Bankruptcy Rules The Federal Rules of Bankruptcy Procedure and any corresponding or other local rules of the Bankruptcy Court.

Bar Date As defined in the LSTA Purchase and Sale Agreement, the last date fixed by the Bankruptcy Court (if any) pursuant to the Bankruptcy Code or the Bankruptcy Rules on which proofs of claim or interest may be filed in a bankruptcy case with respect to transferred rights.

Basis Point (bp) 1/100 of 1 percent. It is the unit of measurement used to describe fees or spreads in most loan transactions.

Best Efforts Syndication A transaction in which the arranging syndicate does not firmly commit to provide all the funds requested by a borrower, but rather commits to using its "best efforts" to raise the money; as a consequence, the related pricing and fees will typically be lower than those for fully underwritten transactions. If other banks elect not to join the deal, then the credit is not closed.

Bid-Ask Spread (Bid-Offer Spread) The difference between the bid and ask (offer) prices.

Bid Price The price at which a potential buyer would agree to purchase an asset.

Bilateral Netting Agreement The LSTA Bilateral Netting Agreement—Par/Near Par or the LSTA Bilateral Netting Agreement—Distressed. The agreements provide that transactions evidenced by two trade confirmations between two parties may be netted against each other to determine the "netting amount" to be paid by one party to the other party.

Borrower The entity that borrows funds under a credit agreement.

Business Day Typically defined in a credit agreement as a day other than a Saturday, Sunday, or other day on which commercial banks in the governing jurisdiction are authorized or required by law to close.

Buy-In / Sell-out A transaction is (1) a buy-in if the buyer purchases the debt specified in a confirmation from a counterparty other than the original seller, and (2) a sell-out if the seller sells debt specified in a confirmation to a counterparty other than the original buyer.

Call The right to buy an asset at a specified price at or prior to a given date.

Cash Flow Loan A type of loan in respect of which the applicable credit agreement gives the lenders the option to ask to receive earlier repayment of the loan if the borrower is performing well. The provision will typically stipulate that some percentage of the cash generated by the borrower's business in excess of a certain amount will be applied to prepay the loans.

Change of Control   A merger, an acquisition of the borrower, a substantial purchase of the borrower's equity by a third party, or a change in the majority of the board of directors. One of the events of default in a credit agreement is a change of control of the borrower.

Closed-End Fund   A fund that has a fixed number of shares outstanding; the shares are generally traded on an exchange. (See also "Open-End Fund.")

Closing Date   The date on which a credit agreement closes or takes effect.

Club Deal   A smaller loan (usually $25 million to $150 million) that is premarketed to a group of relationship banks. The arranger is generally a first among equals, and each lender gets a full cut, or nearly full cut, of the fees.

Collateral   The assets of a borrower that are pledged to secure its loans. Collateral can be specific assets like inventory and receivables or can include all of the tangible assets of a borrower. Leveraged loans are typically backed by pledges of collateral.

Collateral Agent   The agent in a syndicated loan that is responsible for monitoring collateral and ensuring that all liens securing the collateral are properly filed.

Collateralized Debt Obligations (CDOs)   Special-purpose vehicles that are established to hold and manage pools of debt, including bonds and loans. CDOs are typically financed by the sale of numerous tranches of debt that have rights to the CDO's collateral and payment streams in descending order.

Collateralized Loan Obligations (CLOs)   Special-purpose investment vehicles established to accumulate a diversified pool of loans as collateral. The accumulation of the collateral is funded by the issuance of a series of rated notes plus equity. The rated notes are sequentially tranched, with the higher-rated tranches having a priority claim on the cash flows generated by the collateral pool and increasingly higher levels of subordinated capital support to protect against collateral losses. The CLO market is a subset of the broader CDO market.

Commencement Date   In connection with a trade, the date (under LSTA standard documentation) when delayed compensation begins to accrue. The commencement date (with the exception of early day trades) is 7 business days after the trade date in the case of par loans and 20 business days after the trade date in the case of distressed loans.

Commitment   The amount of credit that lenders have collectively agreed to provide to a borrower under a credit agreement.

Commitment Fee   In a revolving credit agreement, the fee paid by borrowers on unused commitments. On term loans, this fee, which applies to the amount of a commitment that has not yet been drawn down, is typically referred to as a "ticking fee."

Competitive-Bid Loan (or Competitive Access Facility)   A type of loan that is most often offered to borrowers with a high credit quality and is tied to a revolving credit facility. Lenders do not commit to make competitive-bid loans; rather, they may be offered by the lenders at their individual option within the aggregate limits of the revolving credit commitments of all revolving credit lenders. Competitive-bid loans allow lenders to provide loans to a borrower at rates lower than those otherwise available under the agreed pricing set out in the credit agreement.

Competitive-Bid Option   A subfacility within a revolving credit loan that allows investment grade borrowers to solicit bids from the syndicate group for short term loans. (See "Competitive-Bid Loan.")

Compliance Certificate   A document delivered under a credit agreement that sets forth certain financial statements and any compliance calculations that are certified by the chief financial officer or a senior financial officer of the borrower. Since the enactment of the Sarbanes-Oxley Act, a practice of requiring two officers to make these certifications has been developing.

Conditions Precedent   The conditions precedent in a credit agreement are in essence a simplified closing list. They specify what the borrower must deliver to the lenders (or the administrative agent), what actions it must take, and what other circumstances must exist in order for credit to be available.

Confidential Information   All nonpublic written, recorded, electronic, or oral information provided to a party by another party in the course of exchange of such information between those parties and identified by the providing party as confidential information.

Confidential Information Memorandum   The information memorandum or "bank book" provided to prospective lenders after the arranger and the borrower have agreed on the basic structure and terms of a proposed loan.

Confirmation   The LSTA Trade Confirmation, which sets out the key terms required for a binding trade based on the LSTA Standard Terms and Conditions for Distressed Trade Confirmations or the Standard Terms and Conditions for Par/Near Par Trade Confirmations as applicable. The terms of the trade are recorded (at the time of the trade) by checking the appropriate boxes and filling in other required information on each of the applicable Confirmations.

Counterparty   The other party to an agreement.

Covenants   Restrictions in credit agreements that dictate, to varying degrees, how borrowers can operate, financially and otherwise. Covenants generally fall into two main categories, affirmative covenants and negative covenants. Affirmative covenants generally include reporting requirements as well as financial benchmarks that must be met periodically. Negative covenants prohibit a borrower from taking certain actions (including, for example, increasing debt beyond a prearranged limit).

Credit Agreement   The agreement entered into between the borrower, the lenders, the agent, and other financial parties that describes the terms and conditions of the loan being made to the borrower and the obligations and requirements for the borrower, its related entities (if any), and the lenders.

Credit Default Swap   A contract that involves the payment of an up-front premium by the buyer of the swap to the seller, in return for the receipt of a cash flow from the seller, which is contingent on the occurrence of a credit event with reference to a preagreed reference obligation.

CUSIP   Committee on Uniform Securities Identification Procedures, which was created in July 1964. The main goal of the CUSIP Committee was to develop specifications for a uniform security identification system. Now the acronym is used to refer to the CUSIP system, which is owned by the American Bankers Association and operated by Standard & Poor's and which facilitates the clearing and settlement process of financial instruments. A CUSIP number consists of nine digits, of which the first six identify the borrower, two others (alphabetic or numeric) identify the credit agreement or the facility and the ninth is the check digit.

Debtor-In-Possession (DIP) Loan Facility A credit agreement entered into by an entity during the Chapter 11 bankruptcy process, Federal Bankruptcy Rule 4001(c)(1), which is secured and has priority over existing debt and other claims.

Deemed Dividends A problem that may arise when a loan to a U.S. borrower is guaranteed by a non-U.S. subsidiary. Under Section 956 of the U.S. Internal Revenue Code, a guarantee of this type is generally deemed to be a dividend by the subsidiary to its U.S. parent (up to the amount of the guarantee) of the earnings and profits of the subsidiary. Although not something that affects the enforceability of the guarantee, a deemed dividend can have potentially terrible tax consequences for the U.S. parent, since the parent will have to include the subsidiary's earnings and profits as taxable income without receiving any cash to pay the associated taxes. As a consequence, most guarantees of debt of a U.S. borrower will be restricted to U.S. subsidiaries.

Default In its most general sense, a breach of, or failure to fulfill or comply with, the terms of a contract or instrument. In the context of loans and other debt obligations, a default is a contractually specified event that allows lenders to demand repayment, in some cases subject to a grace period and right to cure.

Delayed Compensation A component of pricing in the settlement of debt trades that do not close on a timely basis that is intended to put parties in the approximate economic position on the settlement date that they would have been in if they had closed on a timely basis.

Derivative A security whose price is dependent upon or derived from one or more underlying assets. The derivative itself is merely a contract between two or more parties.

Derived Loan Pricing A model based process which is used to derive an indicative secondary market price for a given loan. The model is based on discounting the cash flows of a given loan by first calculating the average market yield on similar loans with the same rating, and then using that average market yield as an input into the discounted cash flow model in order to calculate the derived price. Derived loan pricing is used on loans which are most often smaller in size, less liquid, and not quoted in the secondary market by broker/dealers.

Distressed Loan A loan that is not expected to be paid at the face value and/or is trading at or near a rate that is less than or equal to 90 percent of face value are indicators that a loan may be a distressed loan. For LSTA trades, the debt should be traded with a Distressed Purchase and Sale Agreement and an Assignment and Assumption Agreement. These criteria are indicators only. The market ultimately determines when a loan should commence trading on distressed documentation.

Distressed Purchase and Sale Agreement The Purchase and Sale Agreement for Distressed Trades published by the LSTA as of May 2005, which sets forth, among other things, the representations, warranties, and indemnities made by the seller and buyer with respect to the debt being traded.

Distribution Any payment of interest, principal, notes, securities, or other property (including collateral).

Documentation Agent The bank that handles the loan documentation and selects the law firm that will act as lenders' counsel. (See "Agent.")

Domestic Subsidiary With respect to any entity, a subsidiary that is formed in the same jurisdiction as that entity. (See "Subsidiary.")

Drawdown A drawing made by a borrower under a revolving credit facility or by a beneficiary of a letter of credit under that letter of credit.

DTC The Depository Trust Company, a limited-purpose trust company under New York State banking law; it is a member of the U.S. Federal Reserve System and a registered clearing agency with the Securities and Exchange Commission.

Due Diligence An investigation into the business, legal, and financial affairs of a company that may be undertaken in connection with a financing.

Effective Date The date specified in an agreement as the date upon which the terms of that contract will take effect.

Electronic Settlement The process of closing a purchase / sale of a loan using a Web-based platform.

Electronic Trading The buying and selling of loans using a Web-based platform.

Eligible Assignee A party that is permitted to enter into an assignment and acceptance with a lender with the consent of any party whose consent is required pursuant to the terms of the applicable credit agreement. Most credit agreements will state the eligibility requirements for a potential buyer of debt to become a lender of record in a credit facility, whether or not such a buyer is given the defined term *Eligible Assignee*.

ERISA The Employee Retirement Income Security Act of 1974.

Event of Default A default under a credit agreement that has not been remedied or waived by the lenders after the expiration of any applicable grace period.

Facility Fee A fee that is paid on a facility's entire committed amount, regardless of usage; it is often charged on revolving credits to investment grade borrowers instead of a commitment fee because these facilities typically have a competitive-bid option (CBO) that allows a borrower to solicit the best bid from its syndicate group for a given borrowing. The lenders that do not lend under the CBO are still paid for their commitment.

Federal Funds Rate The interest rate at which depository institutions lend balances at the Federal Reserve to other depository institutions overnight.

Fee Letter The letter that identifies the type and amount of fees payable by a company with respect to a syndicated loan, including arrangement and structuring fees or underwriting fees, administrative agency fees, collateral agent fees, and other amounts payable to the arrangers. The Fee Letter will also generally reflect "market flex" language, which details certain provisions of the facility that may be subject to change if necessary to complete syndication (for example, the structure of the facility and its terms or pricing). (See "Market Flex.")

Financial Covenants   A type of covenant set forth in a credit agreement. They can be divided into two categories: those that test the borrower's financial position at a particular date (such as a net worth or current ratio covenant) and those that test performance over one or more fiscal periods (such as the leverage ratio covenant, interest coverage covenant, fixed charges coverage ratio covenant, and capital expenditures covenant).

Financial Sponsor   An entity that finances the acquisition of a company. In a leveraged buyout, the equity portion is contributed by the financial sponsor, and the debt portion is raised by the company to be acquired.

First Lien   A first attachment on a borrower's asset; it may be a perfected first lien if it is duly recorded with the relevant government body, so that the lender will be able to act on it should the borrower default.

Fixed Rate   An interest rate that does not change.

Floating Rate   An interest rate that resets at specified intervals.

Foreign Subsidiary   With respect to any entity, a subsidiary that is formed in a jurisdiction other than the one in which such entity has been formed. (See "Subsidiary.")

Fraudulent Conveyance   A transaction where (1) an entity undertakes an obligation or transfers property without receiving reasonably equivalent value, and (2) the entity is insolvent at the time of, or would be rendered insolvent as a result of, the transaction.

Fully Underwritten Syndication   A transaction in which the arranging syndicate firmly commits to provide all the funds requested by a borrower. See also "Best Efforts Syndication."

Fund   As used in the LSTA Model Credit Agreement Provisions, any entity that is engaged in making, purchasing, holding or otherwise investing in commercial loans and similar extensions of credit in the ordinary course of its business.

Funded Participation   As used in LMA documentation, a funding arrangement between the lender under the credit agreement and another party, known as the participant. The participant puts the lender, as grantor of the participation, in funds and is repaid principal and paid interest only to the extent that the lender receives such amounts under the credit agreement. Since the participant has only a contractual arrangement with the lender, the participant has no direct rights against the borrower and no beneficial interest in the underlying debt.

G.A.A.P.   Generally Accepted Accounting Principles.

Gold Sheets   Loan Pricing Corporation's publication for syndicated loan and investment product pricing information.

Governmental Authority   As defined in the LSTA Purchase and Sale Agreement, any federal, state, or other governmental department, agency, institution, authority, regulatory body, court, or tribunal, foreign or domestic, including arbitration bodies, whether governmental, private, or otherwise.

Grid Pricing   Possible rates in a credit agreement that are set forth in the form of a grid that varies by type of loan (by tranche and by pricing option) and the relevant financial measure; grid pricing is used when the applicable margin in the credit agreement is dependent on the credit rating and/or leverage of the borrower.

Guarantee A guarantor's agreement to purchase or otherwise become contingently liable for the debts or other obligations of another entity. With respect to a group of companies guarantees can be "upstream" (a subsidiary guaranteeing debt of its parent), "cross-stream" (a subsidiary guaranteeing debt of a "sister" company, where both are ultimately owned by the same parent), and "downstream" (a parent guaranteeing debt of a subsidiary). (See "Guarantor.")

Guarantor The grantor of a guarantee or contingent agreement to purchase or otherwise to become contingently liable with respect to the debts or other obligations of another person.

Hedge Funds Collective investment vehicles, often organized as private partnerships and formed as offshore vehicles for tax and regulatory purposes.

High-Yield Issuer An issuer of a debt obligation that has not earned an investment grade rating. (See "Noninvestment Grade.")

Highly Leveraged Loan Loans regarded as less creditworthy than leveraged loans. Different institutions define a leveraged loan in different ways; for example, for Loan Pricing Corporation, it is any loan with a BB+/ Bal rating or lower bank loan rating (or any loan that is unrated) and that is priced at LIBOR + 250 or greater; for Standard & Poor's, if the loan is unrated, it must have a spread over LIBOR of 225 basis points or more.

Indemnification An agreement that one party will bear the monetary costs, either directly or by reimbursement, for any losses, damages, and expenses incurred by another party.

Indemnified Party The party that enjoys the benefit of an indemnification given by another party. (See "Indemnification.")

Institutional Investors Nonbank investors seeking longer-term capital deployment and higher yields by investing in term loans with longer tenors and limited amortization.

Institutional Term Loan A term loan that is structured to be sold to institutional investors (for example, where interest is paid throughout the term of the loan and the principal is paid back at maturity).

Intercreditor Agreement An agreement entered into by classes of lenders of a borrower that sets forth the arrangement governing how those lenders will exercise their rights and remedies under the applicable credit agreement. For example, first lien lenders and second lien lenders will enter into an intercreditor agreement pursuant to which the second lien lenders may agree (1) not to take enforcement actions (or to limit their right to take such actions) with respect to their liens, (2) not to challenge enforcement or foreclosure actions taken by the holders of the first liens, and (3) to limit their right to challenge the validity or priority of the first liens. Second lien lenders may also acknowledge the first lien lender's entitlement to first proceeds of the shared collateral.

Interest-Rate Risk Risk inherent in certain financial instruments as a result of their fixed-rate nature.

Investment Grade A security with, for example, a rating of BBB or higher by Standard & Poor's and Baa or higher by Moody's.

ISDA   International Swaps and Derivatives Association, a global financial trade association. ISDA represents participants in the privately negotiated derivatives industry.

Lead Arranger   Essentially the "middleman" in the syndication process. In most transactions, the lead arranger drives the deal; sets the terms; interfaces with the client and investors; prepares, negotiates, and closes documents; and manages the syndication process.

League Tables   Tables that rank lenders according to certain criteria, such as submission guidelines, transaction classifications, and eligibility rules. Market share in the syndicated loan market is quoted in league tables published by several companies, including Loan Pricing Corporation, Bloomberg, and Thompson Financial.

Lender   An entity that extends credit to a borrower or borrowers pursuant to the terms of the credit agreement governing a credit facility.

Letter of Credit   An undertaking by the issuer of the letter of credit to pay the beneficiary of the letter of credit a specified sum against delivery of documents during the term of the letter of credit. The issuer is unconditionally obligated to honor a drawing under the letter of credit if the proper documents are presented, without any requirement that the issuer verify the truth of statements in the documents. The borrower (in letter of credit terminology, the "account party") will in turn be unconditionally obligated to reimburse the issuer for the amount paid by the issuer as a result of any drawing under the letter of credit.

Letter of Credit Fee   A fee accruing at an agreed per annum rate that borrowers are obligated to pay to each revolving credit lender on its participation in the undrawn amount of each outstanding letter of credit.

Leveraged Buyout   The process of taking a public company private; the transaction is financed through debt raised by the company and equity contributed by a financial sponsor. (See "Financial Sponsor.")

Leveraged Loan   A loan that is regarded as less creditworthy. Different institutions define a leveraged loan in different ways; for example, for Loan Pricing Corporation, it is any loan with a BB + / Bal, or lower bank loan rating (or any loan that is unrated) and a spread of 150 to 249 basis points; for Standard & Poor's, if the loan is unrated, it must have a spread over LIBOR of 125 to 224 basis points.

LIBOR (or "LIBO Rate")   An acronym for "London Interbank Offered Rate"; it refers to the London-based wholesale market for jumbo U.S. dollar deposits between major banks. Since such deposits are often referred to as "Eurodollar" deposits, the terms *Eurodollar* and *LIBOR* are often used interchangeably.

Lien   The right to retain property of another person until the owner of such property fulfills a legal duty to the person holding such property, for example, payment for work done on the property.

Liquidity   The ease of trading debt in the loan market. Generally, more liquid instruments are priced more cheaply than less liquid ones.

Loan   Credit that is extended by one person to another person for a specified period and that bears interest at a specified rate for that period.

Loan Market Association (LMA)   The association registered in the United Kingdom to promote liquidity in the Euroloan market by, among other things, standardizing the documentation used in loan syndications and debt trading under English law.

Loan Market Participant   An entity that participates in the loan market.

Loan-only CDS   Credit default swaps with respect to which loans are the only deliverable obligation upon default.

Loan Syndications and Trading Association (LSTA)   A not-for-profit organization dedicated to promoting the orderly development of a fair, efficient, liquid, and professional trading market for corporate loans originated by commercial banks and other similar private debt. The LSTA was formed largely in response to the exponential growth in loan trading volume in the secondary debt market.

Long-Term Debt Ratings   An investment grade or noninvestment grade rating assigned to debt obligations of an issuer by one of the rating agencies. Long-term debt ratings are an opinion of a rating agency as to whether an issuer will be able to fulfill its ongoing financial obligations to investors in a timely fashion.

Loss Given Default (LGD)   The loss incurred by a lender in the event that the borrower defaults.

Management Buyout   The purchase of an entity by its management using the value of the entity to secure financing to complete the acquisition.

Mandatory Prepayment   A required partial or total repayment of a loan triggered by the occurrence of certain events specified in the applicable credit agreement.

Margin   An additional amount, sometimes also referred to as the "spread," included in the interest rate on each base rate loan and each LIBOR loan. In some cases, the applicable margin is a flat rate fixed for the life of the agreement, but in other instances, it increases over time or is dependent on the credit ratings and/or leverage of the borrower.

Mark-to-Market   Recording the price or value of an asset, whether it be a loan, bond, stock or other security, portfolio, or account, to reflect its current market value.

Market Flex   A situation in which arrangers and borrowers agree on a targeted and often a maximum price for the loan, but actual pricing is determined through the loan marketing process. Historically, loans were priced by the arrangers at the time the engagement was granted and did not vary as they came to market. Now, loans are announced with a target price, but will either flex up or flex down depending on demand and on general market conditions.

Master Confidentiality Agreement   The Form of Master Confidentiality Agreement published by the LSTA as of July 1999. The agreement sets forth the terms that will apply to the treatment of confidential information relating to a financing that either party to the agreement may supply to the other party.

Material Adverse Change (MAC)/Material Adverse Effect   A clause typically included in a credit agreement that provides a representation and warranty by the borrower that since a specified date, there has been no material adverse change in its business, condition (financial or otherwise), assets, operations or prospects, and subsidiaries, taken as a whole. The continued accuracy of such representations will generally be a condition precedent to new loans under a credit agreement.

Middle Market   Generally regarded as companies with less than $750 million in sales and EBITDA levels of $25 million to $50 million that depend upon the loan market as their primary source of financing.

Moody's Investors Service, Inc.   A subsidiary of Moody's Corporation that issues credit ratings and conducts related research and risk analysis.

Mortgage-Backed Security (MBS)   A security created when a group of mortgages is pooled and bonds (typically guaranteed by the government) are sold to other institutions or the public. The bondholders receive a portion of the interest payments on the mortgages and the principal payments.

Multicurrency Options   A provision in credit agreements that allows loans to be made (or letters of credit to be issued) in currencies other than U.S. dollars. Normally, the available currencies will be specified at closing with an option to add currencies later, subject to certain conditions.

Multilateral Netting Agreement   The "Multilateral Netting Agreement— Distressed" or the "Multilateral Netting Agreement—Par/Near Par" published by the LSTA in April 2004. The agreements contemplate partial or total netting of transactions among several parties that are evidenced by trade confirmations. (See also "Bilateral Netting Agreement.")

National Association of Insurance Commissioners   A national organization of insurance regulators involved in the coordination of solvency and market regulatory activities.

Net Asset Value   The market value of a fund share. NAV is calculated by most funds by dividing total net assets by the total number of shares outstanding.

Noninvestment Grade   A security with, for example, a rating of BB or lower by Standard & Poor's or Ba or lower by Moody's. (See also "Investment Grade.")

Obligor   As defined in the LSTA's Purchase and Sale Agreement, any entity (other than the borrower, the lenders and any administrative, collateral, syndication, documentation, or other similar agent under a credit agreement) that is obligated under the applicable credit documentation.

Offer/Ask Price   The price at which a seller of a loan or commitment offers to sell that loan or commitment in the secondary loan market.

Open-End Fund   A mutual fund with an unlimited number of shares that can be issued, purchased, or redeemed at any time.

Optional Prepayment   Repayment of a loan at the choice of the borrower. Credit agreements will nearly always expressly override the general rule under New York law that a loan may not be prepaid without the consent of the lender and allow the borrower to prepay loans at any time at its option, subject to certain exceptions.

Original Issue Discount (OID)   Debt that is originally issued at a price that is less than its face value.

Par/Near Par Loan   Generally, a loan that is expected to be paid in accordance with the terms of its original credit agreement and/or trades at or near a purchase rate ≥ 90 percent of face value, or par. Debt that trades at or near par is generally transferred pursuant to an Assignment and Assumption Agreement without the LSTA's Purchase and Sale Agreement.

Pari Passu   A Latin term meaning "without partiality" that is used to describe an equal claim by lenders to the assets of a borrower. Typically, the term is used in a representation with respect to "pari passu ranking" to the effect that the obligations of the borrower under the credit agreement rank at least pari passu with all other obligations of the borrower.

Participation   A sale to the participant of an undivided interest in a lender's loan and/or commitment to a borrower with respect to which the selling lender maintains the relationship with the borrower and remains a party to the credit documentation; the transaction is generally not disclosed to the borrower or the public. The lender remains the official holder of the loan, with the participant owning the rights to the amount purchased.

Portfolio Manager   The manager of a fund. A portfolio manager considers investment alternatives and seeks to analyze investments in the portfolio to try to achieve a strong performance.

Prepayment Fee   An additional fee in a percentage equal to the amount of principal being prepaid that a borrower will in some cases be required to pay in addition to any breakfunding payments that may need to be made upon a prepayment.

Prime Rate   The primary benchmark rate publicly announced by a bank for interest on its loans. (Some banks prefer to call their publicly announced rate their "base rate," and others prefer "prime rate.") The base or prime rate is unilaterally determined by the bank based upon its cost of funds, competitive pressures, and other factors.

Prime-Rate Funds   Loan participation mutual funds, originally marketed as an alternative to money market funds, seeking returns that track the prime rate.

Priority   In the context of liens, the order in which liens are treated. For example, a first lien lender enjoys priority over a second lien lender and will be paid out of the proceeds of the collateral secured by its lien before the second lien lender is paid; however, a second-priority lien gives a second lien lender effective priority over trade creditors and other unsecured creditors to the extent of the value of its interest in the collateral.

Private-Side Lender   A lender that receives and uses syndicate information (which may include "material nonpublic information") in loan originating, loan trading, and/or lending and is, therefore, subject to trading restrictions if it is in possession of material nonpublic information.

Pro Rata   A general principle in virtually all credit agreements that the lenders are treated on a proportional basis. Thus, lenders in a tranche make loans of that tranche "ratably," i.e., in amounts that are proportional to their commitments (with an exception for competitive-bid loans). Similarly, principal and interest are paid and prepaid "ratably" in accordance with the outstanding amounts of the relevant tranche. Commitments are reduced, and commitment and facility fees are paid, "ratably" in accordance with the commitments of the particular tranche.

Promissory Note   A note evidencing loans under a credit agreement. Most credit agreements today are so-called note option deals, i.e., promissory notes are not executed except for any lender that requests them.

Proof of Claim   A document filed by a creditor with the Bankruptcy Court setting forth details of the debtor, the creditor, and the claim (for example, the basis for the claim, the amount of the claim, and whether it is secured or unsecured). This serves as notice to the debtor that such property is owed and is being claimed against the assets of the debtor.

Prospective Lender   A lender that reviews and evaluates information and documentation about a borrower and the financing with a view to becoming a lender under the applicable credit agreement.

Public-Side Lender   A lender that has elected to conduct loan trading and/or lending solely on the basis of public information; typically, a public-side lender is also involved in securities trading and sales.

Purchase and Sale Agreement (PSA)   The LSTA Purchase and Sale Agreement for Distressed Trades, published in May 2005. The PSA governs the purchase and sale of distressed loans, commitments, and other rights being transferred in connection with those loans and commitments and contains, among other things, representations, warranties, and indemnities made by the seller and the buyer.

Purchase Price   As used in the LSTA's documentation, the amount to be paid by the buyer to the seller for the amount and type of debt specified in the applicable trade confirmation as calculated in accordance with the LSTA's Standard Terms and Conditions for Par/Near Par Trade Confirmations or Distressed Trade Confirmations, as applicable, or if such calculations produce a negative number, the amount to be paid by the seller to the buyer in respect of such debt.

Purchase Price Letter   As defined in the LSTA's Purchase and Sale Agreement, the letter agreement between a buyer and seller that specifies the calculations determining the purchase price of debt specified in the applicable trade confirmation.

Purchase Rate   As defined in the LSTA's Purchase and Sale Agreement, the rate specified as a percentage of the face value of debt that is set forth in the applicable trade confirmation for such debt.

Recovery Rate   The rate of recovery of principal for lenders in the event of a default by the borrower.

Recovery Value   The market price of a loan immediately following an event of default.

Reference Bank   A specific bank named in a credit agreement whose rates are used to determine the prevailing interest rate offered by banks for a Eurodollar time deposit matching the applicable LIBOR interest rate for a loan under that credit agreement if the applicable rate is not available through a "screen quote" from Reuters or Telerate.

Register   The list maintained by the administrative agent that identifies the names and addresses of the lenders and the amounts of their respective commitments and loan balances. The credit agreement will normally state that the loan register is conclusive and thus is the definitive determinant of who must consent to modifications to the agreement and who are the "required lenders."

Regulation FD An SEC regulation that became effective on October 23, 2000; it eliminated the practice of selective disclosure and is designed to promote the full and fair disclosure of information by issuers, and to clarify and enhance existing prohibitions against insider trading. The rules address issues such as the selective disclosure by issuers of material nonpublic information, and when insider trading liability arises in connection with a trader's "use" or "knowing possession" of material nonpublic information.

Related Parties As defined in the LSTA's Model Credit Agreement Provisions, with respect to any person, such person's affiliates and the partners, directors, officers, employees, agents and advisors of such person and of such person's affiliates.

Representations and Warranties The statements in a credit agreement that affirm the basic understandings upon which the lenders are extending credit. They address legal and financial issues, matters relating to the business and capital structure of the borrower and its subsidiaries, and various other matters of concern to the lenders.

Revolving Credit Loans Loans that "revolve" within "commitments" established by the lenders. The borrower may borrow, repay, and reborrow the loans during the term of the commitments, so long as the applicable lending conditions are satisfied. By contrast, term loans once borrowed and repaid may not be reborrowed.

Risk Participation A participation in which the original party remains liable to the beneficiary for the full amount of an obligation (e.g., a direct credit substitute), notwithstanding that another party has acquired a participation in that obligation.

SEC The United States Securities and Exchange Commission.

Second Lien Loans Loans secured by liens on a borrower's collateral the claims in respect of which are behind those of first lien loans. Second lien loans typically have less restrictive covenant packages, with maintenance covenant levels that are set wide of those for the first lien loans. As a result, second lien loans are priced at a premium to first lien loans. (See "Priority" and "Subordination.")

Secondary Market Trading Trading that occurs after a loan is closed and allocated. Loans trade at a percentage of par, and sales are structured as either assignments or participations, with investors usually trading through dealer desks at the large underwriting banks.

Security/Secured The asset collateral of the borrower pledged to repay the lenders in the event of default under a credit agreement. Secured loans are commonly used in the leveraged loan market.

Seniority The order of repayment. In the event of bankruptcy, senior debt must be repaid before subordinated debt is repaid.

Setoff A situation in which a lender that has a monetary obligation to a borrower, such as a deposit liability or an obligation under a derivative contract, may be able to effect payment on the loan by canceling, on a dollar-for-dollar basis, the lender's obligation to the borrower against the borrower's loan obligation to the lender. The right to do this is referred to as the right of "setoff." The right of setoff arises under common law; however, credit agreements generally include an express contractual right of setoff.

Settled Without Accrued Interest   The interest convention that provides that (subject to any compensation for delayed settlement) interest that has accrued but has not been paid prior to the settlement date of a trade belongs to the seller.

Settlement Amount   As used in LMA documentation, the amount to be paid by the buyer to the seller at the date of the novation, assignment, or participation. The calculation used to work out the settlement amount is found in Condition 11 of the Standard Terms and Conditions and is usually replicated in the Pricing Letter. The seller represents and warrants in the Standard Representations and Warranties that the amounts used in the settlement amount calculation are true and correct.

Settlement Date   The date on which payment of the purchase price occurs against the transfer of the purchase amount of debt.

Spread   The amount of yield the loan pays above a benchmark market interest rate given a particular price in the secondary market.

Standard & Poor's   Standard & Poor's Ratings Services, a division of The McGraw-Hill Companies, Inc. Standard & Poor's is a provider of credit ratings and financial market indices.

Standstill Period   A period during which lenders agree to refrain from taking certain enforcement action in respect of a borrower's outstanding debt so that the borrower may work with its financial advisor to restructure its debt.

Subordination   Giving lower priority to a claim or lien. In traditional debt subordination, the debt claim itself is subordinated; thus, if a holder of subordinated debt obtains anything of value in a bankruptcy from any source, it agrees to turn it over to the holders of "senior debt" until the senior debt is paid in full. In the case of second lien loans, only the liens are subordinated; the underlying debt claim is not.

Subparticipation   An undivided interest in a participation interest.

Subrogation   The substitution of a new creditor for an existing creditor, and the succession by the new creditor to the existing creditor's rights.

Subsidiary   With respect to any person, any corporation, limited liability company, partnership, or other entity of which at least a majority of the securities or other ownership interests having by their terms ordinary voting power to elect a majority of the board of directors or other persons performing similar functions of such corporation, limited liability company, partnership, or other entity is directly or indirectly owned or controlled by such person and/or one or more subsidiaries of such person.

Summary of Terms   A summary of the principal terms and conditions of a loan as agreed to by the arranger and the borrower, and set forth in an information memorandum that is then distributed to prospective lenders. The terms will be documented in greater detail in the credit agreement.

Swap Spread   The spread difference between the Treasury and LIBOR curves or the fixed- and floating-rate markets.

Swingline Loans   Loans made available by a "Swingline Lender." They are an adjunct to the revolving credit facility. Swingline Loans can be made on short notice because they are being advanced by only one lender, usually the same lender that serves as the administrative agent and are typically required to be repaid in a very short period.

Syndication Agent   The bank that handles the syndication of the loan. The title of "Syndication Agent" is often awarded in conjunction with large commitments, but the actual responsibilities of this role may be shared or handled by the administrative agent or the lead arrangers. (See "Agent.")

Synthetic Asset   A value that is artificially created by combining other assets, such as securities.

Tax Gross-Up   A mechanism included in a credit agreement that is intended to protect the lender against taxes that would reduce its yield on the loan. The primary concern relates to taxes that the borrower would be required to withhold from the stated interest that it would otherwise pay to the lender. The provision will, therefore, typically require the borrower to "gross up" the interest payment so that the lender realizes an amount in cash that, after deduction for the withheld taxes (including further withholding taxes on the gross-up payments), is equal to the stated interest on the loan.

Term Loan   A loan that may be drawn down by a borrower during a given commitment period and is then repaid by the borrower in accordance with a scheduled series of installments; once borrowed and repaid by the borrower, term loans may not be reborrowed. Term loans may be made available under commitments that contemplate multiple drawdowns (a so-called standby term loan facility).

Term Loan Conversion ("Term-Out Option")   A credit agreement provision stating that, at the commitment termination date for revolving credit commitments, any outstanding revolving credit loans will convert into term loans (sometimes called a "term-out option"). This type of conversion is normally automatic (i.e., not subject to a bring-down of representations or the absence of a default), but in some agreements those conditions will be required to be satisfied.

Total Return Swap ("Bank Loan Total Return Swap")   A derivative contract between two parties to exchange the return of one or more bank loans. The swaps grew to prominence as a result of the desire for leverage and the lack of a repurchase market where institutional loan market participants could leverage their investment in bank loans.

Trade Date   The date listed on the trade confirmation as the date on which the trade between the buyer and the seller took place.

Tranche   In the context of term loans, tranche refers to either the so-called A loan tranche or B loan tranche. A loans are generally understood as term loans that are made by bank lenders (as opposed to funds or other institutional investors), have a maturity equal to the term of any revolving credit commitments in the credit agreement, and are entitled to the benefit of real amortization, i.e., installments that over the term of the loan will represent sizable paydowns of the facility. By contrast, B loans will typically be made by funds or other institutional lenders, have a maturity longer than any related A loan (usually six months to a year further), and will have only nominal amortization until the last year. Revolving credit and A loans are often referred to as the "pro rata tranches"; B loans are referred to as the "B tranche." The latter is true even though a credit agreement may have multiple series of B loans (Series B, Series C, Series D, and so forth).

Transfer Notice   As defined in the LSTA's Purchase and Sale Agreement, any notice and evidence of transfer, with respect to transferred rights, filed in a bankruptcy case in accordance with the Bankruptcy Rules, including Bankruptcy Rule 3001(e). (See "Transferred Rights.")

Transferred Rights   As defined in the LSTA's Purchase and Sale Agreement, the seller's rights, title, and interest in the loans and commitments and all other amounts payable to the seller under the applicable credit documentation and all related claims, guarantees, and collateral that are being acquired by the buyer under the applicable Purchase and Sale Agreement.

UCC Article 9   The section of the Uniform Commercial Code dealing with security interests and secured transactions. Among other things, Article 9 governs perfection of security interests and the filing of UCC financing statements.

Underwriting Fee   A fee paid to the arranging syndicate for underwriting a loan. The fee will be higher than the fee paid to the arranging syndicate in a best efforts syndication, since, in an underwritten deal, the arranging syndicate must provide the funds even if less than the committed amount is sold.

Unfunded Commitment   The portion of the total commitment that has not been drawn down by the borrower. Such amount is available to be funded at the request of the borrower.

Uniform Commercial Code (UCC)   A uniform act that tries to standardize the laws regulating commercial transactions, in particular those transactions involving the sale of goods and secured transactions in the United States.

Unsecured Loan   A loan in which the lenders do not have a lien against the assets of the borrower.

Up-Front Fee   A fee paid by the borrower to lenders to increase the return on their portion of the loan. While most institutional term loans are sold at "par" (i.e., no closing fees are paid), the pro rata portion of loans typically has an up-front fee associated with it. The fee will vary from transaction to transaction and will frequently vary within the same transaction based on the level of commitment offered by a lender.

Voting Mechanics   Rules covering lender approval of any changes in a credit agreement. The basic rule with respect to voting provisions of a credit agreement is that the "majority" or "required" lenders must approve any modification, waiver, or supplement to any provision of the credit agreement. "Majority" or "required" will normally mean lenders holding more than 50 percent of the aggregate credit exposure, i.e., unused commitments and outstanding loans and letters of credit. Sometimes the credit agreement will break out particular issues and require a so-called supermajority vote for changes in these areas.

When-Issued Trading   Trading following the allocation of a facility by the arranger to committed investors but before closing.

Withholding Tax   A tax that a borrower is required to withhold on an interest payment to a lender. (See "Tax Gross-Up.")

INDEX

A

A loan tranches, 212
ABS (asset-backed securities), 718
Acceleration of payment remedy, 350
Acceptance, 106
Access to loan register, in credit
  agreements, 365–366
Accordion feature (credit agreements), 218
Accounting:
  for hedging activities, 829–830
  LSTA positions on issues, 82–84
  for total return swaps, 708
Accounting changes covenant, 326–327
Accounting standards, 825–842
  Basel 2 regulatory capital requirements,
    842–856
    assessment of, 853–856
    countries adopting, 851
    incentives with, 846–847
    origin of, 843–846
    pillars of, 847–850
    quantification of credit risks, 852–853
    as "regulatory dialect," 847
    regulatory framework changes,
      851–852
    risk types covered by, 850
  FAS 140, 834–842
  GAAP, 294–295
    banking book, 826–828
    credit-related investment products, 829
    for credit-risk hedging activities,
      829–830
    FASB SPE consolidation rules, 830–833
    held for sale, 828
    initial recognition and measurement,
      825–826
    trading book, 826
    transfers between portfolios, 828
Accrual conventions, in credit agreements,
  237
Acquisition(s):
  and global loan market, 862, 864–866
  investments constituting, 318
  limitation on, 315
  of total return swaps, 686

Acquisition debt, 313
Acquisition financing, 23–24
Acquisition liens, 311
Acquisition/equipment lines, 105
Additional debt covenant, 313–314
Additional indebtedness, in credit
  agreements, 150
Additional liens, in credit agreements, 151
Adelphia Communications, 490–491, 586
Administrative agents, 50, 172, 354–355
  delegation of acts, 357–358
  filing of proofs of claim, 358
  no fiduciary duty/exculpation, 356–357
  reliance on sources, 357
  successors to, 358–359
Admission of insolvency, 344
Advisors, in distressed loan restructuring,
  630
Affected lender concept, 361
Affiliate transactions covenant, 324–325
Affirmative covenants, 301–308, 333
  disclosure, 301–303
  further assurances, 308
  hedging transactions, 307–308
  maintenance of insurance, 303–304
  "motherhood and apple pie," 304–306
  substantive consolidation, 306
  in term sheet, 184
  use of proceeds, 307
  visitation rights, 303
Agency provisions, in credit agreements,
  354–359
  agents, 358–359
  appointment, 355–356
  delegation, 357–358
  filing proofs of claim, 358
  no fiduciary duty/exculpation, 356–357
  reliance, 357
  successor agents, 358–359
  syndication, 359
Agents, 50
  administrative, 50, 172, 354–355
    delegation of acts, 357–358
    filing of proofs of claim, 358
    no fiduciary duty/exculpation,
      356–357

Agents *(Cont.)*
    reliance on sources, 357
    successors to, 358–359
  agency provisions for, 358–359
  documentation, 50, 172
  in primary market, 171–174
  successor, 358–359
  syndication, 50, 172
Allocation, in secondary loan settlement,
    425
Alternative fixed income investment
    strategies, 794–797
Altman, Edward I., 819, 820
Amendments:
  to organic documents and other
      agreements covenant, 325–326
  to project documents/credit agreements,
      152
  in restructuring process, 631
Americas:
  M&A lending, 864
  mandated arranger league table, 863
  syndicated lending, 867
  United States' lending percentage in, 867
  (See also United States)
Amicus curiae, LSTA as, 80–82
Amortization:
  of revolving credit commitments, 217
  of term loans, 104–105
Analytics and performance, 509–576
  Credit Suisse Institutional Leveraged
      Loan Index, 548–568
    benchmarks for, 555
    creation of, 548
    loans included in, 549, 551
    price criteria for, 551
    profile characteristics of, 556, 563–566
    rating of loans in, 553–555
    risk and return with, 549–555
    as subindex of Leveraged Loan Index,
        543
  Credit Suisse Leveraged Loan Index,
      541–548
    inclusion rules, 542
    ratings, 545–548
  leveraged senior loan performance
      attribution, 569–579
    combining models for, 575–579
    equity performance attribution,
        574–575
    fixed-income performance attribution,
        571–574
    process for, 569–571

rating agencies in loan market, 521–525
  recovery rate factors, 533–539
  relative value analysis, 513–521
    credit spread optionality, 519–521
    fixed vs. floating interest rate, 514
    interest-rate optionality, 518–519
    recovery rates, 516–518
    risk/return, 515
    term, 514–515
    windfalls from imperfect correlation,
        521
  S&P/LSTA Leveraged Loan Index,
      539–541
  S&P's loan and recovery ratings, 526–533
    empirical data and market practice,
        531–533
    factors determining, 529–531
    marketplace use of, 533
    nominal recovery, 528–529
    types of ratings, 527–528
    yield calculation, 511–513
  Annualized performance, 297
Antifraud liability, 94–96
Applicable margins, 174, 230–232
Appointment, agency provisions for,
    355–356
Appraisal condition, in credit agreements,
    272
Arbitrage CDOs, 713
Arbitrage CLOs, 646, 653–654
Arindo Global, 902
Aristotle, 509
Asia-Pacific region:
  imbalance of lending in, 867–869
  issuance in 2003, 865
  M&A lending, 862, 866
  mandated arranger league table, 863
  post-September 11 market, 864
  secondary loan market in, 886
  syndicated loan market, 898–903
  syndicated loans, 874
Asset-backed securities (ABS), 718
Asset-based lending, 105–106
Assets:
  haircuts for, 692–693
  ratable distribution of, in bankruptcy,
      610–620
    bankruptcy preferences, 611–613
    equitable subordination, 616–618
    fraudulent transfers, 613–615
    reclassification of payments, 618–620
  sale of
    in bankruptcy, 116

bankruptcy code restrictions on, 121
  in credit agreements, 151, 255–256
  as restructuring strategy, 632
  secured borrowing vs., 834–841
secured in CDOs, 716–719
for total return swaps, 692
Assignment(s):
  credit agreement clause for, 153, 366–372
    consent rights, 367–368
    eligible assignees, 368–369
    loan register, 369
    loans covered by securities laws,
      369–372
    minimums, 369
    transfer fees, 369
  FAS 140 applied to, 834–841
  of second lien loans, 135
  in secondary loan settlement, 426–427
  of syndicated loans, 22
Assignment fees, in secondary loan market,
  455
Australasia region, 868
Australia, syndicated loan market in, 898
Automatic stays, in Chapter 11 bankruptcy,
  636
Average trade size, 398
Avoidance powers, in Chapter 11
  bankruptcy, 637–638

B

B loan tranches, 212
B term loans, 6–7
Back-office requirements, in secondary
  market, 406–407
Balance sheet CLOs, 645, 657–658
Banco Espanol de Credito v. Security Pacific
  Nat'l Bank, 596
Bank books, 193–194
Bank credit risk, 3–6
Bank for International Settlements (BIS),
  845
Bank loan debt, 34
Bank loan total return swaps (see Total
  return swaps)
Bank loans:
  as asset class (see Loan asset class)
  default on, 9, 10, 12
    in 1990s through 2002, 18–19
    industry data on, 13
    probability of, 15
    trends in, 533–539

high-yield bonds vs., 55–56
  interplay in market, 52
  in mutual funds, 19
    risk and return with, 16
    Sharpe ratios for, 17
  pro rata vs. institutional tranches, 53–55
  public information on, 188
  ratings of, 529–533
  risks and returns with, 3, 7–21
    bankruptcy, 8–9
    collateral, 9
    default vs. recoveries, 8
    first credit test, 19–20
    historical review of, 9–21
    time line of, 18–19
  securities vs., 87
  speculative grade (see Leveraged loans)
  spreads on, 21
Bank meeting, 180–181
Bank of America, 63, 172, 696
Bank of Montreal, 63
Bank risk, ratings of, 7
Bankers' acceptances (BAs), 106–107,
  216–217
Bankers Trust, 6, 8
Bankers Trust Company, 63
Banking book, loans recorded in, 826
Bankruptcy:
  as bank loan risk, 8–9
  Bankruptcy Code definition of
    underwriter, 599–602
  Chapter 11, 634–641
    automatic stays in, 636
    avoidance powers in, 637–638
    and Bankruptcy Code, 634–635
    commencement of, 635
    creditors' committee in, 636
    debtor in possession in, 636
    disclosure in, 640
    estate creation, 636
    executory contracts and unexpired
      leases in, 638–639
    first-day orders in, 635
    goals of, 635
    plan of reorganization in, 639–641
    U.S. trustee in, 636
    use of cash collateral in, 639
  equity dividends in, 609
  intercreditor arrangements
    documenting, 128
    enforcement of, 128–129
  and interest as "security," 594–597
  new securities issued by debtors, 597–599

Bankruptcy *(Cont.)*
  preferences in enforcing ratable
      distribution, 611–613
  restrictions on asset sales, 121
  second lien loans
      lenders' actions/rights, 129–130
      lenders restrictions, 122–128
      secured creditors' rights in, 114–117
      unsecured creditors' rights in, 117–118
  under-/unsecured claims in, 608–609
Bankruptcy Code, 634–635
Banks, 50–51
  changing role of, 28–29
  commercial vs. investment, 4
  and development of leveraged loans, 6
  funding total return swaps, 695–696
  Japanese, 910–912, 914–915
  Japanese megabanks, 906
  loan pledges by, 373
  primary market investments, 165
  (*See also* Bank loans)
Barclays, 696
BAs (*see* Bankers' acceptances)
Base rate, 224–225
Basel 2 regulatory capital requirements,
      842–856
  assessment of, 853–856
  countries adopting, 851
  incentives with, 846–847
  origin of, 843–846
  pillars of, 847–850
  quantification of credit risks, 852–853
  as "regulatory dialect," 847
  regulatory framework changes, 851–852
  risk types covered by, 850
Basel Capital Accord (1988), 843, 851–854
Basel Committee on Banking Supervision
      (BCBS), 842, 845, 850
Basket CDS, 743–744
BB Index, 540
BCBS (*see* Basel Committee on Banking
      Supervision)
Bear Stearns Cos., Inc., 63, 459
Benchmark CDS indices, 752–756
Best efforts basis, 176–177
Best efforts syndication, 49
Best practices and policy, LSTA
      development of, 78–79
Bid-ask spread, 398–399
Bill of exchange, 106
BIS (Bank for International Settlements),
      845
Bloomberg, 172

Blue-sky laws, state, 96–97
Bond Market Association, 78
Bonds:
  corporate, 25, 26, 718–719
  high-yield, 4–5
      as asset class, 4–5
      bank loans vs., 55–56
      trading in secondary market vs.,
          403–405
  interest rate optionality for, 518–519
  Japanese investments in, 904–905
  recovery rates for, 516–517
  trading in loans vs., 403–413
  volatility of, 408
Book runners, 50, 172
Books and records covenant, 304
Borrower indemnification, in credit
      agreements, 375–377
Borrower Restricted Information, 198
Borrowers:
  distribution of information relating to,
      206–207
  insolvency of, 330
  multiple, credit agreement provisions for,
      261–262
  in project finance, 139
  rights of, in credit agreements, 386–390
  (*See also* Issuers)
Borrowing base, 254–255
Breach of covenants, 339–340
Breakfunding, 76–77, 243–245
Brinson, Hood, and Beebower model, 574
Brinson-Fachler equity model, 575, 577–579
Broker, definition of, 97*n*8
BT Alex Brown, 459
Budget, in credit agreements, 147–148
Business, representations regarding,
      285–288
Business cycle, loan recovery rates and, 588
Business day conventions, in credit
      agreements, 238

C

Call risk, with CDOs, 729, 732
Callable loans, 157, 519–521
Campisi, Stephen, 571
Canada, 867
Capital contributions, in credit agreements,
      147
Capital costs, yield protection clause for,
      242

Capital expenditures, 299–299
Capital structure, of CLOs, 651–652
Capital structure arbitrage:
  distressed loan investing, 592–593
  total return swaps, 698
Capital structure trades, 419
Capital trust pass-through securities (TRUPS), 719
Capitalization representations and disclosures, 285–286
Captions, in credit agreements, 384
Caruana, Jaime, 848
Cash collateral:
  advance consent to sales of, 126–127
  advance consent to use of, 125–126
  in bankruptcy, 116
  in Chapter 11 bankruptcy, 639
  defined, 116
Cash flow:
  projections of, in credit agreements, 147–148
  in settlement of distressed loans, 605–606
Cash flow arbitrage CLOs, 647 (See also Collateralized loan obligations)
Cash flow CDOs, 721–727
  asset quality tests, 722–723
  cash flow coverage tests, 722–723
  coverage tests, 722
  simplicity of, 767–678
  synthetic CDOs vs., 724–727, 766–767
Cash flow waterfall, in credit agreements, 148–150
Casualty events, 256
Catchall condition, in credit agreements, 273
CBOs (collateralized bond obligations), 20
CBOs (competitive-bid options), 104
CDOs (see Collateralized debt obligations)
CDS indices, 670, 749–758
  benchmark, 752–756
  characteristics of, 750–752
  tranches of, 756–758
CDS (see Credit default swaps)
CDX, 670, 676
CDX.EM index, 755
CDX.EM.Diversified index, 755–756
CDX.NA.HY index, 753
CDX.NA.IG index, 752
CDX.NA.XO index, 753–754
Change of control:
  as event of default, 346
  prepayment due to, 257–258
Chapter 11 bankruptcy, 634–641

  automatic stays in, 636
  avoidance powers in, 637–638
  avoiding, 633–634
  and Bankruptcy Code, 634–635
  commencement of, 635
  creditors' committee in, 636
  debtor in possession in, 636
  disclosure in, 640
  drawbacks of, 634
  estate creation, 636
  executory contracts and unexpired leases in, 638–639
  first-day orders in, 635
  goals of, 635
  plan of reorganization in, 639–641
  U.S. trustee in, 636
  use of cash collateral in, 639
Charter Communications, 414
Chase Manhattan, 6, 8, 24
Chemical Bank, 6, 8, 63
China, syndicated loan market in, 899, 900, 902–903
CIP (see Customer Identification Procedure)
Citibank, 6, 63, 459
Citigroup, 172, 696
Clawback clause, in credit agreements, 364–365
Clean-down requirement, 254
Clearing House Association, 81
CLOs (see Collateralized loan obligations)
Closing documentation, in secondary loan market, 430–434
"Club deals," 47, 49, 110
CMBS (commercial mortgage-backed securities), 718
CMOs (collateralized mortgage obligations), 658
CNOOC, 902–903
Co-agents, 50, 172, 174
Co-borrower arrangements, 261
Code of Conduct (LSTA), 79
Collateral:
  bankruptcy restrictions on dispositions of, 119–120
  cash
    advance consent to sales of, 126–127
    advance consent to use of, 125–126
    in bankruptcy, 116
    in Chapter 11 bankruptcy, 639
    defined, 116
  for CDOs, 714
  for CLOs, 653
  enterprise value as, 9

Collateral *(Cont.)*
  perfection of. condition relating, 267–268
  real property, 120
  recovery rate and quality of, 535
  review of, in restructuring process, 629
  for second lien loans, 111
  in settlement of distressed loans, 605–606
  in term sheet, 183
Collateral credit risk, with CDOs, 728, 731
Collateral manager:
  for CDOs, 739–740
  for CLOs, 667–668
Collateral packages, in credit agreements,
    332–334
Collateral security, 332–334, 361–362
Collateral trust agreements, 128
Collateralized bond obligations (CBOs), 20
Collateralized debt obligations (CDOs),
    647, 711–784
  annual issuance of, 659
  benefits of, 715–716
  CDS indices, 670, 749–758
    benchmark, 752–756
    characteristics of, 750–752
    tranches of, 756–758
  CLOs as, 647 (*See also* Collateralized loan
    obligations)
  collateral for, 714
  correlation and tranche pricing, 774–784
  credit analysis of, 729–732
  customization and easy execution of,
    767–773
    investment strategies, 770–773
    market participants, 768–770
  defined, 771
  funded vs. unfunded, 747–748
  Japanese market for, 908–909
  other pooled investments vs., 711, 802
  other structured products vs., 714–715
  parties to transactions, 739–742
  purpose of, 713
  risks with, 728–732
  structures of, 713, 719–728
    cash flow, 721–727
    market value, 727–728
    synthetic, 723–727
  synthetic, 658, 723, 765–767
    and basket CDS, 743–744
    cash flow CDOs vs., 724–727
    customization of, 767–773
    defined, 742
    funded vs. unfunded, 747–748
    and single-name CDS, 742–743

  structure of, 713
  valuation of, 774–779
  synthetic SF CBOs, 758–765
    cash basis of, 762–763
    credit event definitions for, 763–764
    efficiency of, 761–762
    sectors of largest impact, 759–760
  types of assets secured in, 716–719
  valuation of, 732–739
    assumptions used in, 736–737
    discounted cash flow analysis, 733–734
    interest-only, 734–735
    net asset value, 738–739
    principal-only, 734–736
Collateralized loan obligations (CLOs), 51,
    646–670
  advantages of, 648–649
  annual issuance of, 660
  balance sheet CLOs, 657–658
  cash flow arbitrage CLOs, 647
  as CDOs, 647 (*See also* Collateralized debt
    obligations)
  current market conditions, 662–664
  definitions of, 646–647
  and downturn of early 2000, 19–20
  history of market, 658–661
  liability spreads, 661
  and market declines, 18
  market value CLOs, 657
  origin of, 6, 645–646
  reasons for developing, 648
  redemption of, 668–669
  risks with, 666–670
  secondary trading of, 664–665
  as segment of institutional market, 166
  structure and mechanics of, 649–657
    arbitrage, 653–654
    capital structure, 651–652
    collateral, 653
    indenture covenants, 655–656
    payment waterfall, 654–655
    warehouse facility, 656–657
  synthetic CDOs, 658
Collateralized mortgage obligations
    (CMOs), 658
Collections, guarantees of, 328–329
Colony Investments, 902
Commercial banks:
  credit offered by, 3–4
  and high-yield bond market, 4, 5
  mergers of, 7
Commercial mortgage-backed securities
    (CMBS), 718

Commitment fees, 234
Commitment letter, 182
Commitments, 217–219
    conversion of, 219
    increasing, 218–219
    reducing, 217
    several liability, 217
    terminating, 218, 349–350
Competitive bid loans, 212–213, 221
Competitive landscape, 144–145
Competitive-bid options (CBOs), 104
Completeness of disclosures representation, 288
Complexity premium (synthetic SF CBOs), 762
Compliance with law covenant, 305
Compliance with law representations, 279
Computation of interest and fees, in credit agreements, 236–237
Conditions precedent, 333
    in credit agreements, 262–275
        applicable to non-U.S. borrowers, 272
        appraisals, 272
        catchall condition, 273
        corporate and organizational matters, 263–264
        defaults, 275
        to disbursement, 148
        effectiveness, 274
        environmental due diligence, 273
        execution, 262–263
        government approvals, 264
        insurance, 273
        legal opinions, 264–267
        material adverse change clause, 269–272
        ongoing conditions, 274
        promissory notes, 268–269
        relating to perfection of collateral, 267–268
    for representations, 275
    in term sheet, 183
    waiving, 262
Confidence, duty of, 189
Confidential information memoranda, 193–194
Confidential Information Supplement to the Code of Conduct, 79
Confidentiality:
    borrowers' rights to, 389–390
    desire to protect, 189
Confidentiality agreements, for Syndicate Information, 200

Confirmation, 421, 423–425
Consent rights, in credit agreements, 367–368
Consequential damages, in credit agreements, 377
Construction contractors, 139
Construction phase (project finance), 154
Construction risk, 143–144
Constructive fraudulent transfer, 513
Continental Bank, 6
Continental Illinois, 24
Contingent liabilities covenant, 307–308
Continuing guarantees, 330
Corporate bonds, 25, 26, 718–719
Corporate loans:
    for acquisitions, 23–24
    credit management for, 814–815
    investor base for, 28
    issuance of, 25, 26
    in mutual funds, 24
Corporate matters condition, in credit agreements, 263–264
Corporate pensions funds, Japanese, 913
Correlation and tranche pricing (CDOs), 774–784
    base correlation models, 782–784
    effect of correlation on spreads, 779–782
    for investment grade tranches, 778–779
Counterparts, in credit agreements, 383–384
Counterparty credit risk, 141, 143
Covenants:
    breach of, 339–340
    in credit agreements, 291–327
        affiliate transactions, 324–325
        affirmative, 301–308
        amendments to organic documents and other agreements, 325–326
        applied to subsidiaries, 292–294
        categories of, 291
        debt, 312–314
        definitions related to, 294–296
        derivatives, 319
        disclosure, 301–303
        disqualified stock, 314
        dividend blockers, 322–323
        dividends, 320–322
        financial, 297–301
        fiscal periods and accounting changes, 326–327
        fundamental changes, 314–316
        further assurances, 308
        guarantees or contingent liabilities, 319–320

Covenants *(Cont.)*
   hedging transactions, 307–308
   incorporation by reference, 327
   investments, 316–318
   lines of business, 318–319
   maintenance of insurance, 303–304
   modification/prepayment of other
      debt, 323–324
   "motherhood and apple pie," 304–306
   negative, 308–327
   negative negative pledge, 311–312
   negative pledge, 308–311
   sale-leasebacks, 316
   substantive consolidation, 360
   tax-sharing payments, 322
   use of proceeds, 307
   visitation or inspection rights, 303
  for second lien loans, 111, 132–133
  in term sheet, 184
Cover for letters of credit, as remedy, 260,
   351–352
Coverage tests:
  CDOs, 722
  CLOs, 656
Cram-down risk, 606–608
Crammed down creditors, 117
Credit agreements, 146–153, 211–391
  access to loan register, 365–366
  additional indebtedness, 150
  additional liens, 151
  agency provisions, 354–359
   agents, 358–359
   appointment, 355–356
   delegation, 357–358
   filing proofs of claim, 358
   no fiduciary duty/exculpation,
      356–357
   reliance, 357
   successor agents, 358–359
   syndication, 359
  amendments to project documents/credit
     agreements, 152
  assignments, 153, 366–372
   consent rights, 367–368
   eligible assignees, 368–369
   loan register, 369
   loans covered by securities laws,
      369–372
   minimums, 369
   transfer fees, 369
  bankers' acceptances, 216–217
  borrower indemnification, 375–377
  borrower's rights, 386–390

business day conventions, 238
capital contributions, 147
captions, 384
cash flow projections/annual budget,
   147–148
cash flow waterfall, 148–150
class voting under, 624
clawback clause, 364–365
collateral packages, 332–334
commitments, 217–219
conditions precedent, 262–275
  applicable to non-U.S. borrowers,
    272
  appraisals, 272
  catchall condition, 273
  corporate and organizational matters,
    263–264
  defaults, 275
  to disbursement, 148
  effectiveness, 274
  environmental due diligence, 273
  execution, 262–263
  government approvals, 264
  insurance, 273
  legal opinions, 264–267
  material adverse change clause,
    269–272
  ongoing conditions, 274
  promissory notes, 268–269
  relating to perfection of collateral,
    267–268
  for representations, 275
consequential damages, 377
counterparts, 383–384
covenants, 291–327
  affiliate transactions, 324–325
  affirmative, 301–308
  amendments to organic documents
    and other agreements, 325–326
  applied to subsidiaries, 292–294
  categories of, 291
  debt, 312–314
  definitions related to, 294–296
  derivatives, 319
  disclosure, 301–303
  disqualified stock, 314
  dividend blockers, 322–323
  dividends, 320–322
  financial, 297–301
  fiscal periods and accounting changes,
    326–327
  fundamental changes, 314–316
  further assurances, 308

guarantees or contingent liabilities,
    319–320
hedging transactions, 307–308
incorporation by reference, 327
investments, 316–318
lines of business, 318–319
maintenance of insurance, 303–304
modification/prepayment of other
    debt, 323–324
"motherhood and apple pie," 304–306
negative, 308–327
negative negative pledge, 311–312
negative pledge, 308–311
sale-leasebacks, 316
substantive consolidation, 360
tax-sharing payments, 322
use of proceeds, 307
visitation or inspection rights, 303
cumulative remedies, 374–375
deemed dividends, 335–336
dividend distribution tests, 150
electronic execution, 384–385
enforcement provisions, 379–383
events of default, 336–348
    breach of covenants, 339–340
    change of control, 346
    cross-default/cross acceleration,
        340–343
    default in payment, 337–338
    environmental events, 346
    ERISA events, 345
    foreign borrowers, 347
    inaccuracy of representations, 338–339
    insolvency, 343–344
    invalidity of guarantees or liens,
        346–347
    judgment default, 344–345
    material adverse change, 348
    specialized, 34
expenses provision, 375
financial covenants, 150
for first and second lien loans, 132–133
frequency, 221–222
funding mechanics, 222–223
governing law, 377–379
guarantees, 327–332
    continuing, 330
    downstream/cross-stream/upstream,
        331–332
    insolvency of borrower, 330
    of payment vs. collection, 328–329
    reinstatement, 329–330
    subrogation, 329

summary procedure, 330–331
    waivers, 329
indirect damages, 377
and information distribution, 194
insurance proceeds, 151
integration, 384
intercreditor arrangements, 151
interest savings clauses, 247–248
lender indemnification, 359–360
lending offices, 239
for letters of credit, 214–216
limitations on business, 152
loan pledges, 373
for loans, 211–214
minimums, 221–222
for multicurrency facilities, 219–221
multiples, 221–222
no deemed waivers, 374
nonpublic disclosure of, 620–623
notice provisions, 373–374
ownership, 152
participations, 366–367, 372
payments, 248–262
    advancing maturity date, 250
    application of prepayments among
        tranches, 259–260
    cover for letters of credit, 260
    extensions for nonbusiness days, 249
    in immediately available funds,
        248–249
    mandatory prepayments, 253–259
    with multiple borrowers, 261–262
    prepayment opt-outs, 260–261
    prepayment premiums, 261
    scheduled repayment, 249
    stripped loan facilities, 251
    364-day facilities, 250–251
    time of, 248
    voluntary prepayments, 252–253
pricing, 223–237
    accrual conventions, 237
    applicable margins, 230–232
    computation if interest and fees,
        236–237
    default interest, 232–234
    fees, 234–236
    interest, 223–230
    interest payment dates, 232
pro rata treatment, 362–363
for project finance transactions, 137–138,
    146–153
    additional indebtedness, 150
    additional liens, 151

Credit agreements *(Cont.)*
  amendments to project documents or
    credit agreements, 152
  assignment, 153
  capital contributions, 147
  cash flow projections and annual
    budget, 147–148
  cash flow waterfall, 148–150
  conditions precedent to disbursement,
    148
  dividend distribution tests, 150
  financial covenants, 150
  insurance proceeds, 151
  intercreditor agreements, 151
  limitations on business, 152
  ownership, 152
  related-party transactions, 152
  sale of assets, 151
  security package, 147
  voting rights, 152–154
punitive damages, 377
related-party transactions, 152
remedies, 348–354
  accelerate, 350
  cumulative, 374–375
  demand cover for letters of credit,
    351–352
  demand payment from guarantors, 352
  institute suit, 352
  rescission, 352–353
  setoff right, 353–354
  stop lending, 349
  terminate commitments, 349–350
  waterfalls, 353
representations, 275–291
  completeness of disclosures, 288
  conditions precedent for, 275
  financial condition, 281–282
  for foreign borrowers, 289–291
  legal matters, 277–281
  perfection and priority of security, 289
  projections, 283–285
  regarding the business, 285–288
  status as senior indebtedness, 288–289
sale of assets, 151
security, 327–328, 332–336
  collateral packages, 332–334
  deemed dividends, 335–336
  springing liens, 334
  true-up mechanism, 335
security package, 147
severability, 383
sharing of setoffs/other claims, 363–364

  springing liens, 334
  stripped loan facilities, 251
  structuring, 146–153
    additional indebtedness, 150
    additional liens, 151
    amendments to project
      documents/credit agreements, 152
    assignment, 153
    capital contributions, 147
    cash flow projections/annual budget,
      147–148
    cash flow waterfall, 148–150
    conditions precedent to disbursement,
      148
    dividend distribution tests, 150
    financial covenants, 150
    insurance proceeds, 151
    intercreditor arrangements, 151
    limitations on business, 152
    ownership, 152
    for project finance transactions,
      146–153
    related-party transactions, 152
    sale of assets, 151
    security package, 147
    voting rights, 152–153
  survival, 385
  364-day facilities, 250–251
  true-up mechanism, 335
  and USA Patriot Act, 385–386
  voting provisions, 360–362
  voting rights, 152–153
  yield protection clauses, 239–247
    for breakfunding, 243–245
    for capital costs, 242
    for Eurodollar disaster, 242
    for illegality, 243
    for increased costs, 240–241
    for taxes, 245–247
Credit analysis, 169–171, 729–732
Credit default cycle, 27
Credit default swaps (CDS), 60
  basket, 743–744
  indices for, 670, 749–758
    benchmark, 752–756
    and CDOs, 749–758
    characteristics of, 750–752
    tranches of, 756–758
  loan-only, 670–680
    appeal of, 678
    credit events, 677
    participants in, 678–679
    settlement of, 679–680

typical terms for, 676–677
uses of, 671–676
origin of, 645, 646
single-name, 742–743
single-name high-yield, 670
Credit derivatives, 60 (*See also* Credit
default swaps)
Credit enhancer, for CDOs, 741–742
Credit events:
loan-only credit default swaps, 677
for synthetic SF CBOs, 763–764
Credit losses:
allowance for, 826–827
for bank loans, 12, 14
Credit management, 805–813
for corporate loans, 814–815
"5 Ps of credit," 808
in-depth fundamental analysis, 810
inputs into, 807
lessons learned, 811–813
monitoring, 810
screening, 809–810
sourcing of investment opportunities, 809
Credit risk:
avoidance of, 5
bank, 3–6
with bank loans, 7
under Basel 2, 850, 852–853
with CLOs, 666
counterparty, 141, 143
default events, 8
hedging in accounting for, 829–830
management of, 5
measurement techniques and assumption
of, 15, 16
quantification of, 852–853
standards across industries, 170–171
Credit spread optionality, 519–521
Credit spreads, in bank loan market, 12
Credit strategy, in portfolio management,
790–792
Credit Suisse Distressed Loan Index, 542
Credit Suisse Institutional Leveraged Loan
Index, 548–568
benchmarks for, 555
creation of, 548
loans included in, 549, 551
price criteria for, 551
profile characteristics of, 556, 563–566
rating of loans in, 553–555
risk and return with, 549–555
as subindex of Leveraged Loan Index,
543

Credit Suisse Leveraged Loan Index,
541–548
analytics, 543–544
Distressed Loan Index, 542
inclusion rules, 542
Institutional Leveraged Loan Index
subindex, 543
ratings, 545–548
Credit Suisse SAMI (Secured) Index, 670
Credit Support Annex (CSA), 700–701
Creditors:
"crammed down," 117
priority of, 118–119
second lien rights in bankruptcy, 114–121
voting by classes of, 131–132
Creditors' committee, in Chapter 11
bankruptcy, 636
Credit-risk portfolio management, 5
Cross-Border Project, 918–927
claims against third parties, 922–924
delayed compensation, 927
distributions, 925–927
focus areas in, 921–922
historical challenges to convergence,
918–921
settling trades, 924–925
Cross-default/cross acceleration:
as event of default, 340–343
of second and first lien loans, 136
Cross-stream guarantees, 331–332
CSA (*see* Credit Support Annex)
CS, 73
Cumulative remedies, in credit agreements,
374–375
Cure rights, 388–389
Currency:
judgment currency clause, 382–383
local currency tranches, 220–221
multicurrency deal currency adjustments,
259
multicurrency lines, 104
Current ratio, 301
CUSIPs, 73
Customer Identification Procedure (CIP),
82–83

D

Daily value at risk (DVaR), 493, 495–496
Date-specific covenants, 297, 300–301
Dealer, definition of, 97*n*8
Debt:

Debt *(Cont.)*
  bank loan, 34
  definition of, 295–296
  institutional, 103
  pro rata, 103
  types of, in secondary loan settlement, 427
Debt basket, 314
Debt covenant, 312–314
Debt cushion, recovery rates and, 535
Debt prepayment requirement, 256–257
Debt ratio, 298–299
Debt service coverage ratio, 299
Debt subordination, lien subordination vs., 113–114
Debt Traders Association, 63
Debt-for-equity exchange, 632
Debtor in possession, in Chapter 11 bankruptcy, 636
Debtor-in-possession (DIP) financing, 107
  advance consent to, 127–128
  right to approve, 117
Debt-to-equity ratio, 141
Deemed dividends, in credit agreements, 335–336
Default, 8
  on bank loans, 9, 10, 12, 533–539
    in 1990s through 2002, 18–19
    industry data on, 13
    probability of, 15
  credit agreement conditions for, 275
  credit default cycle, 27
  events of
    breach of covenants, 339–340
    change of control, 346
    in credit agreements, 336–348
    cross-default/cross acceleration, 340–343
    default in payment, 337–338
    defined, 336
    environmental events, 346
    ERISA events, 345
    foreign borrowers, 347
    inaccuracy of representations, 338–339
    insolvency, 343–344
    invalidity of guarantees or liens, 346–347
    judgment default, 344–345
    material adverse change, 348
    in payment, 337–338
  under second lien loan agreement, 135
Default interest, in credit agreements, 232–234

Default rate:
  for leveraged loans, 45
  trends in, 533–539
Defaults clause, 333
Delayed compensation, 77
Delayed-draw term loans, 105
Delegation, agency provisions for, 357–358
Delphi, 409, 410
Derivatives, 60, 645–646
Derivatives covenants, 319
Derived Pricing Model, 461 (*See also*
    LSTA/LPC Secondary Mark-to-Market
    Pricing Service)
Deutsche Bank, 8, 696
Development phase (project finance), 153–154
DIP financing (*see* Debtor-in-possession
    financing)
Direct lending, 57–58
Directional trades (CDOs), 772–773
DirecTV, 511–512
Disbursement, conditions precedent to, 148
Disclosure:
  in Chapter 11 bankruptcy, 640
  representation of completeness, 288
  SEC requirements for, 91
  under Securities Act of 1933, 94
Disclosure covenant, 301–303
Discounted cash flow analysis, 733–734
Discounting the draft, 107
Dispositions, limitation on, 315–316
Disqualified stock covenant, 314
Distressed loan investing, 583–641
  and borrower's bankruptcy, 594–602
    Bankruptcy Code definition of
        underwriter, 599–602
    and interest as "security," 594–597
    new securities issued by debtors, 597–599
  Chapter 11 bankruptcy, 634–641
    automatic stays in, 636
    avoidance powers in, 637–638
    and Bankruptcy Code, 634–635
    commencement of, 635
    creditors' committee in, 636
    debtor in possession in, 636
    disclosure in, 640
    estate creation, 636
    executory contracts and unexpired
        leases in, 638–639
    first-day orders in, 635
    goals of, 635
    plan of reorganization in, 639–641

U.S. trustee in, 636
use of cash collateral in, 639
history of, 584–588
portfolio management for, 817–821
access to information, 818
inefficient market, 820–821
restructuring process, 818–819
risk/return characteristics, 817–818
supply and demand, 819
recovery rate factors, 587–590
restructuring process, 625–641
advisors for, 630
alternative paths for, 632–634
Chapter 11 bankruptcy, 634–641
costs of restructuring, 627
decision-making for, 626
exercise of remedies in, 630
information for starting process,
628–630
interim documentation, 630–632
lender group size/composition, 627
severity of borrower's distress, 627–628
strategy formation for, 632
risk considerations in, 602–625
access to nonpublic information,
620–623
enforcing ratable distribution, 610–620
litigation risk, 609–610
settlement of loan obligations, 603–609
voting in syndicated credits, 624–625
and securities laws, 594–602
strategies for, 590–593
types of investors, 593–594
Distressed loan market, 585–587
global, 917–928
claims against third parties, 922–924
conditionality, 924–925
delayed compensation, 927
distributions, 925–927
focus areas for, 921–922
historical challenges to, 918–921
origin of, 858
supply of loans, 585–587
Distressed loans:
closing documentation for, 431–433
and globalization, 917–918
Distressed trade confirmation, 77
Distressed trades/trading, 395, 397
proceeds letters, 454–455
revolving credit, 448–455
delayed compensation, 449–450
delayed settlement, 448–449
negative funding, 452–453

with permanent reductions before
settlement date, 451–452
settled without accrued interest
recurring fee allocation, 450–451
in secondary loan market, 444–455
term loans, 445–448
delayed settlement calculations,
446–448
purchase price calculation, 445–446
trade/settlement date purchase prices
greater than 25%, 453–454
Dividend basket, 322
Dividend blockers covenant, 322–323
Dividend distribution tests, in credit
agreements, 150
Dividends:
in bankruptcy, 609
deemed, 335–336
Dividends covenant, 320–322
DJ CDX, 570, 749
DJ iTraxx, 750
Documentation:
amendments to, 152, 325–326
confirmation, 424–425
for distressed loan closing, 431–433
for distressed loan restructuring, 628–632
for par loan closing, 430, 432–433
primary market, 182–185
commitment letter, 182
fee letter, 182
term sheet, 183–185
for second lien loans, 132–136
intercreditor agreements, 128–129
security documents, 131
for secondary loans, 405–406
standardized, 32, 33, 73, 76–78
for total return swaps, 699–704
for TRS, 699–704
Credit Support Annex, 700—701
investment management agreement,
703–704
ISDA Master Agreement and Schedule,
699–700
swap confirmation, 701–703
voting right agreement, 703–704
Documentation agents, 50, 172
Downstream guarantees, 331–332
Draft, 106
Drexel Burnham Lambert, 4–5
Due authorization representations, 277
Due diligence:
environmental, 273
upstream, 432

Due execution representations, 278
Due organization representations, 277
Duty of confidence, 189
DVaR (*see* Daily value at risk)

E

EBITDA, 296
Economic cycles, 671, 672
Effectiveness of credit agreements, 274
Electronic execution, in credit agreements, 384–385
Eligible assets, in total return swaps, 692–693
Eligible assignees, in credit agreements, 368–369
EMEA (*see* Europe, the Middle East, and Africa)
Employee Retirement Income Security Act of 1974 (ERISA), 283–284, 345
Employee stock plan payments, 321
Endgame strategy, distressed loan investing, 591–592
Enforceability representations, 278
Enforcement provisions:
  control over, in bankruptcy, 119
  in credit agreements, 379–383
Enron, 586
Enterprise value, 9
Environmental due diligence condition, in credit agreements, 273
Environmental liabilities, events of default tied to, 346
Environmental matters representations and disclosures, 288
Equitable subordination, in distressed loan distributions, 616–618
Equity investors, 139
Equity performance attribution, 574–575
Equity prepayment requirement, 256–257
ERISA (*see* Employee Retirement Income Security Act of 1974)
ERISA event of default, 345
Estate, in Chapter 11 bankruptcy, 636
Eurodollar disaster, yield protection clause for, 242
Europe:
  and global loan market, 862
  growth of loan market, 873
  high grade market, 871
  investment grade market, 871–874
  leveraged loan market, 874–876

  primary volume for, 37
  since introduction of Euro, 36
  spreads on, 38–39
  U.S. market vs., 58–60
  volume as percent of global volume, 59
  mark-to-market pricing in, 400
  nonbank lenders in, 876–877
  secondary loan market in, 402–403, 881–886
Europe, the Middle East, and Africa (EMEA):
  issuance in 2003, 865
  lending volume by country, 869
  M&A lending, 864, 866
  mandated arranger league table, 863
  post-September 11 market, 864, 865
  syndicated lending, 866–867
  syndicated loan market, 888–897
    borrower profile for, 888
    evolution of, 888, 889
    geographic diversification of borrowers, 890–891
    growth of, 890
    and leveraged loan market in Europe, 891–892
    secondary market development, 892–893
    U.S. Market vs., 894–897
Evaluation Materials:
  distribution of, 205–206
  production of, 204–205
  receipt of, 206
Event risk, 673
Events of default:
  in credit agreements, 336–348
    breach of covenants, 339–340
    change of control, 346
    cross-default/cross acceleration, 340–343
    default in payment, 337–338
    environmental events, 346
    ERISA events, 345
    foreign borrowers, 347
    inaccuracy of representations, 338–339
    insolvency, 343–344
    invalidity of guarantees or liens, 346–347
    judgment default, 344–345
    material adverse change, 348
  defined, 336
  remedies against, 348–354
    accelerate, 350
    cumulative, 374–375

demand cover for letters of credit,
  351–352
demand payment from guarantors, 352
institute suit, 352
rescission, 352–353
setoff right, 353–354
stop lending, 349
terminate commitments, 349–350
waterfalls, 353
in term sheet, 185
Evergreen option, 104
Excess cash flow, prepayment due to, 257
Exclusivity period, in bankruptcy, 640
Exculpation, 356–357
Execution condition, in credit agreements,
  262–263
Executory contracts, in Chapter 11
  bankruptcy, 638–639
Exide Technologies, Inc., 619–620
Existence and franchises covenant, 304–305
Existing debt/loan representations and
  disclosures, 286
Expenses:
  accounting standards for, 827
  credit agreement provision for, 375
Exposure Draft on SPE Consolidation
  (FASB), 83
Extensions for nonbusiness days, in credit
  agreements, 249

F

Facility fees, 234–235
Farallon, 902
*FAS 140 (see Statement of Financial
  Accounting Standards No. 140)*
FASB (*see* Financial Accounting Standards
  Board)
FASB SPE consolidation rules, 830–833
Federal Reserve Board, 160, 161, 280–281
Federal securities laws, 87–91
Fee letter, 182
Fee payments, 512
Fees:
  accounting standards for, 827
  in credit agreements, 234–236
    commitment, 234
    computation of, 236–237
    facility, 234–235
    letter of credit, 236
    utilization, 235–236
  non-use, 176

in syndication strategy, 176
Fidelity Management and Research
  Company, 621–623
Fiduciary duty/exculpation, agency
  provisions for, 356–357
FIFO (*see* First-in, first-out)
Filing proofs of claim, agency provisions
  for, 358
FIN 46R, 830–831
Finance companies, 51, 168
Financial Accounting Standards Board
  (FASB):
  accounting positions of, 83
  Exposure Draft on SPE Consolidation, 83
  FAS 140, 83, 834–843
    applied to assignments and
      participations, 834–841
    loan securitization, 832–833
    proposed revisions of, 841–842
    qualifying special-purpose entities, 831
  SPE consolidation rules, 830–833
Financial condition representations,
  281–282
Financial covenants, 297–301
  in credit agreements, 150
  in term sheet, 184
Financial statement representations,
  281–282
First Chicago, 63
First lien loans:
  future, limits on amount of, 134
  second lien lenders' purchase of, 130
First-day orders, in Chapter 11 bankruptcy,
  635
First-in, first-out (FIFO), 294, 295
Fiscal periods covenant, 326–327
"5 Ps of credit," 808
Fixed charges coverage ratio, 299
Fixed income performance attribution,
  571–574
Fixed interest rate, floating rate vs., 514
Flat margins, 231
Flexible structuring, 157
Floating interest rate, 40, 157, 514
Floating-rate assets, leveraged loans as, 23
Floating-rate loans, benefits/disadvantages
  of, 55
Forbearance agreements, 631–632
Force majeure risk, 146
Foreclosure, 120
Foreign assets control regulations, 280
Foreign borrowers:
  credit agreement conditions for, 272

Foreign borrowers *(Cont.)*
  representations for, 289–291
  risk of default with, 347
Foreign tax credits, 246
Forms of purchase, in secondary loan
    settlement, 426–427
Forum non conveniens doctrine, 381
France, 869, 891
France Telecom, 891
Fraudulent transfers, in bankruptcy,
    613–615, 637–638
Frequency, in credit agreements, 221–222
Fridson, Martin, 56
Fundamental changes covenant, 314–316
Fundamental value strategy, in distressed
    loan investing, 591
Funded CDOs, 747–748
Funding mechanics, in credit agreements,
    222–223
Further assurances covenant, 308

G

GAAP, 825–833
  banking book, 826–828
  credit-related investment products, 829
  for credit-risk hedging activities,
      829–830
  definition of, 294–295, 326–327
  FASB SPE consolidation rules, 830–833
  held for sale, 828
  initial recognition and measurement,
      825–826
  trading book, 826
  transfers between portfolios, 828
Gains, realized/unrealized, 512
Gehring, Louis, 571
Georgia Pacific, 414
Germany, 869, 891
Getty, J. Paul, 569
Global Crossing, 409, 587
Globalization of loan market, 36–39,
    861–888, 910
  call to convergence in, 917–918
  Cross-Border Project, 918–927
    claims against third parties, 922–924
    delayed compensation, 927
    distributions, 925–927
    focus areas in, 921–922
    historical challenges to convergence,
        918–921
    settling trades, 924–925

  differences in lender classes and
      outcomes, 876–880
  distressed loans, 917–918
  history of global lending, 861–867
  leveraged lending, 874–876
  loan structure similarities across markets,
      869–874
  main dilemma in, 917–918
  and regional/national markets, 867–868
      (See also specific markets)
  secondary markets, 881–886
  trends toward, 887–888
Goldman Sachs, 7, 63, 459–460
Governing law, in credit agreements,
    377–379
Government approvals condition, in credit
    agreements, 264
Government approvals covenant, 305–306
Government approvals representations,
    279
Grandfathered debt, 312
Grandfathered investments, 317
Grandfathered liens, 310
Grid notes, 268–269
Grid pricing, 231–232
Guarantees:
  in credit agreements, 327–332
  demanding, in event of default, 352
  invalidity of, 345–347
Guarantees covenant, 319–320

H

Haircuts (total return swaps), 692–693
Hedge counterparty, for CDOs, 741
Hedge funds:
  CDOs in, 768, 769
  direct lending, 57–58
  of distressed debt, 590–591
  impact on loan market, 415–416
  total return swaps in, 697–698
Hedging transactions covenant, 307–308
Held for sale, accounting standards for,
    828
HIBOR, 230
High-leverage par investing strategy,
    698–699
High-yield bonds:
  as asset class, 4–5
  bank loans vs., 55–56
  trading in secondary market vs.,
      403–405

Hokkaido Takushoku Bank, 907
Hong Kong, 868, 898
Hot market, 417
Hybrid cash/synthetic mezzanine SF
    CBOs, 760

I

IBM, 902
IBOR, 230
IBoxx, 749
Illegality, yield protection clause for, 243
Imetal, 891
Immediately available funds, payments in,
    248–249
Immunity representation, 289–290
In re Adelphia Communications Corp., 623
In re Enron, 623
In re Federated Department Stores, 621–623
In re Global Crossing, 623
In re Mobile, 616–617
In re Till, 607–608
In re Win Dixie, 623
In re WorldCom, Inc., 623
Inaccuracy of representations, as event of
    default, 338–339
Incorporation by reference covenant, 327
Increased costs, yield protection clause for,
    240–241
Incremental facilities (credit agreements),
    218–219
Indenture covenants (CLOs), 655–656
Indirect damages, in credit agreements, 377
Indonesia, 902
Industry Sector Indexes, 540
Inefficient market, 820–821
Inequitable conduct, in bankruptcy, 617
Information:
    control policies and procedures for,
        200–207
        to avoid entering transactions on basis
            of MNPI, 200–201
        key elements in, 201–203
        special issues addressed in, 203–207
        tailoring, 201
    for distressed loan restructuring, 628–630
    for managing portfolio of distressed
        loans, 818
    material nonpublic, 188, 189, 198–199
        defined, 189
        information control policies and
            procedures for, 200–207

    principles for use of, 79
    private information vs., 188, 189
        for securities-market participants, 186
        Syndicate Information vs., 198–199
    private, 188–189, 191–196
    public, 188
    on secondary market investors, 411–412
    Syndicate, 196–207
        Borrower Restricted Information vs.,
            198
        confidentiality arrangements, 200
        defined, 197
        LMP control policies and procedures,
            200–207
        material nonpublic information vs.,
            198–199
        public vs. private side participation,
            199
Information barriers, 202–203
Information distribution:
    architecture of, 186–189
        article organization, 187
        definitional issues, 187–189
    contractual provisions for private
        information, 191
    documents related to private
        information, 191–196
        bank books, 193–194
        credit agreements, 194
        Master Confidentiality Agreements,
            191–192
        splash pages, 194–196
        Standard Trade Confirmation,
            192–193
    practices regarding, 189–190
Information memorandums, 179–180
ING, 63
Insolvency:
    of borrower, guarantee for, 330
    as event of default, 343–344
    fiduciary duties in, 120–121
Inspection rights, 303
Inspection rights covenant, 303
Institutional debt, 103
Institutional investors, 51
    in corporate loans, 28
    direct lending, 57–58
    in European market, 36
    Japanese, 914
    loan portfolios of, 30
    in primary market, 166–169
    secondary liquidity of, 29
Institutional term loans, 105, 717

Institutional tranches, pro rata tranches vs., 53–55

Insurance, maintenance of, 303–304
  covenants for, 303–304

Insurance companies, as investors, 168

Insurance condition, in credit agreements, 273

Insurance proceeds, in credit agreements, 151

Integration clause, in credit agreements, 384

Intellectual property representations and disclosures, 287

Intercompany debt, 313

Intercompany dividend payments, 321

Intercreditor agreements, 128
  bankruptcy role of, 625
  with distressed loan sale/refinancing, 606
  enforceability of, 128–129
  and voting rights, 624

Intercreditor arrangements:
  in credit agreements, 151
  documenting, 128
  enforcement of, 128–129
  relationships without, 118–121

Interest:
  in credit agreements, 223–230
    computation of, 236–237
    default, 232–234
    payment dates, 232
    savings clauses, 247–248
  as "security," 594–597

Interest coverage ratio, 299

Interest expense, 298

Interest rate optionality, 518–519

Interest rate risk:
  with bank loans, 7
  with CLOs, 669–670

Interest rates, 223–230
  base rate, 224–225
  for competitive bid loans, 229–230
  default, 232–234
  fixed, 514
  floating, 40, 514
  LIBOR, 225–229
  spread on, 230–232

Interest treatment:
  in secondary loan settlement, 428–429
  for term loans
    paid in kind, 429
    paid on settlement date, 439

Interest-only CDO valuation, 734–735

Internal Revenue Service regulations, 83–84

International Convergence of Capital Measurement and Capital Standards (Basel Committee on Banking Supervision), 842

International Monetary Fund, 291, 347

International Organization of Securities Commissions (IOSCO), 850

Internet splash pages, 194–195

IntraLinks, 195

Invalidity of guarantees or liens, as event of default, 346–347

Investment banks:
  for CDOs, 740
  and high-yield bond market, 4, 5

Investment Company Act of 1940, 279

Investment grade issuers, 47

Investment grade market, 161, 162

Investment grade sector:
  noninvestment grade sector vs., 42
  syndicated loan market, 41–42

Investment management agreement, for total return swaps, 703–704

Investment philosophy, establishing, 805

Investments basket, 318

Investments covenant, 316–318

Investor meeting, 180–181

Investors:
  in CDOs, 741, 768–770
  in corporate loans, 28
  Japanese, 912–915
  main groups of, 50–52
  meeting of, in syndication process, 180–181
  nonbank, portfolio management by, 803–816
    credit strategy, 805–813
    investment philosophy, 805, 806
    outlook for credit management in loan market, 814–815
  in primary market, 31, 164–169
    diversification of, 37
    for highly leveraged loans, 788

Investors' information, in secondary market, 411–412

Involuntary default, 234

IOSCO (International Organization of Securities Commissions), 850

ISDA Master Agreement and Schedule, 699–700

Issuers:
  defined, 47
  investment grade, 47
  leveraged, 47–48
  middle market, 48
  primary market, 164
  syndicated market, 47–48
  (*See also* Borrowers)
Italy, 891
ITraxx, 670, 676
ITraxx Asia index, 755
ITraxx Australia index, 755
ITraxx CJ index, 755
ITraxx Corporate index, 754
ITraxx Crossover index, 754

J

Japan:
  domination of Asia-Pacific region, 867,
    868
  investment environment, 898–900,
    903–916
    CDO market, 908–909
    environment of, 903–904
    global CDO deals, 910, 911
    Japanese banks' role in, 910–912
    secondary loan market, 907–908
    strategies and methods, 905
    syndicated loan market, 899, 900,
      905–907
    types of investors, 912–915
    in U.S. bonds, 904–905
    in U.S. high yield loan market, 915, 916
    volume of, 899
  mandated arranger league table, 863
  syndicated loan market, 898–900,
    905–907
Joint Market Practices Forum, 79
JP Morgan, 172
  CUSIPS, 73
  merger of, 8
  volume of trades, 413
Judgment currency clause, 382–383
Judgment default, 344–345
Jurisdiction, 379–381
Jury trial, waiver of, 382

K

Kmart, 537–538

L

Labor representations and disclosures, 287
Last-in, first-out (LIFO), 294, 295
Lawsuits, as remedy for default, 352
LBOs (*see* Leveraged buyouts)
Lead arrangers:
  in primary market, 171–174
  in syndications, 50
"Lead manager" title, 49
League tables, 172, 173, 863–864
Lease payments, 299–299
Legal characterization of loans, 87–100
  antifraud liability, 94–96
  loans as securities, 91–100
  and NASD rules, 96–100
  registration requirements, 91–94
  regulation under federal securities laws,
    87–91
  regulation under state blue-sky laws,
    96–97
  "securities" vs., 87–91
Legal form representation, 290
Legal matters representations, 277–281
Legal opinions condition, in credit
  agreements, 264–267
Legal risk, 145–146
Legal standards development (LSTA),
  75–76
Legend, 902
Legislative initiatives, LSTA involvement
  in, 80
Lehman Brothers, Inc., 63
Lender debt, 312
Lenders:
  assignees as, 366–367
  borrowers rights with
    confidentiality, 389–390
    cure rights, 388–389
    to designate additional borrowers,
      388
    that lender act in good faith, 388
    that lender make the loan, 386
    that lender mitigate costs, 386–387
    yank-a-bank provision, 387–388
  differences in classes and outcomes,
    876–880
  and distressed loan restructuring, 627
  indemnification of, 359–360
  liability of, 604–605
  meeting of, in syndication process,
    180–181
  pro rata treatment of, 362–363

Lenders *(Cont.)*
  second lien, first lien loan purchase by, 130
  second lien loans permitted by, 112
  titles for, 49–50
Lending offices, in credit agreements, 239
Letters of credit (LOCs), 105
  credit agreements for, 214–216
  demanding cover for, 260, 351–352
  fees for, 236
Leverage:
  with CLOs, 666
  to generate excess returns, 417–418
Leverage ratio, 298
Leveraged buyouts (LBOs), 584–585
Leveraged Commentary & Data (S&P), 662
Leveraged issuers, 47–48
Leveraged loan funds, total return swaps in, 698
Leveraged loan indices:
  Credit Suisse Institutional Leveraged Loan Index, 548–568
  Credit Suisse Leveraged Loan Index, 541–548
  S&P/LSTA Leveraged Loan Index, 539–541
Leveraged loan market, 21–39
  and credit default cycle, 27, 28
  and globalization, 36–39
  and leveraged loans as alternative investment class, 22–23
  maturation of, 32
  primary market origins, 23–25 *(See also* Primary Market)
  secondary market development, 25–32 *(See also* Secondary loan market)
  second lien loans in, 35–36
  standards for, 32–34
  as submarket, 162–164
Leveraged loans:
  as alternative investment class, 22–23
  default rate for, 45
  defined, 22, 459
  and globalization, 874–876
  and growth of corporate loan market, 25
  institutional debt, 103
  investors in, 788
  origin of asset class, 6–9
  pro rata debt, 103
  risk with, 22, 43
  senior, performance attribution for, 569–579
    combining models for, 575–579

  equity performance attribution, 574–575
  fixed-income performance attribution, 571–574
  process for, 569–571
  syndicated, 22, 42–45 *(See also* Syndicated loans)
  in U.S. vs. European markets, 58–60
  valuation of *(see* Secondary market pricing)
LGD *(see* Loan loss given default)
Liability:
  antifraud, 94–96
  with CLOs, 661
  of lenders, 604–605
  in settlement of distressed loans, 604–605
  several, 217
LIBOR *(see* London Inter-bank Offered Rate)
Lien basket, 311
Lien subordination, debt subordination vs., 113–114
Liens:
  acquisition, 311
  in credit agreements, 151
  first *(see* First lien loans)
  invalidity of, 345–347
  negative pledge covenants for, 310–311
  permitted prior, 134–135
  priority of, with distressed loans, 606
  second *(see* Second lien loans)
  springing, 334
LIFO *(see* Last-in, first-out)
Limitations on business, in credit agreements, 152
Limited waivers, 631
Lines of business covenant, 318–319
Lipper, 15, 16
Liquidity, 26
  of CLOs, 669
  measures of, 398
  of middle market loans, 45
  in restructuring process, 632
  in secondary loan market, 400
  for secondary loans, 399
Liquidity premium (synthetic SF CBOs), 762
Litigation, LSTA involvement in, 80–82
Litigation representations and disclosures, 286–287
Litigation risk, 609–610
LLI *(see* S&P/LSTA Leveraged Loan Index)
LMA *(see* Loan Market Association)

LMPs (*see* Loan mark participants)
Loan asset class, 3–21
  historical risk and return in, 9–21
    current market, 20–21
    first credit test, 19–20
    rebound of 2003, 10
    time line of risk/return, 18–19
  and history of bank credit risk, 3–6
  leveraged loans as new class, 6–9
  syndicated loans, 22
  (*See also specific types of loans*)
Loan derivatives, 60
Loan loss given default (LGD), 533–539
Loan market, lack of definition of, 160
Loan Market Association (LMA):
  and Cross-Border Project, 918–927
  in secondary market development, 892,
    893
Loan market participants (LMPs):
  information control policies and
    procedures for, 200–207
  not using total return swaps, 695
  number of, 413
  in project finance, 139
  public vs. private side, 199
  securities market participation by, 186
  strategies of, 416–420
  and Syndicate Information, 197, 200–207
Loan pledges, in credit agreements, 373
Loan price volatility, 493–506
  average, by pricing category, 496–499
  change distribution for, 494–495
  daily value at risk, 493, 495–496
  distributions, by pricing category, 497,
    499–506
  by pricing category, 494, 495
  short term, 494
Loan Pricing Corporation (LPC), 7, 69, 172
  LSTA/LPC mark-to-market process, 33,
    464–470
  LSTA/LPC MTM Pricing, 69
  LSTA Trade Data Study, 470–479
Loan ratings (S&P), 527
Loan register, 365–366, 369
Loan structures, 103–107
  asset-based lending, 105–106
  bankers acceptance, 106–107
  debtor-in-possession financing, 107
  flexible, 157
  project finance (*see* Project finance)
  second lien loans (*see* Second lien loans)
  similarities across global markets,
    869–874

syndicated loan facilities, 103–105
Loan Syndications and Trading Association
    (LSTA), 61–84
  best practices and policy, 32, 33, 78–79
  Chairs of, 1995–2005, 74
  Code of Conduct, 79
  Confidential Information Supplement to
    the Code of Conduct, 79
  core mission of, 66
  and Cross-Border Project, 918–927
  documentation standardization, 32, 33,
    73, 76–78
  formation of, 7
  future directions for, 74–75
  general market initiatives of, 68–73
    CUSIPs, 73
    mark-to-market pricing service, 68–70
    S&P/LSTA Leveraged Loan Index,
      69–72
    trade data studies, 72–73
  history of, 61–66
  initial goal of, 421
  legal standards development, 75–76
  legislative initiatives, 80
  litigation as *amicus curiae*, 80–82
  LSTA/LPC mark-to-market process, 33,
    464–470
  LSTA/LPC MTM Pricing, 69
  LSTA Trade Data Study, 470–479
  main goal of, 63
  mark-to-market process, 32–33, 460
  minimum assignment amounts, 73–74
  origin of, 25
  regulatory and accounting issues
    positions, 82–84
  standards, 65–68
    best practices and policy, 78–79
    documentation, 32, 33, 73, 76–78
    legal, 75–76
    minimum assignment amounts, 73–74
    for practices, 32, 33
  Trade Checklist, 422–423
Loan-only credit default swaps, 670–680
  appeal of, 678
  credit events, 677
  participants in, 678–679
  settlement of, 679–680
  typical terms for, 676–677
  uses of, 671–676
"Loan-only deliverable" market, 60
Loans:
  covered by securities laws, 369–372
  credit agreements for, 211–214

Loans (*Cont.*)
  trading in bonds vs., 403–413
  volatility of, 408
Local currency tranches, 220–221
LOCs (*see* Letters of credit)
London Inter-bank Offered Rate (LIBOR),
    23, 40, 225–229, 238
Losses, realized/unrealized, 512
"Low covenant" deals, 536
Low-leverage distressed investing strategy,
    698–699
LPC (*see* Loan Pricing Corporation)
LSTA (*see* Loan Syndications and Trading
    Association)
LSTA/LPC mark-to-market process, 33,
    464–470
  creation of, 465–468
  current status of, 468–470
  history of, 462–463
LSTA/LPC MTM Pricing, 69
LSTA/LPC Secondary Mark-to-Market
    Pricing Service (SMPS), 460–461,
    464–465
  average bid-ask spreads, 473, 474
  average mean of the mean and average
      trade prices, 473, 474
  current services of, 468–470
  first quarter 2005 mean difference,
      478–479
  influence of market liquidity and credit
      factors on prices, 477–478
  trade prices and SMPS indicative prices,
      473, 475, 477
LSTA Trade Data Study, 470–479
  growth of, 471
  process used for, 470
  SMPS comparisons, 473–479
LTCB, 907

M

MAC clause (*see* Material adverse change)
Maintenance of insurance covenant,
    303–304
"Manager" title, 49
Managing agents, 50
Mandatory prepayments, in credit
    agreements, 253–259
  asset sales, 255–256
  borrowing base, 254–255
  casualty events, 256
  change of control, 257–258

cross-default clause, 343
currency adjustments, 259
debt and equity issuances, 256–257
excess cash flow, 257
revolving clean-downs, 254
Manufacturer's Hanover, 6, 8
Margins:
  applicable, 174, 230–232
  flat, 231
  regulation of, 280–281
Market risk, 144–145, 850
Market value CDOs, 727–728
Market value CLOs, 657, 698
Markit Group, 479–480
Markit Group model pricing, 462, 480–484
Mark-to-market pricing:
  by LSTA, 32–33, 68–70
  LSTA/LPC process, 33, 464–470
  in secondary market, 400–401, 414–415
Master Confidentiality Agreements,
    191–192
Material adverse change (MAC) clause,
    269–272, 348
Material misrepresentations, 94, 95
Material nonpublic information (MNPI),
    188
  defined, 189
  information control policies and
      procedures for, 200–207
  principles for use of, 79
  private information vs., 188, 189
  for securities-market participants, 186
  Syndicate Information vs., 198–199
Maturities, 40–41
Maturity date, advancing, 250
McLeod USA, Inc., 409, 587
Measurement:
  and credit risk assumption, 15, 16
  of returns, 510–513 (*See also* Analytics
      and performance)
Megabanks, Japanese, 906
Mergers:
  and global loan market, 862, 864–866
  limitation on, 314–315
Merrill Lynch & Co., 63
Merton, Robert, 574
Mexico, 867
Mezzanine SF CBOs, 759–760
Middle East, 895 (*See also* Europe, the
      Middle East, and Africa)
Middle Market Index, 540
Middle market issuers, 48
Middle market loans, 45–47

interplay with other capital markets, 57–58
syndication of, 57
Milken, Michael, 4, 5
Minimum assignment amounts, LSTA standards for, 73–74
Minimum loan amounts, in credit agreements, 221–222, 369
Minmetal, 902
MNPI (*see* Material nonpublic information)
Model Credit Agreement Provisions (LSTA), 240, 242, 251, 365, 373
Model NOL Orders, 78
Modeling risk, with CDOs, 728, 730
Moderate-leverage par investing strategy, 698
Modification of other debt covenant, 323–324
Moody's Investors Service, 517, 524, 525, 539
Moody's ratings, 546–548
Morgan Guaranty Trust Co. of New York, 63
Morningstar, 15, 16
Multicurrency deals, currency adjustments in, 259
Multicurrency facilities, credit agreements for, 219–221
Multicurrency lines, 104
Multiple borrowers, credit agreement provisions for, 261–262
Multiples, in credit agreements, 221–222
Multisector CDOs, 720
Multistrategy distressed loan investors, 593
Multitranche agreements, 360–361
Mutual funds, 6
  for bank loans, 19
    risk and return with, 16
    Sharpe ratios for, 17
  for corporate loans, 24
  long-term results for, 15
  portfolio manager for, 799–803

N

NASD (*see* National Association of Securities Dealers, Inc.)
NASD Regulation, Inc. (NASDR), 97, 98
National Association of Securities Dealers, Inc. (NASD), 91
  broker-dealer requirements, 98–100
  NASDR subsidiary of, 97

rules of, 96–100
National Foods of Australia, 902
National markets, 867–868
NationsBank, 645
NatWest, 645
NAV (*see* Net asset value)
Negative assurance, 266
Negative covenants, 308–327
  affiliate transactions, 324–325
  amendments to documents/agreements, 325–326
  debt, 312–314
  derivatives, 319
  disqualified stock, 314
  dividend blockers, 322–323
  dividends, 320–322
  financial covenants as, 291
  fiscal periods/accounting changes, 326–327
  fundamental changes, 314–316
  guarantees or contingent liabilities, 319–320
  investments, 316–318
  lines of business, 318–319
  modification/prepayment of other debt, 323–324
  negative negative pledge, 311–312
  negative pledge, 308–311
  sale-leasebacks, 316
  tax-sharing payments, 322
  in term sheet, 184
Negative negative pledge, 311–312
Negative pledge, 308–311
Net asset value (NAV):
  in CDO valuation, 738–739
  in mutual funds, 800, 801
Net worth, 300
New York law, 378–379
New York State Statute of Frauds, 80, 421
New York "TriBar" Committee, 265
Nextlink Communications, 587
Niche investors, 168
No burdensome restrictions representations and disclosures, 288
No conflict representations, 278–279
"No covenant" deals, 536
No deemed waivers, in credit agreements, 374
No-action letters, 600
Nominal recovery, 528–529
Nonbank investors:
  in Europe vs. U.S., 876–877
  par trading vs., 397

Nonbank investors *(Cont.)*
  portfolio management by, 803–816
    credit strategy, 805–813
    5 Ds of, 809
    investment philosophy, 805, 806
    outlook for credit management in loan
      market, 814–815
    in primary market, 166–169
    (*See also* Institutional investors)
Nonbusiness days, extensions for, 249
Nonpublic information, access to, 620–623
Nonratable committed loans, 220
Non-U.S. borrowers (*see* Foreign
  borrowers)
Non-use fees, 176
Noranda, 902
Note option deals, 268
Notes, securities vs., 370–371
Notice provisions, in credit agreements,
  373–374

O

O/C ratios (*see* Overcollateralization ratios)
Offering materials, 179–180
*Official Comm. of Unsecured Creditors v. R.F.
  Lafferty & Co.*, 604
Off-takers (project finance), 140
One Form of Action Rule (California),
  374–735
Ongoing conditions, in credit agreements,
  274
Operation phase (project finance), 154
Operation risk, 144, 850
Operators (project finance), 139–140
Ordinary course items, 318
Organizational matters condition, in credit
  agreements, 263–264
Original-Issue B Index, 540
Original-Issue BB Index, 540
Overcollateralization (O/C) ratios, 663–664
Owens Corning, 81–82, 586
Owens Corning, 306
Ownership, in credit agreements, 152

P

Par trades/trading, 395, 397
  closing documentation for, 430, 432–433
  revolving credit
    multicurrency, 443–444

  settlement of, 441–444
  in secondary loan market, 434–444
  term loans, 104–105, 435–441
    delayed settlement compensation
      calculations, 436–438
    interest treatments, 429, 439
    proceeds letters, 439–441
    settled without accrued interest
      treatment, 436
Parent company debt payments, 321–322
Pari passu ranking representation, 290
Participants:
  in collateralized debt obligations,
    768–770
  in loan-only credit default swaps,
    678–679
Participation fees, accounting standards for,
  827
Participations:
  assignments vs., 366–367
  in credit agreements, 366–367, 372
  FAS 140 applied to, 834–841
  in secondary loan settlement, 426–427
  syndicated loans, 22–23
Parties to transactions (CDOs), 739–742
Payment of taxes and obligations covenant,
  305
Payment waterfalls:
  CLOs, 654–655
  as default remedy, 353
Payments:
  acceleration of, 350
  in credit agreements, 248–262
    advancing maturity date, 250
    application of prepayments among
      tranches, 259–260
    cover for letters of credit, 260
    extensions for nonbusiness days, 249
    in immediately available funds,
      248–249
    mandatory prepayments, 253–259
    with multiple borrowers, 261–262
    prepayment opt-outs, 260–261
    prepayment premiums, 261
    scheduled repayment, 249
    stripped loan facilities, 251
    364-day facilities, 250–251
    time of, 248
    voluntary prepayments, 252–253
  default in, 337–338
  demanding, from guarantors, 352
  guarantees of, 328–329
  reclassification of, in bankruptcy, 618–620

in term sheet, 183
Penn Square Bank of Oklahoma, 24
Pension Benefit Guaranty Corporation
    (PBGC), 345
Pension representation, 283–284
Perfection and priority of security,
    representation of, 289
Perfection of collateral, condition relating
    to, 267–268
Performance:
    historical, in secondary market pricing,
        484–493
    measuring (see Analytics and
        performance)
Performance attribution, for leveraged
    senior loans, 569–579
    combining models for, 575–579
    equity performance attribution, 574–575
    fixed-income performance attribution,
        571–574
    process for, 569–571
Performance-based covenants, 297–300
Performing Loan Index, 540
Permitted encumbrances, 310
Permitted investments, 317
Permitted prior liens, 134–135
Personal jurisdiction, 380–381
Personality of loan market trades, 412–413
Philippines, 902
Pilgrim Prime Rate Trust, 24
Plan of reorganization, in Chapter 11
    bankruptcy, 639–641
Policy control, for syndicate information,
    200–207
Pooled investments, CDOs vs., 711, 802
Portfolio management, 787–821
    accounting standards for transfers
        between portfolios, 828
    and credit strategy
        development/application, 790–792
    credit-risk, 5
    and current loan market participants,
        787–790
    defined, 5
    distressed loans, 817–821
        access to information, 818
        inefficient market, 820–821
        restructuring process, 818–819
        risk/return characteristics, 817–818
        supply and demand, 819
    diversification strategies, 791–792
    first applications of, 5
    by institutional investors, 30

investment strategies, 793–799
    alternative fixed income, 794–797
    total return investment, 797–799
liquidity, 26
from manager's perspective, 799–803
market valuation, 791
by nonbank loan investors, 803–816
    credit strategy, 805–813
    investment philosophy, 805, 806
    outlook for credit management in loan
        market, 814–815
secondary market in, 416–417
vendor-assisted, 792
Portfolio total return swaps, 688, 690–691
Postpetition interest, 115
Preference recovery (Bankruptcy Code),
    611–613
Preferential transfers, in bankruptcy,
    637–638
Preferred dividends payments, 321
Prepayment(s):
    in credit agreements
        application of, among tranches,
            259–260
        mandatory, 253–259
        voluntary, 252–253
    of other debt, covenants for, 323–324
    of second lien loans, 135
    without penalty, 41
Prepayment opt-outs, in credit agreements,
    260–261
Prepayment premiums, in credit
    agreements, 261
Pretrade issues, in secondary loan market,
    421–423
Pricing:
    in credit agreements, 223–237
        accrual conventions, 237
        applicable margins, 230–232
        computation if interest and fees,
            236–237
        default interest, 232–234
        fees, 234–236
        interest, 223–230
        interest payment dates, 232
    fees, 176
    grid, 231–232
    mark-to-market
        by LSTA, 32–33, 68–70
        LSTA/LPC process, 33, 464–470
        in secondary market, 400–401
    in primary market, 175–176
    in secondary market, 459–506

Pricing (Cont.)
    evolution of, 459–463
    historical
        performance/distributions/volatil
            ity, 484–493
        loan price volatility, 493–506
        LSTA/LPC mark-to-market process,
            464–470
        LSTA Trade Data Study of, 470–479
        Markit Group model pricing, 479–484
        measuring accuracy of, 470–479
Pricing flex, 175
Primary market, 157–207
    agents, 171–174
    breaking into secondary market, 181
    credit analysis, 169–171
    distinguishing attributes of, 157–158
    diversification by investor type, 31
    forms used, 182–185
        commitment letter, 182
        fee letter, 182
        term sheet, 183–185
    growth rate of, 27–30
    history of loans, 159–160
    information distribution
        architecture of, 186–189
        contractual provisions for private
            information, 191–196
        practices regarding, 189–190
    investors, 164–169
    issuers, 164
    lead arrangers, 171–174
    lender meeting, 180–181
    loan pricing, 174–175
    offering material and preparation,
        179–180
    origins of, 23–25
    pricing flex, 175–176
    ratings process, 178–179
    sales process, 181
    size and scope of, 160–164
    Syndicate Information, 196–207
        Borrower Restricted Information vs.,
            198
        confidentiality arrangements, 200
        defined, 197
        LMP information and policy control,
            200–207
        material nonpublic information vs.,
            198–199
        public vs. private side participation,
            199
    syndication process, 171

    syndication strategy, 176–177
    value in secondary market vs., 417
    volume growth of, 28
Prime funds, 30, 31, 51, 52
Prime rate, 224–225
Prime-rate funds, 166, 167
Principal/agent issue, in secondary loan
    settlement, 425
Principal-only CDO valuation, 734–736
Private equity distressed loan investors, 593
Private information, 188–189
    contractual provisions controlling,
        191–196
    definitions of, 187–188
Private market, loan market as, 158
Private-side LMPs, 199
    advantage of, 411
    receipt of MNPI by, 203
Pro rata debt, 103
Pro rata investors, 165
Pro rata tranches, 52–55, 212
Pro rata treatment of lenders, 362–363
Proceeds Letter, 78
    for distressed trades, 454–455
    for par loans, 439–441
Project finance, 137–154
    credit agreements, 137–138, 146–153
        additional indebtedness, 150
        additional liens, 151
        amendments to project
            documents/credit agreements, 152
        assignment, 153
        capital contributions, 147
        cash flow projections/annual budget,
            147–148
        cash flow waterfall, 148–150
        conditions precedent to disbursement,
            148
        dividend distribution tests, 150
        financial covenants, 150
        insurance proceeds, 151
        intercreditor arrangements, 151
        limitations on business, 152
        ownership, 152
        related-party transactions, 152
        sale of assets, 151
        security package, 147
        voting rights, 152–153
    risk in, 141–146
        construction, 143–144
        counterparty credit, 141, 143
        and debt-to-equity ratio, 141
        force majeure, 146

legal, 145–146
market, 144–145
operation, 144
sovereign, 146
role of participants during project life,
153–154
structuring of, 137–140
unique characteristics of, 137
Project sponsor, 139
Projections representation, 283–285
Promissory notes condition, in credit
agreements, 268–269
Proofs of claim, 358
Properties covenant, 304
Proprietary desks, CDO investments of,
768, 769
PSAs (see Purchase and sale agreements)
PSI Net, 587
Public bank books, 193–194
Public Evaluation Materials, 206
Public information, 187–188
Public Utility Holding Company Act of
1935, 279
Public-side LMPs, 199, 203
Punch Taverns, 891
Punitive damages, in credit agreements, 377
Purchase amount, in secondary loan
settlement, 427
Purchase and sale agreements (PSAs), 77,
431–432
Purchase money debt, 312
Purchase money liens, 310–311
Purchase rate, in secondary loan
settlement, 427

Q

QIBs (qualified institutional buyers), 92
QSPEs (see Qualifying special-purpose
entities)
Qualified institutional buyers (QIBs), 92
Qualifying special-purpose entities
(QSPEs), 831, 832–833
Quiet second liens, 121–122

R

Raffles Holdings, 902
Ratable committed loans, 220
Ratable distribution of assets, enforcing,
610–620
bankruptcy preferences, 611–613
equitable subordination, 616–618
fraudulent transfers, 613–615
reclassification of payments, 618–620
Rating agencies, 521–525, 741
Rating scales, 524–525
Ratings:
B, 547
of bank loans, 529–533
of bank risk, 7
BB, 546
CCC/Split CCC, 547
demand for, 523–524
development of, 33–34
distressed/default, 547–548
investment grade, 546
for leveraged loans, 545–549
process for obtaining, 178–179
S&P, 526–533
split B, 547
split BB, 546
split BBB, 546
RCN, 587
Real property collateral, foreclosure on, 120
Real property representations and
disclosures, 286
Realized gains/losses, 512
Recission, right to, 352–353
Recognition of loans, 825–826
Recovery:
of bank loans, 9
nominal, 529
research on, 8
Recovery rates, 516–518
and active bank management, 536
and business cycle, 588
and debt cushion, 535
on distressed loans, 587–590
factors in, 533–539
and LGD vs. trading price after default,
536–537
for middle market loans, 46
and quality of collateral, 535
on second liens, 36
Recovery ratings, 525–527
Refco, 409, 410
Refinancing loans, 519–520
Refund from foreign jurisdiction, 246
Regal Cinemas, 587
Regional markets, 867–868
Registration:
blue-sky laws, 96–97
legal requirements for, 91–94

Registration *(Cont.)*
  Rule 144A, 89–90, 92–93
  with SEC, 90–91
  syndicated loan facilities, 91–94
Regulation:
  under federal securities laws, 87–91
  LSTA positions on, 82–84
  oversight and regulatory authorities, 790
  under state blue-sky laws, 96–97
Regulation FD (SEC), 82, 190
Reinstatement, guarantee of, 329–330
Reinvestment risk, with CLOs, 666–667
Related-party transactions, in credit
    agreements, 152
Relative value analysis, 513–521
  credit spread optionality, 519–521
  fixed vs. floating interest rate, 514
  interest-rate optionality, 518–519
  recovery rates, 516–518
  risk/return, 515
  term, 514–515
  windfalls from imperfect correlation, 521
Relative value trades (CDOs), 772
Reliance, agency provisions for, 357
Remedies:
  in credit agreements, 348–354
    accelerate, 350
    cumulative, 374–375
    demand cover for letters of credit,
        351–352
    demand payment from guarantors, 352
    institute suit, 352
    rescission, 352–353
    setoff right, 353–354
    stop lending, 349
    terminate commitments, 349–350
    waterfalls, 353
  in distressed loan restructuring, 630
  in second lien deals, 114
  for terminating commitments, 218
Repayment, in credit agreements, 249
Representations:
  in credit agreements, 275–291, 333
    completeness of disclosures, 288
    conditions precedent for, 275
    financial condition, 281–282
    for foreign borrowers, 289–291
    legal matters, 277–281
    perfection and priority of security, 289
    projections, 283–285
    regarding the business, 285–288
    status as senior indebtedness, 288–289
    inaccuracy of, 338–339

in term sheet, 183–184
Rescission, 352–353
Reservation of right letter, 631
Restricted lists, 202
Restricted securities, 89
Restricted subsidiaries, 292–293
Restructuring, 625–641
  advisors for, 630
  alternative paths for, 632–634
  and bank loan risk, 8–9
  Chapter 11 bankruptcy, 634–641
  costs of restructuring, 627
  decision-making for, 626
  defined, 626
  exercise of remedies in, 630
  information for starting process, 628–630
  interim documentation, 630–632
  lender group size/composition, 627
  portfolio management, 818–819
  severity of borrower's distress, 627–628
  strategy formation for, 632
Retail loan funds, 799–803
Returns:
  with bank loans, 7–21
    bankruptcy, 8–9
    collateral, 9
    default vs. recoveries, 8
    historical review of, 9–21
    time line of, 18–19
  measuring, 510–513 *(See also* Analytics
      and performance)
  in portfolio management, 793–794
  on portfolio of distressed loans, 817–818
  in relative value analysis, 515
  total return investment strategies,
      797–799
Reves v. Ernst & Young, 595
Revolvers, 53, 55
Revolving credit lines, 103–104
  clean-down requirement, 254
  conversion of commitments, 219
  distressed trades, 448–455
    delayed compensation, 449–450
    delayed settlement, 448–449
    negative funding, 452–453
    with permanent reductions before
        settlement date, 451–452
    settled without accrued interest
        recurring fee allocation, 450–451
  multicurrency, 443–444
  settlement of, 441–444
    with delayed compensation, 441–442
    purchase at a premium, 443

purchase of nonperforming loans, 442–443
term loans vs., 212
Revolving loans, 157
  non-use fees with, 176
  total return swaps on, 688
Risk:
  with access to information, 620
  with bank loans, 3, 7–21
    bankruptcy, 8–9
    collateral, 9
    default, 15
    default vs. recoveries, 8
    historical review of, 9–21
    time line of, 18–19
  under Basel 2, 850, 852–853
  with CDOs, 715–716, 728–732
  with CLOs, 666–670
  cram-down, 606–608
  credit
    avoidance of, 5
    bank, 3–6
    with bank loans, 7
    under Basel 2, 850, 852–853
    with CLOs, 666
    counterparty, 141, 143
    default events, 8
    hedging activities, accounting for, 829–830
    management of, 5
    measurement techniques and assumption of, 15, 16
    quantification of, 852–853
    standards across industries, 170–171
  in distressed loan investing, 602–625
    access to nonpublic information, 620–623
    enforcing ratable distribution, 610–620
    litigation risk, 609–610
    portfolio management, 817–818
    settlement of loan obligations, 603–609
    voting in syndicated credits, 624–625
  event, 673
  with leveraged loans, 22, 43
  in portfolio management, 793–794
  in project finance, 141–146
    construction, 143–144
    counterparty credit, 141, 143
    and debt-to-equity ratio, 141
    force majeure, 146
    legal, 145–146
    market, 144–145
    operation, 144

sovereign, 146
  in relative value analysis, 515
"Riskless" transactions, 100
Rule 10b–5 antifraud provisions, 95–95, 190
Rule 135c, 94
Rule 144A, 89–90, 92, 96
Russian debt default, 861

S

Safe harbor provision, 614–615
Sale of assets:
  in bankruptcy, 116
  bankruptcy code restrictions on, 121
  in credit agreements, 151, 255–256
  as restructuring strategy, 632
  secured borrowing vs., 834–841
Sale of loans, process for, 181
Sale-leaseback covenant, 316
San Miguel Corporation, 902
Scheduled interest payments, 512
Scheduled repayment, in credit agreements, 249
SEC (*see* Securities and Exchange Commission)
SEC v. Ralston Purina, 88
SEC v. W.J. Howey Co., 596
Second lien loans, 35–36, 108–137
  controversy with, 113
  debt vs. lien subordination, 113–114
  documenting intercreditor arrangements, 128
  documents involved in, 132–133
  enforcement of intercreditor agreements, 128–129
  first lien lenders' reasons for, 112
  future, limits on amount of, 134
  junior creditor's acceptance of, 112–113
  limits on amounts of future first lien loans, 134
  limits on amounts of future second lien loans, 134
  multiple secured creditors' rights, 118–121
  permitted prior liens, 134–135
  pros and cons for borrowers, 110–111
  and purchase of first lien loans, 130
  restrictions before bankruptcy filing, 122–123
  restrictions in bankruptcy proceedings, 123–128

Second lien loans (Cont.)
  secured creditors' rights in bankruptcy,
      114–117
  sets of security documents for, 131
  silent/quiet/well behaved, 121–122
  structuring, 121–136
  unsecured creditors' rights, 117–118
  unsecured creditor-type rights with,
      129–130
  voting by classes of creditors, 131–132
Secondary loan market, 395–455
  breaking into, 181
  for CLOs, 664–665
  development of, 25–32
    changes in loan structure, 31
    corporate loan investor base, 28
    and credit default cycle of 1999–2000s,
        27
    growth rate, 27–30
    institutional investor role in, 28–30
    LSTA and ratings establishment, 32
    prime funds, 30, 31
    volume traded, 25–27
  in Europe, 402–403
  facilitators of trading, 398–400
  and globalization, 881–886
  growth of, 395–398
  liquidity, 400
  mark-to-market pricing, 400–401
  origin of, 25, 26
  pricing in (see Secondary market pricing)
  pricing information availability, 400
  settling loan transactions, 420–455
    allocation, 425
    assignment fees, 455
    closing documentation, 430–434
    confirmation, 424–425
    distressed trades, 444–455
    forms of purchase, 426–427
    interest treatment, 428–429
    par trades, 434–444
    pretrade issues, 421–423
    principal/agent issue, 425
    purchase amount/type of debt, 427
    purchase rate, 427
    Trade-Specific Terms of Trade, 429–430
  trading in, 403–416
    hedge funds, 415–416
    high-yield bonds trading vs., 403–405
    investors' information, 411–412
    lack of short-selling capability, 412
    and market growth factors, 413–414
    marking to market, 414–415

  measuring volatility, 407–411
  personality of loan market trades,
      412–413
  settlement issues, 405–406
  settlement process and back-office
      requirements, 406–407
  strategies for, 416–420
  transparency in, 401
  value in primary market vs., 417
  volume growth of, 28
  volume of, 26, 27
Secondary market pricing, 459–506
  evolution of, 459–463
  historical performance/distributions/
      volatility, 484–493
  loan price volatility, 493–506
    average, by pricing category, 496–499
    change distributions, 494–495
    daily value at risk, 493, 495–496
    and daily value at risk, 495–496
    distributions, by pricing category, 497,
        499–506
    by pricing category, 494, 495
    short term, 494
  LSTA/LPC mark-to-market process,
      464–470
  LSTA Trade Data Study of, 470–479
  Markit Group model pricing, 479–484
  measuring accuracy of, 470–479
Second lien Loan Index, 540
Secured borrowing, sale of assets vs.,
      834–841
Securities (trading instruments):
  federal securities laws, 87–91, 597–599
  information flow issues with, 186–187
  loans considered as, 91–100
  loans vs., 87–91
  notes vs., 370–371
Securities Act of 1933 (as amended),
      87–90
  definition of security in, 370, 594
  Rule 135c disclosure, 94
  Rule 144A registration, 89–90, 92–93, 96
  Section 4(2), 88–89, 91–94
  Sections 11 and 12 material
      misstatements or omissions, 95
Securities and Exchange Commission
      (SEC):
  disclosure requirements, 91
  interpretive letter on valuation
      methodology, 461
  "ordinary trading transactions," 600
  registration with, 90–91

Regulation FD, 82, 190
sale of securities registration, 88
SEC v. Ralston Purina, 88
SEC v. W.J. Howey Co., 596
Securities Exchange Act of 1934 (as
   amended), 87
   definition of security in, 370, 594
   Rule 10b–5 antifraud provisions, 95–95,
     190
   Rule 12g3–2(b) (information to
     investors), 92
   Section 29(a) misstatements in fraud
     context, 95
Securities laws:
   Bankruptcy Code definition of
     underwriter, 599–602
   and interest as "security," 594–597
   loans covered by, 369–372
   on material nonpublic information, 190
   new securities issued by debtors, 597–599
Securitization, 832–833
Security (for loans):
   and bank loan risk, 14
   in credit agreements, 147, 327–328,
     332–336
     collateral packages, 332–334
     deemed dividends, 335–336
     springing liens, 334
     true-up mechanism, 335
   documents for first and second liens, 131
   for leveraged loans, 23
   perfection and priority of, 289
Security agreements, 289
Security documents, with second lien loans,
   131
Security Pacific, 596
Senior indebtedness status representation,
   288–289
Senior SF CBOs, 760
Seniority, bank loan risk and, 14
September 11, 2001 attacks, 488, 864
Servicer/manager risk, with CDOs, 729,
   731–732
Setoff right, 353–354
Setoffs, sharing of, 363
Settlement:
   of distressed loan obligations, 603–609
     cram-down risk, 606–608
     equity dividends in bankruptcy, 609
     inadequacy of collateral/cash flow,
       605–606
     intercreditor agreement risk, 606
     litigation risk-lender liability, 604–605

     under-/unsecured claims in
       bankruptcy, 608–609
   of loan-only credit default swaps,
     679–680
   in secondary market, 406–407, 420–455
     allocation, 425
     assignment fees, 455
     closing documentation, 430–434
     confirmation, 424–425
     distressed trades, 444–455
     forms of purchase, 426–427
     interest treatment, 428–429
     par trades, 434–444
     pretrade issues, 421–423
     principal/agent issue, 425
     purchase amount/type of debt, 427
     purchase rate, 427
     Trade-Specific Terms of Trade,
       429–430
Severability, in credit agreements, 383
Several liability, 217
Shared National Credit Exam, 160–161
Shared National Credit (SNC) Review, 395,
   396
Sharing of setoffs/other claims, in credit
   agreements, 363–364
Sharpe ratios, 17, 20, 486, 487
Shift poll mechanism, 433
Short term loan price volatility, 494
Short-selling, in secondary market, 412
SIBOR, 230
Sight draft, 106
Silent second liens, 112, 121–122
Singapore, 902
Single B Index, 540
Single-name credit default swaps, 670,
   742–743
Single-name total return swaps, 688–689
SMPS (*see* LSTA/LPC Secondary Mark-to-
   Market Pricing Service)
SNC Review (*see* Shared National Credit
   Review)
Solvency representation, 284
South Korea, 868, 898, 899
Sovereign borrowers representation,
   290–291
Sovereign immunity, waiver of, 381–382
Sovereign risk, 146
S&P (*see* Standard & Poor's)
Special-purpose investment vehicles
   (SPVs):
   CDOs as, 711, 742
   CLOs as, 647

Speculative-grade loans, 22 (*See also* Leveraged loans)
Splash pages, 194–196
S&P/LSTA Leveraged Loan Index (LLI), 69, 71–72, 539–541
  criteria for inclusion/deletion, 541
  data sourcing and management, 540–541
  historical returns, 485
  performance calculation formulas, 541
  subindexes of, 540
Sponsor, project, 139
Spread(s), 174
  on bank loans, 21
  bid-ask, 398–399
  for CLOs, 662–663
  on European and U.S. markets, 38–39
  on leveraged loans, 673
  for leveraged loans in Europe vs. U.S., 879
  of pro rate tranches, 5
Springing liens, 334
SPVs (*see* Special-purpose investment vehicles)
Standard & Poor's (S&P), 524, 525
  Leveraged Commentary & Data, 662
  loan and recovery ratings, 33, 525–533
    empirical data and market practice, 531–533
    factors determining, 529–531
    marketplace use of, 533
    nominal recovery, 528–529
    types of ratings, 527–528
  LossStats Database, 531, 532
  S&P/LSTA Leveraged Loan Index, 69–72, 539–541
Standard Terms and Conditions (STCs), 424–425
Standard Trade Confirmation, 192–193
Standards:
  accounting, 825–842
    banking book, 826–828
    Basel 2 regulatory capital requirements, 842–856
    credit-related investment products, 829
    for credit-risk hedging activities, 829–830
    FAS 140, 834–842
    FASB SPE consolidation rules, 830–833
    held for sale, 828
    initial recognition and measurement, 825–826
    trading book, 826
    transfers between portfolios, 828

creation of, 32–34
LSTA development of, 32–33, 65
  best practices and policy, 78–79
  documentation, 73, 76–78
  minimum assignment amounts, 73–74
  ratings, 33–34
State blue-sky laws, 96–97
Statement of Financial Accounting Standards No. 57, 831
Statement of Financial Accounting Standards No. 140 (FAS 140):
  applied to assignments and participations, 834–841
  loan securitization, 832–833
  proposed revisions of, 841–842
  qualifying special-purpose entities, 831
Statement of Principles (Joint Market Practices Forum), 79
STCs (*see* Standard Terms and Conditions)
Stock dividends payments, 321
Stop lending remedy, 349
Strike price, 520
Stripped loan facilities, in credit agreements, 251
Structural risk, with CDOs, 729, 731
Structure of loans (*see* Loan structures)
Structured products, 645–646
  CDOs vs., 714–715
  origin of, 6
  (*See also specific products*)
Subject matter jurisdiction, 379–380
Subrogation, 329
Subsidiaries:
  covenants applied to, 292–294
  investments in, 317–318
  representations and disclosures, 286
  significant, 293–294
Subsidiary debt, 313
Substantive consolidation covenant, 360
Successor agents, agency provisions for, 358–359
Summary procedure, guarantee for, 330–331
SunGard, 414
Suppliers, project finance, 139
Supply and demand, distressed loans, 819
Survival clause, in credit agreements, 385
Swap confirmation, for total return swaps, 701–703
Swingline loans, 104, 213–214
Syndicate Information, 196–207
  Borrower Restricted Information vs., 198
  confidentiality arrangements, 200

defined, 197
LMP control policies and procedures,
    200–207
material nonpublic information vs.,
    198–199
public vs. private side participation, 199
Syndicated loan facilities, 103–105
    registration requirements, 91–94
    "stripped," 251
Syndicated loan market, 39–52
    defined, 23
    general characteristics of, 40–41
    investment grade sector, 41–42
    investors in, 50–52
    issuers in, 47–48
    lender titles in, 49–50
    leveraged loan sector, 42–45
    middle market sector, 45–47
    origin of, 23–25
    secondary, 25, 26
    submarkets within, 161–164
        invest-grade market, 161, 162
        leveraged loan market, 162–164
    subsectors of, 41
    syndicators in, 48–49
    (See also specific topics)
Syndicated loans:
    assignments of, 22
    characteristics of, 40–41
    Federal Reserve definition of, 160
    middle market, 57–58
    participations in, 22–23
    secondary market for, 25, 26
    types of, 103–105
Syndication:
    agency provisions for, 359
    agents, 171, 172
    co-agents, 172, 174
    fees, 176
    lead arrangers, 171, 173
    league tables, 172
    pricing, 174–175
    pricing flex, 175
    process of, 171
    strategy for, 176–177
Syndication agents, 50, 172
Syndication fees, accounting standards for,
    827
Syndicators, 48–49
SyndTrak, 195
Synthetic CDOs, 658, 723
    and basket CDS, 743–744
    cash flow CDOs vs., 724–727, 766–767

    customization of, 767–773
    defined, 742
    funded vs. unfunded, 747–748
    motivation behind, 765–766
    and single-name CDS, 742–743
    structure of, 713
    valuation of, 774–779
Synthetic structured finance (SF) CBOs,
    758–765
    cash basis of, 762–763
    credit event definitions for, 763–764
    efficiency of, 761–762
    sectors of largest impact, 759–760
Systemic risk, with CDOs, 728, 730

T

Taiwan, 868, 899
Tawney, R. H., 509
Taxes:
    representations for, 283, 290
    with total return swaps, 706–708
    yield protection clause for, 245–247
Tax-sharing payments covenant, 322
Telecom defaults, 409
Term loan As (TLAs), 53, 55, 717
Term loan Bs (TLBs), 53–55
Term loans, 104–105, 435–441
    delayed settlement compensation
        for nonperforming loans, 438
        for performing loans, 436–438
    distressed trades
        delayed settlement calculations,
            446–448
        purchase price calculation, 445–446
    interest treatments
        paid in kind, 429
        paid on settlement date, 439
    proceeds letters, 439–441
    revolving credit loans vs., 212
    second lien, 108–109 (See also Second lien
        loans)
    settled without accrued interest
        treatment, 436
Term of loans, 514–515
Term sheet, 183–185
Termination of commitment remedy,
    349–350
Term-outs, 104
Terms, for loan-only credit default swaps,
    676–677
Thomson Financial, 172

364-day facilities, in credit agreements, 250–251
Time drafts, 106, 216
Time of payments, in credit agreements, 248
Title to property representations and disclosures, 287
TLAs (*see* Term loan As)
TLBs (*see* Term loan Bs)
Total rate of return swaps, 60
Total return investment strategies, 797–799
Total return swaps (TRS), 680–708
  accounting treatment for, 708
  acquisition process, 686
    on non-U.S. dollar loans, 687–688
  description of, 682–686
  documentation of, 699–704
    Credit Support Annex, 700–701
    investment management agreement, 703–704
    ISDA Master Agreement and Schedule, 699–700
    swap confirmation, 701–703
    voting right agreement, 703–704
  eligible assets, 692
  funding banks for, 695–696
  haircuts for eligible assets, 692–693
  on non-U.S. dollar loans, 687–688
  operation of, 704–706
  origin of, 645
  portfolio, 688, 690–691
  reasons for using, 696
  on revolving loans, 688
  sample yield for, 696–697
  single-name, 688–689
  tax issues with, 706–708
  trading/investment strategies using, 698–699
  transaction reporting, 681
  users of, 697–699
  uses of, 681
Trac-X index, 749
Trade data studies (LSTA), 72–73
Trade ticket, 423
Trade-Specific Terms of Trade, 429–430
  flip representations, 429–430
  reasonably acceptable documents, 430
  subject to the buy-in, 429
Trading book:
  under Basel 2, 850
  loans recorded in, 826
Trading groups (banks), 29

Trading in secondary market, 403–416
  facilitators of, 398–400
  hedge funds, 415–416
  high-yield bonds trading vs., 403–405
  investors' information, 411–412
  lack of short-selling capability, 412
  and market growth factors, 413–414
  marking to market, 414–415
  measuring volatility, 407–411
  personality of loan market trades, 412–413
  settlement issues, 405–406
  settlement process and back-office requirements, 406–407
  strategies for, 416–420
Trading with the Enemy Act, 280
Tranches:
  CDOs, 774–784
  of CDS indices, 756–758
  pro rata, 52
  pro rata vs. institutional, 53–55
Transaction reporting, for total return swaps, 681
Transfer fees, in credit agreements, 369
Transparency, 401, 522–524, 716
"TriBar" Committee (New York), 265
TRS (*see* Total return swaps)
True-up mechanism, 335
TRUPS (capital trust pass-through securities), 719
Trustees, for CDOs, 740

U

UBS, 696
UCC (*see* Uniform Commercial Code)
Underwriter, Bankruptcy Code definition of, 599–602
Underwritten deals, 49, 176–177
Unexpired leases, in Chapter 11 bankruptcy, 638–639
Unfunded CDOs, 747–748
Uniform Commercial Code (UCC), 120, 267
Unilever, 891
United Kingdom, 869, 891
United States:
  and global loan market, 862
  growth of loan market, 873
  investment grade market, 869–873
  issuance in 2003, 865
  Japanese investments in, 910

leveraged loan market, 874–876
    European market vs., 58–60
    spreads on, 38, 39
    success of, 36
    M&A lending, 866
    nonbank lenders in, 876–877
    percent of lending in the Americas,
        867
    post-September 11 market, 864
    secondary loan market in, 881–886
    and WorldCom default, 865
Unocal, 902
Unrealized gains/losses, 512
Unrestricted subsidiaries, 292–293
Upstream due diligence, 432
Upstream guarantees, 331–332
U.S. trustee, in Chapter 11 bankruptcy,
    636
USA Patriot Act, 280
    Customer Identification Procedure,
        82–83
    regulations for customer issues under,
        385–386
Use of proceeds covenant, 307
Use restrictions, 390
Usury, 247, 618
Utilization fees, 235–236

distributions by pricing category, 497,
    499–506
    loans priced 98 to par, 502–503
    loans priced above par, 500–502
    moderately distressed loans, 503–505
    severely distressed loans, 505–506
historical, 484–493
leveraged loans, 515
measuring, 407–411
in mutual funds, 800–802
by pricing category, 494, 495
short term, 494
Voluntary default, 343
Voluntary prepayments, 135
    in credit agreements, 252–253
    and cross-default to first lien loans, 136
    mandatory prepayments of, 135
    restrictions on assignability of, 135
Voting:
    basic rules for, 360
    credit agreement provisions, 334,
        360–362
    in syndicated credits, 624–625
Voting rights:
    agreement for total return swaps,
        703–704
    in credit agreements, 152–153
    and intercreditor agreements, 624

V

Valuation:
    of CDOs, 732–739
        assumptions used in, 736–737
        discounted cash flow analysis,
            733–734
        interest-only, 734–735
        net asset value, 738–739
        principal-only, 734–736
    corporate, increases in, 588, 590
    in secondary market (*see* Secondary
        market pricing)
    of synthetic CDOs, 774–779
Value, in bankruptcy, 615
Vendor-assisted portfolio management,
    792
Venue requirements, 381
Visitation rights covenant, 303
Volatility, 407–408, 411, 493–506
    average, by pricing category, 496–499
    of CDOs, 774–779
    change distribution for, 494–495
    daily value at risk, 493, 495–496

W

Wachovia, 696
Waiver of jury trial, 382
Waiver of sovereign immunity, 381–382
Waivers, 329
Wall Street Journal, 69, 462
Warehouse facility (CLOs), 656–657
Warranties, in term sheet, 183–184
Watch lists, 202
Waterfalls (*see* Payment waterfalls)
Weighted average spreads (CLOs),
    662–663
Welfare representation, 283–284
Well behaved second liens, 121–122
Wind Tel, 891
Windfalls, from imperfect correlation,
    521
Winstar, 587
Working capital, 301
Working capital debt, 312–313
WorldCom, 484, 490, 491, 586
Wynn Resorts, 902

Y

Yamaichi Securities, 907
"Yank-a-bank" provision, 387
Yield, 511–512
    calculation of, 511–513
    for CDOs, 716
    for floating-rate loans, 55
    for total return swaps, 696–697

Yield protection clauses, in credit
        agreements, 239–247
    for breakfunding, 243–245
    for capital costs, 242
    for Eurodollar disaster, 242
    for illegality, 243
    for increased costs, 240–241
    for taxes, 245–247
Yield to maturity, 511

ABOUT THE EDITORS

Allison Taylor has been the Executive Director of the LSTA since May 1998. As Executive Director, Allison devotes her time and attention to managing the LSTA's activities. Her specific duties are to move the LSTA to its next stage of development in achieving its primary goal of creating an efficient, liquid, and professional market place for loan syndications and trading.

The Loan Syndications and Trading Association (LSTA), is a not-for-profit association dedicated to promoting the orderly development of a "fair, efficient, liquid, and professional trading market for commercial loans and other similar private debt".

From an original membership of 15 institutions in 1995, the LSTA has grown today to over 210 members. Members include commercial banks, investment banks, mutual funds, CLO fund managers, buy-side institutions, sell-side institutions, law firms, accounting firms, brokers and many others. Within these institutions, you are likely to see the following types of people attending an LSTA meeting: loan syndicators, commercial lending officers, portfolio managers, hedge fund investors, loan traders, work out officers, and many others.

Prior to becoming the Executive Director of the LSTA, Allison was instrumental in the creation and establishment of the LSTA. She held the position of Chair of the Association since its inception in 1995 until becoming its Executive Director in 1998.

In 2005, under her leadership, the LSTA was honored with the first Life Time Achievement award for the industry. Allison is a frequent contributor to a number of LSTA's publications, has authored chapters in a number of books on the syndicated loan market, and speaks about the syndicated loan market at numerous conferences a year.

Prior to becoming the Executive Director of the LSTA, Allison was instrumental in the creation and establishment of the LSTA. Beginning in 1995, while Head of Par Loan Trading at ING Barings, Allison held the position of Chair of the Association, the precursor to the LSTA. From 1993 to 1998, while at ING Barings, Allison traded Par and Near Par loans for U.S. domestic and Latin American corporate loans.

Prior to her position at ING Barings, Allison worked as a salesperson of corporate loans in the syndication department of Bank of Montreal, Marine Midland Bank, and Citibank. She received her credit training at Texas Commerce Bank where she also was a commercial lender to Fortune 500 companies in the Midwestern States. She has been in the business since 1982.

Allison is a graduate of Pennsylvania State University. She has a BA degree in International Business.

Alicia Sansone is Senior Vice President of Communications, Marketing and Education for the LSTA, where she is responsible for the development of LSTA publications, seminars, conferences, Web site, and oversees media relations.

Alicia works closely with the LSTA membership in order to increase awareness of the LSTA and promote the loan asset class especially among institutional investors, distressed investors and hedge funds. In addition Alicia works with analysts and authors who specialize in the floating rate corporate loan asset class in order to provide better educational tools for LSTA members.

Prior to joining the LSTA, Alicia worked at Institutional Investor Magazine (II) for over 9 years. Her most recent position at II was Associate Publisher and a member of the II Board of Directors, where she oversaw sales, marketing, circulation and new business development for this international monthly magazine.

Alicia is a graduate of New England College. She has a BA degree in Communications.